The CIA and the Culture of Failure

The CIA and the Culture of Failure

**U.S. INTELLIGENCE
FROM THE END OF THE COLD WAR
TO THE INVASION OF IRAQ**

John Diamond

STANFORD SECURITY SERIES
An Imprint of Stanford University Press
Stanford, California

Stanford University Press
Stanford, California

©2008 by the Board of Trustees of the Leland Stanford Junior University.
All rights reserved.

Library of Congress Cataloging-in-Publication Data

Diamond, John (John M.)
 The CIA and the culture of failure : U.S. intelligence from the end of the Cold War to the
invasion of Iraq / John Diamond.
  p. cm.
Includes bibliographical references and index.
ISBN 978-0-8047-5601-3 (cloth : alk. paper)
1. United States. Central Intelligence Agency—History. 2. Intelligence service—United
States—History. I. Title.
JK468.I6D53 2008
327.1273009'049—dc22
                              2008011826

Typeset by Bruce Lundquist in in 10/14 Minion

Special discounts for bulk quantities of Stanford Security Series are available to
corporations, professional associations, and other organizations. For details and discount
information, contact the special sales department of Stanford University Press.
Tel: (650) 736-1783, Fax: (650) 736-1784

To Celia

CONTENTS

ILLUSTRATIONS

Photographs follow page 188

ACKNOWLEDGMENTS

THE TIME PERIOD COVERED BY THIS BOOK coincides roughly with my tenure as a member of the national press corps in Washington. Within a month of my arrival in the fall of 1989 from previous reporting assignments in Boston, the Berlin Wall was coming down. The next summer Iraq invaded Kuwait, and in December of 1991, the Soviet Union ceased to exist. These events were matched in magnitude at the opposite end of the timeline covered by this work—the 9/11 attacks and the U.S.-led invasion and occupation of Iraq. The intervening years were a decade of contingencies—military emergencies arising in unexpected places for unexpected reasons in a context of rapidly declining spending on intelligence, weapons, and military manpower, and uncertainty about the nature and magnitude of the threats facing the United States. My reporting for the Associated Press, the *Chicago Tribune*, and *USA Today* took me from the corridors of the Pentagon to a pontoon bridge over the Sava River in Bosnia and the back of a Bradley Fighting Vehicle in Baquba, Iraq. These assignments afforded me an eyewitness outlook on the national security challenges of the decade but in no way exposed the full magnitude of the transition through which the United States passed during this period. It was only after 9/11 and the invasion of Iraq that many of the events I had covered in the preceding decade came into clear perspective as episodes in a stormy transition from one paradigm of U.S. national security to another. As a journalist, I covered them for their intrinsic news value at the time. As a historian, I sought to explore not just the events themselves but the channel in which they flowed, and to identify the ways in which developments in the intelligence community during these years of transition contributed to the magnitude of the crises brought on by the 9/11 attacks and the invasion and occupation of Iraq.

Attempting to write authoritatively about intelligence matters with only partial access to the relevant records is a risky undertaking, not unlike the business of intelligence collection and analysis in its inherent incompleteness. In selecting the episodes that form the basis of these chapters I deliberately identified events and subjects for which I knew there was a substantial public record available. One positive offshoot of the painful intelligence lapses surrounding 9/11 and the war in Iraq was the generation of a substantial public record by a variety of internal, congressional, and outside review panels. The process of congressional oversight, though at times deeply politicized and prone to produce excessive caution and overcorrection on the part of the intelligence community, had the beneficial effect of exposing to public view intelligence records that might otherwise have remained secret for years. I selected episodes for study not merely because of the availability of this large body of material. A fundamental part of my argument is that U.S. intelligence, though an inherently secret and secretive enterprise, operates in a highly charged atmosphere of public and political scrutiny that brings to bear pressures that affect everything the CIA does, from the most remote stations overseas to the White House Situation Room. A theme running through every event described in this book is the impact of public scrutiny, second-guessing, criticism (both well founded and exaggerated), and politicization at work on the CIA.

The project I undertook, therefore, required a complete re-reporting of the key events that fit into the stream of the CIA's history from the end of the Cold War to the beginning of the so-called global war on terrorism. This effort required the cooperation of intelligence practitioners, overseers, and policy-makers who gave their time to assist me. This book is based on an examination of the extensive public record of intelligence built up since the end of the Cold War, including recently declassified material, and on interviews with some fifty current and former officials with access to highly classified intelligence and with direct experience in the episodes I cover. Many spoke frankly of their experiences, knowing that my interpretation of events might not paint a flattering portrait of the intelligence community. I am grateful to them for their willingness to share their experiences.

For affording me the time, work space, and grant support to begin this project, I am most grateful to the Woodrow Wilson International Center for

Scholars under Director Lee Hamilton. The center provided early and essential support to my project, and my interaction with fellow scholars and staff members greatly enhanced the quality of my research. Director Hamilton, a former member of the House Intelligence Committee, the 9/11 Commission, and the Baker-Hamilton Commission on Iraq, gave generously of his time and insight into the obstacles confronting U.S. intelligence and the factors contributing to intelligence lapses.

The Nuclear Threat Initiative under the leadership of former senator Sam Nunn provided full-time office space while I was conducting part-time writing and research for NTI, an organization devoted to reducing the dangers posed by nuclear, chemical, and biological weapons. I am also grateful to NTI President Charles Curtis and Brooke Anderson, NTI's vice president for communications.

Professor David Brady of the Hoover Institution at Stanford University supported this project from its inception and opened the institution's facilities to me during my research. I am grateful also to Hoover's Mandy Mac-Calla, who arranged my initial meetings with Stanford University Press editors. Amanda Moran and Norris Pope greeted my initial presentation to the press enthusiastically, and Geoffrey R. H. Burn, director of the press, was both supportive and effective in carrying the project through final drafts and peer review into production.

Staff members of the U.S. Senate Library, the Library of Congress, and George Washington University's National Security Archive were unfailingly helpful as I sifted through the wealth of research material available at these indispensable institutions.

The Central Intelligence Agency did not open its files or provide access to current senior analysts or operations officials. But Agency public affairs officers Paul Gimigliano and Mark Mansfield were helpful in putting me in touch with former CIA officials who played key roles in some of the events I was researching. Particularly helpful were L. Britt Snider, a former professor of mine in Georgetown University's National Security Studies Program and former CIA inspector general; Douglas MacEachin, who held several senior analyst positions in a distinguished career at the Agency; and Bruce Riedel, a senior intelligence analyst and Mideast specialist now at the Brookings Institution.

A number of people provided critical assistance to me at various stages. Foremost among them is Ralph Chipman, the first person to read a completed draft of the book. His skillful editing and keen conceptual insight, informed by a career in international diplomacy, greatly improved the final result. Paul Soucy, a former *USA Today* colleague who has been nationally recognized as one of the best copy editors in the news business, combed through every page and endnote rooting out typos, inconsistencies, dropped first references, and other undesirables with his usual skill and speed. Terence Taylor, director of the International Council for the Life Sciences and a former United Nations weapons inspector in Iraq, read several draft chapters and offered not only his own insights from real-world experience but skillful editing as well. At the opposite end of the project—the beginning—*USA Today* editors George Hager and Bill Sternberg provided both encouragement and practical advice on how to turn a promising idea into a finished product. My longtime friend Greg Bedner offered encouragement and material support in the early going. Peter Osnos, editor of *Public Affairs*, helped clarify my original idea for this book with advice geared to the most important participant in the process, the reader. Professor Richard Russell of the National Defense University and his NDU colleague Michael Mazarr, another former professor of mine, brought their expertise in intelligence and other national security fields to bear in advising me on framing my research. Anthony Cordesman of the Center for Strategic and International Studies and one of the foremost experts on Mideast security issues, gave generously of his time in offering sound advice both on the issues at hand and on the practical problems of honing an argument. Regalle Asuncion of the Associated Press and Mark Brender of GeoEye helped track down images for this book.

I have been lucky throughout my career to have editors who helped me polish my craft as a reporter and writer and entrusted me with reporting assignments that took me to the far corners of the world covering issues of national and international moment. An incomplete list of those people would include Mike Bezdek, Sandy Johnson, Randall Keith, Walter Mears, Mike Tackett, Owen Ullmann, Vicki Walton-James, Jim Warren, and Jon Wolman. I am grateful to the faculty and staff of Georgetown University's Center for Peace and Security Studies, formerly the National Security Studies Program, for helping me close the sometimes nettlesome gap between journalism and scholarship. To the degree that this work succeeds as a history, I owe a great deal to the training I received in the Corcoran Department of History at the University of Virginia, and especially to Professors Charles W. McCurdy and Duane J. Osheim. My beloved parents, Marie and Bill Diamond, taught me to write.

John Diamond
Washington D.C., June 2008

The CIA and the Culture of Failure

INTRODUCTION

THE SHORT DRIVE from the White House to the headquarters of the Central Intelligence Agency can begin on Constitution Avenue. The route crosses the Theodore Roosevelt Bridge into Virginia and merges onto the George Washington Memorial Parkway. After tracing the big bend in the Potomac River, the parkway crosses over Spout Run and begins to climb. In a few hundred yards, the spires of Georgetown University, academic home to many a former intelligence officer, and recruiting ground of many a future one, come into view over the cliffs on the opposite bank. Above them, dominating the skyline of Northwest Washington, D.C., is the white cube of the Russian embassy, a few blocks from a mailbox where CIA turncoat Aldrich Ames and his Russian handlers left chalk marks to signal that he was prepared to drop another batch of secrets at a hiding place nearby, and pick up a bundle of cash. Not far from the parkway, in a drab, unmarked office in the Rosslyn section of Arlington, CIA officials met in 1991 with United Nations weapons inspectors to develop a plan for uncovering and destroying Iraq's weapons of mass destruction (WMD).[1] At the second rest stop on the right, high above the Potomac, a Nixon White House emissary in 1973 offered former CIA officer James W. McCord Jr. executive clemency for his involvement in the Watergate burglary in exchange for his silence. Twice, in late-night meetings at the rest stop, McCord refused. McCord conveyed a message of his own: if President Nixon sought to avoid blame for Watergate and let the CIA take the fall, the Agency and its defenders would fight back, a threat that McCord, in due time, carried out, a major step in the downfall of the Nixon presidency.

After the Chain Bridge Road exit ramp, on the approach to the Agency entrance in Langley, Virginia, a sign marked "WARNING: Restricted U.S. Government Installation" interrupts the pretty suburban scenery. Occasionally, a small cross and bouquet of flowers can be seen placed along the median by the turn lane into the Agency grounds. These tokens of love and mourning mark the scene of a double murder in early 1993 when a lone Pakistani man, enraged by the presence of American troops in Muslim holy lands, opened fire with an AK-47 assault rifle on a line of cars carrying CIA employees and contractors awaiting the turn signal into the Agency grounds.

In the post-9/11 world, with the awareness that the hatred of one killer signaled the intent of a global jihadist movement, the drive into the CIA grounds is a multi-step procedure. Visitors are asked to give their name and affiliation at a squawk box a hundred yards short of what looks like a turnpike toll plaza. If a visitor is expected, his name, Social Security number, and date of birth are already entered into the CIA security service's computer, and he is handed a small color map of the CIA grounds. Trees, shrubs, and lawns designed to give the Agency headquarters a campus feel do not hide the barbed-wire fencing, hydraulic metal barriers, and concrete stanchions that are more evocative of a medium-security prison. From the access road, the complex of headquarters buildings looms in the distance. To the left, a set of smokestacks marks the CIA furnace where classified papers discarded in "burn bags" are disposed of by janitors with security clearances. On a lawn closer to the headquarters stands a chunk of the Berlin Wall, gift of a reunited Germany in recognition of the years during which Berlin had been the central arena of the Cold War. Spray-painted graffiti on the concrete slab includes what appears to be a line from a Jimi Hendrix song: ". . . and the wind cries . . ." Other graffiti, also, oddly, in English, include the words "Freedom" and "Democracy" and a paraphrase of President Ronald Reagan's June 12, 1987, speech in Berlin: "tear down the wall."[2] The words evoke a yearning for freedom from tyranny by people in a place where the CIA fought communism over four decades. In fact, the paint was applied not in Berlin but at Langley, to dress up an otherwise non-descript slab of concrete. As such, it stands as the CIA's last propaganda gambit against the East Bloc, a final psychological operation, an inside joke cooked up at headquarters to enhance an otherwise featureless souvenir of the Cold War.

In the CIA's white marble lobby stands a life-size bronze statue of General William "Wild Bill" Donovan, head of the Office of Strategic Services, the World War II predecessor of the CIA, and symbol of the daring and risk-taking the CIA cherishes and, from time to time, emulates. On the opposite wall, dozens of deeply engraved stars represent the Agency officers killed in the line of duty since the CIA's founding in 1947. Some, though not all, of the names appear in a book of remembrance in a glass case below the stars.[3] Down the corridor is a gift shop where employees and escorted visitors can buy the ever-popular CIA-logo golf balls, money clips, highball glasses, sweatshirts, and towels—not a bad kit, come to think of it, for a fictional, if not actual, spy. There are CIA Christmas ornaments with porcelain portraits of past directors Allen Dulles and Richard Helms, semi-deities at agency headquarters. Another popular ornament features a miniature U-2 spy plane dangling in a gold ring above tiny maps of Cuba and the USSR.

The seventh-floor office suite of the CIA director includes a window-less, wood-paneled conference room decorated with the seals of the various military and civilian intelligence agencies over which, most agreed in the wake of the 9/11 attacks, the CIA director had insufficient control. Here in January of 2003, Secretary of State Colin Powell, CIA Director George Tenet, and a cluster of senior intelligence analysts put together the now-infamous briefing for the United Nations Security Council in which Powell, citing information since discredited as almost entirely erroneous, presented the case that Iraq's arsenal of weapons of mass destruction warranted immediate military action. The office of the CIA director affords a view of the trees, or, one might say, the forest, flanking the parkway. Here in 1961 a young Porter Goss, newly arrived at the Agency from Yale by way of the Army and look-ing ahead to a career as a CIA field officer, chatted with Dulles—a legend even then—and watched in horror as the CIA director nearly ignited his tweed coat while trying to light his pipe. Decades later, Goss would return for a brief and stormy turn as director, an emissary from the White House under orders to make that journey from Washington to Langley and clear out Agency officers who were regarded with deep suspicion among the sec-ond President Bush's inner circle as adversaries of the president.

The short distance between the White House and the CIA appears greater when measured in other ways. And the tension between these two power centers during the course of just over a decade—from about the time that unpainted slab of the Berlin Wall arrived at Langley to the day when Colin Powell and a room full of harried intelligence analysts assembled a case for war in Iraq—is the subject of this book. During the dozen or so years from

1990 to early 2003, from the time of the Soviet breakup and the Persian Gulf War to that of the 9/11 attacks and the war in Iraq, the CIA experienced a series of tremors that weakened its foundation, though the cracks were not always visible at the time. Many of these took on the label "intelligence failure"—sometimes because the CIA had failed, other times because the White House or Congress found it expedient to make it seem as if it had. These controversies—allegations that the CIA missed the collapse of the Soviet Union, the CIA's performance before and during the Persian Gulf War, the Aldrich Ames spy scandal, the belated realization of the al-Qaeda threat, battles over the capabilities of "rogue state" adversaries, the intensifying struggle against Islamic terror, and the near-total misjudgment of Iraq's arsenal—unfolded during a decade of transition and distraction for the United States. The economy, the Republican takeover of Congress, crises in Somalia, the Balkans, and Rwanda, and the Monica Lewinsky scandal and impeachment of President Clinton all deflected the country's attention from the gradual political and substantive weakening of the intelligence community during a time when its services were most urgently needed. Problems at the CIA seemed to be matters for Washington insiders to confront during this period, and while intelligence failure garnered headlines, the consequences of failure seemed detached from the lives of average Americans. The 9/11 attacks and the course of the war in Iraq would change that.

The CIA reports to Congress, the military, and other arms of the executive branch, but most of all to the White House, and specifically the president. And it does so almost always in secret. On most mornings, the first thing a president reads comes from the CIA.[4] These arms of government are the CIA's "customers," in the fashionable term, and the president is first among them. This allusion to the CIA as something akin to a business, with customers who have both needs and demands that must be served, gained in currency during the business-centric 1990s. Intelligence reports freighted with caveats, footnotes, and minority views that ate up the time of busy executives were out, as were estimates of future developments that predicted so many different possibilities as to predict nothing at all. Though the term intelligence "customer" or "consumer" remains in use to this day, the idea that the CIA served only a rarified group of cleared officials within the government was shattered by the 9/11 attacks and by the disastrous miscalculations in the run-up to war in Iraq. More than at any time since the Japanese attack on Pearl Harbor, intelligence failure reached directly into the lives of average Americans. Whereas in the early 1990s intelligence reform panels were driven by presidents and staffed by retired generals and Cabinet officers, in the post-9/11 world intelligence reform was resisted by the White House and driven by average Americans, people who, for the most part, had little connection to the military and intelligence nerve centers in Washington—that is, until their families suffered profound loss in the 9/11 attacks.

Throughout the years between the end of the Cold War and 9/11, warning signs of serious trouble in the intelligence community had been accumulating. Budget cuts were an important ingredient, but there were other stresses as well. Severe turbulence beset the Agency's executive suite, where five directors held the top post in the first seven years of the 1990s. A series of events beginning with the CIA's flawed performance leading up to and during the Gulf War, its failure to predict the collapse of the Soviet Union, and the eruption of the Aldrich Ames spy scandal led to a pronounced drop in confidence in the CIA among both Democratic and Republican leaders in the executive branch and Congress. These and other fissures led to a raft of panel studies and legislative efforts to reform the intelligence community, but with little resulting effect.

For most of the CIA's history, disclosure of its misdeeds or failures have alternately titillated the public, served various political agendas, or fueled conspiracy theories. Some Americans still believe the CIA had something to do with the assassination of President Kennedy and the crack cocaine epidemic of the mid- to late-1980s. The political left spent the latter years of the Cold War focused on the CIA's role in propping up corrupt and abusive Latin American juntas as a bulwark against communism and welcoming hosts for American business interests. The admissions in the mid-1970s about CIA spying on Americans and CIA involvement in a plot to assassinate Fidel Castro gave political traction to the liberal criticism of the agency. On the right, anti-Soviet hard-liners argued that the reining-in of the CIA following the congressional investigations of 1975 had de-fanged U.S. intelligence, leaving it ill-equipped to deal with an aggressive, expansionist adversary. One offshoot of this argument was the Reagan administration's backing of a massive CIA operation to funnel weapons and training to Mujahadin fighters in Afghanistan. At the same time, the right also aired suspicions that the CIA, far from being a tool of reactionary politics in the developing world, was insufficiently aligned with the anti-Soviet agenda and tended to underrate the menace of Soviet military power.

The patterns of intelligence failure and correction did not change with the end of the Cold War. Institutions fail; their failures are exposed to criticism; political pressure is brought to bear; personnel are punished and organization charts redesigned; and bureaucracies alter their behavior, taking extra care not to repeat the mistakes that received the most criticism. The risks inherent in the business of intelligence make it a bureaucratic endeavor particularly prone to failure. On the operations side, it involves covert activity, often in hostile environments against adversaries trying to mislead it. Analysts, meanwhile, struggle to fit the scattered secrets the intelligence community has managed to collect into complex political dynamics and make informed predictions at times when even the adversary may not know his own future course of action. These dynamics existed at the CIA both before and after the Soviet collapse. Nevertheless, several factors make the dynamics of intelligence failure stand out in the post–Cold War period.

With the collapse of the Soviet Union, the mission that had defined the CIA since its creation in 1947 and that had taken up the majority of the intelligence community's energies was suddenly gone. In addition to having to explain its failure to foresee the collapse of the Soviet monolith, the CIA faced the even more daunting challenge of defining a new mission in turbulent and uncertain times, all while its own capabilities were shrinking rapidly with post–Cold War downsizing. It is important to recall that while intelligence failure followed by critical assessment of the CIA occurred at various times throughout the Cold War, the structures of scrutiny were vastly different. The House and Senate oversight committees that serve as arenas for so much criticism of the intelligence community today did not exist until 1975. Before then, the CIA operated in a largely closed world. A budget meeting concerning the CIA in the 1950s was likely to involve a one-on-one conversation between the director and Senator Richard Russell of Georgia, chairman of the Armed Services Committee. The investigations of Watergate and intelligence activities of the mid-1970s by the congressional Church and Pike committees shined a harsh spotlight on the CIA, but the focus was on CIA misdeeds—assassination plots, spying on Americans and the like—not on CIA incompetence at the job it was supposed to be doing.[5] The Reagan presidency saw a strenuous effort to restore public belief in the need for a robust clandestine service that resulted in a temporary revival of morale at the CIA. While there were furious internal debates on questions of intelligence analysis, particularly disagreements over the severity of the Soviet threat, there was a broad public consensus on the importance of countering that threat. Even the Iran-Contra scandal of the late 1980s landed only a glancing blow on the CIA, since the Reagan administration had gone to some lengths to keep the Agency's professional bureaucracy out of the information loop regarding the clandestine arms sales to Iran and the funneling of the proceeds from those sales to anticommunist Contra forces in Nicaragua.[6]

The dynamics of intelligence failure changed with the collapse of the Soviet Union because the geopolitical situation changed. The 1990s began with a debate about whether the CIA was even necessary. Then came the shocking revelation in 1994 that Aldrich Ames, a senior CIA officer in the Soviet espionage division, had been spying for Moscow for nine years and had exposed dozens of Soviet insiders working secretly for the CIA, at least nine of whom the KGB promptly executed.[7] A steady stream of intelligence failures in the 1990s occurred in every facet of CIA activity, from intelligence collection to analysis to counterintelligence to covert operations. The decade saw disclosures of CIA dealings with unsavory Latin American paramilitary groups and drug dealers; the breakup by Iraqi dictator Saddam Hussein of a covert operation to topple him from power in 1996; the ill-considered targeting by the CIA of a pharmaceutical plant in Sudan in 1998 and the unintended targeting of the Chinese embassy in Belgrade in 1999; the failure to foresee India's nuclear test and a North Korean test of a three-stage rocket in 1998; the inability to uncover plots to bomb U.S. embassies in Africa in 1998 or the USS *Cole* in Yemen in 2000; and haste, followed by indecision, in the response to those attacks.

Congressional and public attention to these lapses was amplified by the turbulent political environment in which they occurred, as the White House shifted from Republican to Democratic control and back and Congress went from Democratic to Republican control in asynchronous fashion. Serious though these lapses were, it was possible to view them in one way or another as inconsequential to the well-being of average Americans. However serious Aldrich Ames's treachery, for example, the KGB's liquidation of U.S. intelligence sources did not prevent the Soviet Union from collapsing. The CIA has disputed the charge that it failed to foresee the Soviet collapse. But even if the argument prevails that the CIA failed in this regard, the consequences of that failure seem limited compared to the benefits of the Soviet collapse itself, a development for which the agency must receive at least some measure of credit. By failing to recognize Soviet weakness, the CIA helped the Reagan administration frighten the nation into a far larger defense buildup than was necessary. I believe the claims by Reagan's supporters that the defense buildup "caused" the Soviet collapse and was intended to bring about that end are greatly exaggerated and ignore the arguments they made at the time—that the buildup was needed to counter a strengthening, not weakening, Soviet Union. However, the buildup did contribute to the overwhelming coalition victory in the Persian Gulf War, which reestablished the U.S. military credibility world-wide that had been so badly damaged by defeat in Vietnam. The Gulf War and the U.S. military interventions in Bosnia and Kosovo, though beset by intel-ligence lapses, were ultimately successful operations.

The intelligence lapses prior to the 9/11 attacks and the realization that the war in Iraq had been sold on a foundation of faulty intelligence brought the public into the national debate about intelligence in an unprecedented fash-ion. No official body has unequivocally said that better intelligence could have prevented the 9/11 attacks, but an overwhelming consensus formed around the idea that massive intelligence failure had preceded 9/11 and that massive intel-ligence reform must follow it. The general public could see in the 9/11 attacks and the war in Iraq a straight-line connection between intelligence failure and the deaths of thousands of Americans. The lapses that allowed the 9/11 plotters to keep their deadly plan secret, the gross *over*estimation of the threat posed by Saddam's supposed weapons of mass destruction and *under*estimation of the danger of insurgency and civil war that might follow the collapse of his regime, contributed to events that cost thousands of American lives and hun-dreds of billions of dollars. These devastating events were not caused by the CIA. Osama bin Laden and al-Qaeda launched the 9/11 attacks, and the CIA had warned, generally, that we were in danger; Saddam Hussein adopted the policy of strategic ambiguity that complicated efforts to accurately assess the strength of his armaments; President Bush, not the CIA, made the decision to invade Iraq; some CIA analysts had warned, tentatively, of civil unrest in Iraq after the fall of Saddam, and so on. But the integral role of intelligence in these events and their impact on average Americans brought the public into the debate over how the United States steals secrets and interprets intelligence in a way unimaginable just a few years ago.

THE CULTURE OF FAILURE

The seemingly limited and transient consequences of the earlier post–Cold War intelligence failures and the profound consequences of the failures re-lated to September 11 and the war in Iraq are connected, however. The events of the 1990s both stemmed from and led to a steady erosion of intelligence capability, contributing to a series of intelligence lapses and alleged lapses and to a consequent decline of confidence in the intelligence community that left the CIA critically weakened. These processes fed off and fueled one another, leading to a fatal cycle of error, criticism, overcorrection, distraction, and politicization. The term "culture of failure" refers not to alleged CIA incompetence, which, though it occurs in cases we will explore, is often overstated by the agency's critics. Rather it refers to an atmosphere of declining confidence in the abilities of U.S. intelligence to do its job. This diminished faith in the abilities of the CIA existed at the CIA itself, as well as in the executive branch and Congress.

At the beginning of the 1990s, national security debate focused on managing the "peace dividend" that would come from trimming spending on defense and intelligence that had been overwhelmingly geared toward countering the now-nonexistent Soviet threat. The CIA had indeed failed to foresee the Soviet breakup until it was almost upon us. To Agency critics such as Senator Daniel Patrick Moynihan, this massive failure stemmed from a Cold War mindset that led to gross overspending on weaponry and an unnecessary aggravation and prolonging of superpower tension. It was a mindset with a political history, dating back to the "Team B" exercise of the mid-1970s, in which hawkish critics of the policy of détente toward the Soviet Union brought forth an alternative interpretation of Soviet weaponry and policy to counter the CIA's "Team A" interpretations. Some of these same hawks, having overridden CIA circumspection about the Soviets and implemented a massive peacetime military buildup during the Reagan presidency, would return in the 1990s to push the national missile-defense program, once again beginning their campaign with an attack on CIA analysis that downplayed the missile threat. Many of these same hawks, some now carrying the "neoconservative" label, would hold key levers of power as the second Bush administration made its case for invading Iraq. In the early 1990s, Congress waved off Moynihan's proposals to break up the CIA and distribute its component parts among various government agencies such as the Defense and State Departments. But even before the Soviet collapse, spending on intelligence was declining, and, with the exception of a single year, the trend continued through the 1990s. The way the cuts were made, as much as the cuts themselves, cast a shadow that would reach to the intelligence failures of 9/11 and the Iraq invasion. Training of new field officers ground to a virtual halt by the mid-1990s, as did the recruiting of analysts with expertise and knowledge of languages spoken in the parts of the world that were spawning the nation's emerging enemies.

Though this study focuses on the CIA in the dozen years from the end of the Cold War to the U.S.-led invasion of Iraq, it reaches back into the Cold War to examine some of the CIA's work on the Soviet threat in order to better judge the validity of the charge that the CIA had missed the Soviet collapse. I also look at CIA analysis of Iraq in the 1980s to lay a foundation for understanding the intelligence misjudgments about Iraq at the time of the Gulf War, and the lasting impact of those misjudgments years later as the second Bush administration contemplated going to war against Iraq once again. Both these episodes contributed substantially to the post–Cold War perception that the U.S. intelligence community was woefully underperforming, a perception that prevailed even within the CIA itself. So it was that in the early 1990s U.S. intelligence was struggling to define its post–Cold War reason for being at a time when al-Qaeda, unbeknownst to the CIA, was planning and executing its first attacks on U.S. interests. To be sure, this atmosphere of doubt, this culture of failure, had an impact that was not always negative. Concern about the intelligence community led to earnest though largely unsuccessful efforts throughout the 1990s by congressional oversight committees, blue-ribbon commissions, and the intelligence community itself to redefine and reform the intelligence system.[8] On balance, however, the culture of failure afflicting U.S. intelligence was like an old injury, a weak point that kept hobbling the intelligence community as the decade unfolded toward the 9/11 attacks and war in Iraq, two of the greatest national security disasters in U.S. history. Again and again the episodes examined in this book point to a combination of real intelligence failure and persistent, sometimes exaggerated doubt about the capability of the intelligence community that fueled developments detrimental to U.S. interests.

One of the great ironies of the 1990s was that U.S. intelligence, in combination with U.N. inspectors and a policy of constant military vigilance, *succeeded* in ridding Iraq of its weapons of mass destruction. It was, as we now know all too well, a success that went entirely unnoticed by the intelligence community that helped bring it about. The CIA did not trust its own abilities, and no one else in the national security community, whether Republican or Democrat, was prepared to argue otherwise. The perception of failure, real and exaggerated, led the CIA to a position in 2002 in which its own analysis rested on the assumption that it could not fully perceive what the Iraqi adversary was doing.

Concrete events reinforced this culture of failure. Throughout the 1990s, at repeated turns, the intelligence community, in concert with the U.N. inspectors, was caught by surprise with the discovery of some new secret about Iraqi weapons of mass destruction that had been deliberately concealed by Saddam's regime. Early in the decade it was the discovery of a robust nuclear weapons program, far more advanced than the CIA had estimated. In mid-decade, U.N. inspectors discovered irrefutable evidence that Iraq had embarked in the 1980s on a hitherto unknown biological weapons program. As the inspectors were unraveling the Iraqi biological program in 1995, another Iraq-related controversy enveloped the CIA—the inadvertent detonation by an Army demolition team of Iraqi chemical munitions at a place called Kamisiyah immediately after the Gulf War. The furor among Gulf War veterans over the CIA's failure to adequately share with the military what it knew about chemical weapons at Kamisiyah reenforced the contention that whatever the CIA and the U.N. inspectors were finding in Iraq was a mere hint of what Saddam Hussein was actually hiding.

As the perception of American victory in the Cold War coincided with the perception of intelligence failure, so the swift U.S.-led victory in the 1991 Persian Gulf War, a conflict the CIA had predicted would be lengthy and costly, left the Agency on the defensive. And as with the end of the Cold War, the perception of intelligence failures—whether those failures were real or politically expedient exaggerations designed to cover the mistakes of others—cast a shadow down the decade with negative consequences for U.S. national security. Evident problems in the intelligence community's ability to get the right spy satellite imagery to war-fighters in a timely fashion during the Persian Gulf War led to renewed investment in spy satellites and imagery analysts in the 1990s, forcing steeper cuts in human intelligence manpower and slowing the recruitment of people with new and badly needed skill sets. Politics, a sense of responsibility to the intelligence officers who served through the Cold War, and failure to adequately perceive the emerging terrorist threat meant that staff cuts at the CIA were accomplished by attrition, and hiring of much-needed experts on the new threats was severely constrained. The result was a surplus of Soviet expertise in the intelligence community at a time when the CIA needed a much larger cadre of Middle East specialists.

Amid declining capability and intensifying and politicized scrutiny, the mistakes made by the intelligence community cast shadows forward in time. The failure to see Saddam's aggressive intentions toward Kuwait in 1990 led U.S.

intelligence to see nothing but aggressive intent in Iraq's subsequent foreign policies. The intelligence community's erroneous prediction that the Persian Gulf War would cost thousands of American lives contributed to an atmosphere of optimism a decade later as it evaluated the prospects for the conquest of Iraq. The CIA's embarrassing failure to see how far Iraq had progressed in the 1980s toward nuclear weapons capability fueled the conclusion that failure to detect Iraqi nuclear activity in the 1990s reflected Saddam's deviousness and skill in concealing a continuing and aggressive nuclear program.

Even when adversaries revealed their intentions and capabilities, as in the al-Qaeda bombings of the U.S. embassies in Kenya and Tanzania in 1998, Serbia's suppression of Kosovar Albanians in 1999, and the suicide attack on the USS *Cole* in 2000, intelligence seemed inept at guiding the nation to an appropriate response. Flawed intelligence led to President Clinton's decision to launch cruise missiles on a pharmaceutical plant in Sudan and on a suspected al-Qaeda leadership meeting in Afghanistan after the embassy bombings in Africa. The evidence that the Al-Shifa pharmaceutical plant was manufacturing nerve gas grew shakier by the day after the strike. And the al-Qaeda meeting did not take place, almost certainly because the terrorists canceled it after realizing that U.S. intelligence had detected their plans. The next year, during the Kosovo crisis, a U.S. B-2 bomber targeted 2,000-pound precision satellite-guided bombs onto the Chinese embassy in Belgrade, owing to an almost absurd series of lapses in target identification at the CIA. Chastened by these embarrassing misfires, the Clinton White House, with the concurrence of the CIA's leadership, declined to take military action on several occasions when intelligence reports appeared to pinpoint the location of al-Qaeda leader Osama bin Laden.

The surprise accompanying the Indian and Pakistani nuclear tests and North Korea's three-stage rocket test in 1998 helped foster a belief in the CIA's incompetence. The assumption advanced by Donald Rumsfeld in an examination of the missile threat from North Korea and other "rogue" states was that the CIA could no longer be counted on to detect the threats arrayed against the United States. It was this judgment, and Rumsfeld's role in moving the missile defense program forward, that returned him to prominence and led to his being named secretary of defense in the George W. Bush administration. Adversaries adept at "denial and deception"—the concealment of weapons programs and other secret activities from U.S. intelligence—would be able to spring surprises on Washington, of which the India-Pakistan nuclear tests and North Korean missile launches were but two examples. The only safe thing to do, went the argument, was to assume the worst and act accordingly. It was precisely this philosophy that would guide Bush administration decision-making leading up to war in Iraq.[9]

The Bush team genuinely believed that Iraq had some banned weapons. U.S. commanders on the march north to Baghdad in March 2003 were surprised when Saddam's troops didn't launch chemical projectiles at the coalition forces. But the administration considered Iraqi weaponry to be a manageable threat. The problem was the future and what Iraq might do with its oil money once it was free from the crushing international sanctions imposed by the United Nations after the 1991 Persian Gulf War and aimed at forcing Iraq to get rid of its weapons of mass destruction. North Korea, meanwhile, was far enough along in its nuclear weapons development that it would not be safe to invade, and Iran did not yet have nuclear weapons but was too strong for an easy invasion. The 9/11 attacks, while not linked to a state-sponsored terror group, nevertheless showed how vulnerable the United States was to that type of attack. Without worrying particularly about the quality of the evidence against Iraq, the Bush administration wanted to send a message to would-be state sponsors of terrorism. And if a message of toughness was to be sent to Pyongyang and Tehran, best send it through Baghdad, the weakest spoke on the "Axis of Evil." This, at least, was the internal logic, if not the case actually presented to the American people.

The low regard for the CIA among the officials who came to power with George W. Bush in January 2001 made it easier to use the agency as a prop in the run-up to war on Iraq. And the Agency's embattled posture during the 9/11 Commission's investigation of its failure to uncover the 9/11 plot made it much more politically risky for the CIA to raise skeptical questions about whether the threat posed by Iraq was as serious as the White House alleged. An agency lambasted for missing clues that might have unraveled the deadliest terror plot in history was now handed the mission of interpreting a threat based on abundant clues about deadly weapons in the hands of a murderous dictator. To the White House, there could be no question how to respond, and despite internal arguments over details of the intelligence case, the CIA met the demands of its customer.[10]

Intelligence agencies tend to lean toward the worst-case scenario, so it was not difficult for Rumsfeld and the neoconservatives of the second Bush administration to prod the CIA in the direction of making the WMD case for war on Iraq. But the administration's preemption policy upended the normal calculus of intelligence estimating. Through most of the Cold War, the tendency to overestimate Soviet military power arguably enhanced U.S. security, albeit at the cost of excessive defense budgets that may have exacerbated superpower tension. The stronger Washington thought the Soviets were, the more arms the Pentagon obtained, creating economic incentives for U.S. defense industries and the military. The stronger the U.S. military, the less likely it was to be challenged by the Soviets, who, for decades after World War II, had a vast advantage in conventional forces in Europe. While overestimating the enemy contributed to wasteful spending by the Pentagon, it also tended to reduce the chances of conflict. In the lead-up to the U.S. invasion of Iraq in 2003, the Bush administration's preemption policy turned this formula on its head. For where the worst-case analysis tended to downplay the chances of conflict in the Cold War model, in the preemption model it guaranteed war, for it was precisely the enemy's capability that was given as the reason for going to war. The Bush administration was well aware of this dynamic. The CIA was not.

The Iraq War was largely a self-inflicted catastrophe. The Bush administration's fundamental mistake was its failure to realize that the world's most powerful nation cannot be, or be seen to be, the world's most aggressive nation. If it is seen this way, it tends to destabilize the U.S. position in the world by undermining the view of American power as a benign force for protecting weaker nations and intervening to thwart or shorten conflicts. This mistake existed completely apart from the deeply flawed execution of the war, and as that execution improved with painful experience, the initial flaw in the thinking behind the invasion remained unchanged. The U.S. adventure in Iraq was abetted by the abuse of intelligence by policymakers, an overeagerness to take aggressive action, flawed intelligence collection and analysis by the CIA, insufficient critical reporting by the media before the war, and inattention to the Bush administration's manipulation of intelligence by congressional Democrats, who, with access to classified material, were in a unique position to see the gap between what the White House was saying and what the intelligence community was reporting about Iraq.

The 9/11 catastrophe was enemy-inflicted, abetted by the neglect of intelligence capability in the early 1990s, the failure by intelligence leaders to focus analytic attention on the terrorist threat, the failure by overworked intelligence officers to fully appreciate the adversary's motivations and intentions, a reluctance—owing to past intelligence failures—to take military action against that enemy, and the grandstanding of Republican lawmakers over a sex scandal to the neglect of real threats confronting the nation.

Despite these distinctions, the Iraq and 9/11 failures were linked. In late September 2002, as senior intelligence analysts were rushing to assemble the infamous National Intelligence Estimate on Iraq's weapons of mass destruction, a joint committee of Congress was grilling the CIA on its lapses in recognizing the al-Qaeda threat in the years leading up to 9/11. Pressured by the Bush administration to provide intelligence in support of its war policy, lambasted by Congress for failing to uncover the 9/11 plot from a handful of disparate clues, and laboring under its own mistaken assumptions about Saddam Hussein's motivations and actions, the CIA was not about to dismiss the Iraqi threat within weeks of the first anniversary of 9/11.

The sixty-year history of the CIA is pockmarked with failures, whether botched or illegal covert operations, failures to warn of foreign invasions, or lying by Agency officers in testimony to Congress or to government investigators.[11] What made the post–Cold War period different was that the CIA, beset as always by the imperfections of its political leadership and liable to commit errors in an error-prone business, was operating with declining resources, declining power, and declining expertise all while its very reason for being was in question—and as new and even more challenging missions were emerging. It is, therefore, not coincidental that in the early 1990s, at a time when the CIA was charged with failing to perceive the decline of its longtime adversary, the Soviet Union, the Agency was blind to the rise of a new and deadly adversary, al-Qaeda.

A typical pattern in U.S. national security is for a major failure, or perceived failure, to be studied and investigated for the lessons it can teach, a backward-looking exercise that usually focuses on the events immediately in question, not links between intelligence failures in one arena and national security challenges in another. While such probes bring to light a great deal of information about institutional structures and processes that scholars can use in the study of intelligence, they tend to miss the links between seemingly disparate crises and controversies. The interconnectedness of intelligence failures is a theme that runs through this book. The underlying assumption of this analysis is that readers understand that massive intelligence failures preceded the 9/11 attacks and the invasion of Iraq. The purpose here is to analyze events in the years leading up to those failures to help put the failures themselves, and the intelligence organization that made them, into historical perspective and to show the links between lower-profile intelligence contro-versies of the early post–Cold War period and the high-profile failures whose consequences we live with today.

In the case of 9/11, the CIA failed to uncover the target, timing, and per-petrators of an attack that it knew, in a general way, was coming. In the case of Iraq's alleged weapons of mass destruction, the CIA perceived a threat that was not there. It knew its assessments might be wrong, but decided that the "safe" course of action was to assume the worst. As a result, it helped the Bush administration justify a war that carried the nation headlong into a different disaster. In January 2003, two months before the U.S.-led invasion of Iraq, two intelligence community reports put together by Paul Pillar, then the CIA's senior Mideast analyst, warned the White House and Congress of the pos-sibility of prolonged sectarian unrest in Iraq following the defeat of Saddam's regime. The reports predicted that al-Qaeda might set up terrorist operations in remote parts of Iraq. They cautioned that democracy would not take hold easily in a country accustomed to authoritarian rule. And they said that other states in the region would not abandon their weapons of mass destruction programs based on the military action against Iraq. But the reports were is-sued three months *after* Congress had already voted to authorize war.[12]

The study of intelligence controversies is a hazardous trade because the more recent the event, the more likely it is that vital documentary evidence re-mains classified. That applies to the events examined in this book. In part for that reason, I have chosen events of sufficiently high profile at the time they happened that they generated a considerable amount of public reporting and debate. The congressional investigations, inspector general's reports, press coverage, and scholarly writing on these events, along with the willingness of participants to discuss them, aided greatly in producing a coherent picture. But my purpose is not simply to revisit episodes that drew public notice at the time. Rather, it is to reexamine intelligence controversies through the lens of the post-9/11, post-Iraq-invasion world with an eye toward understanding how the intelligence community's own mistakes, along with the political and budgetary pressure exerted upon it, fueled the massive intelligence failures that so profoundly affect us all at the beginning of the new millennium. My topic, in other words, is not only the tremors that shook the CIA during this period, but more important, the aftershocks.

1 THE CIA AND THE END
OF THE COLD WAR

ON DECEMBER 7, 1988, Mikhail Gorbachev, in an address to the United Nations General Assembly, announced a unilateral plan to reduce Soviet military personnel by half a million troops in the coming two years. The cuts would entail withdrawing six tank divisions from Eastern Europe, including forces specializing in river crossings, an essential combat element for an invasion of Western Europe. The cuts would leave the remaining East Bloc forces in an unambiguously defensive posture. Gorbachev made clear that his aim went far beyond a mere structural shift. The announcement, he said, was "aimed at demilitarization of international relations," and his plan for his own country amounted to "changing over from an economy of armament to an economy of disarmament."[1] Gorbachev had effectively preempted President-elect George H. W. Bush, then still in transition a month after the U.S. presidential election, and set a pattern in which Moscow took dramatic steps and left the Bush team struggling to craft a response.

As Gorbachev spoke in New York, a closed-door hearing was under way in Washington, in a sound-proofed room, SH-219 of the Hart Senate Office Building. A group of Soviet specialists from the Central Intelligence Agency was addressing a task force on the Soviet Union headed by Senator Bill Bradley (D-N.J.) of the Senate Select Committee on Intelligence. One of the analysts, Bob Blackwell, the national intelligence officer for the Soviet Union, excused himself from the meeting and shuttled to an adjacent room to watch portions of Gorbachev's speech on television. The *Washington Post* that morning had reported from sources that Gorbachev was planning to announce major but as yet unspecified force cuts. With evident chagrin, the senior intelligence officers

informed Bradley that the CIA had nothing more of substance on the forthcoming speech than the informed speculation that had appeared in that morning's newspaper.[2]

In due time, Blackwell returned to the meeting room and reported what
Gorbachev had announced, noting that the cut of 500,000 troops represented 10 percent of the Soviet military. The lead CIA witness that day was
Douglas J. MacEachin, then director of SOVA, the CIA's Office of Soviet
Analysis. MacEachin, who had spent much of his career focused on the Soviet
threat and would later rise to head all CIA analysis, reflected on the ground-
shifting import of Gorbachev's policy changes and on the CIA's failure to
foresee them. The problem, MacEachin told Bradley, was that the CIA had
viewed the Soviet Union almost entirely as a threat rather than as a "political entity" with vulnerabilities that could lead to the kind of transformation
Gorbachev was bringing about. No one inside the U.S. government or outside it, he said, had predicted the Gorbachev phenomenon. This was technically true, though he was glossing over the work of some scholars, politicians,
and even intelligence officials who, over the preceding decade, had predicted
trouble ahead for Moscow.

The problem was not merely one of the CIA's mindset, MacEachin said, but
of the political environment in which the Agency worked. Even if senior analysts had foreseen the rise of a Soviet leader determined to follow the path Gorbachev was now pursuing, MacEachin said, "We never would have been able to
publish it anyway, quite frankly. And had we done so, people would have been
calling for my head. And I wouldn't have published it." Nor was this kind of
political pressure confined to the early years of the Reagan administration, before Gorbachev and Reagan began working together to reduce nuclear arsenals.
MacEachin testified, "In all honesty, had we said a week ago that Gorbachev
might come to the U.N. and offer a unilateral cut of 500,000 in the military,
we would have been told we were crazy." The most recent prediction the CIA
had made along these lines held out the possibility that the Soviets might unilaterally cut 50,000 to 60,000 Red Army troops. MacEachin told Bradley that
distributing even that cautious estimate had required a struggle among senior
Reagan administration officials.[3]

One week before the Gorbachev speech, on December 1, 1988, a National
Intelligence Estimate on Soviet strategic forces had found evidence, apparently endorsed across the U.S. intelligence community, that Soviet planning
envisioned the possibility of "longer conventional combat and defensive op-

erations, in order to cope with NATO's improving conventional capabilities."⁴
While this assessment anticipated the emphasis Gorbachev would place on
adopting a defensive posture, its tone hardly pointed to the sweeping and
unilateral force cuts the Soviet premier was about to announce: "To date, as
demonstrated in the strategic force programs and resource commitments we
have examined, we have not detected changes under Gorbachev that clearly
illustrate that either new security concepts or new resource constraints are
taking hold."⁵ Two weeks earlier, another intelligence estimate on Soviet conventional forces in Europe said that Moscow might propose unilateral force
reductions but that the Kremlin's overriding goal in its conventional force
restructuring was neither to save money nor to improve relations with the
West, but "to make units more effective for prolonged conventional combat
operations against NATO."⁶

By asserting that the CIA, even if it had predicted the dramatic moves
being made by Gorbachev, could not have published that prediction without
severe repercussions, MacEachin was making a frank admission—albeit in
closed session—of the dynamic of political pressure on intelligence analysts.
As described by MacEachin, it was not a case of the CIA making bold predictions and being forced to tone them down by an administration accustomed to
regarding everything that came out of Moscow with deep suspicion. Rather, it
was a case of the CIA censoring itself, avoiding bureaucratic trouble by keeping its analysis well within acceptable bounds. Political pressure wasn't really
necessary because the CIA already knew perfectly well what its "customers"
in the White House would tolerate. This admission, coming from MacEachin,
was significant for another reason. In the mid-1990s, MacEachin would lead
an effort by veteran CIA analysts to defend the Agency against the charge that
it had entirely missed the coming Soviet breakup.

NOT INVITED TO THE PARTY

When the Soviet Union passed into history in December 1991 with the declaration of independence by the Soviet republics and Gorbachev's resignation,
the CIA was pointedly not invited to the victory celebration. The wave of self-
congratulation that swept across the U.S. national security establishment in
the early 1990s for "victory" in the Cold War passed over the agency that, more
than any other government body, had as its primary function tracking and,
when possible, countering the Soviet threat. The charge was that the agency
that had been set up to warn the government of major world developments

had failed to predict one of the biggest developments of all—the end of the Cold War and the demise of Soviet communism.

With the two superpowers carefully avoiding direct military conflict during the Cold War, the CIA's operational side, the Directorate of Operations (D.O.), engaged in pseudo-conflict with the Soviet adversary through clandestine and covert means from Latin America to Southeast Asia. The CIA's analytical side, the Directorate of Intelligence (D.I.), had the job of assessing the Soviet threat, using whatever human intelligence the D.O. could collect from spies, information from other national security branches, communications intercepts and (beginning in the late 1950s) U-2 overflights, and (from the early 1960s on) satellites. While the military fought bloody proxy wars against communist forces in Korea and Vietnam and stared down East Bloc forces in Berlin, it was the CIA that was most directly engaged with the Soviet Union throughout the Cold War. By one estimate, the U.S. intelligence community spent nearly two-thirds of its budget on the task of following the Soviet Union.[7] As late as 1990, by which time the Berlin Wall had come down and the breakup of the Soviet empire was well along, the intelligence community was still devoting half its resources to the Soviet Union.[8]

Even before Gorbachev's resignation in December 1991, critics charged that the CIA had failed to detect the transformation of the one country that, above all others, it was supposed to know. While the CIA was busy counting tanks and keeping tabs on which Soviet apparatchiks were standing on Lenin's Tomb for the May Day parade, the empire was falling apart unbeknownst to the analysts at Langley, so the criticism went. Even though the process took several years to unfold, the demise of the Soviet Union still managed to catch the CIA unprepared. As late as October 1988, CIA Deputy Director Robert Gates was asserting that "the dictatorship of the Communist Party remains untouched and untouchable" and that "a long competition and struggle with the Soviet Union lie before us."[9] It was in this climate of perceived intelligence failure and the disappearance of the CIA's primary target that commentators, lawmakers, policymakers, and even CIA veterans in the early 1990s raised the rhetorical question, "Do we need a CIA?"[10]

The charge, moreover, was not merely that the CIA had failed to foresee the Soviet breakup. The Agency had failed even more spectacularly, according to the CIA's critics. For during the two decades preceding the breakup, the CIA had taken its place in the executive branch chorus warning that the Soviet Union was strong and getting stronger. The United States, that chorus went, was falling behind in the arms race and had to catch up or risk a fundamental shift in the strategic balance. In the late 1970s, after the U.S. defeat in Vietnam, Moscow sensed that weakness and was becoming more aggressive in places such as Yemen and Ethiopia and, in December 1979, Afghanistan.

The CIA bore the scars of many a bureaucratic battle for taking somewhat less alarmist positions toward the Soviet Union than the Pentagon's Defense Intelligence Agency, whose self-serving depictions of Soviet military power translated into bigger defense budgets. Nevertheless, the CIA helped make the case for the Soviet threat, and that case became the Reagan administration's basis for accelerating an arms buildup begun under President Jimmy Carter that would grow to become the largest peacetime military expansion in U.S. history. Democrats by no means universally opposed the Reagan defense buildup. But by Cold War's end, many viewed the intelligence community's failures with regard to the Soviet collapse as part of a politicized effort to whip up support for record peacetime defense budgets at the expense of "Great Society" social programs. A leader among these critics was Senator Daniel Patrick Moynihan (D-N.Y.), who came forward several years in a row in the early 1990s with legislation to abolish the CIA. His argument was that the CIA, in its obsession with secrecy and the stealing of adversaries' secrets, forgot to look at developments occurring in plain sight—in this case the growing decrepitude of the Soviet economy and the eroding faith of its subjects in the communist system. He cited the work of demographers who noted growing tendencies toward ethnic and regional identification in the Soviet world, in contrast to the Marxist prediction that such tendencies would disappear under communism, and disturbing trends such as increases in infant mortality. Intelligence had failed to see that the United States was clearly militarily superior to the Soviet Union and vastly superior economically. The CIA, Moynihan argued, had become one of a number of Cold War institutions that "gradually mutated—from informing policy to making it. There was nothing conspiratorial about this. Organizations behave that way."[11] The result, he said, was enormously wasteful defense spending in the 1980s that helped plunge the U.S. government into debt.

The abolish-the-CIA bill went nowhere; Moynihan said he never expected it to do otherwise. Indeed, a CIA veteran has pointed out that throughout the latter Cold War period and into the 1990s, despite his pointed criticism, Moynihan always voted for the funding the CIA requested.[12] Moynihan's point was to force a public discussion of the CIA's failings, and on that score he succeeded, as a number of commentators took up the senator's call to abolish the CIA.[13]

Some reduction in the size of the U.S. intelligence apparatus was inevitable with the collapse of the Soviet Union. In 1992, Franklyn Holzman, an economics professor at Tufts University's Fletcher School of Law and Diplomacy and a leading critic of the CIA, wrote that the Soviet collapse "eliminated the need for a large part of the 'intelligence' that the CIA was designed to provide. It seems quite clear that a substantial reduction in expenditures on CIA activities . . . may well be in order." But the imperative to cut intelligence spending went beyond the mere practicalities of the disappearance of the intelligence community's principal target. In the view of Holzman and others, punishment for the sins of the past was in order. The CIA and the rest of U.S. intelligence had inflated the Soviet threat, driving Congress into approving larger-than-necessary defense budgets. "The slanting of results by an intelligence agency represents an intolerable usurpation of power," Holzman wrote. "The demand for a larger-than-anticipated peace dividend from the Pentagon is justified."[14]

Politicians on the right had no particular incentive to defend the CIA. They were more interested in advancing the theory that the Reagan arms buildup had toppled the nation that Reagan had dubbed the Evil Empire. To be sure, the idea of communism as a fundamentally untenable system fit conservative thinking, and to that extent, conservatives might complain that the CIA should have seen the rot that was undermining the Soviet Union. But the notion of a powerful and menacing dictatorship having been driven out of existence by the forces of freedom, led by President Reagan, better fit the image conservatives wished to advance. Conservatives had expended their energy criticizing the CIA before the Reagan presidency, through the Committee on the Present Danger and the "Team B" exercise in second-guessing CIA analysis of the Soviet Union from a harder-line perspective.

And so at 7:35 p.m. on Christmas Day 1991, as the hammer-and-sickle flag came down the Kremlin flagpole to be replaced by the tsarist white, blue, and scarlet tricolor of the Russian Federation, the CIA stood accused of failing to foresee the fundamental transformation of its primary target—indeed, its reason for being—for the past forty-four years.

As we will see, a vastly more complex reality surrounding U.S. intelligence and the breakup—some call it a collapse—of the Soviet Union underlay the preceding sketch.[15] For example, to simply lump the CIA in with the advocates of the Reagan buildup misses the CIA's resistance to even more dire assessments of the Soviet threat emanating from the Pentagon and from the neoconservative defense hawks who formed the core of Reagan's national security team. Many of the vulnerabilities of the Soviet system that became ingredients in the breakup were carefully tracked, analyzed, and in some cases foreseen by the CIA. Some of those who argued that the CIA's coverage of the Soviet Union in the 1980s constituted a colossal failure justified their contention on the assumption that a weak and tottering empire could not also be a dangerous one. The two concepts were not mutually exclusive; an empire could be predatory, and might become particularly so, if it perceived itself to be in a weakened state.

What historian Alan Moorehead said about the Russian revolution could also be said about the Soviet Union's demise. In the official accounts of the revolution, he wrote,

> An impression of inevitability is given; each event is said to have happened because it had to happen in just that way: an irresistible historical process was at work. This hardly squares with the recollections of more impartial observers who were there at the time. They make it clear that from day to day, nobody really knew what was coming next. . . . In other words, there was nothing inevitable about these days; at every moment, a dozen alternatives presented themselves, and often it was only by chance that one of these alternatives was adopted.[16]

The Soviet breakup, an event easily as complex and historic as the revolution—indeed, an event that has itself been called a revolution—happened largely in plain sight during the years of Gorbachev's rule. In that sense, it was an event not particularly in need of a spy agency to correctly perceive. By the late 1980s, anyone with access to the news could see that a historic shift of some sort was under way. To be meaningful, therefore, a CIA prediction of the end of the Soviet Union would have to have predated Gorbachev's rule. It did not. Even during Gorbachev's reign from March 1985 to December 1991, the CIA seemed reluctant to extricate itself from the view that the Soviet Union would endure and remain a fundamental adversary of the United States for years to come. In a basic sense, then, the critics were right.

This belief—that the CIA "failed to predict" the end of the Soviet Union—took on the mantle of undiluted fact and remains to this day a part of the public perception of the CIA as a bumbling spy agency that can't see straight. Bruce Berkowitz and Jeffrey Richelson have argued that the belief that the

CIA failed to predict the Soviet collapse is a "myth" that has thrived because of the many other all-too-real mistakes the Agency has made.[17] Their analysis correctly identifies a tendency to see the CIA as an agency prone to failure, but they are perhaps too quick to dismiss criticism of the CIA's performance in connection with the Soviet collapse. Past CIA failures such as the Bay of Pigs fiasco were operational failures subject to bad decision-making in the White House and bad execution, or luck, on the ground. Failure to foresee the Soviet collapse stood as a fundamental failure of intelligence collection and analysis, a failure that went to the core of the CIA's mission. While this chapter and the next will contend that the critique of the CIA on the Soviet breakup does not always take account of many overlapping and mitigating factors, there were in the CIA's coverage of the Soviet Union egregious errors driven here by politics, there by a lack of imagination, and elsewhere by a failure to steal secrets.

Part of the problem facing the CIA after the fall of the Soviet Union in 1991 was that key Cold War successes were not credited to the intelligence community. Richard Kerr, who spent a career in increasingly senior positions as a CIA analyst, culminating in the acting directorship just as the Soviet Union passed into history, points up some of those successes:

- No nuclear war with the Soviet Union and no major combat incident pitting U.S. forces directly against Soviet forces anywhere in the world during fifty years of Cold War.[18]

- The slowing and halting of the expansion of communism.

- The development of highly accurate intelligence on virtually all Soviet weaponry—to include acquisition of entire weapons systems, such as fighter planes.

- A transition to representative democracy in Eastern Europe that was, except in Romania, almost entirely peaceful.

"Unless you are willing to conclude that intelligence played no role in the above, [the CIA] must have done something right and consistently right," Kerr says.[19] That conclusion was not the prevailing view at the time the Cold War ended.

In sum, the Central Intelligence Agency began the 1990s with its reputation at a low ebb, its primary mission at an end, its budget in decline, and its relevance to national security in question. This weakness of the CIA's stature would, itself, have grave consequences for the course of U.S. intelligence throughout the decade.

INEVITABILITY

The CIA's first line of defense against the charge that it failed to predict the Soviet breakup is that no one else predicted it either. That assertion is false. Though predictions that the Soviet Union was wobbling toward collapse were hardly dominant, a surprising variety of participants and observers saw serious trouble ahead for Moscow. This is an inconvenient fact for the CIA, but in one sense, the existence of these predictions actually reduces the opprobrium that should be directed at the Agency. Whatever the CIA's failings during the latter years of the Cold War, it cannot be said that intelligence failure prevented the U.S. government from considering the possibility that the Soviet Union might someday collapse. The idea existed in a variety of forms—if not as a formal intelligence estimate, then at least as prognostications by persons of no small credibility in national security circles.[20] The most famous of these dates to the beginning of the Cold War. In February 1946, George F. Kennan, the number-two U.S. diplomat in Moscow during World War II and in the immediate postwar years, wrote his famous "long telegram" to Secretary of State James Byrnes on the prospects for economic, military, and political conflict with the Soviet Union in the coming decades. Writing in clipped telegram-ese, Kennan said that Soviet territorial expansion into Central Europe would subject Moscow to the same "additional strains which once proved severe tax on Tsardom." Not since the end of the postrevolutionary civil war "have mass of Russian people been emotionally farther removed from doctrines of Communist Party than they are today." As a result, "internal soundness and permanence of movement need not yet be regarded as assured."[21] Eighteen months later, now in Washington as head of the State Department's Policy Planning Staff and with the outlines of U.S.-Soviet competition coming into view, Kennan wrote his equally famous "Mr. X" article, published in *Foreign Affairs* magazine and based on the ideas he had laid out in the "Long Telegram." Kennan called it a strong possibility "that Soviet power, like the capitalist world of its conception, bears within it the seeds of its own decay, and that the sprouting of these seeds is well advanced."[22] Accurate though his prediction eventually proved to be, Kennan's long-range forecast was not the sort of construct usually put together in an intelligence report. For the CIA's purposes, its most important element was that the erosion of Soviet power could be helped along by the right combination of Western policies, including clandestine pressure by intelligence agencies.

In the fall of 1979, thirty-two years after Kennan emerged as "Mr. X," *Newsweek* magazine approached several prominent people seeking predictions about the 1980s. Among those asked to give a view on the coming decade was Senator Moynihan. His response: "The Soviet empire is coming under tremendous strain. It could blow up."[23] Not particularly noted at the time, the prediction was entirely overwhelmed in the public consciousness a month later by the Soviet invasion of Afghanistan, an event that greatly strengthened the hand of anti-Soviet hard-liners in U.S. political circles, particularly the Committee on the Present Danger, a group that had been advocating a substantial increase in defense spending and accusing the CIA of underestimating growth in the Soviet strategic arsenal. In the wake of the Afghan invasion, the operative part of Kennan's article was not the prediction of Soviet collapse but the invocation to contain communist expansionism "by the adroit and vigilant application of counterforce at a series of constantly shifting geographical and political points."[24] Still, Moynihan kept at it. On the Senate floor in January 1980, barely two weeks after the Soviet invasion of Afghanistan, Moynihan opined:

> The Soviet Union is a seriously troubled, even sick society. The indices of social disorder—social pathology is not too strong a term—are even more so. The defining event of the decade might well be the break-up of the Soviet Empire. But that . . . could also be the defining danger of the decade.[25]

Four years later, at the height of the Reagan defense buildup, Moynihan told graduates at New York University's commencement that "the Soviet idea is spent" and that "our grand strategy should be to wait out the Soviet Union: its time is passing."[26]

Most of the debate on the Soviet Union in the Cold War fell on one side of the fence or the other. Either the Soviet Union was a dangerous, aggressive, expansionist adversary that must be deterred, contained, or rolled back, or it was a tottering empire, ideologically and financially bankrupt, that the West need only outlast. It was rarely both.

An exception to this pattern occurred on September 3, 1980 when Lt. Gen. William E. Odom, senior adviser on President Carter's National Security Council, contended that the Soviet Union was both powerful and dangerous *and* vulnerable to collapse. He presented his argument in a memo to his boss, National Security Adviser Zbigniew Brzezinski, that outlined a strategy for dealing with the Soviet Union in the coming decade. Timed to give Carter ideas for Soviet policy in a second term, should he win the upcoming election against Republican nominee Ronald Reagan, the eight-page memo portrayed the Soviet threat as worsening. Odom judged the two superpowers as roughly equivalent in military power but with the trend in the Soviet Union's favor. The United States was "ahead" economically, but Moscow was closing the gap in military technology. The Soviet Union was expanding its reach with blatant aggression in Afghanistan and expanding its influence through proxies in the Persian Gulf, the Horn of Africa, southern Africa, and Latin America. Neither containment nor détente would meet this challenge. "The U.S. must neither rely largely on military power nor passively 'contain' Soviet power. The U.S. must *engage* the USSR *competitively*," Odom wrote.[27]

As far back as 1977, Defense Secretary Harold Brown had outlined a new administration policy toward the Soviets to increase defense spending by 3 percent per year in real terms. By the end of the following year, the debate in Congress had turned to how fast the defense budget should grow.[28] Carter's January 1980 budget, which would have been prepared well before the Soviet invasion of Afghanistan a month earlier, requested $162 billion for fiscal year 1981, $34 billion more than Congress had approved for the previous year. Congress added $5.2 billion to that figure. Brown, in his final report to Congress as defense secretary, estimated that between 1968 and 1979 the Soviets had outspent the United States on defense by $270 billion. Reagan would put the gap at $300 billion.[29] Brown warned that the Soviet buildup would bring Moscow "from inferiority to essential equivalence," and he dismissed any notion that Soviet economic weakness would ease the threat:

> There is no evidence to support the contention . . . that the Soviet system or the Soviet economy or the Soviet people will not tolerate or cannot bear the additional increment in defense spending that a renewed, intensified arms competition would necessitate. On the contrary, the evidence, over the last two and a half decades, demonstrates that the Soviet system bears what from a U.S. perspective would be an intolerable peacetime defense burden.[30]

Reagan campaigned on the theme of the urgency of meeting the Soviet threat and on the allegation that Carter had been naive in his attitude toward Moscow and weak in his response to the Afghan invasion. With Carter trying to out-Reagan Reagan, Odom's portrayal of Soviet vulnerability and menace was not in play publicly, though his prescription for how to respond closely tracked with what was to happen under Reagan. Physical containment of the Soviet empire would allow Moscow to consolidate its gains within the borders of that empire, Odom argued. A "competitive approach" to Soviet influence in various parts of the world, on the other hand, would put pressure on the Kremlin:

> The Soviet Union, however militarily strong it is becoming, suffers enormous centrifugal political forces. A shock could bring surprising developments within the USSR, just as we have seen occurring in Poland. The dissolution of the Soviet Empire is not a wholly fanciful prediction for later in this century. U.S. policy should sight on that strategic goal for the longer run.[31]

Odom knew he had a receptive audience in Brzezinski. In 1969, Brzezinski had edited a book of articles on the future of the Soviet Union. Six of the chapters, including one by Brzezinski himself, deemed Soviet collapse a realistic long-term possibility.[32] Brzezinski had posed the question of whether the Soviet Union was at the beginning of a "sterile, bureaucratic phase" in its history leading into "a period of decay."[33] We know that Brzezinski sent Odom's memo on to Carter and that the president read the document closely, marking it up extensively and writing "very interesting," among other comments back to Brzezinski. Many elements of Odom's prescription reappeared as part of the Reagan administration's policy toward the Soviet Union.[34] But there appears to have been no substantive follow-up within the national security establishment on Odom's prognosis of Soviet decline. Given that the CIA was criticized not only for failing to predict the Soviet collapse but also for not even considering the possibility through much of the 1980s, it is fair to point out that Odom, Brzezinski, and Carter could have tasked the intelligence community to address the issue as a long-term forecasting exercise. So could President Reagan, who, more than once, let loose with rhetorical flourishes predicting the Soviet Union's demise.

Would a correct prediction by the CIA of Soviet collapse have made a substantial difference in the formulation and execution of U.S. policy during the 1980s? For a partial answer to that question, it is useful to consider the evolution of Odom's own thinking during the period after he predicted a Soviet breakup. By 1987, two years into Gorbachev's rule, Odom declared himself deeply suspicious of the Soviet leader. A logical result of Gorbachev's economic reforms, Odom argued, would be a reaction of Soviet hard-liners and the end of Gorbachev's rule—a forecast that anticipated the failed coup against Gorbachev in 1991, which came just before the Soviet leader's eclipse by Boris Yeltsin and the Russian independence movement. There was also the possibility, Odom said, repeating the prediction he had made in his memo to Brzezinski, that Gorbachev's reform could set in motion an uncontrolled chain reaction that could lead to the empire's breakup. Since neither result could possibly be Gorbachev's intent, Odom reasoned, it followed that Gorbachev must be insincere in pursuing his reform program, doing it for show and to gain some political advantage over the West.

"Gorbachev himself does not intend systemic change," Odom argued, but was acting with "remarkable energy and cunning" to preserve the old system while appearing to favor reform.[35] This view mirrored that of Soviet analysts in the CIA who were later accused of failing to grasp the significance of Gorbachev and, therefore, of failing to see the breakup coming. Thus a senior military officer who had made the right prediction in 1980 had, by 1987, joined the skeptics in arguing that the Soviet Union remained a formidable adversary that would be around for a while yet. Odom's assessment of Gorbachev did not emanate from the political sidelines. At the time he wrote his 1987 assessment, Odom was head of the National Security Agency, the nation's code-breaking and electronic eavesdropping organization. By the time of the Soviet breakup, Odom had joined Moynihan and other critics questioning the need for a CIA and recommending that the Agency be broken up and its functions distributed to the Pentagon and State Department. His objection had less to do with CIA mistakes than with the CIA's irrelevance to policy decisions. Intelligence analysis—as distinguished from raw intelligence about specific developments, such as troop movements or weapons systems—had little day-to-day impact. "I can think of almost no time when the findings of an NIE [National Intelligence Estimate] caused any policymaker to change his mind on anything or caused a policy to move in one direction or another," Odom said.[36]

Now a senior fellow at a Washington think tank, Odom is less critical than Moynihan was on the issue of the CIA's failure to predict the Soviet collapse. "A prediction is interesting, but it's kind of lucky," Odom said in an interview. The key to the Soviet collapse, he said, was the series of decisions made by Gorbachev. Choices made by leaders in real time amid a welter of short-, medium-, and long-term calculations are inherently impossible to predict years in advance. As Odom put it, "How can I predict free will?" As a practical political matter, it is impossible for an intelligence agency to get too far from the policymakers it serves, he said.[37] The evolution of Odom's thinking on the CIA and the Soviet breakup provides a one-man case study that sheds a clearer light on the debate over whether the CIA's analysis during the late 1970s and through the 1980s constituted a massive intelligence failure.

One reason why Cold Warriors in the United States were slow to recognize the significance of Gorbachev was that the evolution he sought and the revolution he wrought did not neatly fit the model of collapse elemental to their own thinking. The idea that the communist system was fundamentally flawed and would fall of its own weight did not quite match up with the idea of leaders within the communist system making a series of conscious decisions to transform that system and, eventually, to share power to the point where regional leaders could arrange to break it up in a relatively orderly and peaceful process. Reagan's defenders have portrayed the U.S. military buildup as part of a coordinated plan to topple the Soviet Union by confronting it with a burden of military spending its weak economy could not sustain. The problem with this argument is that it rests on the idea that Reagan was trying to provoke greater Soviet spending by undertaking a sustained military buildup on the U.S. side. In fact, the argument advanced by the Reagan administration after the defeat of Carter in the 1980 election was that Soviet defense spending was already a fact of life: it was ongoing and, in all likelihood, unstoppable; it had to be countered with a U.S. buildup. In his first appearance before the Senate Armed Services Committee as Reagan's newly confirmed defense secretary, Caspar Weinberger began his testimony by agreeing with the Carter Pentagon's outlook: "I think my predecessor summed it up well when Secretary Brown said, 'When we build, they build. When we stop, they build.'"[38] Soviet defense spending did not weaken the empire, Weinberger argued; it strengthened it by helping Moscow "consolidate the geographic expansion of Soviet influence and presence in many regions of the world. This expansion of Soviet dominion, in turn, has further strengthened Soviet military power and influence," a trend he described as "mutually reinforcing."[39]

Clearly, then, the Reagan plan, as presented to the public, was to catch up with a Soviet military spending spree that was well under way and likely to continue regardless of what Washington did. It was not a plan designed to goad the Soviets into increasingly detrimental defense spending. Yet the Reagan administration did raise the possibility of Soviet collapse, with Reagan himself the most prominent among those discussing the issue. In 1981, speaking at the University of Notre Dame commencement, Reagan famously said, "The West won't contain communism, it will transcend communism," and the Soviet system would eventually be remembered as "some bizarre chapter in human history whose last pages are even now being written."[40] A year later, Reagan contended that the lumbering Soviet economy would fall further and further behind a vibrant and militarily revived West that would eventually "leave Marxism-Leninism on the ash heap of history."[41] Statements such as this helped Reagan's defenders later claim credit for "victory" in the Cold War based on the contention that the Soviet breakup resulted at least in part from Reagan's strong moral tone and the military buildup he engineered.[42]

In congressional testimony in 1981, even the relentlessly hard-line Weinberger made at least a passing reference to the idea of Soviet vulnerability. He speculated that by the late 1980s the Soviets could be "in a position that is increasingly running against them. This would be just at the time when strains on their economy might indicate some slackening of their consistent buildup of military capabilities. But it is very hard to judge right now exactly how much trouble they may be in economically in the late '80s."[43] This vague notion that the Soviets were in an arms race that they could not win fueled hopes not of a total Soviet collapse, but of the possibility that Moscow would halt its foreign expansionism and return to the negotiating table to consider arms control agreements on terms more favorable to the United States.[44]

The closest thing we have to a documentary policy statement on the demise of the Soviet Union is National Security Decision Directive (NSDD) 75, signed by Reagan on January 17, 1983. The document laid out three elements of policy toward the Soviet Union: resistance to and reversal of Soviet expansionism; weakening sources of Soviet economic strength; and negotiations for arms reductions. The goal was "to promote, within the narrow limits available to us, the process of change in the Soviet Union toward a more pluralistic political and economic system in which the power of the privileged ruling elite is gradually reduced." NSDD 75 adds that if Soviet behavior were to improve, the United States could consider broadening economic engagement "to show the Soviets the benefits that real restraint in their conduct might bring." Such concessions, the directive continued somewhat cryptically, "could not, however, alter the basic direction of U.S. policy."[45] While the Reagan administration argued at times for a comprehensive anti-Soviet economic policy, in practice the policy was more ad hoc, here allowing for grain sales to the Soviets, there blocking exports of pipeline equipment. Statements by officials and administration policy papers indicate that these policies were directly linked to Soviet behavior in places such as Poland and Afghanistan, not part of a grand strategy to bring about Soviet collapse. The administration always held out the possibility of removing trade sanctions if Soviet behavior improved.

One of the intellectual wellsprings of Reagan's idea that the Soviet Union could be both contained and defeated was Harvard professor Richard Pipes, who led an attack on CIA analysis of the Soviet Union and pushed for an increase in defense spending during the 1970s, then became a White House aide in the early years of the Reagan administration. Writing in the mid-1990s, Pipes said it was those who wanted to appease and accommodate Moscow who failed to predict the collapse while Reagan "acted with the conviction that the Soviet Union was not strong but weak" and "did not have long to live."[46]

Presentation of Reagan's policies as part of a master plan to bring about the Soviet collapse is largely a post–Cold War phenomenon. At the time, Reagan's policies were sold to the American people on sharply different premises. Reagan may well have believed the Soviet Union to be weak, and his comments about the eventual doom of the Soviet empire speak for themselves. But any intelligence estimate of the Soviet Union that suggested acute economic weakness, slowing defense modernization, restraint in the use of force abroad, or initiative to accommodate with the West faced stern resistance from those most closely associated with Reagan's anti-Soviet policies. It is odd, in a sense, that this should be so, since intelligence reporting on a weakening Soviet position would have tended to validate Reagan's policies. It is equally notable that by the late 1980s, when Soviet weakness was becoming apparent, congressional Democrats had halted the growth of U.S. defense spending, which peaked in 1986.

ACADEMIA AND PREDICTIONS OF SOVIET COLLAPSE

Moynihan attributed his suggestion in 1979 that the Soviet Union might "blow up" to the work of Census Bureau demographer Murray Feshbach. In research presented to congressional oversight committees, Feshbach documented a rise in infant mortality in the Soviet Union along with declining adult longevity and sharply rising levels of alcoholism as part of a broad and growing social malaise in the empire.[47] The same year that Moynihan posited his scenario of Soviet collapse, Hélène d'Encausse wrote that ethnic hostilities within the Soviet Union proper, let alone the broader East Bloc, along with declining Russian ethnic population and rapidly growing Soviet Asiatic populations portended serious trouble.[48]

Andrei Amalrik and Randall Collins, in articles written a decade apart, focused on rising ethnic and nationalist separatist forces within the Soviet empire and the declining legitimacy of the centralized structure. In 1970, Amalrik documented a growing desire for democratic reform among Soviet elites and growing discontent among the masses. In an experience mirroring difficulties of CIA analysts who sought to document Soviet political and economic vulnerabilities, Collins had difficulty getting his 1980 article published, according to Seymour Martin Lipset and Gyorgy Bence, "because it went so much against the accepted scholarly wisdom." Collins eventually published it in 1986 in a collection of his own essays in which he predicted that the Soviet Union faced "the likelihood of extensive decline becoming very high before the 21st century."[49] However, Collins said that war would be required to bring about the disintegration and that total dissolution of the Soviet empire could take up to three centuries. Thus another who "got it right" misjudged a key aspect of what actually unfolded in the late 1980s, the *peaceful* breakup of the Soviet Union and East Bloc. In academia as well as at the CIA, an inability to see the possibility of a coercive, totalitarian state breaking up by peaceful means, and the absence of a countervailing force powerful enough to physically challenge Soviet state power, were major obstacles to foreseeing what was to unfold.

Such predictions by no means pervaded public policy debate. Indeed, scholars who have documented the instances in which analysts foresaw the collapse have noted how rare such foresight was during the latter decades of the Cold War. The discussion within the academic world focused less on the predictive failure at the CIA than on the question of why various social science theories did not lead scholars to predictions of Soviet collapse. Cold War historian John Lewis Gaddis went so far as to argue that virtually no one foresaw what was to happen.[50] University of Michigan political scientist Ted Hopf has said the problem was not so much that U.S. intelligence and academia considered and then discounted such an outcome, but that they never raised the question in the first place. To even consider the possibility, Hopf contended, might have, in a Cold War context, been considered a proposal bordering on silly: "Can anyone imagine a senior international relations scholar applying to the Carnegie Endowment in 1972 for a research grant to investigate the conditions under which Moscow would most likely voluntarily relinquish control over Eastern Europe? Predicting the end of the Cold War was an unimaginable research question during the Cold War."[51] Commentary along the lines of Gaddis's and Hopf's shows that predictions of Soviet collapse were so rare as to be overlooked entirely by serious scholars of the period.

Preconceptions on both the political right and left in the United States got in the way of a clearer view of what lay ahead for the Soviet Union. The political right viewed the Soviet Union as a totalitarian power that ruled by brute force and in which internal political discontent, while rampant, was of no consequence since the regime was subject to no popular checks and ruthlessly silenced criticism. This went along with the right's view of the Soviet Union as a global adversary, aggressively expansionist, seeking to spread its philosophy and to overcome its own economic weaknesses by the predatory domination of neighboring states. Collins, the scholar whose prediction of Soviet vulnerability ran into resistance in the academic world, recalled giving a talk in 1980 and meeting open hostility from Russian anticommunist émigrés who "did not want to hear of anything that would lessen the motivation for American military arms buildup to match the perceived threat of Soviet power."[52] On the political left, meanwhile, two themes identified by scholars as obstacles to foreseeing Soviet vulnerability were the concern in the arms control community over Moscow's formidable nuclear arsenal and the need to deal with that threat through negotiated force reductions. Too much emphasis on Soviet weakness might slow the momentum of the arms control movement, which by the mid-1980s was getting the upper hand over defense buildup advocates. Also, on the far left there were still pockets of admiration in the West for supposedly progressive aspects of Soviet communism.[53]

The theoretical proclivities and policy preferences of the left did not burden the CIA in its analysis of the Soviet threat. And pressure from the right to view the Soviet Union as uniformly menacing and threatening met resistance at times among Langley's analysts. The important point to note is that the near total absence of public dialogue on the vulnerabilities of the Soviet Union put the question out of bounds as an analytical issue at the CIA and contributed to the Agency's embarrassing position at the end of 1991 when witnesses to the historic events in Moscow turned to the CIA and wondered where the intelligence agency had been all these years.

THE GATES CONFIRMATION

The exchange between senior CIA analyst Douglas MacEachin and Senator Bill Bradley on the day Gorbachev announced massive Red Army troop cuts in 1988 remained secret until three years later, when it became part of the public record of the confirmation of Robert Gates, President Bush's choice to head the CIA. Those hearings began in September 1991, a month after a coup attempt by

Kremlin hard-liners failed to remove Gorbachev from power but set up Boris Yeltsin as the hero of Russia's independence movement. Though it would be another three months before the Soviet Union ceased to exist, the monumental shift occurring in the communist empire was obvious by the time the Senate Select Committee on Intelligence took up the Gates nomination. In the month before the first hearings, Estonia, Latvia, Ukraine, Belorussia, Moldavia, Georgia, Azerbaijan, Kyrgyzstan, Uzbekistan, Tajikistan, and Armenia declared their independence from the Soviet Union.[54] Lithuania had led the way with its declaration of independence a year earlier, and had endured a Soviet military crackdown and protracted negotiations for independence that eventually cleared the way for the wave of declarations, and U.S. diplomatic recognition, in the summer of 1991.

Moynihan was among the first witnesses in the Gates hearing. Earlier in the year he had introduced the "End of the Cold War Act," legislation proposing to break up the CIA and distribute its component parts among several agencies, including the State Department and Pentagon. A former member of the intelligence committee, he reminded his colleagues that he had begun arguing as early as 1977 that the Soviet Union was tottering. Like Kennan, Moynihan based his argument on concepts of historical inevitability. Fealty to the communist system was declining; ethnic loyalties in regions of the Soviet empire were growing; male life expectancy was declining. The promise of communism was a mirage. The Soviet Union, Moynihan had said, confronted a "crisis of belief [that] would lead to the crisis of the regime which would lead to the break-up in the 1980s."[55] The CIA, as far as Moynihan was concerned, simply failed to consider such reasoning. Moynihan blamed in particular the Agency's "incredibly wrong" estimates of the size of the Soviet economy. In the late 1970s, he said, the CIA pegged Soviet gross national product at 62 percent of U.S. GNP. He noted with scorn unclassified CIA data that put East Germany's GNP higher than West Germany's: "Now any taxi driver in Berlin could have told you that wasn't so."[56] The erroneous assessment of the East German economy, it turned out, stemmed from an error in calculating the exchange rate, one that the CIA quickly corrected, a point Moynihan glossed over. This was the thrust of Moynihan's barb: if a senator, an economist, and a taxi driver could see the weakness of the Soviet system, why couldn't the CIA?

The answer, according to Moynihan and other Agency critics, was not institutional blindness but bureaucratic cowardice. A mistake so sweeping as missing the breakup of the Soviet Union had to be the result of willful refusal to see the facts. In 1990, Moynihan had organized a Senate Foreign Relations Committee hearing into "perhaps the most important work which the Central Intelligence Agency had to do," namely, estimating the size and strength of the Soviet economy. The result of that work, Moynihan said, may have been "an enormous mistake. We may have hugely overestimated the size and the growth of the Soviet economy."[57] Senior CIA Soviet analyst George Kolt acknowledged serious problems in estimating the Soviet military and economy, particularly the valuation of the ruble and the secrecy of the Soviet government. But he cited CIA testimony delivered as far back as 1977 to the Joint Economic Committee that the Soviet economy "faces growing strains in the decade ahead." Defense Intelligence Agency analyst William Lee told the committee that the CIA had underestimated Soviet military spending, to which Moynihan replied, "If you are right and if, simultaneously, we have overestimated the size of the Soviet economy, then it would not have been very much beyond the capacities of most people to predict the present collapse of the Soviet system, which was not exactly what people were saying around this place ten years ago."[58]

Gates stood accused by Democrats of being a key part of the Reagan administration effort to inflate the Soviet threat to justify an excessive military buildup. As deputy to CIA Director William Casey under Reagan and as the senior career CIA official, Gates had ensured that analysts hewed to the White House line.

Though Gates won confirmation, the hearings and the Moynihan critique provided a media-saturated forum for a lengthy indictment of the CIA. The charge was not only that it had failed fundamentally in assessing its highest-priority target but that it had done so deliberately, under political pressure. Critics, including a few from within the CIA, charged that Gates, as Casey's deputy, had slanted intelligence reporting to conform with the Reagan administration's alarmist assessment of Moscow's intentions and capabilities. The hearings also provided a forum for re-airing widespread dissatisfaction, particularly among Democrats, with the Bush administration's slow response to the historic changes in the Soviet Union, and an opportunity to blame that slowness on Gates and the CIA.[59] As a career CIA officer serving on Bush's National Security Council staff, Gates had particular influence working with a president who, as a former CIA director, was a keen consumer of daily CIA briefings.[60]

Given the lengths to which defenders of the CIA went later in the 1990s to rebut charges of having failed to predict the Soviet breakup, it is remarkable how much of the case against the CIA relied on CIA officers themselves. The Gates confirmation hearings coincided with the publication in *Foreign Affairs* of an article by Stansfield Turner, CIA director under President Carter, about the need to define new missions for U.S. intelligence with the waning of the Soviet threat. Turner blamed himself, as well as senior CIA analysts, for failing to grasp the implications of information showing that by 1980 Soviet GNP was declining while defense spending increased. "Neither I nor the CIA's analysts reached the conclusion that eventually something had to give: that there would be a political and economic crisis," Turner wrote. Soviet academics and economists whose writings were obtained by the CIA only to be ignored had, for years, been contradicting the official line and warning of fundamental problems in the Soviet economy, Turner wrote. He rejected as "revisionist rumblings" the contention that the CIA had done well in assessing the Soviet Union:

> If some individual CIA analysts were more prescient than the corporate view, their ideas were filtered out in the bureaucratic process; and it is the corporate view that counts because that is what reaches the president and his advisers. On this one, the corporate view missed by a mile.[61]

In Turner's view, the "failure" to predict the Soviet collapse was not a failure at all but a deliberate distortion by higher-ups at the CIA at the Reagan administration's request to help sell the Reagan defense buildup. During the Gates confirmation hearings, no one disputed that the CIA missed the Soviet breakup. The question was whether that failure was the fault of the CIA institutionally or had been the deliberate work of Gates himself.

Support for the latter came from within the ranks of the CIA. Melvin Goodman, by 1991 a former career CIA analyst, testified against Gates at the confirmation hearings. Goodman portrayed Gates as a willing tool of Casey. "Casey seized on every opportunity to exaggerate the Soviet threat," Goodman alleged. "Gates' role in this activity was to corrupt the process and the ethics of intelligence" to serve the Reagan administration's agenda.[62]

Gates's reluctance to recalibrate his thinking in light of the dramatic changes taking place beginning in 1985 under Gorbachev drew particular attention from his critics. Because Gorbachev was so integral to the events leading to the Soviet breakup, a critical question about the CIA's performance in tracking those events was, to what extent did the CIA foresee the Gorbachev phenomenon—the coming of a new generation of Soviet leaders committed to economic reform and to an easing of East-West military tensions—and to what extent did the CIA recognize Gorbachev as a revolutionary leader once he was in power? The verdict of the Gates hearing was that some good work had been done by Agency analysts on these issues, but that Gates, in his key role as gatekeeper of high-level intelligence analysis on the Soviet Union, was an unbending skeptic. Graham Fuller, who had been vice chairman of the National Intelligence Council, the interagency group that drafted intelligence estimates for the director of central intelligence, defended Gates generally but said he had been "far too resistant to recognizing the reality and the import of the Gorbachev revolution."[63]

In his highly readable memoir, *From the Shadows*, Gates wrote that the CIA had been "enthusiastic" about Gorbachev as far back as 1983, two years before his rise from member of the Central Committee to general secretary of the Communist Party. The enthusiasm, however, stemmed from the CIA's assessment that Gorbachev, in his willingness to address chronic economic problems, would avert a crisis in the Soviet Union that could lead to internal chaos and violence or to a "desperate military lunge" westward.[64] That is to say, the CIA valued Gorbachev for his ability to hold the Soviet Union together, not set in motion events that could lead to its breakup. The CIA correctly predicted that Gorbachev would succeed Konstantin Chernenko, whose death on March 10, 1985, came only a year after the death of Yuri Andropov, Gorbachev's mentor, whose rule had been similarly shortened by death two years after succeeding the late Leonid Brezhnev. The CIA still had good sources in Moscow as Gorbachev took power; in March 1985, CIA officer Aldrich Ames was still a month away from beginning his espionage on behalf of the KGB, work that would begin with the disclosure to Moscow of virtually all the human sources the CIA had recruited inside the Soviet hierarchy. Still, even before Ames's treachery, the CIA struggled to develop a picture of goings-on in the Kremlin. Gates claimed the CIA "never recruited a spy who gave us unique political information from inside the Kremlin, and we too often failed to penetrate the inner circle of Soviet surrogate leaders."[65] He reported that the Agency was embarrassed at having to rely heavily on the governments of Canada and Britain in developing even a basic portrait of Gorbachev, who had made official visits to those countries in 1983 and 1984, respectively. And though it predicted Gorbachev's ascension, the CIA missed the fact that it came only after an intense internal struggle pitting a more traditionalist Brezhnev faction against members of the late Andropov's camp, who were more reform-minded. Better intelligence on that struggle might have indicated to the CIA not only the strength of Gorbachev's convictions but also the tenacity with which he intended to apply them. Despite its relatively favorable view of Gorbachev, the initial CIA take on him was that he had "risen to prominence as a standard communist functionary," Gates wrote, and on foreign policy would not likely stray "from long-established Soviet positions."[66]

In presenting the first CIA report to Reagan after Gorbachev was named general secretary, Gates and CIA Director Casey distanced even this cautious assessment from the notion of Gorbachev as an agent of dramatic change. Gates believed that CIA analysts down the chain of command were overly dazzled by Gorbachev. The June 1985 report overseen by Gates described Gorbachev as an agent of change but not of radical reform. The Soviet leader would be disinclined to favor concessions in arms control and would seek to drive wedges between the United States and its European allies. This latter view proved to be enduring: with each passing year, as Gorbachev's reforms appeared increasingly far-reaching and irreversible, the CIA tended to portray them as tactical shifts designed to obtain some sort of advantage in the international arena.

Gorbachev certainly became a radical reformer if he did not necessarily start out as one, and to the extent that he sought fissures in the Western alliance, dramatic arms control proposals were precisely the wedge he chose. Casey, apparently not content even with Gates's scrubbing of the CIA report to Reagan, added a cover note telling the president that Gorbachev and his new team "are not reformers and liberalizers."[67]

In fairness to Gates, there was political pressure from the opposite direction, also from within the Reagan administration. Secretary of State George P. Shultz derided the CIA as hopelessly biased in favor of the hardline view of the Soviet Union. Interestingly, Shultz portrayed the CIA as pressuring the State Department, a reversal of the usual thesis about policy agencies leaning on the CIA to toe the administration line. Shultz's critique focused on the CIA's cautious assessment of Gorbachev. He complained that the CIA's initial take was that the new Soviet leader's positions amounted to "just talk," and that the CIA kept adjusting its position as each of its initial assessments of Gorbachev proved wrong.[68] In his 1993 memoir, Shultz described what sounded like a lengthy and one-sided dressing-down of Gates at a January 1987 meeting, a time when Reagan administration hard-liners were in retreat over the Iran-Contra scandal and Shultz's pro-negotiation line was ascendant. Shultz told Gates that the CIA had been wrong on the Soviet Union, Gorbachev, Iran, and a host of other issues and should keep out of policymaking and stick to the facts, if it could find any. Gates repaid Shultz in kind with a retaliatory drubbing in his 1997 memoir.[69]

CIA analysts had identified Gorbachev as someone to watch before he became general secretary, when he had been a member of the Central Committee and a protégé of Andropov, former head of the KGB, and general secretary after Brezhnev's death. CIA reporting had noted Gorbachev's interest in economic reform and some indications of interest in political reform, reports that had stirred controversy in policy circles. Gates said he had questioned the analysts about whether "Gorbachev was being cast in too rosy terms," but the view of Gorbachev as a reformer, he said, "was accepted and reached policymakers."[70] Gates, however, did not regard the broader possibilities opened up by Gorbachev's reforms as material worthy of the CIA's attention, at least until late 1986. Senator Bradley recounted Gates's reply to his question in a March 16, 1986, intelligence committee hearing when asked whether the CIA should prepare to collect new kinds of intelligence data against the possibility that the Soviet Union might change dramatically: "Without any hint that such fundamental change is going on," Gates responded, "my resources do not permit me the luxury of sort of just idly speculating on what a different kind of Soviet Union might look like."[71] In his memoir, Gates would recall his response as "not a good answer, nor was it the right one."[72] For the time being, though, it reflected the view of the high command at the CIA. It is perhaps worth noting that Defense Secretary Caspar Weinberger, whose worldview utterly ruled out the possibility of some sort of benign evolution in the Soviet Union and whose ability to intimidate the intelligence bureaucracy had already been noted by Gates, was seated next to Gates at the witness table at that 1986 hearing.

In his confirmation hearings, Gates denied the charge that he had based his views on a desire to meet the demands of his political masters. But in the process he confirmed that there was, indeed, political pressure within the Reagan administration to hold to an alarmist view of the Soviet threat. Rather than deny the existence of pressure, Gates asserted that the CIA had successfully resisted it. Gates pointed out, for example, that in 1983, at the height of the Reagan defense buildup, the CIA had presented to the Reagan team a correction of its previous estimates of Soviet defense spending. The new judgment was that the rate of growth had been slowing through the late 1970s and early 1980s. "If you think it was fun to publish that when Cap Weinberger was sitting over in the Pentagon, I think you'll appreciate the situation," Gates told the committee.[73] The report in question, presented publicly to a congressional committee in 1983, undermined Weinberger's notion of a military "spending gap" between the United States and the Soviet Union. The supposed gap was important to Reagan administration efforts to continue the defense buildup and pressure NATO allies to do the same. If Gates, in retelling the story in his 1991 confirmation hearing, created the impression that he had championed the controversial paper, then the Senate committee was misled. As former CIA analyst James Noren has since pointed out, the paper "encountered a great deal of resistance in the upper levels of CIA and in the Department of Defense."[74] Those upper levels would have, of course, included Gates, then the deputy CIA director. George Kolt, who worked on the paper as an assistant national intelligence officer for the USSR, wanted to strengthen the wording of the assessment to include an assertion that the Soviet Union would not be able to sustain high levels of defense spending indefinitely. "But I couldn't get this into the estimate," he told the author of a Harvard case study on CIA analysis of the Soviet Union near the end of the Cold War. The opposition came from the Pentagon, Kolt said; his CIA colleagues supported the stronger statement, but apparently not his superiors, including Gates: "When it came to the top, there was nobody willing to fight for it."[75] Ever the adroit legislative tactician, Weinberger responded to this inconvenient report by ignoring it and helping ensure that the administration did nothing to draw attention to it.[76]

Gates conceded that while CIA analysts reported consistently and accurately on imbalances and vulnerabilities in the Soviet economy, the Agency "overestimated statistically how big the Soviet GNP was, giving a false impression of economic strength." This mistake prevented the CIA from fully appreciating the burden that Soviet defense spending was having on the economy.[77] Indeed, combined with the CIA's downward revision of Soviet defense spending, it tended to undermine any notion that a strategy of forcing Moscow into uncomfortable levels of defense spending was working.

Later in the same year in which he said he had not had the luxury of speculating on what a different Soviet Union might look like, Gates said he had taken steps to correct the CIA's overriding fixation on the Soviet threat. He pointed to a memo he wrote in October 1986 directing CIA analysts to seek "new lines of inquiry" to sharpen the picture of what was happening in the Soviet Union. "I sense that there is a great deal more turbulence and unhappiness in the Soviet Union than we are conveying in anything we have written,"

Gates wrote in his memo to the CIA's director of intelligence analysis. "I am concerned that we are in a rut and may not be recognizing significant change in the Soviet Union even as it is taking place."[78]

Such course corrections notwithstanding, Gates's reputation as a hard-liner on the Soviet Union was fixed. Indeed, by the late 1980s, it was sufficiently well known to have come to the attention of Gorbachev himself. In 1989 Gates, who had spent his career focused on the Soviet Union as an intelligence analyst, traveled to the Soviet Union for the first time as part of an official delegation with Secretary of State James Baker. At a reception, Gorbachev singled Gates out and, perhaps tongue-in-cheek, said he was aware of Gates's work on the National Security Council focused on discrediting the Soviet leader. He suggested that if he, Gorbachev, and Baker could strike a deal, perhaps Gates would be out of a job. As it turned out, it was the other way around. In the fall of 1991, Gates was about to be confirmed as head of the CIA while Gorbachev was within weeks of resigning and seeing the country he led dissolved.

WARPED ANALYSIS

By directing his analysts to take a second look, then, Gates himself confirmed that CIA analysis of the Soviet Union had been too narrowly focused from the late 1970s through the mid-1980s, the very period when a CIA forecast of the possibility of a Soviet breakup would have been meaningful. Once Gorbachev had begun his reforms, dramatic change in the Soviet Union was occurring in plain view; it did not require access to classified information to make the assessment that fundamental change was taking place and to speculate on the possible outcomes. Even in the period after Gorbachev came to power, as Gates himself admitted, Gates and the CIA were reluctant to view his reforms as sincere. It is distinctly possible that academics had an advantage over the CIA in foreseeing the possibility of dramatic change in the Soviet Union by virtue of not having access to classified information. Most of the intelligence the CIA collected and consumed, after all, was focused on the Soviet military and intelligence branches, institutions hardly in the vanguard of the Gorbachev reform movement. For example, by the summer and fall of 1985, a few months after Gorbachev had become general secretary, the CIA's Directorate of Operations was preoccupied with the dawning realization that it had suffered a catastrophic loss of virtually all its sources inside the Soviet government. Though it would take the Agency nine years to discover that one of its own, Aldrich Ames, had betrayed these "assets"—resulting in several of them being tortured and executed—it was immediately clear that Moscow, through whatever means, was taking aggressive action to shut down CIA sources inside the USSR.[79] In other words, from the CIA's point of view, the Cold War in the mid-1980s remained in full flower, with no signs of softening coming from Moscow.

Gates won Senate confirmation with relative ease in a 64–31 vote.[80] His confirmation had been quietly helped along by the Senate Intelligence Committee's then chief of staff, George Tenet, who had worked for both Republican and Democratic lawmakers. Tenet's assistance to the first Bush administration would be repaid by the second a decade later when Tenet, by then President Clinton's CIA chief, became one of the few national security officials from the Clinton administration invited to stay on by President George W. Bush. His confirmation secured, Gates, who had been serving on the elder Bush's National Security Council staff, now returned to Langley to occupy the director's suite. By then, in early November 1991, the Soviet Union that he had spent his career tracking had less than two months to live.

Gates is central to the debate over whether the CIA failed to predict the end of the Soviet Union because of his role as gatekeeper of analytical products throughout the Reagan years. To the extent that the CIA time and again underestimated the magnitude of change occurring in the 1980s in Moscow and missed, or misinterpreted, critical signals, Gates often played the role of final arbiter. The available evidence indicates that Gates was predisposed to view the Soviet Union warily, not that he shaped his view to please his superiors in the Reagan administration. Senior CIA analyst Harold Ford, another of the Agency veterans who opposed Gates's nomination as CIA director (more analysts testified in his favor), said because he had developed an outlook toward the Soviet Union over many years, by the mid-1980s he found it very difficult to change in the face of new realities.[81]

A presidential team can easily avoid the appearance of intimidating the intelligence community simply by selecting analysts for key positions whose views are known to conform with its own. Because CIA analytical shops have typically been forums for heated internal debate among many viewpoints, an administration has a ready supply of career officers with differing views from which it can choose those who best suit its ideological point of view. So it was with Gates, who, though not particularly close to Casey, nevertheless fit the incoming Reagan administration's profile of the "correct" attitude about the Soviet Union. Casey, who saw as his main mission reviving the Directorate of Operations from the damage inflicted by the Church and Pike Committee hearings of the mid-1970s, left Gates with a free hand on the analytical side to determine the tenor of CIA reporting.[82]

Much of the Gates confirmation battle revolved around the charge that Gates had squelched benign interpretations of developments in the Soviet Union written at the staff level and prevented those views from reaching senior decision-makers. Though there were some instances described in his confirmation hearing that fit this description, the evidence supporting this charge was not sufficiently compelling to sway even a Democrat-controlled Senate. One reason for this may have been that self-censorship at the working level of estimate-writing spared Gates the trouble of rewriting the work of his staff. In a November 1985 National Intelligence Estimate, for example, CIA analysts did battle with counterparts at the Defense Intelligence Agency over how to describe the internal stresses confronting the Soviet system. The NIE came as close as any intelligence assessment in the early to mid-1980s to predicting the end of the Soviet Union, albeit as a lower-order possibility. The report stated that economic and separatist political tensions "could eventually confront the regime with challenges that it cannot effectively contain without system change and the risks to control that would accompany such change."[83] One of its authors, Fritz Ermath, national intelligence officer for the USSR, told the Harvard case study author that he was not proud of the document because he and other analysts at the CIA "pulled our punches" in the face of Pentagon opposition and held back from a more blunt assessment of the weaknesses confronting the Soviet Union. This was, he said, "not because Casey said so or Reagan said so, but because it would have been too hard to get coordinated in the bloody intelligence community." As a result, the document's bottom line was that the Soviet Union would endure; a stronger suggestion to the contrary, Ermath said, would have meant that other branches of the intelligence community would not have endorsed the estimate, and it would not have been published with that language.[84]

We have already discussed the CIA's failure to anticipate, or find out about, the dramatic cuts in military force that Gorbachev announced to the U.N. General Assembly in December 1988. Even a year *after* Gorbachev's speech, in an estimate published five days after the Berlin Wall came down, Langley was still worrying about the possibility of an unprovoked Warsaw Pact attack on Western Europe. After acknowledging the dramatic changes wrought by Gorbachev, the intelligence analysts reported, "We cannot, however, rule out the possibility that the pact might initiate hostilities from a condition of partial mobilization if it perceives an opportunity to achieve decisive results against NATO, or a need to forestall NATO from achieving decisive results against the [Warsaw] Pact."[85] In a sober and balanced evaluation of Cold War–era intelligence reporting on the Soviet Union published under the auspices of the CIA, Raymond L. Garthoff called this "probably one of the most bizarre estimates in the history of the Cold War."[86]

TEAM B: THE CIA VS. THE PENTAGON

The central controversy of the Gates confirmation hearings was whether Gates had intimidated his subordinates into slanting their intelligence analysis to please their masters in the Reagan administration. The judgment of the Senate was that he had not or, if he had, the transgression was sufficiently limited to allow for his confirmation. A secondary issue in the Gates hearing—how much he knew about the Reagan administration's shipment of arms to Iran and diversion of the proceeds to Contra rebels in Nicaragua—had, in a way, helped Gates fend off the first set of charges. For Gates was able to demonstrate, notwithstanding skepticism among some senators, that he knew nothing of the Iran-Contra matter even though his own boss, CIA Director Casey, played a central role in the illegal operation. Gates's denial served to underscore his insulation, and that of the rest of CIA, from the political apparatus of the Reagan administration.

What the confirmation hearings failed to fully expose was the degree to which no political intimidation of the CIA was necessary to elicit hard-line reporting on the Soviet threat. That work had, to a large degree, already been done before Reagan took office in January 1981. It was accomplished in what amounted to a decade-long campaign in the 1970s waged by ideological neoconservatives, including many of the same people who would be involved in developing the Iraq invasion policy in the second Bush administration. This was the series of debates that began in the early 1970s and continued through the decade in which like-minded pro-defense conservatives and neoconservatives working under the banner of the Committee on the Present Danger attacked the détente policies of the Nixon and Ford administrations, accused President Carter of naiveté bordering on appeasement, and charged the CIA with repeatedly understating the magnitude and intent of a Soviet military buildup.

The original Committee on the Present Danger dated to 1950 and an effort by anticommunists in both political parties to support the blueprint for

a much more robust U.S. national security posture spelled out in the seminal National Security Council Report 68, a policy view greatly energized by
the North Korean invasion of South Korea in June of that year. After more
than two decades of dormancy, the committee was revived in 1976 by a new
generation of pro-defense conservatives, drawing on work by hawkish Senator Henry "Scoop" Jackson (D-Wash.); by Harvard Professor Richard Pipes,
a Jackson adviser and future Reagan aide; and by a *Foreign Policy* article written in 1974 by Albert Wohlstetter, founder of the neoconservative movement.[87]
The argument developed by these and other key members of the committee
was that détente with the Soviet Union represented a false promise, that the
Soviets were no longer calculating their global position based on the restrictions of mutually assured destruction but were building a force intended to
win a nuclear war. The Soviets, the argument went, were not simply rearming
to get ahead of the United States in the arms race; they were doing so with an
offensive, predatory purpose. To meet this threat, the committee prescribed
a rapid U.S. military buildup and a more confrontational policy toward the
Soviets. Hype was an integral part of the effort to sell this policy program.
Defense hawks, for example, likened Soviet military policies of the 1970s to
Nazi Germany's rearmament of the 1930s. Such ideas then found their way
into the statements of U.S. officials. "Not since Germany's rearmament in the
1930s has the world witnessed such a single-minded emphasis on military expansion by a major power," said General David C. Jones, chairman of the Joint
Chiefs of Staff under Presidents Ford and Carter.[88] U.S. Representative Les
Aspin (D-Wis.), chairman of the House Armed Services Committee, exposed
the exaggerated nature of such claims in a study that showed Soviet defense
spending growing at a very gradual rate in comparison with the dramatic
jump in spending on weaponry by Nazi Germany in the 1930s. Yet even Aspin
conceded that "without a doubt, Soviet power has been increasing. And it has
been increasing at a time when U.S. spending on its military has been declining."[89] Such concessions by a skeptic demonstrate the weakness of the opposition to the hard-line interpretation of the Soviet threat and help explain the
absence of discussion of Soviet vulnerabilities.

Underlying these views was the accusation that U.S. intelligence in general
and the CIA in particular had been consistently underestimating the growth
of Soviet military power. President Ford, faced with a challenge in the 1976
campaign from the right wing of his own party mounted by Ronald Reagan,
proposed the concept of a "Team B" to challenge the CIA's reporting on the

Soviet Union as one way to at least appear to be adopting a harder line. The original idea came from members of the President's Foreign Intelligence Advisory Board; it was quickly embraced by White House Chief of Staff Dick Cheney and by Donald Rumsfeld, who was then serving the first of his two stints as defense secretary. When the idea was initially floated, CIA Director William Colby, a career intelligence professional, opposed it. Colby's resignation in January 1976 cleared the way for George H. W. Bush—a political appointment from the senior ranks of the Republican Party—to assume the top job at the CIA, and presently Bush agreed to the Team B exercise.

There were, in fact, three Team Bs. Two dealt with Soviet air defenses and the accuracy of Soviet ICBMs. Those areas, though technical and highly classified, were nevertheless important to the political point that Team B's sponsors hoped to make. Team B contended that Soviet missiles were more accurate than the CIA had estimated, raising the possibility that they could destroy, or at least that the Soviets might calculate that they could destroy, U.S. ICBM silos. On air defense, Team B argued that the CIA underestimated the expansion of the Soviet air defense network and progress in developing an antiballistic missile system. The broader point stemming from these technical arguments was that the Soviet military buildup appeared to be clearing the way for offensive nuclear war, or at least envisioned the idea of winning a nuclear war, by destroying American missiles in their silos, shooting down strategic bombers, and intercepting ballistic missiles in flight. The third part of the Team B exercise drew the most public attention, thanks in part to a leak to the press of its findings, then classified Top Secret.[90] Chaired by Pipes, it focused on the Soviet Union's objectives for its strategic nuclear force.

The Team B report, in Fred Kaplan's colorful phrasing, "read like one long air-raid siren."[91] Designed and constructed to attack the CIA from the right, Team B did not disappoint its creators. The fifty-five-page report produced by Pipes's panel accused the Agency of "mirror imaging"—that is, of assuming that the Soviets saw the strategic rivalry the way we did, as a standoff, and planned their forces for nuclear "sufficiency" rather than superiority.[92] The problem was not mirror-imaging itself. Team B and its supporters, after all, were arguing for a robust U.S. defense buildup and a change in military strategy to match, or mirror, what was perceived to be the Soviet strategy. The problem, according to Team B, was that the CIA had got the picture wrong, with the result, they contended, that the U.S. military was mirroring the wrong image.

The Team B report opened with the disclaimer, "A certain amount of attention is given to the 'track record' of the NIE's in dealing with Soviet strategic objectives" and "the purpose of these historical analyses is not recrimination."[93] In fact, the entire document amounted to a broad attack on the CIA and the civilian intelligence community, which, by its makeup and location at CIA headquarters, tended to dominate NIE drafting that also included input from military intelligence agencies. In examining National Intelligence Estimates over more than a decade, Team B found that:

> The NIE's tendency to view deterrence as an alternative to war-fighting capability rather than as complementary to it, is in the opinion of Team "B," a grave and dangerous flaw in their evaluations of Soviet Strategic objectives.[94]

Team B ascribed what it viewed as the CIA's consistent underestimation of the Soviet threat to "bureaucratic rivalry" with the Pentagon, though it did not consider the equally logical alternative, that the military's more pessimistic view stemmed from a desire to win approval of its weapons programs. Team B found in the case of CIA skepticism about possible Soviet development of missile defenses that "a strong circumstantial case emerges on the matter of politically influenced intelligence." The source of that influence, though not identified, was understood to be Henry Kissinger, then President Ford's secretary of state and previously, under Nixon, the lead U.S. negotiator of the 1972 Anti-Ballistic Missile Treaty.[95]

The massive Soviet military buildup perceived by Team B carried "considerable economic and political costs and risks," including the possibility of growing economic frustration in the Soviet Union and a countervailing U.S. military buildup that would blunt whatever military advantage the Soviets would be able to achieve.[96] This is as close as the report came to acknowledging the possibility of military and strategic overreach by the Soviet Union. The point Team B emphasized was the need for the U.S. buildup and the danger of a "window of vulnerability" to a Soviet preemptive nuclear attack in the early 1980s.

The atmosphere in the actual Team B meetings with the CIA's Soviet analysts was about as hostile as the tone of the report would suggest. Richard Lehman, a veteran intelligence analyst whose CIA career stretched back to the Kennedy administration, looked back ruefully on the Team B experience in an interview with a CIA colleague published in the Agency's historical review publication, *Studies in Intelligence*. The problem, as Lehman saw it, was that experienced analysts, "who were themselves divided" on issues relating to the Soviet threat, were put up against "a team of howling right-wingers." The "Team A" report that resulted was professional, polished, and competent but, in reflecting internal divisions and seeking some sort of compromise language "certainly made no waves." Team B, in contrast, "produced a coherent inflammatory document." Lehman described Team B meetings with CIA officers as "painful." Following a rather tepid presentation by Team A, Pipes stood to deliver a ringing case for a harder-line approach, a case, Lehman said, "all full of things that were nonsense but which sounded good." One of Pipes's fellow Team B members leapt to his feet and hailed the presentation. "It was really embarrassing," Lehman said. "And some of the more sensible members of the B Team were embarrassed by it, too. But nonetheless, the right wing had their triumph."[97]

In the Team B narrative a number of patterns emerged that would reappear in the mid-1990s in the debate over national missile defense and in the run-up to the 2003 invasion of Iraq. These included: attacking the credibility of existing intelligence analysis; accusing the analysts of political bias while mounting an obviously biased contrary analysis; developing hard-line policy based on threats for which evidence was scant; repudiating arms control treaties and inspection and verification regimes in favor of confrontational policies; seeking at first to force a recasting of intelligence analysis and, failing that, producing alternative analysis as a basis for new policies.

Some of these obvious political dynamics were pointed out at the time. In 1978, Raymond L. Garthoff, then Carter's ambassador to Bulgaria, attacked the Team B effort as a politicized exercise in "worst-case analysis." The emotional appeal underlying Team B, Garthoff argued, was that "to overestimate an enemy's capabilities (or intentions) is merely to cost dollars, while to underestimate can cost lives." Garthoff conceded that there was some validity to this age-old tenet of defense planning, but he said it overlooked the risk that one's enemy would, in turn, overreact to America's overreaction. At the very least, Garthoff said, a worst-case exercise should have been conducted hand-in-hand with a best-case exercise.[98] Pipes responded by flatly denying that Team B represented a worst-case scenario; rather, "all of us were confident that our conclusions accurately reflected the actual state of things."[99]

In light of the subsequent collapse of the Soviet Union, and the role of Team B staffers Paul Wolfowitz and Doug Feith in manipulating intelligence to help sell the second Bush administration's policy of invading Iraq, history's judgment of Team B has been harsh. In what may have been the Agency's revenge, the CIA commissioned Garthoff to write a post–Cold War assessment of the Team B episode. Garthoff did not disappoint, declaring, "In retrospect, and with the Team B report and records now largely declassified, it is possible to see that virtually all of Team B's criticisms of the NIE proved to be wrong."[100] Team B overestimated the range of the Soviet Backfire bomber and the size of the bomber force and the accuracy of SS-18 and SS-19 ICBMs, predicted that the Soviets would field an antiballistic missile system, and tended to regard the absence of information on weapons systems as a sign that the weapons program existed behind a shroud of secrecy.[101]

Professor Steven Rosen, a Harvard colleague of Pipes, defended Team B, saying that while shown to have overestimated several specific weapons systems, Team B was worthwhile in forcing senior intelligence analysts to consider the possibility that the Soviets, in contrast to prevailing U.S. policy, viewed nuclear superiority as an achievable goal.[102] Pipes himself, commenting twenty-seven years later, dismissed the criticism of Team B for being wrong about an array of Soviet weaponry. "Hardware doesn't tell you anything," he said. It was an interesting comment for a man who directed a critique of the CIA based in large part on the Agency's supposed underestimation of Soviet military hardware. The main point of the exercise, Pipes said, was to "see if we could conclude that the actual Soviet strategy is different from ours. It's now demonstrated totally, completely, that it was."[103] Veteran arms control negotiator Paul Warnke was not prepared to concede that point, writing in 1999, by which time extensive information about Soviet nuclear strategy was emerging from the Kremlin archives, "It is now entirely clear . . . that by the early 1970s Soviet leaders had concluded that the Soviet Union could not win, and might not even survive, a nuclear war. Anyone dealing with Soviet officials could readily recognize that they held no illusions about having military superiority."[104]

The battle lines drawn in the Team B debate should not obscure the fact that the CIA's reporting on the Soviet Union, though not sufficiently alarmist to satisfy the defense hawks of the Carter and Reagan years, conveyed the broad theme of a large, powerful, economically sustainable, and expanding empire that would remain a superpower peer of the United States into the indefinite future. And it is not fair to portray the tone of CIA reporting as entirely the product of external political pressure. Former CIA director James Woolsey has pointed out, for example, that during the 1960s and '70s, when James Jesus Angleton, the CIA's chief of counterintelligence, struck fear into Agency employees with his aggressive-bordering-on-paranoid search for a spy within the CIA's ranks, anyone who raised doubts about the Soviet Union's viability risked coming under suspicion. "He came to the view," Woolsey said, "that if you believed in the sign of Soviet split, you may well be suspect."[105]

Since an attack on the intelligence community was seen by the Committee on the Present Danger as vital to advancing its agenda, we must consider that the lasting legacy of the Team B episode is more than just its core philosophy. What came out of Team B, as much as a belief in an aggressive Soviet posture and the need to confront all aggressors with force, was a confirmed distrust of the CIA and a determination that in vital policy areas the Agency should be regarded not as an unbiased collector and interpreter of intelligence but as an obstacle to forward-leaning policies toward U.S. adversaries. The way around that obstacle, according to the Team B model, was to either force a recasting of CIA views or develop alternative views that could compete with the CIA's for the attention of policymakers.

The disdain for the CIA built into this view has a flip side: an assumption that CIA reporting is highly influential. This is remarkable because so often we hear policymakers and intelligence officials alike asserting that intelligence analysis has little impact at the policy level. Gates, in his memoir, describes secret directives issued by President Carter in 1978 to adopt a more competitive military and economic posture toward Soviet advances in the Third World. The directives came in the wake of a National Intelligence Estimate—undoubtedly influenced by the Team B experience—that warned that the Soviet Union saw its growing military strength as opening the way to cautious but persistent expansion of its influence in developing countries. "This was one of the few instances I can recall," wrote Gates, "where a national intelligence estimate provoked such a strong reaction on the part of a president and senior policymakers, and led to actions being taken."[106] It was a revealing statement from a person who had spent a good part of his career crafting, drafting, and redrafting these estimates. I have already mentioned that General Odom joined the ranks of those questioning the need for the CIA after the Soviet collapse. "You could close down the DDI [office of the Deputy Director of Intelligence, the CIA's analysis center] and nobody would miss it."[107]

From the substantial body of work on Team B and the debate about the Soviet threat in the 1970s, a few key points affecting U.S. intelligence for years to come warrant emphasis:

- The CIA did not cave in to Team B by sharply revising its assessments of the Soviet Union.[108] Lehman recalls that the CIA made some adjustments at Team B's prompting toward a conclusion that the Soviets had improved their low-altitude air defenses but did not recast its overall Soviet analysis.[109] But pressure from the right was a constant for the Agency, particularly once the key players brought together by the Committee on the Present Danger and Team B came into senior positions in the Reagan administration.

- With few exceptions, among them Secretary of State Shultz's clashes with Casey and Gates, there was little pressure on the CIA from the left to revise its interpretation of the Soviet threat until the end of the Cold War.

- Team B did not prove that the CIA could be intimidated into changing its views, but did show that the CIA could be effectively sidetracked or gone around.

- Team B established a model for military hawks of a neoconservative bent that they used again in the mid-1990s during the GOP push to build a national missile-defense system and in 2002 during the run-up to war in Iraq.

As the Gates confirmation hearings demonstrated, there were sharp conflicts within the CIA over how to assess the Soviet Union during the 1980s, enough so that at least a few analysts were willing to come forward and publicly oppose the promotion of their former boss. But in the U.S. intelligence community as a whole, the dynamic over assessing the Soviet Union during the Reagan years, when a prediction of a Soviet collapse might have been meaningful, was not so much a battle between points of view within the CIA as a clash between an extremely hard-line outlook at Weinberger's Pentagon and a more balanced outlook at the Agency. Viewed in retrospect, we see a plodding CIA lacking the imagination to grasp how the combination of economic pressures, discontent in Soviet satellite states, and a new generation in the Kremlin more tolerant of discontent might combine to transform and eventually bring down the empire. Viewed through a contemporaneous lens, we see a CIA struggling with the Pentagon and its arms buildup agenda to temper excessively alarmist assessments of the Soviet threat.

I will return to the theme of the CIA cast as a moderating force, resisting more extreme intelligence analysis of the Pentagon in the run-up to the Iraq War in 2003. There again, the CIA found itself stuck in a no-man's land between an administration's ideologically tinged view of reality and the available facts. Choosing its battles carefully, the CIA fought judgments about the Iraq threat it deemed unsound or unsupported, thereby making determined enemies in the White House and Pentagon. Yet both in the Cold War and in the run-up to the invasion of Iraq, the CIA bent in the face of criticism and gave its masters in the West Wing the intelligence findings they demanded. The result was an institutional defeat of major proportions for the CIA but with this difference: in Iraq, the Bush administration's and the CIA's overestimation of the adversary did not simply translate into building a few too many warships and missiles. It translated into war. For under a policy of military preemption, the age-old defense philosophy of better safe than sorry is turned on its head. Under preemption, hyping the threat, to paraphrase Garthoff, no longer merely cost dollars; it cost lives.

2 INTERVENTION, RESTRAINT, AND SOVIET COLLAPSE

NO NOTE-TAKERS WERE INVITED to the meeting of the Soviet Politburo on December 12, 1979, to witness the ratification of a fateful decision. Four days earlier, Premier Leonid Brezhnev had agreed privately to the recommendations of a special Politburo executive committee, consisting of KGB chief Yuri Andropov, Foreign Minister Andrei Gromyko, Defense Minister Dmitri Ustinov, and Central Committee International Department head Boris Ponomarev, on the deepening crisis in Afghanistan. Alarmed by an increasingly violent Islamic insurgency and frustrated by the ineptitude and possible duplicity of the communist government in Kabul, Moscow was preparing to send 50,000 to 75,000 troops across the border into Afghanistan to join a small Soviet security contingent already deployed to that country. Soviet troops were already massing along Afghanistan's northern border, a fact known both in Washington, which had quietly cautioned the Soviets against intervention, and in Kabul, where the government had at various times requested military help from the Soviets. Despite the rather public spectacle of the Soviet mobilization, the proceedings unfolding in the Kremlin in early December took place in utmost secrecy. The Soviet plan for Afghanistan was not simply to come to the aid of the communist government in Kabul and help fight the Islamist insurgents. Rather, Moscow planned to overthrow the communist leadership then in power—in part out of fear that it was about to shift its loyalties to the United States—and install a group more closely aligned with Moscow. With a government in power that they could trust and support, the Soviets would then turn to crushing the uprising.

With secretaries barred from the meeting, Politburo member Konstantin Chernenko scrawled out a two-point memorandum in his own hand under the cryptic heading, "Concerning the Situation in 'A.'" But for the signatures on the document, and for the work of Cold War historians in Russia and the United States who have unearthed and interpreted papers from the Kremlin's once-secret archives, it would be impossible to grasp the import of the memo based solely on its text. The signatories were agreeing to "ratify evaluations and measures set forth by Andropov" and the rest of the special committee. The Politburo empowered the Andropov group to adjust these unspecified measures as circumstances warranted, subject to the approval of the Politburo, and instructed them to keep the Politburo informed. Brezhnev signed the memo, marked "Top Secret" and stamped "SPECIAL FILE." Andropov, Ustinov, Gromyko, and seven other Politburo comrades scrawled their signatures across the text. Since the document went directly from this closed session into a safe, its purpose appears to have been to get the senior Politburo members on record in support of an invasion that all understood could go badly. Mikhail Gorbachev, then a junior Politburo member, did not attend the meeting. In two days, Marshal Sergei Akhromeyev would be at his headquarters just north of the Afghan border at Termez, in what is now Uzbekistan, ready to lead the invasion by the Soviet army, which would begin in earnest on Christmas Eve. Akhromeyev, first deputy chief of the Soviet General Staff, was a highly decorated veteran of World War II. He would go on to be the lead Soviet negotiator in arms control talks with the United States during the 1980s and would, at the end of the Cold War, make one final appearance as one of the plotters of the August 1991 coup against General Secretary Gorbachev. Days after the coup failed, Akhromeyev would be found dead by suicide in his Kremlin office, having left behind a note saying that everything to which he had devoted his life was coming to an end. A dozen years earlier, as commander of Soviet forces entering Afghanistan in 1979, Akhromeyev took on a key role in a disaster that would help bring about the Soviet Union's demise.[1]

Four days before the signing of the document that sealed Afghanistan's— and possibly the Soviet Union's—fate, the *National Intelligence Daily* (*NID*), a classified CIA report distributed to senior U.S. officials in the executive branch not privy to the more sensitive and limited-distribution President's Daily Brief, carried an article discussing the arrival in early December of Soviet airborne troops at Bagram, Afghanistan, and of troop activity north of the Afghan border. The article suggested that the activity might signal Soviet concerns about the security of the Bagram base, or plans to evacuate Soviet military and diplomatic personnel in case of a rapid deterioration of the situation.[2]

TRACKING THE FALL OF A GREAT POWER

Assessing the meaning of Soviet military moves in and around Afghanistan in late 1979 was the job of the CIA's Office of Soviet Analysis, or SOVA, the same group targeted for criticism by the Team B review four years earlier. Although the verdict of historians and the weight of evidence in post–Cold War assessments favors the CIA's analysis over Team B's (as discussed in Chapter 1), at the time, the hard-liners were the dominant power in Washington. President Carter was pressing a defense buildup that Ronald Reagan would accelerate and expand with the help of many of the same neoconservatives who had participated in Team B. Moreover, world events seemed to confirm rather than refute their hard-line point of view concerning the strength and aggressiveness of the Soviet Union.

As the long and tragic U.S. effort in Vietnam was ending in defeat in 1975, the Soviet Union, Hanoi's chief sponsor, was pressing to widen its influence elsewhere in Asia and Africa. In early 1975 the Soviets began shipping weapons to a communist faction in Angola; in 1977, Moscow signed on formally as an ally and sponsor of the communist government in Ethiopia; and the Soviets were also expanding ties with Yemen, Rhodesia, and Libya. Though the CIA did not believe that the Soviet Union engineered the coup in Afghanistan that brought the communist regime to power there in 1978,[3] once in power, that new government gained Moscow's formal support, further reinforcing the perception in Washington of Soviet expansionism.

As I will explore in greater detail in this chapter, the CIA failed until very late in the developing crisis to predict that the Soviets planned to invade Afghanistan. Over the next two years, the CIA followed this failure with a series of alerts that Moscow was preparing a major military incursion into Poland to quell the uprising by the Solidarity labor movement. Once again, on an issue involving intensive analysis of its top-priority target, the CIA missed the mark: there was, of course, no Soviet invasion of Poland.

Examining these events serves several purposes in connection with our topic—narrowly, the performance of the CIA in connection with the demise of the Soviet Union, and broadly, the arc of the CIA in the decade between the Soviet collapse and the 9/11 attacks. Evaluating how the CIA performed in foreseeing and tracking the Soviet collapse requires a judgment about what caused or contributed to that collapse, followed by an evaluation of how the CIA perceived those contributing events. Scholars are only beginning to plumb the vast topic of the end of the Soviet Union, and this study will but touch on the complex crosscurrents that led to the tectonic shifts of the Gorbachev era. Debate will continue for generations over the relative weight to give such factors as Gorbachev's own reformist drive, the decline (not to say unworkability) of the Soviet economy, the Soviets' inability to keep pace with the Reagan defense buildup, ethnic and nationalist pressures that overcame a gradually weakening police state, policies in the West that encouraged Moscow's reforms and eased Cold War tension, a new ethic in Moscow that no longer tolerated violent crackdowns on dissidence, and the unpredictable dynamic of economic reform spinning out of control and leading to results that the reformers never intended.

A few points appear on just about everyone's list: the painful Soviet experience in Afghanistan; the Solidarity uprising and the precedent it set for the coming independence movements in Central Europe; and the rise of Gorbachev. The CIA's interpretations of these episodes are not an uninterrupted catalogue of failure or misperception. Rather, the things the CIA got right and the things it got wrong in connection with Afghanistan, Poland, and Gorbachev tell us a great deal about the political dynamic of intelligence during this turbulent period, the state that the CIA found itself in at the end of the Cold War, and the legacy of these events as the Agency moved forward into the years of declining intelligence budgets, eroding espionage capability, obscure and elusive intelligence challenges, and uncertain leadership.

AFGHANISTAN

When internal power struggles within the communist regime in Kabul raised fears in Moscow that it would turn to the West, and when the Afghan regime's repressive policies intensified an Islamist insurgency, the Soviet Union, in a watershed event, invaded Afghanistan on Christmas Eve 1979. The incursion had the dual purpose of replacing the troublesome regime and putting down the insurgency by blunt force.

The CIA had provided detailed tactical warning to the Carter administration in the days before the invasion, interpreting satellite photos showing long lines of military fuel trucks as signs of a "possible" full-scale ground invasion, not a mere military exercise.[4] Through much of the year, even into late

December, the CIA had considered but, on balance, discounted the possibility of a major Soviet invasion. Nevertheless, the Agency had examined the question repeatedly and in detail, to the point where it could not be said that the Carter administration should have been caught by surprise. CIA reports to then-Director Stansfield Turner had raised the possibility of a Soviet invasion as far back as March 28, 1979, a notable accomplishment since newly available Soviet archives show that the first discussion by the Politburo of military intervention in Afghanistan occurred only eleven days earlier.[5] True, the initial CIA warning discussed invasion only as a possibility, but that's all it was in Moscow as well. And just as CIA reporting through much of 1979 described a massive Soviet invasion as unlikely because of the expected negative worldwide reaction, the difficulty of Afghan terrain and the tenacity and popularity of the insurgents, so these concerns informed Moscow's deliberations.

Not by coincidence were CIA analysts at Langley and Soviet leaders in the Kremlin both, in March 1979, considering the possibility of a Soviet incursion into Afghanistan. The unrest in that country had hit home in Washington a month earlier when, on February 14, 1979, Marxist guerrilla fighters kidnapped the U.S. ambassador to Afghanistan, Adolph Dubs, in Kabul. Hafizullah Amin, then the Afghan defense minister, ordered a rescue operation that resulted in Dubs being killed in the crossfire. Then, on March 15, Islamist forces in Herat, joined by mutinying Afghan army forces, began a major uprising that took more than a week to quell and led to the deaths of some twenty Soviet advisers. The first Kremlin discussion of military options took place March 17.[6]

The CIA's Soviet analysts opined that because invasion carried significant risk for the Soviets, Moscow would seek other means to influence events in Afghanistan.[7] An intelligence memorandum prepared by the CIA but including the views of other branches of the intelligence community stated that one of the principal factors motivating Soviet calculations was avoiding the loss of face that would occur with the overthrow of a communist regime: "The Soviets feel obligated to support such revolutions and embarrassed when they fail. The outcome assumes added importance when the revolution occurs in a country on the USSR's border."[8]

The intelligence memorandum concluded that Moscow's most likely course of action would be to gradually reinforce Soviet security forces already in place in Afghanistan at a pace designed not to attract attention. "Nevertheless, we can foresee contingencies under which the chances of large-scale and long-term intervention would become substantially greater," the report stated.[9] Such a commitment, the memorandum advised, would confront Moscow with "the grave and open-ended military task of holding down an Afghan insurgency in rugged terrain."[10] This was written in September 1979, three months before the invasion.

The extraordinary and chilling Soviet archival material that has been made public since the end of the Cold War contains assessments similar to those from Langley. This suggests not a penetration into Kremlin thinking by the CIA but an ability by two well-established intelligence and security teams, given similar sets of facts, to arrive at similar conclusions concerning an insurgency whose nature was as apparent to Washington as to Moscow. The basic idea of Afghanistan's importance to Soviet prestige, articulated in the September CIA report, shows up early on in the Politburo's discussions. "Under no circumstances may we lose Afghanistan," declared Foreign Minister Gromyko in the March 17, 1979, Politburo meeting.[11] Andropov, even then jockeying to succeed the ailing Brezhnev as premier, agreed, but with a caveat: "Bearing in mind that we will be labeled as an aggressor, but that in spite of that, under no circumstances can we lose Afghanistan."[12] Central Committee Secretary Andrei Kirilenko injected a note of caution: "The question arises, whom will our troops be fighting against if we send them there?" Just the insurgents, he asked, or, more likely, "ordinary people" who support the uprising? "Thus, we will be required to wage war in significant part against the people."[13]

This prediction proved grimly prescient. The Soviet invasion was intended to suppress an insurrection and, in something of a contradiction, replace a brutal and incompetent communist regime with a better one so as to lessen popular opposition. Instead, it unleashed a devastating nine-year civil war that killed or wounded more than a million Afghans, forced some 4 million more into exile as refugees, provoked the very U.S. involvement in the region that the invasion was supposed to prevent, contributed to the breakup of the Soviet Union, and helped nurture a radical Islamic movement that would come to torment both the United States and Russia into the twenty-first century.[14] In the annals of twentieth-century statecraft, the decision to invade Afghanistan in December 1979 must rank among the most thoroughly disastrous for the country that made it.

It should be noted that one of the attendees at the March meeting in which the Afghan problem was discussed was Central Committee member Mikhail Gorbachev, a protégé of Andropov. The future premier, however, was silent on the invasion issue, at least so far as the available Soviet archives show, between March and December 1979—perhaps a consequence of his junior status.

In the March 1979 deliberations, Brezhnev sided with those on the Politburo who opposed intervention, thus settling the issue, at least for the time being. The evolution of the premier's thinking through the rest of the year, to the point of signing the order authorizing invasion on December 12, 1979, brings into play a key point on which there is a notable gap between the CIA's assessment of Moscow's likely actions in Afghanistan and the deliberations going on inside the Kremlin. Ironically, that gap concerned the role of the CIA itself in the crisis.

THE CIA UNWITTINGLY SHAPES EVENTS

After Afghanistan's Deputy Prime Minister Hafizullah Amin seized power in a coup on September 16, 1979, the KGB became concerned that the new premier, sensing Moscow's impatience with Kabul's inability to deal with the Islamic insurgents, was planning a turn to the West. KGB General Leonid Shebarshin recalled at a 1995 symposium on the Cold War that Soviet intelligence was deeply concerned about meetings between Amin and U.S. officials in Kabul in October 1979, two months before the Soviet invasion. The KGB's inability to find out from Amin, a communist and ostensible Soviet ally, what had happened in those meetings only increased Soviet concern. In particular, the KGB worried that Washington, having just lost its technical intelligence monitoring posts in northern Iran after the Iranian revolution in early 1979, was eying Afghanistan as a replacement intelligence base.[15] Those posts were a vital source of technical intelligence on Soviet missile capability; their location was ideal for tracking Soviet missile tests. Moscow was right that the CIA was looking to replace its lost monitoring posts, but wrong about the location: Washington eventually made arrangements with China to establish technical intelligence collection posts for electronic eavesdropping and the tracking of Soviet missile tests. Moreover, U.S. diplomats in Kabul regarded Amin not as a potential ally but as a subject of suspicion. Nevertheless, the concern over U.S.-Afghan cooperation was real to Moscow. More important, the CIA was either unaware of this concern or discounted it, a factor that contributed to the Agency's difficulty in predicting what was about to happen.[16] Andropov, in a handwritten note to Brezhnev in early December 1979 that scholars of the Afghan war view as a decisive document, warned of "Amin's secret activities, forewarning of a possible political shift to the West."[17]

Indeed, fear of creeping American influence in territory that Moscow regarded as part of the Soviet sphere runs through the available Kremlin records on the decision to invade Afghanistan. By early December, we know that Brezhnev's chief foreign policy adviser, Andrei Aleksandrov-Agentov, was telling colleagues that the crisis meant either choosing military intervention in Afghanistan or deciding to "give Afghanistan to the Americans."[18] Given the sycophantic nature of Kremlin politics, this may safely be taken as a parroting of Brezhnev's view. In a pivotal meeting on December 8, 1979, in Brezhnev's private office at the Kremlin, KGB chief Andropov and Defense Minister Dmitri Ustinov—the two leading advocates of invasion—warned of a grand CIA plan to establish a "new Great Ottoman Empire" along the Soviet Union's southern flank. Because Soviet air defenses along that front were weak (despite Team B's emphasis on the Soviet Union's formidable air defenses), American Pershing missiles, if stationed in Afghanistan, could threaten such vital Soviet installations as the Baikonur Cosmodrome, home of the Soviet space and missile programs.[19] We may infer the dynamics of these fateful meetings from an American observer of interactions between Brezhnev and his senior subordinates six months earlier at the SALT II arms control negotiations in Vienna. Robert Gates, attending as a senior member of Zbigniew Brzezinski's NSC staff, noted that Foreign Minister Gromyko and Defense Minister Ustinov "did not hesitate to correct Brezhnev when he misspoke."[20] Though Brezhnev had another three years to live, he was so enfeebled by 1979 that two large KGB officers practically carried the Soviet premier about during the summit, even in front of members of the American delegation.

The CIA and the Carter White House were not privy to Kremlin deliberations, but they still were receiving some indications from the Soviets that a key concern within the Kremlin about Afghanistan was that American influence there was growing. President Carter recalled years later that at the Vienna summit in June 1979, after he had expressed concern about increasing Soviet military activity already apparent in Afghanistan, Brezhnev "made some very disparaging remarks about extending the frontiers of the United States over to the Soviet borders."[21] An account of the Soviet invasion of Afghanistan by J. Bruce Amstutz, the American deputy chief of mission in Kabul at the time, makes clear that U.S. diplomats were aware of Moscow's concern that the Amin government was tilting toward Pakistan and, by extension, the United States.[22] But the CIA and the Carter administration appear not to have taken seriously, or even considered, Soviet concerns about American designs in Afghanistan, and the Soviets appear not to have taken seriously the Carter administration's muted warnings about the consequences of Soviet military intervention. As Amstutz put it, "Though the American Government had publicized the steady Soviet troop buildup on Afghanistan's border, beginning in the summer of 1979, the Soviets correctly concluded that American warnings were more bark than bite."[23]

Soviet assessments grossly exaggerated the CIA's clandestine role in Afghanistan during the pre-invasion months in 1979. The Soviets were right in sensing that something involving the CIA was going on; they were wrong about the nature of that involvement. Responding to overtures from Afghanistan's Islamic insurgents, sometimes conveyed directly, at other times through the pro-insurgent government in neighboring Pakistan, the CIA's Directorate of Operations began considering aid to the insurgents as early as March 5, 1979. Thus the CIA was lining up not with Amin and his communist government, but with Amin's enemies. After months of deliberations and no action—months in which U.S. intelligence reports were documenting Moscow's growing distress over the situation in Afghanistan and considering the possibility that it would respond with military action—the CIA's clandestine plan finally made its way through the National Security Council review process and emerged on July 3, 1979, as a formal intelligence finding signed by President Carter. The plan was modest: about $500,000 in nonmilitary assistance would go to the Islamic insurgents, the Mujahadin, most of it in the form of cash, basic supplies, and support for psychological operations such as radio broadcasts supportive of the insurgents.[24] By comparison, aid to the Mujahadin in the first three years of the Reagan administration averaged $60 million per year and rose exponentially after that. Throughout the 1980s, Reagan administration aid to the Afghan rebels totaled an estimated $2 billion. By the late 1980s, the CIA operation in Afghanistan had gone from covert to overt and was the largest of its kind in Agency history, according to Milt Bearden, who ran it.[25]

What jumps out of the CIA intelligence reporting on the Afghan crisis in 1979 is that neither the U.S. covert aid program nor the Kremlin's exaggerated worries about the U.S. role in Afghanistan weighed in the calculations of U.S. intelligence analysts considering the possibility of a Soviet invasion. Yet we know from the Soviet archive that fear of a growing U.S. role may well have been the deciding factor in the Kremlin's decision to invade. We have the meetings between U.S. diplomats and Amin, which helped spark those fears. And we have the fact of a CIA-run operation, albeit a modest one, to exacerbate Moscow's problems in Afghanistan by helping the insurgents. Also, we know that CIA intelligence analysts knew what their brethren in the Directorate of Operations were doing in Afghanistan. Sometimes the secrecy surrounding U.S. covert operations such as aid to an insurgency group prevents the Directorate of Operations from informing even the CIA's own Directorate of Intelligence of its activities. This was not the case with the aid to the Afghan rebels. We know from Gates's memoir that amid the Carter administration's discussion of whether to launch the covert program to support the insurgents, Arnold Horelick, national intelligence officer for the Soviet Union, sent his boss, CIA Director Turner, a paper weighing the possible Soviet reaction if it sensed Washington was backing the insurgency. Horelick worked for the analytical rather than the operations side of the CIA. He concluded that the modest U.S. effort then being planned would have no impact on Moscow's ability to control events in Afghanistan. As for the concern that a covert operation might provoke the Soviets into military intervention, Horelick advised that it would make no difference: regardless of what course Moscow followed, it would blame CIA meddling whether or not the Agency was actually doing anything in Afghanistan.[26]

Here we have an example of intelligence as a hall of mirrors.

CIA reporting neglected the impact of Moscow's fear of the CIA—a greatly exaggerated fear, yet one the CIA knew Moscow harbored. Moscow, for its part, reflexively blamed "imperialist" meddling through the hidden hand of the CIA for its international problems, missing entirely the CIA's nascent role supporting the Afghan insurgents. In Afghanistan, unbeknownst to the CIA, this reflexive excuse had become a real concern to the Kremlin and a motivating factor behind plans for a major military incursion.

It is unfair, however, to say that U.S. intelligence entirely missed the question of how Moscow would figure the United States into its calculations in Afghanistan. All the work done between March and July of 1979 on the covert operation—work that engaged CIA covert operators, analysts, the NSC and the president himself—concerned what the United States should do in Afghanistan and how the Soviets might respond. Precisely because of the level of White House and CIA activity on the covert action plan, the failure of CIA analysts to consider how the Agency's own actions in Afghanistan would figure into Soviet military planning is the more remarkable.[27]

Even with the transparency provided by post–Cold War access to Kremlin archives, the motivations underlying Soviet decision-making are not entirely clear. Were the Soviets really concerned that Afghanistan was about to go over to the American side and give U.S. intelligence a listening perch on its doorstep? Or was this specter merely a card played by Andropov in the final weeks before the invasion to win over the reluctant Brezhnev? The Soviet archives are something of an echo chamber. Christopher Andrew and Vasili Mitrokhin, in their detailed account of Soviet activities in the developing world based in part on Mitrokhin's own extraordinary archive of smuggled KGB documents, describe the tendency of Soviet leaders to lie and peddle propaganda even in their own highly classified internal memoranda. In trying to sell Brezhnev on war in Afghanistan, Andropov was "economical with the truth," the authors note dryly. Andropov assured the ailing Brezhnev that the job could be done with a modest number of troops even as a much larger Soviet force was poised on the northern border of Afghanistan, ready to enter the country.[28] On December 31, 1979, with the invasion already under way, an internal report to Brezhnev by Andropov and other senior architects of the invasion described Amin as having been killed by an Afghan uprising even though the report's authors had themselves directed the KGB forces who, four days earlier, had attacked Amin's palace and summarily executed the Afghan leader.[29] Yet as Andrew and Mitrokhin demonstrate, the available records indicate that Andropov and his KGB subordinates genuinely feared a U.S. alliance with the government in Afghanistan. With so much misinformation circulating in the Kremlin, small wonder that the CIA had trouble sorting it out.[30]

Douglas MacEachin, a former senior CIA analyst, has conducted two detailed studies of the Afghan case since leaving the Agency.[31] His reading of the Soviet archives—and he must be regarded as among the best-informed Western readers of these documents—is that they reveal internal politicking between moderates and hard-liners for Brezhnev's approval. MacEachin notes, in particular, a sharp change in tone from pro-invasion comments made in a Politburo meeting on March 17, 1979, to anti-invasion comments made by the same people in another meeting the next day. "Clearly, between the first two Politburo sessions," MacEachin wrote, "discussions took place off line, probably informed by additional assessments and information and reflecting Brezhnev's (anti-invasion) outlook." The emphasis on the risk of the United States turning the Afghan insurgency to its advantage clearly formed a central theme of the final appeals of Andropov and Ustinov to Brezhnev. Overall, however, the primary motivation that emerges is preventing a loss of territory that the Soviet Union regarded as part of its orbit, whether that loss be to

Islamic insurgents or to the United States. The bottom-line issue in Moscow was Soviet credibility. Afghanistan was a communist client state on the Soviet Union's southern border threatened by a religious uprising that had already claimed the lives of Soviet soldiers sent before the invasion to provide security assistance to the embattled government. The "loss" of Afghanistan and the forced withdrawal of even the limited pre-invasion Soviet contingent would be seen as a major political setback. Once convinced, Brezhnev took to telling his comrades, "How should the world be able to believe what Brezhnev says, if his words do not count in Afghanistan?"[32]

WERE THE AMERICANS PROVOCATEURS?

Two decades after Brezhnev's fateful, even fatal, decision, Carter's national security adviser, Zbigniew Brzezinski, threw a new twist into the Afghanistan plot, suggesting in an interview that the covert aid to the Afghan insurgents had been designed to provoke, or at least encourage, a Soviet invasion. Brzezinski told a French publication, *Le Nouvel Observateur*, that on July 3, 1979, the day Carter signed the intelligence finding authorizing nonlethal aid to the insurgents, Brzezinski had written the president a memo predicting that "this aid was going to induce a Soviet military intervention." The administration wasn't pushing for an invasion, Brzezinski told the magazine, "but we knowingly increased the probability that they would." He called the clandestine operation "an excellent idea. It had the effect of drawing the Russians into the Afghan trap."[33] Brzezinski told the interviewer that as the invasion was unfolding in December 1979, he wrote that the incursion "could become a South Vietnam" for the Soviets.[34]

The former national security adviser was counting on his French interviewer not doing his homework. For in the memo to Carter the day after Christmas 1979, Brzezinski had said that the Soviet invasion "poses for us an extremely grave challenge, both internationally and domestically. While it could become a Soviet Vietnam, the initial effects of the intervention are likely to be adverse for us."[35] In a 1997 interview with CNN and the National Security Archive, Brzezinski depicted the U.S. aid to the insurgents not as a way to provoke the Soviets into invading but as a way to better position the United States for a Soviet invasion he saw as inevitable.[36] And in a memoir written before the Soviet Union collapsed, Brzezinski lamented that the Soviets might have refrained from invading Afghanistan, "had we been tougher sooner, had we drawn the line more clearly."[37]

Brzezinski's suggestion that the Soviet disaster in Afghanistan sprang from a clever plot by the White House would be easier to dismiss as a boast, crafted with the advantage of hindsight, were it not for the testimony of the Politburo members fretting about creeping American involvement in Afghanistan as a motivating factor behind the Soviet decision to invade. Well before the covert action approved by Carter in July 1979, Moscow directed its official press organs *Pravda* and *Izvestiya* to delegitimize the Afghan insurgents by depicting them as tools of Pakistan, China, Saudi Arabia, and on occasion the United States, and CIA reporting reflected this.[38] This validation from Moscow, however, must be viewed with caution. Keep in mind that the primary concern expressed privately in the Kremlin, as distinguished from Soviet pronouncements through controlled media, was not about U.S. aid to the insurgents, which in any case was negligible and had no discernible impact on the intensity of the uprising before the invasion. Rather, the Politburo worried about closer ties between the United States and the Amin government. That Kremlin fears of an Amin overture to the United States were exaggerated does not discredit them as a motivating factor behind Andropov's decisive support for the invasion.

These worries intensified after the September 1979 coup in which a failed assassination attempt on Amin (probably a botched KGB operation) resulted in Amin engineering a successful coup and taking over sole control of the government.[39] Political rivals of Amin marginalized by the coup then began feeding KGB officers in Afghanistan stories about Amin making deals with the Americans.[40] Those stories fell on receptive ears, for like many in Afghanistan's ruling communist elite, Amin had studied in the United States, earning a master's degree in education at Columbia University in the late 1950s, and was a leader of an Afghan student association that received some U.S. support. Boris Ivanov, the KGB's senior officer in Afghanistan, apparently suspected—erroneously—that the CIA had recruited Amin during his student days. Ivanov's suspicions, shared with Andropov, his boss in the Kremlin, contributed to the alarmist tone of Andropov's memo to Brezhnev that led to the decision to invade.[41]

The meetings between U.S. embassy officials and Amin in the fall of 1979 helped provide just enough reality to the KGB's otherwise groundless fears to fuel concern in Moscow. For their part, U.S. embassy officials reported to Washington that little had come of the meetings; there was some talk of providing U.S. grain to Afghanistan, but Amin offered nothing particular in return, certainly not a place for the CIA to set up a high-tech listening post. U.S. officials in Kabul had regarded Amin with suspicion after his role in the botched rescue mission in February 1979 that resulted in the death of Ambassador Dubs, who had been kidnapped by a shadowy Marxist splinter group. The involvement of Soviet officials in that rescue operation and the Afghan government's refusal to apologize for the bad outcome reinforced the idea in Washington that Amin remained firmly loyal to Moscow.[42] One U.S. embassy dispatch written late that summer indicated that an insurgent victory and the collapse of the pro-Soviet regime "would certainly serve the U.S. interest." It would do so, however, not by provoking a Soviet invasion but by showing other developing countries the hollowness of Moscow's boasts about historical inevitability and the triumph of communism. An opportunity for closer U.S. ties to Afghanistan, the embassy advised the State Department, would come not through the communist government but as a result of its collapse.[43]

Intelligence reporting in 1979 alerted the White House to Moscow's dissatisfaction with its client regime in Afghanistan, even to the point of speculating that Amin's seizure of sole power in September was a preemptive strike against a planned Soviet-backed move against Amin.[44] But U.S. intelligence did not attribute Moscow's dissatisfaction to a Westward tilt on the part of Amin. The CIA's view was that Moscow was frustrated with clumsy, sometimes brutal policies of the Kabul government, policies particularly identified with Amin and that appeared to be alienating the Muslim population and intensifying the insurgency.[45] Given the extreme brutality of the subsequent Soviet military operations in Afghanistan, eventually escalating to include bombings of villages and appalling civilian casualties, it requires a leap of imagination to ascribe the invasion to a Soviet wish to install a more people-friendly government in Kabul, though the absurdity of the idea does not rule it out. Of far greater concern to Moscow than the communist regime's brutal ineptitude in provoking insurgency with unwelcome land reforms and other Stalinist measures was Kabul's inability to crush the insurgency once it began.

A formal report immediately after the invasion by the Politburo's executive committee on Afghanistan, consisting of Andropov, Gromyko, Ustinov, and Ponomarev, derided Amin's "dictatorial methods of running the country, repressions, mass executions, and disregard for legal norms" that "have produced widespread discontent in the country." The thrust appears to have been post-facto justification for the removal of Amin. A clearer picture of what was in store for the abused people of Afghanistan appeared in Andropov's early-December handwritten memo to Brezhnev. While downplaying the need for a massive invasion force, Andropov, with chilling understatement, allowed that, "in the event of unforeseen complications, it would be wise to have a military group close to the border. In case of the deployment of military forces we could at the same time decide various questions pertaining to the liquidation of gangs."[46]

The initial movement of Soviet invasion forces into Afghanistan began on Christmas Eve 1979, with a major Soviet airlift of soldiers and supplies to bases along the northern border of Afghanistan and to key Afghan cities. It was a two-part operation: an overt invasion to emplace troops who could fight the insurgents where Afghan government forces had failed, and a covert coup to replace Amin with a regime more to Moscow's liking. Amin suspected nothing, viewing the initial Soviet incursion as a helping hand in coping with the insurgents. U.S. intelligence had, as already noted, spotted the Soviet troop concentrations along the northern border and alerted the White House to the possibility of an incursion. The idea of a combination invasion and coup to remove Amin was not part of the picture presented by U.S. intelligence. The surprise was complete, therefore, both in Washington and Kabul when, at sunset on December 27, 1979, Soviet paratroopers and accompanying KGB units stormed Amin's palace and executed him along with his brother, nephew, and several aides. A new government headed by Babrak Karmal, an Afghan communist who had been under Moscow's protection, was installed. Soviet-directed propaganda broadcasts announced that Afghanistan had been "liberated" from Amin's rule and denounced Amin as a "bloodthirsty spy of American imperialism."[47] The Soviets convinced no one with their claim that the military incursion was taking place at the request of the new government in Kabul.

INTELLIGENCE FALLOUT

Given the devastating impact of the Afghan adventure on the Soviet Union by the time it ended, it is easy to forget the stunning impact it had on Washington when it began. Coming on the heels of Soviet-backed moves in Ethiopia, Angola, Yemen, and elsewhere, the invasion of Afghanistan—the first full-blown Soviet military offensive outside the East Bloc since World War II, and the first of any kind since the 1968 crackdown on the "Prague Spring" anti-Soviet reforms in Czechoslovakia—appeared to signal a new level of aggressiveness in Moscow and a dismissive attitude toward the consequences of displeasing the United States. Despite documentary evidence that the CIA, the National Security Council, and President Carter personally had been tracking the possibility of Soviet intervention through most of the year, Carter expressed shock publicly over the Soviet invasion. On December 31, 1979, he told ABC News anchorman Frank Reynolds, "my opinion of the Russians has changed more drastically in the last week than even the previous two and a half years."[48] The comment, typical of Carter's tin ear for tone in a key sound bite, implied that he had, until that moment, had a somewhat benign regard for the Soviet Union, an opening that Ronald Reagan, weeks away from the pivotal Republican primaries, jumped on along with his supporters, the hawks of the Committee on the Present Danger. Senator Edward Kennedy (D-Mass.), challenging Carter from the left in the upcoming presidential election, accused Carter of negligence. At the president's first major news conference after the invasion, Carter was compelled to deny a reporter's summation of Kennedy's charge that "Afghanistan might not have happened if you'd paid more attention to the signs and been more resolute in advance."[49] Carter's expression of surprise is mystifying. Even in his memoir, in which he recounts following signs of impending Soviet intervention through most of that year, Carter described the invasion as "another shock to a world which yearned for peace."[50] In his private memo to Carter on December 26, 1979, Brzezinski undermined his later claim that the Soviet invasion of Afghanistan was not only a positive development, but one the Carter White House had worked to bring about. "We are now facing a regional crisis. Both Iran and Afghanistan are in turmoil," Brzezinski wrote the president. Soviet success in Afghanistan could lead to further gains in the region and, eventually, to achievement of "the age-long dream of Moscow to have direct access to the Indian Ocean."[51]

Of immediate concern to the administration was whether those Indian Ocean ambitions would take the Soviet Union in the direction of the vital, oil-rich Persian Gulf. As a result, just under a month after the invasion, Carter laid down an unambiguous warning to Moscow in his 1980 State of the Union address: a Soviet attack on the Persian Gulf region would be regarded in Washington as an attack on the United States. "The implications of the Soviet invasion of Afghanistan could pose the most serious threat to the peace since the Second World War," Carter asserted. "An attempt by any outside force to gain control of the Persian Gulf region will be regarded as an assault on the vital interests of the United States of America, and such an assault will be repelled by any means necessary, including military force."[52] This stand, which became known as the Carter Doctrine, was the most direct threat by a U.S. president toward Moscow since the Cuban missile crisis.

Yet only in passing had U.S. intelligence before the invasion considered the Soviet Union's long-standing quest for a warm-water port as part of the calculus of the Afghan crisis. Because Afghanistan itself is landlocked, further moves by the Soviets would be required to achieve that ambition, and the issue received relatively light treatment in the intelligence documents to which we have access.[53] The post-invasion specter of a Soviet move on the oil-rich Persian Gulf and the Carter administration's corresponding Carter Doctrine, promulgated less then a month after the invasion, point to a more serious intelligence community failure. Even as it doubted that the Soviets would invade Afghanistan, the intelligence community could have and should have considered the global strategic implications were this to happen. According to General William E. Odom, then a top aide to Brzezinski, the president had been concerned about Soviet pressure in the Persian Gulf region as far back as 1977 and had been considering a response that would evolve into a "Persian Gulf Security Framework" in early March 1979.[54] These strategic concerns intensified with the eruption of the Iranian hostage crisis in November 1979. Yet the available intelligence analysis before the Soviet invasion of Afghanistan does not consider the brewing Afghan crisis in the context of broader regional Soviet ambitions. The intelligence community's exculpatory October 1980 evaluation of its own performance did not address this failing, even though the document devoted several paragraphs to the problem of whether further moves by Soviet forces into Afghanistan or Iran could be detected in the preparation stages.[55]

Although the intelligence community reporting on Afghanistan remained classified in the immediate aftermath of the Soviet invasion, there was ample evidence in the public domain that the Carter administration had considered the possibility of a Soviet incursion and had presumably done so based at least in part on what it was being told by CIA. As early as March 23, 1979, the same month when the Politburo first discussed the possibility of invasion, the State Department sent Moscow a formal note that the United States and its allies would "regard external involvement in Afghanistan's internal problems as a serious matter, with the potential for heightening tensions and destabilizing the situation in the entire region."[56] With Carter's approval, Brzezinski in early August 1979 gave a speech denouncing foreign interference on peoples with deep religious and nationalist traditions, remarks that White House sources assured the press were a reference to Soviet interference in Afghanistan. On September 19, the State Department said publicly that it had repeated to Moscow its "opposition to any intervention in Afghan internal affairs." On December 15, the State Department formally asked the Soviet government, both in Washington and Moscow, for an explanation of events in Afghanistan. The requests were brusquely rebuffed. Again on December 21 (after weeks in which U.S. policymakers had been absorbed with the hostage crisis in Iran), administration officials disclosed to the press details of the Soviet troop buildup and said Washington had voiced concern to Moscow several times.[57]

Clearly the performance of U.S. intelligence had been imperfect. The tenor of CIA reporting through most of 1979 was that a full-blown Soviet invasion was unlikely. Even as the attack approached, intelligence reporting said a gradual insertion of limited forces to protect the existing government was the most likely development. The Agency missed the Soviet intent to overthrow Amin as part of an invasion scenario and missed the primary importance the Kremlin placed on the possibility that Afghanistan would shift its allegiance to the West. But the CIA had raised the possibility of a Soviet incursion in March 1979, within two weeks of when the Politburo first discussed the idea, giving the Carter administration time to develop counterstrategies and to signal Moscow that negative consequences would ensue if it carried out an attack. The Agency had tracked the possibility throughout the year and engaged directly with the National Security Council and Carter in developing a covert action plan. Based on Brzezinski's subsequent testimony, he had concluded by early in the year that a Soviet invasion was a strong possibility, enough so that the CIA was instructed to carefully consider whether its covert aid to insurgents might provoke the Soviets to opt for invasion. On September 19, 1979, Brzezinski notified Carter that the likelihood of a Soviet invasion of Afghanistan was increasing and called a meeting for the next day of senior officials to deal with that contingency.[58]

Afghanistan, then, stands as an example of the difference between substantive intelligence failure and perceived intelligence failure. Without question, on the substantive side, the CIA failed to predict the invasion until shortly before it happened. Nevertheless, the Carter administration had—well in advance—all the information it needed to issue a stern warning to Moscow. The Carter administration, not the CIA, made the decision to downplay its warnings. On the perception side, the objective fact that the CIA had guessed that the Soviets would refrain from full-blown invasion opened the door to intense and politicized criticism from the right that lumped the Carter White House and the CIA together as being naive in their view of the predatory nature of the Soviet Union. That criticism then fueled a shift in viewpoint at the CIA that influenced subsequent judgments, as we will explore, and contributed to the degree to which the Agency was slow in perceiving the decline of the Soviet Union. Carter's own expression of shock over the invasion helped reinforce the idea that policymakers had been caught by surprise, and therefore, by implication, had been badly served by the people charged with warning of such threats. Neither Carter nor his adversaries on the political right had any incentive to defend the CIA.

The impression of intelligence failure also held sway at Langley. MacEachin recounts a dark joke then in circulation. The CIA, the joke went, had correctly identified the downside for the Soviet Union of invading Afghanistan—it was the Soviets who got it wrong.[59] That is to say, the CIA correctly foresaw that Afghanistan was a stony Central Asian trap that would absorb Soviet treasure and lives in an open-ended commitment; the Soviet Union had failed to foresee the risks involved and took the reckless plunge.

Brzezinski's NSC ordered CIA Director Turner to produce the classified report on the intelligence community's performance on the Afghan question. The ostensible purpose was to determine whether a Soviet invasion of Western Europe could similarly catch the intelligence community by surprise. The unspoken message was that the White House believed the CIA had failed in the Afghan case.[60] The resulting Interagency Intelligence Memorandum was published at the Top Secret level in October 1980, less than a month before the presidential election. The report reached two key conclusions: first, that "the U.S. intelligence collection system proved equal to the task of providing analysts with sufficiently detailed, accurate and timely data to allow them to reach essentially correct conclusions" so that "no key policymaker should have been surprised by the invasion"; and second, that the Soviets followed in broad outline "their doctrine for mobilization and the initiation of hostilities" that one would expect to see in an invasion of Western Europe.[61] The report also concluded that "the majority of decision-makers," names unspecified, "apparently felt that the flow of intelligence during the fall and early winter of 1979 had given them warning that the Soviets could make a move into Afghanistan."[62] Since its declassification after the end of the Cold War, the document has become our main source of information on what the intelligence community had said throughout much of 1979 about the Soviet threat to invade Afghanistan. Needless to say, no one in the Carter White House, with the election weeks away, was prepared to leak this document to the press. The belief that U.S. intelligence had been caught badly off guard by a surprise Soviet attack would persist.

Four years after this study, the CIA, now under the Reagan administration, with William Casey in charge and Robert Gates, who had been on Carter's NSC staff in 1979, as his deputy, took a sterner view of CIA performance in the Afghan crisis. An article in the classified edition of the CIA publication *Studies in Intelligence* listed Afghanistan among "instances when the intelligence community did not adequately anticipate significant events on the world scene."[63] The authors of the article found that before mid-December 1979, when the Soviet buildup was becoming apparent, virtually every intelligence community report that considered the possibility of a Soviet invasion of Afghanistan judged it unlikely:

> The community held to a premise that the disadvantages of intervention outweighed the advantages and concluded therefore that the Soviets would act rationally in accordance with our perception of Soviet self-interest. As real as the penalties to the Soviets have proved to be, we failed to comprehend the imperatives of Soviet policy as they perceived them. We had a clear understanding of their capabilities. But we misjudged their intentions.[64]

Even years after the end of the Cold War, uncertainty persisted within the intelligence community as to how to evaluate CIA performance in warning of the Soviet invasion of Afghanistan. We have cited frequently MacEachin's detailed study done in 2002 at Harvard's John F. Kennedy School of Government following a CIA career in which he rose to deputy director for intelligence—the Agency's top analyst post. In that study, published by the CIA, MacEachin concluded that "The military intervention the Soviets carried out in the last week of December 1979—particularly its timing and scope—came as a surprise to the U.S. intelligence community."[65] Three years later, MacEachin co-chaired a panel at Georgetown University that rendered a more favorable judgment of the CIA's performance. It concluded, "The case of the Soviet invasion of Afghanistan does not seem to be one of traditional 'intelligence failure.' U.S. leaders were not surprised by the invasion because they lacked clear evidence of Soviet military preparations and movements in and around Afghanistan prior to the invasion." Rather, the problem was that distractions such as the Iranian hostage crisis and the SALT II negotiations, divisions between the hard-line Brzezinski and softer-line Secretary of State Cyrus Vance, and "wishful thinking" about Soviet intentions prevented a more focused response to the building crisis.[66]

A similar duality of opinion has appeared in Gates's writings. In his 1997 memoir, Gates credited the CIA with perceiving early on the risk of Soviet intervention in Afghanistan and cited evidence to back it up.[67] He was, at that point, a former CIA director taking pride in the performance of the place where he spent most of his career. In 1991, with the Soviet Union troubled but still in existence and with his own confirmation as Director of Central Intelligence on the line, Gates told the Senate Select Committee on Intelligence that the CIA "failed to foresee the invasion of Afghanistan in 1979."[68] The daylight between those two assessments clearly reflects timing, politics, and point of view as much as the actual circumstances in 1979. In his confirmation hearing, Gates was defending himself against charges that he politicized intelligence during his time as Casey's deputy during the Reagan administration. Part of his defense involved demonstrating that the CIA during the Carter years had failed to fully appreciate the level of Soviet aggressiveness in expanding its influence in the developing world, in places such as Ethiopia, Angola, Yemen—and Afghanistan—and that he, Gates, took it upon himself to ensure a course correction at Langley to more accurately gauge the Soviet threat.

As we have seen, Brzezinski and Gates, from their NSC posts, had been actively engaged with the CIA through most of 1979 in devising a covert action program intended, however modestly, to exacerbate the Soviet Union's problems in Afghanistan. If the idea was not quite to provoke an invasion, it was to make Moscow's choices more difficult. Brzezinski and two of his senior deputies, Gates and Odom, have taken some pride in claiming, not without justification, that some of the key anti-Soviet policies generally identified with Reagan—the defense buildup and the covert engagement in Afghanistan—actually began under the Carter administration. As hard-liners toward the Soviet Union themselves, they had the same incentive as Reagan's hard-liners to distinguish their own outlook toward Moscow from that of the CIA. In this way, officials in a position to know that the CIA had tracked the Soviet threat to Afghanistan felt in no way compelled to defend the Agency after the invasion against the charge that it had missed the threat.

In retrospect, as Brzezinski has acknowledged, the critical U.S. failure with regard to Afghanistan occurred not at Langley but at the White House in the decision to soft-pedal the remonstrations with Moscow over the possibility of a Soviet invasion. The administration had its reasons. Negotiations on the SALT II treaty were completed in May 1979, and a signing ceremony with Carter and Brezhnev in Vienna was set for June 18, 1979—the gathering at which Gates observed Brezhnev being carried by his bodyguards and corrected by his subordinates. The Senate took up ratification of the treaty, which set limits on offensive nuclear weapons and ICBM launchers, in October. Carter's decision to use relatively quiet diplomatic channels to express concern about the possibility of a Soviet invasion of Afghanistan clearly stemmed from a desire not to upset the SALT II process. Overtaken by events in December, SALT II was never ratified by the Senate, though both nations honored its provisions.

DEFEAT OF THE SOFT-LINE VIEW

The CIA's handling of the Afghanistan case is vital to judging Agency performance in predicting the collapse of the Soviet Union because the Soviet debacle in Afghanistan was one of the key events that hastened that collapse. The episode neatly illustrates the way in which the CIA found itself without allies on the question of the Soviet threat at the end of Carter's presidency and the beginning of Reagan's. Both administrations had incentives to deride the CIA for failing to accurately perceive the threat—Carter to explain his hesitance in adopting a harder line, Reagan to better make that hard line a reality. Gates, one of the few to move from one administration to the other, returned to the CIA, where he made sure the Agency took in the criticism. The result was that the CIA outlook shifted from slowness to perceive Soviet expansionism in the 1970s to a blindness in the following decade to the erosion of Soviet power brought on, in no small part, by the Kremlin's imperial overreach in Afghanistan.

The Afghan invasion buttressed Team B's thesis that growing Soviet strength would manifest itself in a more aggressive and expansionist Soviet policy worldwide. In the view of Washington's anti-Soviet hard-liners, Afghanistan was not a special case brought on by special circumstances but was part of a trend. A National Intelligence Estimate issued in November 1981, at the height of the Solidarity crisis in Poland, reflected this view, stating in its first of several "Key Judgments" that "the Soviet goal is clear-cut force superiority—conventional, nuclear and chemical—with which to fight and win a short war; one in which NATO would be overwhelmed by the scale and violence of the [Warsaw] Pact's offensive before the allies could bring their strength to bear." However, the CIA and the majority of the intelligence community were not ready to accept Team B's thesis in full. In the next paragraph, the estimate cautioned that Kremlin leaders "remain profoundly skeptical that nuclear conflict can be controlled."[69]

By this point, with the Reagan administration in its first year in office, the caveats and nuances of CIA-generated estimates mattered little in Washington Cold War politics. The Reagan military buildup was under way, bolstered not so much by a change in attitude at Langley as by the enthusiastic support of the Pentagon and its intelligence branch, the Defense Intelligence Agency. That year, DIA began issuing an unclassified annual report on the Soviet threat called *Soviet Military Power*, a decidedly alarmist look at what DIA saw as an across-the-board bid for military superiority by Moscow.[70]

That first year of the Reagan presidency provided perhaps the best opportunity—an opportunity missed—for the CIA to have at least begun to get a glimmer of the transformational events that were to come later in the decade. The opportunity was the Solidarity crisis in Poland, an event we can now study in detail thanks to the declassification of intelligence documents and internal deliberations in Washington, Warsaw, and Moscow.

THE CIA AND THE POLISH CRISIS

Within months of the Soviet invasion of Afghanistan, crisis in another communist-bloc state once again tested the U.S. government's intelligence and response reflexes. As in Afghanistan, the intelligence concerning the Solidarity uprising in Poland was impressively thorough in some places but frustratingly imprecise in others, particularly at the critical moment. Once again, the basic question for intelligence was how the Soviet Union would respond to unrest in a client state. Would Moscow leave it to the regime in Warsaw to deal with the Solidarity labor organization headed by Lech Walesa? Or would Warsaw Pact forces, led by the Soviet army, invade Poland and crush the dissident group? In no small part as a result of the CIA's failure to predict Soviet intervention in Afghanistan well in advance, it then failed to predict Soviet nonintervention in Poland, though to its credit in both cases, CIA reporting was thorough enough in considering various contingencies that policymakers should not have been taken completely by surprise. The ubiquitous Douglas MacEachin, centrally involved in the Polish crisis at the CIA and writing years later from an academic post, reached an almost identical assessment of CIA failings in the Polish crisis as he did in his evaluations of Agency analysis concerning Afghanistan. The

CIA had plenty of accurate raw intelligence in both cases, yet both times its mindset, its assumptions about Soviet behavior, proved mistaken, albeit in opposite directions. "The bottom line is that the intelligence deficiency was not in the 'gathering' of information, but in how the information was interpreted, and how its potential implications were portrayed," MacEachin wrote of the CIA's performance in the Polish crisis.[71] Likewise on Afghanistan, the Agency leaned against an invasion scenario, "*not* because of an absence of intelligence information on Soviet preparations for the move. It was that the operation being prepared was contrary to what intelligence analysts had *expected* Moscow would be willing to do."[72]

Many of the elements feeding concern in the Kremlin about the situation in Afghanistan in 1979 also pertained in the Polish crisis a year later, following the rise of the Solidarity movement in August 1980: worry about a powerful and popular "counterrevolutionary" uprising in a communist country bordering the USSR; religious opposition to a secular communist regime; doubts about the loyalty of client-state armed forces; frustration with ineffective countermeasures by the client regime; mid-crisis leadership changes within the client regime; suspicion of CIA meddling to worsen the situation; early consideration of the introduction of Soviet forces; overt signaling through military maneuvers just over the border that invasion was a possibility; and a strong preference in Moscow that the client regime handle the problem on its own. The difference, in Moscow as well as Washington, was that the Polish crisis came *after* the Afghan invasion, the subsequent rift in U.S.-Soviet relations, the highly negative world reaction and the emergence of a stubborn Afghan insurgency. The painful lessons of the earlier events informed analysis and decision-making on the latter, in both capitals, but was seldom acknowledged by U.S. or Soviet leaders, at least in the records we have available to us today. For the Kremlin, the many political and military downsides of the Afghan invasion now becoming apparent, combined with the difficulty of taking on a second major military intervention, led to a decision not to intervene in Poland. For Washington, the intelligence community's failure to see developments through much of 1979 as a likely precursor to a Soviet invasion of Afghanistan and the failure of the Carter administration to loudly warn Moscow of the consequences clearly shaped assessments of and responses to intelligence on Poland over the next two years.

One of the intelligence errors during the buildup to the Afghan invasion was the CIA's failure to perceive the importance of that country, a relatively recent addition to Moscow's stable of client states, to the leaders in the Kremlin. No such doubt clouded analysis of Poland, the largest of the Warsaw Pact countries, with the largest military force, and a bulwark of Soviet bloc forces opposite NATO. In 1977, a year after a sharp increase in food prices provoked worker riots in Poland, the CIA concluded that the Soviet Union obviously preferred not to have to intervene there but that if it perceived a threat to the communist client state, or an unwillingness of Poland's leaders to keep order, "armed Soviet intervention could and probably would take place."[73] The substantial risk of stubborn Polish resistance to such a move would be offset by the assertion of Soviet power and its impact elsewhere in the Soviet sphere. The inevitably negative reaction in the West would be of relatively little concern, according to the CIA's analysis. This pre-Afghan baseline belief that the Soviets would be willing to use force to maintain control in Eastern Europe was no doubt informed by the CIA's failure to predict the Soviet invasion of Czechoslovakia in 1968. Though the Soviets had been less blunt in signaling the level of their concern to Prague than they would be in 1980 and 1981 during the Polish crisis, a classified CIA post-mortem of the crushing of the "Prague Spring" concluded that the Soviets had done little to hide preparation for military intervention and that the intelligence failure at the CIA stemmed from a misreading of Soviet intentions.[74] During the Polish crisis, it sometimes seemed as though the intelligence analysts considered the implications of Afghanistan more in terms of their own perception that they had failed in the earlier crisis than in terms of how Soviet experience in Afghanistan would weigh in Kremlin decision-making on Poland. We see in the available declassified intelligence reports a clear effort to avoid repeating the mistakes of the Afghan crisis but scant mention of Soviet calculations through the lens of their increasingly painful experience fighting the Mujahadin.

It is a testament to the complex dynamics of the Soviet decline and collapse that Moscow's decision to intervene in Afghanistan and its subsequent decision against intervention in Poland each contributed significantly to the collapse of the Soviet empire. The Afghanistan invasion weakened the Soviet Union from within, sapping resources in a no-win war that became increasingly unpopular in the USSR and led to hitherto inconceivable domestic questioning of the competency of the regime in Moscow. The Polish crisis weakened the Soviet Union from without by showing the satellite states that internal dissent would be tolerated to a surprising degree and that a crackdown, if it became necessary, would have to come from within the satellite country; it would not come

from the Soviet Union. Both of these dynamics—Afghanistan as Soviet quagmire, Solidarity as fundamental challenge to Soviet empire—were noted by
senior U.S. officials at the time. We have seen how the CIA viewed the military
challenges in Afghanistan as so serious for the Soviets that Moscow would opt
against invasion; we have seen Brzezinski alerting Carter to the possibility,
albeit a slim one, that Afghanistan could become the Soviet Union's Vietnam.
Likewise concerning Poland, a National Intelligence Estimate, written just
under a year before the Polish premier, General Wojciech Jaruzelski, declared
martial law, opened: "The present crisis in Poland constitutes the most serious
and broadly based challenge to Communist rule in more than a decade."[75] By
June 1981, the intelligence community judged the crisis as one of the USSR's
"most significant and complex foreign policy problems since World War II."[76]
But in the broader stream of intelligence reporting on the Soviet Union in the
late 1970s and early '80s, these flashes of insight appear as exceptions to a general belief in the intelligence community that the Soviet empire was expanding
and that challenges to Soviet hegemony within that empire were manageable
because of Moscow's willingness to deal with them harshly.

There were two distinct phases to the Polish crisis, both in Europe and in
the United States. The first phase, in 1980, came on President Carter's watch
and involved the clearest signals and, declassified Soviet archives show, the
gravest danger of Soviet intervention. The second phase, in 1981, encompassed
the first year of the Reagan administration, culminating with the declaration
of martial law by Poland's communist government on the morning of December 13, 1981, and the sudden crackdown on the Solidarity movement—without
the involvement of Soviet or other non-Polish Warsaw Pact troops.

Stung by the miscalculation of Soviet plans for Afghanistan in 1979, U.S.
intelligence considered the possibility of Soviet intervention on a massive scale
in Poland a more likely outcome than in Afghanistan and reported this view
repeatedly over the course of the crisis in 1980 and 1981. Several times during
the crisis, the CIA would explicitly warn policymakers that a Soviet invasion
appeared imminent. MacEachin, both a senior CIA participant in the intelligence analysis on the Polish crisis and author of a later study using declassified archives, points out that the influence of events in Afghanistan, and the
perception that CIA failed to correctly evaluate those events, "cannot be discounted." Indeed, during much of the first year of the Polish crisis, senior CIA
analysts would have been simultaneously evaluating the risk of Soviet incursion and preparing the report ordered by the NSC on whether, in light of the

intelligence lapses on Afghanistan, the CIA could be relied upon to predict a Soviet invasion of Western Europe. In this environment, observes MacEachin, "There was a clear inclination among senior intelligence officials to 'err on the high side,'"[77] intelligence-speak for emphasizing the worst-case scenario.

To be sure, CIA assessments were based on more than just unpleasant bureaucratic memories of the Afghan crisis. In 1980, the Kremlin undertook concrete planning for an invasion of Poland and made some of that planning overt—in the form of military exercises on Poland's periphery—as a clear warning signal to Solidarity, the Polish government, and the West alike. The CIA interpreted these moves as genuine preparations, and the Soviet archives indicate that they were, at the very least, contingency plans. We have, for example, an August 28, 1980, memo to the Politburo by a special commission of senior Politburo members headed by chief Soviet ideologue Mikhail Suslov and including Andropov, Gromyko, and Ustinov, the three leading advocates of the Afghan invasion. Noting that the Solidarity "strike movement is operating on a countrywide scale," the Soviet leaders outlined plans to mobilize 25,000 troops, and possibly five to seven more divisions, or about 100,000 troops, as an invasion force "if the situation in Poland deteriorates further."[78] This secret planning was matched by public signal-sending in late September 1980 after completion of a scheduled Warsaw Pact military exercise when Soviet Marshal Victor Kulikov, the supreme commander of Warsaw Pact forces, announced that the Pact was "ready to defend the revolutionary achievements of socialism," presumably against all enemies, foreign or domestic.[79]

Even as the Kremlin became increasingly set against sending Soviet forces into Poland, the Politburo strove to maintain the impression that invasion was a possibility. An April 1981 memo from the same Politburo special commission said that to the extent Solidarity had failed to convert its labor organizing power into political power, "that is primarily because of its fear that Soviet troops would be introduced." The commission recommended, "As a deterrent to counterrevolution, maximally exploit fears of internal reactionaries and international imperialism that the Soviet Union might send its troops into Poland."[80] Poland's leaders varied in their views on Soviet intervention. Through most of the two-year crisis, the records indicate that they strove to avoid that eventuality; by December of 1981, however, as Jaruzelski prepared to declare martial law, he sought the Kremlin's assurances that Soviet and Warsaw Pact forces stood ready to intervene if Polish forces proved unable to enforce the crackdown on their own.[81]

The Polish leaders were consistent, like the Soviets, in supporting a display of the potential for Soviet invasion. An April 1981 memo of a meeting of Polish leaders with Marshal Kulikov reports that a military exercise, "SOYUZ-81," was extended "explicitly as a result of the requests of comrades Jaruzelski and [Poland's General Secretary Stanislaw] Kania. They wanted to utilize the exercises to strengthen their position."[82]

In addition to spy satellites and a very active U.S. embassy in Warsaw, the CIA had a source within the Polish hierarchy directly involved in developing plans for declaration of martial law. On December 4, 1980, in a coded dispatch headed "Very Urgent!" this source, Colonel Ryszard Kuklinski, warned that the Warsaw government had decided to clear the way for a Soviet-led incursion into Poland involving eighteen divisions—not the four divisions outlined in the Politburo report unbeknownst to the CIA, or the three divisions U.S. spy satellites detected mobilizing once poor weather in Central Europe finally cleared later that month. The message warned the CIA that three Soviet armies were set to invade Poland on December 8. Contradicting CIA doubts about the reliability of Polish forces in such a circumstance, Kuklinski reported "with bitterness" that "there hasn't even been thought of military opposition by Polish forces to the military action of the Warsaw Pact."[83] Two days before Kuklinski's warning, CIA Director Stansfield Turner had told the White House that another Soviet exercise near the Polish border, unprecedented for that time of year, led him to conclude that "the Soviets are readying their forces for military intervention in Poland."[84] Now, with the Kuklinski warning in hand, Turner was even more explicit. On December 6, Turner said the CIA had concluded that the Soviets were about to invade.[85]

The now-defeated Carter administration, having been reminded almost daily during the presidential campaign of its failure to adequately warn Moscow of the consequences of invading Afghanistan, determined to be clear and public in its warnings on the Polish crisis. The White House released a statement on December 7 indicating that "preparations for a possible Soviet intervention in Poland appear to have been completed" and repeating past warnings that the consequences of such an act for U.S.-Soviet relations would be "very adverse."[86] MacEachin has judged that the Politburo had already decided against invading Poland by the time the White House statement was issued. Thus he discounts the idea that Carter's public and official remonstrations prompted Moscow to reverse an invasion decision.[87] What can't be discounted is how the more active U.S. response to the Polish crisis weighed in Moscow's calculations in the ensuing year during which, we now know from the archives, Moscow moved toward a policy—kept secret from the world but made explicit to Polish communist leaders—that it would not intervene militarily. Moscow's policy was to pressure the regime in Warsaw to handle the problem with harsh measures but measures imposed entirely by the Polish government. As in the Afghan crisis, the CIA was particularly weak in assessing the impact of U.S. policymaking on Soviet thinking, admittedly a highly subjective and constantly shifting sphere of intelligence analysis. Obviously, neither Carter nor Reagan advocated martial law in Poland. But it is worth noting that the outcome Moscow clearly preferred could be said to conform with the policy the Carter administration's State Department laid down in the summer of 1980: "The matter is for the Poles themselves to resolve without any foreign interference."[88]

Whereas Agency analysts had predicted an incremental and modest Soviet military involvement in Afghanistan, if it became necessary at all, CIA reporting on Poland contemplated a massive Soviet invasion, sized to crush any possible resistance from Poland's army, whose loyalty to the communist regime the CIA doubted. In June 1981, a report in the *National Intelligence Daily*, essentially a classified newspaper distributed broadly to cleared officials in the U.S. government, estimated that "at least 50 Soviet and Warsaw Pact combat divisions and additional support units would be needed to invade" and that the ensuing war could yield 600,000 to 800,000 casualties on both sides.[89] There is no evidence in the declassified Soviet archives that anything so massive was ever contemplated during the two-year crisis. The key failures by the CIA lay in discounting the possibility that the Polish government could impose martial law and crush the Solidarity uprising without Soviet military help, and in underestimating Moscow's aversion to intervention.[90] Indeed, the CIA's emphasis on Soviet invasion was premised in no small part on a judgment that the Warsaw government could not handle Solidarity on its own. While it rated Kuklinski's reporting highly, and rightly so because of his position within the Polish government, the CIA discounted his observation in the December 1980 warning that Polish forces were not going to oppose the Soviets. As in the case of Afghanistan, the intelligence failure with regard to Poland was not absolute. In April 1981, with invasion alarm bells once again sounding at Langley, CIA Director William Casey told Reagan in a note accompanying the latest intelligence reporting that Moscow would "move heaven and earth" to avoid having to invade Poland and to get the Warsaw government to crush the Solidarity uprising on its own.[91]

Gates, meanwhile, made the intellectual leap in grasping that the absence of a Soviet invasion was emerging as the most significant development in the crisis. The passing of the April 1981 crisis without a military move by the Soviets prompted Gates to urge his boss, Casey, to consider "the prospect that the Soviets will not intervene in Poland and that the reform movement will continue." Gates went on, "We may be witnessing one of the most significant developments in the post war period which, if unchecked, may foreshadow a profound change in this decade in the system Stalin created both inside the Soviet Union and in Eastern Europe."[92]

It was a brilliant and highly accurate assessment but one that must be understood as an exception in an intelligence flow that continued to see Moscow as both puppet-master and menace. The occasional intelligence commentary that looks good in retrospect also tends to obscure the broader picture being presented by intelligence at the time, which was that the crisis was worsening and that the Soviet Union would be forced to turn to invasion as the solution. The key tactical intelligence failure was in concluding that martial law was not a viable solution because Polish forces could not be relied upon. "Soviet prospects for convincing the Polish regime to declare martial law are limited" because of the regime's reluctance, the CIA judged in June 1981. "There is little chance, moreover, that martial law could be instituted without sparking widespread unrest, which would, in turn, probably trigger a Soviet military intervention."[93] The CIA saw Moscow's ultimate nonintervention as a case-specific choice and, aside from Gates's prescient commentary, did not consider the possibility that a more profound policy Rubicon had been crossed. When Poland declared martial law on December 13, 1981, the primary response in Washington was one of surprise, though in comparison with the Afghan experience, policymakers tended not to be overly harsh in blaming the CIA.

The notion that there could have been any surprise is hard to understand based on the record. By October 1981, the CIA knew from Kuklinski that Jaruzelski had ordered preparations for imposing martial law.[94] Notwithstanding the exceedingly restricted handling of source information from Kuklinski, Bobby Ray Inman, the senior CIA intelligence analyst at the time, has said that some twenty top officials, including President Reagan, were informed of Kuklinski's identity and the substance of his reporting.[95] The Defense Intelligence Agency, in early November, reported that "events suggest martial law may be imposed in Poland this winter."[96] Overall, however, the intelligence community leaned toward Soviet intervention as the more likely outcome.

While in both Afghanistan and Poland the CIA failed to consider the impact of its own actions on events, the failure in the Polish instance is less excusable. In the Afghan case, we have seen that the CIA was unaware of overheated KGB fears of CIA scheming with the Afghan communist government. In the absence of such scheming by the CIA beyond the nascent insurgent aid program, and without access to the Politburo deliberations that we may now read in the open press, it is at least understandable that the Agency did not fully grasp the level of Moscow's concern, or paranoia. In Poland, the failure was more direct. On November 7, 1981, in an operation worthy of a spy thriller, the CIA extracted Kuklinski and his family from Poland amid growing concerns that his espionage activity was at risk of discovery by the KGB. MacEachin has described how the sudden disappearance of Kuklinski and his family from Warsaw would have been interpreted by Jaruzelski as a defection to the West, particularly since the Polish government was already aware that a source within its ranks had leaked the martial law plan to the Americans. The communist government would have immediately understood Kuklinski's disappearance as a defection and reached the logical and correct conclusion that Washington would now be aware of its martial law plans. The CIA, MacEachin reasons, should have understood this as well, and alerted policymakers that Warsaw knew that its plans had been revealed to the Americans. Jaruzelski, the CIA should have understood, would then have been in the position of awaiting a warning from Reagan urging Warsaw to refrain from a martial law crackdown.[97] No such warning arrived because key U.S. policymakers had discounted that possibility in favor of direct Soviet intervention. A decade after these events, with the Berlin Wall down, the Cold War over, and the founders of Solidarity in power in Poland, Jaruzelski—concerned about his standing in his native country given bitter memories of his role in ordering the crackdown—maintained that he interpreted the nonreaction from the United States in November and early December of 1981 as an explicit signal of tacit acceptance of the martial law option. Washington had already made clear that it preferred a Polish solution to the crisis. Martial law, Jaruzelski told a French television interviewer in 1992, "was the lesser evil for everyone. It enabled the Poles to avoid disaster." He rejected as an "insult" the idea that he was acting on Moscow's behalf.[98]

The Soviet Union's skill at what the Russians call "*maskirovka*," the art of deceiving an adversary and denying him critical information as to your intentions, played a role in the intelligence community's performance in both the

Afghan and Polish crises. In Afghanistan, the Soviet Union went to lengths to conceal its extreme displeasure with the Amin regime in Kabul, not so much to keep the United States in the dark as to ensure that Amin himself could be captured by the Soviet special forces and KGB officers sent to remove him by summary execution. In Poland, Moscow, having seriously considered invading for a time, went on threatening invasion even after it had decided internally against it. Educated—one might even say burned—by the experience in Afghanistan, the Carter administration remonstrated loudly to Moscow over the threatened invasion of Poland in late 1980, a move that may well have contributed to Moscow's determination the following year against intervention. It was vital to Moscow that its decision not to invade remain secret, however, because the Politburo wanted to give Solidarity a reason to curb its labor actions and hoped the Warsaw government would be moved to crack down, if for no other reason than to avert Soviet intervention.

Whether intentionally or otherwise, there is some indication that Moscow deceived even its communist ally on this point. For as the imposition of martial law approached, Jaruzelski—far from acting to avoid Soviet intervention—pressed Moscow for a promise that Soviet troops would come to his rescue if needed.[99] In a conversation three nights before the implementation of martial law, Marshal Kulikov assured Jaruzelski, "The question of assisting you in the event that your own resources have become exhausted is being addressed at the General Staff Level."[100] On December 10, 1981, in a Politburo discussion, Andropov averred that the Soviet marshal may have "spoken incorrectly" in assuring Jaruzelski. "We can't risk such a step," Andropov told his colleagues. "We don't intend to introduce troops into Poland. That is the proper position and we must adhere to it until the end."[101]

The Kremlin archives show clearly that nonintervention by the Soviet Union in Poland was a concrete decision made in Moscow, not a possibility cut off by Warsaw's declaration of martial law. In the extraordinary transcript of the December 10 Politburo conversation, certainly one of the most revealing documents of the latter Cold War years to come out of the Kremlin archives, the Soviet leaders' depth of concern over the situation in Poland stands in contrast with their unwillingness to act, not only by military means but even with economic aid to ease Poland's crisis. Nikolai Baibakov, chief of Soviet state planning, briefed his comrades on his just-completed trip to Warsaw for meetings with Jaruzelski, whom Baibakov described as "extremely neurotic." He reported that the Communist Party structure in Poland "no longer exists" and that the Polish military's ability to crack down on Solidarity was all that remained to be salvaged from the situation.[102]

Clearly the political weakness in the Soviet system manifested by the Solidarity crisis was apparent to the CIA and the Reagan administration. The CIA's assumption that the Polish military could not be relied on to crack down on Solidarity, a mistaken assumption, as it turned out, signified—to a fault—that it perceived the cracks in the Soviet empire and the threat posed by the labor uprising. What the CIA appears to have missed, based on its subsequent reporting, was the degree to which the Solidarity crisis and the war in Afghanistan were sapping Soviet resolve.

The nonintervention decision in Poland, in retrospect, appears to be a major turning point in the Cold War. At the time, U.S. intelligence saw it as a pragmatic choice based on the bloodbath likely to ensue in Poland and the potentially exorbitant price Moscow would pay in the international community. So far as U.S. intelligence was concerned, both the Afghan and Polish crises were resolved the old-fashioned way, by brute force. That Moscow had to intervene in Afghanistan while Polish forces managed the crackdown on their own was of relatively minor consequence. The vulnerabilities in the Soviet system exposed by the two crises were not lost on the CIA. In the case of Afghanistan, the Agency embarked on an escalating, decade-long campaign of support for the Mujahadin insurgents that sharply increased the cost of the Soviet occupation and undoubtedly contributed to Gorbachev's decision to withdraw forces. Under the usually aggressive Casey, the CIA's Directorate of Operations, the clandestine service, made a conscious decision to be more reserved in its support for Solidarity. Whereas in Afghanistan the CIA spent liberally on weapons and combat training for guerrilla fighters, aid to Solidarity consisted mainly of printing presses, smuggled books, and propaganda operations.[103]

The intelligence challenges posed by the two crises were considerable, and in some of the hard, day-to-day work of tracking events, the CIA performed well. The CIA can be forgiven for failing to learn the substance of the closed-door sessions in which the Politburo decided firmly against intervention in Poland, for this was a supreme state secret that remained unrevealed until after the Soviet breakup and the opening of Kremlin archives. The CIA's human intelligence network in the Soviet Union was still intact in 1981, four years before its destruction by CIA mole Aldrich Ames. But the Agency's sources did not extend to the Politburo's inner circle.

The Brezhnev Doctrine, it now turns out, was ended not by Gorbachev but by Brezhnev himself. Nonintervention in Poland was indeed a turning point in the Cold War, as historians such as John Lewis Gaddis and Matthew J. Ouimet have argued.[104] But it was a turning point to which the CIA was not privy and that Moscow wished to keep secret. The blind spot at the CIA would continue well into the 1980s. In May 1987, Gorbachev told a gathering of Warsaw Pact leaders that the Soviet Union would not intervene militarily in their countries—a formal renunciation of the Brezhnev Doctrine. The speech, however, took place behind closed doors, and the CIA was unable to steal the secret.[105] The way was now clear for Solidarity to lead the way to the breakup of the communist bloc with its landslide victory in elections in June 1989. The Solidarity crisis of 1980 and 1981 not only set the stage for the earth-shaking events at the end of the decade but also marked the critical turning point. The CIA perceived Afghanistan as a brutal Soviet crackdown and Poland as a brutal Soviet client-state crackdown. While those interpretations were correct, as far as they went, Afghanistan was also the last Soviet military incursion beyond its own borders, and Poland marked the clearest indication that the Kremlin's calculus for intervention had changed fundamentally.

This is a judgment made much easier with the benefit of hindsight.[106] Still, given the great weight the CIA placed on Moscow's determination to hold the East Bloc together with force if necessary, nonintervention in Poland should have occasioned some deep thinking at Langley about whether the Kremlin's outlook had shifted.[107] With the one known exception of Gates's memo to Casey, the CIA can be faulted for failing to speculate on the meaning of Soviet nonintervention in Poland beyond an expedient preference for Poland to handle the crisis on its own. Once events had unfolded in Afghanistan and Poland, a reading of the sweep of intelligence analysis available to scholars suggests a collective failure to fully grasp the significance of events now generally understood to have been major turning points toward the ultimate breakup of the Soviet empire. However, as of 1981, and through most of the rest of the decade, U.S. intelligence would, with occasional exceptions and flashes of foresight, view the Soviet Union not as a crumbling empire but as a predatory superpower.

CIA REPORTING: BLINDNESS, AND PREMONITIONS

Given the huge volume of CIA analysis of the Soviet Union now available to the public through declassification, it is easy for a scholar to find examples of intelligence analysis to make the Agency look either brilliant or foolish, depending on the scholar's predisposition. On the question of whether the CIA failed to predict the collapse of the Soviet Union, it bears reminding that a desire by the U.S. intelligence community and its defenders to rebut this charge served as a major motivator in the declassification of Cold War intelligence analysis.[108] Much of the rebuttal has focused on analysis of the Soviet economy, in part because some of Senator Moynihan's original charges focused on the CIA's tendency to overestimate Soviet gross national product, thus underestimating the burden of Soviet defense spending on the overall economy. MacEachin, in a 1996 article published in unclassified form by the CIA, cites numerous CIA economic assessments throughout the latter decades of the Cold War that portray the Soviet economy as consistently underperforming, not to say sputtering.[109] MacEachin, as we have seen, also wrote more recent monographs on the performance of U.S. intelligence in the Afghan and Polish crises, though his earlier treatment did not consider those events and CIA coverage of them through the lens of whether U.S. intelligence predicted the decline and fall of the Soviet Union. The CIA's rebuttal of Moynihan's charges, coming a full six years after Moynihan first started publicly criticizing the CIA, was more than a little late. And that tardiness did much to cement the charge of failure despite evidence in subsequently declassified material indicating that the CIA had not missed the trends entirely. MacEachin said his purpose was not to prove that the CIA was right but to demonstrate "that charges that CIA did not see and report the economic decline, society deterioration, and political destabilization that ultimately resulted in the breakup of the Soviet Union are contradicted by the record."[110]

All of the factors leading to the breakup had an economic component—the rise of Gorbachev as an agent of change; an atmosphere of greater tolerance of debate within the Soviet system; the rising economic cost of the Soviet empire; declining fortunes and concomitant rising nationalistic unrest in East Bloc countries; the human and economic cost of the Afghan conflict; the pressure of post-Afghanistan economic sanctions; and the U.S. defense buildup—even if the breakup itself was not a simple economic collapse. Still, the back and forth on Soviet economic performance and the CIA's analysis of that performance makes for frustrating reading because the debate presupposes that the breakup of the Soviet Union was primarily an economic collapse. Even MacEachin himself disputes this assumption, though he nevertheless engages in the CIA-Soviet collapse debate on economic terms. Historian Stephen F. Cohen contends that "no large modern state has ever collapsed because its economy collapsed. It didn't happen to us in the 1930s, nor, more significantly, did it happen to Russia in the 1990s when its economy was much weaker than the Soviet economy in the 1980s."[111] One of the factors contributing to the intelligence community's failure to more clearly grasp the general trends gathering in the late 1970s and 1980s was the case-specific nature of intelligence reporting. In July 1981, for example, a National Intelligence Estimate on Warsaw Pact forces found that "the Soviet Union's commitment to improving its military forces will not flag and that, despite changes in the political leadership and problems in the economy, its investment in these forces will continue at the current annual 4-percent growth rate for at least the next four to five years."[112] The estimate was published in the midst of the Solidarity crisis at a time when CIA analysts following events in Poland were predicting a Soviet invasion necessitated by the unreliability of Polish forces to impose their own crackdown on the wayward labor union. Just over two weeks after the intelligence community circulated its robust assessment of Warsaw Pact strength, a CIA analysis of the Polish crisis concluded that a Soviet invasion, which the agency considered an increasing possibility, "would mire some Soviet military units for years in occupation and policing tasks," thus reducing their effective strength for their primary mission as a counterweight to NATO forces in Western Europe. Moreover, "The important role of Poland's armed forces in Warsaw Pact war plans would be seriously undermined even if these forces stood aside and acquiesced in a Soviet invasion."[113] In contrast, the National Intelligence Estimate on Warsaw Pact forces, which reads suspiciously like an argument for the Reagan defense buildup, barely mentions the potential for the Polish crisis to weaken Soviet military posture, and then only to dismiss the idea as a problem that Moscow will overcome with "more sophisticated weaponry."[114]

This tendency to separate internal Warsaw Pact discord from external Warsaw Pact military power would continue throughout the 1980s. In 1987, another CIA paper on the readiness of Soviet forces in Central Europe declared the Warsaw Pact troops of East Germany, Poland, and Czechoslovakia as the most combat-ready, taking no account of the Agency's own past skepticism about the loyalty of Polish troops to Moscow.[115]

Perhaps the most prescient paper on the fortunes of the Soviet empire was produced, significantly, not by the CIA's Office of Soviet Analysis—target of all that Team B pressure—but by its Office of European Analysis. The intelligence assessment was distributed in December 1982, at the end of the Reagan administration's second year in office, with Cold War tension still running high. At this point, a year after the Polish crisis ended without Soviet intervention, the CIA still viewed the threat of Red Army incursion into wayward East Bloc countries as "the ultimate trump card" for keeping the Soviet empire together. But that threat could not make chronic economic problems in the region go away. Andropov, the hard-line former KGB chief who succeeded the deceased Brezhnev in November 1982, as the CIA report was written, would probably be able to avoid further crisis for a time. The next generation of leaders after Andropov, the CIA opined, would be "less likely to be spared." These leaders, the Agency noted, would be "drawn from the post-Stalin generation" and would likely be "much more innovative than their predecessors," including being open to broad economic reform and a greater voice for other communist bloc states. The World War II generation of hard-liners such as Andropov and Gromyko, while more willing to use force, was less able to understand the economic and nationalist pressures at work in Central Europe and the likelihood that significant change would be required in the Soviet system to hold it together: "It hardly needs saying that if these men in fact do not understand these things and will not in the future, then they will not be able to formulate effective policies and implement lasting solutions."[116]

Poland presented the Kremlin with an unprecedented challenge, and the solution, internally imposed martial law, was equally unprecedented in postwar Central Europe, according to the CIA's analysis. But while martial law halted the Solidarity uprising, it also showed that "the aging leadership in the Kremlin was simply not able to respond quickly and effectively and would be hard put to persuade even its most devoted followers that it had handled itself well or resolved its problems in Poland and Eastern Europe in any fundamental, lasting way." The Warsaw regime had "almost fallen apart," under pressure from an unarmed labor group. "And these forces were not counter-revolutionaries or fascists or Western agents but the workers in whose very name the regime professed to rule." Martial law was a "desperation" move and a last resort short of invasion. Though the CIA believed that Moscow remained willing to invade client states in Central Europe, the Kremlin's reluctance to do so "is now generally recognized in Eastern Europe," an ominous development for the future of the communist bloc.[117]

Given the CIA's inability to penetrate the innermost discussions of the Politburo, the paper went about as far as could be expected in speculating on a shift in Soviet calculations on unrest in its client states. "Whether the Soviets will intervene militarily in one or another East European crises is, ultimately, the essential question," the analysts wrote. The Europe desk analysts predicted that, "over time, perhaps in the middle or later years of this decade, a new contender for power in the CPSU will be cast up, probably a younger man, a representative of the post-Stalin generation, more vigorous and less committed to the mores and myths of the past." There would be similar turnover at virtually all levels of the Soviet hierarchy. Viewed collectively, the trends in Eastern Europe were almost entirely negative for the Politburo, with the greatest factor being the woeful state of the region's economy set against "the persistent allure of the West."[118]

This was extraordinarily prescient writing, particularly at this early date, three years before the emergence of Gorbachev and seven before the triumph of Solidarity and the fall of the Berlin Wall. But again, the key word is "extraordinary," for such analysis, though not unique, stands in contrast to the general tenor of CIA and intelligence community writing on the Soviet Union, which favored caution in the direction of overestimating the Soviet threat as opposed to daring in grasping the epic changes then under way.

The growing economic woes confronting the East Bloc were not lost on the CIA in the mid-1980s, but CIA reporting displayed the Agency's reluctance to go too far with economic analysis. In a 1982 report, the CIA's Directorate of Intelligence advised policymakers that hard-currency problems in the East Bloc "give the West an unusual opportunity to influence Soviet Bloc developments" but cautioned against unintended side effects of various policy options. For example, an increase in pressure on Eastern European countries to pay down their debt to the West would increase the economic burden on Moscow and hurt the region's economy but would also tend to "force the Soviet Bloc economies closer together." Liberal Western financial policies toward Eastern Europe might open up political opportunities with Soviet satellite states but would also ease Moscow's economic burden.[119]

By 1983, U.S. intelligence viewed Andropov as consolidating Moscow's hold on the Polish situation and showing no sign of giving up "the new geopolitical position the Soviets have acquired" in Afghanistan.[120] The National Intelligence Estimate accurately identified the pressures on the Kremlin: the Soviet economic slowdown; post-Afghanistan U.S. sanctions; the U.S. defense buildup; the economic and political crisis in Poland. But the combined effects of these, the NIE reported, "appear to have galvanized the Soviets to do what they have long wanted to do: force the East Europeans to tighten their belts and reduce their dependence on Western imports, assume a 'greater' share of the burden of enormous combined Warsaw Pact military bill, and help out as well in problem areas of the Soviet economy."[121]

At times, the inexplicable tendency to see Soviet military power and Eastern European political unrest as two entirely unrelated issues occurred within the confines of a single paper. A 1984 CIA assessment predicted:

> Moscow will have to tighten the economic screws on Eastern Europe, which will almost certainly make East European regimes and publics the point of greatest potential vulnerability to U.S. economic and political initiatives in the 1980s.[122]

Nevertheless, the same paper predicted that even with modest Soviet economic growth, "We project impressive force gains in the 1980s" in the Soviet military.[123]

CIA ANALYSIS AT COLD WAR'S END

That a few individuals such as Senator Moynihan and General Odom foresaw the Soviet breakup and the CIA did not became a source of embarrassment for the Agency in the 1990s, in part because of the extensive CIA resources devoted to Soviet analysis. How could an intelligence organization looking so hard at a single country miss such a sea change? Part of the problem may have been precisely because so many resources were devoted to the Soviet threat. The Agency tended to look at the USSR one problem at a time because it had the resources to do so. As we saw in the Warsaw Pact estimate, the analysis often paid little regard to what was going on in other intelligence channels. The CIA's heavy focus on the military threat was a key impediment to developing a clearer view of the bigger picture. An intelligence estimate of Soviet nuclear forces written in July 1987—by which time Gorbachev was already proposing sharp cuts in strategic forces—is typical of a kind of stovepiping that could occur within Langley. The report predicted that Soviet strategic forces would be "extensively modernized" through the 1990s with an eye toward being able to sustain and win a nuclear war with the United States. The NIE reported debate within the intelligence community over what impact "if any" Gorbachev's economic reform policies would have. It concluded that the difficulty of converting weapons production to civilian lines would mean that modernization of its strategic forces would continue separate and apart from Gorbachev's domestic agenda.[124]

In 1989, the CIA's Office of Soviet Analysis looked back on a decade of National Intelligence Estimates concerning Soviet strategic forces and found a consistent pattern across the intelligence community of overestimating Soviet efforts to modernize its forces. The report attributed the problem not to political pressure from Reagan-era hawks but to a mistaken conclusion that a period of rapid Soviet weapons modernization in the 1960s was standard Soviet procedure rather than an exceptional period of military growth. The result was chronic inaccuracy in estimating Soviet strength: "This tendency to substantially overestimate the rate of force modernization occurred in every NIE published from 1974 through 1986, and it was true for every projected force."[125] Why it took the CIA until 1989 to identify the problem, the report did not say.

On those occasions when the CIA focused on weaknesses in the Soviet system rather than the military threat, it usually concluded that only radical change could hold the communist bloc together. In a sense, the CIA set itself up for later failures of analysis by its occasionally prescient early-1980s assessments of the pressures toward radical change in the Soviet bloc. Once Gorbachev arrived on the scene and began to institute just that sort of change, the CIA viewed it as an essentially preservationist development, designed ultimately to strengthen and prolong the system. While the CIA proved highly accurate in forecasting the risk of a reaction to Gorbachev by hard-liners, culminating in the failed August 1991 coup, the Agency tended to downplay the power of the centrifugal forces unleashed by Gorbachev's liberalizations.

As the Gates confirmation hearing of 1991 revealed, tension within the CIA over how to cast the Soviet threat in analytical reports was resolved, at times, by direct intervention by Gates in favor of a harder-line view. Nowhere was Gates's hand more apparent than in the CIA's exceedingly cautious analysis of Gorbachev.[126] The fastest route to understanding the CIA's reluctance to view changes wrought in the Gorbachev era as truly revolutionary would be to start with one of the more insightful estimates Langley produced on the implications of his tenure and consider the gap between its conclusions and events as they ultimately unfolded. Entitled *Whither Gorbachev*, the NIE judged that the Soviet leader was a traditionalist in the national security arena, bent on "expanding Soviet influence worldwide; and advancing Communism at the expense of capitalism." The difference between Gorbachev and his ossified predecessors was not the goal but the means. The Soviet leader, the report judged, had fixed on a clever plan to advance communism not through crude administration of blunt force but by reaching accommodations with the West and China, deemphasizing military force, and using "the favorable image created by change at home" to win more friends in the underdeveloped world. This formulation was followed by lengthy analysis, some of it cogent and prescient, some equally bewildering. The estimate pointed to "a risk that some of the reforms will set loose centrifugal forces in the Soviet empire." On balance, however, the report found it more likely that the pressure would be in the other direction. The collective and apparently unanimous judgment of the intelligence community was, "We see little chance of nationality unrest sufficiently serious to threaten the regime, but a good chance of tensions that cast doubt on Gorbachev's program and slow the pace of change."[127]

The risk, in other words, was to Gorbachev's right, among the traditionalists on the Politburo who preferred doing business the old-fashioned way. Here the intelligence community foresaw, as it would in even greater detail toward the end of the Gorbachev era, the gathering of forces that would culminate in the abortive Politburo coup in the summer of 1991 that set in motion the final chain of events resulting in the end of the Soviet Union. But note that the centrifugal forces were judged to affect only the Soviet satellites, not the Soviet Union itself. In considering an array of possible outcomes, the NIE judged that the most likely was "rejuvenation of the existing system"— in other words, success of the Gorbachev program in achieving its intended results within the boundaries of the traditional political Soviet structure. The chances of Gorbachev bringing about what the analysts called "systemic reform" were rated lower, about 30 percent, and the risk of a traditionalist reaction creating a "neo-Stalinist" government lower still: "At the other end of the spectrum, we believe the odds of a turn toward *democratic socialism*, featuring a more radical push for a market economy and a pluralistic society than *systemic reform*, will remain virtually nil under any circumstances."[128] Here the intelligence community was ruling out entirely the chain of events that would begin to unfold in less than two years and culminate in another two. By the time this NIE was written, in late 1987, Gorbachev, in power for more than two years, had proposed dramatic cuts in all Soviet and American nuclear weapons, announced troop withdrawals from Afghanistan, ended the internal exile of physicist and Nobel Peace Prize–winning dissident Andrei Sakharov, come to the brink of a radical cut in nuclear arsenals at the Reykjavik summit with President Reagan, announced political reforms including multicandidate elections, and published his book *Perestroika*.[129]

Unless the intelligence community is asked to do so, most of its reporting and analysis avoids wading into U.S. policy. We have seen how the CIA neglected to consider Soviet concerns about CIA activities in Afghanistan in 1979 and how the CIA's extraction of its source, Kuklinski, from Poland was not accompanied by an assessment of what that move signaled to the Polish government, and the Kremlin, about what Washington knew. The Gorbachev NIE was an exception, and here the report provided one of its shrewder judgments: "We believe that the fate of reform will be sensitive to the state of East-West relations. The proponents of reforms that attempt to introduce market forces and political diversity into the Soviet system are more likely to be able to advance their cause in a climate of reduced tensions."[130] This was, in fact, the course that the Reagan administration, under the growing moderating influence of Secretary of State George Shultz relative to Defense Secretary Caspar Weinberger, was beginning to follow and that the elder President Bush would continue. Here, Washington's thinking aligned with Moscow's, for as Gorbachev made clear to his senior aide in the Kremlin, reducing U.S.-Soviet tension was a prerequisite for the success of his internal economic reforms because they were to be financed by reductions in the burden of military expenditures.[131]

While the relative weights of various factors leading to the Soviet collapse are difficult to measure with precision, declining U.S.-Soviet tensions clearly helped ease the path. Tensions eased despite the continued cautious, even suspicious, outlook of the intelligence community and the first Bush administration. Bush's national security adviser, Brent Scowcroft, admitted to being a Gorbachev skeptic, and his doubts contributed to the slow pace the new administration kept in adjusting its policy toward the Soviet Union.[132] Eventually, Washington's outlook toward Gorbachev became so favorable that the White House began to prefer his survival in office to some of the alternatives, such as a shift to a hyper-nationalist Russian state. When Bush asked his policy team shortly after his inauguration in January 1989 whether the United States might urge Gorbachev to grant more concessions on human rights, the advice he got back was not to press the Soviet leader too hard, lest the pressure provoke a reaction from hard-liners still in the Kremlin.[133] Writing in the midst of the elder Bush's presidency, Michael Mandelbaum described Bush as "passive" in his outlook toward developments in the Soviet Union and Eastern Europe and said that passivity was precisely the right approach: "The president kept the United States in the background. In response to the most important international events of the second half of the twentieth century, the White House offered no soaring rhetoric, no grand gestures, no bold new programs. This approach served America's interests well."[134]

The driving force behind this policy of benign neglect may have been opportunism as much as foresight. Once Gorbachev's determination to cut Soviet defense spending became clear, the Bush administration policy was to push ahead toward conventional and nuclear force reduction agreements on the most advantageous terms possible. William Webster, CIA director for most of Bush's presidency, contends that the Agency deserves some of the credit for this outlook, that its warnings of a possible hard-liner reaction against Gorbachev helped the Bush administration focus on strategies that would promote peaceful evolution in the East Bloc rather than violent revolution.[135]

Here we arrive at an important distinction between the end of the Cold War and the breakup of the Soviet Union. Most historians consider these separate, though related, events, with Cold War tensions easing and contributing to the sense of overall safety and security within which the Russian people could contemplate dramatic change.[136] Precisely which event marked the end of the Cold War remains a matter of historical debate, though the key year was 1989, two years before the Soviet breakup. While most tend to cite the fall of the Berlin Wall in November 1989 as the official "end," there are also votes for the Soviet withdrawal from Afghanistan completed eight months earlier and the Malta Summit in December 1989. Neither the collapse nor the breakup was predicted with any kind of certitude by the CIA, though the Agency did better on the question of the wobbliness of the Soviet empire than on the breakup of the Soviet Union itself.

If we accept that easing East-West tension was a critical prerequisite to dramatic change in the East Bloc, we can appreciate the challenge confronting an intelligence agency assigned a predictive mission. "Getting it right," in the case of the Soviet breakup, required foresight about shifts in U.S. and Soviet policy, as well as the interaction between those shifts. Amid the heated internal debate in the Reagan administration through the mid-1980s about how to respond to developments in the Soviet Union, it is not hard to understand that the CIA, directed by hard-line ideologue Bill Casey, with hard-line pragmatist Bob Gates as his deputy, was disinclined to predict Reagan administration shifts toward a less confrontational Soviet policy. The leading exponent of greater accommodation toward the Soviets in the Reagan administration was Secretary of State Shultz, who viewed the CIA as a major obstacle to moving in that direction.

One of many areas of dispute between Shultz and the CIA was over Afghanistan. Having failed to predict the Soviet invasion, the CIA next failed to predict the Soviet withdrawal, or, it seemed at times, to even acknowledge it when Gorbachev made clear his intention to withdraw. As early as February 1986, just under a year after becoming premier, Gorbachev told the 27th Communist Party Conference that Afghanistan was a "bleeding wound." In July, three months after the CIA began supplying Stinger surface-to-air missiles to the Mujahadin, Gorbachev announced troop withdrawals from Afghanistan. By early 1987, the Soviets were signaling to the U.S. ambassador to Moscow a desire to discuss options for Soviet withdrawal from Afghanistan. In April, Gorbachev told Shultz directly that the Soviets wanted out. Shultz recalled that when he consulted with the CIA about Soviet withdrawal, the response was that "the Soviet talk was political deception; we were foolish to take them seriously."[137] In December 1987, Jack Matlock, the U.S. ambassador to Moscow, endorsed a cable drafted by staffer Eric Edelman predicting a Soviet withdrawal. Edelman, speaking to the author of the Harvard study on the CIA and the end of the Cold War, recalled, "The reaction I heard from people back in Washington was that the embassy had gone soft, the embassy had developed client-itis for the Russians. There was an absolute unwillingness to accept the notion that the Russians might be willing to get out."[138]

An X-factor complicating the CIA's task in accurately forecasting major developments in the Soviet empire involved penetrating Gorbachev's personality. Only with time did Gorbachev's now well-documented aversion to violence become clear. The initial indications were his push for an end to the Afghan quagmire, followed, in 1988, by his unilateral troop cuts in Europe, which not only made an attack on NATO forces impossible but dramatically reduced the Red Army's ability to impose its will on client states in the Warsaw Pact. By April 1990, a report by the National Intelligence Council made the connection that its predecessors in the mid-1980s had failed to make. The council, representing the intelligence community, reported that "Moscow can *not* rely upon non-Soviet Warsaw Pact forces; it must question its ability to bring Soviet reinforcements through East European countries whose hostility is no longer disguised or held in check."[139] Threatening NATO was off the table. It was all Gorbachev could do to hold things together. Later that year, the CIA tracked signs of a move by Gorbachev toward a harder-line stance. These events culminated in January 1991 with the seizure by Soviet troops of key government buildings in Lithuania and Latvia to quash an attempt to separate from the Soviet Union. Soviet troops fired on peaceful demonstrators, killing fifteen in Lithuania on January 13 and, in Latvia, four government officials on the 20th. It would be the last violent spasm of a dying empire. Condoleezza Rice, at that time a member of the elder Bush's NSC staff and an expert on the Soviet Union, said of Gorbachev, "Confronted with the bloodshed, he couldn't stomach it, and he backed off."[140] CIA reporting noted Gorbachev's preference for diplomacy over military measures, but had little to go on to reach a judgment about an extreme aversion to violence. Early in Gorbachev's tenure, he actually intensified military operations in Afghanistan in hopes of breaking the insurgency so that Soviet troops could sooner quit the war under circumstances more to the Kremlin's liking. Gorbachev's role as protégé to Andropov, one of the ultimate hard-liners during the Brezhnev years, hardly provided a clue.

Had the CIA somehow gained access to the Kremlin archives, it would have witnessed a leader going through a dramatic transition. In a Politburo session in October 1980, Gorbachev, venturing one of his few comments on the Polish crisis from his position as a junior member of the group, advised Brezhnev to "speak to the Polish friends frankly and resolutely" because "they are taking no appropriate measures and are merely in some sort of defensive position."[141] In May 1989, Gorbachev, now in charge, told his Politburo colleagues, "We have accepted that even in foreign policy force does not help." In internal crises, "we cannot resort and will not resort to force."[142]

Slow to gauge the scope of the Gorbachev revolution, the CIA began to catch up by 1989. An estimate published less than two weeks after the fall of the Berlin Wall took a dramatically different tone from the reporting of previous years. Gorbachev, the NIE predicted, "will be preoccupied with domestic problems for years to come" and will cope by a process of "political liberalization," including greater independence of the legislature and rival political groups as well as more private enterprise. The intelligence community's habitual caution was evident, as the estimate predicted more of the same—continued reform with the occasional retreat to the old ways of doing business: "In a less likely scenario that all analysts believe is a possibility, the political turmoil and economic decline will become unmanageable and lead to a repressive crackdown, effectively ending any effort."[143] Here the analysts were right about the crackdown, wrong about its sustainability. Richard Kerr, then the chief of intelligence analysis at the CIA, found the estimate's conclusions overly cautious and offered a minority view which comes as close to a clear-cut prediction of the Soviet breakup as any we have prior to the final months of the Soviet Union two years later. Kerr's assessment is worth quoting in full:

> Assuming Gorbachev holds on to power and refrains from repression, the next two years are likely to bring a significant progression toward a pluralist—albeit chaotic—democratic system, accompanied by a higher degree of political instability, social upheaval, and interethnic conflict than this Estimate judges probable. In these circumstances, we believe there is a significant chance that Gorbachev, during the period of this Estimate, will progressively lose control of events. The personal political strength he has accumulated is likely to erode, and his political position will be severely tested. The essence of the Soviet crisis is that neither the political system that Gorbachev is attempting to change nor the emergent system he is fostering is likely to cope effectively with newly mobilized popular demands and deepening economic crisis.[144]

Kerr's was a particularly important minority view because of the position he held. As DDI, deputy director for intelligence, Kerr was head of all intelligence analysis at the CIA, including preparation of the President's Daily Brief, the highly classified worldwide intelligence summary. President Bush was a particularly avid consumer of intelligence, owing to his prior experience as CIA director, and, unlike his successor Bill Clinton, he received the brief both verbally, often from Kerr in an Oval Office meeting at 8 a.m., and in written form so that he could jot questions to send back to the CIA for further research.[145] By late 1989, in other words, the intelligence officer with the most direct influence over the information put into the hands of the president each day was predicting a set of events in the Soviet Union that closely tracked what would actually happen.

The majority CIA view, however, showed consistent skepticism toward Soviet reforms and tension-easing measures, even when they were announced publicly or conveyed in face-to-face conversations with U.S. leaders. Yet, in a backhanded way, the Agency acknowledged Gorbachev's seriousness by its keen awareness of the risk of a rightist coup and a return to harder-line policies. As early as September 1989, the CIA predicted just such a coup as would occur two years later.[146] By 1991, relations between the Bush administration and Gorbachev had softened to the point where the White House passed on to Gorbachev intelligence it had collected pointing to the danger of a coup.[147]

President Reagan's team had brought to the White House a deep skepticism about the CIA, a suspicion that the spy agency had been co-opted by soft-liners on the analysis side and stripped of its operational teeth on the operations side by the Church and Pike committee investigations in Congress. The first Bush administration was much more positively disposed toward the CIA, starting with the president. There is no sense in Bush's memoir of his having been misled by the CIA about the Soviet Union. Preparing for the December 1989 Malta summit with Gorbachev, coming two months after the fall of the Berlin Wall, "I found the CIA experts particularly helpful," Bush wrote. He recalled one briefing paper that indicated that Gorbachev's political reforms "were beginning to cause problems he might not be able to control" and that the results would be either a crackdown or an anti-Gorbachev coup by Kremlin hard-liners.[148]

At the working level of the Bush administration, the view toward the CIA's Soviet analysis was similarly favorable, though it acknowledged the failure to predict the Soviet breakup. Condoleezza Rice said that intelligence community guesses about major strategic and geopolitical trends were of little use, but that real-time tactical intelligence could be critical to policymakers. A warning from intelligence that Soviet security forces were about to crack down on protesters in a satellite state could prevent embarrassment in Washington if, for example, the administration was on the verge of announcing summit plans. Overall, Rice rated the intelligence community's performance "magnificent" in the final years of the Soviet Union. To whatever extent the breakup caught the White House by surprise, it was a benign intelligence failure, according to Rice, because the administration did not want to appear to be advocating a breakup: "If it was going to fall, let it fall of its own weight. Because we weren't prepared to deal with the consequences of a collapse that we helped engineer."[149]

Jack Matlock, Bush's ambassador in Moscow, agreed. In a 2006 conference on the fifteenth anniversary of the breakup, Matlock said there are times when an intelligence report is no longer merely an observation but can become an action in its own right capable of influencing events. By 1989, the White House was beginning to regard the possibility of the disintegration of the Soviet Union as a problem rather than an opportunity. An intelligence prediction of Soviet collapse might, if it leaked, create the impression that the United States was fomenting that development, thereby emboldening the reactionary forces in Moscow looking for an excuse to abruptly end Gorbachev's reforms.

> That was the last thing in the world we wanted. Any such prediction would have leaked immediately and it would have stopped the whole reform process.

Under some circumstances, simply by observing something you actually affect the outcome. If the prediction had been made, a second conclusion would have been we wanted it to happen. The implication is we didn't understand what was going on. We did.[150]

All the same, there is no evidence that the CIA consciously calibrated its Soviet analysis to avoid placing the United States in the position of advocating collapse.

One could define the CIA's performance in the latter years of the Cold War as a failure to see the rise of Russia just as easily as one could define it as a failure to predict the breakup of the Soviet Union. To be sure, the CIA tracked the growing influence of Boris Yeltsin and the tension between the Communist Party and Russian nationalism. But by late 1990 the concern was about a violent descent into anarchy. A November 1990 estimate is typical of the mindset: "No end to the Soviet domestic crisis is in sight, and there is a strong probability that the situation will get worse—perhaps much worse—during the next year." The economy would continue to slide, the Soviet republics would continue their push for independence, and the situation would grow so fragile that the sudden death of Gorbachev or Yeltsin "could lead to anarchy and/or the intervention of the military into politics."[151] The notion of Soviet military entry into internal affairs is interesting since it is not clear that the U.S. intelligence community had ever previously removed the Soviet military from politics. No matter, this may be one of those instances where the intelligence community served the government well by being wrong. Warnings of potential chaos helped policymakers develop strategies and send signals to ward off that threat. The key question was whether the creation of a new governmental system in the Soviet Bloc would happen as fast as the dissolution of the old system. U.S. intelligence rated the odds that it would as 1-in-5.[152]

In June 1991, the intelligence community at long last arrived at a firm judgment that the Soviet Union—in no small part the reason-for-being of the intelligence community—was on the way out: "The USSR is in the midst of a revolution that probably will sweep the Communist Party from power and reshape the country within the five-year time frame of this Estimate."[153] In fact it would be more like five months. On December 8, unbeknownst to Gorbachev, the leaders of Russia, Ukraine, and Belarus met at a retreat in Belovezh Forest near Minsk for discussions that resulted in their declaration of the dissolution of the USSR. Gorbachev's position had been rendered untenable by the coup and by Yeltsin's leading role in his rescue. Gorbachev resigned on Christmas Day, a dozen years and a day after the Soviet invasion of Afghanistan. At midnight on December 31, 1991, the Soviet Union ceased to exist. The U.S. intelligence report of the previous June is a fascinating document as a window both into intelligence community thinking at the time and into the complexity of geopolitical developments. The report examines four alternative scenarios—a continued state of chronic crisis in the USSR; peaceful change to a pluralistic system; violent fragmentation; and regression to a hard-line communist dictatorship. What is interesting in reading through the scenarios is the degree to which elements of all four have come to pass. Certainly economic crisis continued and worsened after the Soviet collapse. The change was surprisingly orderly and peaceful, yet, with the war in Chechnya, we have seen an example of fragmentation at its most violent. And, as of this writing in 2008, there are certainly concerns about regression in the Kremlin to the old ways of doing business.

CONCLUSION

At the beginning of the last year of the Soviet Union's existence, Richard Pipes, leader of the Team B assault on CIA analysis of the Soviet Union and one of the intellectual architects of the Reagan military buildup, arrived at a surprising conclusion about the impending Soviet collapse: the United States did not have much to do with it. The problems, Pipes argued, were almost entirely internal to the Soviet system. The meaning of the Soviet system, he wrote in late 1990, was stability, but stability came at the price of economic stagnation. Gorbachev's effort to expose the errors of the past and introduce energetic reform succeeded only in revealing the system's "thoroughly decrepit structure, no part of which could be repaired without causing other parts to totter." Supporting Gorbachev from Washington was irrelevant, according to Pipes: "Events inside the USSR have their own momentum. Our ability to influence them is marginal at best, and all the more since foreign policy plays in them a minor part."[154] These views are in accord with the conservative movement's overriding view of the bankruptcy of Soviet communism. They accord not at all with the argument advanced by Pipes and others on the Committee on the Present Danger in the 1970s about an expansionist, aggressive, ascendant Soviet threat and the importance of U.S. foreign and military policy in countering that threat. If Pipes and the hard-liners were wrong in their emphasis on the Soviet threat over Soviet weakness in the late 1970s, they bear some responsibility for the CIA, under intense political pressure from these same hard-liners, making the same mistake.

The path the CIA followed in tracking the Soviet Union over the last dozen years of its existence amounts to a case study in the inseparability of politics and intelligence. Intelligence reporting, in no small degree, reflects less the views of analysts than the views implied by questions policymakers have asked those analysts to answer. Under Carter in the latter years of détente, the CIA judged that the Soviet Union would not risk disrupting relations with the West and upend a pending arms control treaty with the United States in order to quell an Islamist uprising on its southern flank. Under Reagan, and with the Afghanistan misjudgment fresh in mind along with the Team B experience, the CIA predicted massive Soviet military intervention in Poland. The political tide through much of the late 1970s and early 1980s favored sharp increases in defense spending to close a perceived gap in military capability versus the Soviets. Already embattled by the right, and with the right now in power under Reagan, the CIA was not about to exacerbate its own problems by venturing forth with speculation on questions its masters were not asking about the long-term future of the Soviet empire.

Not surprisingly, the Reagan-era debate about the Soviet Union continued long after the country itself had broken up. Moderates argued that it was precisely the easing of tension that gave the Soviets space to go forward with the messy and unpredictable process of change. Notwithstanding Pipes's view, hard-liners generally took a more determinist view, arguing that the defense buildup and economic pressure exploited built-in weaknesses in the East Bloc and drove the Soviet Union into bankruptcy. The CIA's place in this debate was somewhere in the middle. As the Team B process showed, the CIA stopped short of the Reagan hard-liners in its evaluation of Soviet military capability. On the other hand, the tone of CIA analysis in the early to mid-1980s was unmistakably in the direction of highlighting Soviet military power and the threat of global Soviet ambitions. Though the CIA wrote about structural flaws in the Soviet economy, it consistently overestimated Soviet GNP, thus underestimating the impact of the defense burden on the economy, a point Gates conceded in his confirmation hearings.[155] The United States did apply economic pressure on the Soviet Union in the 1980s with the sanctions imposed by the Carter administration after the Soviet invasion of Afghanistan. This was, however, a punitive policy imposed because of past behavior; it was prospective only to the extent that the goal was to convince the Soviets to withdraw from Afghanistan, not to the extent of driving the USSR out of existence. Nor, as the Reagan administration's lifting of the grain embargo showed, was it an across-the-board policy.[156]

By the mid-1990s, when the CIA was belatedly getting around to rebutting the charge that it had botched its main mission, the performance of U.S. intelligence on the transformation in Moscow had become a salon topic, subject of conferences, seminars, and case studies generating a sizable body of literature. Much of the debate focused on the CIA's erratic record of assessing the Soviet economy. In retrospect, one of the key intelligence misjudgments was in gauging popular tolerance for this chronically underperforming economy. In December 1982, the CIA's Soviet analysts wrote that "popular discontent over a perceived decline in the quality of life represents, in our judgment, the most serious and immediate challenge for the Politburo." But on balance, the CIA judged the threat manageable for the Soviets: "The pervasive police powers at the Politburo's disposal, when coupled with the Soviet populace's traditional passivity toward deprivation and respect for authority, should, however, continue to provide the regime with the necessary strength to contain and suppress open dissent."[157] The transforming event of the Gorbachev years was the spread of discontent over poor economic performance to the Kremlin itself. The Soviet premier was disinclined to crack down on nationalist, separatist tendencies in the East Bloc or on economic discontent at home, not just because of an aversion to violence but because he fundamentally agreed with his constituents.

Neither the political left nor right in America had a particular interest in defending the CIA against the charge of intelligence failure—no one outside the Agency itself, at any rate. Conservatives, of course, adopted the line that their policies—the arms buildup, aid to the Mujahadin, moral pressure on Moscow to halt abuse of dissidents—had caused the Soviet collapse. They didn't overestimate Soviet strength; Moscow was every bit as dangerous as the conservatives had claimed, they argued. The heroic stand of President Reagan ("Mr. Gorbachev, tear down this wall!") and the inherent superiority of free-market capitalism brought the empire crashing down. In this view, the CIA didn't see it coming because the Agency wasn't "on board." The CIA failed to predict the collapse because it didn't understand Reagan's grand plan. In the meantime, it consistently underestimated the Soviet threat, creating more work for Reagan's team to make the case for the buildup and other hard-line policies.

Liberals adopted the same nonsupportive posture toward the CIA for entirely different reasons: they'd been sold a bill of goods by Reagan; the Soviet empire was crumbling, not menacing. Had intelligence provided a clear understanding of what was happening, Washington would have had the opportunity to attempt to manage the outcome in Moscow rather than be caught by surprise, and in the meantime could have spared taxpayers the expense of an arms buildup for an enemy that, soon enough, would cease to exist.

The CIA indeed failed to predict the Soviet breakup, if the word "predict" has any meaning at all. But the scorn heaped on the Agency in the early 1990s—scorn that had a significant and damaging impact on intelligence spending at what we now know was a crucial time of the emergence of militant Islam—is based on the dubious assumption that predicting the breakup should have been an easy call. The Soviet breakup unfolded in a series of events, many of which took place in plain sight, requiring no special intelligence facility to discern. It was also an enormously complex event evolving from the often chance interplay of a vast number of contributing factors leading in a direction that was neither clear nor altogether inevitable even in its late stages. The intelligence failure that occurred in Washington was, to some extent, mirrored in Moscow. As Coit Blacker wrote at the time, "If the rapid disintegration of the postwar order in Europe took Western leaders by surprise, it stunned, confused and demoralized their counterparts in Moscow." An attempt to reform the system "dissolved in the face of an extraordinary political upheaval that the Soviet leadership appears not to have anticipated. As a result, Kremlin leaders now confront the virtual collapse of Soviet power on the continent."[158]

One example of many of the ways in which Kremlin policies designed to bring about gradual improvements within the East Bloc created rather than averted deeper crisis concerns the right to travel. In January 1989, East Germany, under pressure from Moscow, agreed to allow individuals to travel without restrictions.[159] It was this initiative, of course, that started the trickle that led to the flood that, by October of that year, brought down the Berlin Wall. The point is that if the CIA didn't see the Soviet collapse coming, it's also true that neither did Moscow. One could argue that Gorbachev did foresee collapse, or disaster of some sort, and strove to head it off with reforms and, in the end, only succeeded in bringing about a swift and thankfully peaceful transition to a new world order.

While the transition was peaceful, the new world was not. Even before the Soviet Union passed out of existence, the threat to peace in the Persian

Gulf that had worried Washington since the Carter administration finally emerged—not from Moscow but from Baghdad. Like the Cold War, the Persian Gulf War entailed major intelligence failure, yet ended in victory for the United States. A huge conventional force, the product of the Reagan defense buildup intended for a war in Europe against the Soviets, won overwhelming victory in the desert against a forced equipped and modeled after the Red Army. It was, it is now clear, not an absolute victory but a successful skirmish at the beginning of an age of instability. As we learned in *The 9/11 Commission Report*, al-Qaeda's founders saw the deployment of U.S. forces to Saudi Arabia in August 1990 as a new cause arising eighteen months after Soviet forces, at long last, had been expelled from Afghanistan. In 1992 and 1993, al-Qaeda would launch its first strikes on U.S. forces in the region, in Yemen and Somalia. The CIA would not learn of the terror group's hand in these attacks until mid-decade. In the meantime, the Agency, its manpower, budget, and morale in decline, groping to define a new role now that its principal adversary was gone, struggled to prove its relevance.

3 INTELLIGENCE AND
THE PERSIAN GULF WAR

IN LATE JUNE OF 1990, Bruce Riedel, one of the CIA's senior analysts for the Mideast, flew into Saddam International Airport for a week of meetings with members of the Agency's small Iraq Station, based at the U.S. embassy in Baghdad.[1] Riedel traveled under routine diplomatic cover, purporting to be a State Department official with an itinerary that included meetings with the U.S. ambassador to Iraq, April Glaspie. He was under no illusion that his official status fooled anyone in Saddam Hussein's intelligence service. The Iraqi dictator's secret police were well aware of where Riedel worked and, as would become apparent soon enough, intended to watch him closely throughout his visit.

Just over a month after Riedel's trip, Saddam would line up three divisions of his elite Republican Guard along Iraq's southern border with Kuwait and, on August 2, storm the oil-rich emirate, marking the first full-blown invasion of an Arab country by another in the twentieth century.[2] Saddam's solution to disputes over Iraq's enormous debt to Kuwait, border lands, and falling Iraqi oil revenue (due to price declines he attributed to heightened Kuwaiti production) would be to take over the entire country. His way to eliminate disputes with Kuwait, in other words, was to eliminate Kuwait. But at the time of Riedel's visit, an Iraqi invasion of Kuwait, planning for which may have begun as early as January 1990,[3] was not on the CIA's list of concerns. On May 21, 1990, the U.S. Central Command, whose area of responsibility included Iraq, had opined that "Iraq is not expected to use military force to attack Kuwait or Saudi Arabia to seize disputed territory or resolve a dispute over oil policy."[4] Recalls Riedel:

> Nobody in a week of meetings in June 1990 raised the notion of Iraq going to war with Kuwait. That is not to say we shouldn't have. It just was not on the radar screen. That also tells you a lot about our human intelligence on Iraq before the war, which was, there was none—I mean, *nada*. We were totally and completely dependent on technical intelligence.[5]

While human intelligence is usually difficult to obtain in hostile countries, it is markedly less so in countries on friendly or at least polite terms with the United States, ostensibly a description applicable to relations between Washington and Baghdad at the time of Riedel's visit. Diplomatic relations afford the CIA's human intelligence organization, the Directorate of Operations, direct access to a country; diplomats, military attachés, and intelligence officers under official cover attend official functions and interact with their counterparts, exchanges that sometimes yield valuable information. The potential for information exchange is even greater when one country assists another in a military campaign, as was the case with the United States and Iraq for much of the Iran-Iraq War. In 1982, the Reagan administration had dropped Iraq from the list of state sponsors of terrorism.[6] Two years later, the United States reestablished formal diplomatic relations, opening its embassy in Baghdad. Throughout the bloody Iran-Iraq War, from Iraq's invasion on September 22, 1980, to the ceasefire of August 20, 1988, Iraq had been the enemy of America's enemy. It was taking on the Islamist regime in Iran that had thrown out the United States—including highly valuable intelligence listening posts aimed at the Soviet Union to the north—after the 1979 revolution, and had, later that year, condoned the hostage-taking of U.S. diplomats in Tehran by militant Iranian students. During Iraq's increasingly bloody war with Iran, the CIA had shared imagery intelligence with Baghdad showing the placement of Iranian forces. In October 1989, with the Iran-Iraq War over, the Bush administration enshrined the pro-Iraq "tilt" in a formal policy document, National Security Directive 26. NSD-26, a broad statement of U.S. objectives in the Persian Gulf region, favored normal relations between the United States and Iraq and proposed "economic and political incentives" for Iraq to moderate its belligerent behavior toward neighbors such as Kuwait and Saudi Arabia.[7]

A friendly response to these U.S. overtures was not the situation Riedel encountered in June 1990. With the disclosure in late 1986 that the United States had been secretly supplying arms to Iran, in contrast to its public assistance to Iraq, Saddam began to regard the attempted U.S. rapprochement with suspicion. Saddam believed that the CIA, in particular, had been playing both sides of the war, funneling not only arms but also battlefield intelligence to the Iranians. By late 1989, after the end of the war, Saddam was concerned that the CIA was working with opponents of his regime toward his overthrow, always the dictator's paramount security concern. His worry was not put to rest by a Voice of America editorial broadcast on February 15, 1990. In the wake of the transformation of several Eastern European countries to democracy, VOA, the U.S. government-funded world news service, editorialized that "the tide of history is against such rulers" as the dictators of Iraq, North Korea, and other repressive regimes.[8] The State Department approved the editorial for wide broadcast distribution, to include VOA's Arabic networks. The next day, Armando Valladares, the U.S. ambassador to the United Nations in Geneva, denounced Iraq's "abysmal" human rights record. The VOA broadcast provoked a formal protest from Saddam to the U.S. embassy. In April 1990, Senator Bob Dole (R-Kan.), on a visit to Baghdad, gave the Iraqi dictator his personal assurance—erroneous, as it turned out—that the author of the editorial, Bill Stetson, had been fired.[9]

The staff of the CIA's Iraq Station, according to Riedel, reported being routinely subject to overtly hostile treatment by the Iraqi government. One CIA officer, working in Iraq under routine diplomatic cover, was called to a meeting with an Iraqi counterpart at a government ministry building. There was no meeting; instead, the officer was roughed up and left in the desert outside the Iraqi capital. "They would routinely go by the [CIA] chief-of-station's house and whack the mirror off his car or rip the antenna off. It was their way of saying, 'Don't fuck with us,'" Riedel recalled. Riedel's personal initiation into the attitude of Saddam's regime toward the United States in general and the CIA in particular came on the day he drove south to Najaf and Karbala to visit Shiite Muslim holy sites. U.S. government officials had to obtain Iraqi government permission in writing, a week in advance, for travel to Iraqi destinations outside Baghdad. Permission was not always granted. When granted, the Iraqi approval specified the route to be followed and the timetable of the trip. "There weren't many spontaneous picnics, as you can imagine," Ambassador Glaspie noted dryly after the Persian Gulf War.[10] In Riedel's case, no fewer than six cars from the Mukhabbarat, the Iraqi intelligence service, tailed him and his group. When they arrived at the holy sites, the Americans found that Iraqi authorities had closed the mosques minutes earlier, possibly, Riedel speculates, because they suspected that the CIA officer planned to meet with an opposition Shiite group. At one point on the drive to Karbala, Riedel's driver had to stop and ask directions. As they drove on, Riedel remembers that they could see in their mirrors as the secret police stopped and picked up the person they had spoken to: "God only knows what happened to that poor man."[11]

After the Iraqi invasion of Kuwait, the Bush administration would mount a campaign to demonize Saddam, likening the Iraqi dictator to Hitler. Calibrated to whip up support for the war, the public relations assault on the Iraqi regime had the unintended side effect of highlighting American efforts to improve relations with Baghdad over the preceding decade. As embarrassing as the friendly efforts were in retrospect, considering Saddam's long record of brutality toward his own people, let alone his regional aggression, the true scandal may have been how little the United States got for extending its hand to Saddam. It certainly got nothing in the way of increased access to intelligence on Saddam's military, the largest in the Arab world, or on the dictator's plans to use it in a bid for regional hegemony.

As deputy CIA division chief for the Persian Gulf, one of Riedel's responsibilities was to alert senior U.S. officials of a threat of war in the region. Indeed, the CIA was concerned about conflict in the Gulf, a key reason behind Riedel's June 1990 trip. But the feared scenario did not involve an Iraqi invasion of Kuwait. An intelligence community assessment of the state of play in Iraq at the end of the Iran-Iraq War in August 1988 was that the conflict had left the Iraqi military victorious but exhausted, the government some $100 billion in debt, and Saddam inclined to spend the next several years resting and rebuilding his military.[12] A CIA Directorate of Intelligence report in March 1989 forecast "diminished threats to the region" and reduced chances of regional hostilities over the next two years. The assessment did caution that the territorial dispute between Iraq and Kuwait posed "a serious threat" that could lead to requests for "a higher U.S. military profile to support security guarantees" in the region.[13] U.S. intelligence also noticed that Saddam had not demobilized much, if any, of his enormous army, as had initially been expected after the war with Iran.[14]

But the issue on Riedel's mind at the time of his visit to Baghdad was not war with Kuwait but Saddam's threatening attitude toward Israel. On April 1, 1990, Saddam had gone on Iraqi television to announce the development of a more lethal type of chemical weapon and warned, "By Allah, we will make the fire eat up half of Israel if it tries to do anything against Iraq."[15] U.S. spy satellites, meanwhile, had been tracking construction in the western Iraqi desert—

the part of the country nearest Israel—of concrete pads the CIA believed were intended for launching Scud missiles at Israel. In the feared scenario, mobile Scud launchers would be hauled onto the pads, whose precisely fixed location would improve the poor accuracy of the missiles when fired at Israeli cities.[16]

The CIA's assessment that Saddam planned to rest his military for at least a few years after 1988 was based more on logic than on specific intelligence, according to Riedel. The Agency saw Iraq as gravely damaged by the brutal war with Iran and in need of time to heal military and economic wounds. William Webster, the director of central intelligence at the time of the 1991 Gulf War, said the view that Iraq would give its military a rest was shared across the intelligence community. Iraq, Webster said in an interview, "had had a seven-year war, they were all pretty battered. A lot of things had taken place, including chemical attacks, some of which blew back on their own people." It was a judgment, he said, "that was not based on any hard intelligence . . . and has haunted us ever since."[17]

But there was another kind of logic at work in Baghdad driven by the Iran-Iraq War. Iraq had paid dearly in the war, yet had little to show for it. Saddam, though he had been the aggressor, cast his country as the defender of the Sunni Arab world against the Shiite hordes from Iran. His Sunni brethren in Kuwait, the United Arab Emirates, and Saudi Arabia, who had helped finance the conflict but had not shared in its physical costs, were showing no signs that they intended to forgive Iraq's debt. The price of oil, meanwhile, had dropped sharply in 1986, thanks to increased production. That made it all the more difficult for oil-rich Iraq to climb out of its financial hole. Saddam attributed the price decline to a conspiracy involving Kuwait and the United Arab Emirates, working with the United States, to secretly exceed OPEC production limits.

"The conceptual problem people had in dealing with Saddam's intentions vis-à-vis Kuwait was our logic, which was that if you are deeply in debt to the banker, you might intimidate the banker and see if you could shake him down," Riedel said. "Saddam's approach was not to shake the bank down. His approach was to rob the bank, literally. We didn't see that as clearly as we could have."[18]

In the world of intelligence, Riedel was not, strictly speaking, a spy. He was an analyst who spent most of his time at a desk in Langley examining incoming intelligence reports, electronic intercepts, and satellite images to develop a clear picture of his area of responsibility. For that week in June, however, he was an intelligence collector. Though he may not have recognized it as such at the time, perhaps the most significant piece of intelligence he collected in Baghdad was the undisguised hostility of Iraq toward the United States. He did not fully grasp its import; no one in the intelligence community did in the run-up to the Gulf War.

Within three weeks of Riedel's return to CIA headquarters, Saddam would begin to take concrete and visible steps that raised questions about the CIA's logic on Iraq. Even then, for a frustrating period of days leading up to the crisis, the power of logic would, at Langley, outweigh the power of spy satellite photos showing Iraqi troops mobilizing and moving south. Only in the final days before war would the intelligence community step forward with a clear warning: Iraq is about to invade Kuwait. The result was a crucial missed opportunity for the White House to warn Iraq clearly of the consequences of aggression.

There were sound reasons for some of the CIA's prewar assessments, and the record shows that the Bush administration responded sluggishly to the late warnings it did receive. It is a matter of informed speculation, at best, whether Saddam would have been deterred if clearly warned that an Iraqi invasion of Kuwait would prompt a massive U.S. and allied military response. But it is a matter of fact that, owing to intelligence misjudgments and inattention by the Bush White House, the opportunity to issue such a warning was missed. The repercussions of the Gulf War, particularly as a prelude to the invasion of Iraq in 2003, were profound. The Gulf War led to the direct engagement and stationing of U.S. forces in the region and the smoldering resentment of militant Islam to the presence of those U.S. troops in Muslim holy lands. Democrats who opposed the Gulf War found themselves very much on the wrong side of an overwhelmingly popular conflict, a factor that guaranteed that there would be far less opposition a dozen years later when the younger President Bush proposed a very different kind of war on Iraq. The intelligence community's perception of its own mistakes in connection with the Gulf War—failure to predict the invasion; overestimation of the cost of liberating Kuwait; underestimation of Saddam's progress toward a nuclear weapon—led to an overcorrection of assessments during the critical period before the 2003 U.S.-led invasion of Iraq, with disastrous results for the CIA and the country. That all of this might have been avoided if a firm warning to Baghdad from Washington had averted Saddam's reckless invasion of Kuwait makes the intelligence failure concerning Iraq in the summer of 1990 the single most fateful intelligence lapse of the decade.

Eight months before Riedel's visit to Baghdad, Army General H. Norman

Schwarzkopf, newly appointed head of U.S. Central Command, took a tour of his area of responsibility. Schwarzkopf was aware of the menace of Iraqi military power; his command had even begun work on a war-game scenario that posited aggressive Iraqi military moves against Kuwait and Saudi Arabia. Still, as with Riedel, the threat of an Iraqi invasion of Kuwait did not pose a clear and present danger in Schwarzkopf's thinking. Yet Schwarzkopf, like Riedel, also managed to collect a small but significant piece of human intelligence during a tour of Kuwait's modest military installations: all the guns, he noticed, were pointed north, toward Iraq.[19]

INTELLIGENCE FAILURE AND THE GULF WAR

The CIA and the broader U.S. intelligence community made three key mistakes in connection with the Gulf War. Up until a few days before the Iraqi invasion, U.S. intelligence was predicting that Iraq would not invade Kuwait or, if it did, would do no more than grab a small chunk of disputed territory. Once Iraqi forces were in Kuwait, U.S. intelligence overestimated what it would take to drive them out. And U.S. intelligence underestimated the progress Iraq had made toward developing a nuclear weapon. None of these failures was the one that got the most attention at the time. During and after the conflict, the issue of the hour was the charge that CIA support to the war-fighters had been spotty. In particular, Schwarzkopf complained that the CIA refused to acknowledge the bomb damage that the air campaign was inflicting on Iraqi forces.[20] Central Command also alleged that the national intelligence agencies, with the CIA at the head of the list, had not done enough to boil down voluminous and sometimes conflicting raw information into discrete and specific bites that could be used by forces in the field.[21] The CIA and the Defense Intelligence Agency responded that the new precision-guided weapons being used by the Air Force sometimes left little more than a small-diameter hole in the outside of a building while the devastation inside was undetectable.[22] A postwar review by the House Armed Services Committee, which did not appear biased toward either side, supported Schwarzkopf's complaint about technical flaws in the distribution of intelligence and the tendency to overly qualify reporting to the point of making it useless to the war-fighter. The same report, however, vindicated the battle-damage estimates produced by the CIA and DIA, which were far more conservative than those by U.S. forces in the field.[23] This significant intelligence success went largely unheralded because highlighting it would have implied criticism of Schwarzkopf, the victorious commander, by acknowledging the extent to which Iraq had been able to escape Kuwait with its forces intact.

The three key misjudgments cast a lasting shadow, discernible more than a decade later in the bloody occupation of Iraq. In this chapter and the next, I examine each of them in turn:

- Intelligence failed to predict the Iraqi invasion of Kuwait, dismissing Baghdad's hostility toward the emirate as a family feud among Arab brothers. Even in the immediate run-up to the invasion, when menacing Iraqi troop movements were apparent, the weight of intelligence analysis was that Saddam was probably bluffing and would, at most, make a grab for disputed borderlands, perhaps to include some of Kuwait's oil fields, but would not seek to take over the entire country.

- Having underestimated Saddam's hostile intentions, the intelligence community, once Saddam had seized Kuwait, now overestimated the tenacity with which he would hold it. Confronted with the question of what it would take to liberate Kuwait, the answer the intelligence community produced was that it would take a great deal. Different branches of intelligence produced different estimates, and the estimates themselves evolved as the war plan changed, but the overall impression remained constant: Iraq was a battle-hardened foe with the region's largest and most capable army; it was especially adept when on the defensive and was prepared to inflict heavy casualties in a prolonged conflict.

- The intelligence community was unable to fully penetrate Saddam's carefully concealed nuclear weapons development program, with the result that Iraq turned out to be much closer to building a nuclear weapon than U.S. intelligence was estimating at the time Iraq invaded Kuwait.

Each of these misjudgments would become apparent soon enough. Optimistic intelligence assessments that the Iraqi-Kuwaiti dispute would pass peacefully went up with the dust clouds of three crack Iraqi divisions storming into Kuwait; within thirty-six hours, the entire country would be in Iraqi hands. Then, fears that the U.S.-led invasion to liberate Kuwait would deteriorate into "another Vietnam" disappeared after a relentless thirty-eight-day coalition air campaign and a 100-hour land war in early 1991. And by June 1991, U.N. inspectors, guided by U.S. and British intelligence, would discover evidence of a far larger and more advanced Iraqi nuclear program than prewar intelligence had estimated.

What would take longer to emerge was the legacy of these wayward intelligence assessments. Failure to issue a clear and timely warning to Saddam about the U.S. response to an attack on Kuwait might not have stopped Iraq from invading. But that failure complicated the Bush administration's job of building support in Washington for its war policy, for it put the White House in the position of convincing skeptical Democratic lawmakers of the dangers posed by a regime that, only a few months earlier, had been the subject of the administration's friendly overtures.

Overestimating Iraqi military strength had the beneficial effect of fueling the push to deploy overwhelming force to Saudi Arabia. Thus it may be that the rout of Iraq from Kuwait was in part a result of the alarming intelligence assessments of Iraqi strength, prompting the assembly of a coalition force sufficient to quickly crush it—an issue I will explore in more depth. But by "making Iraq ten feet tall," as Riedel described it, the CIA and military intelligence agencies helped solidify Democratic opposition to the war. The political penalties imposed on lawmakers who relied on intelligence warnings in opposing what turned out to be a swift and popular victory would not be forgotten in the fall of 2002 when it came time to authorize the younger President Bush to use force against Iraq. The latter conflict was a far more radical proposition. The United States would be invading another country, then at peace with its neighbors, without direct provocation and without the support of the United Nations. It would not simply be pushing Iraq out of a small country but would be invading and occupying Iraq itself.

Despite all that, congressional opposition to the Iraq War in 2002 was far lighter than to the Gulf War in 1991. Intelligence goes a long way toward explaining why this was so.

In 2002, the intelligence community, perhaps recalling its miscalculation about the fight Iraq would put up in Kuwait, predicted an easy victory. The intelligence community warned of the possible difficulties of occupying Iraq, but did so months *after* Congress had voted to authorize the use of military force. The importance of this dynamic goes beyond whatever political discomfort may have been suffered by Democrats in connection with either war. The legacy of the politics of the first Gulf War dramatically curtailed the appetite to vigorously debate the second. Then, having supported invasion overwhelmingly in 2002, it became all the harder for Democrats to walk their position back to one of skepticism and then opposition once the occupation of Iraq turned sour. Even after the Democrats regained control of Congress in 2006, their past support for the war made it much harder for the public's overwhelming desire to end the conflict to be translated into a meaningful policy change.

The underestimation of Iraq's progress toward nuclear weapons prior to the first Gulf War was understandable given the lengths Saddam went to to hide his program. But it nevertheless embarrassed the U.S. intelligence community when, after the war, U.N. inspectors in the summer of 1991 discovered the full scope of what turned out to be a highly advanced nuclear weapons program. The discovery underscored a point that had been central to the Team B critique of CIA assessments of the Soviet Union and that would reappear in the debate over national missile defense: U.S. intelligence, the hawks charged, could not be counted on to detect the full military potential of an adversary determined to conceal its weapons systems. When national intelligence officers met in the fall of 2002 to prepare the fateful National Intelligence Estimate of Iraq's supposed weapons of mass destruction, the failure to detect the full extent of Iraq's nuclear program in 1990—a failure in which some of those same officers had participated—would be part of the deliberations. It was a mistake they vowed not to repeat.[24]

Before delving more deeply into these intelligence misjudgments, let me first note elements of U.S. intelligence reporting on the 1990 Gulf crisis that were validated by events—the things, in short, that U.S. intelligence got right:

1. The CIA concluded correctly that Iraq was trying to reconstitute its nuclear weapons development program after the Israeli air raid in 1981 that destroyed the Osirik nuclear reactor; however, it misjudged how far along that revived program had come.[25]

2. Intelligence forecasts did not provide warning of an Iraqi invasion of Kuwait until immediately before the war, but the Defense Intelligence Agency, as early as 1989, initiated contingency planning for regional warfare in the Gulf that included an Iraq-invades-Kuwait scenario. As a result of this work, while the Bush administration was caught by surprise by the invasion at the policy level, Central Command, at the professional military level, was in the midst of a table-top war game involving precisely that scenario in July 1990, a month before Iraq attacked.[26]

3. Iraq did not ultimately use the desert launch pads detected in western Iraq by U.S. spy satellites. But Iraq validated the CIA's assessment that Saddam might launch missile attacks against Israel when, two days after the com-

mencement of the coalition air campaign on January 17, 1991, it mounted a series of Iraqi Scud missile strikes on Tel Aviv intended to undermine Arab support for the U.S.-led coalition by drawing Israel into the war.[27]

4. U.S. intelligence satellites spotted and reported the movement of Iraqi troops on July 19, 1990, shortly after it began. Intelligence *collection*, therefore, afforded two weeks for intelligence *analysis* to alert policymakers to the danger, an opportunity lost to misinterpretation of Saddam's intentions.[28]

5. In the final days before Iraq invaded Kuwait, some senior U.S. intelligence officials reached the assessment that Iraq was not bluffing and had assembled a force designed to conquer all of Kuwait, not simply seize a few disputed oilfields.[29] Though these were minority views, they were shared with policymakers.

6. When Saddam announced immediately after the invasion that Iraqi troops would soon pull out, the CIA correctly labeled that assurance a lie and judged that the Iraqi military was digging in to stay.[30]

7. As Congress considered the prospect of war in the Gulf and debated the authorization to use military force, the question put to the CIA was whether sanctions alone would eventually drive Iraq out of Kuwait. The Agency assessment, couched as usual in a degree of uncertainty, was that sanctions alone would not work.[31] The Agency also judged that Saddam would be able to hang on to power despite the suffering of his people under sanctions.[32] Though the sanctions-only policy was not fully tried, Saddam's resilience following the Gulf War under the pressure of more than a decade of crippling sanctions tends to validate the CIA's judgment.

8. A key question during congressional debate on the use of force against Iraq was whether Saddam would approve the use of chemical weapons. In what Riedel conceded was a somewhat convoluted National Intelligence Estimate, the intelligence community assessed that Iraq would probably not use chemical weapons because to do so would provoke retaliation that could threaten Saddam's regime. If the coalition threatened Saddam's survival, the report judged, he might then unleash these weapons. Saddam's non-use of chemical weapons against the coalition vindicated this judgment.[33]

9. Finally, the CIA's skepticism over bomb damage reported by Central Command grew to include doubts about the military's claim to have trapped Saddam's elite Republican Guard forces in the sweeping "left hook" movement of U.S. and coalition troops. The rapid and unexpected surge of

coalition forces into the Iraqi desert west of Kuwait was intended to trap Iraq's forces before they could escape northwest to Baghdad. President Bush and his team of advisers had a strong political incentive to side with Central Command's assurances that the Republican Guard had not escaped. But subsequent intelligence collection showed conclusively that the CIA was right and that Saddam had managed to save the most capable and loyal elements of his still-formidable military.[34]

I now turn to a more detailed examination of the three key intelligence failures outlined previously, starting with the CIA's prewar assessment of the regional threat posed by Saddam Hussein.

"WE HAVE NO OPINION":
U.S. INTELLIGENCE BEFORE THE STORM

On the afternoon of Wednesday, July 25, 1990, the White House Situation Room distributed a memorandum to the senior staff of President Bush's National Security Council relating the content of a cable from Ambassador Glaspie concerning her unexpected meeting earlier that day in Baghdad with Saddam Hussein. Titled "Saddam's Message of Friendship to President Bush," Glaspie's cable sought to reassure the administration that the potential for conflict between Iraq and Kuwait appeared remote, that the crisis brought on by a verbal broadside by Saddam the previous week, and by Iraqi troop movements toward Kuwait, was passing.[35] Whether the exchange between Glaspie and the Iraqi dictator as she described it should have been so interpreted was and remains an open question. Glaspie's much-recounted meeting has been depicted as a serious diplomatic error. The United States failed to sternly warn Saddam of the consequences of aggression and by that omission seemed to tacitly acquiesce to a possible decision by the dictator to go to war. There is some truth to this criticism, and we will consider the contribution of U.S. intelligence to the failure of the Bush administration to develop a tougher stance. But Glaspie's report of her meeting with Saddam may be viewed as a failure of human intelligence in her apparent determination to cling hopefully to the conciliatory portions of Saddam's message, and ignore the threatening signals he was sending.

A series of events deeply intertwined with U.S. intelligence-gathering had led to the unprecedented conversation with Saddam. On July 17, Saddam had accused Kuwait and the United Arab Emirates of engaging in a conspiracy with the United States to depress oil prices by exceeding OPEC production quotas, to the great detriment of Iraq's economy, still prostrate from the eight-year Iran-Iraq War.[36] That same day, the Defense Intelligence Agency picked up a rumor, later determined to be true, that elements of two Iraqi Republican Guard divisions had begun moving out of garrison and heading south toward the Kuwaiti border. The rumor probably came from Kuwait, where the U.S. military maintained a liaison presence. As Republican Guard forces started to deploy southward, the Kuwaiti military went on full alert to defend Kuwait City. The next day, July 18, following another Iraqi warning to Kuwait, the U.S. Central Command requested an increase in spy satellite coverage of Iraq and Kuwait. By July 19, thanks to the added spy satellite coverage, the DIA received its first clear indication of the Iraqi troop movement.[37] The imagery was "startlingly clear," recalled General Colin Powell, then chairman of the Joint Chiefs of Staff, who saw the photographs at his Pentagon office. In the direct sunlight of the Iraqi desert in summertime, Soviet-made T-72 tanks—a signature of the Republican Guard—could be seen in formations along the border with Kuwait.[38] What the spy satellites were seeing from space, the U.S. military liaison officer in Baghdad confirmed on the ground. Alerted by the DIA, the officer got permission from the Iraqi government to travel south and watch Republican Guard forces on the move. Baghdad, not willing to let U.S. officials go wherever they wanted, was evidently eager to show the world that its threats to use force were more than just rhetoric.[39]

Amid these developments, Glaspie for several days had been personally relaying to the Iraqi Foreign Ministry the U.S. government's concern about menacing Iraqi troop deployments to the Kuwaiti border and equally threatening statements by Saddam about the intransigence of Kuwait and the United Arab Emirates concerning Iraq's grievances about oil production, war debt and disputed lands. U.S. diplomats in Washington had been conveying the same messages to the Iraqi ambassador there.[40]

Nothing seemed to particularly resonate with Saddam until the afternoon of July 24, when the Bush administration announced that it would participate in a joint military exercise, dubbed "Ivory Justice," with the United Arab Emirates. The maneuvers hardly entailed an intimidating show of American force. Two Air Force KC-135 tankers and one transport plane arrived in the Gulf on the 24th to participate in the event.[41] But the Iraqis apparently believed it might involve more U.S. force than that, and the public announcement clearly got Saddam's attention. At about midnight on the night of July 24, Iraqi Foreign Ministry officials asked Glaspie to provide details about what forces were deploying to the region; the next morning, without warning, she was summoned to one of the presidential palaces in Baghdad and ushered into the presence of Saddam.[42]

The two-hour meeting between the American ambassador and the Iraqi dictator has been portrayed as a diplomatic blunder on the part of Glaspie or, more likely, her Bush administration masters in Washington.[43] The charge, aired publicly after the war, was that by telling Saddam that the United States had no position on the Iraqi-Kuwaiti dispute, the United States effectively gave Iraq the go-ahead to invade. In lengthy testimony before House and Senate committees shortly after the Gulf War, Glaspie displayed a sharp intellect and a keen understanding of both the international situation and the internal Washington politics surrounding the war. A strong impression that the Bush administration was only too happy to let whatever blame there be fall on Glaspie rather than on the administration's inner circle, particularly on Glaspie's boss, Secretary of State James A. Baker III, actually worked in Glaspie's favor. A bipartisan consensus formed after Glaspie's testimony that the ambassador had made clear to Saddam that the United States wanted the conflict resolved peacefully. If there was a failure, it was in the Bush administration's not instructing Glaspie to warn Saddam that the United States would defend the sovereignty of Gulf states by force; had she made such a comment without instructions from Washington, "I would have been fired," Glaspie stated flatly.[44] Moreover, she argued, the U.S. participation in the Gulf military exercise, the event that prompted the audience with Saddam in the first place, had already conveyed the possibility of the use of American force more eloquently than Glaspie could have with words.

Pressed by Glaspie to explain the intent of Iraqi troop deployments to the Kuwaiti border, Saddam said negotiations were being arranged with Kuwait to take place in Saudi Arabia around the end of the month. "Nothing will happen" before then, he said. If the Kuwaiti emirs were reasonable and gave Iraq hope that they would reduce oil production, resulting in higher oil prices and relief from Iraq's debt to Kuwait, then the matter could be resolved peacefully, Saddam said. Glaspie reported to Washington that she told Saddam that "we can never excuse settlement of disputes by other than peaceful means" but that, as for the Iraq-Kuwait dispute, "we took no position on these Arab affairs."[45] Glaspie's exact words to Saddam—"we have no opinion on the Arab-Arab conflicts, like your border disagreement with Kuwait"—appeared to some in retrospect a signal that Iraq could, at least, grab disputed territory and the United States would not intervene.[46] According to Glaspie, the comment simply restated something she had told the Iraqi government repeatedly. The intent was to convey neutrality on the details of any agreement worked out *peacefully* by Iraq and Kuwait. Accused of encouraging Iraqi aggression, however inadvertently, Glaspie protested that a partial transcript of the conversation produced by the Iraqi government and released to American news organizations left out key passages in the conversation so as to make her presentation appear weaker. The Glaspie transcript was leaked by Iraq in September 1990, after the Iraqi invasion but before the U.S.-led coalition had begun Operation Desert Storm to liberate Kuwait. Saddam's apparent intent in authorizing the leak was to suggest some justification on Baghdad's part for believing the United States had tacitly agreed to Iraq's military action against Kuwait, thus undermining U.S. efforts, then ongoing, to build a coalition against Iraq. In her congressional testimony after the war, Glaspie said that one key omission from the Iraqi transcript was her statement to Saddam that the United States would "insist that you settle your disputes with Kuwait nonviolently." She said Saddam assured her that he would.[47]

Glaspie's post facto version of events does not quite square with the language of her cable, which came to light later. The word "insist," which she so strongly emphasized to lawmakers, does not appear in the July 25 cable. After the war, Glaspie portrayed the U.S. participation in the joint military exercise as an American show of strength and a signal to Iraq of American determination to protect its vital interests in the Gulf. President Bush and his national security adviser, Brent Scowcroft, said the same thing in their memoir, characterizing the UAE exercise as "a sign of our displeasure with Iraqi bullying."[48] But in her cable to Washington the day of the meeting, Glaspie added a comment section in which she observed that "Saddam suspects our decision suddenly to undertake maneuvers with Abu Dhabi is a harbinger of a USG [U.S. Government] decision to take sides" with Kuwait and UAE against Iraq. This being her view, Glaspie's own "we have no opinion" statement to Saddam must have come across as an attempt to assuage the dictator's concern on that very score. In this fashion Glaspie would appear to have undercut the supposedly intended message of the joint military exercise.

Criticism of Glaspie's handling of the meeting with Saddam focused on her role as a diplomat and the allegation that her disavowal of a U.S. stance in the territorial dispute between Iraq and Kuwait represented a tacit acceptance of the possibility of war. Glaspie's critics overlooked her accomplishment in simply bringing about the meeting in the first place. While it was Saddam's decision to summon her, Glaspie's vigorous diplomacy, her repeated visits to the Iraqi Foreign Ministry to personally convey U.S. messages of concern about the troop buildup and the dispute with Kuwait helped get the Iraqi regime's attention and signaled that she was a diplomat of substance and rank to whom Saddam could deign to speak with a reasonable assurance that his message would be received in Washington. True, Glaspie could have stated the U.S. position more forcefully. The United States, in fact, *did* have a position on the Iraq-Kuwait dispute, the position being that it should be resolved peacefully. This and only this point should have been emphasized; the statement of "no opinion" on the substance of the dispute served only to muddy the main message.

There was virtually no discussion of Glaspie's other role in her meeting with Saddam, that of human intelligence collector. Here her performance is more open to criticism. In this rare, indeed unprecedented, opportunity for the chief U.S. diplomat in Iraq to speak directly to the dictator in a time of crisis, Glaspie's role as collector of intelligence was, if anything, more important than her role as rote conveyor of a diplomatic message formulated in Washington, which she was powerless to amend. Perhaps it is not surprising that Glaspie misread Saddam, since this was her first face-to-face encounter with the Iraqi leader. In nearly two years in Baghdad, Glaspie had only met Saddam in ceremonial group gatherings. Indeed, none of Glaspie's colleagues in the diplomatic corps in Baghdad could recall Saddam ever calling in a foreign ambassador for a substantive meeting dating back to 1984, when the demands of the Iran-Iraq War caused him to cancel all such parleys. Saddam, in Glaspie's words, was "totally isolated and extremely ignorant." But then, Glaspie was isolated as well in Baghdad, and ignorant, for lack of access to him, of the dictator's methods of signal-sending.[49] What to Glaspie was an effort by Saddam to reassure the Bush administration that Iraq wanted to avoid war and would negotiate with Kuwait, reads in retrospect more like an ominous warning from a powerful dictator at the end of his tether. Saddam broke away from the meeting with Glaspie to take a phone call from President Hosni Mubarak of Egypt and returned to tell the American ambassador that he had promised Mubarak that Iraq would send negotiators to meet Kuwaiti counterparts at the end of the month and that "nothing will happen until the meeting"—hardly a blanket assurance that the use of force was being taken off the table. According to Iraq's transcript of the meeting, Saddam, after speaking with Mubarak, told Glaspie, "We are not going to do anything until we meet with them [the Kuwaitis]." The operative word, of course, was "until." If the negotiations resulted in reasonable compromise, Saddam said, "then nothing will happen. But if we are unable to find a solution, then it will be natural that Iraq will not accept death."[50]

Saddam ran down his list of grievances with the United States, "chief among them Irangate," Glaspie reported, referring to the Reagan administration's secret arms shipments to Iran during the Iran-Iraq War. He pointed an accusing finger at the CIA and the State Department, charging those agencies with quietly looking to find new leaders of Iraq who might replace Saddam. The famous "we have no opinion" remark by Glaspie, depicted by Bush administration critics as a green light for Iraq to invade Kuwait, must have sounded to Saddam like a curious and hardly credible denial that Washington had any hand in Iraq's troubles. The notion that the United States was a passive observer of the Iraqi-Kuwaiti dispute, far from being the go-ahead sign Saddam was looking for, may be better understood as an unconvincing denial of U.S. complicity with Kuwait and the UAE in suppressing oil prices. It was a denial that Saddam could reasonably disregard in light of the ongoing joint exercises. Far from being reassured that the United States would stay out of the conflict, Saddam appeared resigned to the likelihood that the United States would intervene, and so he leveled thinly veiled threats by way of warning. Acknowledging America's overwhelming military power, Saddam, according to Glaspie's cable, "asks that the USG not force Iraq to the point of humiliation, at which logic must be disregarded," a cryptic statement, possibly alluding to the use of chemical weapons against U.S. forces. Saddam depicted the United States not only as a co-conspirator with Kuwait and the UAE, but as the guiding hand, describing those two countries as "the spearheads" of U.S. foreign policy against Iraq. It was Iraq that had defended the integrity of the oil-rich Gulf in the Iran-Iraq War, Saddam said, and, in perhaps another veiled threat, he said the United States could not have confronted its archenemy, Iran, directly because it was "impossible for the Americans to accept 10,000 dead."[51] Saddam did say that Iraq did not want war, that it was tired of war after the bloody eight-year conflict with Iran, but by no means did he say that therefore Iraq would not wage war.

"Do not push us to it," was his message to Glaspie. "Do not make it the only option left with which we can protect our dignity."[52] Saddam's language in the Iraqi transcript, which Glaspie criticized only as incomplete, not inaccurate, is even more blunt: "If you use pressure, we will deploy pressure and force."[53] Saddam, as described to the White House by Glaspie, sounded frustrated, saying almost in desperation, "How can we make them [Kuwait and the UAE] understand how deeply we are suffering?" He claimed to have "tried everything," had even "begged" the UAE's leader to change his oil policies, all to no avail.[54]

Much of this, no doubt, was bombast by Saddam. But whatever else it was, it hardly read—even in Glaspie's telling the day of the meeting—like a disavowal of war. After the invasion, Glaspie depicted Saddam as having engaged in "deception on a major scale" by lying to Arab leaders such as Mubarak about his desire for peace.[55] Indeed, he did lie. But to the extent that his remarks, both as described in Glaspie's cable and as represented in Iraq's partial transcript, can be taken as a warning that war remained an option if Iraq did not get relief in negotiations with Kuwait, then Saddam was being honest. Thus Glaspie, the intelligence community, and the George H. W. Bush administration fell into the same trap U.S. intelligence and the George W. Bush administration would encounter in 2002 when Saddam insisted that he had no weapons of mass destruction: their own refusal to believe that Saddam could possibly be telling the truth.

Glaspie's failing was not in delivering a muddled message to Saddam but in failing to receive the very clear message Saddam was giving her. Even after the fact, Glaspie was unable to perceive her own role as that of intelligence collector and interpreter rather than diplomatic messenger. Lamenting some of the consequences of the failure to anticipate the invasion, among them the failure to warn the thousands of American citizens in Kuwait and Iraq to leave, Glaspie, in her postwar congressional testimony, pointed her finger at U.S. intelligence. "Now, you know, Washington, which is responsible for providing intelligence, did not come to the conclusion that Iraq was going to invade," Glaspie said. "That was intelligence failure."[56] That is true. But as the ambassador to Iraq and the only U.S. official to speak directly with Saddam just before the war, Glaspie herself was a critical part of that intelligence reporting.

MINORITY REPORT

Glaspie made a convenient scapegoat for the Bush administration's failure to recognize the danger of war and the resultant missed chance to warn Saddam more directly that it would face massive U.S. force if Iraq invaded Kuwait. After her meeting with Saddam, Glaspie regarded the crisis as sufficiently defused to depart Baghdad for a break in London and then go on to Washington for long-planned consultations. She would not return to Iraq. By September, with Iraq now in possession of Kuwait, Glaspie found her career sidetracked. Highly knowledgeable about Iraq and the Middle East and one of only two Bush administration officials who had met Saddam, she was, nevertheless, relegated to a State Department desk job for the duration of the war.[57]

"Obviously, I didn't think—and nobody else did—that the Iraqis were going to take all of Kuwait," Glaspie told a reporter a month after the invasion.[58] In this Glaspie was wrong, and it is telling of the intelligence community's failure to share minority views of analysts that she was unaware of it. U.S. intelligence, particularly the CIA and DIA, agreed with Glaspie that an attack by Iraq on Kuwait was unlikely. But some within the intelligence community held a contrary view. On July 25, the day of Glaspie's meeting with Saddam, one intelligence analyst "attempted to warn senior administration and military decision-makers about potential Iraqi aggression," according to the *Gulf War Air Power Survey*, the Air Force's comprehensive six-volume history of the Gulf War.[59] Perhaps with an eye toward avoiding embarrassing some of the policymakers who received this warning, U.S. security censors who reviewed the *Survey* before its release in 1993 deleted any further discussion of this analyst's minority view, identifying neither the analyst nor his agency. They also blacked out the footnote identifying the intelligence report in which this minority view was expressed.

The cryptic passage refers to a report by Kenneth Pollack, then a junior CIA analyst who had been tracking the Iran-Iraq War and now was following events along the Iraq-Kuwait border with growing alarm. Pollack's July 25 warning, distributed to senior policymakers most likely in the National Intelligence Daily and President's Daily Brief, said that Iraq was not bluffing and that it had amassed enough force to take all of Kuwait. Pollack's bosses disagreed, and as a result he had to engage in heavy internal lobbying simply to get a "watered down" version of his assessment out of the CIA and into the hands of decision-makers. A second attempt by Pollack to "publish"—the CIA's term for issuing an internally vetted piece of intelligence analysis to recipients in key government positions—a longer piece on the brewing crisis got held up for nearly a week in internal debate and ultimately was not presented to the National Security Council until the afternoon of August 1, 1990. Later that evening—early the next day in Iraq—Saddam's forces invaded Kuwait.[60]

After filing his own report on July 25, Pollack got a look at the Glaspie cable and saw in it only further confirmation of his concern. Pollack's view was that

Glaspie "had completely misread the importance of what Saddam was telling her": that Kuwait and the UAE were strangling Iraq with U.S. help, that Saddam was prepared to break the stranglehold by force if necessary, and that the United States should stay out because Americans would not tolerate the casualties involved in such a war.[61]

A decade later, Pollack, having left the CIA, recounted these events in an influential book that advocated an invasion of Iraq to eliminate the threat of weapons of mass destruction. Though he may not have intended to do so, Pollack, in his critical assessment of Glaspie's performance, effectively blamed the CIA for failing to predict the invasion of Kuwait. For as Pollack himself points out, the raw material needed to assess Saddam's intentions was present in Glaspie's cable and available to the CIA's Mideast analysts above Pollack in the chain of command who continued to assess the chance of war as unlikely. As human intelligence goes, a spy agency could not do much better than reporting a direct conversation with an adversary dictator on the eve of war. As had been and would be the case on so many occasions, the problem was not getting the information, but understanding it.

Glaspie and the intelligence community were moving in circles in the weeks leading up to the Iraqi invasion of Kuwait, as Glaspie read intelligence reports written in Washington downplaying the possibility of war, then wrote her assessment of her meeting with Saddam in Baghdad and sent her low-probability-of-war assessment back to headquarters, where it went into the mix of material being evaluated by U.S. intelligence officials. Glaspie was echoing intelligence reporting going back at least a year. In November 1989, for example, a DIA assessment titled "Iraqi Military Developments Through 1992" determined that "Iraq is unlikely to launch military operations against any of its Arab neighbors over the next three years with the possible exception of Syria. . . . To protect its image of moderation, Iraq is unlikely to take military action against Kuwait." On July 20, five days before Glaspie's meeting with Saddam, the DIA produced a *Defense Intelligence Digest* article assessing that "Iraq is unlikely to use significant force against Kuwait, such as the occupation of Warbah and Bubiyan Islands. . . . Small-scale incursions are possible."[62] This too was the assessment of the CIA almost until the eve of invasion, though precisely what the Agency was saying will remain shrouded in uncertainty until its prewar assessments of the risk of war are declassified. Charles Allen, the national intelligence officer for warning at the time of the Gulf War, testified after the war that the "prevailing view" at the CIA, as at the DIA, was that Iraq would not invade its Arab neighbors.[63] Both Allen and Riedel said that Saddam's April speech threatening Israel and the U.S. spy satellite coverage showing Scud launch-site construction in the western Iraqi desert directed concern in the intelligence community about Iraq westward, toward Israel, not southward toward Kuwait.

"All we had was intelligence about Iraq's capability," Riedel said. "The president had good data from the CIA on Iraqi capability but no data on intentions."[64] The information concerning Saddam's intentions appeared to point to continued tense negotiations with Kuwait, but not to an invasion. The Bush administration was in direct contact with Mubarak of Egypt and Jordan's King Hussein, both of whom assured the White House that Saddam had pledged to them that he would not invade Kuwait. W. Patrick Lang, one of the first intelligence officers to shift gears and state flatly that the Iraqi troop movements appeared to presage a full-blown invasion, attributed the myopia, in part, to wishful thinking.

"There wasn't anything like unanimity in the intelligence community," Lang recalled. Aside from individual exceptions such as Pollack, the CIA and the State Department's Bureau of Intelligence and Research advised that invasion was unlikely. In the Bush administration, they had a receptive audience. "The policy guys didn't want invasion. They wanted a nice quiet transition" from the Cold War to peacetime, Lang said. "They convinced themselves the Iraqis were bluffing."[65]

Why a threatening speech toward Israel and the construction of missile launch sites in the Iraqi desert would trump threatening speeches toward Kuwait and the deployment of more than 100,000 troops to the Kuwaiti border is difficult to fathom in hindsight—especially because, for nine months, the U.S. military had been conducting detailed contingency planning for precisely the scenario now unfolding.

WAR GAMES

In 1932, nine years before the most spectacular failure in the history of U.S. intelligence, Rear Admiral Harry E. Yarnell, playing the role of a Japanese admiral in the U.S. Pacific Fleet's annual spring exercise, used two aircraft carriers in a virtual raid on Pearl Harbor. Yarnell positioned his carriers in the remote waters north of Hawaii to guard against their discovery by accident or by patrol craft. In the war game, called Fleet Problem XIII, the attack inflicted considerable damage on the U.S. fleet, but the high command dismissed the carrier strike as infeasible owing to doubts about the ability of the Japanese navy to project power over such great distances and to the underestimation— by battleship-minded admirals—of the striking power of carriers.[66] As it turned out, of course, the exercise predicted with remarkable accuracy the attack the Japanese were to launch on December 7, 1941.

"Warning intelligence" is a particular specialty within the intelligence profession. It is a science or an art, depending on the circumstances, that involves weighing incomplete evidence, reaching a conclusion, or perhaps acknowledging divergent opinions, and then carefully couching a report in language that gets the attention of policymakers but doesn't sensationalize. The point of warning intelligence is to enable policymakers to prepare for an international shock, or better yet, to give them an opportunity to take action that might avert the shock. It is an area of intelligence that has developed its own body of literature, most of it involving retrospective assessment of events the intelligence community failed to anticipate.[67] There is, however, the opposite problem, of warning of events that do not occur, a hazard well articulated by I. William Zartman:

> The biggest problem in the early warning debate is not whether an event is preceded by warning signals but whether warning signals are followed by an event. There are many more prior indications than there are ensuing events; many warning signals simply fizzle and seemingly impending events work themselves out. . . . What is needed is tornado warnings that announce tornados but also that do not announce non-tornados. The corridors of policymakers reverberate with cries of 'wolf!'[68]

The further in advance of a hostile event a warning comes, the better the chance that the U.S. government could issue a formal démarche or some other diplomatic warning designed to deter the other party from acting. CIA veteran Douglas MacEachin has spoken of the critical importance of developing warning intelligence on an undesired event before the other side makes the final decision to act. It is much easier, MacEachin points out, to get an adversary to refrain from doing something he has not yet decided to do than to reverse a decision already made.[69] There is, of course, the corollary: the further in advance of an event, the more difficult it is for intelligence to predict. As Charles Allen, head of warning intelligence at the CIA at the time of the Gulf War, told an oversight committee after the invasion, "We can always warn at the last minute when it's obvious that war is going to occur. But if you warn early enough, you can truly give the policymakers the tools to avert, diffuse a crisis."[70] Intelligence community success in providing warning well in advance of a crisis is no guarantee that policymakers will respond appropriately. As the scholars Alexander L. George and Jane Holl have pointed out, "early warning does not necessarily make for easy response" because such warning sometimes forces uncomfortable decisions at a time when an administration may not be ready to make them. In the case of the Iraq crisis, for example, it would have required the Bush administration to abandon its policy of seeking improved relations with Baghdad.[71]

Warning of an event is not the same as planning for an event or anticipating an event, a point illustrated not only by Fleet Problem XIII but also by the Iraq-Kuwait crisis of summer 1990. For even as the CIA and DIA downplayed the possibility of an Iraqi invasion of Kuwait, U.S. Central Command, in part at the DIA's behest, was engaged in extensive contingency planning revolving around the possibility of Iraqi aggression against Kuwait or Saudi Arabia, or both. Here again, institutional politics played a role. The Bush administration, its hands full with the world-changing events in the Soviet Union, wanted a period of quiet elsewhere in the world and hoped, as much as believed, that the Persian Gulf was due for calm after the Iran-Iraq War. In contrast, Central Command, an organization established in 1983 to counter a feared Soviet sally from Afghanistan through Iran and into the Persian Gulf, now actively sought a new, post–Cold War mission to justify its existence. In April 1989, Central Command, under General Schwarzkopf, judged that Iraq represented the most likely threat to U.S. interests in the region now that the Soviet threat had receded and the Iran-Iraq War had ended. In August of that year, DIA analysts who had been studying the Iraq problem presented a war-game scenario to Central Command based on a notional Iraqi invasion of Kuwait.[72] General Colin Powell, chairman of the Joint Chiefs of Staff, embraced the concept and urged Schwarzkopf in October 1989 to revise war planning for the Gulf region as part of a worldwide reexamination of U.S. military strategy that Powell was directing amid the decline of Cold War tensions.[73]

"We were doing scenario-driven war games for six or seven months before" Iraq started to threaten Kuwait, the DIA's Lang said. "When this came up, Schwarzkopf really liked it because it gave him a raison d'être for his command." The DIA had built up a substantial base of knowledge about Iraqi forces and order of battle during the Iran-Iraq War. Intelligence analysts knew how quickly Saddam's forces could mobilize, how long it took them to get into position to launch a strike, what clues signaled the use of chemical weapons, and what battlefield tactics they used. Lang found little interest in the scenario at the CIA or the Pentagon. People he approached were uninterested because they didn't believe Iraq would invade Kuwait.[74] Nevertheless, planning moved ahead. By the spring of 1990, Central Command had a Concept Outline Plan for the defense of allied states in the Gulf, and by July, a draft operations plan that included deployment and logistics schedules, target lists, and a command blueprint, all tested in a tabletop exercise called "Internal Look—90" that was still in progress when Iraq invaded Kuwait.[75]

Among the civilian leadership of the military, there was little appetite for identifying and taking on a new mission. The Bush administration was inclined to study the situation and develop new policy only after extensive interagency review. Much as 9/11 caught the second Bush administration just beginning to study options for a new policy on terrorism, so the Iraqi invasion of Kuwait fell in the beginning days of the first Bush administration's reassessment of global military posture. The new strategy would be based on possible "regional contingency" wars rather than a big war with the Soviets in Western Europe. Before a planned major speech by President Bush, Defense Secretary Dick Cheney, in the summer of 1990, asked for a private meeting with Senators Sam Nunn (D-Ga.) and John Warner (R-Va.), the chairman and ranking Republican, respectively, on the Senate Armed Services Committee, to discuss the new strategy. The meeting did not take place; when the appointed hour arrived, Cheney and other senior administration officials were busy watching the unfolding crisis as Iraqi forces took possession of Kuwait.[76]

READING SADDAM'S MIND

When Saddam had given his set-Israel-afire speech in April 1990, senior officers at CIA headquarters took notice. Charles Allen, the national intelligence officer for warning, recalled reading and rereading the speech several times, "just to get the sense of what this man really had in his brain."[77] By July 1990, mind-reading was not required to understand the situation confronting Kuwait and the oil-dependent West. With Saddam's threatening words, the movement of thousands of troops, a long-standing historical feud between Iraq and Kuwait, Iraq's crushing debt from the war with Iran, and the ominous statements from Baghdad in the latter weeks of July 1990, there was nothing in the substantive intelligence reporting to prevent a judgment that invasion was imminent. With some 100,000 Iraqi troops massing on the Kuwaiti border by the third week of July, it was anyone's guess whether Saddam would invade, but that was a lot of troops to put into the desert simply to make a point. In the Bush administration, and most of the intelligence community, the prevailing guess was that he would not. The guess was no war, not because it was the likely outcome but because it was the desired outcome. The obstacle was not primarily the difficulty of divining Saddam's intentions but the mindset of the Bush administration and the intelligence community. As demonstrated in numerous other cases from Cuba to Prague to Poland, mindset is a formidable obstacle to overcome. Former CIA director Webster recalled a gradual split developing between the White House and the intelligence community as analysts became increasingly concerned that a troop deployment so massive could not be a mere feint. "At that particular point, the National Security Council folks were more inclined to view it as saber-rattling than we were," Webster said in an interview. "Every morning when I went into the White House, if I had new Iraqi troop numbers, I would add that to the President's Daily Brief."[78] The mindset shift came in the final days of July. On the 27th, a day when the news on the diplomatic front pointed to an easing of the oil production dispute between Iraq and Kuwait, imagery intelligence showed evidence that logistical support elements of the Republican Guard Forces Command were moving south toward Kuwait. To military professionals such as Powell, this was an ominous sign. Three days later, a *Defense Intelligence Digest* item opined, "Saddam will probably maintain Iraq's military stance until Kuwait agrees to his demands. Some military action is likely if Kuwait is resolute." That same day, Lang e-mailed the director of the DIA warning that, in his opinion, Saddam was not bluffing. On the 31st, with other elements of the intelligence community still hedging, Lang told the DIA chief that Iraq had assembled forces sufficient to take all of Kuwait and the oil-rich eastern portion of Saudi Arabia. The first DIA warning that invasion was "imminent" came on August 1 in Washington, a few hours before Iraqi forces, eight hours ahead in the Gulf, crossed into Kuwait at 1 a.m. August 2, 1990, Iraqi time.[79]

The CIA's official take on the July 1990 crisis was that it was an intelligence success story. In June 1997, the Agency issued a report on its performance in the Gulf War. The report came at a time when the Agency was facing criticism by Gulf War veterans for delays in confirming their belief that some Gulf War–related illnesses had been caused by inadvertent exposure to Iraqi chemical weapons blown up unwittingly by U.S. troops along with conventional munitions after the liberation of Kuwait. "CIA's activities are usually secret, and the Agency rarely publicizes its successes," the Agency report stated. "Nevertheless, CIA believes that Gulf War veterans may benefit from knowing the extent—albeit in summary—of CIA efforts to support Operations Desert Shield and Desert Storm." The week before the invasion, the 1997 report recounted, the CIA had reported that an Iraqi attack with a force large enough to take all of Kuwait and penetrate deep into Saudi Arabia was "highly likely" if Kuwait failed to yield to Iraqi demands. On August 1st, the CIA judged it "possible . . . that Saddam has already decided to take military action against Kuwait."[80] This was almost certainly a reference to Pollack's minority opinion that a major invasion was imminent. Richard Kerr, CIA deputy director at the time of the Gulf War, insisted, "We did predict the invasion." He said that specific analysts, certainly a reference to Pollack, among others, "in senior forums said the Iraqis were going to invade."[81]

Others remember it differently, describing the CIA as frustratingly unwilling to declare flatly that a massive invasion was about to occur almost until the moment the Iraqi troops crossed into Kuwait.[82] Most accounts have the CIA issuing its emphatic warning on August 1.[83] By that afternoon, Powell and Cheney were discussing recommending that Bush call Saddam directly and warn him not to invade or issue a stern, attention-grabbing warning. "But it was too late," Powell recalled. "Before we could fire a diplomatic warning shot, eighty thousand of Saddam's Republican Guards were across the border rolling toward Kuwait City."[84]

IMPACT OF FAILURE

In both World War II and the Gulf War, the U.S. military saw war coming and planned for it, but failed, along with civilian intelligence agencies, to discern the precise time and place the enemy would attack.[85] The distinction is between tactical intelligence—knowing when, where, and how an adversary plans to strike shortly before it does so—and strategic intelligence, involving an emerging understanding of the potential threat posed by an adversary and of how to counter that threat, or prepare for it well in advance.[86] If it had to be one or the other—adequate preparation for war based on long-term strategic intelligence or foreknowledge of a specific attack based on solid, short-term tactical intelligence—I believe most national security professionals would prefer the former. The United States would have been worse off if it had learned sometime late in 1941 of a Japanese plan to bomb Pearl Harbor on December 7th, but had not spent the preceding decade building aircraft carriers and battleships and engaging in fleet exercises against a theoretical Japanese adversary. In the event, the United States suffered a terrible surprise attack and grievous losses, but, even after the damage inflicted in the raid, it retained the fleet, officers, and strategy to win the war. Iraq's invasion of Kuwait was not an entirely analogous surprise: the buildup of U.S. conventional forces during the 1980s had unfolded as a counter to perceived Soviet strength and a possible war contingency in Europe, not in anticipation of a ground war against Iraq in the desert. It was a matter of good luck for the Bush administration that when war came in the Gulf it involved an adversary fighting largely with Soviet weapons and tactics against U.S. forces at their peak of capability after a decade-long buildup. Still, the U.S. military had been preparing for the possibility of war against Iraq for two years by the time war came. That must be regarded as an intelligence success, even though the surprise regarding Iraq's actual attack was an intelligence failure. In no small part because of this preparation, Operation Desert Storm ended in a swift and domestically popular victory for coalition forces at a cost far less than predicted. The U.S. combatant commands, though not immune to political influence, functioned at a remove from Washington and could conduct quiet contingency planning—usually with a worst-case mindset—without running afoul of policymaker preferences. Warning intelligence of an attack provides an opportunity, however fleeting, to dissuade an adversary from attacking; long-term preparation for battle enables a nation to deter an enemy from attacking. Neither one guarantees that an enemy will stand down. Strategic intelligence for war planning is the more important factor for winning a war if war becomes unavoidable.

As a consequence of the relatively easy victory, recriminations after the war for the prewar failure to predict the invasion were relatively mild, particularly as measured against the bitter feuding a decade later between the CIA and the second Bush administration over the prewar intelligence on Iraq's weapons of mass destruction. In the seven months from the Iraqi invasion of Kuwait to the coalition liberation of Kuwait in Operation Desert Storm, both the elder Bush's administration and the intelligence community shared the blame. The intelligence community had made a judgment following the Iran-Iraq War that Baghdad had no appetite for another war and wanted time to recover economically and militarily. The CIA was reluctant to budge from that position even when signals of trouble grew strong. For the Bush administration, the crisis arrived at a time when it was trying to improve relations with Iraq, having badly misread Saddam's level of anger toward Washington. Shifting into the language of a stern warning to Saddam required a greater transformation of thinking than the administration was capable of making until Iraqi forces were actually in Kuwait. The administration's political task of generating public and congressional support for the war was made all the greater by this miscalculation, since it had to expend time and energy explaining why an erstwhile object of U.S. diplomatic overtures was now to be considered a sworn and dangerous enemy.

Regardless of the level of recrimination, there were serious short- and long-term consequences of the failure to provide earlier warning of invasion. Among the most immediate results of the intelligence failure, some 3,000 U.S. citizens remained in Kuwait after the invasion and 500 in Iraq, having received no warning to evacuate, as would have been automatic had the U.S. government expected war. By mid-August, Iraq was barricading these and other Westerners in their hotels, or, more ominously, moving them to strategic sites regarded as possible targets of U.S. air strikes, to be used as human shields. With the declaration by Saddam that Kuwait was now the nineteenth province of Iraq, Baghdad ruled that diplomats in Kuwait would no longer enjoy immunity. The U.S. embassy staff in Kuwait City was besieged for three months by Iraqi troops. Saddam's strategy, though crude, caused severe consternation in the Bush White House and uncertainty about whether a military campaign could proceed under the circumstances.[87] After months of international outcry, on December 6, 1990, Saddam announced that all detained foreigners would be released, a move that most Gulf War postmortems regard as laudable, but that was from Saddam's point of view a serious strategic mistake. For the coalition, it was a fortuitous ending to a problem created by the misreading of Iraqi intentions by the administration and the CIA.[88]

Another short-term consequence of the lack of warning was the mortal threat to Saudi Arabia posed by the sudden presence of Iraqi forces on a largely undefended border. In the immediate aftermath of the Iraqi conquest of Kuwait, there was little but a badly overmatched Saudi military to prevent Saddam from extending his gains into the kingdom. That threat motivated the Bush administration's rapid-fire and highly effective diplomacy, in which Defense Secretary Cheney, on August 6, won agreement from Saudi Arabia's King Fahd—a fateful decision, conveyed with a single word, "Okay"—for thousands of U.S. troops to begin flowing into Saudi Arabia to defend the kingdom and use it as the base of operations against Iraq.[89] Those troop movements began immediately, though Saudi Arabia remained in serious danger for the better part of a month until the heavier American forces began arriving. It remains unclear whether the swift Saudi decision thwarted an Iraqi invasion or whether Saddam had gone as far as he intended to go in taking Kuwait. In mid-August, an Iraqi defector presented himself to Egyptian authorities bearing what purported to be an Iraqi invasion plan of Saudi Arabia. Schwarzkopf said he never was able to determine if it was genuine, but he regarded it as credible, saying that the attack plan was just as he would have designed it had he been an Iraqi commander.[90]

Even King Fahd's ready approval of Cheney's request for permission to deploy American forces did not immediately ease the threat to his regime. The heavy U.S. Army units that would be needed to stop an attack by Iraqi armored columns were in Western Europe, still oriented toward the Warsaw Pact nearly two years after the fall of the Berlin Wall. In summer 1991, the Pentagon was still maintaining its Cold War "Europe first" strategy.[91] Thus the plodding response of the U.S. military and intelligence community to the Soviet breakup had the effect of leaving the United States badly positioned to cope with crisis in the Persian Gulf. The Bush administration further contributed to the failure to better prepare for what was certainly a possibility of war in the Gulf by adopting a policy of avoiding moves that might provoke Saddam. The intelligence community's failure to provide meaningful warning of war, along with the Bush administration's failure to respond once warning signs were obvious, meant there was no chance of repositioning those forces ahead of an Iraqi invasion. After the war, Cheney recalled the acute nature of the crisis of August 1990. If Saddam's forces had pushed on an additional 200 to 250 miles, they would have seized the Saudi air bases and port facilities that were vital to the U.S. troop deployment. Instead of the orderly deployment that eventually occurred, he said, coalition forces would have had to storm the Saudi coast in an amphibious assault: "In August all we had over there initially was the ready brigade of the 82nd Airborne and [one] wing of F-15s from Langley [Air Force Base] in Virginia and relatively small forces at the outset, so it really wasn't until the end of August that we began to feel fairly comfortable with the size forces we were getting there."[92]

The interval between the Iraqi invasion of Kuwait and the arrival of substantial U.S. forces was, Cheney said later, one of the "moments that we have been concerned about of potential significant danger." Yet as Cheney himself acknowledged, Iraq did not need to run the risk of an invasion of Saudi Arabia in order to achieve the strategic objective of de facto control of world oil. In strategic terms, the damage had already been done. Iraq had 10 percent of the world's oil reserves before the invasion of Kuwait; with the takeover of Kuwait, Saddam doubled Iraq's control of world reserves to 20 percent. By merely taking Kuwait and positioning his huge army on Saudi Arabia's doorstep, Cheney told lawmakers, Saddam, without further offensive action, "was clearly in a position to be able to dictate the future of worldwide energy policy, and that gave him a stranglehold on our economy and on that of most of the other nations of the world as well."[93]

It is in light of the dangers posed by Iraq's takeover of Kuwait—the threat to Saudi Arabia, complications for U.S. force deployment, Iraqi dominance of global oil—that the Bush administration's tentative responses to the warnings of war are all the harder to understand. The contrast between the Bush administration's pre-crisis quietude and postinvasion alarm echoed the contrast between the Carter administration's muted statements before the Soviet invasion of Afghanistan and its postinvasion fears of a Soviet takeover of the Persian Gulf. As we have seen, the Bush administration's hesitance was largely a problem of its own making, but it was aided and abetted by intelligence that was equally slow to see the danger. Weeks before some intelligence analysts such as the DIA's Lang and the CIA's Pollack sounded the invasion alarm, the intelligence community, notwithstanding its uncertainty about Iraq's intentions, could have been putting together contingency analysis pointing out the dire consequences that might flow from an Iraqi invasion of Kuwait. Even in a state of continued uncertainty about the tactical intelligence, the administration would have thus been alerted to the approaching danger and might have calibrated its diplomacy, rhetoric, and military preparations accordingly.

In an example of the circularity of national security emergencies, the slow recognition of the Iraqi threat led to the poor positioning of the intelligence community as well as the military to deal with the crisis once it erupted. U.S. intelligence had been watching Iraq, and the observations had led to some timely contingency planning by the military. But the overall picture that would emerge from postmortem examinations of intelligence community performance made clear that the intelligence community viewed Iraq as a relative backwater on the collection-and-analysis priority list. A House Armed Services Committee study of intelligence in the Gulf War found that, as of July 1990, the Defense Intelligence Agency had forty-two people assigned to collecting information on prisoners of war and soldiers missing in action from previous wars, particularly Vietnam; the DIA had two analysts assigned full-time to Iraq. The same study found that the intelligence organization within Central Command, the command that would run the Gulf War, "was a shell, with few trained personnel, no collection assets under its direct control and no joint intelligence architecture."[94] Better long-term intelligence would have afforded the opportunity to build up some of these intelligence analysis and operations nodes, but with insufficient people assigned to the Iraq problem, better intelligence was not forthcoming. The *Gulf War Air Power Survey* was similarly unsparing in its assessment of the prewar intelligence effort on Iraq:

> Intelligence analysts were caught in the post–Cold War transition from Soviet-European emphasis to smaller, but more numerous regional threats. As a result of the region's relatively low priority before Desert Storm, their information on Iraq was less than comprehensive and woefully out of date. Even when those analysts who were watching the Arabian Peninsula detected early signs that Baghdad might be preparing for military operations, they were unable at first to capture the attention of senior policy makers who, up until the summer of 1990, had been advised that Iraq had been exhausted by its war with Iran and would limit its bellicosity to the diplomatic arena.[95]

The hearings on the nomination of Robert Gates to be CIA director, which began seven months after the Gulf War, brought to light information suggesting that Iraq's "relatively low priority" had not been a recent development. The Iranian revolution and the taking of American hostages in 1979, the Soviet invasion of Afghanistan later that same year, the Iraqi invasion of Iran in September 1980 and the subsequent eight-year Iran-Iraq War, and fear of Soviet military ambitions in the oil-rich region—all these combined to cause a sharp increase in the U.S. intelligence focus on the Persian Gulf in the 1980s. Indeed, the Reagan administration had created Central Command in 1983 out of concern that Moscow would seek to exploit U.S. difficulties in Iran with an expansionist military move from Afghanistan through Iran and into the oil fields of Kuwait, Iraq, and Saudi Arabia.[96] During the Iran-Iraq War, Gates testified, U.S. spy satellites and, more important, the analysts who interpret the thousands of images they produce, devoted extensive attention to the Gulf region. That emphasis, Gates said, "had imposed some limitations on our satellite capabilities in terms of some long-standing problems in the Soviet Union and elsewhere. And so, when the war was over, we tried to address some of those issues and problems." Gates, who was deputy CIA director in 1988 when the Iran-Iraq War ended, based the resource shift away from the Gulf in part on his own intelligence community's assessment that "Saddam Hussein and Iraq would be spending the next several years rebuilding."[97] Senator Bill Bradley (D-N.J.), a member of the Senate Intelligence Committee who opposed the Gates nomination, dismissed the shift as one more example of the CIA's refusal to let go of the Soviet threat even in the late stages of the Cold War. The CIA, at Gates's direction, Bradley charged, turned away from an emerging threat and opted for "monitoring Soviet military power more closely just as the Soviet Union was being squeezed by a shrinking economy and a decaying political system."[98] Gates himself would have to bear the consequences of this miscalculation, for when Iraq invaded Kuwait, Gates was a member of Bush's National Security Council staff scrambling to respond to the emergency.

LEGACY OF A CRISIS

Notwithstanding the emphatic ejection of Iraqi forces from Kuwait by the coalition in January and February of 1991, the Iraqi invasion of Kuwait was the signal event that defined much of what was to happen in the region in the coming decade. To build an international coalition to liberate Kuwait and overcome domestic concern about the cost of war, the Bush administration chose the fateful course of demonizing Saddam. This was by no means an unreasonable position given Saddam's appalling human rights record and his unique role as regional aggressor. But it was a jarring shift from the administration's own friendly overtures of just weeks before. So successful was the demonization campaign that Saddam's continuation in power after the war, combined with his brutal suppression of uprisings in the Shiite south and Kurdish north, helped spark the dissatisfaction in some circles that the war aims had not included regime change in Baghdad. Severe international sanctions imposed on Iraq put an already weakened economy in a stranglehold in the 1990s, with the result that in some quarters, such as France and Russia, there was a push to ease the sanctions and, possibly, return Iraq to a normal international footing. The unacceptability of that course led the Clinton administration to emphasize Iraq's failure to fully cooperate with arms inspections. It caused the White House to press the case, based on long experience with Iraqi perfidy, that Saddam had retained, or was secretly reestablishing, his arsenal of weapons of mass destruction.

The arrival of U.S. forces in Saudi Arabia beginning August 7, 1990—the military called it "C-Day"—would be an event of profound importance to the militant jihad movement, which was then little-known outside the Middle East. Al-Qaeda would choose August 7, 1998, to bomb U.S. embassies in Kenya and Tanzania, the pivotal development in the war on terrorism before the 9/11 attacks. What to Americans seemed a selfless defense of one Arab ally and liberation of another by U.S. troops would be portrayed by al-Qaeda as the beginning of the Western military occupation of the Muslim holy land, home of the two holy cities of Mecca and Medina. Having, in its eyes at least, vanquished the Soviet presence in Afghanistan, leading to the Soviet Union's later collapse, al-Qaeda would now take on the remaining superpower and make the removal of American forces from the Arab region its rallying cry.

These sweeping events cannot all be laid to the intelligence failure of summer 1990. Rather, the magnitude of the Gulf War's impact in a number of geopolitical arenas intensifies the spotlight on what might have been done to avoid conflict in the first place and highlights the stakes underlying key intelligence community judgments. Better intelligence collection and analysis—not only by the intelligence community but also by the policy community, beginning with the U.S. embassy in Iraq—would not have guaranteed avoidance of war, nor could it have ensured correct judgments by policymakers at critical junctures in the crisis. Even with the flawed intelligence that it had, the Bush administration had enough information to take stronger measures to deter Iraq from attacking weeks before the Republican Guard surged into Kuwait. Nevertheless, in the forty-eight hours before the invasion, when the intelligence warning of war suddenly became unambiguous, the administration belatedly realized the seriousness of the situation and discussed—too late, as it turned out—the option of a direct presidential warning to Saddam. This sudden awakening in the White House suggests what might have been had the administration been presented with that same unambiguous reporting days or weeks earlier. This, in the view of then-Senator David Boren, chairman of the Senate Intelligence Committee, was the signal failure of intelligence in connection with the Persian Gulf War.[99]

Another lasting legacy of the failure to predict the invasion was the view of key policymakers on the reliability of U.S. intelligence. On September 11, 1990, not yet a date of infamy, Defense Secretary Cheney was under the klieg lights on Capitol Hill explaining to the Senate Armed Services Committee why the invasion had come as a surprise. "What we could not know, and what no intelligence system could tell us, was what the intentions of Saddam Hussein were at the time," Cheney testified. "All the reports we received from those most directly affected focused specifically on the proposition that Saddam Hussein will never invade Kuwait."[100] That was a reference not only to the intelligence community but also to the nation's Gulf allies, including King Hussein of Jordan and Egypt's Hosni Mubarak, who later were left to lament that they had been deliberately misled by Saddam. From direct and painful experience, therefore, we see Cheney articulating a lesson he would carry forward to the second Bush administration: that the intelligence community and America's allies cannot be relied upon to fully appreciate the threat posed by a devious enemy.

4 IRAQ IS TEN FEET TALL

WHEN IRAQ INVADED KUWAIT on August 2, 1990, Arnold Punaro, the stocky, klaxon-voiced staff director of the Senate Armed Services Committee, was in the midst of another Capitol Hill budget cycle, working in the marble chambers of the Russell Senate Office Building on the details of annual authorization and supplemental defense bills for his boss, Senator Sam Nunn of Georgia, the committee chairman. Punaro did not realize it, but his life was about to change dramatically, for he had another job: brigadier general in the United States Marine Corps Reserve.

As the U.S. posture in the Persian Gulf evolved in the fall of 1990 from a defensive deployment protecting Saudi Arabia to an offensive stance geared toward the liberation of Kuwait, the dominant concern became the cost of a frontal assault on dug-in Iraqi forces. House and Senate Democrats who favored giving U.N. sanctions more time to weaken those forces or pressure Baghdad to leave Kuwait without a fight saw the initial war plan as a possible meat grinder. Even under General Norman Schwarzkopf's "left-hook plan," U.S. Marines would have to go straight at Iraqi forces who had been digging in to layered entrenchments in Kuwait. Though lawmakers were not being briefed in detail about the war plan, they knew that at least some frontal assaults would be required to dislodge Iraqi forces. Anxiety about casualties did not reside exclusively in Washington. Marine commanders in particular were concerned about their portion of the mission—driving straight from northeastern Saudi Arabia into southern Kuwait through layers of Iraqi defenses.

Military protocol dictated that the Marines simply salute and follow orders, which is what they eventually did. Washington, however, is a city crisscrossed by unofficial back channels, and among the four services, the Marines were undisputed masters at navigating them. Standard procedure for a backchannel campaign typically would involve a private meeting on Capitol Hill between a general and a lawmaker or senior staffer where concerns could be aired, but no fingerprints taken. The Marines decided to take this strategy to another level: the Corps ordered Punaro activated and immediately deployed to the Gulf theater to give him a firsthand look at what lay in store for the Marines. The Marines could then count on Punaro to carry this report directly back to Nunn, then the single most influential lawmaker in Congress on military matters.

"General Al Grey, commandant of the Marine Corps, was worried about the extreme casualties the Marines would suffer," Punaro recalled. "They were going to have to go through what they thought was a huge triple-concertina-wire defense into Kuwait, so that while the Army was doing the big 'left hook,' the Marine Corps was going right into the heart of Iraqi forces." Punaro got a full raft of briefings in Saudi Arabia and was flown by helicopter along the now heavily fortified frontier between Saudi Arabia and Kuwait, where he could see examples of the kinds of obstacles the coalition forces would confront. The message the Marine field commanders conveyed to Punaro during his tour of the battlefront was unambiguous: "Arnold, you better make sure people back in Washington know about this," Punaro said he was told. He duly reported back to the committee. "How can you ignore information like that?"[1]

Punaro was one spoke in a large, slowly rotating wheel involving the CIA, the Defense Intelligence Agency, frontline military intelligence, and Congress that was rolling toward the conclusion that the United States could well be in for a difficult and costly war. What the Marines and other ground commanders did not fully appreciate at the time was the ferocity of the air campaign the U.S.-led coalition was about to unleash. The Marines did go straight at Iraqi forces and did encounter some stubborn fighting, particularly near Kuwait City's main airport, according to Defense Intelligence Agency Mideast analyst Patrick Lang. But the pounding of the thirty-eight-day air campaign, declining morale among Iraqi troops, Saddam Hussein's realization that he had to withdraw his army or lose it, and the overwhelming superiority of coalition ground forces backed by air power with complete control of the skies translated into an overwhelming victory.

MINDSET ON THE ENEMY

U.S. intelligence about Iraqi troop dispositions and weaponry did much to enable that victory, as Schwarzkopf, despite his complaints about bomb-damage assessments, made clear.[2] But victory seemed a long way off when the critical question confronting U.S. intelligence was what it would take to get Saddam to let go of Kuwait. Answering that question required a clear assessment of Iraqi military capability and political will, compared with the military capability and political will of the nascent U.S.-led coalition. Complicating this question was the constantly changing situation on the ground. After its initial invasion, Iraq began pouring tens of thousands of additional troops into Kuwait, far more, it was apparent, than necessary simply to pacify the emirate. Were they reinforcing against counterattack or preparing for a further offensive into Saudi Arabia? The coalition's force profile and war plan also changed dramatically in the months following the Iraqi invasion. The initial troop deployments sought to secure Saudi Arabia against attack. Only on November 8, 1990, did President Bush approve a major reinforcement of 200,000 additional troops that signaled his intent to liberate Kuwait. Likewise, the war plan underwent major revision as Schwarzkopf, at Colin Powell's insistence, crafted the "Left Hook" plan to cut off the retreat of Iraqi forces. According to the DIA's Lang, U.S. intelligence analysts trying to assess the coming conflict were not privy to the war plan beyond the broadest generalizations. "They were so obsessed with operational security, they wouldn't tell us what their plan was," Lang said. "We knew from the huge [coalition] force assembled that we weren't going to fool around, but we didn't know the plan."[3]

Bruce Riedel, a senior CIA Mideast analyst at the time, said there was a division of labor in the intelligence community following the invasion of Kuwait: the CIA would assess the overall Iraqi military situation, as well as geopolitical questions such as the chance that sanctions alone might persuade Saddam to withdraw, while the DIA had the job of assessing how Iraqi forces would stand up to a U.S.-led onslaught. "We got accused in retrospect of making the Iraqis ten feet tall," Riedel said. "What we were trying to do was to tell the American military that compared to other Arab armies, the Iraqis were the best." He called it "entirely understandable" that lawmakers who received CIA briefings came away with the impression that Iraq represented a formidable adversary for the coalition force, but he added that Pentagon intelligence briefings, also given in abundance in the months before the vote to authorize the use of military force, should have provided a level of confidence about the enormous capability assembling in the Gulf under the coalition banner. "We hadn't told them that the U.S. military was more capable than the Iraqi military," Riedel said. "We thought that they could have figured that out."[4]

Richard Kerr, deputy CIA director at the time, says in retrospect that the CIA "gave the Iraqis more credit for military competence than they deserved. There was no question that the U.S. could drive them out of Kuwait, but we expected stiffer resistance and, perhaps, the use of chemicals."[5]

In the intelligence community, the biggest obstacle to accurately assessing the coming conflict was not the rapidly changing circumstances in the Gulf theater, but the sudden shift in mindset at Langley over Saddam's intent to hold his new acquisition. Having underestimated Iraqi readiness and aggressiveness before the invasion, the CIA now judged that Iraq would fight tenaciously to hold Kuwait, and that the Iraqi forces, which only a few months earlier were said to be in need of a long rest after the war with Iran, were now highly capable and extremely dangerous.

Immediately after the invasion, Saddam put forth the cover story that Iraqi intervention had been requested by a hitherto unknown political entity in Kuwait, that Iraqi forces had come to the aid of this group, and that once order was restored they would withdraw. CIA Director William Webster, pointing to satellite photos showing Iraqi troops digging in, advised President Bush to dismiss these absurdities. "All the intelligence shows he won't pull out," Webster told the president. "He will stay if not challenged within the next year."[6] Already in possession of the world's fourth largest army, Saddam would now have oil wealth sufficient to pour vast sums into upgrading his military, Webster said. The Iraqi leader had no credible military rival in the region. Events quickly validated the CIA's rejection of the Iraqi withdrawal rumors: on August 8, Saddam declared the annexation of Kuwait; Iraq was no longer the occupier of Kuwait because Kuwait no longer existed. The CIA's new assessment of Iraqi strength and aggressiveness would color intelligence judgments of Iraq during months of public and congressional debate about whether to go to war.

Worrisome estimates of Iraqi military strength were based on several considerations. Where the CIA had once judged Saddam's forces to be exhausted from the Iran-Iraq War, it now portrayed them as battle-hardened and experienced at desert warfare. Iraq was regarded as particularly adept at defense-in-depth. Satellite imagery of Iraqi forces digging in along the Saudi border in southern Kuwait supported that view. Iraq had an estimated 5,000 main battle tanks, including modern T-72s, modern MiG-29 and Mirage F-1 fighter aircraft, Scud ballistic missiles, sophisticated air defenses, and strong artillery, with some 3,000 pieces larger than 100mm. Iraq's combat engineers, the ones in charge of digging frontline fortifications, were rated among the best military engineers in the world. Saddam positioned his elite Republican Guard units in northern Kuwait, a disposition U.S. intelligence interpreted as part of a classic counterattack strategy. Once coalition forces engaged, the Republican Guard, instead of being struck in the opening battle, would be poised to hurl itself against the point of attack, so the reasoning went. As the Pentagon's postwar report to Congress stated, "Strong, mobile, heavily armored counterattack forces, composed of the best elements of the Iraqi army, stood poised to strike at Coalition penetrations of the initial lines of defense." Iraq's coastal defenses were equally formidable, with layers of barriers, sea and land mines, and troops stationed in fortified positions within coastal highrise buildings, turning them into giant coast fortresses.[7] From those force dispositions, the intelligence community extrapolated what was likely to happen once the fighting began.

"The estimates were based on assumptions," Webster said. "One assumption was he'd use his army. The Republican Guard stayed to the north. He put all his crummy stuff along the border." But U.S. intelligence had misread the meaning of Saddam's troop dispositions, or at least had not considered an alternative. What the CIA failed to perceive was that "Saddam intended to survive," not fight, Webster said. The Republican Guard was poised not to counterattack but to retreat: "Everything he did was to protect his assets if needed."[8]

Few in Washington questioned that Iraq represented a formidable enemy. The most controversial judgment the CIA made prior to Operation Desert Storm was that sanctions alone would not drive Iraq from Kuwait. The evolving debate on Capitol Hill about the Bush administration's war strategy focused not on "war or no war" but on "war now or war later." Democrats lining up against the administration plan wanted to give sanctions more time to work. There was at least a chance that Saddam would quit Kuwait; if not, Iraq's forces would be that much weaker when coalition forces attacked. The sanctions on Iraq were the most severe ever imposed on a country by the United Nations, according to Riedel, affecting everything from oil and durable goods to food and medicine. Iraq, one of the world's largest oil producers, had to ration gasoline, and Saddam decreed that anyone caught hoarding food for profit would face the death penalty.[9] The inflationary impact of sanctions in some areas of the economy was reminiscent of 1920s Weimar Germany. In August 1990, a fifty-kilogram bag of sugar cost $32 in Iraq; by November the same bag cost $580.[10] The sanctions shut off 90 percent of imports and 97 percent of exports, slashing Iraqi foreign exchange by $1.5 billion in hard currency earnings per month, roughly one-third of Iraqi national product. All Iraqi and Kuwaiti international financial holdings were frozen.[11]

Still, by about October, the CIA had come to the conclusion that sanctions alone would not drive Iraq from Kuwait. U.S. intelligence knew that Iraq, with its irrigated, highly productive farmlands, expected a bumper crop in 1990 and had large quantities of wheat in storage.[12] The Iraqi people had become inured to material deprivation by the long war with Iran. And Saddam was not particularly sensitive to the comforts of the average Iraqi anyway. This was not what Democrats deeply skeptical of the idea of a large-scale war in Iraq wanted to hear.

"This was pretty explosive stuff," Riedel said. In an almost daily series of private and closed-door briefings on Capitol Hill, "We were grilled pretty hard." Most of the private briefings were for Democrats, Riedel recalled, since Republican lawmakers had lined up solidly with Bush's policy and knew how they were going to vote. Riedel called the briefings "endless" and viewed them as "an enormous diversion of resources from actually working on the target."[13]

The Agency resisted pressure from lawmakers for a more positive assessment of the sanctions option. On December 5, 1990, CIA Director Webster told lawmakers that the sanctions and blockade had prevented Iraq from "cashing in on higher oil prices" resulting from the destabilization in the region, but he judged that "Saddam apparently believes that he can outlast international resolve to maintain those sanctions. We see no indication that Saddam is concerned at this point that domestic discontent is growing to levels that may threaten his regime or that problems resulting from the sanctions are causing him to rethink his policy on Kuwait."[14] And on January 10, 1991, two days before the House and Senate voted to authorize the use of force to liberate Kuwait, Webster again addressed the sanctions issue in a letter to House Armed Services Committee Chairman Les Aspin (D-Wis.). The letter, cited repeatedly in floor debate in the House and Senate, went a step beyond his December testimony that Iraq could weather sanctions. Here Webster addressed whether more time under sanctions would make Iraq a weaker foe, an argument the Democrats were making, or would give Iraq time to strengthen its position. Webster concluded that "the ability of Iraqi forces to defend Kuwait and Southern Iraq is unlikely to be substantially eroded over the next six to 12 months even if effective sanctions can be maintained." This would be especially true, Webster wrote, if Saddam knew that at least for a time he did not have to worry about a coalition attack. Sanctions would have no impact on Iraq's ability to supply ammunition to its frontline forces; Saddam had conventional ordnance in abundance and a considerable arsenal of chemical weapons as well. Whatever erosion of Iraqi military preparedness would occur under sanctions would likely be offset by Iraq's use of the additional time to improve its formidable defensive positions in Kuwait, the CIA chief judged.[15]

Concern about casualties cost the administration Democratic votes on the authorization to use force. On balance, however, the prospect of a powerful Iraq in control of Kuwait and menacing Saudi Arabia—with a strong enough military to outlast sanctions—strengthened rather than undercut the administration's case for war. The portrayal of a powerful Iraq buttressed the administration's argument that even a successful sanctions-only policy that resulted in Iraq's withdrawing from Kuwait without a fight would leave unresolved the dangerous and destabilizing influence of an Iraqi military that, whatever its shortcomings, was far more capable than any other force in the Gulf region. The White House favored the portrayal of Iraq as ten feet tall because it helped justify the massive deployment of forces begun on August 7, 1990, and the major troop reinforcement ordered by Bush in November—after congressional elections—as the coalition strategy shifted from defensive to offensive. Senator Dennis DeConcini (D-Ariz.), a member of the Senate Intelligence Committee and its future chairman, was convinced that the Bush administration was deliberately exaggerating Iraqi military capability as a scare tactic designed to win public support for the war.[16]

The dynamic among the U.S. military services further bolstered the belief that Iraq would fight the coalition tenaciously and effectively. The Army and Marines emphasized the strength of Iraq's forces as a rebuttal to Air Force claims that air strikes alone might break Iraqi resolve to hold Kuwait. Air commanders wanted to prove their point about the impact of modern air power. And since minimizing coalition casualties was an explicit top priority of the war plan, they had a go-ahead to unleash truly frightful violence on the enemy, particularly with B-52 strikes on entrenched Iraqi forces. Ground commanders, naturally, argued that only "boots on the ground" would eject Iraq from Kuwait, and the more boots the better. Aspin, the House Armed Services chairman, observed,

"Advocates of air power will likely get a full opportunity to see if air power can win it by itself. But the U.S. military has made sure that sufficient ground force capability is available to do the job."[17] Powell, chairman of the Joint Chiefs of Staff, observed dryly that U.S. ground forces would not be thrown headlong at Iraqi military strengths "until they are no longer strengths."[18]

The intelligence community saw no downside to a worst-case analysis of Iraqi forces. Intelligence analysts were less concerned with winning political support in Congress (though they were heavily involved in Hill briefings) than they were about not underestimating the enemy and achieving rapid victory. In their reasoning, the alarming assessments of Iraqi capability energized the push to deploy the overwhelming force needed to deliver victory.

"Our rule is very simple," said the DIA's Lang: "In anything like this, you worst-case the situation. If they ask you what the worst case is, you tell them the worst case. We told them. We'd discussed this with Colin Powell, that if the Iraqis stood and fought in Kuwait, you could have 5,000 U.S. casualties. That was probably the upper range—dead, wounded, and missing. We actually felt that would be acceptable."[19]

CASUALTY ESTIMATES DRIVE THE DEBATE

For the Bush administration, the high casualty estimates that began to circulate in the months before Desert Storm were the one political downside to the portrayal of Saddam's formidable, dug-in military. In public, the Pentagon was closed-mouthed about its casualty estimates, in part because the numbers fluctuated wildly as the war plan and assessments of Iraqi combat readiness evolved. Some estimates were shared privately with lawmakers, but there was a public information vacuum filled by outside experts who, at times, offered some truly scary numbers that did nothing to win the Bush administration support for the war in Congress.

On October 30, President Bush met with House Speaker Tom Foley, Senate Majority Leader George Mitchell, and members of an eighteen-member bipartisan team created to monitor events in the Gulf during the recess for the November 1990 elections. The Democratic leaders handed Bush a letter signed by eighty-one Democrats warning of "catastrophic" consequences, including 10,000 to 50,000 American deaths, a far higher figure for killed-in-action than any official body produced during the run-up to war.[20] It was unclear where some critics of the war policy were getting their numbers: Representative Barbara Boxer (D-Calif.) quoted predictions of as many as 15,000 U.S. casualties, which would include soldiers killed, wounded, and captured. Former defense secretary Robert McNamara estimated at least 30,000 casualties; former senator George McGovern said as many as 50,000 American soldiers might be killed. The most authoritative Democratic estimate came from Nunn, who said military and civilian intelligence officials, as well as outside experts, were estimating 10,000 to 20,000 casualties.[21]

President Bush claimed in his memoir that the Pentagon casualty estimate that he had in hand in late 1990 was below 2,000.[22] According to Schwarzkopf, by October, military analysts had given him what he regarded as a "rather optimistic" estimate of 8,000 U.S. wounded and 2,000 dead, assuming Iraq did not use chemical weapons.[23] In October, at a war planning meeting at the Pentagon, U.S. commanders using standard military computer models estimated 10,000 casualties, including 1,500 killed in action.[24]

Through most of the run-up to Desert Storm, Saddam did his best to instill fear of high casualties in hopes of sapping American public support for war. Though his remark in his July meeting with U.S. Ambassador April Glaspie that it was "impossible for the Americans to accept 10,000 dead" seemed like an ominous hint of the dictator's belligerent intent, Glaspie said she paid it little mind because it was something the Iraqis said to her frequently. "It has also appeared in the Iraqi-controlled press," Glaspie told lawmakers after the war. "It was a very common misapprehension about us."[25] At the end of August, Saddam boasted on Radio Baghdad, "The harm that will be inflicted on the invaders will be even more severe than what they experience in Vietnam, and Iraq will come out on top."[26]

Debate in Washington in the ensuing months made clear that however flawed Saddam's geopolitical calculations or his strategic thinking, his public information strategy of instilling doubt about the Bush administration's war plan was at least partially effective. By December, as it became clearer that war with the United States and its allies was coming, Saddam asserted, "If President Bush pushes things toward war . . . once 5,000 of his troops die, he will not be able to continue the war."[27] In January, a few days before the war began, Saddam said his troops were well protected in underground bunkers and would rise up against the enemy to inflict mass casualties.[28]

President Bush visited troops in Saudi Arabia over Thanksgiving. With the war plan basically settled, Schwarzkopf gave Bush best- and worst-case scenarios of the duration of the war, from three days at the low end to a stalemate that could last months; the general's in-between scenario was three to four weeks.[29]

In mid-December, retired Army Colonel Trevor DePuy presented lawmakers with his estimate that the air campaign would produce 1,800 U.S. casualties, including 300 dead, while the ground campaign would yield 9,000 casualties, including 1,500 dead. DePuy, whose casualty estimates for the 1989 U.S. incursion into Panama had proved highly accurate, based his Gulf War estimate on the assumption that U.S. forces would mount a frontal attack on Iraqi defensive positions in Kuwait.[30]

On December 5, 1990, Defense Secretary Dick Cheney told lawmakers in a public session that it was "difficult to say" how long the war would last or how many coalition casualties it would produce. A decision to go to war, he said, would activate a strategy "that guarantees success, that makes it as short a campaign as possible and keeps casualties to the absolute minimum."[31] Just fifteen days later, however, Cheney secretly signed off on the final plan for Operation Desert Storm. Included in the "operational imperatives" outlined in the plan was a requirement that Schwarzkopf "accept losses no greater than the equivalent of three companies per coalition brigade." That represented about 10 percent of the coalition ground force, or 10,000 soldiers killed, wounded, and missing.[32] Powell recalled a conversation with Bush at the Holly Cabin at Camp David on Christmas Eve 1990:

> The worst-case scenarios were truly frightening, our troops advancing against hundreds of thousands of entrenched Iraqis, a sea of mines between them and the enemy, ditches full of oil that were to be set ablaze as our men advanced, and hanging over our heads the unknowable elements of chemical and biological warfare.[33]

There had been press leaks that the Pentagon had ordered 15,000 body bags. The move, it turned out, had nothing to do with Desert Storm. Schwarzkopf, reluctant to be pinned down, eventually estimated 5,000 casualties; Powell estimated 3,000.[34]

The actual American casualties, of course, fell far below all of these estimates: 148 killed in action, 458 wounded.

IRAQ'S VULNERABILITIES

Amid the general mood of dread concerning the upcoming war to liberate Kuwait, a steady stream of intelligence pointed to the possibility that Iraq might not be as tenacious an adversary as many believed. Military analyst William Arkin has recounted how U.S. Army Lieutenant Colonel Fred C.

Hart, a liaison officer to Kuwait's armed forces who was in Kuwait at the time of the invasion, observed Iraqi forces scavenging for food and water once they got to the Kuwaiti capital. To Hart's professional eye, it bespoke the lack of an established logistics chain for troop support.[35] U.S. commanders, with their access to crystal-clear satellite imagery of Iraqi military emplacements in Kuwait along the Saudi border, quickly realized that those positions, though heavily fortified, could be easily flanked to the west through the Iraqi desert. As Lawrence Freedman and Efraim Karsh wrote in a postwar analysis, the Iraqis made some efforts to extend their defensive line, but "only limited results were achieved and the resultant gap was later exploited mercilessly."[36]

Even before the air campaign began to grind down Iraqi forces and before the ground campaign to go around rather than through Iraqi defenses took shape, there was reason to question the size as well as the capability of the Iraqi force in Kuwait. Pentagon intelligence analysis in October 1990 estimated that Saddam had deployed more than 435,000 troops to Kuwait, "dug in and arrayed in mutually supporting defenses in depth." By January, according to intelligence estimates, more than half a million Iraqi troops were in Kuwait.[37] Shortly after the war, however, U.S. Central Command reported in a partially declassified debriefing that "most infantry divisions were sent to the Kuwait theater undermanned, short of equipment . . . and with little or no idea of what they were to do upon arrival in their areas of responsibility, other than to dig in and await orders."[38] The Gulf War Air Power Survey stated flatly that "none of the Iraqi units deployed in theater were at full personnel or equipment strength." Regular Iraqi army units, the ones dug in along the border with Saudi Arabia, were down to 75 to 85 percent. Figuring in the wholesale desertion rates prior to the commencement of Desert Storm, these units were at roughly half strength by mid-January 1991. The tide of desertions appears to have been only marginally stemmed by Saddam's order that execution squads be organized in each unit. Hundreds of Iraqis not only deserted their positions but chose to defect to the coalition side, providing a stream of human intelligence about wavering troop morale and readiness on the Iraqi side, in addition to the mute testimony of their own desertions.[39] As the Air Power Survey put it:

> The Iraqi army that U.S. and coalition forces faced on the eve of the war suffered from numerous self-inflicted wounds which put them at a significant disadvantage. The dramatic expansion of the army before the war had weakened Saddam's army rather than strengthened it. Although the Republican

Guard was at nearly full strength, the regular army divisions were not. This situation adversely affected the confidence of his troops. In addition, the regular army—recently bolstered with large numbers of untrained recruits—was weary from a decade of combat against Iran and the Kurds and demoralized by the prospect of a war against the coalition.[40]

Although the extent to which Iraqi divisions were undermanned did not become clear to U.S. intelligence until after the war, many of the shortcomings of Saddam's invasion force in morale, equipment, and capability were known before the liberation of Kuwait began. And doubts about the capability of Iraqi forces were not kept locked up in drawers at the CIA and denied to lawmakers weighing whether to support the use of force against Iraq. The point was being made publicly. Defense Secretary Cheney, for example, noted in a Sunday talk-show appearance in November that the reinforcements Saddam was sending to Kuwait "are not very high-quality forces, and not necessarily an asset for him."[41] But as a point of emphasis in intelligence briefings, the size, unconventional armaments, and recent combat experience of Iraq's forces got the most play.

While tanks and artillery pieces are easily counted by satellites, individual soldiers are not; U.S. intelligence appears to have calculated Iraqi troop strength by multiplying the estimated thirty-eight Iraqi divisions deployed to Kuwait by 15,000, the standard Iraqi complement for a division. The end result was a gross overestimation of Iraqi numeric strength; by one postwar estimate, the actual number of Iraqi troops in Kuwait as of January 15, 1991, was 350,000, nearly 200,000 fewer than the 547,000 the intelligence community was estimating.[42] Postwar analysis by the House Armed Services Committee showed an even more dramatic disparity. By the beginning of the coalition ground war, Iraqi units were reduced by a further 185,000, including 153,000 troops who had deserted, 17,000 who had been injured in the air war, and 9,000 who had been killed. By February 24, 1991, when the ground war began, that left 183,000 Iraqi troops facing a coalition force of 700,000—a force that had better equipment and training and total control of the air.[43]

Contributing to the inaccurate estimates of Iraqi strength were limitations in technical intelligence collection. The spy planes and satellites in the U.S. inventory at the time of the Gulf War were positioned and designed for the Soviet threat. Their mission was "close-look" intelligence—imagery that would show details of weapons, missile silos, and the like. These assets were not capable of "wide-look" intelligence for such missions as searching the desert for mobile Scud launchers or accurate estimates of troop formations.[44] Also, Iraqi commanders observed strict discipline in the use of communications—and suffered severe punishment if they failed to do so. Iraq's army used buried communications cables and motorcycle runners for sensitive communications, reducing the intelligence "take" from signals intercepts. The White House, meanwhile, had banned reconnaissance aircraft flights over enemy territory to avoid an incident that could spark war before the coalition force was ready to go.[45] Compounding these problems, the urgent priority of finding Iraqi mobile Scud launchers, which arose even before the first Iraqi strike on Israel on January 19, 1991, drew the focus of satellite intelligence and analysis to the far western Iraqi desert, away from Iraqi troop concentrations in Kuwait.[46]

THE CASUALTY DEBATE WITHIN THE MILITARY

Schwarzkopf was aware of many of the weaknesses of Iraq's army but told his own commanders, "You can take the most beat-up army in the world, and if they choose to stand and fight, you're going to take casualties." His "nightmare," as the coalition ground attack began, was that U.S. forces would be halted before Iraqi obstacles and then hit with a chemical attack. This "possibility of mass casualties," Schwarzkopf wrote in his memoir, was behind the decision to set up sixty-three field hospitals, two hospital ships, and 18,000 hospital beds within the war zone.[47] U.S. intelligence reporting on the 1980–88 Iran-Iraq War produced frightening estimates of the effectiveness of chemical weapons. A 1988 intelligence memorandum reported that in one campaign Iraq inflicted 30 percent casualties on the enemy, of which 3 to 4 percent were deaths. The report declared that the U.S. "Intelligence Community believes that in some cases during specific battles Iraqi chemical employments have been tactically effective."[48]

Here as elsewhere, however, intelligence reporting tended to overemphasize Iraqi capability without differentiating the force Iraq would be up against. Les Aspin, the House Armed Services Committee chairman, was one of the most influential Democrats to vote in favor of the authorization to use force. A series of hearings chaired by Aspin in December 1990 brought forth witnesses who largely discounted the threat of chemical weapons against U.S. forces much better equipped than had been their Iranian counterparts a few years earlier. In a resulting report, Aspin wrote that there was "little doubt" that Saddam would use chemical weapons, but much doubt as to how much damage they would inflict. Chemical agents tend to dissipate quickly in a hot desert environment. Expert witness Brad Roberts, then of the Center for Strategic and International Studies, testified that chemical weapons would have primarily a psychological effect and that the Iraqi military could not sustain a chemical weapons barrage for any significant time.[49] However, the mere threat of chemical weapons imposes practical as well as psychological burdens, since troops have to wear cumbersome and uncomfortable protective gear, a particularly unpleasant task in desert heat. Beyond the issue of the questionable effect of chemical weapons on prepared troops, Aspin noted that the Iraqi army "has never come under sustained, heavy air attacks," such as those Central Command was then preparing. In one of the more accurate predictions of the war to come, retired Army general William DePuy, former head of the Army's Training and Doctrine Command, told the House Armed Services Committee, "If [coalition] attacks are in general effective, quick, devastating and lethal, the word will get around, and the second- and third-class troops will begin to fade away."[50]

Though there were serious shortcomings in CIA analysis relating to the Persian Gulf War, the Agency did not accommodate the Bush administration's desire to win congressional support either by reducing its estimates on chemical weapons or by telling lawmakers the war would be easy. The institutional mindset that prevailed was fear that intelligence would predict a quick and easy conflict only to have the fight bog down into a protracted and costly war. And this fear was not limited to the intelligence community. The Marine Corps's concern about its mission of mounting a frontal assault on Iraqi entrenchments has already been noted. Joint Chiefs Chairman Powell, while publicly supporting the Bush administration policy, was privately tilting toward Sam Nunn's position of giving sanctions more time to work.[51] Speaking to Nunn's committee in December 1990, Powell derided the "experts, amateurs and others" in Washington who believed Iraq could be dislodged from Kuwait by air power alone.[52]

In fact, the dispute was not so much between experts and amateurs as between ground-force generals and air-force generals. Some of the officers working on the air campaign, such as Brigadier General Buster Glosson and his boss, Lieutenant General Chuck Horner, were concerned that Powell was raising doubts about the war plan by heightening fears of an arduous ground campaign. They worried among themselves that Powell, with his

Army background, had no concept of what modern air power could do and was squandering an opportunity to frighten Iraq into withdrawal by touting the awesome firepower that coalition warplanes were about to unleash on the Iraqis.[53] Schwarzkopf used concern about casualties raised by the initial frontal-assault plan to lobby President Bush for the major reinforcements Bush approved in November, which enabled Schwarzkopf to design the more complex flanking operation that he dubbed the "Hail Mary" pass. At least some in the Bush administration had chafed at proposals to enlarge the force. Robert Gates, then a senior National Security Council adviser to Bush, made a crack after an October briefing on the earlier ground-war plan, likening Schwarzkopf to General George B. McClellan, the Civil War commander with a reputation for being reluctant to fight until every possible preparation—and then some—had been made. Gates also suggested that military warnings of high casualties had been calibrated to cause Bush to rethink his strategy and consider giving sanctions more time.[54]

As the air campaign unfolded, the doubts of Schwarzkopf, Powell, and other Army commanders melted away, to be replaced by confidence that the ground forces would encounter a heavily damaged and demoralized Iraqi force. The CIA dissented, arguing that pilots were succumbing to the natural tendency to claim damage far beyond what they were actually inflicting. According to a congressional examination of intelligence in the Gulf War, Schwarzkopf was "irate that people in Washington were plotting to blame him if the attack went poorly by positioning themselves to claim that he acted on data they knew to be wrong." Schwarzkopf himself told the investigative panel that there had been "some distancing on the part of some agencies from the position of Central Command" as to the level of destruction wrought by the air campaign.[55] He was charging that the CIA had adopted a skeptical posture toward bomb-damage assessments, or BDA, as a prudent hedge against the possibility that the war would go badly. In the end, both the Agency and Schwarzkopf were vindicated. The CIA was right that the military's bomb-damage reports were grossly inflated. Indeed, even the CIA's far more conservative damage assessments proved overly optimistic, as later detailed examinations of the amount of Iraqi hardware and targets destroyed came in at far lower levels than estimated.[56] Meanwhile, Schwarzkopf, while wrong about BDA, was right about the bigger issue, decisive victory in the war itself.

"CENTCOM said the Republican Guard was 80 percent destroyed; we said 40 percent destroyed," the CIA's Riedel recalled. "As you can imagine, that created a great deal of tension with the war-fighters. This fed the complaint that we made Iraq look ten feet tall. At the end of the war, we look like the stubborn brothers who won't acknowledge success."[57]

This rancor between the military and the Agency over bomb damage doubtless contributed to the military's sparing postwar praise for the support it received from the intelligence community, even as it celebrated its own brilliant victory. But the issue went beyond the apportionment of credit for the victory. In addition to liberating Kuwait, a key objective of Operation Desert Storm was establishing the "security and stability of Saudi Arabia and the Persian Gulf."[58] In theory, it sounded like a benign goal. In practice, it entailed inflicting massive destruction on Iraq's military. The point was not just getting Iraq out of Kuwait but also destroying as much of the Iraqi military machine as possible so that nothing similar could happen again. As translated into an operational order, this meant that the coalition would seek to "destroy Republican Guard Forces in the [Kuwaiti Theater of Operations]" and "destroy known nuclear, biological and chemical (NBC) production, storage, and delivery capabilities."[59] Thus, bomb damage and battle damage assessments became issues far beyond the point of pride over how many "kill" or "strike" symbols a fighter pilot could paint on the side of his aircraft. It went to the issue of how well CENTCOM had executed the mission it had been given, and how big a threat Iraq would continue to pose to the region. The CIA's greater skepticism, helped along by being one step removed from an investment in gaining credit for the execution of the war, evolved from an intelligence failure before the war, the overestimation of Iraqi strength, to an intelligence success afterward, the correct assessment that a great deal of Iraqi military power had survived intact. Schwarzkopf and the Pentagon were reluctant to admit it, but inevitably it became a point impossible to ignore: the Republican Guard had largely escaped Iraq and lived to fight another day. After taking over Kuwait, Saddam had positioned his elite forces in the northern part of the country, well behind the front line opposite Saudi Arabia, allowing them to be withdrawn when threatened.

Saddam chose to save his best forces rather than lose them, as surely would have happened had he chosen to throw them at the coalition attack. Devastating though the air campaign undoubtedly was on Iraqi troops, its real impact was to sap Iraq's will to resist and prompt a determination by Saddam to save his main forces rather than lose them in the sands of Kuwait and southern Iraq. The vindication for the CIA on the bomb-damage question was not complete, however. The operational order had laid out the need to destroy "known" nuclear, biological, and chemical weapons sites. As I will lay out in greater detail, what became clear after the war with the arrival of U.N. weapons inspectors was the degree to which Iraq's WMD facilities were unknown to Western intelligence, including the CIA. Thus the failure to more completely degrade Iraqi military power was in part an intelligence failure that could not be laid entirely at the feet of Central Command.

After the war, Gates said Schwarzkopf's request for more troops stemmed from the military's understandable reluctance to replay the Vietnam experience in which U.S. troop strength escalated in increments carefully controlled by Washington, enabling the enemy to keep pace. "There was very little enthusiasm in the American military for, in fact, throwing Saddam out of Kuwait militarily," Gates said. In the post-Vietnam era, Gates said, commanders "try, perhaps even unconsciously, not only to exaggerate the level of forces that will be required to accomplish a specific objective but the casualties as well, in the hope of forcing a sanity check."[60] In early January, as Congress debated whether to go to war, the concerns among U.S. ground commanders spilled over into the debate on Capitol Hill.

A RELUCTANT CONGRESS SAYS YES TO WAR

Both the American Civil War and Vietnam seemed to be on lawmakers' minds as Congress, in January 1991, took up the resolution to authorize force in the Gulf—the first congressional vote for outright war since the 1964 Tonkin Gulf Resolution that authorized the Vietnam War. In the fall of 1990, PBS had broadcast filmmaker Ken Burns's series on the Civil War, a television event that became a national phenomenon, with its emphasis on the war's unexpectedly protracted duration and immense cost in death and suffering. Virtually all the key players in the Bush White House had watched the series, starting with Powell, who had received an advance set of tapes from Burns. Powell was so moved by the series that he told the president about it, and Bush, busy with war planning and diplomacy, found time to watch. Cheney gave a set to Schwarzkopf as a Christmas gift, and the war commander later wrote that as a result of watching the series he redoubled his effort to reduce U.S. casualties.[61]

Intelligence warnings of heavy casualties and of a drawn-out war in the Gulf permeated the congressional debate. "Many of my constituents in Georgia have written and called and asked me whether this is another Vietnam," Sam Nunn told his colleagues during his Senate floor speech a day before the vote. Nunn said he did not believe so—that the open, desert terrain and exposed positioning of the enemy favored American firepower. But he made clear that intelligence briefings on the strength of the Iraqi military and its defensive positions in Kuwait, and intelligence community uncertainty about the cost of liberating Kuwait, heavily influenced his decision to argue for giving sanctions a chance to work: "What guarantees do we have that war will be brief, American casualties will be light? . . . I have not seen any guarantees on any subject from the intelligence community."[62] Nunn did not blame the CIA for this; it was in the nature of the business. As chairman of the Senate Armed Services Committee, Nunn had done more, perhaps, than any other member of Congress to establish the modernized conventional forces and joint command structure that would play so critical a role in the coalition's overwhelming victory. Nunn had no doubt the coalition would prevail, and he advocated the unsparing application of firepower that Schwarzkopf, in fact, employed in the Desert Storm campaign. But ultimately, Nunn did not consider the liberation of Kuwait a sufficiently vital U.S. interest to warrant the casualties that might be involved in commencing war immediately. As both a respected pro-military voice in Congress and chairman of a key committee privy to extensive intelligence and military briefings, Nunn was a senator to whom other Democrats looked for guidance as the final vote approached. In a series of televised hearings in December, Nunn had provided a forum not only for the administration to defend its policy but also for a host of skeptics to voice their concerns about the proposed war. Thirty-four fellow senators joined Nunn as co-sponsors of an alternative resolution supporting continued international sanctions but leaving open the use of force at a later time.[63]

Among the co-sponsors was Senator David Boren (D-Okla.), an influential voice in the war debate in his own right given his chairmanship of the Senate Select Committee on Intelligence. Boren, who had been privy to CIA briefings emphasizing Iraqi military strength, said too much of the financial and military burden of the campaign was to be borne by the United States for the less-than-vital purpose of restoring to power a fabulously wealthy Arab emir: "While all of us hope that war would be short, decisive, and with few casualties, there is also a considerable risk, according to most experts I have heard in both open and closed classified sessions, that it could last for months rather than for days and could be extremely costly."[64]

In the House, the equally influential Armed Services Committee chairman, Les Aspin, supported the war. Aspin revealed detailed knowledge of the plan for the forthcoming Desert Storm campaign in the outline he presented to colleagues during floor debate in the House. The fight would begin with an intensive air campaign, he said. "Those who think air power alone will win the war will have their chance," Aspin said. "We do not want more casualties than is absolutely necessary." In the end, Aspin argued, the key issue was not so much Iraqi capability as coalition capability relative to Iraq. Here the odds strongly favored the coalition: "I believe our forces are capable of achieving our goals." Aspin also pointed out that Democrats who supported the idea of working in concert with the United Nations now had a chance to put the idea to the test in the Kuwaiti desert. The U.N. Security Council had voted on November 29, 1990, for Resolution 678, which required Iraq to withdraw its forces from Kuwait by January 15.[65]

Three days before the deadline, the Senate voted narrowly—52 to 47—to authorize the use of force. It was the closest vote for war by a chamber of Congress in U.S. history.[66] In the House, with Aspin's influential support, a larger percentage of Democrats went along with the administration, and the margin in support of war was wider, 250 to 183. Among Senate Democrats, 82 percent opposed the authorization; 67 percent of House Democrats opposed it. Republican support was solid in both chambers; only 2 of 44 Republican senators opposed authorizing the use of force; 3 out of 167 House Republicans opposed it.[67]

The politics of the congressional votes to support the liberation of Kuwait have been studied extensively by scholars and political analysts.[68] Certainly numerous factors besides the briefings by intelligence officials weighed in the voting. Among them: for Republicans, loyalty to the Bush administration; for members of both parties, a belief that the administration and U.S. allies had already committed so much that to back down would be disastrous; a genuine view that Saddam represented a menace to the region and the world's oil supplies; fear that Saddam's newly stolen oil wealth would translate into an even greater military menace; and support for the principle that a country, even a small, oil-rich emirate, should be secure within its borders and safe from foreign invasion, that the precedent of a total, forcible takeover of one country by a predatory neighbor could not be allowed to stand. Lawmakers, of course, were aware of the U.N. resolution and its January 15 deadline for Iraq to quit Kuwait, and they knew that a defeat by Congress of the authorization to use force would undermine the credibility of the U.N.

For opponents of the war, there was concern, not exclusively driven by intelligence briefings, about taking on so large and heavily armed an adversary and about the threat of chemical warfare. There were doubts that Kuwait represented a sufficiently close ally or vital interest that it had to be liberated—the view, in other words, that Kuwait was little more to the United States than a gas station that had now come under new management. There was sentiment for the proposition that war should be an absolute last resort and that all alternatives, particularly sanctions, should be tried to the fullest before resorting to war. Opinion polling on war varied from state to state, but nationwide showed a roughly even split.[69] For politicians, therefore, a key motivating factor was not the risk of angering a large constituency *before the fact*—that was unavoidable regardless of the vote. The larger political concern for supporters was the political cost, *after the fact*, of a bad outcome. The overriding fear was that things might turn out far worse than hoped, that the U.S. military might become bogged down in "another Vietnam"—a phrase heard frequently that fall and winter. Michael Barone has written that some of the antiwar speeches made on the floor of the House and Senate in January 1991 made little sense as commentaries on the immediate crisis and "much more sense as retrospective comments on the Vietnam War: These Democrats were taking the stand they wished they or their elders had taken some 25 or 30 years before."[70] In a sense, a reverse of this dynamic would influence Democrats in 2002 as they lined up to support the George W. Bush administration's push to war against Iraq, ruefully aware of what their opposition to the Gulf War had cost them just over a decade earlier.

James Baker, secretary of state at the time of the Gulf War, said years later that his final attempt at direct diplomacy with Iraq—a dramatic meeting in Geneva with Iraqi Foreign Minister Tariq Aziz on January 9, three days before Congress voted—helped sway key support in Congress.[71] Baker had no expectation that the meeting would produce a breakthrough that might avert war. The point was to show Congress, particularly opponents of war, that the United States had tried all avenues to avoid war. Aziz quickly made clear that he had no leeway from Saddam to negotiate a withdrawal of Iraqi forces from Kuwait, and Baker was bound by the inflexible terms of the Security Council resolution to demand total and immediate Iraqi withdrawal. Regardless of the intelligence community's worrisome assessments of Iraqi military strength, Baker made clear to his Iraqi counterpart in the closed-door session that the Bush administration's top officials were confident in the overwhelming superiority of coalition forces over Iraq's army. The upcoming fight "will not be another Vietnam," Baker warned Aziz.[72] "I said that they should not make the mistake of assuming that they would control the terms of the battle, as perhaps they might have assumed in their war with Iran, that this would be a totally different situation, that our technological superiority was overwhelming and would be brought to bear," Baker recalled. "I think as it turned out our assessments of what our overwhelmingly superior military forces could do were correct."[73] Baker brought with him a letter from President Bush that conveyed an explicit warning that Saddam not only risked losing Kuwait; he risked losing his own army as well. The letter also contained an implicit threat of massive retaliation if Iraq resorted to chemical attacks on U.S. forces or engaged in terrorist attacks. "The American people would demand the strongest possible response," Bush wrote.[74] The language of the letter was so blunt that Aziz, who read it in Baker's presence, refused to convey it to Saddam.

The meeting in Geneva, rather than the congressional votes three days later, seemed to decide the issue of war in the public mind. Baker emerged from six hours of meetings with Aziz and gave an anxious press corps a long recitation of the back-and-forth discussions. At length, Baker said, "regrettably . . . I heard nothing that suggested to me any Iraqi flexibility whatsoever." With the utterance of the word "regrettably," there was an audible gasp in the briefing room.

Still, the outcome of the vote in Congress mattered to the administration as a statement to the world of American resolve and as a vote of confidence in the administration's policy. Baker made clear the administration was prepared to go to war without the support of Congress, but doing so would have been awkward at the very least and potentially highly problematic. With both the House and Senate under Democratic control in 1991, the vote came about not because President Bush asked for it—the White House view, advocated particularly by Defense Secretary Cheney, was that it had authority in law and precedent to launch Desert Storm without an act of Congress. Nor was it an attempt by the Democratic majority to block Bush, since the party leadership in Congress made clear that there was no party line on the question, that each member could vote his or her conscience. Rather, the congressional leadership was asserting the right and power of Congress to have a voice in a decision as momentous as war.

With so many factors in play, it is difficult to isolate any one as critical to the outcome of the vote or to the voting pattern of a particular group in the House and Senate. But it is important to recognize how intelligence was used in the decision-making of key lawmakers who, in turn, influenced the votes of others. Since so much depended on the intelligence community's assessment of what was likely to happen in Desert Storm, Nunn, chairman of the Senate Armed Services Committee and a member of the Senate Intelligence Committee, and Boren, the Senate Intelligence chairman, became particularly important voices on the Democratic side. Looking back on these events, both remembered the sobering tone of the prewar intelligence briefings, the emphasis on Iraq's layered defenses, the capability of the Iraqi military, the risk of chemical weapons attack, and the likelihood of substantial U.S. casualties. As already noted, Nunn recalled estimates of 10,000 to 20,000 casualties. All but two of the Democrats on the Senate Armed Services Committee voted with Nunn against authorizing Bush to use force immediately. None of the Democrats on the Senate Intelligence Committee supported the authorization to use force.[75]

George Tenet, then the Intelligence Committee's chief of staff, arranged almost daily intelligence briefings on the crisis in the Persian Gulf, usually given by senior CIA analysts—the "endless" parade to Capitol Hill not so fondly recalled by the CIA's Riedel. In a monograph on intelligence community relations with Congress, L. Britt Snider, general counsel to the committee at the time of the Gulf War, wrote that the briefings predicted a "prolonged conflict of at least six months' duration involving many casualties." According to Snider, intelligence officials later insisted that they were well aware of the Iraqi military's vulnerabilities but chose not to highlight them in congressional briefings for fear that the information would leak and indicate to Saddam where U.S. forces intended to strike.[76] The real problem, however, was the failure to consider U.S. military capability in comparison to Iraq's. Riedel's answer to this criticism was that the CIA left it to military briefers, who appeared before the Armed Services committees, to describe U.S. capability. It was the CIA's job to describe the foreign threat, the military's to calculate the cost of dealing with that threat. In any case, Riedel said, the CIA assumed that lawmakers could figure out on their own that U.S. forces were superior.[77]

It was, Snider wrote, "largely on the basis of these dire predictions" that Boren and Nunn opposed the rush to war. "Later, when it turned out that coalition forces achieved immediate air superiority and the ground war ended in a matter of days with relatively few American casualties, the Senators who had voted in the negative were understandably upset."[78] Indeed, Snider put it more bluntly in an interview, saying Boren was furious with the CIA following the Gulf War, not only because of his own difficulties with his constituents caused by his vote but by the damage to his credibility among colleagues who had turned to him for guidance in casting their votes.[79] Snider said that Boren, Nunn, and other Democrats on these committees—members whose views influenced the votes of colleagues—felt "sandbagged" by the CIA. Boren himself confirmed this account, recalling his anger at the CIA—which he shared in no uncertain terms with Agency officials—when Desert Storm became a rout, since prewar briefings that had indicated a quite different outcome had so influenced his vote and those of many other Democrats against the authorization to use force.[80]

Nunn was less inclined to blame the intelligence community and was more circumspect about being wrong about Iraqi military capabilities and the estimates of casualties in Desert Storm. "It wasn't just the CIA, it was DIA, it was defense, it was the service intelligence," Nunn recalled. "Intelligence exaggerated the strength of the Iraqi military, without any doubt, but I also think the intelligence missed how stretched out they were logistically. . . . The sanctions had done them more damage than we realized."[81] Nunn echoed Riedel's view that it was the Pentagon's responsibility, not the CIA's, to assess how much damage air power was likely to do to Iraqi forces before the ground war began. From his Senate Armed Services Committee position, Nunn had been a key player in the military modernization of the late 1970s and 1980s. During the Carter presidency, Nunn and Cheney, then a U.S. representative, had co-written a study on ideas then being developed by the military for more accurate, stealthy striking power from the air. It had to do with a war against the Soviet Union in Western Europe and the need to make up for the Soviet advantage in manpower with lethal, survivable striking power from the air. But until 1991 it had all played out in war games and paper studies. "The military had been working on that, the Air Force had been doing that, but nobody had plugged all that in to how that was going to affect a ground operation," Nunn said.[82] Nunn was hearing primarily from ground commanders who were deeply concerned about casualties in a war to liberate Kuwait. He had also, of course, heard directly from Arnold Punaro, his staff director on the Senate Armed Services Committee, on returning from his Marine Reserve stint along the front lines in Saudi Arabia. And he had heard witnesses from military and defense think tanks echoing many of these same concerns.

In an example of how small things can sometimes influence positions, Nunn also spoke privately with a Saudi businessman who told him that members of the Saudi royal family were demanding kickbacks from Saudi hoteliers who were housing thousands of U.S. soldiers while the base logistics for the arriving troops were being set up:

> Here we were protecting Saudi Arabia and . . . the top officials of the govern-
> ment we were protecting were getting kickbacks from American tax money.
> You can believe it or not believe it. I happen to believe it. What it said to me [is
> that] it tied in to the casualty business, not that we should change the mission.
> But should we be in a big hurry about this at the expense of what I thought
> was probably four or five thousand American lives? It turned out I was wrong
> [about the casualties], and thank God for that.[83]

The political cost to Democrats who opposed the war was indirect, affecting reputations and influence as opposed to resulting in wholesale defeat of
Democrats in the next election. Many faced much tougher opposition than
they would have otherwise, and the party overall was subject to renewed accusations that it was soft on national security affairs. For Nunn, a southern
senator and leading advocate of a strong military, political fallout from the
vote on the Gulf War was ironic and painful, but also limited. Nunn had been
an instrumental champion of conventional force modernization as far back as
the mid-1970s and had been a key architect of the congressionally mandated
reorganization of the U.S. military command structure under the Goldwater
Nichols Act of 1986, which promoted joint operations among the military services, weakened the political power of the individual services, and gave field
commanders such as Schwarzkopf much more sweeping authority over troops
under their command. Yet a highway sign in Georgia called Nunn "Saddam's
Best Friend."[84] Nunn's poll numbers in Georgia dipped modestly—from the
high 70s in approval to the high 60s—following the Gulf War, and quickly
rebounded. Nunn had largely ruled out running for president by that point
in his career, but if he still entertained any notion of doing so, he believed his
chances had been hurt nationally because of his opposition to the war.[85]

Some lawmakers were opposed to the war on principle and seized on the
concern about casualties as the best political justification for their position.
Others entered the debate genuinely undecided and, on getting the intelligence briefings, determined to vote against the war. The CIA's Riedel had the
distinct impression that many lawmakers he briefed already knew how they
were going to vote and, among those opposed to war, were looking for ammunition to support their arguments.[86] Given the sharp partisan split in voting
on the Gulf War resolution between Republicans and Democrats who had

access to the same intelligence briefings, it is clear that party affiliation, home state or district leanings, and members' own predispositions heavily influenced the results.[87] Lawmakers in key committee leadership positions, such as Nunn and Boren, also influenced how their party colleagues voted. Nunn called the leadership factor "a mixed bag." Some members genuinely looked to Nunn and Boren for guidance on how to vote. Others knew how they were going to vote, Nunn said, but "used Boren and me, because we were both strong on defense and intelligence, as a little bit of a shield."[88]

Nunn and Boren sponsored the chief alternative to the Bush administration request that Congress authorize the use of force. Their measure, which would have given sanctions more time to work, was defeated 53–46 largely along party lines shortly before the final vote on January 12 to authorize force.[89] After the measure to continue sanctions failed, Nunn considered throwing his support behind the authorization to use force on grounds that a more unified Senate would send Iraq a stronger message and possibly convince Saddam to give up Kuwait. Here Nunn's influence over his fellow Democrats worked in reverse—for now the rank-and-file influenced how the chairman voted. When Nunn told Senate Majority Leader George Mitchell that he was considering voting for the authorization, Mitchell portrayed the move as a switch and said Nunn "would be leaving a lot of Democrats out on a limb" if he now supported the White House. Nunn relented, and immediately regretted doing so because of the divided message the Senate sent in the close vote, 52–47, for war.[90]

Clearly intelligence assessments were an ingredient, although not the only ingredient, in determining views in Congress on the use of force. This much we can say:

- Intelligence estimates of casualties heavily influenced the views of influential Democrats who led party opposition to authorizing the use of force against Iraq in the Persian Gulf.

- After the war, Boren, the chief Senate overseer of the CIA, with Tenet as his chief of staff, let the CIA know of his unhappiness in no uncertain terms. Tenet, of course, would be in charge of the CIA in 2002 when the Agency issued sanguine briefings predicting the U.S. military would have little difficulty in defeating Iraq.

- Democrats did not pay a heavy price in the 1992 elections for their votes against war in 1991, but they did suffer a substantial blow, individually and party-wide, to their reputation on national security issues, and they found themselves, after the conflict, on the "wrong" side of what turned out to be a popular war. They were, figuratively speaking, not invited to the victory parade.[91]

ECHOES OF AN EASY VICTORY

Considering the many ways in which the U.S.-led invasion of Iraq in 2003 was a far more risky proposition than the Gulf War, the substantially stronger support in Congress for the Iraq War is remarkable. In 1991, the United States waged the Gulf War in defense of the principle of national sovereignty and in opposition to aggression by one state against another. The invasion of Iraq a dozen years later repudiated these principles. In the latter war, it was the United States that was proposing to do to Iraq in 2003 what Iraq had done to Kuwait in 1990, namely, resolve long-festering disputes by means of invasion, removal of the government, and occupation.

The procedures as well as the principles were reversed. The 1991 Gulf War vote in Congress came six weeks *after* the United Nations had set a deadline for Iraq to leave Kuwait. By January 12, 1991, the day the House and Senate voted for the Gulf War, the Bush administration had put together a coalition of thirty-two nations. In October of 2002, by contrast, the United Nations had not yet voted on the U.S. proposal to invade Iraq, and it was already clear that far fewer countries were interested in joining a coalition in offensive action to oust Saddam's regime. Indeed, one reason for the timing of the 2002 congressional vote five months before the U.S.-led force invaded Iraq was the hope that it would prod the United Nations into action, an effort that, of course, failed. The Persian Gulf War sprang from the invasion and occupation of Kuwait, an overt act by Iraq. Intelligence reports about Iraqi atrocities in Kuwait—some of them true, others not—were used to heighten political support but were secondary to the principle that one country had invaded another and proceeded to annex it. In 2002, the Bush administration's drive to war in Iraq rested on allegations that Iraq had weapons of mass destruction and was a threat to the United States. Other than no-fly zones in the north and south that prompted occasional and ineffectual Iraqi anti-aircraft fire and immediate U.S. reprisal strikes, the two countries were essentially at peace until U.S. forces invaded. Finally, while the Gulf War followed a set of limited objectives—removing Iraq from Kuwait; restoring Kuwait's government; and preventing Iraq from further threatening its Gulf neighbors—the Iraq War involved the invasion and open-ended occupation of a much larger territory. For all of these reasons, the authorization of force in 2002 should have aroused more political opposition.

One reason for the greater support for war in 2002 was the memory of easy victory in the 1991 Gulf War. The resolution authorizing force and clearing the way for the U.S.-led invasion of Iraq passed overwhelmingly. The House voted 296 to 133 for war on October 10, 2002; the Senate, 77 to 23 the next day.[92] Once again, Republican lawmakers lined up solidly behind their president, with only one GOP senator and six House Republicans opposing the resolution. The wider margin in favor of war stemmed entirely from a shift on the Democratic side, particularly pronounced in the Senate. In 1991, only ten of fifty-six Senate Democrats, 18 percent, had supported the war resolution to liberate Kuwait; eleven years later, a majority of Democrats, twenty-nine out of fifty, or 58 percent, supported the invasion of Iraq. In the House, support for war rose less dramatically, from 32 percent of House Democrats for war in 1991 to 39 percent in 2002.[93]

This shift was due in no small part to Democrats recalling the difficulties of their predecessors a decade earlier. Aides of the younger President Bush lobbying for votes for the war resolution reminded lawmakers, particularly Democrats, of Nunn's "mistake" in opposing the 1991 Gulf War resolution.[94] Members whose careers spanned both wars needed no reminding. Of the Democrats in the House in 1991, sixty-six were still there in 2002. Most were consistent in their position, either supporting use of force on both occasions or, more often, opposing it. But thirteen Democrats switched their positions from opposing the use of force in 1991 to supporting it eleven years later. Only five went the other way, from support for the Gulf War to opposition to invading Iraq. The trend was even stronger in the Senate; of twenty-two Senate Democrats who participated in both the 1991 and 2002 votes, nine who voted nay to war in 1991 voted aye in 2002. Only one, Sen. Bob Graham of Florida, went the other way.[95]

The geopolitical context was dramatically different too. The overwhelming victory in the first Gulf War itself influenced voting the second time around, whereas in 1991, the defeat in Vietnam was the freshest memory of a major war. In the fall of 2002, just over a year after the 9/11 attacks, attitudes about the use of military force in general and against Mideast targets in particular had changed sharply in the direction of supporting aggressive action. And while the intelligence estimates before the Gulf War raised fears of a costly conflict, in 2002 the CIA and Defense Intelligence Agency were predicting easy victory over Iraq.

To be sure, the intelligence community in 2002 was again "making Iraq ten feet tall," but only in the context of its weapons of mass destruction. Iraq's conventional force was presented as greatly weakened by a decade of severe sanctions, as indeed it was. While the depictions of Iraqi strength in 1991 increased pressure to delay war in favor of continued sanctions, in 2002 the reports about Iraqi weapons accelerated the push toward war. The intelligence community's confidence that Iraq's conventional military forces could be easily defeated reflected a calculus based on the first Gulf War in combination with military developments since. Unlike the evidence on weapons of mass destruction, there were solid facts underlying the conventional military estimate of Iraqi strength in 2002. The CIA and Defense Intelligence Agency knew the improvements in U.S. military capability and had been watching Iraq's military closely for a dozen years. Accompanying the objective evidence of Iraqi conventional military deterioration was the memory of how easily Iraq had been defeated in 1991, and of the mistake the intelligence community had made in assuming the Gulf War would be arduous. The intelligence community was determined not to make that mistake again.

In the Gulf War, the *casus belli* had been obvious: Iraq had invaded a neighboring country and taken it over, along with its rich oil reserves. The issue in dispute was the cost of liberating Kuwait. In 2002 it was the *casus belli* that was in question, since Iraq had committed no overt act of war. The cost of "liberating" the people of Iraq from Saddam's rule got far less attention since it was generally assumed that U.S. forces would rout their Iraqi adversaries. The calculus used by the Pentagon and the CIA in arriving at this judgment was simple: Iraq's military had been cut roughly in half by the 1991 Gulf War and, during a decade of sanctions, had struggled to maintain its combat equipment and battle readiness. The U.S. military, though markedly smaller in 2002 than it had been in 1991 owing to post–Cold War cuts, had improved its capability considerably, particularly that of its precision-guided weapons, which played such an important role in the Gulf War. Intelligence community assessments of Iraq's weakened conventional military state were consistent through the Clinton and Bush administrations and were not affected by the intelligence distortions seen in other Iraq assessments. An April 1999 National Intelligence Estimate reported that Saddam's military was "smaller and much less well-equipped than it was on the eve of his 1990 invasion of Kuwait." In April 2002, the intelligence community's assessment was the same: "Iraqi military morale and battlefield cohesion are more fragile today than in 1991."[96] Iraq's weakened military state made war a more attractive option for the Bush administration; this assessment also tended to support concerns about Iraq's unconventional weapons since, by the logic of the U.S. national security establishment, weapons of mass destruction are attractive as a relatively inexpensive way to make up for conventional military vulnerabilities.

Since the coalition had had little trouble defeating Iraq in 1991 under better circumstances for Saddam, it stood to reason that the job would be that much easier the second time around. Air Force General Richard Myers, chairman of the Joint Chiefs of Staff during the Iraq invasion period, made this point explicit in testimony before the House Armed Services Committee less than a month before the Senate authorized the use of force in Iraq:

> In a contest between Iraq's military forces and our Nation's armed forces, the outcome is clear. Our joint war-fighting team, in concert with our partners, can and will decisively defeat Iraqi military forces. Many will remember the results of the last encounter between our coalition forces and Iraq eleven years ago. Since then, U.S. combat power has improved. Today, our nation's joint war-fighting team enjoys improved intelligence, command and control, is more deployable and possesses greater combat power.[97]

From the point of view of a commander prudently accounting for the risks of a major military operation, particularly the risks of a protracted and costly occupation that many were warning of before the war, Myers's presentation must, in retrospect, be regarded as an embarrassment. Putatively the beneficiary of "improved intelligence" capability, Myers devoted two sentences in his prepared testimony to the postwar environment in Iraq. His recitation of improvements in U.S. military capability did not include mention of body or vehicular armor; to the extent that he spoke about U.S. armored combat vehicles at all it was to extol their superior firepower, as if that were the only issue. Other than raising the possibility that Iraq might use chemical or biological weapons against U.S. forces and assuring lawmakers that his troops were ready for this, Myers's presentation barely considered the possibility that anyone might fight back. And Myers did not discuss the fact that the U.S. military, while more capable and better equipped in certain areas, was smaller by one-third than the force in place at the time of the Gulf War, down from an "end strength" of about 2.1 million active-duty, guard, and reserve troops at the time of the Gulf War to 1.4 million soldiers, sailors, airmen, and Marines a decade later. In his testimony, Myers did not discuss the anticipated duration of the mission in Iraq, other than to say that the United States had sufficient forces to accomplish that mission while maintaining its other combat commitments, particularly the global war on terrorism. He did not consider the possibility that war in Iraq could become protracted. The only contingency he discussed was the possibility that "our operations in the war on terrorism are expanded" elsewhere by some future emergency, and how such demands might affect the Iraq mission.[98] Iraqi forces, by contrast, suffered from poor morale, aging weapons systems, and low levels of training. Neither Myers nor Defense Secretary Donald Rumsfeld was so foolish as to say it would be easy to conquer Iraq. They paid lip service to the notion that war brings unexpected challenges. But their presentations to the committee radiated confidence. The common denominator with intelligence and military assessments of a decade earlier was their assertion that waiting would only make war more costly.

"Time is not on our side," Rumsfeld told the Senate Armed Services Committee the next day. "The longer we wait, the more deadly [Saddam's] regime becomes." Breezing over the postwar occupation issue, Rumsfeld conceded, "it is likely that international forces would have to be in Iraq for a period of time," without discussing what that period would be or describing the composition of the international forces. The burden, he said, would be a "small one" when compared with the risk of not going to war.[99]

Intelligence community estimates of the difficulty of conquering Iraq were far less sanguine about the possibility of civil unrest following the defeat of regular Iraqi army forces. But detailed intelligence assessments of likely postwar scenarios in Iraq would not be forthcoming until January 2003, three months after Congress had already voted to authorize the use of force and at a time when the Bush administration's course toward war had been settled.[100] In February 2002, the possibility of war in Iraq was sufficiently in play that CIA Director George Tenet was asked in written questions following his annual presentation on worldwide threats to assess "the likeliest scenario for Iraq when Saddam is removed from the scene." Tenet replied two months later:

> Any new regime in Baghdad would have to overcome significant obstacles to achieve stability. If Saddam and his inner circle are out of the picture and internal opponents of the regime band together, we assess that a centrist Sunni-led government would be pressed to accept an Iraqi state less centralized than Saddam's. Iraq's restive sectarian and ethnic groups, however, would probably push for greater autonomy. Decades of authoritarian rule have deprived Iraqis

of the opportunity to build democratic traditions and paramilitary experience that could help them master the art of consensus building and compromise.[101]

It is a statement that holds up well in light of subsequent events, though Tenet was wrong in assuming that a Sunni-dominated government would succeed Saddam. But note what is missing: there is no discussion of how Iraq's "restive sectarian and ethnic groups" would react to U.S. occupying forces, perhaps because the assumption was that there would be no need for a long occupation. As in the Gulf War, the Pentagon, not the CIA, was responsible for assessments of relative military strength between the United States and Iraq. Still, Tenet repeatedly mentioned that Iraq's military was less than half the strength of Saddam's Gulf War force without mentioning the decline in the size of the U.S. military over the ensuing decade.

The floor speeches of long-serving House and Senate Democrats who opposed the Gulf War in 1991 but supported the invasion of Iraq eleven years later betray an awareness of some of the many elements of the latter conflict that made it a much riskier and more radical proposition. But there was relatively little discussion of the possibility of extensive U.S. casualties. To the contrary, in 2002, the point of war in Iraq appeared to be to avoid the long-term risk of casualties since the underlying assumption was that maintaining the status quo risked the day when Saddam would use weapons of mass destruction on the United States. These lawmakers sought to portray the vote in 2002 to use force as part of a policy continuum rather than a radical break. Representative Henry Waxman (D-Calif.) said he had opposed the Gulf War use-of-force resolution because "I thought then that more time should be given to diplomacy, and to the enforcement of sanctions against Iraq." In 2002, he had concluded, "time has run out." Citing no evidence, Waxman asserted that "inspections have failed." And while he noted that, unlike in 1991, the United Nations had not yet authorized the use of force, he hoped that a vote in Congress would help generate international support. House Democratic Leader Dick Gephardt (D-Mo.) said war in Iraq should be seen as part of an effort to "do everything in our power to prevent further terrorist attacks and ensure that an attack with a weapon of mass destruction cannot happen."[102] Senator Joseph Biden (D-Del.), then the ranking member of the Foreign Relations Committee, rejected assertions that the invasion of Iraq amounted to U.S. military "preemption." Rather, the attack was simply a resumption of hostilities that suspended the Gulf War in 1991. It was justified because Iraq had violated the terms of the ceasefire agreement by stonewalling inspectors and secretly reviving his weapons-of-mass-destruction programs, Biden contended.[103]

Biden's was a strained interpretation of the end of the Gulf War hostilities. Neither the U.N. nor Congress had authorized a full-blown invasion of Iraq to overthrow Saddam's regime. The "or else" clause of the ceasefire agreement was the threat that hostilities against Iraqi forces could be resumed if Baghdad failed to comply with the agreement's terms, not that resumption would entail a march to Baghdad and the overthrow of Saddam's regime. In legal terms, there was no connection between violating the ceasefire agreement and overthrowing Saddam's regime, the explicit purpose of the war in Iraq that began in March of 2003.[104]

Senator Jay Rockefeller (D-W.Va.), who opposed the war resolution in 1991 and supported the 2002 version, was among the few to acknowledge the risk of a protracted and costly occupation of Iraq. As ranking Democrat on the Senate Intelligence Committee, Rockefeller was one of the better-briefed lawmakers participating in the debate. He acknowledged, "we defeated Saddam quickly and conclusively in 1991. In the decade since, our force effectiveness has improved dramatically, while many of Saddam's capabilities have deteriorated." But Rockefeller warned that an all-out invasion of Iraq "will be very different and much more difficult." Victory might be "quick and painless" as many intelligence and military briefers were predicting, Rockefeller said, but he added, "The American people need to know a war against Saddam will have high costs, including loss of American lives."[105]

Rockefeller was one of five Democrats on the Intelligence Committee to support the invasion of Iraq, in contrast to the unanimous opposition of Intelligence Committee Democrats to the Gulf War. Lawmakers on the committee continued to receive intelligence briefings on the upcoming war in the months between the Senate vote and the invasion and, on occasion, raised questions reflecting unease about what was to come. In February, Rockefeller raised the concern that, if the United States invaded Iraq, "a regime change will not be enough and that the follow-up is what will really tell the story for the future."[106] Vice Admiral Lowell E. Jacoby, head of the Defense Intelligence Agency, assured the panel that "Saddam's conventional military options and capabilities are limited" owing to the damage to his forces in the Gulf War and the difficulty of recovering in the intervening time under sanctions. He warned that Saddam might engage in a "scorched-earth" strategy as he retreated from U.S.-led forces, and would inflict "quite a bit of infrastructure damage" on his own country. The longer-term circumstances in Iraq, Jacoby said, "are dependent on freeing up the Iraqi people to bring their energy to bear on putting in place a better way of life." The key, he said, would be rapidly putting in place a new government and a stable flow of basic services such as food and health supplies.[107] Aside from these brief remarks in a hearing dominated by talk of weapons of mass destruction, there was little more on the challenges of postwar Iraq.

Intelligence Committee members did submit written questions about the postwar environment in Iraq. In responding to these, Tenet discussed the importance of a military force adequate to grapple with sectarian violence and of setting up a viable, functioning government. Carl Ford, head of the State Department's Bureau of Intelligence and Research, warned that jihadist groups would attract more recruits in light of the American troop presence and said the troops themselves would provide "more targets" for al-Qaeda and other anti-U.S. terrorists. And he cautioned that Arabs were concerned about the possible length of the U.S. occupation. Before the war, the State Department was deeply involved in postwar planning, though lamentably much of this work was discarded when the Pentagon under Rumsfeld seized control of postwar policy. The responses from these intelligence officials, though they raised critical issues about the postwar environment, came too late to influence how Congress voted on the war or even provide an opportunity to air concerns that might improve U.S. preparations for the conflict, for by the time the intelligence community leaders sent their written answers in, the United States had already toppled Saddam's regime and was struggling, against growing insurgent resistance, to establish any semblance of order.[108]

The intelligence community's 1991 misjudgment that Saddam would hold Kuwait tenaciously, drag out the war, and inflict substantial casualties on the coalition had both short-term and long-term repercussions. It contributed both to the closeness of the votes in the House and Senate before the Gulf War and to the large majorities eleven years later in favor of invading Iraq. In 2002, overconfidence among Pentagon and CIA analysts about U.S. military capability to defeat Iraq and an institutional recollection of how the intelligence community had sold the U.S. military short in 1990 contributed to briefings that gave lawmakers confidence that the conquest of Iraq would be relatively easy. To an extent, of course, the 2002 war assessments were right: getting to Baghdad and removing Saddam from power was a fairly quick and relatively painless operation. But the mission did not end there. Democrats who, because of political circumstances, were once again positioned to be the only voices of caution against a push to war, remembered well what had happened to them in 1991, partly because of the alarming intelligence briefings they received on the impending conflict. It was an experience they did not want to repeat. And the second time around, the intelligence briefings tended to instill in them confidence in the outcome rather than dread. This collective memory effect—fear at the CIA of bureaucratic pain for giving an inaccurate assessment, and fear among Democrats of political punishment for appearing "soft" on Saddam—drove down the number of opponents of war and helped the younger President Bush create the impression that he was taking the country to war with bipartisan support. The greater unity behind the war policy contributed to the lackluster congressional floor debate in 2002. Warning flags in the intelligence briefings about Iraq, particularly postwar Iraq, received scant treatment in public hearings compared with the relentless hammering by administration and intelligence officials on the weapons of mass destruction issue. Intelligence reports, though mistaken in their assessment of Iraq's weapons of mass destruction, were not nearly as definitive as the Bush administration in depicting that threat. Yet House and Senate Democrats who, unlike the press and public, were privy to these classified reports neither mentioned nor even noticed the gap between unqualified administration rhetoric regarding WMD and intelligence reports that were heavy with caveats. It was not because Democrats didn't think the issue was important before the war; it was because they weren't aware of the problematic nature of it. The famous October 2002 National Intelligence Estimate of the Iraqi WMD threat, a document requested by Congress, may have been read by fewer than a dozen out of 535 lawmakers before the votes authorizing invasion.[109] Only after the invasion, when no weapons of mass destruction were found, did Democrats seize on an issue they should have taken up back when it mattered, before Congress gave its support for war. By that time, with the war in Iraq going badly, it was too late for Democrats to generate the political headway to force a rethinking of Bush's policy since, in a sense, it was their policy as well. The intelligence community's overestimate of what it would take to liberate Kuwait in 1991 cast a long shadow, one we live with to this day.

BUSH AND CHENEY INVOKE THE MUSHROOM CLOUD

In the debate during the months before Operation Desert Storm, the fear of Iraqi weapons of mass destruction became a powerful argument *against* war for lawmakers concerned about high casualties. Rather than fight these fears,

the Bush administration sought to redirect them with an even more frightening specter: the possibility, if the United States decided to do nothing to help
Kuwait, of a nuclear-armed Iraq. Intelligence lay at the center of the debate.

The consensus in U.S. intelligence as of August 1990—in reports accessible
to lawmakers as well as the White House—was that Iraq was still years away
from acquiring the ability to build a nuclear weapon, possibly as long as a
decade. For most of the 1980s, U.S. intelligence had judged that Iraq's nuclear
program had suffered a near-fatal setback in the 1981 Israeli air strike on Iraq's
Osirak nuclear reactor at its sprawling Tuwaitha nuclear research complex.
By the late 1980s, Western intelligence agencies had developed some evidence
that Pakistan and Brazil had helped Iraq build a uranium gas centrifuge enrichment facility, but not on an industrial scale.[110] In March 1989, the CIA
said that without acquiring bomb-grade uranium from an outside source,
"Iraq may be able to build a nuclear weapon in less than 10 years." With outside help, including provision of the all-important fissile material, Iraq could
have a bomb in two to four years, the CIA said.[111] In September 1989, the CIA
produced a more detailed report stating that Iraq still needed to acquire an
extensive list of technology to develop its own nuclear weapons production
capability, but was aggressively trying to get that technology without attracting international attention. Specifically, the CIA reported that Iraq needed
technology for the production of fissile material—most likely centrifuges for
enriching uranium. Iraq also needed diagnostic equipment such as high-speed
cameras; oscilloscopes and X-ray machines; high-explosive, hydrodynamic,
and neutronic computer programs for weapons modeling; and sophisticated
electronic components for building the weapons. The purpose of the report
appeared to be to alert U.S. government agencies to the aggressive nature of
Iraq's nuclear program and to ensure that export controls on materials relating to these technologies were strictly maintained. At the same time, however, the report conveyed a sense of how much work remained before Iraq
would have its own nuclear weapons capability.[112] In July 1990, just as the
Iraq-Kuwait crisis was brewing, the CIA produced an unrelated report recommending that the Department of Commerce block the sale of "dual-use furnaces" that might be used to process uranium or plutonium compounds into
forms useful in nuclear weapons production. While cautioning that Iraq was
clearly giving high priority to nuclear weapons development, it went on, "we
have no indication Iraq currently has sufficient material available" to make
a weapon.[113] Thus it came as a stunning surprise to the CIA when President

Bush, in a Thanksgiving 1990 visit with the troops in Saudi Arabia, addressed the foes of his war policy back in Washington:

> And let me say this: Those who would measure the timetable for Saddam's atomic program in years may be seriously underestimating the reality of that situation and the gravity of the threat. Every day that passes brings Saddam one step closer to realizing his goal of a nuclear weapons arsenal. And that's why, more and more, your mission is marked by a real sense of urgency.[114]

In a move that foreshadowed the second Bush administration's playbook for selling a war policy, Defense Secretary Cheney followed up the initial statement about Iraqi nuclear capability with an appearance on the Sunday talk shows. On CBS's *Face the Nation* program on November 25, 1990, host Terrence Smith summed up the issue of the day as, "What's the hurry here?" Replied Cheney: "It's not clear whose side time is on."

Asked whether there was some new intelligence altering the picture of Iraq's nuclear program, Cheney dodged the question, saying only that the administration had long known "from public sources" that Saddam was trying to acquire nuclear capability and "from intelligence sources" that he was "working this problem very hard." The "worst-case assumption," Cheney said, was that Saddam could have a crude nuclear capability in less than a year. Not coincidentally, this was roughly the amount of time war opponents were advocating be given to see if sanctions alone could drive Iraq from Kuwait.[115] The same Sunday, again foreshadowing the second Bush administration's "flood the zone" tactics, National Security Adviser Brent Scowcroft went on another morning talk show to assert that Saddam could have a nuclear weapon in "months." Conceding that there were experts who said Iraq could be up to a decade away from a nuclear weapon, Scowcroft said, "the point the president is making is that for those who say, 'Let sanctions run a year or two years, whatever,' raises the possibility that we could face an Iraq armed with nuclear weapons." Unlike rational leaders who feared massive retaliation, Saddam might take a chance. That, Scowcroft said, "could dramatically change the casualties we might face."[116] The administration statements were based on a special National Intelligence Estimate, still classified, that warned that Iraq could, in a crash program, develop a crude nuclear weapon in as little as six months to a year.

Skeptics of the Bush administration's case for war immediately cried foul, accusing the administration of blowing the Iraqi nuclear threat out of proportion and of ordering a suspiciously timely and sudden shift in intelligence analysis on the threat. Nunn, the Senate Armed Services Committee chairman, focused one of his prewar hearings on the nuclear issue, asking rhetorically whether the near-term threat of an Iraqi nuclear weapon was "a plausible scenario or an extremely remote scenario."[117] Gary Milhollin, director of the Wisconsin Project on Nuclear Arms Control, told Nunn's committee, "Given that President Bush has been under pressure to clarify the objectives of Operation Desert Shield and justify this massive commitment of force, I think it is important to ask why his administration revised its assessment of Iraq's nuclear program in the way that it did and at the time that it did."[118] Democratic Senator John Glenn of Ohio did just that, and came as close as he could, without divulging classified information, to accusing the Bush administration of going beyond existing intelligence reports to arrive at its alarming estimate. Glenn told colleagues that a few days after the administration's Thanksgiving weekend media offensive, intelligence officials briefed the Armed Services Committee in closed session on Iraqi nuclear programs and conveyed a substantially less alarmist message. The Bush administration had not offered the briefing; the White House was content to let its own public statements stand. Rather, skeptical senators who had received intelligence briefings previously and had never heard so dire a warning on Iraq acquiring a nuclear weapon demanded the briefing in the wake of Bush's Thanksgiving statements. Attendance required a "Q" security clearance, signifying discussion of atomic weapons intelligence. For a counterpoint to the Bush administration's "overblown" public statements about the Iraqi nuclear threat, Glenn urged senators to read the transcript of the classified briefing for themselves to get a sense of the views of intelligence officers "who work this day in and day out and who are up to speed on it as of today." Though Glenn could not spell it out, the implication was clear enough: the intelligence briefers had rated the possibility of an Iraqi nuclear capability emerging in the short term as extremely remote. The Bush administration was playing the weapons-of-mass-destruction card to argue for war, and exaggerating the intelligence.[119]

The 1990 U.S. intelligence estimates underlying the Bush administration's unexpected warnings of Iraq rapidly acquiring a nuclear capability remain classified. But a contemporaneous British assessment, almost certainly done in coordination with the CIA, gives us a window into the low degree of probability the intelligence community was giving to this scenario. A September 1990 assessment by Britain's Joint Intelligence Committee concluded that Iraq was, at a minimum, three years from establishing production capacity for enriching natural uranium into bomb-grade material, an additional year from producing enough highly enriched uranium to make a bomb, and a further year from being able to stockpile three to four weapons. The report touched on the possibility of a "crash programme" in which Iraq might illegally divert uranium fuel from its civilian nuclear program, recover uranium from reactor fuel and make rapid progress on the firing systems and conventional-explosive components of a nuclear device:

> If and only if all of these conditions were met, and assuming that reprocessing of diverted fuel started at the time of the invasion of Kuwait, then it is conceivable that Iraq could have the capability to make an untested nuclear weapon (though not a series of weapons) with a yield of approximately 20 kilotons by the end of this year.[120]

By December 1990, British intelligence regarded this unlikely scenario as even less likely, because the International Atomic Energy Agency had inspected Iraq's civil nuclear facilities in November and found that no uranium fuel had been diverted. If, after the IAEA inspection, Iraq had diverted the uranium, it could, under the above scenario, have had an untested bomb by mid-1991.[121]

Unclassified and nongovernmental analysis reached similar conclusions about Iraq's nuclear program, assessing that Saddam was five to ten years away from acquiring the critical mass of weapons-grade uranium for a nuclear device unless he was able to acquire it from an outside source.[122] The Congressional Research Service, in a report to lawmakers days after Bush's Thanksgiving speech, cited unclassified sources in finding that Iraq "has no industrial-scale capacity to produce weapons-grade plutonium or uranium." As of 1990, Iraq had 12.3 kilograms, or twenty-seven pounds, of uranium enriched to 93 percent U-235, the form of the metal needed for an atomic bomb. This material was subject to periodic IAEA inspection. But the quantity was likely not enough to make even a single weapon, CRS concluded, unless Iraq was much more advanced in weapons design and technology than was then believed.[123]

The administration had its defenders on the nuclear worst-case scenario. A decade later, before the invasion of Iraq, a key point would be the inherent uncertainty and historic unreliability of intelligence estimates about threats that enemies wanted to keep secret from the United States. Physicist William R. Graham, a former presidential science adviser, told lawmakers that the Bush administration's six-month "worst-case scenario" might be overly optimistic.

U.S. intelligence, Graham said, has tended to estimate that it will take longer for adversaries to develop and test nuclear weapons than it has actually taken. This was true of Russia's first nuclear test in 1949 and the first Chinese test in 1964. "I would say that it is not obvious to me that Iraq has no nuclear weapons today, and I do not see the benefit of waiting until they have nuclear weapons or have more nuclear weapons . . . before we take action."[124]

The nuclear specter did not constitute nearly as much of the first Bush administration's case for war in Iraq as it did a decade later. The more controversial claims coming from the White House in 1990 concerned reports of Iraqi atrocities in Kuwait. Some were accurate, such as the systematic looting of Kuwait City and the summary execution of captured military and civilian leaders. Some of the charges, particularly the sensational stories about Iraqi soldiers pulling the plugs of infant incubators in hospitals, were later said to be part of a sophisticated Kuwaiti public relations campaign for war, a campaign not firmly grounded in the truth.

TARGETING IRAQ'S NUCLEAR PROGRAM

Not until after Desert Storm, when U.N. weapons inspectors arrived in Iraq, would it become clear that the first President Bush was closer to being right about Iraq's nuclear threat than he knew prior to the Gulf War. His Thanksgiving warning had been based not so much on intelligence as on extrapolation of evidence of what Iraq could do if it pushed aggressively toward constructing a crude nuclear device. Bush and Cheney, though they based their claim on intelligence reports that presented the six-month scenario as a worst case, were actually working against the trend of intelligence reporting, which had Iraq years away from acquiring a nuclear weapon.

Having made an issue of the Iraqi nuclear threat before Desert Storm, Bush had to appear to be dealing with that threat once coalition combat operations began. Since the coalition war plan envisioned the liberation of Kuwait but not a march to Baghdad to end Saddam's regime, it became all the more imperative that the air campaign target and destroy Iraqi nuclear facilities. At the beginning of the war, Central Command's "Black Hole" command center in Saudi Arabia listed only two Iraqi targets as related to nuclear weapons development: Tuwaitha and the remote Al-Qaim uranium mine in northwest Iraq. The strikes focused initially on Iraq's sprawling research center at Tuwaitha, about ten miles southeast of Baghdad and scene of the 1981 Israeli air raid. On January 23, 1991, a week into the air campaign, Bush declared,

"Our pinpoint attacks have put Saddam out of the nuclear bomb-building business for a long-time to come."[125] In fact, by war's end, Iraq still retained key equipment and facilities for its secret nuclear research. As the *Gulf War Air Power Survey* put it, "By the end of the Gulf War, American intelligence had only begun to realize the extent of Iraq's nuclear weapons development beyond Tuwaitha." Intelligence developed during the air campaign had added seven nuclear-related targets to the strike list: "U.N. inspection teams eventually found three times that many nuclear facilities after the war."[126]

The lesson of this experience was not lost on those in the administration, particularly Cheney, who would play a lead role in making the case for the invasion of Iraq eleven years later: U.S. intelligence couldn't be relied on to find all there was to know about Iraq's weapons of mass destruction; policymakers—the people responsible for national security—should be free to go against the evidence of intelligence reporting if they believe it to be in the national security interest; and air power alone, guided by that incomplete intelligence, could not be relied on to fully destroy a well-concealed nuclear program.

As the thirty-eight-day air campaign wore on in January and February 1991, strikes on what were thought to be Iraqi missile-related facilities yielded intelligence suggesting connections to nuclear weapons research. These targets then rose on the priority list. One of the sites that moved from the conventional weapons list to the nuclear list was a facility, first suspected of making missiles, at Tarmiya, twenty-five miles north of Baghdad. U.S. warplanes first struck Tarmiya on February 15, 1991, almost by accident. According to David Kay, co-leader of the first U.N. nuclear inspection team into Iraq after the war, a group of U.S. fighters that had not been able to drop all their bombs and did not want to return to base with live bombs under their wings were redirected to Tarmiya by the airborne warning and control systems (AWACS) aircraft on patrol at the time. Satellite intelligence photographs taken after the bombing to assess the damage showed a beehive of activity at the site as hundreds of people pored through the wreckage and large cranes worked to extract large circular objects from the rubble. A subsequent B-52 raid cut a swath of destruction through Tarmiya that looked to Kay after the war as if a highway project had come through. But further strikes intended to completely destroy the Tarmiya facility were hampered by poor weather.[127]

More than weather hampered the efforts to destroy Iraq's nuclear capability with air power. The flurry of activity spotted by imagery analysts provided a clue that something important resided at Tarmiya. But precisely what was going on there remained unclear until after the war, when U.N. inspectors found that the Iraqis had been scrambling to move large ring magnets, part of a hitherto unknown uranium enrichment effort, out of the facility and thus out of harm's way. The result was that many air strikes judged successful by post-strike bomb-damage assessments had succeeded only in destroying empty buildings. The important assets—the hardware related to uranium enrichment—remained intact, and hidden away.[128]

U.N. INSPECTORS UNCOVER IRAQ'S PROGRAM

The bombing of Tarmiya and the satellite imagery showing an Iraqi scramble to pull equipment from the facility proved fortuitous for the post–Gulf War inspections. In May 1991, as inspectors began their work, U.S. intelligence adopted a supporting role, ordering up spy satellite passes over sites of interest to the inspectors. The effort produced photographs showing large round objects being moved, buried in sand, dug up, and reburied repeatedly. By coincidence, one of the CIA analysts looking at these pictures turned out to be the same one who had seen the flurry of activity at Tarmiya after the mid-February air strikes. U.N. inspectors on the ground traced the objects to a facility near Abu Ghraib outside Baghdad, but by the time they got in they found nothing.[129]

On his way to Iraq with his U.N. inspection team in the spring of 1991, David Kay picked up a copy of a book about the Bush presidency. He was not planning on reading up on the forty-first president while in Iraq. Rather, he was acting on instructions from U.S. intelligence, which planned to use an identical copy of the book to send the inspectors coded messages to guide their search for the Iraqi nuclear weapons program. It was a simple and time-tested code-book arrangement: U.S. intelligence, through a field office in Bahrain, would communicate information to the inspectors via unencrypted fax. The fax would contain a series of seemingly random numbers that the inspectors' communications officer knew corresponded to page, line, and word numbers in the Bush book. Through this time-consuming process, the CIA was able to work in tandem with the U.N. inspectors. Field inspections by the U.N. team would prompt Iraqi concealment activity, which CIA could pick up via spy satellites and then relay back to the inspectors. It was this method that brought the inspectors to the gate of a military transport compound outside Fallujah on June 28, 1991. Through some deliberately vague information provided to his Iraqi minders, who traveled in separate vehicles, and some sudden driving maneuvers, Kay's inspectors arrived at the facility well ahead of the minders. In response to the base commander's initial refusal to let them in, Kay decided to bluff, and he made a show of setting up a satellite field phone and threatening to call President Bush if they were denied admission. The commander said that there was nothing of interest at the site, but that the inspectors were welcome to climb an adjacent tower to see for themselves. It was a fatal mistake on the commander's part, for he was, within a day, executed at Saddam's orders, something Kay has felt bad about ever since. The inspectors scrambled up the tower with binoculars and cameras and saw some 100 trucks loaded with large round objects on flatbed trailers beating a fast retreat out a back gate of the compound. "They were kicking up a huge amount of dust," Kay said. "It was like dinosaurs in heat."[130]

One of the three inspectors who had climbed the tower, Major Richard Lally, scrambled into a U.N. vehicle and gave chase, eventually pulling alongside the fleeing trucks and snapping a few pictures before Iraqi guards in the convoy opened fire on him. Returning to the main group of inspectors, now joined by angry Iraqi minders, Lally was ordered to give up his camera. He refused, saying it was not a camera but a telescope, thus preserving the evidence. Kay related that Lally had brought an expensive family camera from home. When asked by Kay why he didn't simply hand it over to the gun-wielding Iraqis, he replied that if he didn't return home with it his wife would kill him. "He was more afraid of his wife than of the Iraqis," Kay joked.[131] From such spot decision-making, major breakthroughs in revealing Iraq's secret arsenal were achieved.

The confrontation outside Fallujah marked the beginning of the unraveling of Iraq's nuclear weapons development program. Under intense pressure from the international community, including threats to resume military operations, Iraq acknowledged its ambitious uranium enrichment efforts. The Iraqis eventually took the inspectors to a remote desert site where the large round objects had, once again, been buried. They were cast magnets for a massive Iraqi electromagnetic isotope separation plant—the Tarmiya facility. Iraq, it turned out, had not one uranium enrichment program but three. The electromagnetic isotope separation (EMIS) plant was furthest along. It was modeled after the Manhattan Project–era plant at Oak Ridge, Tennessee, but with some custom features designed to deceive Western intelligence agencies looking down from spy satellites. Iraq had a second one at Ash Sharqat some 200 miles north of Baghdad. EMIS plants consume enormous quantities of electricity; the Iraqis, having learned a great deal about spy satellite capability from the imagery that U.S. intelligence shared with Baghdad during the Iran-Iraq War, had buried the power lines in the plant while running decoy lines out of a transformer station into a nearby town.[132] Subsequent inspections in the summer of 1991 took Kay and his team to a facility called Al Furat west of Baghdad that housed a hitherto unknown uranium centrifuge plant. A September 1991 inspection led to the famous confrontation in which Kay and some forty-five nuclear weapons specialists were detained in a Baghdad parking lot for four days, their pockets stuffed with hundreds of pages of seized documents, among them papers indicating that Iraq was much further along than previously known toward developing a sophisticated implosion-type bomb, one that could deliver a bigger explosive yield while using less of the precious fissionable material.[133]

British intelligence, in October 1991, estimated that had the Gulf War not intervened, Iraq would have had its first nuclear weapon by 1993, at least two years earlier than estimated by Western intelligence before the war. Four years later, another British intelligence report confirmed the suspicions raised by Bush in his Thanksgiving 1990 speech to the troops: that Iraq indeed had a crash nuclear weapons program as of August 1990 that it later abandoned that might have produced a nuclear weapon within a year.[134] The Federation of American Scientists, a Washington-based security and arms control think tank, estimated that the Sharqat and Tarmiya enrichment facilities would have been operational in 1992 or 1993, had the Gulf War not occurred. The group said Iraq had indeed begun a crash program in late summer 1990 that would have continued but for that largely accidental strike on Tarmiya. Had that program not been interrupted, Iraq might have had enough enriched uranium for a low-yield weapon by the end of 1991.[135] A 1997 United Nations report was somewhat more cautious, concluding, "there are no indications to suggest that Iraq was successful in its attempt to produce nuclear weapons," but that "Iraq was at, or close to, the threshold of success" in enriching uranium.[136]

As the *Gulf War Air Power Survey* summed up: "The Iraqi nuclear program, in short, was massive, for most practical purposes, fiscally unconstrained, and closer to fielding a weapon than was generally realized when Desert Storm began."[137] U.N. inspectors estimated the total value of the Iraqi program in terms of equipment and the committed manpower of some 7,000 scientists and 20,000 workers at between $5 billion and $10 billion.[138]

REPERCUSSIONS OF INTELLIGENCE FAILURE

The U.N. inspectors had done more than discover a massive Iraqi nuclear pro-gram. They had, with the help of U.S. intelligence and other contributors, uncovered a massive intelligence failure, one that would have far-reaching consequences. A decade later, when senior intelligence officers, some of whom had worked on intelligence issues in the Gulf War, sat down to assess Iraq's weapons programs, the memory of the failure to detect Iraq's progress to-ward a nuclear weapon was a silent presence at the proceedings. Intelligence officials were keenly aware of Saddam's past success at hiding his activities. And in retrospect, they realized they had been guilty of "mirror imaging" in 1990—that is, guessing at Iraq's progress toward a nuclear weapon based on the assumption that Iraq would proceed in step-by-step fashion the way U.S. weapons scientists would have done given similar technology.

By December 2003, the U.S.-led coalition had been in Iraq for nine months and had organized a team of more than 1,000 to find Iraq's weapons of mass destruction. With each passing day, it was becoming clearer that there were no such weapons to be found. That dawning realization put the National In-telligence Council (NIC), which had produced the October 2002 National Intelligence Estimate that gave the second Bush administration the findings it wanted to justify the war, on the defensive. Eager to explain the reasoning and evidence on which the 2002 estimate was based, NIC members took the extraordinary step of discussing with journalists the process of producing the estimate. Looking back on their deliberations of summer and fall 2002 before the war, the senior analysts recalled the experience of the Gulf War and its af-termath, when Saddam had turned out to have so much more than the CIA had believed. "We didn't want to get burned again," was how one member of the National Intelligence Council put it. Guarding against another intelligence failure, the analysts adopted a strategy that had become increasingly common in the eleven years between the two wars with Iraq: they would doubt their own capabilities. The guiding assumption in 2002 was that whatever the CIA could see happening in Iraq on weapons of mass destruction was a tiny fraction of what Saddam was doing. Stuart A. Cohen, who was vice chairman of the Na-tional Intelligence Council at the time and the man in charge of the October 2002 NIE, said, "The lesson of '91 was that he [Saddam] was much more effec-tive at denial and deception than we understood, and consequently he was a lot farther along than we understood. That's the lesson we took away [from the Gulf War], and that's the right lesson to have taken away."[139]

It was a lesson that had been reinforced at the CIA in the 1970s during the Team B debate about Soviet military power, and, seven years after the Gulf War, by the Rumsfeld Commission on rogue-state intercontinental missile capability, a panel made up of Team B veterans such as Rumsfeld and Paul Wolfowitz who would go on to play key roles in bringing about the Iraq War. Concern that the CIA wasn't seeing everything going on in Iraq was hardly unreasonable given Saddam's record of hiding his activities from Western intelligence. The tortuous process by which the U.N. inspectors on the ground had gradually unearthed what had really gone on only tended to confirm the fear that there was much more to find. The missing element in the CIA calculations was even a passing consideration of the possibility that ambiguous intelligence on Iraqi weapons of mass destruction stemmed not from *poor* intelligence but from *accurate* intelligence that pointed to the possibility that there were no weapons of mass destruction remaining, that the inspections, supported by U.S. intelligence, had succeeded. What the intelligence community failed to even consider, to turn a favorite phrase of Rumsfeld's on its head, was that the absence of evidence *was* evidence of absence.

As with the other intelligence failures we have examined in connection with the Gulf War, those concerning Iraq's nuclear programs had short- and long-term consequences. Insufficient intelligence on Iraq's nuclear program meant that some nuclear-related sites never got on the coalition target list. The lesson derived from this experience was that the only sure way to get rid of a rogue state's nuclear capability was to knock over the government by military force and occupy the country. Another lesson of the nuclear intelligence failure was the realization by policymakers that their own judgments were sometimes superior to those of the intelligence community. The 1991 postwar discoveries by U.N. inspectors in Iraq vindicated prewar warnings by President Bush and Defense Secretary Cheney that Iraq could, in a crash program, produce a nuclear weapon in less than a year. As a tactic, Bush's warning about a fast-track Iraqi bomb demonstrated the effectiveness of using nuclear fear to generate support for military action. For Cheney, who as vice president would become the most energetic advocate of war in the second Bush administration, the experience drove home the notion that the intelligence community's cautious assessments of an enemy need not constrain the White House and the Pentagon in trying to convince Congress and the public to support a war policy. Bush and Cheney were clearly pushing to the outer limits of the available intelligence in suggesting that Iraq could get the bomb so quickly. That subsequent discoveries proved them right, or at least closer to right than the CIA, would be a lesson Cheney would carry into the second Bush administration, with disastrous results.

The U.N. Special Commission discoveries in the summer of 1991 of nuclear weapons-related equipment that had been obtained from Western manufacturers and suppliers pointed up the CIA's ability to collect information that it did not always fully understand. As the inspections yielded new intelligence on the advanced state of Iraq's nuclear program, the CIA went back over its files and found that many of the weapons production components discovered by U.N. inspectors had been purchased by Iraq in transactions monitored by U.S. intelligence but not understood at the time as being linked to nuclear weapons.[140] Failure by the CIA to fully understand the meaning of its own data contributed to the erosion of confidence in the ability of U.S. intelligence to uncover an adversary's secret weapons activities. Clever Iraqi concealment of its true intent, the use of unwitting or unsavory middlemen, and the dual-use nature of some of its key purchases helped the process along. The CIA's sharing of imagery intelligence with Iraq during the Iran-Iraq War taught Baghdad how to hide its activities from the CIA.

In 2002, Iraq would be busy with a concealment strategy once again. Only this time Baghdad would be hiding its *lack* of weapons of mass destruction, possibly in hopes that a policy of strategic ambiguity would deter the United States from invading.

CONCLUSION

Between the 1991 Persian Gulf War and the 2003 Iraq War, the CIA reversed itself on the three intelligence misjudgments explored in this chapter and the previous one. In 1990, the CIA saw clear, overt evidence that Iraq posed a threat to its neighbor but did not reach the conclusion that Iraq would act on that threat. After the invasion of Kuwait, the intelligence community warned that defeating Saddam in battle would be a costly and protracted affair. And the CIA and the rest of the intelligence community did not believe Iraq was very far along toward a nuclear weapon. All these judgments were wrong: Iraq invaded Kuwait; the liberation of Kuwait was accomplished in a short campaign with low coalition casualties; and Iraq was discovered to be much further along toward developing a nuclear weapon than U.S. intelligence believed before the war.

In 2002, the CIA had no clear evidence of Iraq threatening the United States or its neighbors but judged that Iraq nevertheless posed a clear threat to both. Having underestimated Iraq's nuclear progress in 1990, intelligence analysts determined not to be caught in the same embarrassing mistake a second time and concluded, based on scant evidence—and some evidence to the contrary—that Iraq had maintained or revived its nuclear and chemical weapons capabilities. On that basis, the Bush administration formed its public argument for war, a conflict the intelligence community believed would be over fairly quickly and with relatively low U.S. casualties. As of this writing, U.S. fatalities in the Iraq War are at 4,079 and counting.

It was not unreasonable for the CIA and the Pentagon to assume that a modern, capable, U.S.-led force would make short work of an Iraqi army much smaller than the force Saddam fielded in 1990—though these assessments should have taken greater notice of the smaller size of the U.S. military in 2002 and of the vastly different challenge posed by invading and occupying a large country than by simply forcing Iraqi forces out of a small neighboring country. The intelligence community's grave mistake on Iraq's nuclear program in 2002 was heavily influenced by the failure to perceive Iraq's progress toward a nuclear weapon in 1991. But the CIA had a history of intelligence failures in the nuclear arena—underestimating when the Soviet Union and China would first test a nuclear weapon, doubting the Soviets would place ballistic missiles in Cuba, and failing to predict the Indian and Pakistani nuclear tests of 1998, to name just a few. Given that Iraq faced a much stronger adversary in the United States, U.S. intelligence analysts reasoned that Saddam's choice would be to acquire the trump card of a nuclear weapon. This example of mirror imaging missed the importance Saddam placed on strengthening his weakened conventional forces to cope with enemies closer at hand, particularly Iran, not to mention Kurdish and Shiite elements within his own country. It also missed the thoroughgoing nature of the sanctions and the effectiveness of counterproliferation efforts to prevent Iraq from importing sensitive technology.

As with the Soviet collapse, victory in the Gulf in 1991 generated more criticism than plaudits for the CIA. Both these cases brought home the inextricable links between politics and intelligence. There is no mistaking the similarity of CIA assessments of the Soviet Union and Iraq in 1989 and 1990 to the policy preferences of the Bush administration at that time. Yet service to an administration's foreign policy agenda brought no lasting gain for the Agency. The left blamed the CIA for being overly alarmist on the Soviet threat and for overstating Iraqi capability. The Bush administration found it convenient to shift blame for its prewar policy miscues on Iraq to faulty intelligence that missed the menacing intent of Saddam's regime. This falling away of support happened at a time when political pressure was moving strongly in favor of a "peace dividend" at the end of the Cold War. Trained and staffed to meet an enemy that no longer existed, straining to perceive new threats that could justify its own existence, unable at that time to see the new terrorist enemy just then emerging, beset by criticism from the left and right, and grappling with sharply declining budgets, U.S. intelligence moved into the 1990s on shaky ground.

Figure 1. Russian President Boris Yeltsin and Soviet Premier Mikhail Gorbachev appear before the Congress of People's Deputies in Moscow in September 1991. The CIA had predicted the previous month's coup attempt on Gorbachev by Soviet hard-liners. But the subsequent Soviet breakup cast the Agency's alarmist assessments of the Soviet threat over the preceding decade in a harsh light. Part of the CIA's failure to see the collapse of the Soviet Union was its failure to see the rise of Russia. This misperception of its prime intelligence target led to calls to abolish the CIA. The Agency survived but started the 1990s on the defensive—and remained there. (AP Images, photo by Alexander Zemlianichenko)

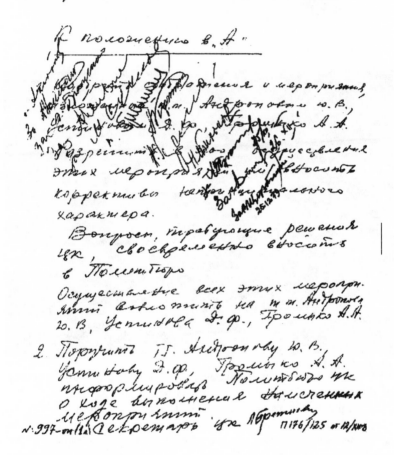

Figure 2. This document from the Politburo archives sealed the fate of Afghanistan, and possibly the Soviet Union. Titled "Concerning the situation in 'A,' " it authorized the Soviet invasion of Afghanistan in December 1979. Hand-written so that no secretaries or aides would learn of the plan, the document went into a Kremlin safe, its purpose simply to create a record of the Politburo members who backed the risky operation. Their scrawled signatures can be seen across the page. On December 8, 1979, four days before this document was signed, the CIA was reporting that the Soviets were planning to evacuate their small force from Afghanistan. When the Soviets invaded on Christmas Eve, the joke at CIA headquarters was that the CIA had correctly assessed the situation in Afghanistan; it was the Soviets who got it wrong. (Politburo document, Bukovsky's Soviet Archives at INFO-RUSS)

Figure 3. The Polish premier, General Wojciech Jaruzelski, meets Polish troops in 1982. Burned by the Afghan experience, the CIA predicted in 1980 and 1981 that the Soviet Union would invade Poland, assuming, incorrectly, that Polish troops would not forcefully halt the Solidarity uprising. The Agency was slow to grasp the dramatic shift represented by the Politburo's decision not to intervene. It was the beginning of the end of Soviet domination of Eastern Europe. (AP Images)

Figure 4. Senators Sam Nunn (D-Ga.) and David Boren (D-Okla.) at the confirmation hearing of Robert Gates to be CIA director in October 1991. Nunn and Boren had been the two most influential Democrats arguing against the authorization to use military force in the Persian Gulf. CIA predictions of a costly war to liberate Kuwait heavily influenced their positions. When the coalition routed Iraqi forces, Boren, in particular, was furious with the CIA for overestimating Iraq's combat power. The perception that these two influential lawmakers had erred in favoring continued sanctions against Iraq weighed on Democrats eleven years later when Congress overwhelmingly authorized the U.S.-led invasion of Iraq. (AP Images, photo by John Duricka)

Figure 5. Aldrich Ames's desire to protect his wife, Rosario, from a lengthy jail sentence for espionage led to his guilty plea and agreement to cooperate with CIA officials trying to calculate the damage he did in nine years of spying for Moscow. But for the Rosario factor, Ames stood a good chance of acquittal by challenging evidence collected without a court-approved warrant. The realization that they might have blown the prosecution of the most damaging spy in CIA history led Justice Department officials to erect a new procedural wall between intelligence and criminal investigations, a barrier that would hinder the pursuit of al-Qaeda by the CIA and FBI before 9/11. (AP Images, photo by Mark Wilson)

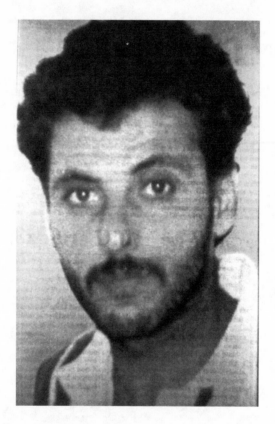

Figure 6. The arrest of Mohammed Sadeeq Odeh by Pakistani authorities on August 7, 1998, was a bad break for U.S. intelligence. Odeh, one of the planners of the al-Qaeda terrorist bombing of the U.S. embassy in Nairobi, Kenya, fled Africa on the eve of the attack en route to a rendezvous of senior al-Qaeda members with their leader, Osama bin Laden, set for August 20. Odeh's arrest tipped bin Laden off to the likelihood that U.S. intelligence knew of the meeting. When U.S. cruise missiles slammed into an al-Qaeda camp on the 20th, neither bin Laden nor any of his senior cohorts were on hand. (AP Images)

Figure 7. Smoldering ruins of the Al-Shifa Pharmaceutical Industries plant in Khartoum, Sudan, August 20, 1998. The CIA played a critical role in U.S. retaliation for the embassy bombings in Africa, reporting intelligence about the supposed al-Qaeda leadership meeting in Afghanistan and recommending Al-Shifa as another target based on intelligence suggesting the plant was manufacturing nerve agent VX. CIA officials said they had no information that the plant had any legitimate function, a statement belied by the containers of human and veterinary medicine strewn all over the neighborhood after the raid. (AP Images)

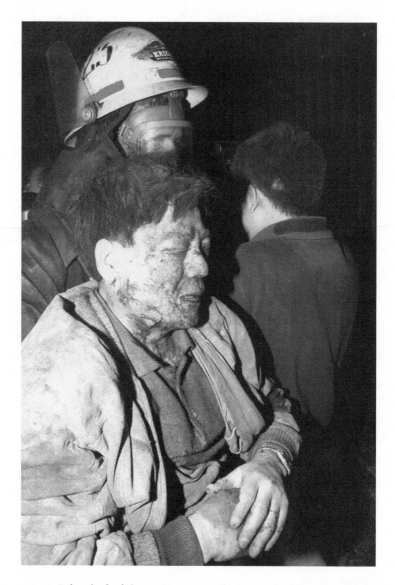

Figure 8. A Belgrade firefighter assists an unidentified Chinese official bloodied in the mistaken bombing of the Chinese embassy in Belgrade by a U.S. B-2 bomber. Coordinates for the May 7, 1999, strike were provided by the CIA after an agency analyst mislocated a Serb military procurement headquarters, which turned out to be several hundred yards from the embassy. CIA lapses in targeting the Al-Shifa pharmaceutical plant and a supposed meeting of al-Qaeda leaders in 1998, and the China embassy bombing in 1999, contributed to the reluctance of CIA leaders to recommend strikes on bin Laden on several occasions before 9/11 when U.S. intelligence believed it had located the terrorist leader. (AP Images)

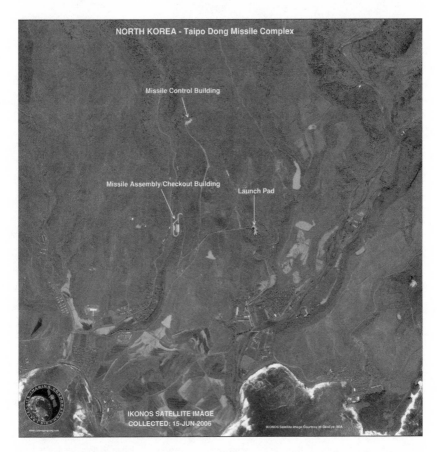

Figure 9. The CIA tracked North Korean preparations for a missile launch from this site in eastern North Korea in the summer of 1998. What the CIA didn't know was that the North Koreans were assembling a three-stage rocket. The test of the three-stage rocket, though not entirely successful, suggested North Korea was close to fielding an intercontinental ballistic missile. Donald Rumsfeld, head of a commission that criticized the CIA's work on the missile threat, cited the test as proof that the CIA couldn't be counted on to identify threats before they emerged. (IKONOS satellite image by GeoEye)

Figure 10. Secretary of State Colin Powell presents the Bush administration's case for war in Iraq to the U.N. Security Council, February 5, 2003. CIA Director George Tenet, left, backed up Powell literally and figuratively. Only the intelligence Powell and Tenet considered solid made it into the presentation, yet almost all of it was wrong. The CIA's principal intelligence failure on Iraq was its inability to conceive that a decade-long effort by the U.N., backed by the CIA, to disarm Saddam had succeeded. To Tenet's left is U.N. Ambassador John Negroponte, who would go on to become the first director of national intelligence. (AP Images, photo by Elise Amendola)

5 ALDRICH AMES AND THE DECLINE OF HUMAN INTELLIGENCE

IN DECEMBER 1988, two senior staff members of the Senate Intelligence Committee traveled to Moscow to meet with CIA chief-of-station Jack Downing, the man in charge of recruiting and running spies for the United States inside the Soviet Union. The trip was a first. Until then, the House and Senate Intelligence Committees, established in the mid-1970s in the wake of congressional investigations of excesses by U.S. intelligence agencies, had confined their oversight activities to Washington. A crisis concerning a new U.S. embassy building in Moscow had set the trip in motion. In 1980, during construction of the embassy, U.S. security officials had discovered that the KGB had wired the building for electronic surveillance from the attic to the subbasement. After five years of fretting over what to do, the Reagan administration concluded that the wiring was so pervasive that the structure could not be reliably cleansed of KGB sensors, and construction was ordered halted. By October 1988, the departing administration had decided to demolish the building and start over, at a cost of nearly $300 million. Congress had to agree before that money could be spent, and the Senate Intelligence Committee sent the two senior staffers to Moscow to get Downing's view and see the complex firsthand.[1]

Taking no chances against an evidently aggressive KGB eavesdropping program, the group met in a building-within-a-building in the old U.S. embassy—a vault-like, soundproof room called "the bubble" on an upper floor of the chancery. When the meeting began, the Senate staffers learned that Downing had something else to discuss besides the KGB bugging. He was concerned about a KGB penetration of the Moscow Station, he told the visitors, but not by means of eavesdropping. Downing said the station had sustained a sudden and unexplained loss of several of its best clandestine sources inside the Soviet intelligence and military apparatus. The agent losses had occurred in close succession in 1985 and 1986 and could not all be explained by the treachery of CIA turncoat Edward Lee Howard, a disgruntled former Agency employee fired because of a polygraph examination that indicated continuing illegal drug use.[2] Howard had come under suspicion as a spy after some unguarded remarks, but he escaped FBI surveillance and fled to Moscow in September 1985 after selling the KGB the identities of several CIA agents inside the Soviet security apparatus.[3] Now it appeared to Downing that a more extensive compromise of sources had occurred, attributable to a CIA mole with even deeper access than Howard. To make matters worse, Downing said, CIA headquarters did not seem to be treating the breach with any particular urgency. No aggressive mole hunt was under way, and Moscow Station could not seem to make Langley understand, or respond to, the serious nature of the problem. The penetration had implications for compromising not only past CIA sources and operations but also future ones. If the CIA had suddenly lost its human sources reporting on its No. 1 intelligence target, the Soviet Union, it was imperative to develop new sources. But if a well-placed mole had informed Moscow of the identities of CIA sources inside the Soviet system and remained in a position to do so, there was nothing to prevent the immediate compromise of newly recruited sources, or "assets." Until the source of the breach was identified, espionage directed at the Soviet Union was effectively shut down.[4]

INKLINGS OF DISASTER

Downing had not told the visitors everything. In fact, the CIA had suffered a catastrophic loss of its intelligence sources in the Soviet Union. In rapid succession, virtually every human source the CIA had in the Soviet government, perhaps twenty-five in all, had been arrested; at least nine were executed.[5] The scope of the loss was not immediately apparent to the Moscow Station and the CIA's Directorate of Operations, to which it reported. It started with a seeming trickle: a few Soviet officials stationed overseas who had been working with CIA were abruptly recalled to Moscow.[6] Sources inside the Soviet Union began failing to make their appointments with CIA handlers or to pick up and drop off materials at "dead drops" used to convey information in the espionage trade. Then the CIA began to pick up intelligence that some of these sources had been arrested, tried, and executed for espionage. For the most part, these events did not make the Moscow newspapers, and so the roll-up drew no U.S. press attention. The few Soviet press accounts mentioning the execution of officials for espionage appeared long after the fact, in most cases.[7] In time, the CIA began to see these developments in their full scope. Indeed, by late 1985—three years before the Senate staff trip to Moscow—then-CIA Director William Casey was informed of a major breach in the Directorate of Operations' Soviet espionage cadre.[8] Two years later, Downing, newly arrived in Moscow, was personally initiated into the scope of the agent losses in an encounter on the Moscow-to-Leningrad train that unfolded like a scene in a spy novel. A man the CIA later identified as Aleksandr "Sasha" Zhomov, the KGB agent assigned to shadow Downing, silently stuffed an envelope in the CIA officer's pocket while brushing past him in the train's passageway. The note identified the man as a KGB officer volunteering to spy for the CIA. Given the CIA code name PROLOGUE, Zhomov was later judged to be a double agent—that is, a spy still under Moscow's control feeding carefully selected information to the CIA. It is standard procedure for such "dangles" to be allowed to give the enemy spy service valid information, the better to convince the other side that they are genuine spies. In the case of PROLOGUE, the KGB came up with a particularly clever ruse: Zhomov would warn the CIA that the KGB was preparing to send several officers offering to spy for the U.S. who would, in fact, be double agents controlled by Moscow. The warning proved accurate, needless to say, since the entire operation was being controlled by the Soviets. And it served its purpose in helping convince the CIA, temporarily at least, that PROLOGUE was a genuine spy. PROLOGUE offered something else: in a subsequent meeting with Downing, he handed over a list of the CIA's Soviet sources who had been arrested and, in some cases, executed in the great KGB roll-up of 1985 and 1986. The CIA already knew it had suffered a major loss, but the material from the new spy confirmed what had become known to a narrow circle in the CIA as "the 1985–86 losses." For Downing, it drove home the extent of the catastrophe over which he was now presiding.[9]

None of this, in its scope and magnitude, was shared with the Senate Intelligence Committee staffers. But Downing had given them enough so that on their return to Washington they arranged to meet with Gardner "Gus" Hathaway, the CIA's top counterintelligence officer, at Agency headquarters in Langley, Virginia. L. Britt Snider, then the general counsel to the Senate Intelligence Committee, had been one of the two staffers on the Moscow trip.

When he and his Senate colleague related what they had learned in Moscow, Hathaway turned pale, betraying his shock that so sensitive a piece of information had moved outside the innermost circle of senior officials at the CIA. "Gus was just horrified that we had been told about this," Snider recalled. "He said, 'Britt, Britt, don't start looking into this. You are going to muck it up if you start messing around in this.'" Hathaway told the staffers that the matter was in hand and asked for assurance that the Senate committee would stay out of it. After a briefing on the meetings in Moscow and at CIA headquarters, Senator David Boren (D-Okla.), chairman of the committee, acceded to the CIA's request.[10]

In fact, the search for a CIA mole was not at all in hand. Rather, it had come to a virtual halt a few months earlier with a small counterintelligence team that had been investigating the losses, unsure whether the breach had been caused by a human turncoat, a technical penetration of CIA communications, or sloppy tradecraft by the CIA's spy handlers. The CIA's leadership in that late-1980s period was embroiled in congressional investigations into the Iran-Contra scandal; the CIA's counterintelligence team, after no success in three years of probing, was put onto other missions. Even in the wake of the Howard case, there was a cultural refusal within the Agency to believe that one of the CIA's own could betray his organization, let alone his country.[11]

Just over five years later, at 8 a.m. on February 21, 1994, Snider was at his desk in the secure wing of the Hart Senate Office Building when he received an unexpected call from the FBI. It was Presidents' Day, a federal holiday, and most of official Washington was shut down. A senior counterintelligence officer with the Bureau was calling to deliver formal notification to the oversight committee that an arrest was about to be made in a major espionage case. Snider asked how serious a case this was; the special agent replied, "Let's put it this way: He was a 30-year employee of the D.O." The suspect, the FBI officer said, had been a Soviet specialist for most of his career in the Directorate of Operations, the D.O., also known as the clandestine service, the espionage arm of the CIA. Just over ninety minutes later, CIA officer Aldrich Hazen Ames, having been ordered under false pretenses to interrupt his day off and drive to Agency headquarters, pulled up to an intersection near his Arlington, Virginia, home and was suddenly surrounded by unmarked cars and brusquely arrested by FBI agents. Investigators had wanted to get Ames out of his house, fearing that he might use his training as a clandestine officer to destroy evidence as the dragnet came down on him. Despite multiple warning signs, including Ames's unexplained wealth, it had taken nine long years to catch one of the most dev-astating spies in U.S. history. The arresting officers handcuffed Ames at the side of his shiny $40,000 1992 Jaguar XJ6, the third Jag he had purchased with some of the $2.5 million in cash the KGB had paid him for secrets.[12]

As details of the Ames case began to spill forth, Snider realized that the crisis described to him by Downing in Moscow in 1988 had been a first glimpse into what became the Aldrich Ames spy scandal. That conversation had been the first inkling outside a closed circle of CIA and FBI insiders of a case that crashed on the Agency like a wave. Virtually every detail of Ames's treachery and the subsequent mole hunt devastated the CIA's reputation, from Ames's personal profile as an overt alcohol abuser and middling performer who nev-ertheless had access to the CIA's most sensitive secrets, to the damage he did by the secrets he sold, to the details of the halting and misdirected efforts to find the source of the 1985–86 losses. Given the criticism that came down on the CIA, the ruin of careers and reputations, and the precipitous loss of confi-dence in the Agency in general and the Directorate of Operations in particu-lar, it is not at all unreasonable to conclude that the fallout from Ames's arrest did as much damage to U.S. intelligence as Ames's spying itself.

THE LID COMES OFF

The Senate staffers learned several important things in that initial conversa-tion with Downing in Moscow: first, that the CIA had suddenly lost Soviet assets and that there was probably a mole betraying the Agency's sources to the KGB; second, that CIA headquarters was doing little or nothing to find out about the losses; and third—information amply confirmed by the follow-up meeting at Langley—that the Agency wanted to keep this intelligence disaster under wraps, even from the people charged with overseeing the intelligence community. These three elements, established in that winter meeting in Mos-cow, well before Ames was revealed as a spy, would form the main storyline of the Ames case as it unfolded following his arrest in the early months of 1994. The Senate Select Committee on Intelligence, when it pieced together the in-formation gathered by its staffers in 1988 with subsequent details of the Ames case after his arrest, was officially outraged at the failure of the CIA to inform the oversight committees of what intelligence officials knew had been a devas-tating blow to anti-Soviet espionage operations in the mid-1980s.

The natural reaction in Congress to an adverse or scandalous situation of which members have not been apprised is official indignation. The complaint "we were not informed" is a constant refrain on Capitol Hill. The anger is more intense where the Intelligence Committees are concerned, for these are "select" committees, whose members are chosen for their seniority and relative experience in national security matters. They, as distinct from rank-and-file lawmakers, are privy to the nation's secrets, and the rest of Congress counts on them to be their watchdogs. When the oversight committees are caught by surprise by disaster or scandal, they not only have been ignored by the intelligence community, but also have let their colleagues down.[13]

At least the Senate committee had heard something about the asset losses. Its counterpart, the House Permanent Select Committee on Intelligence, reported in the aftermath of Ames's arrest, "The Committee believes that the compromise of assets in the Ames case was among the worst intelligence failures in CIA history. Yet the Committee has no evidence that it was informed, either collectively or through the chairman and ranking Republican." The panel called the failure to notify particularly "inexcusable" because from 1985 through 1988 the committee had conducted scores of hearings focused specifically on counterintelligence issues—that is, efforts by adversary spy services to spy on the United States, and U.S. efforts to stop them.[14] In 1990, Representative Bob McEwan (R-Ohio), then the ranking Republican on the Intelligence Committee, had asked CIA Director William Webster and his deputy, Richard Kerr, about a newspaper account of a KGB general who had revealed the execution of Soviet citizens for espionage. Their written response "can best be described as artful" and did not discuss the loss of Soviet assets.[15] Among the Intelligence Committee members who, in the mid-1980s, had asked CIA officials specific and pointed questions that should have yielded some disclosure of the asset losses was Representative Dick Cheney of Wyoming.[16] The withholding of information on the precipitous loss of Soviet sources seemed all the more deliberate because the committee was aware, through its counterintelligence investigations, of other source losses and penetrations across the U.S. intelligence community.[17]

The House committee's pique over "a pattern of a lack of candor by senior CIA officials" overlooked the fact that some of those same officials were, themselves, in the dark about the asset losses and the mole hunt. The list of people with whom information about the asset losses and investigation was shared inadequately, late, or not at all included Webster; his successor as CIA director, Robert Gates; the FBI; CIA officials who administered a polygraph to Ames in 1991; and British intelligence, which also suffered damage from Ames treachery.[18] A 1997 review of the Ames investigation by the Department of Justice found that "FBI's senior management was almost entirely unaware of the scope and significance of the mid-1980s losses and of the FBI's limited efforts to determine their cause."[19] Indeed, one of the ironies of the Ames case is that in a saga marked by the catastrophic loss of secrets and secret sources by the CIA to its principal adversary, the KGB, U.S. intelligence succeeded in keeping the disaster secret from the public, congressional overseers, and even some of its own bosses, for years.

On August 5, 1994, months after pleading guilty to espionage, Ames consented to an interview in the Alexandria City Jail with Senator Dennis DeConcini, who was then the chairman of the Senate Intelligence Committee; he was accompanied by Snider, a second committee aide, and Plato Cacheris, Ames's attorney. DeConcini, who had been incensed that the CIA had "stonewalled" the committee staff over the asset losses, asked Ames whether he and others in the Directorate of Operations had been aware of the asset losses and that an investigation was under way. At least within his own part of the CIA, the Soviet–East European Division of the D.O., Ames said, "Yes. The compromises, the disaster of '85, '86 became relatively common knowledge."[20]

CRISIS IN HUMINT

The Aldrich Ames spy case was a milestone in the history of the CIA, particularly during the "interwar years" between the end of the Cold War and the beginning of what the second Bush administration would call the Global War on Terror. The Ames case cast shadows both forward and back in time: back to the Cold War years for the secrets it revealed about the accomplishments and failings of the clandestine service, accomplishments destroyed by Ames's treachery and the failings exposed by it; and forward to the rise of the al-Qaeda threat and the coming of the U.S.-led invasion of Iraq. Both cases showed how few human intelligence, or HUMINT, sources the CIA had managed to recruit from the ranks of the new terrorist adversary or the old Iraqi foe.

For some, including John Deutch, the CIA director in 1995 and 1996 when most of the work assessing the damage caused by Ames was done, the loss of virtually all the CIA's Soviet sources in the mid-1980s helped explain why the Agency failed to fully grasp the dramatic changes taking place in the Soviet Union under Mikhail Gorbachev, beginning with his rise to power in 1985 just weeks before Ames began spying.[21] This belief that the CIA became misdirected in the late 1980s by deliberate acts of the KGB intensified when the CIA's inspector general, at Deutch's direction, revealed that controlled intelligence fed to the CIA by Soviet double agents during the years of Ames's espionage may have included bogus reports that inflated U.S. assessments of Soviet military capability.

Concern in the mid-1990s over the viability of the CIA's human sources and the Agency's ability to distinguish good sources from bad coincided with congressional and public attention focused on the CIA's dealings with sources in Latin America known to have engaged in human rights abuses. On both issues—the Soviet double agents and the Latin American sources—the fine print of intensive oversight investigations tended to exonerate the CIA, at least partially. Human intelligence reports from the Soviet Union were but one small ingredient in the calculations that went into decisions on the development of U.S. military capabilities during the Cold War. In Latin America, the CIA was doing business with known human rights abusers, but some of the most sensational allegations of direct CIA involvement in human rights abuses were found after lengthy investigation to be false.

It made no difference. By the mid-1990s, the CIA's clandestine service had almost no defenders. It was encountering intense criticism both from Capitol Hill and from its own seventh-floor executive suite, as Deutch, a chemist and mathematician partial to technical intelligence and suspicious of the D.O.'s loose-cannon methods, used these controversies to rein in what he viewed as a rogue division within the CIA. One result, the now infamous "Deutch scrub" of intelligence sources, which was actually begun by his predecessor, James Woolsey, stripped the CIA of hundreds of intelligence sources and added a layer of bureaucracy to the already obstacle-prone process of recruiting new ones. When a somewhat defensive Deutch was questioned by 9/11 Commission member and former Navy secretary John Lehman in 2003, Deutch explained the decline of U.S. human intelligence this way:

> There's no question that human intelligence capability, especially in the CIA, suffered dramatically in the early '90s. No question about it, including during my time. But the overwhelming reason for that fact, Mr. Secretary, had nothing to do with technical or non-technical [intelligence]. It had to do with one thing, and that was Aldrich Ames.[22]

Deutch was right, but what he left out was his own involvement in ensuring that the Ames case hurt the reputation and morale of the Directorate of Operations as had nothing in CIA history going back to the Bay of Pigs fiasco in 1961. Even the exposure of CIA misdeeds in 1975 by the Church and Pike committee investigations, and in the CIA's own "family jewels" compilation of past violations of law, cast the Agency in a nefarious but not incompetent light. Nothing like the exposure brought on by the Ames case had ever happened to the CIA. More than the damage Ames inflicted by exposing the CIA's Soviet sources, Ames's own history as a chronic underperformer and a problem drinker, the CIA's tolerance of that behavior to the point of giving Ames unrestricted access to the nation's most sensitive secrets, and its inability to catch a spy who was as sloppy in his work for the KGB as he was for the CIA— these were the aspects of the case that so damaged the CIA's reputation.

As *New York Times* reporter Tim Weiner, co-author of a book on the Ames case, put it at the time, "The CIA is a laughingstock. When they laugh at you in Washington, you're dead."[23]

Even as the embarrassment over the Ames debacle faded, the legacy of the Ames case carried on. Concern that investigators almost blew the Ames prosecution by collecting evidence outside the rules of criminal procedure prompted the erection of a procedural "wall" between the intelligence and law enforcement. The wall between intelligence gathering and criminal investigations was an overreaction to a near intelligence failure, as opposed to an actual one, since Ames pleaded guilty, rendering mute the concern about evidentiary issues. Against the emerging terrorist threat, the wall greatly complicated the pursuit of terrorists by placing a barrier between investigators working specific cases, such as the USS *Cole* bombing of October 2000, and intelligence officers trying to stop terrorists before they attacked. Post-9/11 rejection of the wall, in turn, led to excesses in the opposite direction, as the second Bush administration unilaterally rewrote the rules of apprehension, detention, and interrogation to an extent that it became a major source of anti-American sentiment around the world and, doubtless, further incentive for acts of terrorism.

THE SPY WHO CAME INTO THE BAR

If the pop-culture image of the international man of espionage was a suave James Bond at a high-class establishment drinking a shaken, not stirred, vodka martini, then the real-life spy as embodied by Ames was that picture, except at a dive bar two or three hours, and several martinis, later. Perhaps no single element of Ames's own background was more embarrassing to the CIA than the exposure of his excessive drinking. The episodes recounted in

Ames's personnel file were bad enough. There were "long liquid lunches" that frequently rendered Ames unable to perform any meaningful work after noon.[24] During his posting to Mexico City in the early 1980s, he engaged in a loud argument with a Cuban official at a diplomatic function and, in another incident, was so drunk at the scene of a traffic accident that he was unresponsive to a police officer's questions. In the summer of 1984 or 1985 (investigators weren't able to pin down the date), Ames drank too much at a softball game and left behind his CIA badge, a wallet containing his alias identification, and some cryptic notes. The beginning of his career as a mole for the Soviets in the spring of 1985 did nothing to curtail his drinking habits. On his very first day as a Soviet spy, April 16, 1985, Ames had gone to the Mayflower Hotel bar in downtown Washington and downed "two or three double vodkas just to relax."[25] He was waiting to meet Sergey Chuvakhin, a KGB officer working out of the Soviet embassy, a sanctioned meeting that Ames had led the CIA and FBI to believe would involve his trying to recruit Chuvakhin as a spy for the United States. In fact, Ames was prepared to volunteer to spy for the Soviets. Chuvakhin failed to show up, and so Ames, who by then must have been quite relaxed, walked the two blocks to the Soviet chancery, strode through the gate, asked the security guard to see Chuvakhin, and handed over an envelope containing his proposal to spy for the KGB. Stationed in Rome from 1986 through 1988, Ames was typically drunk on duty at least three times a week throughout his overseas tour, according to one supervisor. Ames admitted to investigators after his arrest that he was often drunk for meetings with his KGB handlers in Rome.[26] Ames's CIA personnel record was replete with stories of Ames arguing with foreigners, passing out at diplomatic functions, and being unable to perform basic work tasks after lunch.[27] But the truly shocking thing about Ames's drinking was that, within the CIA, it was seen as nothing unusual. As Ames himself described it to members of the House Intelligence Committee in a jailhouse interview, "my problems with alcohol were not glaring and were not exceptional. They were noticed from time to time and, from time to time, mild action was taken."[28] What might have been dismissed as an effort by Ames to downplay an embarrassing truth was borne out by the criminal and congressional investigations, which documented Ames's migration from one sensitive assignment to another despite obvious performance problems. Thus the House and Senate overseers of the intelligence community, already irate at the CIA for keeping them out of the loop about this extraordinary case, had before them the specter of the CIA having its most closely guarded secrets stolen from under its nose by a patently incompetent employee.

The controversy went beyond Ames's theft of secrets to the question of how such an employee could have had access to them in the first place. The CIA's own inspector general offered this devastating assessment:

> By and large his professional weaknesses were observed by Ames's colleagues and supervisors and were tolerated by many who did not consider them highly unusual for Directorate of Operations officers on the "not going anywhere" promotion track. That an officer with these observed vulnerabilities should have been given counterintelligence responsibilities in Soviet operations where he was in a prime position to learn of the intimate details of the Agency's most sensitive operations, contact Soviet officials openly and then massively betray his trust is difficult to justify.[29]

Ames's job at the time he began spying for the KGB in April 1985 was as a case officer in the Soviet–East European Division of the Directorate of Operations. In this post it was part of Ames's responsibility to meet occasionally with KGB officers in hopes of recruiting one or more of them to spy for the CIA. Following standard procedure, these meetings were conducted under authorized circumstances and reported to the CIA and FBI as a routine part of the espionage trade in Washington, Moscow, and capitals around the world. After July 1985, Ames stopped reporting these contacts regularly, as was required, and although the FBI occasionally complained to Ames's CIA superiors, nothing much was done about it.[30] The deep flaw in the system in which Ames operated was his easy access to the case files on those Soviets who had already been successfully recruited by the CIA. All the CIA's security fences, vehicle barriers, soundproof rooms, surveillance-resistant windows, and so on provided no security against the will of an individual CIA officer sitting across a luncheon table from a KGB counterpart. If that officer's loyalty wavered, the CIA was defenseless. Such was the case with Aldrich Ames.

This weakness in the system—the ability of CIA officers who regularly met with the KGB to gain easy access to the identities of those Soviets already spying for the CIA—did not flow both ways. KGB case-file information was much more closely held. For a time, the vast quantity of information Ames was able to hand over, and the ease with which he was able to obtain it, had the KGB wondering whether Ames was really a double agent, controlled by the CIA. The Soviets simply couldn't believe it could be that easy to steal the CIA's secrets. When Ames began handing over bagfuls of top-secret files, his KGB handlers were shocked that he was able to walk out of CIA headquarters without being searched. Such a thing would have been unthinkable in Moscow.[31] While stationed in Rome, Ames said after his arrest, he was handing over so much material to the KGB that they "had a lot more than they could use, and they weren't eager for more." Investigators struggled to quantify the secrets Ames gave away. His most damaging disclosure, the so-called "big dump" of files identifying perhaps two dozen Soviets working for the CIA, was measured in weight. On June 13, 1985, Ames walked into Chadwicks Restaurant on K Street in Georgetown carrying an estimated five to seven pounds of highly classified paper.[32] Another delivery of secrets was measured in height. According to Deutch's unclassified summary of the damage sustained by the CIA, Ames fulfilled one assignment by giving the KGB documents that would have made a pile fifteen to twenty feet high.[33]

Though the ease with which Ames stole secrets bespoke a tolerant, old-boy atmosphere at the CIA, it had not always been so easy to walk out of CIA headquarters or an embassy with classified information. In the late 1970s, Admiral Stansfield Turner, President Carter's CIA chief, instituted a spot-check program that Ames said became extremely unpopular. A friend of Ames's had received a two-week suspension without pay for trying to leave CIA headquarters with classified documents.[34] This reform contributed to Turner's unpopularity within the insular and clubbish Directorate of Operations. It was a security measure that did not outlast Carter's presidency. Under William Casey, brought in by President Reagan to breathe life and a renewed élan into the D.O., the CIA scrapped the spot-check system, leaving the door out of the CIA wide open for Aldrich Ames.

Ames told investigators he began spying for the KGB as a "con game or a scam to get money from the KGB." Ames was going to outsmart everyone. In his own colorful phrase, "instead of robbing a bank, I decided to rob the KGB." He viewed it as a "one-time thing" and decided to continue only when he realized, after receiving a sack of five hundred $100 bills on May 17, 1985, that he had passed the point of no return.[35] In August 1984, Ames had married Maria del Rosario Casas Dupuy, a Colombian diplomat he met in 1982 while stationed in Mexico City. The marriage was irregular for a CIA officer on two counts: Rosario was a foreign national, and she was a CIA asset. Divorce from his first wife had left Ames in debt; remarriage had put him at the head of a new family, with a free-spending wife, all to be supported on Ames's pedestrian government salary.[36] This, at least, is how Ames described his motivation as he began spying for the KGB.

Of course, it was the CIA that Ames was robbing, and the big score came when Ames handed over the bag heavy with cable traffic and code names that would enable the KGB to identify virtually every Soviet spying for the CIA. To this day there are aspects of the "big dump" that remain shrouded in uncertainty. Ames, who had already received one payment from the KGB, did not ask for money for this, by far his most valuable contribution to Soviet espionage. He later would tell American investigators that he did it to protect himself. The most likely way Ames would be caught would be if someone in the KGB chain of command who was reporting secretly to the CIA got wind of a CIA operations officer working for the Soviets. And the best defense against that threat was to liquidate those spies within the KGB.[37] This the Soviets proceeded to do with ruthless efficiency—so much so that Ames himself was shocked at the speed with which the KGB hunted down, arrested, and executed at least nine people whose identities he had given away.[38]

In spite of his desire to get rid of any Soviets who might finger him, Ames claimed he was angered by the swift response. "I knew that this was turning into a potential danger, that the signals were lighting up," Ames said after his arrest. "I mean, the KGB might as well have taken out an ad in the *New York Times* saying, 'We got a source.'"[39] Yet Ames, who claimed to be one of the foremost CIA experts on the KGB, also said he knew from experience that the KGB maintained tight operational security around its spy operations; the number of Soviet officials who would know of his approach to the KGB would be kept to an absolute minimum—of this Ames said he was quite certain, a direct contradiction of his sense of urgency that people who might identify him be put out of business.[40] "What I did in June was irrational," was Ames's only explanation.[41] It seems likely that Ames knew full well that the information he provided in the "big dump" was by far the most valuable material he could obtain and would guarantee payment of large sums without his having to make that demand. After his arrest, he may well have wanted to rebut any suggestion that he profited from abetting the execution of CIA sources.

One of the factors that slowed the CIA mole hunt was the inordinate number of people with access to the case files on Soviets spying for the United States. In August 1991, a joint FBI/CIA investigative unit looking into the 1985–86 losses identified 198 CIA employees with access to the case files concerning Soviets working for the CIA.[42] The FBI became involved in the Ames probe not by being notified by the CIA but because it learned in 1986 that two KGB officers it was running, Valery Martynov and Sergei Motorin, had been arrested. Ames had given up their identities in the spring of 1985, possibly in his very first meeting with the Soviets in April. In October of that year, FBI mole Robert Hanssen also passed information to the KGB fingering them as spies.[43] Both Martynov and Motorin were executed. Initially the FBI was unable to determine who had access to the Martynov and Motorin cases.[44] Eventually, it determined that as many as 250 employees in the FBI's Washington Field Office had knowledge of these cases. (Both Martynov and Motorin were stationed in Washington during the time they were spying for the United States.)[45] In contrast, as few as seven and no more than twenty KGB officers would have known Ames by name as a spy working for the Soviet Union.[46]

Ames described a meeting in Rome in which his KGB handler, Vladimir Mechulayev, apologized for the peremptory roll-up of KGB spies, a move certain to alert the CIA that it had a security problem, and possibly a mole.[47] Mechulayev explained that the Soviet spy service, which normally rolled up moles gradually to avoid compromising its source, had been ordered by political higher-ups to move quickly.[48] If this scene happened as Ames described, it appears likely that he was being deceived. According to Victor Cherkashin, the KGB colonel who oversaw the Ames case, Vladimir Kryuchkov, Cherkashin's boss as head of Soviet intelligence, lied to his superiors and concealed Ames's role to avoid embarrassment. "Instead of telling his bosses in the Politburo that a CIA mole" had revealed the identity of spies and CIA eavesdropping operations on Moscow, "the head of intelligence took the credit himself. Kryuchkov made it appear that the exposures resulted from hard work by the KGB under his leadership,"[49] Cherkashin wrote. To report that a CIA mole—and not even a man recruited by the KGB, but a "walk-in" who had volunteered to spy— had fingered some two dozen turncoats infesting the Soviet security apparatus would have been a career-ending, possibly life-ending disclosure for the key KGB people involved. Author Pete Earley has provided a somewhat different account. Earley quotes an unidentified aide to Kryuchkov as saying that the KGB briefed Soviet Premier Mikhail Gorbachev on Ames, though without naming the CIA officer, and claimed that Ames was a KGB "plant" rather than a walk-in. If this version of events is true, the false information given to Gorbachev would have depended on the Soviet leader's complete ignorance of espionage, since planting someone in the CIA who could have gained access to the kind of secrets Ames was divulging would have been a near impossibility.[50] Nevertheless, both accounts depict the KGB's leadership as trying to deceive the Politburo about Ames to prevent their own embarrassment.

To Ames, all the spy-versus-spy tension was little more than a game. How galling it must have been for CIA veterans, several of whom had their careers and reputations ruined by Ames, to read his expansive comments to investigators and lawmakers about how unimportant and shallow the espionage game was. In the statement of facts Ames gave in federal court in Alexandria on April 28, 1994, nine years to the month after he began spying, Ames observed, "I do not believe that our nation's interests have been noticeably damaged by my acts, or, for that matter, those of the Soviet Union or Russia notably aided." Ames portrayed himself as a political dissenter "from the decades-long shift to the extreme right" in the United States, suggesting, presumably, that through his espionage he was seeking to somehow redress this superpower imbalance. Ames told the court he had "come to believe that the espionage business was a self-serving sham, carried out by careerist bureaucrats who managed to deceive several generations of American policymakers about the value of their work."[51] Ames said he hoped his case would spark a new debate about what all of the money spent in the name of national security really bought. Ames told Pete Earley that the problem wasn't so much the worthlessness of the secrets the CIA stole as the unwillingness of policymakers to heed them. The essence of the clandestine information the CIA had been collecting from the Soviet sources he exposed, Ames said, "was that with only the most minor exceptions, we were consistently superior militarily to the Soviets."[52] To the House Intelligence Committee, Ames said that most of the information the CIA gathered from Soviet sources was about the KGB; very little had anything to do with Soviet foreign policy or political developments within the Kremlin. Ames portrayed himself as something of a stealth secretary of state and said he hoped by his own efforts to show the KGB that Moscow's paranoia about U.S. intentions and activities was overblown.[53] Ames insisted he had not switched loyalties from the United States to Russia but had abandoned his loyalty to the CIA because of his disdain for its role in perpetuating the Cold War.[54]

Apparently with a completely straight face, Ames even inserted himself into the post–Cold War "whither intelligence" debate, telling the lawmakers with power over the CIA's budget that the Agency was far too large and that the clandestine service was perhaps ten times as big as it needed to be. He called Senator Moynihan's proposals on disbandment of the CIA "okay," though he allowed that some residual intelligence capability would probably be needed. Surprisingly, the members of Congress seemed interested in what he had to say.[55]

All this indicated not only that the CIA had incompetents working in sensitive positions who were able to rob the Agency blind, but also that the underlying work that all this trouble was about was of little if any consequence. The timing of Ames's espionage appeared to bear this out. Many officials stated that the Ames case was one of the worst intelligence disasters in CIA history, and yet the Soviet Union collapsed in the face of pressure from the United States halfway through Ames's tenure as a spy for Moscow. It was difficult to see the Directorate of Operations' clandestine mission as particularly critical to national security if it could suffer a total loss of its Soviet sources a few years before the Soviet Union ceased to exist. And while CIA officers were derisive of Ames's jailhouse critique of the Agency, some in the CIA were making similar comments. In November 1995, Richard Kerr, by then the former deputy director of intelligence, told the House Intelligence Committee, "The clandestine service of the Cold War does not serve present needs. It probably got too big, too walled off, and too isolated. Much of its 'culture'—independence and flexibility—must be maintained. But, like the U.S. military after Vietnam, it needs an overhaul."[56] The committee, in a sweeping report recommending changes in the intelligence community, detected across the community "no absence of *schadenfreude*"—delight in another's misfortune—over the difficulties experienced by the Directorate of Operations in the wake of the Ames case. The committee reported that within the intelligence community the D.O. "has been viewed as elitist and deserving a comeuppance."[57]

AMES AS AN EMBARRASSMENT TO THE KGB

The KGB's evident embarrassment over what Ames had revealed pointed to an element of the case largely overlooked by Congress at the time and by historians since. The Ames case had revealed not only that the CIA had suffered a devastating loss due to a mole whom the Agency had taken far too long to catch, but also that the clandestine service had had enormous success in spying on the Soviet Union before Ames's treachery. Colonel Oleg Gordievsky was one of the few KGB officers fingered by Ames as a spy for the West who managed to escape after coming under suspicion. Britain's MI-6, to whom Gordievsky reported, smuggled him out of Moscow in a daring escape operation on June 18, 1985, just five days after Ames, in the "big dump," had handed over confirmation of what the KGB already suspected concerning Gordievsky's work for the

British.[58] When he met with CIA officers for a post-escape debriefing, Gordievsky said he was amazed at the depth of the Agency's knowledge of the KGB. Listening to the CIA officers discuss KGB affairs, Gordievsky recalled, "It was as if I were sitting among my KGB friends."[59] Even Ames, though generally dismissive of the value of information obtained from moles, acknowledged the importance of Gordievsky as a spy. In the early 1980s, Gordievsky had alerted the British that the Soviet government feared that President Reagan was going to start a nuclear war. Awareness of the Kremlin's paranoia led to discreet signals of reassurance that, whatever the hostility between East and West, Washington was not about to start World War III.

British author Christopher Andrew, who perhaps knows more about the KGB and its Cold War operations than any other Western scholar, rates the CIA's clandestine performance as "far better" than the KGB's. The Ames debacle, he said, represented "weaknesses within a system that has been vastly superior to its opposition."[60] Ames's revelations to Moscow represented a KGB coup, to be sure, but also stood as an enormous embarrassment for the Soviet spy service, which suddenly realized the extent to which it had been penetrated by the CIA. The lengths to which the KGB went to keep the Politburo in the dark about how these Soviet moles were being uprooted—to make it look like dogged gumshoe work by KGB spy hunters rather than an unsolicited one-day dump carried out of the CIA in a bag by a walk-in spy—testifies to the flip side of the Ames case, one that neither the CIA's leadership nor congressional overseers cared to emphasize.

The focus in the Ames case after his arrest was on the human spies he betrayed, understandably so since the betrayal resulted in at least nine being put to death. But according to Cherkashin, Ames's KGB case manager, Ames showed the Soviets, to their chagrin, far more about the degree to which U.S. intelligence had penetrated their secret channels through technical means. "If the number of CIA agents in the KGB caused dismay" in Moscow, Cherkashin wrote, "Ames's information about American eavesdropping operations inside the Soviet Union simply astounded."[61] The operations blown by Ames revealed not only the depth of penetration the CIA had achieved against the Soviet target but also the ingenuity involved. Mirroring the audacious tapping of undersea Soviet military cables, the CIA had mounted an operation called TAW to tap an underground link between Moscow and a nuclear weapons research institute southwest of the Soviet capital. Ames also divulged to the KGB that the CIA had installed listening devices disguised as tree branches near selected Soviet research institutes. And he disclosed an operation code-named ABSORB involving a shipping container loaded with CIA-designed sensing equipment. Ostensibly a shipment of consumer goods to be sent by rail across the Soviet Union from the Pacific coast to Leningrad, the container's actual purpose was to measure sources of radioactivity at various points along the way and to photograph passing rail cars for information about Soviet military shipments.[62]

Fixing the precise number of human assets and highly classified technical operations Ames exposed to the Soviets has been as much art as science because investigators have had to rely largely on Ames's memory and his willingness to tell what he knows, and because other turncoats, particularly FBI mole Robert Hanssen, gave away information that overlapped with what Ames compromised. The picture is further muddied because some of the human agents given up by Ames, as well as some of the technical operations, were already under suspicion by the KGB by the time Ames volunteered as a spy.[63] But the most recent authoritative estimate is that Ames compromised roughly thirty human agents and more than a hundred covert operations.[64]

TO CATCH A SPY

Beyond the grievous damage Ames inflicted on the CIA, how Ames remained undetected for so long, particularly given his sloppy tradecraft, became the primary focus of attention and "lessons learned" investigations following his arrest. Once Ames had been caught and the record of his espionage reviewed, it seemed so obvious he had betrayed the CIA that, to overseers and even the Agency's own top management, it was difficult to understand how he had escaped detection for so long. The professionals knew better. As with the 9/11 investigations, the clues seemed obvious only in hindsight. The East German master spy Markus Wolf observed of the Ames case, "The thankless and exhausting task of tracking down a traitor always seems much easier in retrospect than in prospect. The clues always seem so obvious—but only after the hunt has caught its prey."[65]

Missteps by CIA and FBI counterintelligence investigators were not the only reason it took so long to catch Ames. The rules under which Ames and other CIA case officers operated allowed for frequent encounters with KGB officers, a circumstance that left the CIA dependent almost entirely on the honesty of these officers to avoid catastrophic loss. Once Moscow began rolling up the agents exposed by Ames, the KGB went to lengths to throw U.S.

counterintelligence investigators off Ames's trail by leaking false information that offered alternative explanations for the CIA's asset losses. By coincidence, there were in the mid-1980s several other espionage cases that distracted investigators seeking to explain the losses. All these factors received attention in the Ames postmortem. None buffered the blow to the CIA.

The first tip to CIA officials raising a question about Ames's unexplained wealth came in November 1989 when CIA counterintelligence officer Diana Worthen (who knew of the 1985–86 losses, was a friend of Ames, and knew Ames would have had access to the compromised cases) reported on Ames's extravagant spending habits to counterintelligence investigators. Worthen also knew that Rosario's family was not wealthy, contradicting the cover story Ames had used to explain his sudden, post-divorce wealth. An inquiry turned up several large transactions, including the cash purchase by Ames of a $540,000 home in suburban Washington, but it went no further.[66]

Indeed, the entire effort to explain the 1985–86 losses had ground to a halt in the period 1988–90. As a sign of the desperate state of the hunt for the traitor, Gus Hathaway, the recently retired head of CIA counterintelligence, took the extraordinary step in May 1990 of contacting the equally retired East German spy Markus Wolf at Wolf's dacha outside Berlin. Hathaway, who had been so upset to learn in 1988 that Senate staffers knew about the CIA asset losses, was not, in fact, inactive in the hunt for the mole, as the CIA's Moscow Station had feared. In May of 1990 he approached one of the leading figures on the other side with an offer: come to the United States, live comfortably at taxpayer expense, and in return, help the CIA find out who had betrayed its Soviet sources in the mid-1980s. Wolf refused on two grounds: even after the fall of the Berlin Wall, he didn't want to work for the CIA, and he did not know the identity of the spy—or so he claimed.[67]

In December 1990, Dan Payne, an official of the CIA's Counter-Intelligence Center looking into the 1985–86 losses, urged the CIA's Office of Security to open an investigation of Ames's personal finances and the sources of his wealth. His December 5, 1990, memo reported "a degree of urgency involved in our request" because Ames, by then already under suspicion, had been assigned to a desk in the Counter-Intelligence Center with severely limited access to sensitive information. The center reported that it was "quickly running out of things for him to do without granting him greater access."[68]

In April 1991, Ames was given a polygraph examination and passed, with the help of both the KGB and CIA. Ames was alarmed about the upcoming test, particularly about whether he might be asked about his finances. The KGB coached Ames on how to prepare for the test by getting plenty of rest and how to relax during it to avoid tripping the machine. The CIA helped out unwittingly by failing to question Ames in detail about his finances, asking only a few general questions. Perversely, the reason for this was to make the test seem like a routine security check, not part of a mole hunt, and so the CIA avoided questions that might have signaled the fruits of the investigation of Ames that had been sparked by the December 1990 memo. In fact, none of the derogatory information about Ames generated by that investigation—his sloppy work habits, his excessive drinking, his expensive house and cars—was shared with the officials administering the polygraph. Even despite these deficiencies, the polygraph officer noted, "I don't think he's a spy, but I am not 100% convinced because of the money situation."[69] Not until July 1991 did the CIA make a half-hearted attempt to determine whether Rosario's family was independently wealthy, nearly two years after the tip from Worthen.

The key breakthrough in the Ames case did not come until the summer of 1992, when CIA investigators were able to match large bank deposits by Ames with the dates of authorized meetings he had with Sergey Chuvakhin, who handled most of the direct exchanges with Ames involving stolen CIA documents and cash payments from the KGB.[70] A year later, on September 15, 1993, members of an FBI task force working the espionage case picked up Ames's trash outside his Arlington home and found a torn-up Post-it note in Ames's handwriting setting up a meeting with someone the investigators were sure was his Russian contact, further testimony to Ames's sloppy tradecraft.[71] This discovery set in motion the massive FBI surveillance operation that led to his arrest the following February.

The story of Ames's apprehension as told by FBI and CIA participants in the investigation focuses on a painstaking process of narrowing the field of suspects followed by an equally painstaking process of investigation and surveillance of Ames, culminating in his arrest. The accounts vary only in the apportionment of credit to either CIA or FBI counterintelligence investigators. There has been speculation, particularly from the Soviet side, that Ames was given up by a traitor, a contention vigorously denied in Washington and one surely designed to absolve Russian intelligence officers of charges of poor tradecraft on their part contributing to Ames's arrest. Author Ronald Kessler, who had extensive access to CIA sources, attributes the identification of Ames as a spy to a Russian source the CIA code-named AVENGER, who offered up information in 1993 that helped narrow the focus to Ames. After the fall of the Berlin Wall in 1989, access by Western intelligence agencies to the archives of the East German secret police, the Stasi, reportedly provided clues that helped identify Ames. But Milton Bearden, who ran the Soviet–East European Division of the D.O. at the time of the Soviet collapse, and who was in a position to know, has endorsed neither of these accounts.[72]

Whether or not the CIA and FBI received help from Stasi files or a clandestine Russian source, the long timeline of the Ames investigation, the missed signals, and the slow turning of bureaucratic wheels fed the portrayal of the case as an almost uninterrupted catalogue of CIA incompetence. Though the investigation involved both CIA and FBI officials, most of the blame fell on the CIA. The CIA had failed to put enough people on the case. The Agency's insular Directorate of Operations had refused to believe there could be a spy in its midst. The excesses of counterintelligence sleuth James Jesus Angleton in ruining CIA careers in a fruitless search for a CIA mole in the 1960s and 1970s had produced an overreactive commitment never to repeat that mistake, and so on. Lost in this irresistible big picture of the drama were details about the workings of espionage that added texture and nuance to the issue of why it took so long to catch Ames.

As already noted, the most pressing counterintelligence concern in Washington before the KGB's liquidation of the CIA's Soviet sources was the bugging of the new U.S. embassy in Moscow. Some CIA counterintelligence officers, Paul Redmond most notable among them, believed from the beginning that a human penetration of the CIA lay behind the 1985–86 losses. But the early guessing favored some sort of technical penetration in which the KGB had figured out a way to intercept and decode communications between CIA stations around the world and headquarters. Redmond devised a test of this theory involving the transmittal over those same putatively secure lines of false information about CIA recruitment of KGB sources. If the Soviets were reading this traffic, the theory went, these sources would likely be recalled immediately to Moscow for interrogation. Like an angler, Redmond put out his signals and waited. Nothing happened.[73]

The 1985–86 period encompassing the asset losses became known as "The Year of the Spy" because of a flurry of high-profile espionage cases, which could have accounted for some of the asset losses. In August of 1985, KGB officer Vitaly Yurchenko defected to the United States after walking into the U.S. embassy in Rome. Hustled to Washington for debriefings conducted by, of all people, Ames, he immediately provided information confirming CIA suspicions that former CIA officer Edward Lee Howard was a spy. Howard had been fired in 1983 on the eve of an assignment to Moscow after a polygraph indicated he was using illegal drugs. In the fall of 1984, according to Yurchenko, a man code-named ROBERT who fit Howard's profile met with KGB officers in Austria and gave up information about Soviet officials spying for the CIA.[74] U.S. investigators later concluded that Howard had met KGB handlers in January and May of 1985, timing that coincided with the asset losses.[75] Further investigation found that three of the Soviet sources arrested by the KGB in the 1985–86 purge could be attributed to Howard.

Yurchenko also fingered a former National Security Agency employee, later determined to be Ronald Pelton. The low-level employee at the nation's electronic eavesdropping center had told the Soviets of the Navy-NSA program called IVY BELLS that involved tapping undersea cables for unencrypted Soviet military communications.[76] It was an extraordinary loss for U.S. intelligence, but not one that explained the recent loss of the CIA's human sources. Then, in December 1986, Clayton Lonetree, a U.S. Marine security guard at the embassy in Vienna who had previously worked at the Moscow embassy, confessed to having given classified information to the KGB, including drawings of the embassy in Moscow. Lonetree had been seduced into spying by Violetta Siena, a Russian woman under KGB control. For a time, the investigators searching for the reason behind the asset losses suspected Lonetree of enabling the KGB to gain access to secure portions of the U.S. embassy. Indeed, the KGB's prime motivation in recruiting Lonetree may have been to distract attention from their main source of secrets, Ames.[77] It took a year to determine that the Lonetree case probably could not explain the asset losses.[78] Further adding to the noise was the arrest in May 1985 of former Navy communications specialist John Walker, who organized a ring involving family members and colleagues that fed U.S. communications code information to the Soviets from 1962 until 1975, when he retired.[79] Though unrelated to Soviet espionage efforts, the arrest in 1985 of Jonathan Pollard, an employee of the Naval Criminal Investigative Service, for spying for Israel, only added to the impression that the U.S. intelligence community was being robbed blind.

The KGB was doing everything it could to protect Ames, having risked exposing him by the abrupt arrest of the spies he compromised. The KGB spread the story among its own ranks that Howard was the source of most of the recent compromises, assuming correctly that the information would filter its way back to the CIA. It fed misinformation on the arrests to Soviets known, via Ames, to be working for the CIA before they were arrested, confident those sources would be unwitting conduits for the misinformation to reach Langley. Knowing that the CIA would be able to figure out that Howard could not have known of all the Soviets exposed since some had been recruited after Howard's firing, the KGB also spread the story that it had been able to exploit sloppy CIA tradecraft to learn the identities of some of the moles.[80] Indeed, the account of the Ames case by retired KGB Colonel Cherkashin makes clear that several of the spies compromised by Ames were already under KGB suspicion by June 1985 when Ames handed over the "big dump" of asset information. The KGB and Ames developed a subtle strategy in which he was able to report to the CIA enough progress in his CIA-authorized meetings with Chuvakhin so that his U.S. bosses would want these meetings to continue, but not so much progress that the case would draw attention that might expose it as a ruse.[81] The Soviets were further aided in their deception efforts by a fortuitous coincidence: the CIA had selected Ames to debrief the defector Yurchenko. Thus the KGB knew of everything Yurchenko was divulging to the CIA and could plan its disinformation campaign accordingly. Yurchenko eventually re-defected to the Soviet Union, roiling the pot still further, though the key CIA officers involved believe that his defection to the United States was genuine and not part of a KGB disinformation plot related to Ames.[82]

To careful observers at the CIA, the KGB's actions had the unintended effect of helping the U.S. mole hunt by signaling through all this activity that something truly unusual was afoot and that the Soviets were prepared to go to lengths to protect an important intelligence channel. But the process took time. And with senior FBI and CIA managers largely ignorant as to the extent of the losses, and Congress completely in the dark, there were no higher-ups driving the bureaucracy to solve the mystery, and so from time to time the investigation simply ground to a halt.

In putting the difficulty of the Ames mole hunt into perspective, consider that FBI turncoat Robert Hanssen began spying for the Soviet Union in November 1979, first came under suspicion within the Bureau in 1990, yet was not arrested until February 2001, two months before his mandatory retirement date. During that entire time he never submitted to a polygraph examination, never completed a financial disclosure form, and underwent one background investigation. In August 1990, ten years and six months before his arrest, Hanssen first came under suspicion—like Ames, on financial grounds—when his brother-in-law, FBI Special Agent Mark Wauck, reported to his supervisor that Wauck's sister, Hanssen's wife, had found large amounts of unexplained cash in a dresser drawer. The supervisor did nothing.[83] In comparison, the time elapsed from the first report to CIA authorities of Ames's unexplained wealth and his arrest was four years and three months.

The Hanssen case is more than a comparative study to help us put the Ames case in perspective. Hanssen's espionage itself became a factor in the delays in the capture of Ames. One reason given for the slow tempo of the Ames investigation was the CIA's success in recruiting new Soviet sources after the 1985–86 losses. That recruiting success fed the belief that whatever the cause of the losses, the bleeding had been stopped. That confidence was short-lived, however, when in the late 1980s the Soviets began rolling up sources later determined to have been given up by Hanssen. The capture of Ames, in turn, slowed the realization by investigators that another significant mole remained at large. Between 1987 and 1991 the FBI was suffering a series of losses of human sources and technical operations aimed at the Soviet Union of a magnitude similar to what the CIA had experienced in 1985 and 1986. Yet the joint Special Investigative Unit formed by the CIA and FBI in 1991 focused almost entirely on the possibility, and then the reality, of a CIA mole, overlooking the possibility that the Soviets might have recruited an FBI agent. A report written about a year before Ames's arrest, when he was a definite suspect, contained a detailed list of CIA officers, including Ames, with access to some of the compromised assets. No similar list of FBI officers with the same access was compiled. A decade later, in the aftermath of Hanssen's arrest and prosecution, the FBI determined that in connection with the 1987–91 losses, "We now know that Hanssen compromised most of the significant operations."[84]

THE POLITICS OF HUMINT

From the Clinton administration's point of view, the Ames case had at least one positive political aspect: Ames had started spying during the Reagan administration. Most of the damage he inflicted and the mistakes the CIA made in its wake occurred under Republican presidents. Bill Clinton had taken office in January 1993; the big break in the investigation occurred the following September when the FBI went through Ames's trash; and the spy was under arrest in February of 1994.[85] The Clinton administration could take the credit for cracking the case while the damage Ames had inflicted and the bungling of the early years of the investigation could be debited to prior—Republican—administrations. Not by coincidence, then, the assessment of the damage Ames wrought went forward in full public view and with particular energy. The assessment also occurred at the same time as a separate controversy also involving the Directorate of Operations and its human clandestine sources, this one in Latin America where the issue was not espionage against the United States but the use by the CIA of sources with abominable human rights records. Energized by these two public controversies, it was now the Democrats' turn to use CIA mistakes as a vehicle to advance a political agenda. The technique in both cases was the same: take the CIA's serious mistakes and exaggerate them still further, gaining short-term political points at the expense of the long-term well-being of the CIA.

The Latin American and Ames investigations moved forward on separate tracks, but converged in the negative and public light they shone on the Directorate of Operations and in the subtle but recognizable political agenda underlying that negative attention. The investigation by the Ames Damage Assessment Team began by focusing on the main issue, the compromise of human and technical operations, a process that involved the painstaking reconstruction of blown operations and the extensive debriefing of Ames. From there it moved on to the question of whether, during Ames's tenure as a Soviet and Russian spy, Moscow had fed the CIA tainted or controlled intelligence that worked its way into reports distributed to policymakers without warnings that the information might be tainted. The investigation concluded that Moscow had engaged in a disinformation campaign, and that the CIA had been taken. The CIA's sudden loss of Soviet spies just as Gorbachev's reign was beginning, and the planting of false intelligence that exaggerated Soviet military prowess, led CIA Director John Deutch, appointed by Clinton, to assert that Ames contributed to the CIA's failure—under Republican administrations—to foresee the Soviet collapse. In the case of Latin American intelligence sources, the CIA's reliance on civilian and military officers in Guatemala and Honduras with records of human rights abuses provided a vehicle for reviving debate about the Reagan administration's support for these regimes and its use of the CIA to achieve policy aims by questionable means.

Ostensibly, the damage assessment entailed sober, nonpartisan examination of Ames's impact on intelligence and the intelligence community. But there was an underlying partisan slant to the findings that conformed with the Democratic worldview of the time: the CIA had helped perpetuate the Cold War in its blindness to the changes in the Soviet Union; tainted intelligence had contributed to Pentagon overspending on weapons; and misplaced moral values caused the CIA to pay sources in Latin America known to have been complicit in torture, murder, and other human rights abuses.

Not all the political damage of the Ames case was offloaded onto Republican administrations. While Ames had done his worst on the watch of Republican presidents, the Clinton administration came under pressure to ensure that there would be no whitewashing of the results of the Ames probe. The intensity of that pressure became clear when Deutch's predecessor as CIA director, James Woolsey, who had been appointed by Clinton in 1993, came under intense criticism from Congress for failing to more severely discipline CIA officers involved at various critical junctures in Ames's career and in the subsequent mole hunt. Woolsey said the right words, calling the Ames case "a systemic failure of the CIA . . . a failure of management accountability, in judgment, in vigilance."[86] But his actions did not match the magnitude of the failure, in the view of the CIA's critics. Woolsey told congressional overseers that he reprimanded twenty-three current and former Agency officers, eleven in writing, but only one publicly, and that one mildly. Ted Price, head of CIA counterintelligence during part of the mole-hunt period—before 1991 when the inquiry stalled—and, at the time of Ames's arrest, the head of the D.O., received a written reprimand for failing to devote more resources to the mole hunt. Of the eleven formally reprimanded, only four still worked at the CIA by the time discipline was being meted out. None of the CIA officers cited in the initial damage assessment report by CIA Inspector General Frederick Hitz was fired, demoted, suspended, or reassigned, a response that the Senate Intelligence Committee dubbed "seriously inadequate."[87]

The generally accepted explanation for Woolsey's resignation as CIA director in January of 1995 was his frustration over lack of access to President Clinton. The oft-repeated joke was that a small plane that had crashed on the White House grounds in September 1994 was Woolsey trying to get in to see the president. His relations with at least one key lawmaker were little better. Woolsey clashed with Senate Intelligence Committee Chairman DeConcini almost from his first day on the job in early 1993. Britt Snider, the committee's general counsel, described the two as "barely on speaking terms."[88] It was not from lack of familiarity. Woolsey recalled that in 1994 he made 205 appearances before congressional oversight committees, many of them on the Ames case, an average of about one per day in which Congress was in session. Woolsey said the friction stemmed from his refusal to endorse deeper cuts in intelligence budgeting advocated by DeConcini and other Democrats pushing

the "peace dividend" agenda after the Cold War. "We basically stopped hiring," Woolsey said. That was partly because of budget cuts and partly because
Woolsey refused to lay off CIA officers who, in his view, had helped win the
Cold War: "These were folks, Soviet specialists many of them, who'd sacri-
ficed a great deal throughout their careers to be intelligence officers. It seemed
morally wrong to put them out on the street. I wouldn't do it. The result was
no new hiring." DeConcini, Woolsey said, "fought us on everything," particularly Woolsey's desire to protect large budgets for spy satellites. Satellites
were a priority of Woolsey's in part because of the criticism after the Gulf War
about the CIA's inability to feed the right satellite intelligence to the right war-
fighters in a timely fashion.[89]

DeConcini claims he sought increased spending on human intelligence
and cuts elsewhere in the intelligence budget. Woolsey, DeConcini wrote in
his memoir, "became enamored of the CIA culture and quickly grew defensive about the agency." The rift widened when Woolsey accused DeConcini
of leaking classified information, a charge the senator fended off by saying
that his staff had leaked the material and that it wasn't classified anyway.
On one thing the two agreed: Woolsey was, in DeConcini's words, "an isolated bureaucrat," embattled in Congress and receiving little help from a
largely uninterested White House.[90] Author Tom Powers said it was Hitz's
400-page classified damage assessment that ended Woolsey's career, since
Hitz had recommended more than a dozen Directorate of Operations officers for punishment ranging from dismissal to reprimand, and Woolsey
wound up firing no one.[91] This was the dominant lesson brought to the job
by the successor Clinton eventually chose, then–Deputy Defense Secretary
John Deutch.

THE DIRECTORATE OF OPERATIONS AND LATIN AMERICA

On March 22, 1995, during the four-month interval between Woolsey's departure and Deutch's confirmation, Representative Robert Torricelli (D-N.J.), a
member of the House Intelligence Committee, wrote to Clinton concerning allegations that Colonel Julio Roberto Alpirez, a Guatemalan intelligence officer
and paid CIA informant, had ordered the killings in Guatemala of American
citizen Michael Devine in 1990 and guerrilla leader Efrain Bamaca Velasquez,
the husband of American lawyer Jennifer Harbury, in 1992. The letter was somewhat disjointed: Torricelli said the CIA learned of the killings and of Alpirez's
role and covered up its knowledge for years. But he went on to charge, without

citing specific evidence, that "the United States government was complicitous in these murders" and that "the direct involvement of the Central Intelligence Agency in the murder of these individuals leads me to the extraordinary conclusion that the Agency is simply out of control and that it contains what can only be called a criminal element."[92] The following June, a month after Deutch was sworn in as director of central intelligence, the *Sun* of Baltimore published a four-part series alleging that hundreds of Honduran citizens suspected of involvement in leftist subversive activity had been kidnapped, tortured, and murdered by a Honduran military unit called the 316th Battalion that had been trained and financed by the CIA, and that the CIA knew of these crimes and participated in interrogations involving torture. Stories detailing human rights abuses in Honduras had also been published by the *New York Times*.[93]

In a preliminary response to the Guatemala charges, Acting CIA Director William O. Studeman told the Senate Intelligence Committee in April 1995 "emphatically that the CIA is not complicit in the murder of Mr. Devine nor in the apparent killing of Mr. Bamaca." The CIA obtained information about the Devine killing in August 1990 and developed evidence linking Alpirez to the interrogation of Devine in October 1991. In both cases, that intelligence was distributed to key agencies in the executive branch, though not, Studeman admitted, to congressional oversight committees. The CIA learned about Bamaca's capture and apparent murder at the hands of a Guatemalan army unit, and, in early 1995, learned that Alpirez had interrogated Bamaca. This information was briefed to "appropriate U.S. government agencies" and, in February 1995—before Torricelli had written to Clinton—was shared with staff of the House and Senate intelligence oversight committees.[94]

Detailed government investigations of the Guatemala and Honduras controversies would not be completed until 1996 and 1997, respectively. But under Deutch, the CIA did not wait for those results to take action. Indeed, the "scrub" of sources with questionable human rights records had begun under Woolsey and was formalized into a much more thoroughgoing review and new set of policies outlined by Deutch in July 1995.

"Let me be clear: We will continue to need to work with unsavory people," Deutch said in a speech outlining the asset policies. "What will be different is that we will not do these things blindly, without thorough vetting and established procedures for accountability. We will not fool ourselves or fool our customers about the risks we have taken." A new, more formalized "scrub" than the one instituted by Woolsey, would focus, Deutch said, on whether a given human intelligence source was providing information that was still relevant and was worth the risk associated with dealing with that source: "If questions of human rights violations or criminal involvement outweigh the value of the information to our national interest, then we will end the relationship with the asset." Human rights violations would now, for the first time, be taken into consideration before recruiting a source, allowing CIA managers "to make informed decisions" on recruitment.[95] It was a message designed to please both sides of the human intelligence debate, the side angry at the CIA for dealing with nefarious characters, and the side that recognized that good intelligence sometimes came from bad people.

Deutch's response to concern that CIA field officers consorted with unsavory sources without guidance from headquarters has been depicted in the wake of the 9/11 attacks as a key element in the decline of CIA human intelligence collection in the 1990s. This may well be so, though proving it would require deeper access to Directorate of Operations files than is now available. But a critical element has been missing from the debate. The equation, as presented after 9/11, was simple: to stop terrorists, the CIA must recruit terrorists. Deutch's rules made it harder to do so by creating bureaucratic barriers to dealing with unsavory people. There is, however, a fundamental difference between what the CIA was doing in Latin America and what it purports to do in fighting terrorism. Latin American sources with abhorrent human rights records were people whose cause the United States, and therefore the CIA, nevertheless supported. In the case of the notional terrorist recruit, the circumstances are reversed. Yes, the CIA would still be working with a source of unsavory background, but the cause would be the utter defeat of the terrorist group to which that source belonged. Two radically different types of source recruiting were being lumped together under the heading "dealing with unsavory characters."

Given the media attention devoted to the Latin American cases and the heat directed at the CIA by critics on Capitol Hill, the findings of two lengthy investigations of CIA activity in Honduras and Guatemala were underwhelming. A report in June 1996 by the President's Intelligence Oversight Board found that the CIA had worked closely with Guatemalan security forces going back at least to the early 1980s, even though the human rights records of those forces "were widely known to be reprehensible." The report, ordered by Clinton in response to the Torricelli letter, found that the CIA paid too little heed to the well-known record of abuse of some of the government sources or "assets" it was paying. In a key finding, the board reported that "several CIA assets were credibly alleged to have ordered, planned, or participated in serious human rights violations such as assassination, extrajudicial execution, torture, or kidnapping while they were assets—and that the CIA was contemporaneously aware of many of the allegations."[96] But the report debunked many of the most sensational charges against the CIA. The main thrust of criticism of the oversight board concerned a failure by the CIA to accurately report what was going on in Guatemala or to pass on, particularly to congressional overseers, information about known or suspected human rights abuses by some of its sources.

Before the furor begun by Torricelli, the CIA had instituted "asset validation" programs, but they focused not on the human rights pedigree of the source but on whether the source was providing worthwhile information and on the risk that the source was a double agent controlled by his government or organization. In 1989, for example, the Directorate of Operations had instituted an asset validation system whose goal was to "cut ties to assets believed to be counterintelligence risks and to end relationships with assets whose information production was not worth the payments they received." Even this asset review, lacking as it did any focus on human rights concerns about CIA sources, was never fully completed.[97]

Just over a year later, in August 1997, CIA Inspector General Hitz issued a report of his investigation into CIA activities in Honduras in the 1980s. Hitz's starting point was the Baltimore *Sun* series of June 1995 that reported that the CIA had trained and supported the Honduran 316th Battalion, which, through the use of a death squad called ELACH, had kidnapped, tortured, and killed thousands of Honduran citizens in the 1980s. There were widespread reports in Honduras in the early- to mid-1980s that one of the Honduran army's routine methods of dealing with captured guerrillas was to take them aloft in helicopters and shove them out the door. The newspaper also alleged that the CIA knew of these crimes and that CIA officers had participated in some interrogations and torture of Honduran military prisoners. Like the oversight board's report on Guatemala, the Hitz report on Honduras largely cleared the CIA of direct involvement in violent crimes such as participation in torture. Hitz found no evidence substantiating the charge that any CIA officer "was present during sessions of hostile interrogation or torture."[98] But he found indications that senior political appointees concerned with intelligence in Latin America in the 1980s—particularly CIA Director Casey and Reagan's ambassador to Honduras in the early 1980s, John Negroponte (who became the first director of national intelligence after the post-9/11 intelligence reforms) had been less than fully forthcoming in reporting on human rights abuses out of concern that it might undermine the Reagan administration's policy of supporting anticommunist regimes in Latin America.[99]

As journalist and author Tom Powers summed it up, "The abiding theme of Deutch's tenure at CIA was a kind of ongoing guerrilla war between the DCI's office on the seventh floor and the clandestine folks, marked by disrespect on Deutch's side and increasing dislike on the D.O.'s."[100] By his actions in office, Deutch made it increasingly clear that he was not merely predisposed as a scientist and mathematician to prefer technical intelligence over human; he was actively hostile to the Directorate of Operations and, for good or ill, his reforms remained in place through the end of the decade and even beyond the 9/11 attacks.

Snider, who spent much of his career in the role of critical overseer of the intelligence community, including the trip to Moscow that first alerted the Senate Intelligence Committee to the catastrophic loss of human assets inside the Soviet Union, said the conclusions of the intensive investigations into CIA activity in Latin America were remarkably mild. Multiple investigations had yielded a fairly narrow dispute over when and in what fashion Congress had been briefed on human rights abuses in the region, abuses that were, in any case, the subject of daily media coverage. The longer-term consequences for the CIA, however, were more substantial. "There was continued fallout. Morale plummeted," Snider said years later. "It was oversight gone berserk."[101] As in the Latin American controversies, the fallout from the Ames case continued apace and followed the same pattern of sensational charges followed by investigations that reached tepid findings, by which time the damage to the CIA's reputation had been done.

THE AMES DAMAGE ASSESSMENT

When Aldrich Ames walked through the gates of the Soviet chancery on 16th Street, a few blocks north of the White House, on April 16, 1985, he carried a note that he was certain would prove his claim that he was a high-level CIA officer. Ames included in the envelope the identities of two KGB officers the Soviets had assigned to approach the CIA station in Moscow the previous year and volunteer as spies. This was part of what Ames called his "scam" to get money from the KGB. Ames knew that the CIA had realized that these "walk-ins" were, in fact, double agents still under KGB control—"dangles" is the term used in the intelligence community. The information he was giving, therefore, had no real value since the Soviets already knew perfectly well who they were, and so did the Americans—thus the scam. For the moment, Ames was giving the KGB an incomplete account, saying that the men had volunteered to spy, but not that the CIA knew they were double agents. Ames reasoned correctly that this information would confirm that he had access to the top-secret world of the Directorate of Operations, since no outsider would have such sensitive and recent information. Not yet fully committed to a career of spying for the Soviets, Ames rationalized that supplying this information would not hurt the CIA because he would be exposing "spies" whose information was useless due to Soviet control.[102] Moreover, there would be no consequences for the two men, because they were acting on KGB orders. Later on, as Ames began reporting regularly to the KGB and receiving bagfuls of cash, he would complete the loop by passing on to the Soviets the valuable information that the CIA knew the walk-ins were double agents. With this information, Ames was helping the Soviets improve their techniques for feeding controlled information to the CIA.[103]

Two key points in this initial episode would have implications for the investigation that followed Ames's arrest: first, the Soviets had been sending double agents over to the CIA even before Ames started spying; and second, the CIA was adept at identifying them. The KGB's penchant for ultra-secrecy and tight control of information worked to its disadvantage where double agents were concerned, for the CIA knew that under strict KGB doctrine, certain types of people and certain types of information would never be shared with the CIA in a double-agent operation. This was a handicap for the KGB since an elemental part of running a double agent lies in convincing the other side that the information the agent is peddling is true. Accomplishing this means that some of the agent's information must be valid. No apparatchik in the unforgiving KGB bureaucracy wanted to take the responsibility for using as bait intelligence that someone might later say never should have been shown to the CIA. "Even if a document were of no real value," Ames later explained, "no one in the Soviet military was willing to sign off on releasing it, knowing that it was going to be passed to the West. They were afraid that a few months later, they would be called before some Stalin-like tribunal and shot for treason."[104]

Just how good the CIA was at identifying Soviet dangles Ames himself made clear in his jailhouse interview with the Senate Intelligence Committee chairman, DeConcini. The CIA had not merely concluded that the two KGB officers who had approached the Agency's Moscow Station in 1984 were double agents; it had learned of it *before* the approach was even made. Ames later said the tip had come from "one of our sources in the USSR"—quite likely from one of the agents he later compromised.[105] By whatever source, in early 1984 the Directorate of Operations' Soviet–East European branch learned that the Soviets were preparing to send two KGB officers to the CIA as "volunteers" who would, in fact, remain controlled by the KGB. "Towards the middle or towards the end of 1984, two volunteers did appear who appeared to fit that previous description we had to a tee," Ames said.[106] According to the Ames damage assessment, it was partially due to coaching from Ames that the Soviets were able to improve their techniques so that, for a while at least, some of these dangles were taken by the CIA as genuine spies.[107]

Having made an approach to an adversary's intelligence service, a double agent may hope that the service begins requesting particular types of information, usually tailored to that agent's access and field of expertise. In so doing the controlling spy organization learns what the enemy wants to know, valuable intelligence in its own right. Oftentimes a double agent's main goal is to learn how the adversary spy agency operates. The ostensible spy will be given the identity of various handlers, as well as instructions on communications, setting up clandestine meetings with handlers, using dead drops for exchanges of documents and money, operating radios for secret communications, and so on. This information then helps the controlling spy service detect and arrest actual spies. Another function of double agents is to feed false information from the controlling spy agency to the adversary.

On October 31, 1995, Deutch touched off a media firestorm when he emerged from a closed-door briefing for the Senate Intelligence Committee and issued a statement about the damage inflicted by Aldrich Ames. As the damage assessment by CIA Inspector General Hitz unfolded, Deutch said it was becoming clear that Ames had had an impact far beyond the CIA itself. Ames had profoundly harmed U.S. national security in multiple ways. "By revealing to the Soviet Union the identities of many assets who were providing information to the United States, he not only caused their executions, but also made it much more difficult to understand what was going on in the Soviet Union at a critical time in its history." Ames made it difficult for the CIA to recruit new spies by helping the KGB understand how the CIA operated, what inducements it used to recruit assets, and what types of information it sought.

The final point was most explosive of all: "By revealing to the Soviet Union identities of assets and American methods of espionage, he put the Soviet Union in the position to pass carefully selected 'feed' material to this country through controlled assets."[108] In contrast to the leniency that got Woolsey into so much trouble, Deutch announced that he was sweeping out the top level of human intelligence management at the CIA and replacing it with a new team to run operations, counterintelligence, and human resources. Deutch said he would demand "that new emphasis be placed on the quality of agent recruitments and agent handling, rather than on the quantity of recruitments." This responded to a long-held critique of the D.O. that it rewarded field officers for the number of assets they recruited rather than for the quality of intelligence those assets provided.[109] It was a practice that made the CIA more susceptible to double agents by creating a motivation to be less than vigilant in assessing the validity of a recruit. In addition to the asset scrubs already under way stemming from the Latin American controversies, Deutch's new management team would conduct a "complete scrubbing" of personnel standards—an oblique reference to Ames's ability to drink his way through a CIA career. And he would impose a "revitalized system within the Directorate of Operations to validate assets," or ensure that human intelligence sources were genuine and were providing solid information.

The lawmakers Deutch had briefed were shocked to learn that the CIA had disseminated intelligence reports based on source material it knew or suspected came from double agents, yet failed to warn recipients of that concern. "It's just mind-boggling, the scope of what went on here," said Senator Arlen Specter (R-Pa.), then-chairman of the Senate Intelligence Committee. Intelligence reports from known or suspected double agents went to the Pentagon, even the president, without proper warnings, Specter said, and as a result, the government made decisions on U.S. weapons systems such as the F-22 fighter and Seawolf attack submarine based on a knowingly inflated assessment of the enemy's capability. Specter said the tainted intelligence had potentially affected billons of dollars of weapons procurement decisions.

The outrage was bipartisan. "There is no question in my mind that it affected judgments that were made by both elected and appointed representatives of the people," said Senator Bob Kerrey (D-Neb.), the ranking Democrat on the intelligence panel.[110] Kerrey said "The intent was to distort our view of what was going on in the Soviet Union and to alter either our planning for weapons systems or for the deployment of our forces, or for the negotiation posture that we would take in arms control treaties." Deutch, who had apparently authorized the lawmakers to speak publicly about some elements of his closed-door briefing, told reporters that the damage assessment laid out "a devastating record that will take us years and years to recover from."[111] Having delivered this body blow to his own agency, Deutch said his aim was to "rebuild confidence" in the CIA.

The next day's front-page story in the New York Times echoed the outrage of the previous day's news conference. Ames had coached the KGB on how to run double agents by offering "craftily mixed" valid and bogus information. The story equated what the CIA had done to a journalist fabricating a story. "It is as if reporters built an exclusive on the word of liars because they thought it made a good story," the Times reported.[112] The latest disclosure, the story stated, "threatens the CIA's foundation; its central mission is to speak the truth to those in power."

On November 9, 1995, Inspector General Hitz testified before the Senate Intelligence Committee that from 1985 to 1994, the period of Ames's espionage, "the D.O. did not inform consumers that some of its most sensitive intelligence reporting came from sources known or suspected to be controlled by an opposition service." The failure to notify intelligence recipients was described as pervasive: "Except in one case, Department of Defense consumers assert that they were not informed concerning sources [the Central Europe] Division knew or suspected were controlled." And Hitz found that the directors of central intelligence during the period in question—Casey, Webster, Gates, and Woolsey—had failed to insist that intelligence reports be forwarded to policymakers with proper caveats.[113] Webster, Gates, and Woolsey wrote a sharply worded letter to Deutch denying responsibility for the failure to warn lawmakers about the questionable human intelligence reporting during the 1985–94 period. They agreed that failure to flag potentially tainted human intelligence reports was a major offense. They emphasized that they had remained unaware of the failure to warn intelligence consumers of possibly tainted reports, a line of argument hardly likely to lessen congressional dismay over the CIA's inner workings. The three directors then turned their ire on the inspector general, noting that in April 1991, three years before Ames's arrest, the inspector general had written a report on issues concerning the D.O.'s Soviet–East European Division that included a discussion of "the reliability of information from sources possibly controlled by the Soviets." But the report contained no recommendations to the CIA director, at that time

Webster, about the issue of notifying consumers. Another IG report in 1993 on human intelligence from Russia contained no discussion of controlled sources at all, the three former directors complained. Of course, Webster, Gates, and Woolsey could easily, based on the 1990 report, have raised questions about the problem and ensured that reports carried the proper caveats.[114]

From the beginning of this controversy, however, there were major problems with the tainted intelligence storyline. The Ames Damage Assessment Team's key point was the link between Ames and the KGB's use of double agents. Ames was said to have helped the Soviets hone their double-agent techniques to enable the strategy of feeding bogus information to the CIA. Yet what the Hitz report described was a failure by the clandestine service to alert policymakers to potentially tainted intelligence that it *knew* or *suspected* came from controlled agents. Whatever coaching Ames was providing the KGB, it wasn't preventing the CIA from identifying probable double agents. The KGB had run double agent operations against the CIA long before Ames began spying; the damage assessment did not explain whether or how Moscow's disinformation efforts increased during Ames's years as a Soviet and Russian spy.

We know of a few instances in which the KGB used the agents Ames compromised to pass tainted information. The KGB tried to keep the arrest of Sergei Motorin secret from the CIA after he was ordered back to Moscow by having Motorin call his girlfriend in the United States to say that all was well.[115] But Motorin's brief turn as a double agent operating out of a KGB prison was intended only to protect Ames by delaying the CIA's realization that it had a problem. Motorin was not used to feed the CIA controlled information about submarines and fighter planes. But for the most part, as already noted, the agents Ames compromised were not dangled; they were liquidated.

Hitz revealed to the Senate Intelligence Committee that there was a counterargument to his criticism about failure to notify intelligence consumers about possibly tainted sources. Hitz recounted the testimony of a CIA officer who recalled that occasionally, during the period of Ames's espionage, he urged Pentagon officials to use caution in connection with some questionable sources. The officer stopped short of explicitly telling Pentagon officials that certain CIA sources were suspected of being double agents. "He acknowledged, however, that this was *not a departure* from the routine interaction he had with intelligence consumers throughout his tenure," Hitz told lawmakers. The officer said that including too many caveats risked causing intelligence consumers to discount or disbelieve reports the CIA believed were valid, notwithstanding the controlled nature of the source. Hitz noted that his staff made no attempt to reach a judgment on the validity of intelligence reports that came from known or suspected double agents.[116] The consternation on Capitol Hill about presidents and defense secretaries making decisions based on supposedly tainted information, therefore, was based on a conclusion that Hitz himself had not made.

This far into the Ames debacle, none of the key players—not Deutch, not the White House, and neither Republican nor Democratic overseers in Congress—had anything to gain by sparing the CIA a harsh assessment. For Hitz, a hard-hitting report validated his role as a tough overseer of the CIA. For Deutch, it advanced his agenda of gutting and rebuilding a clandestine service to bring it under tighter control. For President Clinton and congressional Democrats, it drew attention to wasteful defense spending by Clinton's Republican predecessors. DeConcini, the former chairman of the intelligence committee, said the inspector general's report validated Senator Moynihan's post–Cold War charges that the CIA had deliberately exaggerated the Soviet threat to overcome political opposition to the Reagan defense buildup. Hitz, DeConcini said, had "uncovered the mother lode" and "deserves to be canonized" for proving this long-held suspicion about the CIA. It was the same technique the CIA had used before the Gulf War, DeConcini said, when the CIA "exaggerated the capacity of the Iraqi army . . . so the president could get public support for that war."[117] For the congressional intelligence committees, the story produced headlines highlighting their watchdog role. And for Republicans, it suggested that past misjudgments about the Soviet Union may have stemmed not from inflexible ideology in the White House but from bad information coming from Langley.

A few commentators in a position to know something about the controversy stepped in to add some perspective, not that it made much difference for the CIA. Defense specialists at think tanks around Washington got a good laugh out of the notion that the Pentagon needed any outside help—let alone a fiendishly clever KGB plot—in order to make wasteful spending decisions on gold-plated weapons programs. "The military services put pressure on their own intelligence services to exaggerate the threat," said Anthony Cordesman of the Center for Strategic and International Studies. "The notion that the Russians could have done more to worsen that particular tendency is a little bit disingenuous." Cordesman dismissed the idea that any single human intelligence report could sway decision-making on a major defense program. The

United States pursued a major qualitative advantage in military technology not because a human intelligence report inflated Soviet capability but because the Pentagon saw technology as a way to make up for the Soviets' strength in numbers.[118] Defense Intelligence Agency analyst Bill Lee detected no surge of human intelligence reporting on startling new Soviet military capability around the time that Ames began spying for the Soviets. What Lee recalled was a sudden drop-off in any sort of human intelligence reporting on the Soviet Union at all. Such reporting as he saw did contain warnings to treat the source material with care.[119] And Air Force General Joseph Ralston, then head of the Air Combat Command, pointed out that the requirements for the next-generation F-22 stealth fighter were written in 1980, five years before Ames started spying. Intelligence reporting, Ralston said, "was a factor, but not *the* factor" in determining what kind of plane to build.[120]

As the head of Pentagon acquisition programs in the late 1980s when the Soviet double-agent operations were said to be at their height, Donald Yockey was uniquely positioned to comment on the CIA inspector general's findings. Yockey said intelligence estimates written by individual military services, rather than by the CIA, had the most impact on weapons decisions. Decisions to go forward with advanced-technology weapons usually had much more to do with a particular type of technology becoming available than with countering a specific Soviet capability. And throughout the period when, according to Deutch's narrative, the U.S. government was being duped by the KGB into wasting money on weapons, the political pressure on defense spending in Washington was emphatically downward, Yockey said: "My whole tenure was based primarily on bringing the [weapons] requirements back down." The decision to go forward toward production of the F-22 fighter, for example, was made during Yockey's tenure, but throughout that period, he said, adjustments made by the Air Force in the design of the plane involved incremental *reductions* in its capability in response to budgetary pressure and the easing of Cold War tensions. If intelligence reports on Soviet weapons were influencing plans for the F-22, Yockey said, the result would have been to reduce cost pressures on the fighter program.[121]

The CIA had certainly been guilty of grossly inflating Soviet military capability at various times in history, leading, for example, to the "bomber gap" of the mid-1950s and the "missile gap" of the late '50s and early '60s. Nevertheless, as a broad generalization, one of the success stories of the CIA in the Cold War was the ability to acquire highly detailed and highly accurate intelligence on

Soviet weapons capability. What the CIA found out when it obtained detailed information on a Soviet weapon—as on the occasion in 1976 when a defecting Soviet pilot flew his MiG-25 jet to Japan, where American intelligence officials spent nine weeks taking it apart—was that Soviet weapons technology was based on American or Western weapons technology. That was worrisome, in that it pointed to the susceptibility to Soviet espionage of the sprawling U.S. defense industry. But it was reassuring, in the sense that it confirmed that the United States would almost always have the technological edge.[122]

No one seemed to focus on the one aspect of the double-agent story in which the CIA might be open to criticism: its apparent failure to consider the KGB's motivation for feeding the CIA controlled intelligence that exaggerated Soviet military capabilities. On its face, it would seem counterproductive for the Soviets to give the CIA such false intelligence, the effect of which would be to cause the Pentagon to design and build better weapons, putting the Soviets and then Russia farther behind in the military technology race. Deutch himself pointed out this anomaly without explanation: "I believe the net effect of the Soviet/Russian 'directed information' effort was that we overestimated their capability. Why the Soviet/Russian leadership thought this was desirable is speculative."[123] CIA analysis of possible reasons why the Soviets would have sought to make themselves look stronger than they were would have helped policymakers understand Soviet motivations and fears late in the Cold War, and Russian plans at the beginning of the new government's rule. Retired Air Force general Charles Horner, former head of the U.S. Space Command, said the Soviets may have fed the CIA exaggerated intelligence about the strength of their missile silos so that the Pentagon would needlessly spend money improving U.S. missile accuracy.[124] The Soviets may also have been trying to strengthen a weak hand at the arms control negotiating table. Focusing on the purpose of the apparent Soviet disinformation campaign in the late 1980s would have highlighted an understandable sense of insecurity and unease in Moscow as Gorbachev's reforms and the Soviet empire's declining economic and political fortunes left the Soviet military far behind its American counterpart.

Dick Kerr, one of the CIA's top officials through the decline and fall of the Soviet Union, says the Agency was well aware of the Soviet motivation to inflate its military capability during this vulnerable period.[125] This may be so, but it is not evident in the declassified intelligence estimates, and the CIA inspector general's findings suggest that while some at the Agency may have been aware of the disinformation campaign, that awareness did not inform policy discussions at the White House.

On closer examination, the issue of tainted reporting from controlled Soviet sources seemed less of a problem than it had originally. On December 7, 1995, Deutch reported that the inspector general's Damage Assessment Team had identified some 900 Soviet and Russian human intelligence reports between 1985 and 1994 that key policymakers recalled as being particularly influential. Those 900 reports probably were generated by no more than two or three dozen individuals, since each source likely provided grist for multiple intelligence reports over that time span. Narrowing the field to just over 450 reports, the team then looked at CIA records on the Soviet and Russian sources. Out of 450 human intelligence reports, there were ninety-five in which "the CIA did not provide adequate warning" that the source was either controlled or suspected of being controlled. That phrase suggested that reports included at least some language warning intelligence consumers to be wary of the source but that the inspector general regarded the warning as inadequate. Of the ninety-five inadequately flagged reports, "at least three formed the basis of memoranda that went to the President." Some of the reports "were accompanied by warnings." Deutch said the tainted reports had played a "substantial role" in sustaining the view in Washington "of the USSR as a credible military and technological opponent," which, it should be remembered, it was. Deutch conceded that "the impact of such information on actual decisions . . . was not significant."[126]

Whatever the specifics of the Hitz findings, Deutch wanted to ensure their impact remained undiluted:

> The fact that we can identify only a relatively few significant reports that were disseminated with inadequate warning does not mitigate the impact of Ames's treachery or excuse the CIA's failure to adequately warn customers. We believe that, whatever the numbers of such reports, the provision of information from controlled sources without adequate warning was a major intelligence failure that calls into doubt the professionalism of the clandestine service and the credibility of its most sensitive reporting.[127]

With the completion of Hitz's report, Deputy Defense Secretary John White ordered Lieutenant General Kenneth A. Minihan, head of the Defense Intelligence Agency, to examine the possible impact of human intelligence reporting from the CIA to the military that may have come from controlled sources. "This is an issue that causes us a lot of consternation and great concern," Captain Michael Doubleday, a Pentagon spokesman, said the day the review was announced.[128] Veteran CIA analysts must have found the notion of such Pentagon "consternation" amusing. In the 1980s, after all, it was the CIA that stood accused of consistently underestimating Soviet military power while the Pentagon took the alarmist position, the better to generate support for growing budgets and more weapons programs. Now the Pentagon was suggesting that the CIA was to blame for overstating the Soviet threat.

Then a surprising thing happened: the issue disappeared entirely. There were no public follow-up reports from the Pentagon on the Minihan review. The Senate Intelligence Committee moved on to other issues. By December 1996, Deutch had resigned from the CIA to return to his teaching post at the Massachusetts Institute of Technology. The controversy that had dominated the headlines in November and December of 1995 simply dropped from view.

Much of the key documentary information remains classified, including Minihan's report. Deutch declined to be interviewed for this book; Minihan did not respond to a request for an interview, but said through an intermediary that his review confirmed Deutch's earlier acknowledgment that major weapons decisions were not appreciably affected by a few tainted human intelligence reports.[129] Although the documentary trail ends at this point, interviews with some of the key participants indicate that the reason the issue went no further was that the Pentagon's examination of the controlled intelligence problem found little to warrant significant concern. White, the deputy defense secretary who ordered the DIA review, said that while the specific results of the Minihan review remain classified, he agreed with many of the senior military and intelligence officials and outside experts who assessed the issue at the time that, on the whole, controlled human intelligence reports had minimal impact on Pentagon weapons procurement decisions.[130]

Two former CIA Directorate of Operations officials who worked in Soviet intelligence discussed the issue—one, Milton Bearden, on the record, the other on condition of anonymity. They said that, in most cases, the CIA believed it was successful in identifying Soviet double agents and passed on warnings to consumers accordingly in instances when information they provided seemed valid enough to disseminate. Many of the problems described in the damage assessment stemmed from assets the CIA deemed valid up until the spring of 1985 but who were then compromised by Ames. Because of the ruthless fashion in which the KGB rolled up the sources identified by Ames, the CIA was able to pinpoint fairly accurately when an agent had been compromised. Any intelligence provided by these sources after their exposure—and, because of the rapid KGB roll-up, there was not much of this—was considered controlled by Moscow. However, in many of these cases, some of the intelligence provided by such an asset before his arrest might not have been disseminated to the Pentagon and other consumers until after he had been arrested. This was due to the often technical nature of the intelligence, concerned as it often was with specific weapons designs and capabilities. In such cases, the CIA might hold intelligence to allow time for technical specialists to go over it and, when possible, verify its accuracy; thus the delay in its release to consumers at the Pentagon and elsewhere.

The Directorate of Operations took the position that intelligence disseminated to consumers *after* a validated asset had been arrested but which contained information collected *before* the asset's arrest should be considered valid and need not be accompanied by a warning. Bearden insists that the controlled agents the KGB plied to the CIA after Ames started spying "never gave us anything good." It wasn't that the information was tainted; it simply was of no value. In the vast majority of cases, the intelligence on Soviet or Russian weapons went to the Pentagon through long-established channels between the CIA, the DIA, and the individual service intelligence branches, Bearden said. In this world, written warnings were not necessary because the CIA officials and their military counterparts were in constant communication. Where a certain human intelligence report needed to be handled with caution, that warning was conveyed, usually verbally, according to Bearden.[131] Bill Lee, the former Defense Intelligence Agency analyst, agreed, saying that caveats and warnings about sources were constant and were unambiguously transmitted to intelligence consumers at the Pentagon.[132] And former deputy CIA director Kerr also supported the view that "the information of concern probably would have made little or no impact on U.S. decision-making regarding weapons programs." Some tainted data may have found its way into a threat assessment, Kerr said, "but it is hard to believe that it would have made an impact on the huge data base we had on Soviet strategic programs."[133]

In a 2007 interview, Hitz said Ames coached the Soviets not on the spycraft of using double agents against the CIA but on the type of information the CIA was seeking. Ames helped the Soviets identify the gaps in the CIA's knowledge, thus making it easier for the KGB to prepare controlled information that would pass muster and be judged valid by the Directorate of Operations. The

CIA's mistake was in failing to raise the bar on the validation of human intelligence once the 1985–86 losses became apparent. "The operating assumption after '85 had to be that everything we've gotten in the Soviet era is gone, is known to them, so we'd better be very leery of anything we get back. . . . You have to have the working assumption that that information is suspect."[134] In retrospect, Hitz acknowledges that "the story got stretched" in the implication that the CIA passed on information it was certain was tainted. "We were fairly clear," Hitz said. "We thought that the reports people in the Soviet area knew or should have known of the likelihood that this [intelligence] was being fed to us. It should have been their working assumption that there was a mole." The press, Hitz said, "took it further and said [the CIA] knew for a fact that this had been fed."[135] However, if indeed the press took the story further than the still-classified facts supported, they did so at the behest of the CIA director.

THE AMES DAMAGE ASSESSMENT

If John Deutch's agenda was to strengthen the clandestine service, the best that can be said is that it didn't turn out that way. The Directorate of Operations that Deutch handed over to his deputy and successor, George Tenet, would be, in the words of veteran CIA analyst John McLaughlin, "in Chapter 11."[136] It was to the benefit of Tenet and his deputy, McLaughlin, to spread the idea in the wake of the 9/11 attacks that the CIA they took over after Deutch's resignation in December of 1996 was all but broken, particularly in that part of the organization on which so much of the frontline war on terror would depend, the clandestine service. The stronger the case they could make that they took over a broken CIA, the less blame would fall on them for the intelligence lapses before 9/11. However, this position skipped over the inconvenient fact that, as Deutch's deputy, Tenet had taken on the Directorate of Operations as an area of particular focus. He had been Clinton's intelligence adviser on the National Security Council through the first two years of the administration, and had influenced intelligence oversight and budgeting as staff director of the Senate Intelligence Committee for four years before that. He could not portray himself as having arrived on the scene at the end of 1996 with Deutch's departure. But whether Tenet, in his earlier posts, bore any responsibility or not, his assessment of the sorry state of CIA human intelligence operations in the mid-1990s was beyond question. The Directorate of Operations had sustained steep cuts in manpower and budget and public ridicule for failures both real and exaggerated, and had been harnessed to a new set of rules that would raise barriers to its overriding priority, the recruitment of sources knowledgeable about the key emerging threats facing the country.

According to Tenet, human intelligence manpower declined by 25 percent in the 1990s, and most of that reduction in force had occurred by mid-decade. Recruitment of new CIA "case officers," as the D.O.'s overseas staff are called, ground to a virtual halt between 1995 and 1997. In 1995 the CIA graduated two classes of case officers, with a dozen graduates in each class.[137] The lead-time involved in training a CIA officer for overseas duty, providing the officer with a first foreign tour and beginning to see the benefits of that training pay off meant that the recruiting dip would be felt most heavily in the years immediately after the 9/11 attacks. Even after a major hiring surge in the late 1990s and in the immediate aftermath of the 9/11 attacks, the Directorate of Operations in 2004 had about 1,000 operations officers—about one-third of its total manpower—in counterterrorism assignments worldwide, fewer than the number of FBI officers assigned to New York City.[138] The savings to taxpayers involved in those early 1990s cuts was insignificant. Out of a total U.S. intelligence budget of about $27 billion per year in the mid-1990s, the CIA budget, though classified, was estimated at about $3.2 billion, and the Directorate of Operations' share was a small fraction of that total, almost certainly less than $1 billion.[139]

As weaknesses in the clandestine service drew renewed attention in the late 1990s, the legacy of Ames loomed large. A sweeping House Intelligence Committee blueprint for improving the intelligence community blamed post-Ames attempts at reform for "a proliferation of systems meant to ensure the accountability of D.O. personnel for their professional judgments." These checks, the committee staff report opined, were not always in the hands of people qualified to critique the performance of field officers "in an organization that demands its officers take risks, involves the use of highly specialized skills, and by definition will have numerous false starts and failures for each major success."[140] Some of the damage, particularly budget and personnel cuts, would have happened without Ames. Beginning in 1990, the National Foreign Intelligence Program, the part of the intelligence budget that includes the CIA, National Security Agency and imagery intelligence functions, underwent seven consecutive years of reduced spending. That was four budget cuts authored by the Bush administration and three by Clinton before five years of level budgets, with the exception of 1999, when then–House Speaker Newt Gingrich pushed through a supplemental intelligence spending package.[141]

After the 9/11 attacks, amid the recriminations over poor human intelligence from within al-Qaeda, the bitterness among operations officers at the CIA was palpable. "After the deep, debilitating cuts of the 1990s, when any thought that the end of the Cold War would bring us a safer, more predictable world, one in which intelligence was not important, a world in which intelligence officers were no longer (regarded) as necessary, we now continue to rebuild," James Pavitt, then the CIA's operations chief, told Duke University law students seven months after the 9/11 attacks.[142] In his memoir, Tenet, who was the CIA's fifth director in seven years, said the clandestine service was in an "appalling state" in the mid-1990s and morale Agency-wide "was in the basement." Mid- and upper-level CIA officers feared not only tough congressional oversight, but also legal jeopardy if they were to be brought to court and asked to defend Agency actions. This period saw the growth of a practice of CIA officers buying their own liability insurance to pay legal fees in such a contingency.[143]

But the manpower problem was not simply a function of post–Cold War spending cuts. In the two years after Ames's arrest, the Directorate of Operations was well under its authorized manpower ceiling and was "having tremendous problems recruiting qualified new employees." The problem, in the view of the House Intelligence Committee study, was a "climate of public opinion" running strongly against the CIA.[144] Aggravating the damage to the CIA's reputation and morale that was affecting recruiting was a tightening of security restrictions in the wake of the Ames case that made it more difficult for recruits with foreign connections such as a foreign parent or spouse to get security clearances for work at the CIA. People with such backgrounds, particularly in the Arab world, were of course precisely the sort of people the CIA would need, and sorely lack, in the coming war against al-Qaeda.

As investigations into the intelligence failures related to the 9/11 attacks and the U.S.-led invasion of Iraq unfolded, a recurring theme was the near-total lack of high-quality human intelligence coming from sources within al-Qaeda or Saddam Hussein's hierarchy. No one questioned the difficulty of finding someone on the inside of Saddam's regime, the North Korean hierarchy, or Osama bin Laden's inner circle willing to steal secrets for the United States. But that was the CIA's job. The time to have penetrated al-Qaeda would have been in the mid-1990s, precisely when CIA recruiting was at its lowest ebb. In Iraq, the CIA had relied on United Nations weapons inspectors for a picture of what was happening on the ground, a flow of information that made it seem pointless to try to recruit spies. In late 1998, when the weapons inspectors left Iraq amid a standoff between the Clinton White House and Saddam over "unfettered" inspections, the CIA, according to McLaughlin, had to start from scratch in building sources inside Saddam's regime.[145] It made little headway. Tenet claims that in the years before the 9/11 attacks the CIA had some seventy sources and subsources reporting on al-Qaeda.[146] Senior decision-makers didn't see it that way. In 2004, with Osama bin Laden still at large and no weapons of mass destruction turning up in Iraq, Deputy Defense Secretary Paul Wolfowitz vented that his intelligence briefings amounted to a daily reminder that the CIA had no sources supplying information on the highest-priority targets. "Part of our problem was we didn't have any human intelligence at all. Part of our problem in al-Qaeda is we don't have any human intelligence at all. How many times do you want to get briefed on al-Qaeda and be reminded we don't have any human sources? So we're making some guesses here."[147] And Tenet's own defense against charges that in 1998 and 1999 he had held off on recommending attacks that might have killed al-Qaeda leader Osama bin Laden was that the CIA's sources in Afghanistan, however numerous, couldn't provide "actionable" intelligence that could give President Clinton confidence that an attack would succeed.[148]

It would be an oversimplification to portray Deutch as the outsider who attacked while CIA insiders circled the wagons. Criticism of the Directorate of Operations was widespread in the mid-1990s and remained so through the 9/11 attacks, the invasion of Iraq, and beyond. Much of that criticism came from within the professional ranks of the CIA. Richard Russell, a National Defense University professor and former CIA intelligence analyst, has accused the D.O. of failing to penetrate any of its top-priority targets during the 1990s, in part because it was stuck in a Cold War mindset that relied on field officers working out of embassies instead of officers working under deeper, "non-official" cover. Indeed, Russell says the D.O.'s performance during the Cold War was little better in recruiting sources in places like Beijing, Hanoi, and Pyongyang. "There is a systemic failure of the D.O. to produce exactly what it's supposed to do best," Russell said.[149] Former CIA operations officer Reuel Marc Gerecht has critiqued the Directorate of Operations extensively, rejecting the idea that various rules and restrictions imposed on the clandestine service from the mid-1970s on had emasculated CIA foreign operations. "There simply is no such thing as a case officer who didn't try to recruit a Middle Eastern terrorist because of concerns about the possible legal blow back from associating with someone who may have engaged in criminal behavior," Gerecht wrote.[150] Though it was D.O. heresy to say so, Gerecht was not alone in observing that, "In practice, the good old days were mostly a myth."[151] The problem in the Directorate of Operations was not lack of personnel, in Gerecht's view, but an overabundance of people contributing little to the CIA's understanding of its adversaries.

Deutch's departure from the CIA was an unhappy one, despite his assiduous efforts to please his congressional overseers by coming down hard on the Agency's real and perceived failings. He spent his final months in office fending off greatly exaggerated charges that the CIA had aided and abetted the crack cocaine epidemic in America's inner cities in the 1980s, a lie built on the truth that the Agency had consorted with known drug traffickers in some of its dealings with Contra forces in Nicaragua. One of Deutch's last official acts presented the extraordinary spectacle of the American intelligence chief, surrounded by heavy security, fending off hostile accusations at a raucous community meeting in South Los Angeles at which the CIA was accused of contributing to the crack problem. Clearly unprepared for the onslaught, Deutch promised that the government would get to the bottom of the matter. He was on his way back to MIT the next month. As usual, the CIA was painstakingly slow in coming forward with a detailed response to the charges. It took Inspector General Hitz and a seventeen-person team eighteen months, hundreds of interviews, and an exhaustive review of hundreds of thousands of documents to conclude that there was "absolutely no evidence to indicate that CIA as an organization or its employees were involved in any conspiracy to bring drugs into the United States." Many of the detailed charges contained in a *San Jose Mercury News* series that brought the issue to light were flatly refuted, and the newspaper itself later backed off some of its findings.[152] But Hitz did acknowledge that his team found "instances where CIA did not, in an expeditious or consistent fashion, cut off relationships with individuals supporting the Contra program who were alleged to have engaged in drug trafficking."[153]

On September 19, 1996, three weeks after Saddam Hussein's forces crushed a nascent Kurdish paramilitary movement that was seeking, with little success, to recruit Iraqi military defectors, Deutch told the Senate Intelligence Committee that Saddam's action had strengthened his hold on power.[154] Those frank comments embarrassed the Clinton administration, hastening Deutch's departure, and served as an object lesson to his successor, George

Tenet, about the risks of crossing the White House. The notion of a strengthened Saddam also helped energize a Republican push to shift U.S. policy from containment of Saddam to regime change. But the CIA had suffered spectacular operational failures before the Ames scandal came to light and before the post–Cold War intelligence cuts began to take hold. In 1989, for example, Iranian security forces executed what Gerecht has called "the great Iranian takedown" of a CIA spy network in Iran, rolling up a network of some thirty Iranians working for the Agency.[155]

Deutch, having built a reputation for coming down hard on CIA wrongdoing, ended his tenure under a cloud of his own making. On December 17, 1996, three days after Deutch's last day at the CIA, Agency security officials discovered classified information on his unsecured home computer. Among the 17,000 CIA files on a personal computer Deutch also used to access the Internet were top-secret documents on covert actions and classified memos from Deutch to Clinton. Deutch had used his Macintosh computer throughout his eighteen-month tenure as CIA director, refusing to have a secure CIA computer installed in his home or to be accompanied by a security detail while at home. Among other concerns, Deutch apparently was worried about CIA officials accessing his work through the Agency's internal computer network. In an echo of the mishandling of the Ames case, top CIA officials then neglected to inform the Justice Department for more than a year about the security breach. That lapse ensured there could be no special prosecutor appointed to investigate, since by statute, such a probe would have to begin within a year of Deutch's resignation.

Tenet, who succeeded Deutch as director, ordered that the probe go forward. But CIA internal investigators found that Deutch's top aides who remained at the CIA impeded the internal probe to protect their former boss, that Deutch had refused to be interviewed by CIA security officers, and that initially he had been more concerned about protecting his own privacy than cooperating with an investigation designed to track down the possibility of another catastrophic leak of CIA secrets.[156] The most damaging details about the case were contained in a report by the CIA inspector general, the same office Deutch himself had used in his post-Ames assault on the Directorate of Operations. As unsparing as Hitz had been in his criticism of the clandestine service, so was his successor in assessing the actions of Deutch and his senior aides. Indeed, Hitz himself came in for criticism for failing "to ensure the timely and effective resolution" of the case, which surfaced while Hitz was still in office. The probe did not confirm that any classified information had leaked to foreign governments but said the computers Deutch used were "vulnerable to attacks by unauthorized persons." Deutch claimed he had been unaware until a year after he left office that his home computer might be vulnerable to hackers, a claim of ignorance that did not conform with his own public testimony as CIA chief in which he raised concerns about the growing vulnerability of government computers to hackers. Deutch eventually had his security clearance stripped by Tenet and, faced with possible federal prosecution for mishandling classified documents, endured the indignity of a presidential pardon in the final days of the Clinton administration.[157] The author of the report on Deutch was the new CIA inspector general, L. Britt Snider, who had first heard about what would become the Ames spy case during that winter visit to Moscow in 1988.

Months after Deutch's departure, the impact of his recruiting rules began to leak out. Press reports said that a worldwide scrub of sources had stripped some 1,000 informants from the CIA's payroll, between a quarter and a third of the Agency's total stable of human assets.[158] But while it would be tempting to attribute the decline in the Directorate of Operations to the Ames case and Deutch's restrictions on asset recruiting, it was the plummeting confidence in the clandestine service's ability to do its job that caused the most lasting damage. As we have seen, this decline in confidence rested on a foundation of facts, but also on politically motivated charges and exaggerated public criticism. The piling on had the effect of crippling the clandestine service to the point where it was badly positioned to meet the threats the United States faced by the end of the 1990s. Almost a decade after the end of the Cold War, the CIA was still training its case officers using methods developed in the Cold War for recruiting from an embassy under light "diplomatic cover," working the diplomatic social circuit in search of foreign officials willing to sell or donate secrets to the United States. The challenges confronting human intelligence in the post–Cold War world would require an entirely different approach. But this was a realization the CIA confronted only after the 9/11 attacks.[159]

6 KNOWN UNKNOWNS

That which is unknown is assumed to have great potential.
—Tacitus

PREPARATIONS BY NORTH KOREA in the summer of 1998 to conduct a test launch of a missile were no secret to the CIA. As of early August, regular passes by U.S. spy satellites over the reclusive communist regime's single missile test site along a remote stretch of the northeast coast were returning photographs showing preparations under way. On August 7, spy satellites detected North Korean technicians beginning preparations to test a modified Taepo Dong 1 space-launch vehicle at the Musudan-ri Launch Facility. By August 27, U.S. spy satellites in their thrice-weekly passes over the Korean Peninsula had detected the final launch preparations. An array of national and regional military intelligence assets were thus put on alert. These included geostationary satellites in high orbit with infrared equipment capable of registering the hot plume of a rocket launch; imagery satellites photographing the activity on the ground; and signals intelligence aircraft and satellites carrying equipment to detect the telemetry signals transmitted by a rocket or missile after launch—signals that gave U.S. intelligence precise characteristics of the launch and ascent.[1]

But while U.S. intelligence could congratulate itself for detecting Pyongyang's missile test preparations, there was one aspect of the launch the CIA did not anticipate: the addition of a third stage to the Taepo-Dong missile, entailing a solid fuel booster carrying a small test satellite payload.[2] Reflecting the importance the communist regime gave to the test, the payload was named Kwangmyongsong-1, or "Bright Light Star," the name the late dictator Kim Il Sung had given his son and successor, Kim Jong Il, in 1991 on the occasion of the latter's fiftieth birthday. Third stages generally have two associations in the world of rocket science. One is the placement into Earth orbit of a satellite, such as a manned space capsule or communications satellite. The other is a ballistic warhead of intercontinental range.

With every available U.S. and allied intelligence sensor trained on the target, the Taepo Dong 1 lifted off from Musudan-ri at 12:07 local time on August 31, 1998. First-stage separation occurred ninety-five seconds after launch, and the launch rocket or "bus" splashed into the Sea of Japan about 157 miles due east of Korea. Forty-nine seconds later, having passed over Japan's main island of Honshu, a shroud protecting the payload atop the rocket peeled away and splashed down in the Pacific Ocean 676 miles downrange. Four minutes and twenty-six seconds into the flight, the spent second stage separated, the debris splashing down 1,021 miles from Musudan-ri. Based on the expectations of U.S. intelligence, this should have been the end of the flight. But a third stage, demonstrating for the first time North Korea's ability to deploy a solid-fuel rocket, continued to put out telemetry signals until it began to burn up in the outer reaches of the atmosphere, sending down debris some 2,500 miles east of the launch site.[3]

Five days after liftoff, Pyongyang proclaimed the satellite launch a success. With bombast typical of the communist regime, the North Korean government put out the false story that Kwangmyongsong-1 was in orbit, transmitting revolutionary songs praising the two Kims. Eight days after the launch, U.S. Space Command, quite possibly armed with better flight-tracking data than the North Koreans, concluded that the third stage payload had not reached orbit.[4] On at least four counts the test showed that major obstacles remained to be cleared before Pyongyang would be able to field an intercontinental ballistic missile:

- The payload carried by the rocket was much lighter than the likely weight of a first-generation nuclear weapon.
- The payload, light as it was, still failed to reach orbit.
- The satellite, apparently intended to remain in orbit, had no re-entry heat shield, technology the North Koreans would need for a nuclear warhead and that they have yet to test to this day.
- And the technology displayed in the test indicated that even had the satellite gone into orbit, North Korea lacked the know-how to reliably hit even a city-sized target with a warhead.[5]

Nevertheless, despite the burn-up of the third stage, defense specialists regarded the North Korean test as a stunning and ominous technological breakthrough, one that had caught U.S. intelligence by surprise.

"Until August 1998, the DPRK was known to have developed only a two-stage Taepo-dong 1 ballistic missile. The third stage and satellite capabilities came as a surprise, indicating that the program was further along in developing ICBMs than had previously been estimated," wrote Joseph S. Bermudez Jr. of the Monterey Institute of International Studies.[6] "This is a totally new threat," declared Henry Sokolski, a proliferation specialist in the first Bush administration. "What is alarming is that they are working on a three-stage missile at all."[7]

The missile test itself did not change the global strategic balance or shift the distribution of military and political power in the Pacific. It did not represent the emergence of a North Korean ICBM arsenal capable of threatening the U.S. homeland. The reaction to the test in Washington, however, helped bring about a profound change in America's military posture toward the world, a change that would push aside arms control as a guiding philosophy of nuclear weapons management, open the door to the spending of tens of billions of dollars on an unproven national missile-defense system, undermine faith in U.S. intelligence, and clear the way for an offensive rather than defensive global military strategy. It would also reinforce a precedent for the manipulation of intelligence already seen two decades earlier in the Team B exercise, a precedent that would be taken up once again in 2002 and 2003 as the new Bush administration used uncertain intelligence to make a case for war.

A WELL-TIMED TEST

The North Korean test could not have happened at a better time for advocates of national missile defense. The test confirmed two points these advocates had been trying for years to drive home: the threat of missile attack from a "rogue" state was more immediate than U.S. intelligence has estimated, and U.S. intelligence could not be counted on to detect ominous weapons advancements by rogue states. More important, the test came a month after the release of a special commission report on the threat that a small, unpredictable adversary state such as North Korea could acquire an intercontinental ballistic missile capability that could threaten the United States. The report by the Commission to Assess the Ballistic Missile Threat to the United States, headed by former defense secretary Donald Rumsfeld, had made precisely these same points.

The idea of building a huge although scaled-down successor to President Reagan's Strategic Defense Initiative had formed a pillar of the Republican foreign policy agenda going back to the 1994 GOP victory in congressional elections. National missile defense was a provision of Newt Gingrich's "Contract with America," which had helped his party end a half-century of Democratic dominance in the House of Representatives. Floyd Spence of South Carolina, the newly installed Republican chairman of the House Armed Services Committee, and Curt Weldon, a vocal hawk from Pennsylvania who headed a key subcommittee, stood ready to carry the missile-defense agenda forward.

Almost immediately, however, the Republican majority encountered resistance to turning the missile-defense clause of the Contract with America from a campaign promise into law. On February 15, 1995, a month after the swearing-in of the new Congress, the House voted down the missile-defense portion of the GOP's "National Security Restoration Act" by a vote of 218–212. Democratic opponents viewed the issue as a political distraction from the more pressing task of shoring up the readiness of conventional U.S. forces. They also opposed the national missile-defense program as a threat to the arms control agenda, embodied by the 1972 Anti-Ballistic Missile (ABM) Treaty with the Soviet Union and now with Russia. The theory behind the ABM Treaty had been twofold: first, that missile defenses would accelerate the arms race as each side built more numerous and sophisticated weapons to defeat the other's defensive shield; second, that the side possessing a workable missile defense could take more aggressive actions with a sense of invulnerability to retaliation. The two dozen Republicans who helped defeat the national missile-defense provision included Representative John Kasich of Ohio, a leader of the "deficit hawks" whose main agenda was cutting federal spending.[8] Later in the year Spence and Weldon succeeded in inserting somewhat modified missile-defense language into the defense authorization bill, prompting a veto threat from the Clinton administration. A political critical mass had not yet formed to support spending money on missile defense on a large scale.

In November 1995 the U.S. intelligence community issued a National Intelligence Estimate of the ballistic missile threat facing the United States. Classified "Secret NOFORN," meaning that distribution even to cleared foreigners working for allied governments was forbidden, the report was issued to recipients in the Clinton administration and Congress by the National Intelligence Council, a group representing the collected opinion of the U.S. intelligence community. Its opening line was remarkably declarative for an intelligence branch with a long-established habit of padding predictions and assessments with a thick layer of caveats. "No country, other than the major declared nuclear powers," the NIE stated, "will develop or otherwise acquire a ballistic missile in the next 15 years that could threaten the contiguous 48 states and Canada."[9]

The focus of the all-important opening line on the lower forty-eight states implicitly left Hawaii and portions of Alaska under the shadow a rogue-state missile attack, presumably North Korean. For the time being, however, the intelligence estimate gave the Clinton administration a powerful argument that there was no need to upset the carefully constructed arms control edifice of treaties by spending billions of dollars on unproven technology to meet a nonexistent or at least distant threat. The estimate also sent a powerful message to Republicans pushing the party's agenda: to advance the missile-defense program, the intelligence community's assessment of the threat would have to change.

Bringing about that change became a multiyear effort that not only succeeded in reversing congressional and White House opposition to national missile defense, but also amounted to a dress rehearsal, a political war game, that foreshadowed the second Bush administration's selective use of shaky intelligence to advance its agenda for war against Iraq. In the years following the 1995 intelligence estimate, the Republican majority in the House would engineer a systematic attack on the U.S. intelligence community, an attack that would ultimately be spearheaded by Donald Rumsfeld, helping the former Ford administration defense secretary elevate his profile among conservatives and clear the way for a second stint in the top Pentagon post under the younger President Bush, a post Rumsfeld would use to advocate and then run the war in Iraq.

It is worthwhile to pause here and consider an important point: an element underlying both the Democratic and Republican responses to the 1995 intelligence estimate was the assumption that U.S. intelligence reporting was highly credible and that a policy course contrary to an intelligence assessment was therefore ill-advised. Despite the abuse heaped on the U.S. intelligence community after the Soviet collapse and the exposure of Aldrich Ames's treachery, an assumption persisted that U.S. intelligence reporting remained the most authoritative source for assessing national security threats. This assumption meant that if an intelligence report stood in the way of a certain policy course, advocates of that policy would have to compel the intelligence community to change its judgment in order for the new policy to go forward. In certain circumstances, therefore, the very credibility of the CIA's conclusions set the Agency up for attack by policymakers.

Thwarted by a conclusive intelligence finding that the threat of missile attack by "rogue" regimes was at least fifteen years off, if it existed at all, advocates of national missile defense set about to change the intelligence. In the same fashion, the advocates of war on Iraq, when confronted with ambiguous or inconclusive intelligence reports on Iraq's arsenal and Saddam Hussein's supposed ties to al-Qaeda, did not reconsider the war policy; they set about reconfiguring the intelligence so as to support a course toward war. Virtually all of the elements of politicization of intelligence used by the Bush administration to sell the Iraq War were field-tested in the campaign for national missile defense, just as they had been in the Team B exercise of the mid-1970s:

- Selective leaking of classified information.
- Asserting, falsely, that the hard-line policy was not based on ideology but on threats that became clear once excessive caution in intelligence reporting was swept away.
- Attacks on the credibility of the intelligence community's threat reporting.
- Establishing alternative "authorities" that could portray an alarming threat in those areas where the intelligence community would not oblige.
- Blurring or in some cases erasing the distinction between qualified probable threat assessments and worst-case scenarios.
- Developing worst-case intelligence analysis: if a state was hostile to the United States and it was theoretically possible for that state to develop certain types of weapons, it was assumed it was doing so even if the available intelligence did not support that assumption.

Maria Ryan has called this last point a "hypothesis-based methodology" of intelligence analysis.[10] First tested by the neoconservatives in the Team B exercise and perfected by Rumsfeld in the missile-defense debate of the 1990s, the final, tragic result of this approach was a deadly, protracted war in Iraq based on intelligence concerning supposed Iraqi weapons of mass destruction— intelligence that turned out to be almost entirely wrong. As Ryan put it:

> The now discredited intelligence presented by the Bush administration on Saddam Hussein's WMD was neither a mistake nor an aberration. It was the product of a deliberate and particular style of intelligence analysis that did not rely exclusively on the facts at hand, but instead constructed a worst-case

scenario by surveying additional possibilities that *might* be available to adversaries. Such scenarios, however distant or unlikely, were then presented as probabilities.[11]

But making such hyped, worst-case scenarios believable depended on a factor beyond the control of dedicated ideologues. It required an underlying doubt about the accuracy and reliability of best-evidence interpretations based on straight, unhyped intelligence. And introducing that doubt depended on some sort of event, ideally a highly visible intelligence "failure" that could validate and justify the use of a different, worst-case intelligence formula. In the late 1970s the Soviet invasion of Afghanistan, unanticipated by the CIA until a few days before, served this purpose. In the late 1990s it was the North Korean missile test and the CIA's failure to predict that Pyongyang was capable of designing a three-stage rocket. In the case of Iraq, the intelligence community's failure to penetrate the 9/11 plot served this purpose.

THE 1995 NIE ON MISSILE THREATS

When the 1995 debate on national missile defense shifted to the Senate, Senator Carl Levin, a senior Democrat on the Armed Services Committee, wrote the CIA to find out what the intelligence community was planning to say in its upcoming National Intelligence Estimate on the rogue-state ICBM threat. The Agency shared with Levin the key conclusion of the report: no ICBM threat from North Korea, Iran, Iraq, and other rogue states for at least fifteen years.[12]

The missile-defense advocates played the game of politicizing intelligence with great skill. Their opening gambit was to charge the Clinton administration with politicization, accusing the White House of orchestrating a carefully timed leak to Levin and other anti-missile-defense lawmakers. In the spring of 1996 a "President's Summary" of the classified 1995 intelligence estimate was leaked to the press.[13] Republicans again cried foul, saying the administration was playing politics with state secrets to advance its anti-missile-defense agenda. The appearance of the secret document in the pages of the *Washington Times*, a leading conservative newspaper run by a vehement opponent of North Korea, the Reverend Sun Myung Moon, suggested a source other than someone in the Clinton administration. But that minor point was lost amid the louder noise that the Republican Congress, in a presidential election year, was making about national missile defense.

Whoever leaked the document, the publication of the 1995 estimate summary benefited the proponents of national missile defense by enabling them to go public with their criticism of the CIA and the broader U.S. intelligence community. Where disagreements about interpretations of classified intelligence reporting would normally take place in the secure confines of CIA headquarters, the White House situation room or the soundproofed meeting rooms of the House and Senate Intelligence Committees, now the debate could play out in floor speeches and hearings in the House and Senate. The result was an unprecedented public examination of how intelligence works, possibly the most detailed public look at a recent intelligence assessment in the history of the CIA, up until the war in Iraq.[14]

Republican-led committees ordered the General Accounting Office, the investigative arm of Congress, to examine the missile-defense estimate. In due course the GAO reported that the estimate "overstated" its main conclusion that no non-nuclear power would develop an ICBM within fifteen years with "100 percent certainty" despite indications in the estimate itself that there was reason for concern. The GAO advised that intelligence estimates "should develop and explore 'alternative futures,'" involving "less likely (but not impossible) scenarios that would dramatically change the estimate if they occurred."[15]

Somewhat surprisingly, the assault on the CIA by the Republicans pushing the missile-defense agenda ran into strong resistance from the Agency, at least initially. On December 4, 1996, veteran CIA analyst John McLaughlin, then the vice chairman of the National Intelligence Council, who would later play a key role in assembling evidence of Iraqi weapons of mass destruction, told the Senate Intelligence Committee that he stood by the 1995 National Intelligence Estimate. "After a year of criticism, we still regard this Estimate as a sound intelligence product—one that clearly reports results of analytic work in response to the questions of those who requested the NIE. Its judgments are still supported unanimously by intelligence community agencies and their analysts," McLaughlin testified.[16]

McLaughlin based his confidence on two key factors: first, that the ability of U.S. intelligence to detect activities related to missile testing, such as flight tests and ground-based "bench" tests of rocket motors, would ensure years of warning before an adversary could field a viable ICBM; second, the U.S. intelligence community believed that "no country that currently has ICBMs will sell them."[17] By way of offering a slight concession to critics of the estimate,

McLaughlin acknowledged the declarative, unqualified tone of its principal conclusion and accepted the criticism that readers of the report would have to delve deeper into the text to find caveats and alternative views. This unqualified tone, he said, came in response to past criticism from precisely the opposite direction.

"One of the most frequent criticisms of Estimates is that they are too long and detailed for busy, often harried readers," McLaughlin said. "In response to that criticism, we have sought to keep them to a manageable length." Another common criticism, McLaughlin said, was that intelligence estimates too often "avoid clear positions, that they waffle." The 1995 estimate had been couched in such a way as to avoid a repeat of past criticism by getting straight to the point—that there is no immediate rogue-state ICBM threat and none foreseeable as far off as fifteen years into the future—and to leave the caveats and qualifiers for the finer print further into the report.

Pressure to please "customers" by presenting them with clear, slap-in-the-face conclusions caused the CIA to lurch from one extreme—wishy-washy, cover-your-rear reports that offered little clarity to policymakers—to another: overstated assessments that papered over gaps in the intelligence or plausible alternative scenarios. It was a problem that would reemerge in the prewar assessments of Iraq, though in that case the intelligence community did include minority views about some of the conclusions. The difference was that, while in the missile-defense study the CIA stood accused by GOP critics of understating the ICBM threat, in the Iraq instance it pleased those same critics by overstating the WMD threat.

It was McLaughlin's first high-profile appearance at an open congressional hearing, and he prepared extensively for his testimony. He was unapologetic about the CIA's work in his presentation and defended the positions the Agency and the rest of the intelligence community had taken on the rogue-state missile threat. McLaughlin recalled being teased by colleagues at the Agency who were more used to seeing CIA witnesses grovel under pressure of congressional oversight committees and bend in the face of politically charged criticism.[18]

The day McLaughlin testified before the Senate Intelligence Committee, the second congressionally sponsored report critical of the 1995 intelligence estimate was presented to the committee in classified form; the CIA would make public a scrubbed version of the document three weeks later, on December 23, 1996. The earlier General Accounting Office report had criticized the

NIE, much as its congressional sponsors desired, but the GAO complained it had limited access to classified material. The missile-defense advocates wanted a stronger critique of the intelligence assessment, one done by an outside group that would be able to review the classified intelligence underlying the document. CIA Director John Deutch chose a predecessor from the first Bush administration, Robert Gates.

If the backers of missile defense hoped that an appointee from a Republican administration would carry their water for them, they were disappointed. The panel headed by Gates offered some criticisms of U.S. intelligence but endorsed the basic conclusion of the 1995 estimate, saying the intelligence community "has a strong case that, for sound technical reasons, the United States is unlikely to face an indigenously developed and tested intercontinental ballistic missile threat from the Third World before 2010."[19]

The Gates panel described the 1995 estimate as something of a rush job. If anything, the panel said, U.S. intelligence underplayed the strength of evidence behind the conclusion that rogue-state ICBM threats were a long way off. U.S. intelligence is particularly good at tracking missile threats because so much of missile development and testing must be done out in the open, in rocket engine tests and flight tests that can be observed by U.S. spy satellites and other collection assets. The intelligence estimate could have said more clearly that no working ICBM could be deployed without first being tested, a long, complex process that would give U.S. intelligence substantial warning time before a threat emerged. On the other hand, the Gates panel also found that the National Intelligence Council that prepared the 1995 estimate failed to consider "the consequences of being wrong."[20]

Far from finding that the estimate had been politicized by a Clinton administration seeking support for its case against missile defense, the Gates panel judged the report to be politically naive, written hastily and in a vacuum, with little if any awareness that the topic, and the report itself, was bound to become a political football. "Senior intelligence analysts," the Gates panel found, "failed adequately to alert analysts to the sensitivity of this Estimate, to the uses to which it might be put in the policy debate, and thus the need to err on the side of comprehensiveness."[21]

Virtually all of the flaws identified by the Gates panel in the 1995 missile-defense estimate would reappear in the October 2002 estimate of Iraq's arsenal.

In the spring of 1997, with the Clinton administration still limiting national missile defense to a research program, Pennsylvania Republican Curt Weldon, the leading proponent of missile defense in the House, seized on a report by the independent Institute for Foreign Policy Analysis, which took a sharply critical view of the intelligence community's assessment of the rogue state missile threat. "It is with alarm and genuine concern for the intellectual soundness and credibility of the intelligence community that I compare and contrast the findings" of the two assessments, Weldon said. "If the intelligence community has become intellectually homogeneous, or if different credible views go unrepresented or are suppressed, then we as a nation are in real trouble."[22]

The period 1996–97, encompassing the shutdown of the U.S. government because of a budget standoff between the Clinton White House and the Republican Congress over taxes and spending, was a difficult time to be trying to shove a multibillion-dollar defense program through the system unsupported by intelligence reporting. So, having failed twice to use "independent" reviews to undermine the 1995 intelligence estimate, congressional Republicans tried again. This time, House Speaker Gingrich turned to Rumsfeld— and Rumsfeld, with significant and timely help from the North Koreans, delivered.[23]

A former Navy pilot and Chicago-area congressman who had been ambassador to NATO under President Nixon and secretary of defense under President Ford, Rumsfeld had moderate Republican credentials tracing back to his support for civil rights legislation in the early 1960s and his work on Nixon's domestic policy team. He had largely missed out on the Reagan revolution, having held no senior positions—other than a brief assignment as special envoy to Iraq, where he was famously photographed shaking hands with Saddam Hussein—in either the Reagan or first Bush administrations. He had helped set the stage for the Reagan-era defense buildup as a member of the Committee on the Present Danger, arguing the case that the Carter administration had underestimated the Soviet threat.

Unlike Team B, the roster of Rumsfeld's Commission to Assess the Ballistic Missile Threat to the United States was not entirely stacked with neoconservative ideologues, though they were well represented. Joining Rumsfeld were two retired Air Force generals, Lee Butler and Larry Welch; Barry Blechman, a former arms control negotiator and co-founder of the internationalist Henry L. Stimson Center; Richard Garwin of the establishment Council on Foreign Relations; William Schneider Jr., a State Department official in the Reagan administration; William Graham, a former science and technology adviser to the Reagan White House; former CIA director

James Woolsey; and Paul Wolfowitz, a senior defense official in the first Bush administration and a leading neoconservative scholar and advocate of an aggressive brand of American foreign policy. The commission's staff director was Stephen Cambone, who would become the top Pentagon official in charge of intelligence under Defense Secretary Rumsfeld during the second Bush administration.[24]

The Rumsfeld Commission assembled and encamped at CIA headquarters at the beginning of 1998, a vulnerable time for the agency. George Tenet had been confirmed as director the previous July, but only after Anthony Lake, Clinton's national security adviser, had withdrawn from a bruising confirmation process. After Lake's experience, the administration wanted no more trouble filling the CIA post and went with Tenet, anticipating correctly that his background as staff director to the Senate Intelligence Committee would smooth his way in confirmation hearings before that same committee. Thus, in early 1998, the Rumsfeld Commission was entering an intelligence community structurally weakened by budget and staff cuts, distracted by turmoil at the top as it adjusted to its third director in four years, and politically chastened by the defeat of the administration's first choice for the job. In this environment, it set about to prove the case that intelligence about weapons of mass destruction programs was inherently unreliable because nations pursued those programs in secret and did their best to deny sensitive information to U.S. intelligence.

Given the makeup of the commission, Rumsfeld had to proceed cautiously. He was, Blechman recalled, "very careful to stick to the mandate, to focus on the threat as opposed to what to do about it."[25] Rumsfeld avoided discussion of what the commission should say until months into a process of gathering highly classified data and interviewing senior government officials and experts. Rumsfeld began to move toward findings by putting up only the most general conclusions that he was sure all the commissioners could agree on. "It was a brilliant performance, really," Blechman said. "He was determined to get a consensus report."

Though couched as a nonpartisan, scholarly examination of a national security problem, the report had a clearly partisan agenda: promoting the Republican-backed concept of building a national missile-defense system and undermining faith in arms control as the route to easing nuclear tensions. To do this, it had to undermine faith in the U.S. intelligence community. If a sense of CIA authority had endowed the 1995 National Intelligence Estimate with the power to stop the missile-defense movement, that sense of authority would have to be replaced with one of CIA unreliability. The commission quickly discovered it had plenty of material on which to build a case that the CIA could not be relied on to fully perceive the threats confronting the United States around the world. Because North Korea, even before the August 1998 test, was the rogue state furthest along in developing ballistic missiles, the commission devoted extensive attention to that country—and found much to be desired in the intelligence the United States was producing about the reclusive communist regime.

"It was shocking, what we saw," Blechman said. "I've never seen the intelligence community as closely as I did on that commission. I couldn't believe how little we knew about North Korea." Rumsfeld set up a side-by-side comparison for commissioners to examine, with intelligence community assessments about North Korea over the years on one side and events in North Korea as they later came to be understood on the other. The comparison showed that the CIA and other intelligence agencies had been three years behind actual military developments in North Korea that could threaten the region and the United States. While the commissioners fully understood the paranoid backwardness of Kim Jong Il's regime, they also noted the presence of thousands of American troops on the peninsula since the Korean War, a large population of Korean Americans who could provide recruits to U.S. intelligence with the requisite language skills and cultural knowledge to be effective human intelligence collectors, and the small but steady stream of defectors from North Korea who could be debriefed. However, the CIA had only a disappointing trickle of intelligence on anything that couldn't be observed from space.[26]

THE INDIAN NUCLEAR TESTS: AN INTELLIGENCE FAILURE

In the midst of Rumsfeld's carefully orchestrated investigation, the commission was handed a case in point on the risks of relying on intelligence to warn of emerging proliferation threats.

At 3:44 p.m. local time on May 11, 1998, India set off three nuclear devices buried 500 to 650 feet underground in mine shafts in the northwestern Indian desert near the town of Pokhran, Rajasthan, about 70 miles from the Pakistani border. The blasts registered 5.4 on the Richter scale, the equivalent of a mild earthquake and strong enough to crack the walls of brick-and-mud homes in the nearby village of Khetolai.[27] Despite efforts to contain the radioactivity resulting from the explosions, plumes of dark smoke rose from three mineheads set about two-thirds of a mile apart. The most powerful of the blasts, a boosted thermonuclear device, or hydrogen bomb, left a crater 262 feet across and 50 feet deep. From the nearby command center, a call on a secure phone went to the residence of newly elected Prime Minister Atal Behari Vajpayee that Operation *Shakti* (Power)—98 had been a success. When an aide to the prime minister answered, by one account, he heard a voice declare simply, "Done!"[28] Another version has it that the test-site official conveyed the prearranged coded message, "The white house has collapsed."[29] Though the tremor registered on quake-sensing seismographs around the world, U.S. intelligence remained ignorant of the test until four hours later, when Vajpayee went on television to announce the test. According to author Jeffrey Richelson, John Lauder, the U.S. intelligence community's nuclear counterproliferation chief, responded to word of the announcement by asking, "Is this some sort of joke?"[30]

While there was general condemnation of India's action, its first nuclear test since 1974, the main thrust of anger in official Washington pointed not at New Delhi but at Langley. The White House let it be known that it held the CIA responsible for not providing warning that might have enabled President Clinton to threaten or cajole the Indians out of conducting the tests. "A lot of people were blind-sided by this, and they're not happy," one unidentified administration official told The *Boston Globe*.[31] Senator Richard Shelby (R-Ala.), chairman of the Senate Intelligence Committee, declared that the CIA's failure to warn of the test was the "colossal intelligence failure of the decade," possibly the greatest failure since the collapse of the Soviet Union.[32] The political right, ever suspicious of arms control as an answer to U.S. national security concerns, wasted no time pointing to the intelligence failure as an example of why arms control agreements were unreliable. The conservative *Washington Times* reported the day after the tests, "The intelligence failure has heightened concerns among U.S. officials about the ability to monitor cheating on a proposed international nuclear testing ban being considered for ratification by the Senate."[33] Newly installed CIA Director Tenet launched an investigation, as did Shelby's committee and its counterpart in the House. On May 13, the Indian government announced that it had conducted two more nuclear tests, these at the sub-kiloton level. Even these, with the CIA now on full alert, had been missed by the Agency's analysts. Adding to the intelligence community's embarrassment, Lauder, the day before this second round of tests, had given lawmakers in closed-door briefings no indication of further Indian test activity.[34]

A flurry of media reporting revealed that India had managed to conceal its test preparations from detection by U.S. imagery intelligence satellites until the last hours before the May 11 tests. Tenet told lawmakers that India had deliberately chosen sandstorm season in Rajasthan so that winds would conceal vehicle tracks, a tell-tale sign of activity at the test site, which was routinely photographed by one or more of the half-dozen U.S. intelligence imagery satellites in orbit. Some bulldozer activity had been spotted at least three days before the tests. At 3 a.m., Washington time, on May 11, the day of the tests, an imagery analyst with the Priority Exploitation Group at "Area 58," the secret spy satellite receiving station at Fort Belvoir, Virginia, about fourteen miles south of Washington, noticed that fencing around the test site was being removed and panels, possibly monitoring devices, installed. The analyst marked the images for further analysis by a more experienced officer on the day shift who specialized in the Indian nuclear program. By the time that officer was getting to work, the tests had already happened.[35]

Three weeks later, retired admiral David Jeremiah, who had been named by Tenet to investigate the intelligence issues surrounding the Indian tests, presented unclassified portions of his findings on what was now generally accepted as a major U.S. intelligence failure. Among other deficiencies, Jeremiah reported that the CIA had only one analyst assigned full time to monitor India's nuclear program.[36] Jeremiah also confirmed that the Clinton administration's success at persuading India not to test in late 1995 and early 1996, when the CIA had managed to detect test-site activity at Pokhran, may have contributed to the intelligence failure the second time around. In preparing for the 1998 tests, Indian engineers "took pains to avoid any characteristics that they may have learned were of value to us" from the 1995 episode.

Jeremiah was not explicit, but he was referring to a story published a week earlier by the *New York Times* that suggested the United States may have inadvertently helped India conceal the 1998 tests by revealing what U.S. intelligence had observed at the Pokhran test site in December 1995. U.S. spy satellites had picked up indications of tunneling, the laying of cables, and the setting up of a control center. Frank Wisner Jr., then the U.S. ambassador to India, had gone to Indian officials on December 15, 1995, and shown them satellite imagery to signal to New Delhi that the United States was watching, and that Indian government denials were not credible.[37] Equally significant, the Clinton administration had also gone public, leaking to the *New York Times* and *Washington Post* on the day of Wisner's meeting in New Delhi its suspicion that India was preparing to test a nuclear weapon. By making the issue public, the United States opened India to domestic and international criticism, making it much more difficult for the Indian government to go ahead, since there were potential domestic political repercussions in Parliament that could complicate a decision to test by creating the opportunity for outcry against the move.[38] The Indian prime minister at the time was Narasimha Rao, a moderate whose political rivals would be the party in power three years later directing the nuclear weapons tests. The pressure from Wisner, in the words of Sumit Ganguly, led "the infamously indecisive prime minister to call off the tests."[39]

Jeremiah, obviously striving to avoid being too helpful to future proliferators, nevertheless had to acknowledge that Wisner's use of satellite imagery in his démarche to the Indian government had not made it easier for the CIA to continue detecting activity at the Pokhran site. "I think whenever there is an opportunity to look at what someone else is looking at in your territory, it gives you some insights into what you would want to do to cover that [up]," Jeremiah said. On the other hand, he said that intelligence is of little use if it remains perpetually locked in drawers at the CIA and is never brought out for tactical or strategic advantage when a crisis arises.[40]

The Wisner episode amounted to a repeat of another intelligence coup in 1982, when test activity spotted by U.S. intelligence satellites enabled Undersecretary of State for Political Affairs Lawrence Eagleburger to spring a similar surprise on Indian officials. In a meeting in Washington, Eagleburger asked a senior Indian official, "What are you doing at Pokhran?," then responded to the official's denials by pulling out satellite photos showing the evidence of test preparations.[41] Indeed, the Pokhran site had been a priority intelligence target since 1974 when the CIA had missed India's first nuclear test. An intelligence community report attributed that failure in part to Pokhran not being a sufficiently high priority on the intelligence satellite target list.[42] That earlier remonstration, and India's flirtation with a test as recently as 1995, added to the intensity of criticism directed at the CIA, for it underscored that India had managed to conceal activity from U.S. intelligence at a site the Agency was supposed to be watching closely.

Another embarrassing element of the intelligence failure was the disclosure by Pakistani officials after the test that they had repeatedly warned the Clinton administration in early 1998 that India was preparing a test. On March 19, 1998, two months before the Indian test, the Pakistani government voiced concern at a meeting of the Conference on Disarmament about the intent of

India's governing Bharatiya Janata Party (BJP, or India People's Party) to integrate nuclear weapons into India's arsenal. On April 2, four days before its own Ghauri missile test, Pakistan warned the five declared nuclear powers that India was preparing a nuclear test. Four days before the test, a Sikh separatist group distributed a paper in Washington quoting reliable sources describing nuclear test preparations at Pokhran in some detail, including "feverish nighttime activity" that would have been invisible to imagery satellites. It is not clear if anyone in the CIA or the Clinton administration was aware of the paper.[43] Jeremiah sought to deflect this criticism in a news conference on his investigative report of the intelligence failure. When reminded that Pakistan had been warning the U.S. government, he replied, "Since about 1974, I think," suggesting a cry-wolf phenomenon in which constant Pakistani allegations about India were no longer informative but became part of the general background noise of Indian-Pakistani tension.[44] But the combination of the BJP's campaign promise, Pakistan's warnings, the near-test of 1995, and the bulldozer activity at Pokhran on May 8, 1998, should have put the CIA on a higher state of alert for any activity of the kind that the U.S. imagery analyst spotted early in the morning of May 11. Since active concealment would have been a predictable part of any Indian test preparations, U.S. intelligence should have intensified nighttime radar imaging of Pokhran that might have spotted the stepped-up activity. If any such imagery was collected and yielded useful intelligence, it was not disclosed publicly by Jeremiah.

Postmortems of the 1998 tests showed that India had engaged in an extensive campaign of what is known in the intelligence world as denial and deception, some of it specifically to conceal what was going on at Pokhran from detection by U.S. intelligence satellites. India kept knowledge of the impending tests limited to a bare minimum of officials. Among those in the dark were Indian diplomats who, in a number of exchanges before the tests, had assured their American counterparts that nothing destabilizing on the nuclear front was being contemplated by the newly elected Indian government. By 1998, publicly accessible Internet sites managed by space buffs were carrying detailed information on the orbital schedules of known or suspected U.S. intelligence satellites, whose polar orbital paths made them easily distinguishable from other satellites. These databases informed governments when intelligence satellites were passing overhead, allowing them to time secret activities for periods when they could not be observed. The Indians took special care to conceal their nighttime test preparations, ensuring that trucks were returned to their original parking places by daybreak to suggest no recent activity. Strong winds in May kept the sand and dust moving, covering the vehicle tracks that imagery analysts look for at nuclear test sites. Nighttime earthmoving efforts as the bombs were buried were concealed by dumping dirt in piles shaped to mimic the sand dunes in the surrounding terrain. "It's not a failure of the CIA," Indian nuclear researcher G. Balachandran told the author. "It's a matter of their intelligence being good, but our deception being better."[45]

The suggestion that the CIA had been bested by a foreign government thought to be far less sophisticated than the United States in military and intelligence matters fell on receptive ears in Washington. CIA-bashing had become frequent sport among officials on the right, eager to brand Clinton as presiding over an incompetent security team. And once again, the old formula applied, for while the right attacked, the administration did nothing to defend, preferring that the CIA, not its own diplomats, who were perfectly capable of reading the clear signals coming from India, absorb the blame. It is possible, however, that too much was made of Indian cleverness in evading spy satellite detection. After all, New Delhi had been caught preparing for a test in 1982 and shown satellite photos proving it, but had not learned from that episode sufficiently to foil U.S. intelligence in 1995. John Pike, a national security analyst with GlobalSecurity.org, has offered a different explanation. The test preparations observed in 1995, particularly the digging out of the mine shafts and laying of cables, essentially completed the most visible and overt preparations for a nuclear test. All that remained to do in 1998 was to place the weapons in the shafts, seal them over and turn the firing keys. The CIA may have seen very little because there was very little to see.[46] Richelson's authoritative account of intelligence issues surrounding the Indian nuclear tests differs somewhat from the initial disclosure in the New York Times concerning Wisner's 1995 démarche. According to Richelson, Wisner showed only one spy satellite photo in a meeting with A. N. Varma, private secretary to then–Prime Minister Rao, and did not let the Indian official keep the image. If India "went to school" on the photographic evidence shown by Wisner, it would have done so based on the memory of a single ministerial aide with no particular expertise in imagery intelligence or the mechanics of nuclear testing.

Yet the CIA was not merely the subject of criticism in the wake of the Indian tests, but was also an active participant in that criticism. "There's no getting around the fact that, in this instance, we missed and did not predict the particular test involved," Tenet said, speaking to reporters after a closed-door briefing of the Senate Intelligence Committee.[47] L. Britt Snider, the former staff counsel to the Senate Intelligence Council and, in 1998, Tenet's inspector general at the CIA, called the Indian nuclear test episode "a significant intelligence failure." In an interview, Snider questioned the thoroughness of Jeremiah's three-week investigation, noting that his group did not even travel to India to explore nuclear issues in greater depth. In the early 1990s, while still on the intelligence committee staff, Snider had traveled to India to meet with U.S. intelligence officers there. At that time he said, "The issue of the possibility of India conducting nuclear testing was *the* number-one issue for intelligence in that country. When it happened without us knowing about it, it really blew my mind."[48]

Linda Millis, a former senior intelligence analyst at the CIA and the National Security Agency, said analysts had spotted suspicious activity but not enough to announce suspicions of an impending test. "There were some indications something was going to happen," Millis recalled. Imagery intelligence might show, for example, more trucks on the test site than were usually expected to be there, and evidence of the laying of cable, but "It's not like somebody's getting on the phone and saying 'We're about to test.'"[49] The activity was enough to prompt CIA analysts to request an intensified focus on Pokhran, but by the time that machinery had been set in motion, the bombs had gone off. John McLaughlin, who was head of CIA intelligence analysis at the time of the test, said the Agency expected India to conduct a nuclear test but believed it would do so after first testing a new line of intermediate-range missiles. In an interview, McLaughlin offered a new interpretation of the 1995 incident, saying that the CIA, in effect, "raised the bar on ourselves" by detecting India's test plans that year. Before 1995, contrary to Snider's assertion, CIA had not been required to closely track activity at India's nuclear test site, last used in 1974. "Because we detected that in '95, people said that's part of our mission. Previously our mission was, if there was a bang in the world, was it seismic or was it nuclear?"[50]

Polly Nayak, an India specialist at the CIA at the time of the 1998 tests, wrote in 2004 that the intelligence community had brought to the attention of the Clinton administration the possibility that India might conduct a nuclear test, particularly after the April 6, 1998, flight test by Pakistan of its new Ghauri missile, which had a range of more than 900 miles. After the Ghauri test, intelligence reporting of activity at Pokhran in daily products, presumably including the National Intelligence Daily and President's Daily Brief, "was brought repeatedly to the attention of senior policymakers—perhaps even to the point of numbing them to its potential significance," Nayak wrote. Even before the BJP won 26 percent of the popular vote in elections on March 10, 1998, and formed a coalition government including some thirteen other political factions, Nayak wrote, "Washington observers," a term that presumably includes intelligence analysts such as herself, "anxiously monitored the rise of the hawkish, nationalistic Bharatiya Janata Party (BJP) with a view to how the U.S. might influence a BJP government's nuclear choices."[51] Nayak cited a letter from the CIA to Jeremiah at the outset of his investigation pointing out that "the potential for . . . Indian nuclear tests" had been known for years, "and the issue was addressed once again following recent Pakistani missile tests."[52] Documentary evidence backing up this claim has not yet been declassified. The one CIA product to come to light concerning India in the weeks before the Pokhran tests was devoted almost entirely to political analysis of the new Indian government and barely mentions the nuclear issue. The intelligence report, dated April 13, 1998, a week after the Ghauri missile test, predicted that Pakistan's action "is certain to exacerbate tensions between [Indian] moderates and hardliners who differ sharply on policy toward Pakistan."[53] Conspicuously missing from the CIA assessment is any mention of the BJP's public declaration that it intended to "induct" or incorporate nuclear weapons into India's active military arsenal, a move that would almost certainly require testing. Instead, the CIA determined that BJP would likely delay any significant strategic military decisions and instead set up a national security council to examine policy options. The newly elected government, the Agency advised, "is likely to use the Council to 'buy time' before making decisions on issues that will affect India's relations with the West, such as nuclear policy."[54] The unavoidable fact was that the CIA had considered but discounted the possibility of an Indian nuclear test in the near term. The tone set by Tenet in the post-test review was that the Agency had made a serious mistake, had misinformed the government, and needed to conduct a lessons-learned exercise to ensure that the mistake was not repeated.

There was, however, a perceptible undercurrent of opinion that the Clinton administration had badly served the CIA, as well. For, as we have seen in the Soviet invasion of Afghanistan, the Polish Solidarity crisis and the Gulf War, administrations are producers as well as consumers of intelligence. In this case, the intelligence that senior Clinton administration appointees were producing discounted the campaign promises of the BJP to energize India's strategic position and deemed credible India's private diplomatic assurances that no nuclear testing was in the offing. Admiral Jeremiah addressed the issue this way:

> I suppose my bottom line is that both the intelligence and the policy communities had an underlying mindset going into these tests that the BJP would behave as we behave. For instance, there is an assumption that the BJP platform would mirror Western political platforms. In other words, a politician is going to say something in his political platform leading up to the elections, but not necessarily follow through on the platform once he takes office and is exposed to the immensity of his problem.[55]

BJP had been quite clear in the election campaign on the nuclear issue, an issue the CIA appeared to catch up to only after the nuclear tests. In its national security manifesto, issued in February, the BJP rejected "the notion of nuclear apartheid," the idea that only the "great powers" were entitled to nuclear weapons while the rest of the world cowered in their shadow. It said India would expect the United States to be more sensitive to India's security and economic interests and conduct a strategic defense review and would "exercise the option to induct nuclear weapons" while also increasing the range and accuracy of a new line of ballistic missiles.[56] According to Nayak, the former CIA India specialist, the BJP's vow to declare India a nuclear weapons state was understood in Washington merely as implying the possibility of nuclear testing.[57] Senator Daniel Patrick Moynihan, by 1998 having moved on from his close-the-CIA proposal, rose to the agency's defense. "Why didn't the CIA find this out?" asked Moynihan, a former ambassador to India. "The question is why don't we learn to read? What's the State Department for? The political leadership in India as much as said they were going to begin testing. There's a tendency in the State Department to say, 'Gee, the CIA never told us.'"[58]

The Clinton administration, in fact, had brought up the issue of nuclear testing with the Indian government; indeed, it had been a key bullet point in their discussions at least since late 1995, the previous time that preparations for testing had been detected. The Clinton administration was angry both at India, for deceiving it about the plans for testing, and at the CIA, for depriving the White House of the opportunity to challenge the Indian assertions. State Department spokesman James Rubin, reacting to the May 1998 nuclear tests, had accused India of waging "a campaign of duplicity" and cited twenty recent high-level contacts in which Indian officials had assured U.S. counterparts that there were no immediate plans for nuclear testing.[59] As already noted, some of these assurances were made by senior Indian officials who were themselves unaware of the test plans. But on April 14, Bill Richardson, then the U.S. ambassador to the United Nations, met at the U.N. with Prime Minister Vajpayee and emerged from the meeting believing that India had no plans to conduct nuclear tests. Richardson then traveled to India in preparation for a proposed visit to the country by Clinton. The Richardson delegation left reassured that India was reacting in a low-key fashion to Pakistan's Ghauri missile test and that some progress had been made toward convincing India to participate in arms control regimes.[60]

Although the Clinton administration raised the nuclear issue from time to time, it appeared to place less emphasis on it, having made its own determination, with the CIA's concurrence, that testing was not a near-term possibility. If India did anything, the administration concluded, it would counter Pakistan's Ghauri test with a missile test of its own. In March, in a phone conversation with Vajpayee, Clinton reportedly did not mention the BJP's platform of keeping open India's nuclear options.[61] On May 1, National Security Adviser Sandy Berger did not raise the issue of nuclear testing in a meeting with Indian Foreign Secretary Krishana Raghunath.[62] In fact, Vajpayee had made the decision to conduct the nuclear test no later than April 9, three days after Pakistan's Ghauri test launch, though Raghunath was probably not in the small circle of people let in on the decision.[63]

The recurring themes of intelligence failure are present in abundance in the India case:

- The link between intelligence success and failure; in this case, the Clinton administration's confidence that, having spotted nuclear test preparations in 1995, the CIA would be able to do so again.
- Clear, overt Indian warning statements that U.S. intelligence chose to discount.
- The "mindset" problem; in this case, a belief that India would not jeopardize its improving relations with Washington for the gratification of a nuclear test.
- A growing understanding among foreign governments of how to defeat U.S. imagery intelligence.

As in the case of the run-up to the Soviet invasion of Afghanistan, there was nothing in CIA intelligence reporting on India in early 1998 that would have prevented the Clinton administration from issuing strong warnings to the Indian government not to conduct nuclear tests, warnings that would have made diplomatic sense given BJP's truculent campaign promises on the nuclear issue. The Indian nuclear case presents an interesting study of the dynamics of secrecy, intelligence, and diplomacy. India knew the U.S. government's position on nuclear testing all along. Intelligence shortcomings did not, in this case, result in any misunderstanding; nor did they deprive the U.S. government of the opportunity to make its opposition to testing clear as, it could be argued, happened in the case of Iraq's invasion of Kuwait.

Why, then, the secrecy? If the Clinton administration had confronted India's leaders with a direct warning not to test, India could have simply defied Washington and gone ahead with nuclear testing. Two possibilities present themselves: first, that the Indian government preferred to present the world with a surprise *fait accompli* rather than openly defy explicit, prior admonitions against testing from Washington. Secrecy increased the chances that there would be no such warnings. Nayak, and the CIA, offered a second explanation: that while the Indian nuclear tests were overwhelmingly popular in India—post-test polls showed 91 percent support[64]—the BJP nevertheless was worried that disclosure of its plan to test would fracture its governing coalition, which included factions less enthusiastic about the party's nuclear weapons posture.[65] The available public record of U.S. intelligence reporting on India indicates that the CIA did not fully appreciate the motivations behind the tests or the decision to keep the test plans secret.

In addition to an evident desire, driven by domestic Indian politics, to adopt a harder line toward Pakistan and a less submissive posture toward the established nuclear powers, India may well have conducted the tests to learn more about Pakistan's nuclear capability. For it must have been part of India's calculation that its tests would push Pakistan to test its weapons. Tests by Pakistan would, of course, reveal the capabilities and shortcomings of Islamabad's nuclear program, valuable intelligence for India.[66] This, of course, is precisely what happened, as Pakistan on May 28, 1998, conducted five tests—the same number as India, and also a mix of high- and low-yield blasts. This time, U.S. intelligence spotted the test preparations, and the Clinton administration issued warnings. But the government in Islamabad was not listening to pleas for restraint.

The United States would pay a heavy price for the tension thus generated between Washington and the Subcontinent, the Pakistani government in particular. Throughout the Mujahadin wars against the Soviets and in the years since, Pakistan had been the U.S. government's sole point of access to Afghanistan. The post-test tension now called that access into question, at least temporarily. In later chapters I examine the pivotal bombings of the U.S. embassies in Kenya and Tanzania on August 7, 1998, three months after the Indian and Pakistani nuclear tests. In the critical days after those attacks, the United States needed, and got, cooperation from Pakistan on the apprehension of one of the bombing suspects. But when the United States struck al-Qaeda camps in Afghanistan with cruise missiles two weeks after the embassy bombings, Pakistan's government was informed, not consulted, even though the cruise missiles flew over Pakistani territory. The full story of shortcomings in the U.S.-Pakistani relationship during that pivotal period remains classified, but Tenet lamented in testimony to the 9/11 Commission in 2004 that "Pakistan's nuclear tests of 1998 and the military coup in 1999 strained relations with Pakistan, the principal access point to Afghanistan."[67]

Members and staff of the Rumsfeld Commission, working out of CIA headquarters throughout this period, had an unobstructed view of the Agency in the throes of a failure to warn of a country's nuclear plans. The events surrounding the Indian nuclear surprise fit perfectly with the Rumsfeld Commission's emerging thesis, that intelligence could not be counted on to fully appreciate an enemy's capability. If the CIA could not find out what was going on in a friendly state with a large U.S. diplomatic and intelligence presence, how could it reliably monitor the activities of adversaries such as North Korea or Iraq, with whom the United States had no diplomatic relations?

RUMSFELD AND THE WORST-CASE MODEL

With the Indian case fresh on the minds of the national security establishment, the Rumsfeld Commission propounded a new concept, the idea that because there were threats that U.S. intelligence was incapable of detecting, whether due to shortcomings within U.S. intelligence agencies or clever deception techniques on the part of adversaries, the only sensible position was to assume the worst. No sound national defense posture could be based solely on threats that U.S. intelligence could identify. Unpleasant surprises should be regarded as inevitable, and the nation should prepare its defenses accordingly. Through what the Rumsfeld Commission called an "expanded methodology," a far more alarming assessment of the threat of missile attack by rogue states emerged than had been advanced by U.S. intelligence agencies. The key issue, the commission argued, was not merely detecting what a potential adversary was up to, but doing so far enough ahead of time to develop countermeasures. "The question is not simply whether the U.S. will have warning of an emerging capability, but whether the nature and magnitude of a particular threat will be perceived with sufficient clarity in time to take appropriate action," the commission warned.[68]

Drawing on the ever-lengthening list of intelligence "failures"—or at least strategic surprises—the commission endowed adversaries with powers of deception capable of overcoming concerted collection efforts by human spying and technical intelligence systems, particularly spy satellites. Both forms of collection are more difficult "in those countries where the U.S. has limited access, which include most of the ballistic missile countries of concern."[69] The difficulties were compounded, the commission found, once the information that could be collected was pulled together by analysts back at CIA headquarters. Intelligence analysts had what the commission apparently regarded as a stubborn and annoying habit of insisting on basing their judgments on facts. "In a large number of cases examined, Commissioners found analysts unwilling to make estimates that extended beyond the hard evidence they had in hand," they reported. As a result, U.S. intelligence neglected to develop and test alternative hypotheses about the threats they were studying.[70]

The solution to the problem, the key to what the commission called its "expanded methodology," was to make assumptions about threats. "This approach," the commission said, "requires that analysts extrapolate a program's scope, scale, pace, and direction beyond what the hard evidence at hand unequivocally supports."[71]

This remarkable statement encapsulated what would be the second Bush administration's attitude toward intelligence assessments of the threat of Iraqi weapons of mass destruction. Waiting for certainty was reckless, under this philosophy. The safe course was to assume the worst, even if it required intelligence analysts to envision threats they could not prove.

No one seems to have regarded these ideas as radical at the time.

It was the Rumsfeld Commission that gave us a phrase we would hear again in the run-up to war in Iraq: the absence of evidence is not evidence of absence. A threat could exist, even if U.S. intelligence couldn't prove it. A corollary of this argument was that if intelligence could find signs that an adversary was concealing its activity—"denial and deception"—then the evidence of concealment could stand in as proof for the missing evidence of a threat. In this sense, the Rumsfeld Commission helped set the stage for the Bush administration's skillful campaign to give a sinister tilt to the missing evidence of Iraqi weapons. The commission also anticipated Rumsfeld's famous line about "knowns, known unknowns, and unknown unknowns." The idea Rumsfeld seized upon during the missile study, and retained during the run-up to war in Iraq, was that intelligence analysts tended to write judgments based on what they knew, and often failed to consider the gaps in their knowledge and to look at the probabilities behind those gaps. The answer, according to Rumsfeld and the commission, was to "extrapolate" by examining what a nation with a given technical capability could be expected to accomplish. "When strategically significant programs were assessed by narrowly focusing on what is known, the assessments lagged the actual state of the programs by two to eight years and in some cases completely missed significant programs," the commission concluded.[72]

The beauty of distrusting intelligence reporting, from the Bush administration's point of view, was that the concept could be applied flexibly. Once articulated by the Rumsfeld Commission, the Bush administration—including Rumsfeld as secretary of defense—would apply the principle not only to endow one threat with greater menace, but also to argue that another threat was being overblown. The 9/11 Commission documented how the incoming Bush administration, briefed on the terror threat by its Clinton administration predecessors, put the issue aside through the spring and summer of 2001. A new detail emerged from the reporting of Bob Woodward. Rumsfeld, according to Woodward, had voiced skepticism about a steady stream of intelligence reporting about terrorist attack plans during the summer of 2001 leading up to September 11. Rumsfeld posited that the raw intelligence intercepts from the National Security Agency and other sources might reflect not an impending attack but an effort by al-Qaeda to deceive Washington or to learn more about how the United States might respond to the threat.[73] After 9/11, the fact that these intelligence warnings had been prescient was brushed aside by the Bush administration in favor of a focus on the things the intelligence community had gotten wrong. In Rumsfeld's construct, dating back to the missile-defense debate, one could ignore intelligence, or use it selectively, to steer a policy agenda before the fact. After the fact, to whatever extent the intelligence turned out to be correct, policymakers could obscure that fact by focusing on the places where the intelligence had been wrong.

THE CIA BUCKLES UNDER PRESSURE

For advocates of national missile defense, the timing of the Rumsfeld Commission report, issued July 15, 1998, could hardly have been better. Six weeks later, Pyongyang provided Washington with a live-fire demonstration of the inadequacies of U.S. intelligence. The considerable shortcomings of the North Korean test, the obviously long technical road between failing to put a lightweight third stage into orbit and the deployment of a viable ICBM, figured little when compared with the failure of U.S. intelligence to predict that a three-stage North Korean rocket was even possible. The change in attitude at CIA headquarters was immediate and palpable.

Seventeen days after the North Korean test, Robert D. Walpole, a veteran CIA analyst and the national intelligence officer for strategic and nuclear programs, made a rare public appearance to discuss missile-defense issues. Appearing at the Carnegie Endowment for International Peace, Walpole, whose position made him the leading hand in the writing of intelligence estimates on nuclear and missile threats, displayed a contrite and accepting attitude toward the Rumsfeld Commission. Less than two years earlier, John McLaughlin, a step higher in the chain of command than Walpole, had staunchly defended the 1995 intelligence estimate. Now, in an appearance before an arms control advocacy group ideologically inclined to oppose national missile defense, Walpole was signaling a wholly new posture.

"The Commission made a number of excellent recommendations for how we can improve our collection and analysis of foreign missile developments," Walpole said. "We're looking differently at how we characterize uncertainties." The work of U.S. intelligence had been exposed to "legitimate criticisms." Regarding the threat posed by North Korea, Walpole said, "We are in basic agreement with the Commission."[74]

Indeed, Walpole revealed that the CIA had been moving in the direction of the Rumsfeld Commission even before the release of the report or the North Korean test. A classified report issued in March 1998 and discussed publicly for the first time by Walpole showed that the intelligence community had sharply elevated its assessment of the risk posed by missile technology transfer. Anticipating a key Rumsfeld Commission recommendation, the March 1998 report downplayed the fairly long-term timelines required for a rogue state to develop an ICBM indigenously and raised the specter of one rogue selling key technology to another. It should be noted that this change of tone in the March report may have been more than prescience on the part of the CIA. The Rumsfeld

Commission, as part of its work, was practically installed at CIA headquarters, accessing documents and interviewing analysts. The Agency knew the direction the commission was taking well before publication of the report.

Walpole borrowed whole phrases from the commission in saying, for example, that "despite the lack of evidence in some areas, our analysts make judgments and projections," a point he highlighted "to allay concerns that we would consider the absence of evidence to be the evidence of absence." What had been, four years earlier, a distant and slowly evolving threat, one that U.S. intelligence felt confident it could accurately track, had now become a near-term and unpredictable threat, prone to unpleasant surprises such as the August 31 North Korean launch. Where countries in possession of ICBMs had been deemed unlikely to sell them, now the transfer of missile technology was judged an unpredictable and dangerous possibility, creating "plausible scenarios" that could result in attack on the U.S. mainland. A shorter-range missile mounted on a ship could be used to attack the homeland "with little or no warning."[75]

The tone of the U.S. intelligence assessment of the ICBM threat had changed sharply as a result of the Rumsfeld Commission's involvement. But the fine print—even after the North Korean test—was remarkably unchanged from the 1995 assessment. Only parts of Alaska and Hawaii were even theoretically reachable by any rogue state based on current capabilities, and then only with a lightweight and highly inaccurate payload. North Korea faced considerable technical hurdles, and further testing, before turning the flawed test of August 1998 into a deployed ICBM that could threaten the United States. And an accidental or unauthorized launch of a Chinese or Russian missile—another threat cited by missile-defense advocates—remained a highly unlikely scenario, according to Walpole. In passing, Walpole mentioned that the revised intelligence estimate noted another kind of attack scenario, one that a national missile-defense system would do nothing to avert. "Non-missile delivery of weapons," Walpole said, "pose[s] a serious and immediate threat."[76]

Even before the North Korean missile test, House Republicans had reached a compromise with Democrats on legislative language supporting the deployment of a national missile-defense system. Now, after the test, the issue, in the words of author and *Washington Post* reporter Bradley Graham, came "crashing down" on the Clinton administration. Strobe Talbott, Clinton's senior adviser on arms control issues, said the one-two punch of the Rumsfeld Commission report and the unexpected three-stage missile test by North Korea "blind-sided" the administration.[77] By March 1999, Congress had passed the National Missile Defense Act requiring deployment of national missile defense "as soon as technologically possible." Clinton signed the bill into law in July 1999.[78]

A month later, and just over a year after the Rumsfeld Commission Report and the North Korean missile test, the success of the Republican-controlled Congress and the national missile-defense caucus at eliminating the obstacle posed by the intelligence community became clear in the National Intelligence Council's updated assessment of the ballistic missile threat to the United States. By now, these assessments were an annual exercise; the 1995 report had been a special-order job in response to a request by the military organizations in charge of military space assets. And no longer was there any pretense of keeping the key points secret. The full estimate was classified, but the Clinton administration made public a summary of the key findings. It was almost as though the Clinton White House wanted to show how it was complying with the wishes of the missile-defense advocates. In so many words, the administration, hobbled by the impeachment drama, girding for Vice President Gore's effort to carry on after Clinton, was declaring an end to the fight over missile defense.

Remaining true to form, if not content, the new intelligence estimate opened with a stark declarative assessment of the situation:

> We project that during the next 15 years the United States most likely will face ICBM threats from Russia, China and North Korea, probably from Iran, and possibly from Iraq, although the threats will consist of dramatically fewer weapons than today because of significant reductions we expect in Russian strategic forces.[79]

The caveats were now largely dropped: the report was talking about the possibility of catastrophe. "Emerging systems potentially can kill tens of thousands, or even millions of Americans," the 1999 report warned. The report referred to "North Korea's three-stage Taepo Dong-1" space-launch vehicle, though it downplayed the fact that the third stage had failed to put its payload into orbit. Even a two-stage North Korean rocket could threaten Alaska and Hawaii with a "several-hundred kilogram payload" and half the mainland United States with a lighter payload. How much a North Korean nuclear weapon might weigh was an issue most likely left to the classified portion of the report.

Finally, missile-defense advocates had what they needed to bring their dream to reality: a U.S. intelligence report that laid out a threat that could be addressed with a limited national missile-defense system. Republican advocates of national missile defense were triumphant. "It was the largest turnaround ever in the history of the [intelligence] agency," Weldon said.[80]

Using step-by-step reasoning, the authors of the 1999 intelligence estimate said that the ability of the United States to detect a missile launch using heat-detecting satellites meant that adversaries contemplating launching an ICBM at U.S. territory could count on massive retaliation aimed at ending the regime that made the decision to launch. Why not use other nationally anonymous means, such as a nuclear weapon smuggled into U.S. territory or launched on a cruise missile from a commercial ship or plane? The possibility could not be ruled out. But such methods would not bring with them the national prestige flowing from the fielding of an ICBM force. The goal for these states, presumably, was not merely to possess weapons of mass destruction and the means to deliver them, but to ensure that their enemy *knew* they had these weapons. For the rogue states, as for the major nuclear powers, nuclear weapons would be more effective as deterrents than as attack weapons. The behavioral change their possession would bring about—the increased reserve and caution a superpower would have to exhibit toward a country with these weapons—was precisely the goal of possessing them. The NIE explained:

> Though U.S. potential adversaries recognize American military superiority, they are likely to assess that their growing missile capabilities would enable them to increase the cost of a U.S. victory and potentially deter Washington from pursuing certain objectives. . . . With even a few such weapons, these countries would judge that they had the capability to threaten at least politically significant damage to the United States or its allies. They need not be highly accurate; the ability to target a large urban area is sufficient. They need not be highly reliable, because their strategic value is derived primarily from the threat (implicit or explicit) of their use, not the near certain outcome of such use.[81]

This passage is highly revealing. By explaining that the goal of a rogue state's development of ICBMs and nuclear weapons was to give pause to Washington or other strong adversaries before intervening against that state, the U.S. intelligence community implied the purpose for the United States of acquiring national missile defenses. If the ICBMs were designed to keep us *out* by presenting a deterrent threat, then the purpose of missile defenses was to get us back *in*, by neutralizing that threat. Missile defense would eliminate or reduce the cost in casualties and damage for the United States to go on the offense, to take the fight to its adversaries, to preserve the option to intervene in distant lands without fear of retaliation on the U.S. homeland.

But neither the missile-defense advocates nor the CIA wanted to grapple with the implications of a problem touched on in the estimate's explanation of motivations. The missiles *need not be highly accurate*; they *need not be highly reliable*. The estimate could just as well have said that the missiles need not be certain of penetrating an American missile-defense shield. A rogue state simply needed to have a passable chance of landing a warhead on U.S. territory to achieve its strategic purpose: making the U.S. government think twice before deploying superior conventional forces in their neighborhood. In other words, the United States could invest tens of billions of dollars in researching and building a national missile-defense system. But if the system was anything short of perfect against incoming missiles, or if a rogue state could field a weapon with at least a chance of penetrating the system, the huge investment in missile defense would have bought only a marginal increase in the flexibility to intervene. Even with a missile shield, the United States would have to enter into its intervention calculations the possibility that an enemy missile could penetrate that shield. The stage would be set for precisely the sort of no-win arms race predicted by the drafters of the 1972 ABM Treaty. One country would field defenses; the other country would improve its offensive systems. The cycle could continue indefinitely, except that the cost advantage would always lie with the rogue states because the cost of developing national missile defenses, and upgrading them to keep them effective, would far outpace the cost of upgrading ICBMs to defeat the latest generation of defenses. U.S. technological superiority would be able to gain advantages, but they would be temporary, as the technology to defeat missile defenses is generally regarded as less sophisticated than the technology needed to establish them.

HOLDING OPEN THE DOOR TO INTERVENTION

In the Rumsfeld Commission report, the goal of preserving U.S. options for intervention was presented as secondary to the main aim of defending the nation against attack. The commission, for example, reported in bold type in the opening pages of its findings that rogue states armed with ICBMs and weapons of mass destruction "would be able to inflict major destruction on the U.S. within about five years of a decision to acquire such a capability. During several of those years, the U.S. might not be aware that such a decision had been made." Several pages later, in standard type, the commission noted that rogue states "want to place restraints on the U.S. capability to project power or influence into their regions. . . . For those seeking to thwart the projection of U.S. power, the capability to combine ballistic missiles with weapons of mass destruction provides a strategic counter to U.S. conventional and information-based military superiority."[82]

Because the issue was framed primarily as a matter of simple domestic security—of defeating an enemy attack, not creating or preserving an opportunity to use U.S. military force to influence events—U.S. intelligence did not evaluate missile-defense strategies for their effect on U.S. intervention options. This pattern of avoiding explicit description of the intent to use U.S. military force aggressively and to exploit the nation's status as the sole remaining superpower would continue, with a few exceptions, through the 1990s and into the first years of the Bush administration, ending only with publication of the Bush administration's "pre-emption doctrine" in September 2002, seven months before the invasion of Iraq.[83]

One of these exceptions occurred on June 28, 2000, in testimony on the ABM Treaty before the House Armed Services Committee by Robert G. Joseph, then a professor at the National Defense University, the Pentagon-funded postgraduate institution at Fort McNair in Washington, D.C. Joseph, who would take a key post on Bush's National Security Council the following year and play a significant role in developing the case for war in Iraq, was discussing the volatile nature of rogue states and the challenges they posed for U.S. foreign policy. "These states," Joseph told the committee, "are governed by individuals that are much more prone to taking risks than were Soviet leaders. That does not make them irrational—only gamblers like Hitler and the Japanese militarists in the 1930s."[84] Rogue-state gambling, however, is local, rather than global, Joseph said. Rogue states would develop weapons of mass destruction and missiles, not with an eye toward a surely suicidal strike on the United States but with an eye toward preventing the United States from intervening in their regions, leaving them free to use their inferior but still formidable conventional militaries to intimidate neighbors and affect regional events to their advantage:

These states see weapons of mass destruction as their best means of overcoming our technological advantages that they know will defeat them in a conventional conflict. . . . In this context, long-range missiles become particularly valuable as instruments of coercion to hold American and allied cities hostage, and thereby deter us from intervention. The tremendous disparity in our favor in both conventional capabilities and nuclear weapon stockpiles simply does not matter to this type of calculation. They need only hold a handful of our cities at risk. This is not irrational. In fact, it is very well thought out. If you cannot compete conventionally and you have territorial or political or religious goals that require the use of force, you must find a means of keeping the United States out of the fight.[85]

Even if the United States were to decide to intervene against a country possessing such weapons, the rogue state would have gained an advantage, for in such a circumstance, weapons of mass destruction could be used against U.S. forces at reduced risk of massive retaliation. It might be militarily problematic for the United States to retaliate with its own forces nearby. Or it might be politically difficult to annihilate a large portion of a country's civilian population in retaliation for a repressive regime's WMD attack on invading U.S. forces. "This is what it is all about," Joseph said. "It is not about North Korea's conducting a first strike against us—that is a straw man being put up by NMD opponents as a debating point."[86]

The idea of using a nuclear force to deter a much more powerful conventional military power was indeed well thought out—by U.S. defense theorists of the Cold War. Before the enlargement and modernization of NATO forces in Europe in the 1980s, nuclear weapons had been the key element in a relatively low-cost strategy to deter or stop the enormous Red Army seemingly spring-loaded to invade Western Europe from its Soviet satellite bases in Central Europe. Nuclear weapons were the West's answer to the fear instilled by the juggernaut-like performance of Soviet forces in defeating Germany in World War II. In the 1990s, rogue states were simply applying that same American-made, Cold War–era thinking to the equally dominant performance by U.S. forces in ousting Iraq from Kuwait in 1991.

The tactic among missile-defense advocates of avoiding public dissertations as frank as Robert Joseph's succeeded in muffling awareness on the left of what was really at stake. A paper written in the spring of 2000 by the Carnegie Endowment's Joseph Cirincione, a perceptive critic of the U.S. intelligence community, was representative of the anti-missile-defense position. Cirincione challenged many of the assumptions and conclusions of the 1999 intelligence estimate but did so largely in the terms of missile defense itself, not the issue of U.S. intervention. So, for example, Cirincione properly criticized the CIA and the rest of the intelligence community for "lowering . . . previously established intelligence agency standards for judging threats."[87] He pointed out that the ICBM threat from states such as North Korea, Iran, and Iraq was hypothetical but that once such countries obtained missiles, modest technological advances would enable them to defeat state-of-the-art missile defenses. Cirincione's main aim, true to Carnegie's arms-control agenda, was to oppose a program that necessitated scrapping a cherished pillar of the arms control community, the Anti-Ballistic Missile Treaty. This approach to the missile-defense debate ensured that the two sides were talking past each other, arguing over the emergence of a threat, debating its seriousness and disagreeing over how to respond. The real agenda, preserving the U.S. military's freedom to intervene in smaller countries free from fear of nuclear attack, went largely undiscussed.

THE ROGUE-STATE THREAT

A natural offshoot of the Rumsfeld Commission's success in transforming the missile-defense debate was the broader idea that if intelligence could be manipulated and shaped to better highlight one threat, it could be manipulated and shaped to better highlight another. Thus the missile launched from a remote base in northeastern North Korea on August 31, 1998, and the furor sparked in Washington by the CIA's failure to anticipate the characteristics of the missile to be tested, made an important contribution to the U.S. campaign to invade Iraq five years later, a campaign in which Rumsfeld would again play a central role. To understand how this happened, an examination of the concept of the "rogue state" is useful.

The coinage may go back as far as William Pitt the Younger in reference to France during the Napoleonic wars. For our purposes, the concept emerges with the rise of state-sponsored terrorism in the 1980s, the 1990–91 Persian Gulf War and the collapse of the Soviet Union at the end of 1991. President Reagan used the term "outlaw" states. The elder President Bush talked about "renegade" states.[88] President Clinton first used the term "rogue states" in 1994, but the idea had already been under development in the first year of his administration by General Colin Powell, at the time chairman of the Joint Chiefs of Staff, Defense Secretary Les Aspin, and National Security Adviser Anthony Lake.[89] The term was never given a precise definition but came to refer to smaller powers, averse to the United States, intent on developing weapons of mass destruction and prone to operating outside accepted norms of international behavior. The rogues' gallery came to include Iran with the taking of American hostages, Libya with its role in terrorist attacks such as the downing of Pan Am Flight 103 and its challenges to U.S. fighter jets in the Gulf of Sidra, Syria with its open sponsorship of terrorist groups, Iraq with its use of chemical weapons on its own people and the invasions of Iran and Kuwait, and North Korea with its development of nuclear weapons and warlike posture toward South Korea and the United States.

The idea took hold that rogue states have their own, less predictable calculus and may not bend to traditional deterrent pressure. In November 1999, Pentagon spokesman Kenneth Bacon summed up the concept, saying that "in the new global environment of smaller, more radical states, deterrence may not work with the same effectiveness that it has over the last 40 years."[90]

Though developed by an administration that regarded national missile defense with deep skepticism if not outright hostility, the concept of the rogue state ably served advocates of missile defense, for the term also came to mean an aggressor state, hostile to the United States, which, because of irrational and unpredictable decision-making, could not be deterred by the threat of assured destruction. Yet, in theory as well as in practice, rogue states, though sometimes capable of major miscalculation, operate along fairly predictable lines of deterrence behavior. Their development of weapons of mass destruction, after all, drew from ideas developed in Washington during the Cold War. *They* were trying to deter *us*. And national missile defense, though ostensibly based on the unpredictably dangerous nature of rogue states, also operated on traditional deterrence assumptions: rogue states sought to deter U.S. intervention in their regions by the threat, however implausible, of long-range nuclear attack. Missile defense, so the argument went, neutralized that gambit, thus reopening the door to U.S. intervention.

Though the Bush administration clearly exaggerated the Iraq WMD threat in 2002, it also genuinely believed such a threat existed—witness the earnest and elaborate preparations by invading U.S. forces against the possibility of a chemical or biological attack. But equally clearly, at least in retrospect, the administration viewed the threat as sufficiently limited and local as to make invasion a feasible course. The administration's notably more cautious approach to Iran and North Korea reflected in part the more potent WMD threats fielded by those countries, though, as of mid-2008, they still lacked full-blown ICBM capability. Thus the anomaly of the administration pressuring Iraq based on weak intelligence about WMD programs while largely ignoring North Korea in the face of strong intelligence on nuclear programs was not an anomaly at all. Viewed through the lens of the deterrence/intervention calculus that underlay the national missile-defense program, the policies, though not articulated in this fashion for political reasons, were entirely consistent.

In an analysis of national missile defense written in 2005, long after the key decisions on the program had been made, and with U.S. forces engaged in Iraq and Afghanistan, Nathan Voegeli of the Monterey Institute succinctly described the dynamic imposed on policymaking by national missile defense:

> Fielding NMD would alter not just the way other countries relate to the United States, but it undoubtedly would have effects on how the United States relates to the rest of the world. If U.S. politicians believe that they have an effective shield against an ICBM attack, it could be manifest in their actions. This could cause the United States to treat a rogue state or regional crisis with less tact than is due the situation. The United States may react much more belligerently if it believes it has a credible defense against ICBMs than it would if it had no defense.[91]

The U.S.-led invasion of Iraq cannot be ascribed to a more belligerent White House posture enabled by a defensive shield because the shield had not yet been deployed. Rather, it amounted to leaping through a window opened in part by the September 11 attacks on the United States, a window—which the Bush administration perceived as rapidly closing—for offensive action against a rogue state. But the warping of intelligence by the Bush administration, and the intelligence community's compliance in providing the administration with the "evidence" of a WMD threat it needed to sell the war, flowed from the precedent set by the Rumsfeld Commission's forcible reversal of U.S. intelligence analysis of the missile threat.

With the United States embroiled in wars in Afghanistan and Iraq, spending on missile-defense research and hardware went on largely unnoticed in the policy community. It was no longer necessary to conduct a hard sell about the missile threat because the program was getting little public attention. That the United States was attacked on September 11, 2001, not by missiles but by hijacked commercial airliners did not spark a rethinking of the national missile-defense concept. Rather, missile defense would now be considered simply one layer, albeit a very expensive one, in a multilayered defense of the homeland. The cost overruns, test failures, missed deadlines, and uncertain capability of a program costing $10 billion per year would have been a scandal under quieter circumstances. But by 2006, the money being spent annually on missile defense, a program aided and abetted by the distortion of intelligence, was dwarfed by the $80 billion annual cost of the war in Iraq, a venture that similar distortions helped bring about.[92]

And so a startling remark by Rumsfeld at the end of 2004, when the first national missile-defense interceptors were to have been made operational, drew almost no public attention. Because of a string of failed tests of missile intercep-tors, the timetable recommended by the Rumsfeld Commission and established as policy by the Bush administration had to be extended. Test failures were to be expected in a system as complex as missile defense, Rumsfeld said. If a sudden threat were to emerge, the schedule could be accelerated, he said: "But we don't see that threat. Therefore we're not pressured. Our task in the immediate period is to get it right and keep working on it."[93] The Rumsfeld Commission would have regarded such a statement as heresy. Now, with U.S. forces already com-mitted in the Middle East, perhaps the situation seemed less urgent to Rums-feld. And yet the spending continued.

As of this writing in the spring of 2008, the 1995 National Intelligence Estimate on the rogue-state missile threat is two years away from correctly predicting that no rogue state would acquire the ability to strike the lower forty-eight states of the U.S. mainland with an ICBM for fifteen years.

As it turned out, the National Intelligence Council produced another NIE in 1995 that has since been vindicated by events. In this document, the council warned that international terrorist groups would attempt to strike the U.S. homeland, particularly targets in Washington and New York, and might target U.S. commercial aviation. The document was flawed: it did not name Osama bin Laden as a threat to mount terror attacks; at that time, the CIA still regarded bin Laden primarily as a terrorist financier. The organization called al-Qaeda would not turn up by that name in formal intelligence com-munity reporting until 1999, even though al-Qaeda itself was formed in 1988 and conducted its first attack on U.S. interests with simultaneous hotel bomb-ings in Aden, Yemen, in December 1992. But in 1995, this document, whether in its accurate predictions or its misjudgments about the emerging terrorist threat, did not draw the attention of the newly elected Republican majority in Congress.[94]

BAD INTELLIGENCE AS A WEAPON

A year after the U.S.-led invasion of Iraq, it became clear that there were no weapons of mass destruction to be found there. With the Iraqi insurgency now entrenched, Representative Henry Hyde (R-Ill.), then-chairman of the House Committee on International Relations, welcomed then–Secretary of State Colin Powell to a hearing on the State Department's budget. Before getting down to the numbers, Hyde, a more enthusiastic supporter of the invasion than Powell, addressed the war in Iraq with a speech he had worked on intently over several weeks. Hyde observed with evident scorn that the critics of the Bush administration's war policy were crowing triumphantly, claiming that the failure to find weapons of mass destruction undercut the entire justification for the invasion. America had lost credibility around the world, first by initiating the war without the consent of the international community, then by basing the invasion on what turned out to be false pretenses.

These critics, Hyde said, were missing the bigger point. The war was about more than Iraq. It was about sending a message to America's enemies. The message was that the United States would not wait until it was certain of a threat before taking action; it would not stay its hand if the United Nations or large parts of the international community objected. To the extent that intelligence about Iraq was imperfect and to the extent that America acted alone, or nearly so, the message of the Iraq War was strengthened, not weakened, Hyde contended. Intelligence failure, he said, was inevitable. Echoing the Rumsfeld Commission, Hyde said intelligence could not be counted on to unerringly expose emerging threats. "It is a mistake, or evidence of an alarming naiveté, to talk of intelligence failures as shocking surprises, as though these estimates and extrapolated predictions could ever be more than imperfect," Hyde said. Given the unavoidable imperfections of intelligence collection and analysis, it was always safer to err on the side of caution, and the side of caution, he argued, was the side that said the threats are out there, they are real, and they must be thwarted or, better still, preempted.

In Hyde's view, the intelligence failure in Iraq, regarded by many as one of the most spectacular and consequential failures in the CIA's history, was hardly surprising, and the fact that a war had been justified based on that flawed intelligence was something to highlight, not to scorn.

Now making the rounds is the view that the United States has lost credibility around the world due to its failure to find evidence of weapons of mass destruction in Iraq. I suggest the exact opposite is true. We have in fact gained enormous, immensely valuable, even decisive credibility from our actions. For the next time the U.S. or at least this President, warns some foreign despot to cease actions we believe are threatening to our security, my hunch is that he will listen carefully. The fact that we went into Iraq virtually alone, excepting our courageous partner Great Britain, not only without the sanctions of the international community but in blunt defiance of its strenuous efforts to stop us, is far from the ruinous negative it is often portrayed as. In fact it is all to the good, for it is unambiguous proof that *absolutely nothing will deter us*, that the entire world arrayed against us cannot stop us. The message to those on the receiving end could not be clearer, and unless they are suicidal they will understand that their options have been radically narrowed.[95]

This remarkable statement by a close ally of President Bush, and an energetic supporter of national missile defense, marked the first and perhaps the only time that the broader agenda embodied by the invasion of Iraq was so boldly stated. Gone were fuzzy odes to the spread of democracy. This was foreign policy in schoolyard terms. The United States was sending a message and the message was as follows: We will take action against you if you threaten us; in fact, if we even *think* you are threatening us, we will take action. We won't wait until all our friends are on board. And we won't wait until we can prove through solid intelligence that you are a threat. Under this construction, the *weaker* the intelligence on weapons of mass destruction, the *stronger* the message. It was the preemption doctrine taken a step further. Under preemption, as designed by the neoconservative movement, the United States was legally justified in taking military action against adversaries before an adversary attacked. In the wake of the Iraq invasion, administration critics declared preemption dead because the concept depended on reliable intelligence, and intelligence was inherently unreliable. Hyde was breaking down this last barrier. The intelligence was of little consequence. The message was everything. If a given act of preemption turned out to be based on false or erroneous information, that fact did nothing to dilute—indeed, it did much to enhance—the message to other adversaries calculating what might be in store for them.

"Action long dreamed of is finally being taken," Hyde said. "We are no longer bystanders wringing our hands and hoping that our intelligence will be good enough to somehow uncover it all, no longer waiting for some international court to issue a reluctant warrant or grudging permission to allow us to take measures to protect ourselves."[96]

Hyde's argument was that the United States, having been embarrassed by the collapse of its case for war and embattled by a surprisingly stubborn insurgency, stood eager to jump into new preemptive adventures and to have our adversaries see us as eager. Of course, by 2008, five years after the invasion of Iraq, the exact opposite was true. It was all the Bush administration could do to withstand growing American impatience to leave Iraq, let alone take on other preemptive adventures against adversaries such as North Korea. And Hyde's prediction that other adversary states would cower before the fear of "action long dreamed of" was undermined over the ensuing years by North Korea's decision to go forward with a nuclear weapons program and Iran's decision to continue developing a uranium enrichment capability. What clearer incentive than the Iraq invasion could these countries have had to hasten their development of nuclear weapons capability? Despite the bluster about Iraq's phantom arsenal, it was plain to Tehran and Pyongyang that that United States had picked the weakest spoke in the axis of evil as a demonstration to stronger foes. Clearly the United States wanted to topple Saddam's regime *before* it obtained nuclear weapons.

Hyde's statement is debatable on a number of fronts. America's credibility around the world was indisputably tarnished by the Iraq invasion, the subsequent course of the war, and the failure to validate the weapons of mass destruction charges. But whatever the congressman's misjudgments about the strategic import of the invasion, he performed a valuable service by stating in unvarnished terms what the Bush administration believed but hesitated to say quite so directly. The invasion of Iraq wasn't a response to alarming intelligence. If anything, it was the other way around: intelligence about Iraq, made to look as alarming as possible, was brought to bear in support of a decision to go to war that had been made for other reasons. As U.S. forces grappled with an intensifying urban war in Iraq, the story behind the Bush administration's early determination to invade Iraq gradually came out in exposés such as Bob Woodward's *Bush at War*, Ron Suskind's *The Price of Loyalty*, and Richard Clarke's *Against All Enemies*. On February 11, 2004, it was stated on the record, in public by an elected official and close ally of the Bush administration. Hyde left no doubt.

The attack on U.S. intelligence commenced by Team B and taken up by the Rumsfeld Commission was driven by the neoconservative vision of the

United States using its power to transform the world, to defeat adversaries and guide events, by force if necessary, to the nation's advantage. The idea was not to wait until threats emerged as crises, or even to wait until intelligence, with its inherent limitations and flaws, detected real threats, but to assume the worst and act accordingly. The culmination of these efforts was the distorted case for war in Iraq, a campaign that did not so much preempt a threat as create one.

7 TARGETING BIN LADEN

JUST AFTER 8 A.M. ON AUGUST 7, 1998, Sohail Anjum, a Pakistani immigration officer at Karachi International Airport, stopped a man arriving on an overnight flight from Nairobi, Kenya, carrying a Yemeni passport in the name of Abdullbast Awadah. The clean-shaven man did not match the bearded face in the passport photo. "I was convinced this passport was not his," Anjum later testified. "He couldn't even look me straight in the eyes." The passport was quickly determined to be forged, and the man arrested at the airport gate was identified as Mohammed Sadeeq Odeh, a 34-year-old Palestinian. [1] Just over four hours later, at 10:35 a.m. local time in Nairobi, a Toyota truck with a padlocked rear cargo bay pulled up to the gate of the U.S. embassy and erupted with the force of 1,500 pounds of TNT. Minutes later, another truck bomb shattered the area around the U.S. embassy in Dar es Salaam, Tanzania. When news of the attacks reached Pakistan, the new arrival from Nairobi sitting in the airport holding cell with a false passport became even more interesting to the authorities. A sweep of Odeh's belongings turned up traces of explosives residue, thus beginning five days of interrogation under suspicion of terrorism.

The embassy attacks left 224 people dead and more than 4,000 injured. A dozen U.S. foreign service officers and dependents died in the Kenya attack, as did thirty-two Kenyans working for the U.S. government, making it the deadliest single incident in State Department history. A stun grenade used by one of the attackers against a guard at the gate of the Nairobi embassy drew people in nearby offices to their windows to see what was going on. For some 150 of them, the view out the windows would be their last sight, as flying glass from the main explosion left them blinded. Most of the dead had no connection with the U.S. government; they were students and staff at a Nairobi secretarial school near the embassy that collapsed under the force of the bomb. The Tanzania bomb was just as powerful, but a tanker truck loaded with water stood between the attackers and the embassy. The blast threw the tanker thirty feet into the air; ceilings in the vacant U.S. ambassadorial residence 1,000 yards away collapsed.[2]

Odeh, who later claimed he was subjected to abuse and threats of torture by the Pakistanis, at first denied knowing about the bombing plot. Confronted with the traces of TNT found on his travel bag, he admitted participating in the al-Qaeda cell in Kenya that carried out the attack, described himself as a member of al-Qaeda, and offered up a critique of the bombings themselves, opining that the deaths of so many Kenyans were the result of sloppy execution by the suicide driver. Showing a woeful understanding of American criminal justice, he seemed to be under the impression that if he could convince authorities that he had not actually planted the bomb, but had merely built it, he would escape conviction.[3]

Odeh had flown into Pakistan with an al-Qaeda colleague who made it through airport customs and who saw him being detained, an important detail, since that meant the people Odeh intended to meet learned almost immediately that he was in police custody. Odeh's travel served two purposes: it got him out of Kenya on the eve of a terrorist attack he helped arrange as the explosives expert, and it got him to Pakistan, stopping-off point for travel to Afghanistan and a meeting called by al-Qaeda leader Osama bin Laden. The embassy bombings, carried out on the eighth anniversary of the day in 1990 when U.S. forces began arriving in Saudi Arabia after the Iraqi invasion of Kuwait, were a long-planned escalation of violence by al-Qaeda against the United States' infidel presence in the Muslim holy land. As early as March 1998, bin Laden began telling key field operatives to be ready to return to Afghanistan by the beginning of August for a leadership meeting in which the next phases of the war on the United States would be planned.[4]

The issue of primary interest to investigators was Odeh's knowledge of the embassy bombings, his al-Qaeda history, and his connections to bin Laden's network. In terms of lasting impact, however, the most important piece of information Odeh carried was his rendezvous plan with bin Laden. Odeh's arrest and resulting inability to make any contact with cohorts in Karachi,

and the passage of his traveling companion through Pakistani customs, ensured that al-Qaeda was alerted immediately that one of its own—someone
with knowledge of the embassy bombings and of bin Laden's planned leadership meeting—was in the hands of Pakistani authorities. If al-Qaeda's leaders
somehow missed those warning signals, any doubt was removed when accounts of Odeh's interrogation, including direct quotations provided to journalists out of the notebooks of Pakistani authorities, began appearing in the
Pakistani press on August 17, three days before the U.S. launched "Operation
Infinite Reach" with retaliatory strikes on targets in Sudan and Afghanistan.
The Afghan half of the U.S. strikes sought to destroy the al-Qaeda leadership
meeting to which Odeh had been summoned.[5]

The CIA learned of the planned al-Qaeda meeting the day after the embassy bombings, while Odeh was in Pakistani custody. The intelligence indicated that the meeting was set for August 20 at a terrorist training camp near
Khowst in eastern Afghanistan. Hundreds of al-Qaeda operatives were expected to attend in order to plan future attacks.[6] This intelligence, obtained
from a signals intercept, according to former CIA Director George Tenet, led
to the only pre-9/11 U.S. military attack, or attempted attack, on Osama bin
Laden.

The reason why Operation Infinite Reach failed to kill bin Laden and remained the sole attempt on the terrorist leader's life before 9/11 can be traced
back to the alert Pakistani official who stopped Odeh at the airport. The CIA
never divulged precisely how it learned about the al-Qaeda meeting planned
for August 20, but the two most likely sources are National Security Agency
intercepts—and we know that the NSA had been tapping at least five suspected al-Qaeda phone lines in Kenya for two years before the bombing—
or Odeh himself, a would-be attendee at the meeting.[7] What is clear is that
Odeh's arrest gave bin Laden a clear signal that any plans for a meeting that
were in Odeh's possession were now compromised. Bin Laden got the message. The White House did not.

Pakistan turned Odeh over to authorities in Nairobi, where he was interrogated by Kenyan police and the FBI before being sent to the United States
for trial. Born in Saudi Arabia and raised in Jordan, Odeh became interested
in Islamic jihad while studying architecture and engineering in Manila. In
1990 he traveled to Pakistan and then Afghanistan, where he trained at al-
Qaeda's Farouq camp, near Khowst. It was the Farouq camp that U.S. cruise
missiles targeted eight years later in Operation Infinite Reach. Refusing an

initial overture to join al-Qaeda, Odeh served as a medic for Arab forces supporting the Taliban during the Afghan civil war. In 1992, after more religious training, he pledged "bayat," or loyalty, to al-Qaeda, at which point his training switched from religious topics to high explosives. In March 1993, bin Laden dispatched Odeh to Nairobi, a staging area for both al-Qaeda and the United States for operations in neighboring Somalia, where the United States was providing overt famine relief as well as security and al-Qaeda was providing covert weapons and training for operations against U.S. and other international troops. After the hasty departure of U.S. forces from Somalia following the October 1993 "Black Hawk Down" debacle, in which al-Qaeda-trained Somali militia fighters used tactics borrowed from the fight against the Soviets in Afghanistan, downed two U.S. Black Hawk helicopters, and killed eighteen soldiers, Odeh relocated to Mombasa, Kenya, where he set up under light cover as a fisherman. The actual purpose of his small boats was smuggling explosives into Kenya in anticipation of an attack on U.S. interests.[8] Odeh also learned al-Qaeda techniques for secure communications, including the use of crude code words, such as "goods from Yemen" for fake passports, "working" for jihad, "tools" for weapons, and "potatoes" for hand grenades.[9]

By 1998, the embassy bombing operation that Odeh had been put in place to help coordinate was ready to be carried out. As early as June, Odeh was under instructions to have his "goods from Yemen" in order. But Odeh, who had a wife and son in Mombasa, was apparently reluctant to leave a comfortable, al-Qaeda-subsidized life in Kenya, for by the eve of the embassy bombing he still had not obtained his travel documents. This mistake forced his al-Qaeda handlers to slap together the bogus Yemeni passport that drew the attention of the customs officer in Pakistan and led to his arrest. From documents made public as part of the 2001 trial of Odeh and three other embassy bombing suspects in U.S. District Court in New York, we know that Odeh told the FBI he had received urgent instructions to leave Kenya no later than August 6 and to come to Afghanistan for a meeting with bin Laden. Meeting that morning, the day before the bombings, at the Hilltop Hotel in Nairobi, Odeh was told by the Kenya cell leader, Abdullah Ahmed Abdullah, known by his nom de guerre "Saleh," that all key al-Qaeda operatives were being evacuated from Kenya. According to Odeh, Saleh told him, "We're expecting retaliation by the United States Navy; we're expecting their warplanes to start hitting us and we're expecting missile attacks."[10] Al-Qaeda's intelligence, or at least its educated guess, was correct in every respect except the warplanes. The al-Qaeda leader, Odeh told the FBI, had vacated his Kandahar headquarters in the first few days of August against the possibility of retaliatory strikes by the United States.[11]

Odeh sought, unsuccessfully, to convince the FBI that he was aware of the plot but not directly involved. He told the FBI he suspected an operation of some kind was about to happen; his al-Qaeda comrades were in a state of high tension, speaking cryptically about a "small job" they were about to do; Saleh scolded Odeh for not having his passport in order. It was Saleh who relayed the instructions for Odeh to travel to Afghanistan by August 6, adding that bin Laden had ordered jihadists from all over to come to Afghanistan for the meeting.[12] Here al-Qaeda showed that it, too, was capable of intelligence failure, or at least of poor tradecraft. Saleh ordered Odeh to shave his beard for the trip to Afghanistan, a routine al-Qaeda travel precaution designed to avoid attracting the attention of customs officials used to scrutinizing Muslim men. The precaution backfired, for it was Odeh's clean shave, in contrast to the bearded man in the photo in his doctored passport, that gave him away to the Pakistani immigration officer.

At Odeh's trial in early 2001, FBI Special Agent John Anticev testified at length about Odeh's statements under questioning. Anticev traveled to Kenya immediately after the embassy bombings as part of a massive FBI investigative team and questioned Odeh in a Nairobi jail cell on August 15. That Anticev, a criminal investigator, was unaware of the U.S. plans to strike bin Laden's camps on August 20 is not surprising; he had no need to know. What is surprising is that the entire FBI was unaware of the strike plan—surprising because the FBI was the lead agency in the bombing investigation, and Operation Infinite Reach was planned and launched based on the determination by the FBI and the CIA that al-Qaeda had been responsible for the embassy bombings. In the wake of the embassy attacks, the Clinton White House established a decision-making cell called the "Small Group," sized to ensure absolute secrecy of the strike planning and the incoming intelligence that informed the plan. The scheme was a failure on two counts: It did not succeed in preventing information from getting out, for al-Qaeda had multiple sources indicating an impending U.S. attack, and it also prevented vital information from getting in. Kept out of the Small Group, the FBI was unaware that the White House was planning a retaliatory strike or that the plan was based on specific information about an al-Qaeda meeting; the FBI therefore was not in a position to grasp how the intelligence it was collecting as part of the investigation

might bear on the U.S. strike plans. The FBI pursued the bombing investigation aggressively and reported up the chain of command. But exclusion from
the Small Group prevented the Bureau high command from seeking and reporting to the White House elements of the probe that would be particularly
relevant to the strike plans, such as bin Laden's near-certain awareness that
the security of al-Qaeda's August 20th meeting had been compromised.

The exclusion had another, more concrete consequence. In the days after
the embassy bombings, FBI Special Agent Jack Cloonan, a member of the FBI-
CIA task force that tracked bin Laden, received information from an intelligence source that one of bin Laden's top lieutenants, Mohammed Atef, had
used bin Laden's satellite phone to call a number in Khartoum, Sudan.[13] The
receiving phone in Khartoum, it turned out, belonged to the owner of a local
tannery, which was then on the White House list of Infinite Reach strike options. Sudan's government, which had been quietly seeking a rapprochement
with Washington, worked with Cloonan on the information and arrested two
Afghan men who had use of that phone. The men had recently been in Nairobi,
staying at the Hilltop Hotel, the same one where the Kenya embassy bombers
had stayed—information already available to the FBI. But when Cloonan's
boss, John O'Neill, sought permission from the White House to send an FBI
team to Khartoum to interview the men, he received a cryptic reply from White
House counterterrorism coordinator Richard Clarke directing him to back off
and stay out of Khartoum. Clarke did not explain the reason to Cloonan: that
the sprawling Al-Shifa pharmaceutical plant in Khartoum, Sudan, was on the
strike list because of suspicions that it was producing chemical weapons, and
that Operation Infinite Reach was to take place in two days. After the destruction of Al-Shifa, the Sudanese regime sent the two suspects to Pakistan, whose
government dismissed them as drug traffickers with no involvement in the
embassy bombings. The FBI never got to question them.[14]

The arrest of Odeh in Pakistan was a major break in the embassy bombings
investigation. But through al-Qaeda's own information network and press
leaks about Odeh's interrogation, the arrest gave al-Qaeda valuable intelligence as well. Bin Laden could assume that everything Odeh knew, Pakistan
and the CIA knew, including the purpose of Odeh's travel to Afghanistan to
meet bin Laden, along with the time and place of that meeting. It is distinctly
possible that Pakistan was both a CIA source for bin Laden's plan to hold a
leadership meeting on the 20th, and bin Laden's tip-off that U.S. intelligence
had found out about the meeting.

Bin Laden and his retinue of senior associates, of course, were not killed by the U.S. cruise missiles that struck the Khowst camp in August 1998. Accounts vary as to what happened. National Security Adviser Sandy Berger said an immediate after-action review concluded that the Afghan strikes killed twenty to thirty people, some of them possibly members of al-Qaeda, but had missed bin Laden and his leadership group by perhaps a few hours. Clarke recalled seeing intelligence that bin Laden had reportedly left less than an hour before the strike.[15] Others suggest that bin Laden was never at the camp. Lawrence Wright, in *The Looming Tower*, a history of al-Qaeda, describes a scene in which bin Laden and his bodyguards arrive at a crossroads in Afghanistan and decide at the spur of the moment to go to Kabul instead of Khowst so that they could visit friends.[16] The 9/11 Commission staff reported an intriguing item suggesting that bin Laden's decision was based on more than a whim. According to this account, Hamid Gul, the former head of Pakistani intelligence, the Interservices Intelligence Directorate, or ISID, may have alerted bin Laden allies to the U.S. strike. With deliberate vagueness as to its source, the 9/11 Commission staff wrote that "the U.S. government had information" that Gul had contacted the Taliban rulers in Afghanistan in July 1999 to assure them that the United States was not then planning to attack Afghanistan. "He assured them," the staff reported, "that, *as he had 'last time,'* he would provide three or four hours of warning should there be another missile launch."[17] The implication was that "last time" referred to the August 1998 strikes and that the Taliban, thus alerted, had warned off its ally, bin Laden. This theory is problematic because the victims of the cruise-missile strike on the Afghan camps in Operation Infinite Reach reportedly included some members of the ISID, the very organization that purportedly tipped off the Taliban about the strikes.[18]

From Steve Coll's *Ghost Wars*, we know that Pakistani intelligence was aware of the planned Khowst meeting at least a day ahead of time.[19] Another source of speculation about whether word of the strike leaked to the intended victims was a meeting between Air Force General Joseph Ralston, vice chairman of the Joint Chiefs of Staff, and General Jahangir Karamat, Pakistan's army chief of staff, on August 20, the evening of the strikes. Attacking Afghanistan meant flying missiles over Pakistan. U.S.-Pakistani relations were already strained because of Pakistan's nuclear tests earlier in 1998 and punitive moves in response by the Clinton administration. The White House wanted to avoid worsening relations further. Also, the Clinton administration feared that Pakistan might misinterpret unidentified missiles flying over its territory as an Indian nuclear attack. However, the theory that Ralston's heads-up gave Pakistan time to alert its neighbor has problems because Ralston, well aware of the ties between Pakistani intelligence and the Taliban, carefully timed his meeting to begin just before the arrival of the cruise missiles over Pakistani territory, leaving no time for Pakistan to get word to the Taliban, let alone bin Laden.

Pakistani officials cannot have been taken totally by surprise by Ralston's disclosure. As early as August 17 the Islamabad press had been rife with rumors, spread by officials privy to the Odeh interrogation, that the United States planned to use Pakistan as a base of operations for a strike on bin Laden's compounds in eastern Afghanistan. The rumors, reported in American newspapers on August 19, had been sparked by increasingly solid evidence of al-Qaeda responsibility for the embassy bombings and, on August 18, by the announcement in Islamabad that more than half the U.S. embassy staff, along with dependents, were being sent home on a chartered plane, ostensibly because of concerns about more al-Qaeda attacks.[20] In retrospect, William Milam, then just arriving in Islamabad as the new U.S. ambassador to Pakistan, concluded that the U.S. decision to evacuate its embassy and subsequent media coverage signaled to bin Laden that an attack was about to happen and led the al-Qaeda leader to call off the Khowst meeting.[21] Another possible tip-off to the U.S. military strikes occurred when Pakistani patrol boats approached the U.S. missile-launching ships in the Arabian Sea as August 20 neared.[22] Given the press reporting in Pakistan and other information available to many there, a valid question would be why the White House retained any hope that bin Laden, who had access to that information, would have gone ahead with his planned meeting at the Khowst camp on August 20.

Bin Laden's non-presence at the camp does not mean that the intelligence about the August 20 meeting was faulty. Every indication in public testimony is that the intelligence about the plan for bin Laden and associates to meet on August 20 was solid. As it was prospective or predictive intelligence, it was subject to change by the participants, which is apparently what happened. But the combination of worldwide criticism of the bombing of the Al-Shifa Pharmaceutical Plant in Sudan based on flawed intelligence, the somewhat silly spectacle of a global superpower blowing up some makeshift terrorist obstacle courses and canvas tents in Afghanistan with Tomahawk cruise missiles that cost about $750,000 each, the failure in that attack to kill any significant al-Qaeda personnel, and poor predictive intelligence on bin Laden's likely response to available information—all these contributed to a palpable chilling impact on subsequent decision-making in the Clinton White House concerning proposed attacks on al-Qaeda.

CIA AT CENTER STAGE

Operation Infinite Reach would be the only U.S. military action directed at al-Qaeda until after the 9/11 attacks.[23] According to testimony by participants in the Clinton administration, a combination of fear of further public criticism for errant strikes and low confidence in the ability of intelligence to provide accurate, "actionable" information led to a hesitancy to try again to attack al-Qaeda's leaders. Precisely who was most hesitant is difficult to pinpoint because of the warping effect of the 9/11 attacks. After 9/11, no one wanted to admit to being timid about attacking bin Laden. The evidence points particularly to CIA Director George Tenet, though he was not alone in hesitating. Clinton's national security adviser Sandy Berger and other administration officials recalled multiple occasions in the two years before 9/11 when Tenet would come forward with tantalizing information about bin Laden's whereabouts, only to return hours or days later with word that the information was inaccurate or too soft to justify an attack. The focus of this chapter—the mistakes made in the 1998 strikes on al-Qaeda targets following the embassy bombings and the errant bombing of the Chinese embassy in Belgrade the next year—are the reasons underlying that hesitancy to strike.

At the time of the embassy bombings, no agency of the U.S. government was more focused on al-Qaeda than the CIA, and so it was to the CIA that the Clinton administration turned for proposals of what to bomb in retaliation. To a degree highly unusual in a conventional U.S. military operation, the CIA played the key role in picking the targets for Operation Infinite Reach. Within three days of the embassy bombings, the CIA's Counterterrorism Center, working with the Pentagon's Joint Staff and United States Central Command, had developed a list of 20 targets in Sudan, Afghanistan, and a third, as yet undisclosed country. Further research, however, eliminated all but a handful of those targets, either due to a lack of evidence connecting them to bin Laden or because of the probability of unacceptable collateral damage, a major concern to Clinton.[24]

Six years later, during the investigation into the 9/11 intelligence failures, Tenet would describe al-Qaeda's preparation for the embassy bombings as "careful, patient and meticulous."[25] Indeed, al-Qaeda began planning the attacks in 1993, at a time when the CIA was unaware of the existence of an organization called al-Qaeda.

Al-Qaeda had planned the 1998 embassy attacks over five years. The Clinton administration planned its response over 13 days.[26] Work on a response began at 5 a.m., Washington time, the morning of the embassy bombings, with a White House meeting involving Clarke's Counterterrorism Security Group, or CSG. Clinton got word of the terrorist attacks in a wake-up call from Berger. With Clinton embattled by the Monica Lewinsky sex scandal, it was Berger who made the critical early decision to limit the discussion of a response to the embassy attacks to a select group of senior national security advisers, the Small Group.[27]

As the discussions unfolded, a few priorities became clear. The United States needed to respond forcefully and quickly to show that such terror attacks would not go unpunished. The idea of striking multiple targets was critical, in the administration's thinking, to demonstrating that the United States, as well as al-Qaeda, could hit multiple targets simultaneously. Al-Qaeda's recruiting and training camps in Afghanistan were well known to the CIA. The Agency, after all, had helped set them up in the 1980s when the Reagan administration had provided not-so-clandestine support to the Mujahadin fighting the Soviet invaders. With the embassy bombings, the Clinton administration finally had the political critical mass needed to justify an air strike on the camps. If al-Qaeda leaders who had planned the bombings happened to be present, so much the better. The Al-Shifa Pharmaceutical Plant entered the picture for several reasons. The CIA had analyzed a soil sample taken some months earlier from near the plant that suggested the purported medicine factory was producing nerve agent. The combination of the suspicious plant, suspected ties between bin Laden and Sudan's government, a concern about follow-up al-Qaeda attacks, and a desire to send the message that states that sponsored terrorism would pay a price along with the terror groups that actually mounted the attacks drove the Sudan half of the operation. Members of the Small Group also shared a vague sense that striking a single set of targets in Afghanistan would be an inadequate response to the simultaneous bombings of two U.S. embassies.[28]

The strikes would hit multiple targets far from the United States and far from each other and do so at the same time to prove that Washington, like al-Qaeda, had global reach. The day before the strikes, top administration officials made a round of courtesy calls to congressional leaders to notify them of the impending action. Senator Bob Kerrey, as vice chairman of the Senate Intelligence Committee, was on the list to get a heads-up call from Tenet. Kerrey touched on the mood of the moment—the desire to make a statement with the attacks—telling Tenet, "I hope it's big enough that they know the United States of America has done it."[29] Albright's opening words in public about the cruise missile strikes emphasized this point: "At the time of the latest tragedies, we said that our memory is long and our reach is far. Today, we reached into two locations on the far side of the world."[30]

The biggest intelligence failures are usually the product of accumulating misjudgments and lapses at both the policy level and the level of the intelligence professional. Three key elements contributed to the intelligence lapse that led to the unjustified destruction of a medicine factory in one of the world's poorest countries: haste, excessive internal secrecy, and the conflicting demands for the two target sets to be attacked. Under pressure to present the president with military options in the wake of the embassy bombings, the intelligence community and the Pentagon rushed to produce a list of viable targets. The Small Group immediately confronted a problem that would beset the Bush administration three years later in the wake of the September 11, 2001, terror attacks: the difficulty of identifying any physical asset of al-Qaeda's that could be bombed. Given enough time, the CIA should have been able to discern at the very least that Al-Shifa was a legitimate producer of medicines for animals and people—whatever secret weapons activities might also be going on there. But the national security bureaucracy, only recently awakened to the scope of the al-Qaeda threat, had not been thinking in terms of military targeting options. The Afghan portion of Operation Infinite Reach depended on total secrecy, since any leak would tip off al-Qaeda to evacuate the camps and cancel the leadership gathering. In that sense, restricting information to the Small Group made sense. But the small numbers of people researching the targets and making key decisions contributed to the research lapses in connection with Al-Shifa.[31]

Intelligence failure is paired frequently and incongruously with intelligence success. So it was in the wake of the embassy bombings. The rapid collection of information on the embassy plot by African and American investigators and the tip that al-Qaeda leaders would be meeting at one of the Afghan training camps on August 20 were notable intelligence successes. Those successes, which followed the embassy bombings within days, told the Clinton administration two things: The party responsible for the embassy bombings was al-Qaeda, and the best opportunity to strike back was rapidly approaching. Thus, intelligence success threw the strike planning into high gear and greatly compressed the time available for evaluating targets, thus contributing to intelligence failure.

According to Berger, the Pentagon presented Clinton with options, including the Afghan camps and Al-Shifa, on Wednesday, August 12, a mere five days after the embassy bombings.[32] Two days later, Tenet presented Clinton with what the CIA judged was conclusive evidence of al-Qaeda complicity in the bombings. In a scene he would repeat four years later with President Bush, Tenet—a devoted fan of Georgetown University basketball—confidently told Clinton that the intelligence underlying the conclusion that al-Qaeda had bombed the embassies "is a slam dunk." In this case, at least, Tenet was correct. His use of the same phrase four years later to reassure Bush about the intelligence on Iraqi weapons of mass destruction would haunt him.[33]

Tenet told the Small Group that intelligence pointed to a meeting of al-Qaeda's senior leadership on August 20.[34] With Tenet's confirmation of al-Qaeda involvement on August 14, Clinton gave the go-ahead for strikes, and the timetable for action was set.[35]

Administration officials have not disclosed precisely when Al-Shifa first appeared on target lists presented to Clinton by the CIA and the Joint Chiefs of Staff, but it was under consideration at least nine days before the strikes.[36] It is known that Clinton decided on Al-Shifa as the lone target in Sudan only hours before the attack. One media account reported that the plant was added to the target list the weekend of August 15–16. None of the possibilities are particularly flattering to the CIA or the Clinton administration. If Al-Shifa was on the list from the start, it got there after a maximum of five days of consideration by the Pentagon and CIA, and received little critical scrutiny thereafter. If Al-Shifa was added days before the attack and chosen at the last minute by Clinton, it indicates that there would have been almost no time to run checks on the plant for reasons *not* to bomb it.[37]

CIA knowledge of the meeting of al-Qaeda principals planned for August 20 at Khowst was the primary driving factor in the timing of the U.S. reprisal strikes. Another factor was the alarmingly specific reporting about planned al-Qaeda attacks on more U.S. embassies, leading some to speculate that the August 20 meeting had something to do with these threats. Aside from the desire to kill senior al-Qaeda members, the administration was anxious to strike before al-Qaeda could mount further attacks, possibly involving nerve gas manufactured at Al-Shifa. Some have even advanced the argument that the U.S. strikes were not retaliation but rather pre-emption, designed to stop the terror group before it could act again. Participants in the Small Group have admitted to haste in preparing the Infinite Reach operation but argued that it was haste driven by fear of catastrophic follow-up attacks by al-Qaeda and of the condemnation that would fall on the administration if it failed to do everything in its power to pre-empt such attacks.[38]

The Pentagon recommended simultaneous strikes as a way of preventing one Infinite Reach strike from tipping off the enemy about the other. Simultaneous strikes would also have the symbolic effect of showing al-Qaeda that it was not the only force that could strike in distant locations at the same time. But while the al-Qaeda schedule in Afghanistan drove the timing of the Al-Shifa bombing, the reverse was also true. Clinton's insistence that the Al-Shifa bombing occur after closing time to minimize casualties at the plant forced a delay of a few hours in the Afghan strikes. Though the weight of evidence indicates that bin Laden simply canceled the leadership meeting because he suspected a U.S. attack was in the offing, the delay in striking the camps, by some official accounts, may have ensured that no al-Qaeda leaders would be killed in the strike. Here, as elsewhere in the story of Operation Infinite Reach, the administration's various explanations for the design of the attack don't quite add up. If, as the administration alleged, Al-Shifa was an al-Qaeda front involved in making deadly nerve gas and had no legitimate function making medicine, why the squeamishness about killing the day shift? In fact, why wouldn't killing people engaged in making deadly weapons for use in terror attacks against the United States be regarded as one of the goals of the strike? This point was never addressed by the administration.[39]

Unfortunately for the CIA, hasty decision-making at the White House cannot absorb all the blame for the bombing of Al-Shifa. The agency had been concerned about goings-on in Khartoum long before the African embassy bombings. From 1992 to 1996, bin Laden had made the Sudanese capital his base of operations. Perhaps coincidentally, perhaps not, this was the same time period in which the Al-Shifa plant was built.[40] U.S. intelligence had reason to believe that Khartoum had been a staging ground for at least some of the plotters of the embassy bombings. The CIA had been collecting information on the Al-Shifa plant for at least 18 months prior to August 1998.[41] The facility was viewed with suspicion as an arm of bin Laden's network and a manufacturing plant for deadly chemical weapons. The fact that the equipment at a modern pharmaceutical plant could be used as easily to turn out biological weapons as medicines added urgency to the concern.[42]

In the spring of 1996, U.S. intelligence scored a major coup when Jamal Ahmed al-Fadl, an al-Qaeda member in trouble for stealing from al-Qaeda's accounts, walked into the U.S. Embassy in Eritrea and volunteered to tell U.S. intelligence what he knew about the terror group. His debriefings to CIA and FBI officers in the ensuing months amounted to a trove of information on bin Laden and represented the first detailed description of al-Qaeda obtained by U.S. intelligence and the first presentation of bin Laden as not just a terrorist financier but also a militant organizer of terror attacks.[43] Al-Fadl's defection and cooperation with the CIA were not publicly known until early 2001, when he testified in public in the trial of plotters in the embassy bombings. We know from that testimony that some of the information he had provided to the CIA starting in 1996 concerned linkages between bin Laden and Sudan's Islamic government, particularly the dominant party, the National Islamic Front, and its leader Hassan at-Turabi.[44] A *New York Times* report a month after Operation Infinite Reach, which raised questions about the intelligence used to justify bombing Al-Shifa, said the CIA had relied heavily on "a report from a 'sensitive source' who said bin Laden had asked Sudanese officials to help him obtain chemical weapons that could be used against U.S. installations."[45] We know from al-Fadl's later testimony that he was the sensitive source.

"Sudan, during that period, was about the worst government in the world," Clinton counterterrorism adviser Richard Clarke testified in 2002. "They had invited every terrorist group that you can imagine to set up shop in Khartoum."[46]

In trial testimony as well as in his earlier debriefs, al-Fadl told of his efforts to buy chemical weapons that the Sudanese government was producing for use in the long-running war with rebels in the southern part of the country. In answering questions about Al-Shifa years after the fact, Clarke cited an "often overlooked" passage from the trial testimony in which al-Fadl described being sent to Khartoum by bin Laden to keep an eye on the chemical weapons factory.[47] But al-Fadl, a native of Sudan, did not mention Al-Shifa in his public testimony; he described another location a few miles away in northern Khartoum at which the government allegedly made chemical weapons. Al-Shifa was still under construction at the time al-Fadl claims to have been visiting a chemical weapons production site in Khartoum.[48]

Nevertheless, Al Fadl's debriefs after his defection set in motion a CIA effort to find the manufacturing and storage sites of chemical weapons in Sudan, which would eventually point to Al-Shifa. In the summer of 1997, an informant had told the CIA that the Al-Shifa plant might be one of two sites in Khartoum involved in the production of chemical weapons. In December 1997 an Egyptian operative in the pay of the CIA had taken several soil samples from sites in Khartoum that might be linked to chemical weapons. Only one tested positive for weapons-related substances: a soil sample taken across the street from Al-Shifa's main gate on land not owned by the plant owners. The sample contained 2.5 times the normal trace amount of a substance called EMPTA, an ingredient in pesticides—but also a building block of the deadly nerve gas VX.[49]

Two weeks before the embassy bombings, the CIA had issued its first intelligence report on Al-Shifa, focusing on the implications of the soil sample as well as the Agency's interpretation of what it viewed as unexpectedly extensive physical security at the plant. Two days before the embassy bombings, NSC staffers working for counterterrorism coordinator Clarke wrote that bin Laden not only had invested in the plant but had access to its production of VX.[50] In the wake of the bombings, this intelligence report loomed large as Clinton's advisers sought to identify targets for retaliatory response.[51] At some point never specified publicly by administration officials, U.S. intelligence obtained intercepts of phone conversations from inside the Al-Shifa plant indicating some involvement with chemical weapons production. The intercepts were never made public; at least one unnamed senator who attended a closed-door briefing in which the intercepts were discussed and spoke to a reporter afterward remained skeptical of the evidence linking Al-Shifa with chemical weapons.[52]

Missing from CIA briefings on Al-Shifa was any information on who owned the plant. This is odd since the plant's ownership was a key part of the administration defense of the strikes—specifically, that bin Laden had financial ties to the plant and that Al-Shifa was part of Sudan's military production network. Four years after these events, Clarke acknowledged to a House-Senate investigative committee that during the CIA–Joint Staff briefings on the target list, "I don't recall that they briefed us on who owned it."[53] After the Infinite Reach strikes, the Treasury Department, acting on information provided by the CIA, froze the assets of Saudi businessman Saleh Idris, who had bought the Al-Shifa plant four months before the strikes—meaning that he took ownership *after* the CIA had collected the suspicious soil sample. Idris denied allegations of ties to bin Laden or jihad and retained the powerful Washington law firm of Akin Gump Strauss Hauer & Feld to win release of $24 million in assets frozen in Bank of America accounts worldwide. The government agreed to unfreeze Idris's accounts in May 1999, a tacit admission that it could produce no evidence supporting the allegations about his links to terrorism.[54]

Another key piece of information seems to have escaped the Agency's notice: the fact that Al-Shifa actually produced legitimate pharmaceuticals. The absence of this prosaic fact lies at the heart of the blundering that led to the selection of Al-Shifa for destruction. A senior intelligence official, briefing Pentagon reporters on condition of anonymity the day of the raid, said, "We have no evidence, have seen no commercial products that are sold out of this facility."[55] Within days, crews sifting through the wreckage of Al-Shifa were finding pills, bottles, labels, and other evidence of medicine strewn all over the streets.

A constant complaint about U.S. intelligence is that it forever hedges its bets, afraid to be wrong. "Their favorite verb is 'may.' Everything is qualified," says Lee Hamilton, a former House Intelligence Committee chairman and co-chairman of the 9/11 Commission.[56] In August 1998, however, the qualifiers were nowhere to be found. The intelligence was solid: al-Qaeda had bombed the embassies; Al-Shifa was part of a bin Laden weapons network; and bin Laden was expected at his camps on the 20th. The intelligence official described it with deliberate understatement to the Pentagon press corps: "It's an unusual pharmaceutical facility."[57]

INFINITE REACH

By 7:30 p.m., local time, on August 20, 1998, the day shift at Al-Shifa had gone home, leaving a skeleton crew on duty at the plant. The whine of low-flying jet engines broke the early-evening quiet in Khartoum. These were not commercial airliners flying in to the Sudanese capital but the near-simultaneous arrival of thirteen Tomahawk cruise missiles launched by two U.S. Navy destroyers some 500 miles to the northeast in the Red Sea. The Pentagon gave few details of the attack, refusing even to release the names of the warships that participated. But the cruise missiles were launched from a point where they could enter Sudanese territory over the country's coastal stretch along the Red Sea so that the missiles would not have to violate the airspace of any other country. Witnesses along the Nile River north of Khartoum, the city where the Blue and White Niles converge, reported low-flying jets breaking the sound barrier. To achieve a simultaneous hit—what military tacticians call "time on target"—some of the lead missiles appear to have circled Khartoum for a few moments; at least one was seen flying toward the plant from the west, suggesting a circular path to the target. At impact, the missiles collapsed the structure of the three-story plant and touched off a towering blaze. By the time a local reporter arrived on the scene, the largest supplier of medicine in Sudan was a flaming ruin.[58]

Meanwhile, some 2,500 miles to the east, two U.S. guided missile cruisers, a destroyer, and at least one attack submarine[59] in the Arabian Sea about 120 miles south of Karachi, Pakistan, launched sixty-six Tomahawk cruise missiles at six suspected al-Qaeda camps and training grounds about ninety miles south of Kabul, Afghanistan.[60] The cruise missiles made a mess of the training camps and killed about twenty people, perhaps some of them members of al-Qaeda. The terror group's leadership cadre was untouched.

At the initial news conferences announcing and describing the cruise missile strikes, Clinton administration officials referred to the Al-Shifa plant as a chemical weapons factory in disguise. The United States had attacked "terrorist-related facilities," Clinton announced in a hastily arranged news conference on Martha's Vineyard, where he was vacationing. In Washington, the senior intelligence official said Al-Shifa had suspiciously robust security fences around its perimeter; it was part of Sudan's Military Industrial Corporation, a government controlled weapons procurement agency; U.S. intelligence could find no evidence of legitimate pharmaceutical production; bin Laden had contributed to financing the Al-Shifa complex and was known to be seeking chemical weapons; and, "We know with high confidence that Shifa produces a precursor that is unique to the production of VX," the deadly nerve gas.[61]

Only much later would the public learn that not everyone involved in the strike planning regarded the intelligence on Al-Shifa as unimpeachable. The 9/11 Commission reported that Mary McCarthy, the National Security Council official responsible for intelligence, warned Berger, "We will need much better intelligence on this facility before we seriously consider any options." Attorney General Janet Reno, who was excluded from the Small Group, was briefed on Infinite Reach one day in advance. She warned of the repercussions of attacking two Muslim countries at the same time and urged delay to allow time for more information to be developed linking bin Laden to Al-Shifa and al-Qaeda to the U.S. embassy bombings in Africa. She was also concerned about the justification for the attack under international law, specifically, whether the strikes could be plausibly explained as "self defense," given that they were based on inevitably sketchy intelligence about possible future attacks. Reno did not share her concerns directly with Clinton but conveyed them through Berger. In response, Berger articulated the prevailing view of the Small Group. If the White House failed to act in the face of the intelligence it had on the Al-Shifa plant, and if a terrorist attack involving nerve gas followed, "What will we say then?"[62]

Information about the plant's legitimate function available on the Internet evidently escaped the CIA's notice. Westerners easily accessible to the CIA, such as European diplomats stationed in Khartoum, knew, or could have easily found out, that pharmaceutical products in Al-Shifa's distinctive blue boxes were sold all over Khartoum. These readily available nonsecrets never entered into the administration's calculations. In the days after the attacks, as media reports uncovered information about Al-Shifa's legitimate activities, the State Department belatedly sought to fend off the queries. On August 24, spokesman James B. Foley told reporters that the key issue was not who owned the plant but who had invested in it; and while he conceded that "that facility may very well have been producing legitimate pharmaceuticals," that did not alter the concern about chemical weapons production. Back when it might have mattered—before the decision to bomb the plant—no one appears to have told Clinton that the plant he was ordering destroyed was the largest provider of medicines in Sudan.[63]

Journalists reporting from Khartoum after the bombing had an advantage over the CIA: direct access to the Sudanese capital. The State Department had closed down the U.S. embassy in Khartoum in February 1996 because of growing concerns about terrorist threats and fears that Sudan's National Islamic Front government was sponsoring anti-U.S. terrorists. U.S. diplomatic personnel, including members of the CIA's Khartoum Station, were moved to Nairobi, Kenya. This occurred despite a conclusion reached at about the same time by the CIA that one of its key human intelligence sources in Sudan, who had been reporting rumors of impending terrorist attacks, was a fabricator. In January 1996, the CIA took the unusual step of pulling from circulation more than 100 classified intelligence reports based on this source.[64]

The administration's public certitude surrounding the presentation of intelligence started to weaken in the ensuing days and weeks as the story underlying the Al-Shifa allegations began to unravel. In January 1998 the Al-Shifa plant had won a contract under the U.N. oil-for-food program to ship to Iraq 100,000 cartons of a veterinary medicine called Shifazole. The transaction escaped the CIA's notice even though it involved not one but two subjects of intense interest to the CIA: bin Laden and his ties to the Sudanese regime, and Iraq and its alleged efforts to rearm. As in the run-up to 9/11, government agencies weren't talking with one another. Such transactions required U.N. Security Council approval and were subject to veto by permanent members, including the United States. State Department officials monitoring the U.N. program had reviewed and approved the deal. Seven months after one executive branch department had approved allowing Al-Shifa to produce medicines, another executive branch agency, the CIA, was asserting to Clinton's Small Group—which included the State Department's top official—that there was no evidence of any legitimate production at the Al-Shifa plant.[65]

After the strikes, intelligence officials confronted with the CIA's failure to notice any legitimate activity at Al-Shifa offered the excuse that they had always regarded the pharmaceutical factory label as a cover story for illicit activity, and so never looked particularly hard to find proof that the plant engaged in some legitimate production. Had they done so, they might have learned that the plant was primarily a pharmaceutical packaging facility that took in supplies of medicines manufactured in Europe and bottled them for retail sale and hospital use. This information might have undermined suspicion about the use of medicine-manufacturing labs for making chemical weapons.[66]

Within a month of the strike, the possibility that severely flawed intelligence underlay Clinton's decision to target Al-Shifa had gained wide circulation. As the *Washington Post* editorialized, "how could the CIA not have known more about the factory—not have known what so many ordinary citizens apparently knew?"[67] On September 15, 1998, in a letter to President Clinton, Human Rights Watch raised "serious concerns . . . about the thoroughness of the target-selection process." The letter, from a group that had criticized the Sudanese government for its chemical weapons programs, cited Geneva Convention protocols, accepted as legitimate by the U.S. Navy, requiring attack planners to do "everything feasible" to establish that a target is a valid military objective.[68]

The CIA's logic chain underlying the decision to bomb Al-Shifa contained some solid links but also major breaks. It was true that bin Laden had ties to Sudan's Islamist government and had extensive commercial investments in Sudan. The CIA had collected intelligence pointing to bin Laden's interest in weapons of mass destruction. But the available evidence did not support the assertion that Al-Shifa was connected to Sudan's Military Industrial

Corporation or that bin Laden or al-Qaeda had any ownership link to the plant. CIA reporting indicated that the plant had an elaborate security fence, many armed guards, and was considered off limits to those not authorized to see it.[69] Yet after the bombing, Westerners reported that government officials liked to show off Al-Shifa to VIP visitors to the capital and that no elaborate walls, fences, or out-of-the-ordinary security were in evidence. British engineer Thomas Carnaffin, a technical manager during the plant's construction, rejected allegations that the plant was under tight security. "You could walk around anywhere you liked, and no one tried to stop you," he said.[70] Though the United States had pulled its diplomats from Sudan two years earlier, it was still a country accessible to Westerners. Even without on-the-ground access to the plant, the absence of elaborate security structures should have been apparent. Patrick Eddington, an imagery analyst with the CIA from 1988 to 1996 and later a critic of the Agency, wrote that he examined the satellite photos of Al-Shifa, which "clearly showed" that there was "no fencing, no guard towers, no specialized area for hazardous materials storage—all of which would likely be present at a chemical weapons facility."[71]

The soil sample was problematic on several fronts. The sample had been taken not from the grounds of Al-Shifa itself but from a location across a street from the plant's main gate. The circumstances in which the sample had been collected, stored, and analyzed were not fully disclosed, raising questions about the chain of custody and possible tampering. And the Clinton administration's assertion that EMPTA had no uses other than as a component for nerve gas was questionable. EMPTA, in fact, could be used to produce certain pesticides, though it was not known to be used in any commercial products. The substance would need to be put through two additional complex processes to be turned into VX. Some experts speculated that the soil sample may not have contained EMPTA, but a commercial insecticide widely available in Africa called FONOFOS.[72]

As problems with the administration's justification of the Al-Shifa bombing gained more attention in the weeks following the strikes, some Clinton administration officials shifted footing and advanced the argument that Al-Shifa had ties to Iraq's ambitions to reconstitute its arsenal of weapons of mass destruction. A senior U.S. intelligence official told reporters that Emad al-Ani, a senior figure in Iraq's past development of chemical weapons, had ties to Sudanese officials at the plant.[73] This allegation, if true, raised serious questions about intelligence reporting and interagency communication behind the

Clinton administration's approval the previous January of Al-Shifa for export-ing pharmaceuticals to Iraq under the U.N. oil-for-food program. Five days after the cruise missile strikes, Undersecretary of State Thomas Pickering told reporters that the administration had had concerns about weapons-related ac-tivity at Al-Shifa "for at least two years." Yet those concerns went unnoticed by Pickering's own department at the time the administration signed off on the oil-for-food deal. Pickering also cited "evidence that we think is quite clear on contacts between Sudan and Iraq. In fact, Al-Shifa officials, early in the com-pany's history, we believe were in touch with Iraqi individuals associated with Iraq's VX program."[74] Six years later, however, in testimony before the 9/11 Commission, Pickering stated that he "was not aware of any Iraqi connection until after the [cruise missile] attack."[75]

Fourteen months after Operation Infinite Reach, a report in the *New York Times* by James Risen quoted administration officials, some on the record, as saying there had been serious doubts about the intelligence reporting on Al-Shifa. The article depicted Tenet, who had been so confident about the quality of the intelligence, appearing to back away from responsibility for recommend-ing the strike. The story quoted an anonymous participant in White House planning meetings on the strike—and we know those meetings were restricted to the "Small Group" and a few senior aides—as saying that Tenet cautioned that the intelligence linking Al-Shifa to bin Laden was not solid. The State Department's Bureau of Intelligence and Research had written a report for Secretary of State Albright before the strikes raising concerns about Al-Shifa. Apparently those concerns did not include the awareness of the State Depart-ment's U.N. office that the plant actually did produce medicine. The Bureau of Intelligence and Research, which would reemerge in 2002 as a doubter of some of the intelligence about Iraq and weapons of mass destruction, drafted a follow-up report after Infinite Reach reiterating these concerns and question-ing the CIA's evidence. On learning of the draft, the *Times* reported, Pickering ordered it killed, saying it contained nothing new that had not been brought to Albright's attention before the strikes.[76]

Tenet's reported pre-strike doubt about the links between Al-Shifa and bin Laden shows up nowhere in the recollections of former defense secretary William Cohen presented to the 9/11 Commission: "At the time, the intelligence commu-nity at the highest level repeatedly assured us that 'it never gets better than this,' in terms of confidence in an intelligence conclusion regarding a hard target."[77] The phrase "at the highest level" is almost certainly a reference to Tenet.

Years later, Richard Clarke, out of government and making headlines for a book depicting the Bush administration as slow to wake up to the al-Qaeda threat, cast the decision to strike Al-Shifa not as a case of incomplete intelligence sloppily applied but of aggressive leadership in the face of a clear and present danger. In ordering the August 1998 strikes against Sudan and Afghanistan, Clinton was following the guidance of his own Presidential Decision Directive of June 21, 1995. In PDD-39, concerning "U.S. Policy on Counterterrorism," Clinton had decided, Clarke said, "that there should be a low threshold of evidence when it comes to the possibility of terrorists . . . getting their hands on chemical weapons. And he acted on that basis."[78] Under this construct, destruction of Al-Shifa was justified by the mere possibility that the plant was a terrorist chemical weapons manufacturing site, coupled with credible intelligence about threats of further attacks on U.S. embassies. After the criticism of Operation Infinite Reach, this aggressive posture would lie fallow until the 9/11 attacks. The idea of acting aggressively based on weak evidence would be revived not in response to a terrorist attack but in a preemptive move against Iraq and its supposed arsenal of weapons of mass destruction.[79]

FALLOUT

The destruction of the Al-Shifa plant drew criticism from around the world, particularly from the Muslim world. The plant's output accounted for more than half of Sudan's pharmaceuticals for people and animals and 90 percent of the medicine used in treating Sudan's seven leading causes of death. Werner Daum, Germany's ambassador to Sudan at the time of the attack, said it took three months for imported supplies to make up for the loss of Al-Shifa's production. "It is difficult to assess how many people in this poor African country died as a consequence of the destruction of the Al-Shifa-factory," Daum wrote some years later, "but several tens of thousands seems a reasonable guess."[80]

The Clinton administration was slow to admit error in the Al-Shifa bombing, but rather quickly acknowledged that attacking al-Qaeda camps when no al-Qaeda leaders were present made the United States look silly. The unintended bombing of the Chinese embassy in Belgrade a year later, resulting in the death of three Chinese nationals, severe damage to the embassy complex, and a serious rift in U.S.-China relations, added to the sense that there were major problems with the CIA's target-selection processes. In both the Al-Shifa and Chinese embassy cases, conspiracy theories arose, abetted by the central role played by the CIA in selecting the targets, alleging that the destruction of Sudan's indigenous ability to produce medicine and of China's embassy in Belgrade had been deliberate acts, not intelligence errors.[81] However dubious those theories, they were part of the very real collateral damage to America's reputation resulting from the use of military force based on faulty intelligence.

The most significant damage caused by the errant attacks of August 1998 and the bombing of the Chinese embassy in Belgrade, which are discussed below, was internal to the national security decision-making apparatus itself. The intelligence failures involved in these strikes undermined confidence in the CIA's ability to identify targets and produce timely "actionable" intelligence on terrorist adversaries. That erosion in confidence extended beyond the White House. The CIA itself lost confidence in its ability to find actionable intelligence on al-Qaeda and lost faith in the quality of that intelligence once it was obtained. In part because of the failures involved in these strikes, the CIA—specifically Director George Tenet—stopped short of recommending the use of military force on at least three occasions when intelligence presented opportunities to kill bin Laden in an air strike.[82]

In the mid-1970s, in the wake of the Church and Pike committee investigations of the CIA, the U.S. government had formally rejected political assassination as a tactic.[83] In the 1990s, the rise of al-Qaeda and the persistence of the Iraq problem gave rise to new thinking on the issue in the Clinton administration. The killing of a foreign head of state or a leader of an enemy organization by military means in the midst of a conflict, so the new thinking went, could be regarded as a legitimate act of war. The day after the embassy bombings, Tenet brought to a meeting of top administration officials at the White House a report on the whereabouts of Osama bin Laden that gave the Clinton administration the opportunity to "go operational" with this thinking.

The intelligence indicated that a gathering of al-Qaeda leaders was to take place at the Zhawar Kili Al-Badr base camp about seven miles southeast of Khowst, Afghanistan, on August 20. They were to discuss follow-on attacks on U.S. interests, possibly including more embassy bombings.[84] In this instance, it appeared, the CIA had met a particularly stubborn challenge for intelligence. For a military strike aimed at killing terrorist leaders requires not knowledge of where a particular terrorist leader *is* at a given moment, but where that leader is *going to be* in a matter of hours or days, and how long he will remain in that location. Berger, briefing reporters at the White House shortly after Clinton announced the strikes, chose his words carefully, saying that the intelligence had indicated the possibility of "a gathering of bin Laden's terrorist network" at the camp.[85]

The way the Clinton administration described the Afghan portion of the attack at the time contrasts sharply with its description after the 9/11 attacks. Asked in the White House news conference whether bin Laden had been killed in the cruise missile strike, Berger replied, "We have no idea . . . of bin Laden's whereabouts or whether he was in a camp at this time. Our intent was to target an infrastructure related to bin Laden and his groups, an infrastructure of equipment, of people, of munitions, of training facilities." It was much the same at the Pentagon briefing that day. Asked whether bin Laden had been in any of the camps hit with cruise missiles, Defense Secretary Cohen replied, "That was not our design." And asked whether the attack had targeted bin Laden personally, Cohen said, "No. We were targeting these facilities and his infrastructure."[86]

After the 9/11 attacks, when killing bin Laden had become a fervently pursued and officially sanctioned policy goal instead of a thorny problem of international law, the description of Operation Infinite Reach would change entirely. On March 23, 2004, senior Clinton administration officials testified before the 9/11 Commission. Secretary of State Albright said the Afghan strikes had been based on "credible, predictive intelligence that terrorist leaders, possibly including bin Laden, would be gathering at one of the camps." By the next day, it was clear that "our primary target, bin Laden, had not been hit, so we were determined to try again." Secretary of Defense Cohen was blunt: "We were trying to kill him, or anyone else who was there at the time. That was, you know, what they call a warning shot to the temple."[87] The witnesses were clearly responding to the commissioners' angle of attack, which was, "Why didn't you do more to stop bin Laden?" Despite the efforts of the commission co-chairmen, Tom Kean and Lee Hamilton, to keep partisanship at bay, Republicans on the panel were advancing the theory that a weak Clinton-era policy allowed bin Laden to survive as a problem for President Bush to take on. Democrats argued that it was Clinton who mounted the only U.S. effort to take direct aim at bin Laden before the September 11th attacks. At the next day's 9/11 Commission hearing, former national security adviser Berger tried again, expressing bewilderment at the confusion about whether Clinton had or had not approved killing bin Laden: "There could not have been any doubt about what President Clinton's intent was after he fired 60 Tomahawk cruise missiles at bin Laden in August '98. I assure you, they were not delivering an arrest warrant. The intent was to kill bin Laden."[88]

The Al-Shifa bombing grew into an international embarrassment for the Clinton administration as a steady stream of reporting appeared to support claims by the Sudanese government and the plant's owners that the chemical weapons charges surrounding Al-Shifa were false. The debate reached a painfully awkward low point when the White House was forced to oppose calls in the United Nations for an independent investigation into the plant to determine the truth. At the very time when the administration was pressuring Iraq to submit to unfettered inspections of its suspected weapons sites, it was contending that there was no similar need to examine the decisions underlying the Al-Shifa strike.

The embarrassment did not stop at the White House. The CIA in the weeks following the plant attack was treated to a steady stream of reporting by journalists and researchers with no security clearances who nevertheless managed to find extensive information about the plant that had escaped the Agency's notice during the run-up to the attack. Michael Barletta, a senior research associate at the Center for Nonproliferation Studies in Monterey, California, produced one of the most detailed accounts for *The Nonproliferation Review*'s Fall 1998 issue. Barletta's bottom line was that while it was possible that some chemical weapons production or development had gone on in a secret location within the plant complex, "the balance of available evidence indicates that the facility probably had no role whatsoever in CW development."[89] Barletta appears to have worked on the report for less than a month after the Sudan and Afghan strikes before submitting it for publication. This work by a single outside analyst put to shame the combined product of the CIA's Directorate of Intelligence, Counterterrorism Center, bin Laden desk, and Sudan specialists who contributed to the pre-strike intelligence reporting on Al-Shifa. In the face of overwhelming evidence that the Al-Shifa bombing was a mistake, at least some former Clinton administration officials stood by the decision. "I believed and continue to believe that the plant in Sudan was connected to this network that Osama bin Laden had in Sudan and that it was an appropriate strike," Albright told the 9/11 Commission in 2004. Cohen echoed that conclusion: "I was satisfied, even though that still is pointed [to] as a mistake, that it was the right thing to do then. I believe I would do it again based on that kind of intelligence."[90]

Two years earlier, Clarke acknowledged the problems with the intelligence but stuck by the decision: "This was one of the great controversies, as you know," Clarke told the House-Senate Joint Inquiry into 9/11. "I believe, and I think the DCI [Tenet] believes that we hit a factory that was associated with al-Qaeda, that we hit a factory that was associated with a unique precursor chemical that its only known use is for a particular kind of nerve agent. I think we did the right thing."[91]

Besides the CIA bungling of basic research on the target, the Al-Shifa case provides a vivid example of the interaction of politics and intelligence. As Barletta noted, before the August 20 strikes, no U.S. official had publicly labeled Sudan as a suspect country for illicit development of chemical weapons. After Operation Infinite Reach, the CIA included a single sentence about Sudan and chemical weapons in its twice-yearly reports on global proliferation of weapons of mass destruction: "In the WMD arena, Sudan, a CWC [Chemical Weapons Convention] States Party, has been developing the capability to produce chemical weapons for many years. In this pursuit, it historically has obtained help from entities in other countries, principally Iraq. Sudan may be interested in a BW [biological weapons] program as well." The allegation that Sudan's chemical weapons production was tied to bin Laden—a critical part of the public justification for the Al-Shifa bombing—went unmentioned. Then, after the 9/11 attacks, with Sudan now cooperating in the hunt for members of the terror group, mention of Sudan and chemical weapons disappeared from the CIA reports altogether.[92]

COLD FEET

On December 20, 1998, four months after the failed cruise missile strikes, Michael Scheuer, head of the CIA's bin Laden unit, sent an e-mail to colleague Gary Schroen headed, "Urgent, re UBL,"[93] with word that bin Laden was expected to spend the night at an official residence in Kandahar in eastern Afghanistan. Schroen replied, "Hit him tonight—we may not get another chance."[94]

Even with U.S. warships ordered to remain within striking distance off the Pakistani coast, the use of cruise missiles against al-Qaeda in a follow-up strike would require considerable lead time—easily six hours—between the receipt of actionable intelligence and the delivery of a Tomahawk missile on a target. Once the National Command Authority (the military's term for the president of the United States and his senior advisers) gave the go-ahead for a strike, orders had to be transmitted through the regional command responsible for the Middle East—Central Command, based in Tampa, Florida—and on to the ships on station. Precise coordinates had to be programmed into the Tomahawk missiles and the weapons prepared for launch. The variant of Tomahawk carried by Navy attack submarines could be programmed with the coordinates of multiple rather than single targets. Global-positioning data for known al-Qaeda camps, training grounds, and meeting places were keyed into the guidance systems of the weapons well ahead of time. If bin Laden was located at one of those sites, the preparation time would be reduced accordingly.[95] But bin Laden was cautious about his movements and deliberately unpredictable about where he visited. More than likely, the Navy would have to enter targeting information by hand under time pressure to launch while bin Laden was still at a known location.

Cruise missiles are a closer cousin to pilotless aircraft than to rockets. When launched from the tube of a warship they are propelled aloft by a solid rocket booster but within a few seconds convert to jet-powered flight and then fly with small wings at the speed of a subsonic fighter aircraft—about 550 mph.[96] So there is flying time involved in covering the distance from the Arabian Sea to an al-Qaeda camp in eastern Afghanistan, perhaps upwards of two hours, depending on the distance of the warships from shore. If new information comes in about bin Laden's location, the missiles cannot be retargeted in flight.

Whatever the flaws of the Clinton administration's decision-making in the hunt for bin Laden, an ability to quickly assemble the key people to discuss military options was not one of them. Within hours of the initial report on December 20, 1998, Berger and Clarke were conferring either in person or teleconference from the White House Situation Room with the key people in the chain of command. The overriding concern was collateral damage. General Anthony Zinni, head of Central Command, estimated that more than 200 innocent people would be killed or wounded, some at a mosque adjacent to the residence where bin Laden was expected to be staying in Kandahar. John Maher III, the senior military intelligence officer on the Pentagon's Joint Staff, told the 9/11 Commission that he considered Zinni's estimate to be "shockingly high." But the key officials, including Tenet, regarded the intelligence about bin Laden's supposed plans as questionable, and the "principals," as the most-senior national security officials in the administration were called, decided against a strike.[97]

THE DESERT CAMP

For at least a thousand years, winter in the Arab desert has meant hunting with falcons. Before the hunters can set out in desert caravans, the birds must be captured and trained to get used to their human handlers. Falcons are the world's fastest birds, capable of speeds up to 55 mph in horizontal flight and reaching speeds up to 200 mph in dives. They can catch hares and fowl, but the true sport of falconry centers on a migratory bird called the houbara bustard, known in the Middle East as MacQueen's Bustard. The houbara can run along the ground at up to 40 mph. Although it can't match the falcon's air speed, the houbara can dive, twist, and turn rapidly and, in a tactic that brings James Bond's Aston Martin to mind, can spray a foul-smelling sticky green secretion in the direction of a pursuing falcon.[98] Air battles can go on for miles, and careening after the birds across the desert in four-wheel-drive vehicles embodies the thrill of the hunt.

In the modern Middle East, falconry is the sport of kings, princes, sheiks, emirs, and other potentates who take to the desert with small armies of servants, handlers, global positioning equipment, radars, and customized 4x4 luxury vehicles for wild chases through the desert. In his memoir, General Norman Schwarzkopf, commander of U.S. and coalition forces in the Gulf War, included a photo of himself falconing in the United Arab Emirates desert with Sheikh Mohammed Bin Zayed al-Nahyan, deputy chief of staff of the UAE's armed forces. In winter, it is not uncommon to see one or more Mercedes SUVs, their occupants hanging out the windows looking for houbara tracks, bouncing through the desert. A powerful Arab hunting in his own country or as a guest in another state in the region might receive a permit giving him exclusive access to hundreds of square miles of desert. A typical gratuity for servants and guides in a hunting party might be a gift of the vehicles used in the hunt.[99] As the houbara sightings in Saudi Arabia, the United Arab Emirates, and other Persian Gulf states have declined with overhunting, the sheiks and princes have sought more distant hunting grounds. The departure of Soviet invaders from Afghanistan in 1989 opened that territory to Arab hunting parties. Royals from the UAE in particular came to Afghanistan in search of the houbara and did so, as the 1990s wore on, in increasingly lavish style. By 1999, they would typically come in military transport planes carrying hunting vehicles and air-conditioned tents.

In February 1999, one such camp area south of Kandahar became the focus of intense U.S. intelligence attention. From a human intelligence source that the CIA had cultivated through Afghan intermediaries, the White House learned that Osama bin Laden was a frequent visitor to the area.

The reporting tended to confirm persistent rumors of links between bin Laden and members of the royal family of the United Arab Emirates, a U.S. ally in the Persian Gulf. Now, for the second time since the failed attempt at bin Laden in Operation Infinite Reach, intelligence led to consideration of a missile strike against bin Laden. On February 2, 1999, a CIA situation report written by the Agency's bin Laden unit alerted senior officials to information coming from Afghan tribal sources.[100] The tribal source network had recruited a key contact close to bin Laden, a member of the al-Qaeda leader's security detail provided by the ruling Taliban. Reports from this source on February 7 indicated that bin Laden was frequenting a particular camp south of Kandahar that was near a hunting camp called the Sheikh Ali Camp used for falconry by prominent members of the UAE royal family.[101] The CIA regarded the human intelligence as solid; the Pentagon's initial view was that the target was ideal because it was isolated from population centers.[102] Moreover, the CIA had a clandestine tracking team on the ground observing the camps from a distance and using global positioning beacons to obtain their precise coordinates.[103]

On February 9, 1999, satellite imagery not only confirmed the position of the hunting camp but also showed a U.S.-built C-130 transport plane with UAE military markings at a nearby airfield built by the emirs expressly for their hunting expeditions. What U.S. imagery intelligence analysts couldn't determine was the precise location within the camps where bin Laden would be staying. As the situation unfolded, the best option for killing bin Laden appeared to involve striking not his own nearby camp but the UAE hunting camp at a time when bin Laden would be known to be there. That meant that others at the hunting camp, possibly including members of the UAE royal family, would almost certainly be killed. The timing was particularly awkward. Richard Clarke, Clinton's counterterrorism adviser, had just returned from a trip to the UAE to discuss, among other things, the Emirates' agreement to buy 80 F-16 aircraft for $8 billion. UAE officials had denied rumors that some of the country's emirs had been in Afghanistan recently, but this was contradicted by the satellite photographs.

The 9/11 Commission reported that the military was prepared to strike by February 11. Bin Laden was expected to be visiting the hunting camp that morning. The presence of CIA observation teams nearby enabled near-real-time reporting of bin Laden's movements. When bin Laden visited the

adjacent hunting camp, his whereabouts was reported to the CIA's counterterrorism center within the hour.[104] Strike planning progressed far enough that
House Speaker Dennis Hastert was briefed. But the 11th came and went with
no strike, and by the 12th, new intelligence indicated that bin Laden was no
longer at the camp. The obstacle appeared to reside somewhere between the
CIA operatives providing the intelligence from the field and Director Tenet.
Mike Scheuer, running the bin Laden unit, and Gary Schroen, the agency's
lead officer in Afghanistan, regarded the reporting on bin Laden as solid.
Tenet, according to the 9/11 Commission, doubted the reliability of the intelligence. Clarke was concerned that a strike would cause collateral damage of
a particularly harmful kind—killing members of the royal family of a close
U.S. ally in the region.

In his testimony to the 9/11 Commission, Clarke pinned the decision not to
strike on Tenet. "What I did was to call the director of Central Intelligence and
say that I had finally been presented with satellite photography of the facility,"
Clarke recalled. "And it was very clear to me that this looked like something
other than a terrorist camp. It looked like a luxury hunting trip. And I asked
him to look into it, personally. When he did, he called back and said he was
no longer recommending the attack." When pressed, Clarke admitted that the
tone of his phone call must have made it clear to Tenet that Clarke opposed a
strike. But in an assertion that runs contrary to the notion of the president as
decision-maker on matters of military force and of the CIA director as an information provider one step removed from making policy recommendations,
Clarke insisted, "The decision ultimately was George Tenet's, and George Tenet
recommended no action be taken."[105] Berger likewise depicted the White House
as deferring to Tenet on decisions to strike bin Laden based on fleeting intelligence about the al-Qaeda leader's whereabouts.[106] Testifying before the 9/11
Commission, Tenet described as a "collective decision" the judgment that the
intelligence on the desert camp was insufficient to warrant a military strike.
"I can't recall who made the call, but I know we were all in the same place
about it," Tenet said, the "we" referring to both the CIA and the Clinton White
House.[107] In his memoir, Tenet recalled harried scenes in which he would be
asked to make a snap recommendation on launching a military strike. One
such occasion occurred in the middle of his son's lacrosse match when Tenet
was summoned by his security detail to the secure telephone in his official SUV.
"That's no way to do business," wrote Tenet, who, in retrospect, criticized the
policy of relying on cruise missiles rather than troops to pursue bin Laden.[108]

Even with bin Laden's departure from the desert hunting camp on February 12, 1999, Scheuer and the CIA's bin Laden unit regarded the camp as a place to watch, since it appeared to be a place frequented by the al-Qaeda leader. Within a month, however, a call by Clarke to UAE officials to express concern about their apparent socialization with bin Laden in the Afghan desert appears to have removed the Desert Camp from the list of places where the United States might hit bin Laden. Clarke's call to the UAE officials, which he insists was cleared by the CIA, took place on March 7. Within a week, according to the 9/11 Commission, satellite imagery showed the camp being dismantled. At around the same time, the Taliban security guard who had been feeding information on bin Laden's whereabouts to members of the tribal groups working for the CIA was reassigned. CIA officials denied clearing Clarke's call, and Scheuer and his boss, Deputy Director for Operations James Pavitt, were irate over what they regarded as a tip-off of UAE officials and an apparent subsequent leak to bin Laden that the United States knew about the camp.[109] The dismantling of the hunting camp following the call from Clarke could have been coincidence: hunting season for the houbara bustard ends in March.

UAE officials later denied to U.S. diplomats that any members of the royal family had been at the camp in February. They also claimed that bin Laden had not been there either, though they did not explain how they could have known that without having been there themselves. During the 9/11 Commission investigation, members of Clinton's team repeatedly pointed to after-action reports in this and other cases indicating that bin Laden had not, after all, been where the CIA said he was, as vindication of the decisions against striking.[110] The commission did not appear to support this view, stating as a matter of fact that bin Laden had been at the camp and had left at about the same time the Clinton administration was deciding not to launch missiles.

Former defense secretary Cohen insisted that the flood of public criticism of Operation Infinite Reach—that it blew up a medicine plant on faulty intelligence, that it made bin Laden a hero across the Middle East, that it made the United States look silly to blow up cheap tents with expensive missiles—cast no shadow on subsequent decision-making on opportunities to strike at bin Laden. "It had no impact," Cohen stated flatly. "We would take action against bin Laden or his associates wherever we thought we could do so successfully."[111] Cohen's assessment does not square with that of Clinton's national security adviser. Sandy Berger said that the view in the White House was hardening that firing expensive missiles to knock down a few al-Qaeda tents "would have made bin Laden look stronger, glorified him in the Islamic world, created more terrorists and not made us look stronger or advanced the cause of fighting terrorism."[112]

In the aftermath of Operation Infinite Reach, Tenet was distinctly on the defensive about the quality of intelligence underlying the strikes on Sudan and Afghanistan. As 9/11 Commission member Bob Kerrey recalled, Tenet was all but accused of being a war criminal for the destruction of the pharmaceutical plant in Khartoum.[113] The aftermath of 9/11 presented Tenet with an unchanged set of facts as to the previous opportunities to attack bin Laden but an entirely transformed political environment. Now he was being asked to explain why the CIA had not done more, why he had been so reluctant to recommend strikes when later opportunities to hit bin Laden arose. The problem, Tenet explained, had to do with the difficulty of "predictive" intelligence. "Even if we again sighted bin Laden, we did not have a timely response option," Tenet told the 9/11 Commission. "Targets in Afghanistan were hours away from conventional attack, even if the policy decision had been made and the weapons were positioned and ready."[114] Finding out where a target was going to be "many hours in advance" and killing that target with a missile strike required "close-in access," Tenet said. "That we did not have."[115]

In a defensive appearance before the 9/11 Commission, Tenet conveyed something of the pressure confronting anonymous target analysts at CIA or the Pentagon when the issue at hand is whether to strike. The host of questions to be addressed is truly forbidding: Who is the source of the information about the location of the target? Is it a single source or several? If the target is a terrorist leader, will he be under U.S. surveillance constantly? What track record for accuracy have the sources established? Will the target be in a single location for the four to six hours it will take to get approval and strike that location with a cruise missile, especially bearing in mind the fact that Tomahawk cruise missiles, once launched, cannot be redirected? If the target is believed to be somewhere within a complex of buildings, where within that complex should the strike be aimed? All of these questions, Tenet said, had to be answered in rapid fashion, sometimes in a matter of hours, by the top national security officials in the government.[116]

To the Clinton White House, it was critical that bin Laden or some combination of senior al-Qaeda leadership be present at the target at the time of attack. Berger said the president's team discussed serial or random strikes on al-Qaeda infrastructure. The problem was, Berger said, there wasn't enough infrastructure to justify a sustained bombing campaign. To blow up make-shift camps and not kill the leaders, Berger told the 9/11 Commission, "would actually have strengthened bin Laden and al-Qaeda, glorified him and made us look weak."[117] But it is important to recall that, at least according to the testimony of Berger and others in the Clinton White House, as well as the conclusion of the 9/11 Commission, it was Tenet—Clinton's intelligence chief—not the president's policy advisers such as the secretaries of state and defense, Berger, or the generals, who effectively put a stop to strikes on three key occasions when the intelligence indicated a fix on bin Laden's location.

"In each of those cases," Berger testified, "the director of the CIA would come back to me and say, 'I do not believe we have reliable enough intelligence to recommend going forward.'"[118] The cost of mistaken judgments on previous targets was weighing heavily at Langley.

After 9/11, former members of Clinton's national security team portrayed themselves as straining against the leash to get at bin Laden, and refraining from taking action only out of sober, case-by-case analysis of the facts as they came in with each new potential opportunity to kill or capture the al-Qaeda leader. The 9/11 Commission, carefully avoiding direct political criticism, laid out the narrative and let the public make its own judgment. The commission's staff, in its report on the attempts to strike at al-Qaeda, said the flaws of Operation Infinite Reach, and the avalanche of criticism that followed, took their toll. While absolving Clinton of mounting the August 1998 strikes as a distraction from the Lewinsky scandal and ensuing impeachment crisis, the commission staff nevertheless concluded:

> The impact of the criticism lingered, however, as policymakers looked at pro-posals for new strikes. The controversy over the Sudan attack, in particular, shadowed future discussions about the quality of intelligence that would be needed about other targets.[119]

Though concern about bin Laden increased steadily at the CIA from 1998 to 2001, the top officials at the Agency responsible for overseeing attack options—Tenet and James Pavitt, the chief of CIA's clandestine service—came to doubt the utility of killing bin Laden. In a meeting in 2000 with President-elect Bush, Pavitt recalled highlighting the seriousness of the threat posed by bin Laden and al-Qaeda. But he said that when asked by Bush whether killing bin Laden would solve the problem, both Pavitt and Tenet responded that it would have an impact but not stop the threat of terrorist attack.[120]

Then, before the next bin Laden sighting created another opportunity to use missiles to kill the terrorist leader, a spectacular intelligence failure in the use of precision air power would intervene, deepening the reluctance to opt for stand-off military force in the campaign against al-Qaeda.

AN ACCURATE MISS
("WE SHOOT A WHOLE LOT BETTER THAN WE AIM")[121]

In late March 1999, a few weeks after the desert camp in Afghanistan had been hastily packed up, officials at the CIA's Counter-Proliferation Division assigned to the burgeoning Kosovo crisis began considering a target in Belgrade, the capital of Yugoslavia, for inclusion on the NATO strike list. The CIA analysts, who had no particular expertise in the Balkans or knowledge of Belgrade, focused their attention on the Federal Directorate for Supply and Procurement, Yugoslavia's weapons development and purchasing branch.[122] Also known as Yugoimport, the directorate had been variously described as a military procurement organization as well as a state trade agency dealing in agricultural products and civilian goods as well as weapons. Intelligence analysts were interested in the directorate not only for its military role but also because of its suspected status as the key source of Yugoslavia's hard currency.[123]

Seven months after the terrorist attacks on the U.S. embassies in Africa, and three months after the Operation Desert Fox strikes against Iraq for noncompliance with U.N. sanctions, crisis in the Balkans once again occupied the Clinton administration. Over the preceding ten months, the Yugoslav government forces of President Slobodan Milosevic had mounted a military crackdown on ethnic Albanian separatists in the Yugoslav province of Kosovo, just south of Serbia proper. The crisis, with its claims and counterclaims of massacres and ethnic cleansing by ethnic Albanians and Serbs and the displacement of some 300,000 ethnic Albanian civilians and 200,000 Serbs, appeared to the Clinton administration and NATO as a looming repeat of the Bosnian civil war, which was belatedly settled in December 1995 with the signing of the Dayton Peace Accords after what just about everyone agreed was far too much bloodshed. Now the fear in Washington and European capitals was that Yugoslav-Serb forces under Milosevic would engage in "ethnic cleansing" of Kosovo and that, once again, the international community would stand accused of doing nothing in the face of atrocities bordering on genocide. Reports of massacres by Serb forces and the uprooting of entire ethnic Albanian communities indicated that just such a program—or pogrom—was under way. Milosevic cast his moves as defending Yugoslavia's territorial integrity along with the Serb minority in Kosovo that stood at equal risk of abuse at the hands of ethnic Albanians, who were a minority in Yugoslavia but a majority within Kosovo. Prodded by the Clinton administration, NATO entered the conflict decisively, using air strikes to attack Serbian forces in defense of the ethnic Albanians. Operation Allied Force, as the campaign was called, would mark the first extensive use of NATO air power in attacks on a sovereign European country in the history of the Atlantic alliance.

The seventy-eight-day NATO air campaign had relatively little impact on tactical developments in Kosovo or on Yugoslavia's overall war-making capability. Instead, the Clinton administration and the U.S.-led NATO high command designed the campaign to target strategic assets—particularly the Yugoslav military infrastructure—of sufficient value to Milosevic that the threat of their continued degradation would make him accept NATO's demand that Serb forces withdraw from Kosovo in favor of a NATO and United Nations force.

The campaign was not supposed to last seventy-eight days. The initial planning by U.S. and allied officers under U.S. Army General Wesley Clark, NATO's Supreme Allied Commander-Europe, called for two nights of air strikes on an approved list of just over fifty targets, mostly Yugoslav air defense batteries and military command-and-control bunkers.[124] Air Force Lieutenant General Michael C. Short bridled at the limited nature of the campaign and lobbied unsuccessfully for a much more robust series of initial strikes that would knock out Serbian power stations and bridges. Rejecting this advice, Clark approved a three-phase campaign, beginning cautiously with attacks on air defense assets—almost always the first move by U.S. air forces in action against a country with modern military forces. This would be followed, if necessary, by strikes on other Serb military targets and, if Yugoslavia continued to defy NATO's demands, on "leadership" targets in and around Belgrade. Later, Short complained that NATO commander Clark "had us all convinced we didn't need very many targets, and we didn't need an air campaign, and Milosevic just needed a little bit of spanking."[125]

Problems with this strategy emerged immediately following the commencement of strikes in late March 1999. Serb forces in Kosovo proved skillful at avoiding air attack, and strategic targets were in short supply. As the campaign wore on, a familiar problem confronted strike planners: an acute shortage of targets of high value to the Yugoslav government and military that did not also run the risk of harming civilians. Bombing of population centers was not an acceptable option to American decision-makers.

Precision munitions and bombs reduce pressure on the Air Force by reducing the munitions required to destroy each target and thereby increasing the number of targets that can be hit in each sortie. But a strategy of precision strikes increases the pressure on intelligence analysts and target planners, requiring them to study large numbers of targets and determine whether and how they can be destroyed with minimal collateral damage. During the Kosovo campaign, President Clinton, who sometimes made the final call on approving target sets, demanded highly detailed estimates on the destructive patterns expected to be caused by various types of bombs. He sometimes ordered changes in weapons loads and even delivery angles. Data sent to the White House included such details as how far from an impact point window breakage, and even damage to eardrums, would extend.[126]

When the campaign opened, NATO had amassed a list of 219 targets, mostly air defense systems and military command and communications centers. The plan was to strike by night and pause by day, reducing risk to NATO pilots and affording Milosevic intervals during which he would have an opportunity to yield to NATO's demands. On the first night, NATO hit fifty-one targets; three nights into the campaign it was halfway through the initial target list with no sign of Milosevic yielding.[127] Clark's reluctance to mount a more damaging air campaign, the difficulty of finding Serb forces in Kosovo, poor weather, and the challenge of finding strategic targets that could meet the limiting criteria of the White House and gun-shy NATO allies left little choice but to bomb some targets multiple times. Air Force Lieutenant Colonel Paul Strickland, who worked at NATO's Combined Air Operations Center in Vicenza, Italy, during the Kosovo campaign, recalled that "for the initial 40 days of the campaign, numerous insignificant targets were repeatedly bombed into rubble due to a lack of freshly approved target sets."[128] By the end of the campaign, NATO had flown more than 9,300 strike sorties in attacking just over 900 targets.[129]

Months later, in the aftermath of the accidental bombing of the Chinese embassy in Belgrade, Deputy Defense Secretary John Hamre did not try to conceal the pressure on the military and intelligence community at the beginning of the campaign to find Milosevic's pressure points:

Yes, of course we were trying to find additional targets because we were trying to find additional leverage places where we could try to bring the Yugoslav government to a point where it couldn't continue to prosecute this violence against the people of Kosovo.[130]

It was in this context that the CIA joined in the target selection process that normally would have been entirely the purview of the Pentagon and NATO.

While there was pressure to come up with more targets, two points are important to remember when looking at the bombing of the Chinese embassy. First, the CIA began working on a target proposal to destroy what it thought was the Yugoslav Federal Directorate for Supply and Procurement in late March, about six weeks before the strike took place. There was no shortage of time to check and double-check the selection of this target for destruction. Second, the procurement directorate was the only target the CIA nominated during the entire campaign out of more than 900 targets attacked. Although the agency was supporting the Kosovo operation in other ways, it can hardly claim overwork as a factor in the targeting error.[131] Precisely because target selection was so unusual for the CIA, planners at the agency were in a position to go to lengths to check and double-check their work, precautions that, quite evidently, were not taken.

As with the Al-Shifa bombing, the CIA failed to obtain publicly available information that would have alerted it to its misidentification of the target. In the Al-Shifa case, it was readily available information that the plant did, in fact, produce pharmaceuticals; in the Chinese embassy case, it was the fact, well known by U.S. diplomats who had been stationed in Belgrade, that the embassy had moved to a new location in 1996, the location the CIA nominated for destruction. The embassy and its new address were in the Belgrade phone book.[132] Unfortunately for the Clinton administration, the new address had not found its way into another book, the one the U.S. government uses to ensure that it does not bomb hospitals, orphanages, schools, mosques, and embassies. American intelligence officers and diplomats familiar with Belgrade were not consulted in the target planning phase. Imagery analysts failed to notice that a building they described as a warehouse for the supply directorate did not look at all like a warehouse.

A combination of bad data, bad procedure, and bad luck resulted in the destruction of the Chinese embassy in Belgrade on May 7, 1999.

BAD DATA

Initial media reporting attributed the mistake to faulty maps used by the CIA in selecting the target.[133] The Pentagon and CIA labeled these explanations misleading. Yes, the map used in planning the strike was outdated and placed the Chinese embassy in its former location. However, the fault lay not with the mapmakers but with the people responsible for updating the database used by U.S. intelligence and the military in identifying what *not* to bomb. The laborious task of combing building and construction records and cross-referencing maps with satellite imagery in any city the United States could conceivably bomb—work that got short shrift during the years of declining personnel in U.S. intelligence—underlay the inadvertent destruction of the embassy, the administration explained.[134]

Critics in Congress pointed to the 1996 reorganization of the imagery intelligence bureaucracy as a contributing factor. It was a major merger that combined the Defense Mapping Agency, Central Imagery Office, Defense Dissemination Program Office, National Photographic Interpretation Center, and imagery intelligence units of the CIA, Defense Intelligence Agency, and National Reconnaissance Office. Formation of the new National Imagery and Mapping Agency entailed some disruption and controversy. Coinciding with the leanest years of post–Cold War defense spending, the reorganization reportedly led to numerous protest resignations, particularly among CIA imagery analysts reassigned to the new organization.[135] Writing in the wake of the embassy bombing, former CIA imagery analyst Patrick G. Eddington warned that the "loss of key personnel" and poor coordination between intelligence analysts and war-fighters had left the United States and its allies "vulnerable to making catastrophic errors" on a similar scale.[136]

Updating no-strike lists, Tenet told the House Intelligence Committee months after the bombing, "is one of those basic elements of our intelligence effort, but it is also one that has suffered in recent years as our work force has been spread thin." Tenet stopped short of blaming the mistake on budget cuts. Rather, he said the problem stemmed from the diversion of intelligence resources "away from basic intelligence and database maintenance to support current operations."[137] Tenet's point was indisputable, and had been underscored by independent and congressional reviews of intelligence throughout the 1990s. Still, it was an odd allotment of blame since one might assume that a shift of resources toward support of intelligence operations would have entailed improved performance at the operational level.

Tenet himself touched on the serious flaws in execution of the targeting nomination during his House testimony. The bad-data argument, he conceded, overlooks a key point. The critical mistake had less to do with unreliable data than with the CIA's assumption that the data were reliable. A brief reflection on the scale of the task of tracking every school project, every new hospital wing, every embassy or consulate relocation, and so on, in hundreds of cities around the world makes clear that the CIA needed to carefully vet each target and update lists of sites not to be bombed with new research. During the Persian Gulf War, strike planners circled do-not-bomb locations in red ink on their maps, and they took positive steps to ensure the accuracy of the no-strike list, including contacting foreign governments to verify the location of their embassies. Working with reduced manpower and facing pressure to come up with more targets, planners for the Kosovo campaign were far more trusting of existing databases and less inclined to double-check.[138]

BAD PROCEDURE

The mistaken bombing of the Chinese Embassy in Belgrade began with an accurate piece of information: a street address. The CIA knew that the Yugoslav Federal Directorate for Supply and Procurement was at Bulevar Umetnosti 2 in Belgrade. For an air attack using satellite-guided munitions, the address had to be translated into global positioning coordinates. The CIA was using a 1997 map of Belgrade that did not show specific street addresses.[139] Two other Belgrade maps, one from 1996 and the other from 1989, did have some street numbers. Neither showed the address in question, or the location of the military procurement office. The 1989 map predated the Chinese embassy's move from "Old Belgrade" to its location in "New Belgrade" four miles across town; the 1996 map did not show the Chinese embassy in either its new or its previous location. At this point, a CIA officer made a serious error in judgment. The officer found nearby, on parallel streets, buildings with known addresses that were labeled on the 1997 map, including the Hyatt and Intercontinental Hotels and the Serbian Socialist Party headquarters. By drawing parallel lines across the street grid in this section of the city as shown on the map, the official then attempted to extrapolate the precise location of Bulevar Umetnosti 2.[140]

Delivering President Clinton's formal apology to the Chinese government in Beijing, Undersecretary of State Thomas Pickering, flanked by senior officials from the Pentagon, State Department, and CIA, acknowledged that the method used to extrapolate the coordinates of a bombing target was "seriously flawed." The so-called "resection and intersection" used by the CIA analyst drew on a land navigation technique used by the Army in the field for establishing general geographic locations, but was not intended for use in planning a precision air strike. The CIA analyst was drawing lines across a map of a modern European city to find the coordinates of a building on which the

Air Force would drop five tons of high explosive. Compounding the mistake, the analyst assumed that the Belgrade street-numbering sequence would be identical as long as the streets were parallel, that even- and odd-numbered addresses could be on the same side of the street, and that the numbering would continue in sequence even if the name of a street changed. "Unfortunately," Pickering told the Chinese in what must have been an excruciating session, "a number of these assumptions were wrong."[141]

Having used a dubious extrapolation method to fix the location of the target, the analyst then shrouded his work in a pretty package, downloading from a military intranet site a highly detailed targeting form and filling in the particulars of the strike. The targeting nomination went up the chain of command without further inquiry and was sent on to NATO over the signature of Brigadier General Roderick J. Isler, the CIA officer in charge of intelligence support for military operations. John Hamre, the deputy defense secretary at the time of the attack, later told the *New York Times*, "This target came with an aura of authority because it came from the CIA."[142] Given the number of errors involved in the designation of the target, it is remarkable that the intended target was only about 400 yards away from the Chinese embassy, on a small side street.[143]

Just as there were officials in the U.S. government who knew that Al-Shifa had a legitimate function as a producer of medicines, so there were State Department and CIA officials who had been stationed in Belgrade until just before the bombing who knew perfectly well the new location of the Chinese embassy. None of them were consulted as part of the CIA's strike planning. In the Al-Shifa case, whether the factory was or was not a legitimate pharmaceutical plant was a central question for strike planners. Not so in the case of the embassy bombing in Belgrade. As Tenet put it, "the location of the Chinese Embassy was not a question that anyone reasonably would have asked when assembling this particular target package. . . . We were not looking for it."[144] The job of identifying what not to bomb, according to Tenet, was not an operational matter. If it were not done ahead of time, it would not be done at all.

BAD LUCK

The CIA came close to avoiding the destruction of the Chinese embassy. By chance, a mid-level intelligence officer detailed to the CIA from the National Security Agency but not involved in target planning learned of the CIA "nomination" of the Federal Directorate of Supply and Procurement headquarters for destruction. Equally by chance, this officer knew something about the directorate and recalled having seen information a few years earlier placing that building in a slightly different location from the one the CIA was proposing to bomb. Unaware that the strike had been scheduled for May 7, 1999, the intelligence officer on May 4 contacted a military officer responsible for the target at NATO's Joint Task Force headquarters in Naples, Italy. The intelligence officer did not realize that the targeted coordinates were the site of the Chinese embassy. Rather, he contended that a site identified by the CIA as the Yugoslav directorate's headquarters was merely a support building, and that the headquarters was a few blocks away.

"He, in fact, thought that the building that was targeted was a valid military target," Pentagon spokesman Kenneth Bacon told reporters. "But he didn't think it was as high a value target or as lucrative a target as the Federal Directorate of Supply and Procurement." As recounted by Bacon, the message from the intelligence offer at CIA headquarters to the strike planner in Italy was, "I believe you're going after an appropriate target, but maybe not the best target." The military officer in Italy, according to Bacon, "thought that the CIA analyst was questioning whether the target was labeled correctly."[145]

The intelligence officer tried to arrange a meeting at CIA headquarters with agency officials supporting the Kosovo mission, but without success. Additional information gathered by the intelligence officer only raised his concerns, but he did not immediately convey them before departing for a two-day training program May 6 and 7. The officer returned to CIA headquarters the afternoon of Friday, May 7, to find that the procurement directorate was on that night's target list. The laws governing things that can go wrong remained in effect. The intelligence officer was unable to reach the military officer he had spoken to three days earlier and had to explain his concerns to another strike planner in Naples. Officials at the air operations center interviewed after the fact during the CIA investigation into what went wrong reported that they believed the intelligence officer was telling them that the targeted location was indeed part of the directorate, just not the headquarters building. The intelligence officer took his concerns across rather than up the chain of command. This was an unfortunate choice. While going directly to the NATO command in Naples, Italy, made sense from the point of view of getting quick action from the people making the final call, the officer failed to grasp that key strike decisions were being made at a much higher level, namely, the White House. Almost as the conversations between Langley and Naples were taking place, a brace of 2,000-pound satellite-guided bombs was zeroing in on the Chinese embassy.[146]

THE MISSION

In the predawn hours of May 7, 1999, a single B-2 "Spirit" bomber took off from Whiteman Air Force Base in Missouri for the fifteen-hour flight to Belgrade.[147] The highly trained two-member crew, the radar-evading "stealth" plane they flew, and the payload of satellite-guided 2,000-pound bombs represented the cutting edge of U.S. air power. With an average delivery cost of $2 billion, the B-2 bomber's price tag was the highest ever for an airplane and closer to what the Pentagon was accustomed to paying for a Navy destroyer or submarine than for a warplane. In its initial schemes, dating back to the Cold War, the Air Force had planned to deploy multiple wings of B-2 bombers, their mission to penetrate Soviet radar and deliver nuclear weapons. The Air Force had taken to naming the bombers after states, prompting defense analyst John Pike of Globalsecurity.org to quip that the Air Force was hinting it at how many bombers it wanted: "This would seem to place an upper limit of 50 on the number of aircraft that can eventually be expected to be produced," Pike observed, "though one imagines that additional states can be admitted to the Union if the need arises."[148]

With the steady decline of defense spending that started late in the Reagan administration and continued through the Soviet breakup and the push to balance the budget in the 1990s, Congress choked on the B-2's price tag and uncertain mission and cut the program off at twenty-one aircraft.

The Kosovo campaign represented the unlikely combat debut of the B-2 eight years after the breakup of the Soviet Union. The Air Force reserved the bat-winged B-2 for particularly sensitive missions in the Kosovo crisis, such as attacking heavily defended targets in and around Belgrade in relative safety thanks to its radar-evading shapes and surface coatings.

The thirty-hour mission involved two midair refuelings en route and two more on the return. The designers of the B-2 had made little provision for creature comforts. As with virtually all warplanes in the U.S. arsenal, the interior was functional and cramped. Confronting the prospect of round-the-clock missions in a cockpit seat, B-2 crews at Whiteman developed a low-tech scheme for solving the rest problem on this most high-tech of aircraft. It was a cheap lounge chair bought at a local hardware store that just fit the crawl space behind the pilot seats.[149]

In the bomb-bay of the B-2 for missions to Yugoslavia were up to sixteen GBU-31s, which are MK-84 2,000-pound fragmentation bombs fitted with JDAM satellite guidance systems. Translated at least somewhat out of

Pentagon-ese, that refers to a bomb load of sixteen so-called guided-bomb units consisting of the bomb itself, in this case the Mark-84, jacketed with a Joint Direct Attack Munitions guidance kit. The JDAM is a fairly inexpensive way of turning a dumb bomb into a smart bomb. Developed in the mid-1990s after the spectacular performance of precision-guided munitions during the 1991 Persian Gulf War, the JDAM consists of a tail fin assembly that jackets the bomb and two guidance systems that can deliver the weapon accurately at night and in adverse weather. The B-2 that departed Whiteman on May 7, 1999, had in its on-board computer the coordinates of what the CIA had calculated as the location of Bulevar Umetnosti 2. The same information was entered into the memory of the global positioning system and inertial navigation system guidance devices on the bombs. Late-developing information on new or corrected target coordinates could be dispatched to the bomber in-flight and the bombs reprogrammed for different targets. Through umbilical connections to each of the bombs, the weapons also received constantly updated information on the precise location of the bomber itself. The mission of the B-2 crew was to fly the aircraft into airspace the Air Force calls a "launch acceptable region" within which the bomb can be dropped with enough falling time to use its adjustable fins to guide itself into the target. Depending on the altitude, speed, and flight angle of the plane, a 2,000-pound JDAM can be dropped up to fifteen miles from its target.[150] As the bomber approaches, its synthetic aperture radar can cast a beam at the target and process the reflections into an image that gives a near-photographic representation of the building shapes and sizes. Those images are then checked against the target images brought by the crew.[151] Upon release, the GPS equipment on the weapon checks its position relative to the target and signals for adjustments in the fins. If this works, and in the Kosovo campaign it almost always did, the bomb falls within forty-three feet of its target.[152]

Unfortunately for the Clinton administration and the CIA, the attack on the Chinese embassy turned out to be no exception.

THE STRIKE

The possibility that a stray bomb might hit their embassy in Belgrade had occurred to the Chinese as far back as late March, when NATO tactics shifted from a focus on deployed Serb forces in Kosovo to strategic targets throughout Yugoslavia. Routine precautions, including sending most embassy staff home and housing others in a basement area, paid off at 11:46 p.m., Belgrade time,

May 7, 1999, when the single B-2 bomber, having arrived from Whiteman at its launch-acceptable region, released five MK-84s fitted with JDAMs aimed at a glass-and-concrete building complex five and six stories high.[153] Most of the thirty embassy staffers and relatives still at the compound for the night had gone to bed in the basement as a precaution against what had become nightly air attacks on targets in Belgrade. One, possibly two, of the bombs did not detonate, which probably saved at least a dozen lives. The bombs hit the embassy complex at different points, a feature of air strikes launched by B-2s using JDAMS. One bomb that failed to detonate was recovered from an area directly below the ambassador's office. Another bomb exploded between the main embassy building and the ambassador's residence. Two bombs hit close together on the embassy's roof and plunged to the ground floor. A fifth hit the embassy just below the roof line along a side wall.[154]

Initial news reports described ear-splitting explosions that shattered windows up to 400 yards away. Eyewitnesses were under the impression that the embassy had been attacked by guided missiles, not bombs. One of the bombs demolished a military and intelligence section of the embassy and seriously injured the embassy's military attaché, Ven Bo Koy. It was in this section of the embassy that the three people killed by the bombing were found, journalists Shao Yunhuan and Xu Xinghu and Xu's wife, Zhu Ying. Chinese media reported that the journalists were covering the war and using the embassy's facilities to file stories.[155] U.S. officials later suggested privately that at least two of the three victims were actually intelligence officers, a claim the Chinese denied.[156]

Reaction in Beijing was instantaneous. China accused the United States of deliberately destroying its embassy, an ominous charge implying that one nuclear power had committed a deliberate act of war on another. Secretary of State Madeleine Albright telephoned Pickering, the No. 3 official at State, seeking advice on whether they should go to the Chinese embassy in Washington to immediately offer regrets and whatever explanation they could develop on short notice. The two diplomats, joined by Air Force General Joseph Ralston, vice chairman of the Joint Chiefs of Staff, did go to the embassy that night. As they left a short and uncomfortable session with the Chinese, the three were confronted by what Pickering described as "a group of Chinese newspaper people who were very unruly." The Americans had not brought any security detail with them, and Ralston and Pickering had to push their way through to get Albright out safely.[157]

In the initial aftermath of the bombing, neither the Pentagon nor the CIA was clear on what had happened. The intelligence officer who had worried about the CIA having mislocated the Yugoslav supply directorate in its target planning did not immediately make the connection when he heard news reports about the embassy bombing; like other military and intelligence officers, he assumed the incident was an errant bomb, and he did not understand that the mission that destroyed the embassy was the very one about which he had been raising concerns.[158]

Many features of the incident—the CIA's unique involvement in choosing this target; the use of a U.S.-based B-2 in the attack; reports that part of the embassy destroyed in the attack housed intelligence and military offices; the general accuracy of the NATO raids; and the fact that this was the first foreign embassy hit in the Kosovo campaign—contributed to suspicion in China that the strike had been deliberate. At least one Western news organization, Britain's *Guardian* newspaper, alleged that the Pentagon suspected the Chinese of allowing the Serbs to use embassy facilities to transmit signals to deployed Serb forces—the Serbs' own military communications links having been severed by NATO raids—possibly in exchange for information to Beijing on how the Serbs managed to down a U.S. F-117 Stealth fighter on March 27, 1999.[159]

Beijing did nothing to quell these rumors, opting to exploit the errant bombing for whatever diplomatic advantage it could get.[160] The Chinese government had been hostile to the NATO operation in Kosovo to begin with, viewing it as a hegemonic move by the West into Russia's traditional sphere of influence, with a presumed move farther into Asia as a logical follow-up. In this context, some Chinese commentators saw the strike as punishment of Beijing for its hostility to the operation, and even as a relatively safe way to test Chinese reaction to a military provocation.

Beijing evinced greater faith in the competence of the CIA than did the Agency's own leadership. The Chinese regarded such a blunder as too colossal for the CIA, and the meticulous care behind NATO's strike planning undermined the notion of the embassy bombing as an accident.[161] U.S. imagery intelligence analysts surely noticed that the intended target looked more like a formal office building with spacious grounds than the military warehouse described in papers presented to President Clinton, so the argument went. And the *Guardian* pointed out that no-strike lists maintained by NATO and Britain included the Chinese embassy in its correct location.

Even within U.S. military circles there were rumors suggesting possible motives for the embassy bombing. Unnamed U.S. officials, while rejecting allegations that the bombing had been intentional, told an investigative reporter with the *New York Times* that China's embassy in Belgrade was considered Beijing's major intelligence-collection base of operations for all of Europe. Military analyst William Arkin, a former Army intelligence officer, said he was told by a high-level U.S. intelligence source that the Serbs had given China parts of the F-117 Stealth fighter downed earlier in the campaign and that the embassy had been bombed to signal U.S. displeasure.[162] There is nothing in the public record to support these various charges and much to refute them. The investigation by the *New York Times* found that NATO and Britain both mislocated the Chinese embassy in their target databases, as had Washington. It is neither sinister nor surprising that a European capital of a formerly communist country, but one that had distanced itself from Moscow, would serve as a European intelligence base for China. And U.S. military and intelligence officials, whether in public or on background, have reported no evidence that the embassy stood in as a Serb military communications platform, or even had the proper equipment to do so. The point in describing the persistence of such rumors is to highlight the seismic shock of this major intelligence failure and add weight to the contention that the targeting error in the Chinese embassy case cast a shadow over subsequent deliberations when opportunities to target bin Laden arose.

THE AFTERMATH

Adding to the considerable embarrassment centered at the CIA following the embassy bombing was the fact that the May 7 target was the only one of the entire Kosovo campaign selected by the Agency. Nominations for the roughly 900 other targets struck had come from the Pentagon or NATO. It was not the only target the CIA had planned to nominate. At least two other CIA-selected targets were in the pipeline, but immediately after the embassy bombing the CIA suspended participation in targeting for the Kosovo campaign as it tried to sort out what had gone wrong.[163]

The NATO high command, meanwhile, revamped its targeting procedures to reduce the chances of another mistake. General Wesley Clark, the overall commander, also temporarily halted attacks on targets in Belgrade and strategic targets such as bridges, roads, and power plants. New rapid-response procedures were instituted for updating no-strike lists.[164]

While struggling to assure Beijing that the incident was an accident, the State Department also had to cope with violent demonstrations in China that threatened the safety of U.S. diplomats. For three consecutive days demonstrators threw stones, paint, and eggs at the U.S. embassy in Beijing; Ambassador James Sasser and other embassy staff were, for a time, reportedly trapped in the compound. The Clinton administration, seeking to calm things down, said Sasser wasn't trapped but had simply decided to stay because there was important work to be done.[165] Beijing suspended human rights and arms control talks with Washington and demanded a formal apology even after President Clinton had already apologized. The White House struggled to justify the continuing bombing campaign in Yugoslavia amid the furor: "Again I want to say to the Chinese people and to the leaders of China, I apologize. I regret this," Clinton said. "But I think it is very important to draw a clear distinction between a tragic mistake and a deliberate act of ethnic cleansing, and the United States will continue to make that distinction."[166]

Into this environment, Pickering led a delegation of six senior U.S. officials to Beijing's Foreign Ministry in June 1999 to formally brief the Chinese government on the findings of an internal U.S. investigation of the errant bombing. The meeting began at 8 a.m. and lasted six hours. "The Chinese had a spiel, and the spiel was, 'We don't believe you,'" Pickering recalled. Beginning on that discouraging note, Pickering proceeded to walk the Chinese through what even he conceded was an unbelievable story of out-of-date maps and databases, faulty targeting procedure, and missed signals on the eve of the bombing. "They asked a lot of questions. They were very disciplined—no ranting or raving," Pickering said in an interview. Perhaps concluding that he had little to lose, Pickering at one point tried humor—and it worked. "I said if we were making this up, this was certainly the most convoluted story we could possibly manage, that we'd certainly have come up with something more plausible," Pickering said. "They laughed a little bit." The most important thing he brought to the meeting was not the detailed story of intelligence failure but a reiteration of President Clinton's apology. A formal presidential apology is a rare thing, and even the Chinese could not ignore it. Back at the U.S. embassy that evening, a staff member brought Pickering a Chinese press statement issued after the meeting. It was a four-paragraph recitation of what had happened in the meeting, quite accurate and without editorial comment from the Chinese government. The meeting had been a success for the Americans, if that word can be used. It was, Pickering said, "the only ratification we were going to get" of Chinese acceptance of the American explanation.[167]

REPERCUSSIONS

The Pentagon tabulated thirty instances of unintended damage in the Kosovo campaign. Of those, ten involved attacks that unintentionally killed civilians while damaging the intended target; three involved human error in identifying the intended target; two involved mechanical failure or malfunction; fourteen involved either human error or mechanical failure. The Chinese embassy bombing was the only instance in the seventy-eight-day campaign in which NATO hit the target it aimed at, but had aimed at the wrong target.[168] Overall, the Kosovo campaign was remarkable for how little collateral damage it inflicted, considering the scale and duration of the campaign. As the Pentagon reported to Congress, "No military operation of such size has ever inflicted less damage on unintended targets. And all of this was accomplished without a single combat fatality to NATO forces—an incredible and unprecedented achievement for an operation of this scale."[169] Of course this fact tended to work against the Clinton administration, making it all the harder to claim that the embassy bombing was an accident.

Just under a year later, CIA Director George Tenet fired one agency officer and disciplined six others in connection with what CIA spokesman Bill Harlow said was "clearly a tragic accident."[170] An internal investigation by then–CIA Inspector General L. Britt Snider found that "numerous CIA officers at all levels of responsibility" had failed to ensure that the intended target had been correctly located before the targeting information had been forwarded to the military. Of all the intelligence failures on his watch before the failures concerning Iraq and weapons of mass destruction, this one affected Tenet the most, according to Snider, a friend of the director. "It was a major error," a rueful Tenet told the House Intelligence Committee. "I cannot minimize the significance of this."[171]

ANOTHER CHANCE TO GET BIN LADEN

On May 14, 1999, exactly one week after the bombing of the Chinese embassy, the CIA began receiving another flurry of intelligence on the precise whereabouts of Osama bin Laden. Multiple human intelligence sources reporting through the CIA team on the ground in Afghanistan placed bin Laden in or near Kandahar in eastern Afghanistan. By May 25, the CIA's deputy director, John Gordon, sitting in for Tenet, who was traveling, was briefing the "Principals Committee"—Clinton's team of senior national security advisers—that the Agency was confident of bin Laden's location, and the Navy was standing by to launch cruise missiles. While there would always be uncertainties in such circumstances, the intelligence on bin Laden's location was about as solid as they were ever likely to see, Gordon reported. The CIA people in the field who were producing the intelligence, and the military people using it to prepare the strike, were convinced.

"This was in our strike zone," John Maher III told the 9/11 Commission five years later. Bin Laden, he said, "should have been a dead man."[172] The commission would call this "the last, and most likely the best, opportunity" to kill bin Laden with a missile strike that would arise prior to the September 11 attacks.

Aboard one of the submarines that had been ordered to remain on station in the Arabian Sea for just such a contingency, the "missiles were spinning in their tubes," to use the jargon for final preparation for a cruise-missile launch. Over a span of a day and a half, the CIA three times had a precise fix on bin Laden's location and in each instance the Agency field team recommended attack. Finally, as in the other instances since the Al-Shifa bombing and the strike on the Afghan training camps in 1998, word came back from the White House: there would be no strike.

Still reeling from the aftermath of the Chinese embassy bombing, neither Tenet nor the White House was prepared to launch another military attack based on CIA-generated intelligence. After 9/11, no one was particularly eager to claim credit for a decision that was ultimately Clinton's to make. Gary Schroen, the CIA station chief in Pakistan and the person responsible for the effort to find bin Laden, says that in the desert camp episode it was Clarke who was dubious about launching missiles, while Tenet was pushing hard for action.[173] In the Kandahar case, as in the past instances when the principals considered launching missiles against bin Laden, Berger recalls that it was Tenet who had the most doubts. Tenet could not recall details of the Kandahar episode in conversations with the 9/11 Commission other than to say that the reporting on bin Laden's whereabouts came from a single source. The commission report contradicts Tenet on this point, asserting that the CIA had "very detailed" reporting that came from "several" sources.[174]

Regardless of which senior official leaned most heavily against the option of striking, the overall theme was unmistakable: the decision not to attempt a strike on bin Laden derived from a lack of confidence in the quality and accuracy of the intelligence. The concern was twofold: that the United States would miss bin Laden and appear to the world a toothless giant while ennobling the al-Qaeda leader; and that the attack would kill many innocent civilians and appear to be nothing more than a sophisticated act of terrorism.

But where the picture presented was of low confidence in intelligence leading to concern over the consequences of shooting and missing, the actual sequence appears to have been the other way around. That is, the political consequences of previous intelligence failures fueled a lack of confidence in fresh intelligence. Cohen, testifying before the 9/11 Commission, asserted, "The military gun was cocked for an extended period, but only once was the intelligence adequate to pull the trigger." In the subsequent instances in which the CIA believed it had a fix on bin Laden, the information "was often from sources of questionable credibility, frequently fragmentary and packaged in inference."[175] Albright had similar recollections. The intelligence reported where bin Laden had been recently or where he was at the moment, or, in some cases, reported on the location of someone who looked like him. "It was truly maddening," she told the 9/11 Commission.[176] While the CIA undoubtedly collected dubious information on bin Laden's whereabouts, the instances described here in which the Clinton administration considered ordering a strike sprang from intelligence reporting that was detailed and persistent.

The CIA was caught in a cycle of error, embarrassment, and hesitation. Poor intelligence procedures contributed to faulty decisions that drew public criticism and in turn fueled painful after-action review at the CIA so that when new intelligence flowed in, neither the CIA's leadership nor the White House was prepared to act. In Khartoum, eastern Afghanistan, and Belgrade, the CIA had aimed America's gun and missed badly.

8 THE MALAYSIA MEETING
Tracking the Hijackers

MOHAMMED RASHED DAOUD AL OWHALI was supposed to die on the morning of August 7, 1998, but at the last moment he decided to live. At 9:19 that morning, from a hotel in Nairobi, Kenya, Owhali telephoned what was to have been his final good-bye to a comrade-in-arms at a number in Sana'a, Yemen. The slim, 21-year-old Owhali, born in Liverpool, England, to a wealthy Saudi family, schooled in fundamentalist Islam, and hardened by fighting for the Taliban in Afghanistan, had asked al-Qaeda leader Osama bin Laden for a martyrdom assignment. After Owhali fought bravely in the Taliban's struggle to control Afghanistan, bin Laden personally chose him for a key role in a suicide bombing mission targeting the U.S. embassy in Nairobi. Bin Laden ordered him to coordinate his work through Ahmed al-Hada, whom he had fought beside in Afghanistan. It was al-Hada's number that Owhali called on the morning of August 7, the day of the attacks on the U.S. embassies in Nairobi and Dar es Salaam, Tanzania.[1] Bin Laden had dubbed the Nairobi attack the Holy Ka'ba Operation, after the sacred, black-draped stone cube at the center of the Great Mosque of Mecca. He had chosen August 7 in order to send a message. The date marked the eighth anniversary of the arrival of the first U.S. troops in Saudi Arabia, the seat of Islam, in response to the Iraqi invasion of Kuwait five days earlier on August 2, 1990. The presence of infidel troops in the Muslim holy land was an affront that the jihadists led by bin Laden were prepared to kill to rectify. It also presented bin Laden and his nascent terror group with a new superpower foil to replace the vanquished Soviets, who had departed Afghanistan in 1989. Attacking the U.S. embassy in

Nairobi served bin Laden's purposes in multiple ways. In the early 1990s it had been the United States' diplomatic base of operations in support of the troop deployment to Somalia. In October 1993, that humanitarian effort had turned into a deadly clash between U.S. Army Rangers and Somali fighters backed, unbeknownst to Washington at the time, by al-Qaeda. In the mid-1990s, most of the U.S. embassy staff in Khartoum, Sudan, had relocated to Nairobi in response to growing fears of a terrorist attack. Bin Laden had operated out of Khartoum in the early to mid-1990s until the Sudanese government, under U.S. pressure, had evicted him. Finally, Nairobi and Dar es Salaam were easy logistical reaches for al-Qaeda, close to Sudan and the Gulf states from which the terror group drew its forces, yet outside the Muslim world, making them more comfortable places to mount attacks that would almost certainly kill many innocents.[2]

Owhali's assignment was to ride shotgun in a stubby Toyota Dyna truck driven by a fellow al-Qaeda operative, Jihad Mohammed Ali, also known as Azzam. Once at the embassy, Owhali was to leap out of the truck, force an embassy guard at gunpoint to raise the gate, and toss a few stun grenades to scatter passersby just before Azzam pushed the button that set off the bomb.[3] En route to the embassy, Owhali removed his jacket, forgetting that he had his gun in it, so that when he went into action he had only the stun grenades, which he tossed ineffectually at the guard shack. Considering his mission accomplished and seeing no reason to die along with the victims of the attack, Owhali ran. He had just managed to round a corner at 10:35 a.m. local time when a 1,500-pound concoction of TNT and aluminum nitrate in the padlocked rear section of the truck erupted. Owhali's sudden will to live applied only to himself. The murder half of his murder-suicide mission went ahead more or less as planned. The blast killed 212 and wounded more than 4,000, most of them Kenyans. Among the dead were a dozen Americans and thirty-two Kenyan employees of the embassy. Four minutes later in Dar es Salaam, Tanzania, a similar bomb, this one surrounded with empty oxygen canisters that the attackers hoped would create more deadly shrapnel, exploded outside the U.S. embassy there in what bin Laden had labeled the "Al Aqsa Mosque Operation," after the mosque in Jerusalem that is the third-holiest site in Islam, after Mecca and Medina in Saudi Arabia. A nearby tanker truck blocked much of the force of that blast, limiting the toll to a dozen killed and eighty-five injured.[4]

Owhali's last-second decision to flee proved fateful for the CIA and the entire U.S. intelligence community. It set in motion a chain of events that would put

U.S. intelligence on the trail of two of the future 9/11 hijackers, including the second-in-command of the terror cell, bringing the Agency and the FBI very close to the core of the 9/11 plot. U.S. intelligence and law enforcement turned a scrap of information from Owhali into a massive, globe-spanning counter-terrorism operation that ended in a frustrating near-miss. U.S. intelligence failed to detect and stop the 9/11 plot because of multiple breakdowns within and between agencies. More important, U.S. intelligence failed to fully focus on the nature of the gathering terrorist threat, specifically its intention to strike the U.S. homeland. The intelligence community's terrorist tracking effort, beginning with a fragment of information from the suicide bomber who decided to live, continuing to a terrorist meeting in Malaysia in January 2000, and extending finally to a belated manhunt in the United States in the weeks before September 11, 2001, came to be seen as the signal intelligence failure of the 9/11 catastrophe.

The events set in motion by Owhali's arrest have been examined intensively by a multitude of government and outside investigative organizations and individuals. Yet as I will argue in this chapter, they remain misunderstood and oftentimes misinterpreted. The basic charge—that branches of the intelligence community failed to communicate with each other—is true, but it does not explain the critical failures that prevented a highly complex, and in many ways commendable tracking effort from succeeding. Arguably the critical failure lay not on the operations side, where tracking efforts of terror suspects reside, but on the analysis side in the failure by the CIA and the broader intelligence community to devote analytical resources to repeated in-depth looks at bin Laden and al-Qaeda. Such an effort might well have resulted in more effective counterterror operations, since they would have been informed by a deeper understanding of the adversary.

Beyond the story of the Malaysia meeting, other missteps by U.S. intelligence in the run-up to 9/11 have been documented. As noted earlier, there were missed chances to kill or capture bin Laden in Afghanistan. An FBI agent in Phoenix noticed suspicious patterns by Muslim men at flight schools. There were periodic intelligence reports, lacking any specificity, suggesting that al-Qaeda was interested in targeting planes for terrorist actions, possibly including suicide attacks. A French national, Zacarias Moussaoui, detained in Minneapolis by the FBI and immigration authorities, was in flight training and also a terror suspect before the September 11 attacks. However, that line of inquiry faltered when FBI headquarters ruled that prosecutors lacked probable cause to conduct a search of his computer.[5]

But the series of events that began with Owhali's decision not to be a martyr became the central focus of post-9/11 inquiry into what had gone wrong in the intelligence community before that tragic day. Multiple agencies, committees, and commissions found that a great deal had gone wrong as investigations revealed to the public the inner workings of recent intelligence operations to a level of detail unprecedented since the arrest of Aldrich Ames seven years earlier. The narrative as laid out by a joint congressional investigation, by the 9/11 Commission, and by several other official investigative bodies fit comfortably into the well-established storyline of post–Cold War intelligence oversight. It was a tale of bumbling, of tragicomic miscommunication, of failure—or refusal—to share information, and of interagency rivalry and the hoarding of vital information in "stovepipes" that kept it from the officials who needed it most.

The official critique of the intelligence community to emerge from this self-examination after the 9/11 attacks emphasized barriers, "walls," administrative obstacles, and institutional insularity as the main underlying features of the intelligence failure. The House-Senate Joint Inquiry Committee, which conducted the first major examination of 9/11 intelligence failures, focused on systemic problems built into the bureaucracy, particularly "serious problems in information sharing."[6] The shorthand version of the 9/11 Commission investigation was that U.S. intelligence and law enforcement agencies had failed to share information. It was a version of the Pearl Harbor critique: the government was in possession of vital intelligence about an impending attack, but the people best positioned to act on the information didn't receive it. The 9/11 Commission went somewhat beyond that surface conclusion, focusing on both a lack of information sharing and a lack of coordinated joint action:

> The agencies cooperated, some of the time. But even such cooperation as there was is not the same thing as joint action. When agencies cooperate, one defines the problem and seeks help with it. When they act jointly, the problem and options for action are defined differently from the start. Individuals from different backgrounds come together in analyzing a case and planning how to manage it.[7]

The verdict reached in media reporting and academic analysis bore much the same emphasis. *Newsweek* broke the story of the Malaysia meeting, under the headline, "The Hijackers We Let Escape," detailing the failure by the CIA to follow up on information it had in January 2000 indicating that at least one terror suspect tracked to Malaysia had a multiple-entry visa for travel to the United States.[8] Scholars such as Amy Zegart emphasized structural and institutional flaws in the U.S. intelligence system as the underlying cause of the failure to follow up on information from the Malaysia meeting.[9]

In fact, the terrorist tracking operation that would begin with Owhali was an extraordinarily complex example of interagency and international cooperation among intelligence and law enforcement organizations. Precisely because of its complexity and scope, stretching from Kenya to Yemen to Southeast Asia and to the United States, because of the number of organizations involved in sharing information, and because of the press of other events that at the time seemed just as important or even more important, the operation developed weak points that broke the flow of information. The result was that when the September 11 attacks occurred, U.S. intelligence already had extensive files on two of the hijackers, including surveillance photos of them taken at the Malaysia planning meeting some twenty months earlier. But it had no intelligence on the plot itself. The media, academic reporting, and government investigations were not wrong: there were severe breakdowns in the sharing of information between intelligence and law enforcement agencies. But as I will argue, the interagency coordination in this saga, despite all its faults, was quite impressive. The critical breakdowns happened *within*, not *between*, intelligence organizations. The operational failure, as in so many intelligence cases stretching back to the Cold War, started with a mindset failure. U.S. intelligence and law enforcement agencies, having taken up the trail of two future 9/11 hijackers based on information with roots tracing back to Owhali, failed to follow those hijackers to the United States until it was too late because they did not expect an attack in the United States. But for that mindset failure, many of the systemic or human problems contributing to the breakdown probably would not have occurred.

A PHONE NUMBER

A combination of chance and some good street work by the FBI turned Rashed Daoud al Owhali's decision to live into an operation that almost unraveled the 9/11 plot. Because Owhali decided to run only at the last minute, he did not escape injury in the explosion. Slammed to the ground by the blast, Owhali suffered lacerations to his forehead, back, and hands that required immediate medical attention. Because he had planned to die, he had no money, no passport, no arrangements for getting out of Kenya. He would need to turn to his contact in Yemen for help. At the M. P. Shah Hospital in Nairobi, Owhali realized that he still had three bullets in his pocket and a set of keys to the padlock of the rear section of the truck that held the bomb. In a hospital washroom, Owhali tried without success to flush them down a toilet, then washed the items to remove fingerprints and left them on a shelf in the men's room. His demeanor at the hospital and his early arrival—before victims of the blast started to pour in—touched off suspicion, as did his injuries. The wounds to his back might have been inflicted because he was simply a passerby, fortunate to be facing away from the explosion, but they were also consistent with injuries that might be suffered by someone who knew that a bomb was about to go off and was running for safety. The wounds, the trip to the hospital, the suspicious behavior, the items left in the men's room—all these drew attention. Leaving the hospital after receiving first aid, Owhali took a cab to the Ramada Hotel about a half-hour outside central Nairobi, a hotel where he had stayed for a day on August 2. He told the desk clerk that he had been a guest some days previously, had been injured in the bombing, and needed money on credit to pay for his cab and to get a room until he could wire relatives for more. This drew more attention and led to a call to a tip line, set up by Kenyan authorities after the bombing, reporting someone at the hotel who did not fit in. From his room, Owhali placed another call to the same number in Yemen that he had called the morning of the bombing, 967-1-200578. Concerned that the line was being tapped, he spoke cryptically about what had happened but conveyed the message that he needed money and help in getting out of Kenya. He asked al-Hada, his Yemen contact, to convey word to a Saudi named Khalid, who was an al-Qaeda trainer and his contact in Pakistan, that he had not become a martyr: "Tell Khalid I did not travel."[10] That was not the only call placed to the Yemen number that day. Another came in from a satellite phone known by the U.S. National Security Agency to have been used by Osama bin Laden.[11]

Within days of the attacks, the FBI dispatched some 375 agents, bomb experts, and crime-scene specialists to East Africa.[12] One of them, Special Agent John Anticev, came from the bureau's New York City field office, where he had become an expert on Islamic jihad and al-Qaeda through his work on the 1993 World Trade Center truck bombing case and the prosecution of Omar Abdel Rahman, the "Blind Sheik," who was convicted in 1995 of plotting to blow up New York City landmarks. Anticev arrived in Nairobi about a week after the first wave of U.S. investigators. His assignment was to handle the questioning of Mohammed Sadeeq Odeh, the al-Qaeda explosives expert who had helped build the bomb and fled Kenya the night before the attack with a bad passport that landed him in jail in Pakistan. (As we have seen, it was Odeh's arrest en route to a meeting with bin Laden that alerted the al-Qaeda leader to the probable compromise of his plans to confer with his key field operatives after the embassy bombings and led him to change his plans, with the result that the U.S. air strike on August 20, 1998, blew up tents and obstacle courses, but not the al-Qaeda leadership. For more on Odeh's arrest and interrogation, see Chapter 7.) After initial questioning in Karachi, Pakistan, about the false passport, Odeh was held over for further interrogation about the Nairobi embassy bombing. Pakistani authorities then handed Odeh over to their Kenyan counterparts, who turned him over to Anticev. In the meantime, investigators were getting nowhere with Owhali, though they strongly suspected him of involvement in the attack. They called in Anticev to try his luck.

"He said he had nothing to do with it. [But] none of his story really made all that much sense," Anticev recalled. Among other things, Owhali had checked out of his Nairobi hotel five days before the bombing, then checked back in hours afterward after being treated at the hospital, a move that drew the attention of hotel personnel and almost certainly helped bring about his arrest. "I wasn't getting anywhere in the interrogation, so I took it off-topic. I said, 'Did you get a chance to pray?' He said 'I prayed five times today.' I said, 'You're very devout.' He talked about Islamic religious personalities," names that Anticev knew from his earlier work but were little-known to the general public. Among the figures Anticev discussed with Owhali were Sayyid Qutb, one of the intellectual founders of the modern jihadist movement, and Abdullah Azzam, one of the leaders of the Arab Mujahadin in Afghanistan and an early ally of bin Laden.[13] To Anticev, Owhali came across as both knowledgeable about these figures and approving. Anticev asked if Owhali had fought in Afghanistan. "He said yes. Once he admitted that, I knew this is definitely our guy," Anticev said. "I asked where in Afghanistan. He said, 'I fought in Jalalabad,'" scene of particularly hard fighting in the post-Soviet Afghan civil war. "Then I knew, because Jalalabad is like Iwo Jima to us."[14]

Having gone through the roster of militant Islamic founding fathers, Anticev turned the conversation to bin Laden. Still wary, Owhali's eyes narrowed and he smiled slightly. Recalled Anticev, "That's when I put a pencil in his hand, slid a piece of paper next to him and raised my voice sternly, slapping my hand on the table, and told him to write down the first number he called when he returned to the hotel."[15] Owhali scribbled 967-1-200578, the number in Yemen that he had called on the morning of the bombing and the same one he called afterward as he sought to get money and help in getting out of Kenya.[16]

In an investigation already focused on al-Qaeda, Anticev hoped the number might lead to others involved in the embassy bombing plot. His question had been a shot in the dark that paid off. But not even Anticev understood the importance of the information Owhali had given him. Not until after the 9/11 attacks would he realize that this sliver of information, a single phone number, almost led to the cracking of the terror plot.[17]

The phone number that Anticev got from Owhali under interrogation opened up a mother lode of intelligence on al-Qaeda—so much that it became known as the "Yemen Switchboard." Armed with information Anticev had provided, U.S. intelligence would learn that Al-Hada, the man on the other end of the line, was a recruiter for Islamic jihad. He also turned out to be the father-in-law of Khalid al-Mihdhar, a future 9/11 hijacker. The National Security Agency, as it turned out, had already intercepted communications to this number in its monitoring of al-Qaeda operatives in Afghanistan, Pakistan, and East Africa, but did not fully understand the number's significance prior to the embassy bombings. As far back as August 1996, NSA had been continuously monitoring five Nairobi telephone lines used by suspected al-Qaeda operatives and through that monitoring had picked up the Yemen number.[18] But the events immediately following the African embassy bombings, particularly the realization that both Owhali, a terrorist field operative, and bin Laden, al-Qaeda's leader, had called the same number on the same day shortly after the bombings, identified it for the first time as a communications hub for terrorist operations. It was through this realization that sketchy information the NSA picked up in late December 1999 about people known only by their first names and planning to meet in Malaysia the next month drew the attention of the U.S. intelligence community. The cryptic conversations registered with U.S. intelligence because analysts knew that if a meeting was being discussed on *that* phone line, it was safe to assume that it was significant and had to do with al-Qaeda and terrorism.[19] The problem with most NSA intercepts involving terror suspects lies in separating routine communications from significant ones. The CIA can't possibly investigate every meeting being arranged by people being monitored by the NSA; most would turn out to have nothing to do with terrorism. Identification of the Yemen phone number as a terrorist switchboard was a critical piece of information. And it was while monitoring this switchboard in late December 1999 that the NSA, the electronic ears of the U.S. intelligence community, eavesdropped on phone calls about a meeting in Kuala Lumpur, Malaysia, that would turn out to be one of the key planning events for the 9/11 attacks.

INTERAGENCY COOPERATION

A year after the 9/11 attacks, Cofer Black, head of the CIA's Counter-Terrorism Center from 1999 to May 2002, made an observation to congressional investigators about the job of tracking and collecting intelligence on terrorists. "The essence of counterterrorism, the problem of counterterrorism," Black said, "is that the harder you work and the more effective you are, the more work you create for yourself."[20] That statement applies amply to the task that unfolded for the CIA and FBI at the end of 1999 with the arrival of intelligence from the NSA about the upcoming meeting in Kuala Lumpur. The popular understanding of the pre-9/11 intelligence failure—that the main fault lay in a failure of different intelligence branches to cooperate and share information—is belied by the narrative of the Malaysia meeting. The monitoring of this meeting, one of many operations under way during an increasingly active period for counterterrorism intelligence, involved extensive links among U.S. intelligence agencies and foreign governments. In the following timeline, the element to note is how many different U.S. and foreign government agencies become involved in this single operation. The breaks in the intelligence chain are discussed below:[21]

AUGUST 7, 1998. The U.S. embassies in Kenya and Tanzania are bombed in suicide truck attacks attributed almost immediately to al-Qaeda. The FBI is the lead U.S. government agency assigned to the investigation.

MID-AUGUST 1998. The FBI, with the Kenyan police, obtains the "Yemen Switchboard" number from interrogation of Owhali and shares it with other U.S. intelligence agencies, including the NSA.[22]

DECEMBER 29, 1999. The NSA, through surveillance of the Yemen number, reports to the CIA, FBI, and other intelligence branches information about the upcoming meeting in Malaysia, including plane ticket and travel itinerary of someone identified only as Khalid, and information on other participants, identified only as Nawaf and Khallad.[23] U.S. intelligence doesn't know it yet, but Khalid is Khalid al-Mihdhar, an al-Qaeda operative and son-in-law of

Ahmed al-Hada, owner of the Yemen phone number. NSA does not check its own database and overlooks the fact that it has on file from previous intercepts one Nawaf al-Hazmi, a suspected al-Qaeda operative.[24]

JANUARY 4, 2000. From the intercepts, Mihdhar is known to be planning to pass through Dubai, United Arab Emirates, en route from Yemen to Malaysia. The CIA Directorate of Operations' Counter-Terrorism Center works with UAE customs officials in Dubai and CIA personnel stationed there to obtain as much information on Khalid as possible. The CIA officers in Dubai obtain a photocopy of the passport of Khalid al-Mihdhar, whose itinerary matches that of the "Khalid" on the NSA intercept. The CIA's Dubai Station faxes copies of the passport to headquarters.[25]

JANUARY 5, 2000. Copies of the passport faxed to the Osama bin Laden unit of the CIA's Counter-Terrorism Center touch off CIA cable traffic, read by both CIA and FBI officers at CTC, discussing the Malaysia meeting and information that Mihdhar's passport contains a valid multiple-entry visa to the United States. U.S. consular officials in Jeddah, Saudi Arabia, where the visa was issued, verify the accuracy of reporting on Mihdhar's visa.[26]

JANUARY 5–8, 2000. Alerted by the CIA, Malaysia's secret police, the Special Branch, tails Mihdhar in Kuala Lumpur, taking photographs of him and others attending the meetings.[27]

JANUARY 8, 2000. Mihdhar and an associate, still identified only as "Nawaf," travel to Bangkok, Thailand. CIA-Malaysia alerts its counterparts in Thailand, but too late to catch the pair at the airport as they arrive. Thai authorities place Mihdhar on a travel watch list, and the CIA's Bangkok Station begins an unsuccessful search for him.[28]

JANUARY 2000. Nawaf, though not definitively identified, is believed to be Nawaf al-Hazmi. Saudi intelligence officials tell their U.S. counterparts that Mihdhar and Hazmi are al-Qaeda members.[29]

MARCH 5, 2000. CIA-Bangkok positively identifies Nawaf as Nawaf al-Hazmi but reports to headquarters that Hazmi has departed Thailand and traveled to Los Angeles on January 15. CIA headquarters takes no action on the information. In a significant failure by CIA-Bangkok, Mihdhar's presence on the same flight is not discovered; it will be learned later, in the summer of 2001, that he too went to Los Angeles, left the United States for the Mideast in June 2000, and returned, flying in to New York, on July 4, 2001.[30]

OCTOBER 12, 2000. The Aegis guided missile destroyer USS *Cole* is bombed in a suicide attack in Aden Harbor, Yemen, killing seventeen sailors. The attack is later attributed to al-Qaeda.

DECEMBER 16, 2000. A joint source of the CIA and FBI, probably in Afghanistan, identifies Khallad as mastermind of the Cole bombing.[31]

JANUARY 4, 2001. A follow-up meeting with the source yields to the CIA, but not the FBI, the information that the "Khallad" who organized the *Cole* attack also had attended the Kuala Lumpur meeting.[32]

AUGUST 21, 2001. An FBI review of CIA cables from the Malaysia meeting reveals that Mihdhar and Hazmi traveled to the United States after the meeting.[33]

AUGUST 24, 2001. At the behest of an FBI officer detailed to the CIA's Counter-Terrorism Center, the State Department places Mihdhar and his travel companions on a watch list. Immigration and customs officials are also alerted and confirm the likely presence of Hazmi and Mihdhar in the United States.[34]

AUGUST 29, 2001. The FBI's New York Field Office begins searching for Mihdhar and Hazmi.[35]

SEPTEMBER 11, 2001. Al-Qaeda attacks the United States.

This single tracking operation, sparked by the intercept of suspected terrorist phone conversations mentioning only first names, involved the coordination of at least six U.S. government agencies—NSA, CIA, FBI, State Department, Immigration and Naturalization Service, and U.S. Customs—and authorities from at least five foreign countries—Kenya, the United Arab Emirates, Saudi Arabia, Malaysia, and Thailand. Since we already know the end of the story, it hardly needs to be said that the coordination was far from perfect. A close reading of the above chronology reveals some of the flaws. Most glaring is the time lag between the acquisition of information that a terror suspect has a U.S. visa and the placement of that suspect's name on a terrorist watch list, so that if he crossed a border into or out of the United States, he could be stopped for questioning. United Arab Emirates customs officials in Dubai provided the CIA with a photocopy of Mihdhar's passport on January 4, 2000, including the U.S. visa.[36] His name was placed on the terror watch list on August 24, 2001, twenty months later. For this failure the CIA has issued an unambiguous mea culpa. Of perhaps even greater importance was the CIA's failure to stay on the trail of the terrorists after the Malaysia meeting. Word to the CIA's Bangkok Station that the Malaysia meeting participants were headed their way arrived too late to stop them at the Bangkok airport. But it arrived in plenty of time to enable the CIA and Thai authorities to be on the alert for their departure from Thailand. Mihdhar and Hazmi left Bangkok on January 15, 2000, for the United States. But the Bangkok CIA station did not report this fact until early March, a gap of nearly two months. Still more glaring, when the CIA's Bangkok station cabled headquarters on March 5, no one seems to have read the message. As a chagrined CIA Director George Tenet explained to lawmakers, the cable was labeled "information only," and his overworked counterterrorism staff had too many higher priorities to have time to read information-only cables:

> The cable that came in from the field at the time, sir, was labeled "information only," and I know that nobody read that cable. . . . Sir, we weren't aware of it when it came to headquarters. We couldn't have notified the [FBI]. Nobody read that cable in the March time frame. . . . Of course it should have been.[37]

Before we delve more deeply into these and other breaks in the pre-9/11 intelligence chain, let me briefly recount what we now know the Malaysia meeting was about from post-9/11 reconstructions based on intelligence information.

DRY RUN

Khalid al-Mihdhar and Nawaf al-Hazmi, both Saudi nationals born in the holy city of Mecca, joined al-Qaeda in the mid-1990s. Both went to Bosnia in 1995 to assist Bosnian Muslims in resisting Serb ethnic cleansing. Sometime between 1996 and 1998, Hazmi traveled to Afghanistan and swore allegiance to Osama bin Laden. He and his brother, Salem al-Hazmi, another of the 9/11 hijackers, fought for the Taliban in the late 1990s against the Northern Alliance, the coalition that would, with U.S. help, oust the Taliban from power in the fall of 2001 after the 9/11 attacks.[38] Mihdhar went to Afghanistan in 1996 to undergo al-Qaeda training and indoctrination at bin Laden's camps. He swore allegiance to the terror group in 1998.[39]

In March or April of 1999, bin Laden summoned Khalid Sheikh Mohammed, the lead planner of the 9/11 attacks, to a meeting outside Kandahar, Afghanistan, where the al-Qaeda leader said he had selected four operatives— Mihdhar, Hazmi, Khallad, and Abu Bara al-Yemeni—for what al-Qaeda was calling "the planes operation," then in the planning stages. Mihdhar, 24 at the time of the Malaysia meeting, and Hazmi, 23 at that time, had been bucking for assignment to a high-profile martyrdom attack. They were so eager to participate that they had obtained U.S. visas in Jeddah, Saudi Arabia, in April 1999, before they knew what mission they might be assigned.[40] Khallad was a nom de guerre of Tawfiq bin Attash; calls by Khallad to the Yemen Switchboard seeking to make contact with Mihdhar—calls intercepted by the NSA—later touched off U.S. tracking of the Malaysia meeting.

In the fall of 1999 the four went to al-Qaeda's Mes Aynak training camp at a former Russian copper mine near Kabul. The site was used by al-Qaeda for elite training and, in the wake of the August 20, 1998, U.S. strikes on the camps near Khowst, was the only al-Qaeda training center then operating in Afghanistan. In December, three of the four received training in Western culture under Khalid Sheikh Mohammed's tutelage in Karachi. Mihdhar did not attend for reasons that are still unclear. His non-attendance proved significant, as it required Khallad to seek him out by phone to coordinate their rendezvous in Malaysia, calls that alerted U.S. intelligence to the meeting. Khalid Sheikh Mohammed, or KSM, as the CIA came to call him, was developing a two-part suicide hijacking attack: part one was the 9/11 attacks, more or less as they happened; part two was other hijackings that were to take place in Southeast Asia at the same time. The Asian portion of the "planes operation" was later dropped because of the difficulties involved in coordinating hijackings a dozen time zones apart. But for the time being, the upcoming trip to Southeast Asia was intended to give the hijacker-trainees an opportunity to take several flights in the region and observe cabin crew and airport security procedures. The three were also shown movies built around hijacking dramas, though Khalid Sheikh Mohammed first had to figure out a way to cover up the female characters in the movies in deference to Islamic sensibilities. Kuala Lumpur was chosen as the meeting site for several reasons: citizens of Persian Gulf states were not required by Malaysia to obtain visas; it was a hub for flights in Southeast Asia; and Yazid Sufaat, a member of the radical Jamal Islamiya group, an al-Qaeda ally, was able to provide private accommodations for the meeting in his condominium in Kuala Lumpur. The Malaysian capital was also home to the Endolite clinic, which specialized in prosthetic limbs and had helped jihadis in the past with few questions asked. Khallad, who had lost his lower right leg in fighting in Afghanistan, scheduled an appointment.[41]

In mid-December 1999, their training complete, Khallad and Abu Bara flew from Pakistan to Malaysia; Hazmi joined them, also from Pakistan, on December 25. Mihdhar would make the trip in the first week of January, traveling from Yemen. It is unclear whether the Malaysia "meeting" was, in fact, a meeting or simply a resting place between flights around the region as the future hijackers studied air travel security procedures. For Khallad, the real work would occur on December 31, 1999, and New Year's Day, as he took flights from Kuala Lumpur to Bangkok, to Hong Kong, and back to Kuala Lumpur. Khallad, it would later turn out, was denied a U.S. visa and removed from the roster of 9/11 hijackers; he would go on to mastermind the attack on the USS *Cole* in October 2000 and was eventually arrested in Karachi, Pakistan, in April 2003. Still, Khallad played a significant role in the planning for 9/11. Under interrogation, Khallad said he had been able to get a box cutter past airport security consistently during the Southeast Asia trip by tucking the weapon into a shaving kit next to toothpaste and shaving cream containers with metal exteriors. He also carried art supplies to create a plausible reason for having a box cutter. That lone finding of Khallad's may have been the most significant development to come out of the Malaysia meeting, from the terrorists' point of view, since box cutters became the weapon of choice for the 9/11 hijackers in taking control of the planes.[42]

At this point, the participants knew that they had been assigned to a suicide mission involving hijacking airplanes and that at least one part of the attack was to take place in the United States. Khallad later told interrogators that he and Mihdhar, who would be second only to Mohamed Atta among the team of nineteen hijackers sent to the United States, speculated about hijacking planes and crashing them into buildings or holding passengers hostage.[43] Khallad briefed the other attendees on the results of his research into how to sneak box cutters onto a plane and about onboard routines of flight crews.[44]

The trip from Malaysia to Thailand was something of an accident. Khallad needed to meet with an al-Qaeda courier, Fahd al Quso, who would deliver $36,000 to distribute among the participants in the planes operation. That exchange was to have happened in Singapore, but Quso was unable to obtain a visa, so they met in Bangkok. As a result of this last-minute switch, the intelligence gathered by the NSA in December on the Malaysia meeting had included nothing about Thailand. That information gap proved important when the CIA, reacting with insufficient speed to the meeting participants' travel from Kuala Lumpur to Bangkok, lost the trail of the hijackers in Thailand. Some of the money delivered by Quso went to Mihdhar and Hazmi to finance their travel to the United States and cover living expenses once there. Thailand served as well as Singapore in fulfilling another purpose of the Southeast Asia trip: providing Mihdhar and Hazmi with a less suspicious point of origin for their travel to the United States than a Mideast country.[45] On January 15, 2000, Hazmi and

Mihdhar flew from Bangkok to Los Angeles, their passports stamped with U.S. B-1/B-2 multiple-entry visas good until July 14, 2000.[46] Hazmi and Mihdhar proceeded to San Diego, where they were assisted in finding an apartment by Omar al-Bayoumi, subject of an earlier FBI intelligence investigation that had subsequently been closed. The two eventually rented a room in a residence owned by an FBI "asset," or source, living under their own names with a phone number listed in Hazmi's name. They obtained drivers' licenses, took flying lessons, opened bank accounts, and obtained credit cards. In June 2000, Hazmi moved to Phoenix, where he stayed with another hijacker, Hani Hanjour; in April 2001, those two moved to New Jersey, where they stayed until the September 11 attacks.[47]

The day Hazmi moved to Phoenix, Mihdhar, against the wishes of KSM, left the United States on a Lufthansa flight from Los Angeles to Frankfurt and on to Oman. Khalid Sheikh Mohammed told interrogators after his post-9/11 arrest that he considered Mihdhar's decision to leave the United States and return shortly before the 9/11 attacks a serious breach of operational security. Unlike most of the 9/11 hijackers, who had been carefully selected for having records clean of any past terrorist associations, Mihdhar was known to Saudi authorities as a jihadist, a vulnerability of which al-Qaeda was aware, and he had been known to U.S. intelligence since January 2000. Mihdhar spent a year in the Mideast shuttling between Yemen and Afghanistan, apparently assisting in getting the non-pilot hijackers ready for their travel to the United States.[48] His visa expired, Mihdhar obtained another on June 13, 2001. Coincidentally, the visa was issued two days after FBI and CIA officials met in New York to discuss the Malaysia meeting in general and Mihdhar's travels in particular. But because his name was not on a terrorist watch list to alert State Department officials, Mihdhar got his visa and flew to New York on July 4, 2001. He had no trouble getting through U.S. Customs. As the *9/11 Commission Report* noted pointedly, "No one was looking for him."[49]

In fact, KSM's fears notwithstanding, Mihdhar's departure from and return to the United States in the year before 9/11 worked to al-Qaeda's advantage. In August 2001, with the FBI now belatedly focusing on the travel of Mihdhar and Hazmi to the United States following the Malaysia meeting, information in the Immigration and Naturalization Service database showing Mihdhar's yearlong absence led FBI intelligence officer Dina Corsi to assume that Hazmi had left the United States with Mihdhar in June 2000 and had, unlike Mihdhar, not returned. It was a mistaken assumption.[50]

EYES, BUT NOT EARS, ON THE TERRORISTS

Of the preceding sketch of the Malaysia meeting and its aftermath, U.S. intelligence was aware of only a small fraction, mainly having to do with the travel of the participants to and from Malaysia. The key gap in intelligence was about the purpose of the meeting, a gap the CIA never was able to close. CIA veteran Douglas MacEachin, who examined the Malaysia meeting as an investigator for the 9/11 Commission, said the CIA succeeded in putting eyes on the meeting, but not ears. The behavior of Mihdhar and his companions fit the profile of conspirators and confirmed the CIA's belief that the meeting was some sort of terrorist planning event: they made phone calls from pay phones and used Internet cafes rather than personal Internet connections. Working with Malaysian authorities, the CIA's Malaysia station had been prepared to plant listening devices in hotel rooms, assuming the travelers would be staying in hotels. The CIA had not counted on the four being hosted by Yazid Sufaat, the militant Jamal Islamiya member. Special Branch, the Malaysian secret police, tracked Mihdhar doggedly.

"They met him at the airport with cameras. They followed him to the meeting. They literally tracked these guys in and out of men's rooms," MacEachin said.

The photographs they obtained would prove valuable, particularly after the October 2000 bombing of the USS *Cole* in Yemen. Yemeni authorities briefly detained Khallad after the *Cole* bombing and got his mug shot. Though they released Khallad without understanding his role in the attack on the ship, the photograph proved valuable. From it, a joint CIA-FBI source was able to identify the man as a key operational planner of the attack. That same source later viewed the Malaysia surveillance photographs and spotted Khallad among the attendees. The importance of the Malaysia meeting thus grew in retrospect, but did so in a misleading way. The CIA mistakenly believed that the purpose of the Malaysia meeting was to plan the *Cole* attack. In one of the many frustrating miscues associated with these events, the FBI did not learn of Khallad's participation in the Malaysia meeting, even though an FBI officer attended the January 2001 interrogation of the joint source. The source was speaking a Middle Eastern language that the CIA interrogator understood but the FBI officer did not. It appears that the FBI officer was out of the interrogation room dealing with cumbersome translation and transcription duties when the source identified Khallad from one of the surveillance photos taken in Malaysia.[51] Khallad's *Cole* connection turned out to be unlucky for

U.S. intelligence in another respect: while underlining the importance of the Malaysia meeting and prompting U.S. intelligence to refocus on it in late 2000, the Cole link also reinforced the presumption that the Malaysia meeting had focused on terrorist actions on foreign soil.

Lacking any hard intelligence on the purpose of the meeting, the CIA was left to make guesses. The initial assumption was that the gathering had something to do with terrorist attacks around the turn of the millennium, with a focus on overseas attacks, particularly in Southeast Asia and Yemen.[52] This assumption does not appear to have been undermined by the discovery of a planned attack within the United States. In mid-December 1999, Ahmed Ressam, an Algerian jihadist, was arrested trying to cross the border from Canada into Washington state carrying bomb-making materials intended for an attack on Los Angeles International Airport. Later, the coincidence of Ressam's attempted millennium attack and the arrival of Mihdhar and Hazmi in Los Angeles in January 2000 suggested the possibility that the pair had somehow been involved in the LAX plot. As CIA Director Tenet told the House-Senate Joint Inquiry, success in thwarting the millennium plot contributed to failure in breaking up the 9/11 plot. Over the millennium, Tenet said, "There were no attacks. There were no Americans killed. We didn't have any hearings. We didn't talk about failures. We didn't talk about accountability. We just assumed the system would keep working because it prevented the last attack." The appropriate response within U.S. intelligence and law enforcement following the arrest of Ressam, Tenet acknowledged in retrospect, should have been growing concern rather than satisfaction. One lesson of the Ressam case was that vigilance, such as that shown by the alert Customs agent who stopped Ressam at the Canadian border, could thwart a terror plot. But the more important message was the desire of the jihadist movement to strike the U.S. homeland. "Hindsight is perfect," Tenet said, "but it is the one event that sticks in my mind."[53]

For months, the weight of intelligence indicated that the most likely terrorist scenario would involve an al-Qaeda attack on an overseas target. Linking the arrival of Mihdhar and Hazmi in Los Angeles to Ressam's millennium plot pointed the intelligence community in the right direction in that it suggested a domestic terrorist purpose to their travel—though, as it turned out, Mihdhar and Hazmi had no connection with Ressam. But the foiling of the millennium plot tended to lessen the concern about Mihdhar and Hazmi when the coincidence of their arrival in Los Angeles in January 2000 and the Ressam arrest a month earlier was finally noticed on August 21, 2001, by an FBI analyst reviewing old cable traffic at the CIA's Counter-Terrorism Center. The millennium threat had come and gone. And even in that critical August 2001 time period, less than a month before the September 11 attacks, with "the system blinking red," in Tenet's evocative phrase, the general mindset in U.S. intelligence revolved around finding Mihdhar—not before he struck in the United States but before he had a chance to leave U.S. territory for someplace where it would be harder to find him.[54] Some outstanding analytical work had gone into focusing the CIA and FBI's attention on the presence of terrorists on U.S. soil, particularly by the FBI analyst, a detailee to the CIA's Counter-Terrorism Center identified in government reports as "Mary" to protect her undercover status. But the intelligence community was too late in focusing on the U.S. travel of Mihdhar and Hazmi, a circumstance that arose from flaws in the handling of the Mihdhar-Hazmi intelligence at every step, from the NSA's first key intercept on December 29, 1999, until the 9/11 attacks. The period in late August and early September 2001, when the FBI learned and grasped the importance of their U.S. travel, was no exception. The search for the pair was opened at the "routine" level within the FBI. Its focus was on Mihdhar because of the mistaken assumption that Hazmi had left the United States and not returned. Indeed, other than technical immigration violations, there were no grounds to detain the two suspected al-Qaeda operatives. And because of a procedural concern that dated back to the Aldrich Ames spy case, the search was conducted not by the FBI criminal division, which could have devoted substantial nationwide manpower to the effort, but by the Bureau's intelligence branch. These officials took appropriate initial steps to find Mihdhar and Hazmi, post-9/11 reviews found, but the FBI was only beginning its effort, and not close to finding them, when they struck on September 11.[55]

ALDRICH AMES, "THE WALL," AND THE 9/11 ATTACKS

On October 9, 1993, the FBI, finally closing in on the long-sought CIA mole, searched the Arlington, Virginia, home of Aldrich Ames—the home Ames had bought for cash with his KGB earnings. Electronic surveillance of Ames's telephone had picked up plans by Ames and his wife, Rosario, to attend a wedding in Florida. A special team set up by the Bureau, working in coordination with CIA counterintelligence specialists, had been looking for an opportunity to search Ames's house. A month earlier, the FBI had secretly collected Ames's trash, switching sidewalk bins in the middle of the night, and found a draft message in the CIA officer's handwriting to his Russian contacts about a clandestine exchange. Now certain that Ames was a spy and, in all probability, the mole who had so thoroughly devastated the CIA's stable of Soviet human assets in 1985, the FBI carried out a "black bag" operation—a secret search—at the CIA officer's home. The take from the search was considerable, in part thanks to Ames's habitual sloppiness as a spy, whether working for the KGB or the CIA. A scrap of paper found in the pocket of a tobacco-stained jacket bore, in Ames's handwriting, the initials "A.B." and a Vienna phone number that rang the home of KGB officer Aleksandr Belinkov. The note, dated from 1991, before the Soviet breakup, was still in Ames's pocket two years later to be found and photographed by the FBI search team. The main body of incriminating evidence consisted of messages from Ames to his Soviet handlers extracted from the hard drive of Ames's laptop computer in files Ames thought he had deleted.[56]

The material gathered in the weekend search was a counterintelligence officer's dream, but not necessarily a prosecutor's. The search was conducted not under a standard warrant issued by a federal court but on the authority of Attorney General Janet Reno. Because of the obvious problem that an overt search would cause in alerting Ames—in all likelihood sparking a Russian intelligence extraction operation to get their most valuable spy out of the country—the FBI needed to search the home secretly.

The closest thing to a legal basis for such a secret search was the 1978 Foreign Intelligence Surveillance Act (FISA), which set up a special court to review clandestine surveillance being conducted against intelligence targets in the United States without standard court warrants. But the FISA law as it stood in 1993 covered electronic, not physical searches. Executive Order 12333, signed by President Reagan on December 4, 1981, empowered the attorney general to approve warrantless searches against "a foreign power or agent of a foreign power" inside the United States. But the constitutionality of this procedure for physical searches had not been tested in the courts.[57] The Clinton Justice Department's position was that the search of Ames's house was for intelligence, as opposed to criminal, purposes. At the time Reno approved the search, the case against Ames had not yet solidified sufficiently to be properly called a criminal probe. The Justice Department had likewise certified nine separate times to the FISA court that electronic surveillance of Ames was for intelligence purposes. Now all the evidence gathered from what had been, purportedly, an intelligence investigation conducted outside normal criminal procedures was to be used in a criminal prosecution.[58] According to L. Britt Snider, then the legal counsel for the Senate Select Committee on Intelligence, Reno had approved the search with great reluctance, concerned about jeopardizing the eventual prosecution of Ames.[59]

After Ames's arrest in February 1994, the legality of the October 1993 search of his home loomed as the central element of the defense being prepared by his attorney, Plato Cacheris. A veteran Washington trial lawyer, Cacheris urged his client to fight the charges, despite the weight of evidence, telling Ames there were "significant legal issues which in my judgment should be tested."[60] Ames, however, was not alone in legal jeopardy; Rosario, had been arrested at the same time. She had learned of her husband's espionage long before his arrest and had been caught on tape discussing his activities. Ames's desire to protect her from a long prison term undermined Cacheris's advice to bring the case to trial. Aware of their vulnerable position, prosecutors were eager to obtain a guilty plea and get a promise from Ames to cooperate in their assessment of the damage he had inflicted. Toward that end, federal prosecutors let Ames and his wife hear some of the incriminating surveillance tapes, whereupon she, not Ames, insisted that there not be a trial. That decided the issue for Ames; Rosario got a reduced sentence in exchange for Ames's guilty plea and promise to cooperate.[61]

Prosecutors were well aware of the vulnerability of their case at trial based on the unusual authority the FBI had invoked in conducting its searches. In a case already weighed down by a long list of spectacular failures of performance and procedure at both the CIA and the FBI, the possibility that the most damaging spy in CIA history might be acquitted on a technicality was painful to contemplate. After the Ames case, determined not to run that risk again, the Clinton administration won congressional approval in 1995 to amend the FISA law so that its secret investigative authority would cover physical searches.[62] However, the change in law did not eliminate the question of the potential damage that could be done to criminal prosecutions by actions taken under the auspices of an intelligence investigation. It was, in fact, only the beginning.

Even before Ames's arrest, Mary Lawton, head of the Justice Department's Office of Intelligence Policy Review, raised a concern that the FBI was asserting that its searches and surveillance in the Ames case were focused on foreign intelligence when the clear intent was to bring about a criminal prosecution.[63] Lawton's successor, Richard Scruggs, also voiced concern internally prior to

Ames's arrest about the lack of guidelines governing interaction of FBI intelligence officers with investigators in the criminal division. A judge might rule that none of the evidence collected against Ames under the auspices of an intelligence investigation could be used against him in a criminal prosecution, resulting in Ames going free. Scruggs proposed the concept of parallel investigations, where circumstances required, one criminal in focus, the other concerned with intelligence, and that a "Chinese wall" exist between the two so that a criminal prosecution would not be jeopardized by evidence collected by means that did not meet Fourth Amendment standards.[64] A bureaucratic squabble ensued over who should administer that wall, but there was little debate that there should be one. By early 1995 a new set of procedures was in place, drafted by Deputy Attorney General Jamie Gorelick, who would go on to be a member of the 9/11 Commission. Though they did not follow precisely what Scruggs had recommended, the procedures created new, formalized barriers between intelligence activity and criminal investigations at the FBI. Perhaps more important than the details of the rules was the sentiment behind them. Gorelick wrote that the new guidelines went "beyond what was legally required."[65] The serious concern over possibly losing the Ames case combined with the intense internal debate that accompanied the new rules created what a post-9/11 Justice Department examination termed an atmosphere of fear about crossing the line between intelligence and criminal probes, to the point that some FBI investigators said they worried that a mistake in this area could cost them their jobs.[66]

In this book I have discussed several examples of the profound impact of intelligence failure or perceived intelligence failure on the CIA's conclusions in subsequent cases. The unexpected Soviet invasion of Afghanistan in 1979 was followed by the expectation of military intervention in Poland the next year, which did not happen. The embarrassment over finding in 1991 that Iraq was much closer to building a nuclear weapon than the CIA had estimated contributed to the overestimation a decade later of Iraq's nuclear program. The gross overestimation of Iraqi military strength in 1991 led to an underestimation of the difficulty U.S. forces would encounter in Iraq after the 2003 invasion. An unexpected three-stage rocket launch by North Korea in 1998 pushed the CIA to amend its conclusion that rogue-state adversaries were fifteen years from developing intercontinental missiles and cleared the way for the national missile-defense program. And the failure to put together clues about al-Qaeda's pre-9/11 activity into a coherent picture of the devastating terrorist attack plan made it that much harder for the CIA to downplay the many clues—false clues, as it turned out—that Iraq had weapons of mass destruction.

The long-term legacy of the legal concerns surrounding the search of Ames's home is different in that insofar as prosecution of Ames was concerned, there was no underlying intelligence or national security failure. Ames was sent to prison for life, and prosecutors won his commitment to cooperate. Yet what might be called a near-miss intelligence failure—the possibility that, had the Ames case gone to trial he might have won acquittal by challenging the legality of the search—was enough to spark a shift in intelligence and law enforcement policy that would have long-term consequences, creating what came to be known as "the wall."

As played out in the tracking of Hazmi and Mihdhar in 2000 and 2001, the problem was not the wall between intelligence and criminal investigations as envisioned by the Clinton Justice Department but the wall as overzealously applied to the case of the al-Qaeda plotters by participants on both the criminal and intelligence sides. The most famous example uncovered by the 9/11 Commission as well as earlier probes of the terror attacks occurred in a June 11, 2001, meeting at the FBI's New York Field Office between CIA and FBI intelligence officers working on terrorism and FBI criminal investigators working on the USS *Cole* case. In that meeting, called for the express purpose of exchanging information between officials working on the terrorist threat in different agencies, an FBI intelligence specialist refused to share with the FBI's *Cole* criminal investigators detailed information about the CIA's surveillance of the Malaysia meeting. After 9/11, it appeared that this strict adherence to the rules separating intelligence and criminal work might have prevented the *Cole* prosecutors from learning about Mihdhar's U.S. visa and also about the identification of Khallad, a key suspect in the *Cole* bombing, as an attendee of the Malaysia meeting. There is some disagreement about whether the FBI intelligence officer deliberately withheld this information or simply didn't know it. But a CIA terrorism analyst with detailed knowledge of the intelligence on the Malaysia meeting also attended the New York gathering and did not disclose what he knew to the criminal investigators, later telling post-9/11 investigators that he was not authorized to share CIA information with criminal investigators.[67]

After 9/11, the priority was not to avoid jeopardizing criminal prosecutions but to uncover plans for terrorist attacks before they happened. Considered in that context, the pre-9/11 withholding of information to the *Cole* investigators was important not so much as a barrier to their solving the case or as a way of preserving the integrity of an eventual criminal prosecution in the ship bombing. In the post-9/11 context, the dismay over the New York meeting stemmed from the missed opportunity for the *Cole* criminal investigators, with their special knowledge of the details of that al-Qaeda operation, to have seized on the importance of elements of the Malaysia meeting intelligence that were not fully understood by the intelligence analysts.

This was but one of several episodes in which the wall, which appeared in so many forms that one FBI officer referred to it as a "maze," affected the tracking of Mihdhar and Hazmi. The wall was a barrier in both directions.[68] With the ostensible goal of protecting the integrity of potential criminal prosecutions, it may have, as in the example of the June 11, 2001, CIA-FBI meeting, kept important intelligence information from criminal prosecutors. In the case of the joint CIA-FBI source who identified Khallad as attending the Malaysia meeting, the CIA was concerned that a valuable long-term intelligence source might be lost if forced to testify in a criminal prosecution.[69]

There were wall issues, as well, between the NSA and the FBI around the summer of 2001. The NSA was then requiring that intelligence-sharing with the FBI go through an extra approval procedure if the information the NSA was sharing involved a FISA warrant and hence came from intelligence-gathering rather than from a criminal investigation. When the NSA determined that sorting out such intelligence would slow down its delivery, it decided to impose the extra procedure on all the counterterrorism information provided to the FBI, including the material it had gathered in late 1999 and early 2000 relating to the Malaysia meeting. Among the valuable intelligence obscured behind the wall as set up by the NSA was the record of calls between the Yemen Switchboard and a number in San Diego—the phone listed in Hazmi's name.[70]

Yet another example of the wall impeding the tracking of Mihdhar and Hazmi occurred in August 2001, when intelligence and law enforcement finally focused on their travel to the United States. As already noted, in late August, with the FBI focused on Mihdhar's U.S. travel and uncertain about Hazmi's whereabouts, a debate arose within the FBI as to whether the intelligence or criminal division should handle the search. The debate became heated when Steve Bongardt, one of the lead FBI criminal investigators on the *Cole* case, received a forwarded e-mail, somewhat by accident, indicating that Mihdhar's presence in the United States would be investigated as an intelligence matter.[71] Bongardt emerges as one of the few officials involved in the

Mihdhar saga to cut through the false leads and the background noise and see clearly the danger implied by Mihdhar's presence in the United States. In an e-mail on August 29, 2001, two weeks before 9/11, Bongardt wrote to his counterparts on the intelligence side of the FBI:

> Where is the wall defined? . . . I think everyone is still confusing this issue. . . . someday someone will die—and wall or not—the public will not understand why we were not more effective and throwing every resource we had at certain "problems."[72]

It is telling that an FBI criminal investigator, whose prosecutions the "wall" was presumably designed to protect by preventing acquisition of evidence via means that could compromise a trial, reacted so vehemently against those very protections prior to 9/11. After the September 11 attacks, the concerns that motivated the Justice Department at the time of the Ames investigation faded into insignificance compared with the imperative of finding and stopping terrorists in the United States bent on inflicting attacks that would cause massive casualties. No one was eager at this point to defend the wall between intelligence and criminal investigations. Michael Rolince, head of the FBI's Washington field office, lamented in testimony a year after 9/11 that the difficulties of keeping intelligence and criminal probes separate were particularly acute in terrorism cases, where the process of approving the sharing of information "became so complex and convoluted that in some FBI field offices, FBI agents perceived walls where none actually existed." Senator Carl Levin (D-Mich.) among others, was incredulous after hearing testimony from Bongardt, Rolince, and others in this September 2002 hearing. "This is truly unbelievable, I've got to tell you all. This is extraordinary. This has got nothing to do with information which can't cross a wall. This has to do with leads which are not shared with the FBI, just simple leads, information which is so critical."[73]

THE 9/11 FAILURE, STRUCTURE VS. MINDSET

The public understanding of pre-9/11 intelligence failures—that there were critical breakdowns in information sharing between the FBI and CIA—is by no means wrong. There were numerous opportunities for the CIA, which knew much more about Mihdhar and Hazmi than the FBI, to share that knowledge with the FBI, opportunities missed either deliberately because of the wall or through apparent negligence. But as the above narrative already suggests, the most critical obstacles to the flow of information in the Mihdhar-Hazmi case existed *within* agencies, not *between* them. Here I discuss these instances and their significance:

- The NSA got the first critical intelligence about the Malaysia meeting by monitoring the Yemen Switchboard, but failed to check its own database, thus missing the possibility that the "Nawaf" whose name came up in pre-Malaysia conversations was Nawaf al-Hazmi, who had been identified through previous NSA intercepts as a likely al-Qaeda operative.

- The failure to track the pair from Malaysia to Thailand, the failure to find them once in Thailand, the delay of two months in reporting their departure from Thailand, and the failure of headquarters personnel to read the cable reporting that departure—all in early 2000—were entirely CIA failures. The systemic problem here was that the CIA Counter-Terrorism Center was responsible for tracking the participants in the Malaysia meeting, but the field work was being done by CIA officers who answered not to CTC but to its parent organization, the Directorate of Operations.

- The FBI had several officers working out of the CTC, presumably for the express purpose of making sure the Bureau was aware of all CIA intelligence relating to terrorism that might also interest the FBI. Yet because these officers had no clear set of procedures from FBI headquarters, they each defined their jobs differently, the result being that not every FBI officer in the CTC considered it his or her task to read all incoming CIA cable traffic. This problem was exacerbated by the tendency of CIA officers to believe that the presence of FBI officers in the Counter-Terrorism Center absolved the CIA of information-sharing duties, since the FBI officers were presumably taking care of that task themselves.[74]

- The controversy in August 2001 over whether the search for Mihdhar should be a criminal or intelligence probe occurred entirely within the FBI. The CIA information-sharing problems contributed to the delay in the FBI focusing on this mission, but were not part of the dispute over how the FBI should carry it out.

- And the CIA's failure to place Mihdhar and Hazmi on the State Department's terrorism watch list, while ostensibly an information-sharing matter, had to do with poor training and faulty procedures at the CIA, not institutional reluctance to share information with the State Department. A post-9/11 review of CIA intelligence reporting on terrorism identified nearly sixty individuals in addition to Mihdhar and Hazmi who should have been added to the watch list.[75]

A great deal of investigative energy after the 9/11 attacks went into apportioning blame between the FBI and CIA. Multiple probes focused on a flurry of cable traffic to and within the Counter-Terrorism Center around the time of the Malaysia meeting. The conclusion of the inquiries was that, protestations to the contrary, the CIA shared intelligence on Mihdhar's U.S. visa only with the FBI officers who worked side by side with CIA counterterrorism officers in the bin Laden unit within the Counter-Terrorism Center and who had daily access to CIA counterterror cable traffic; the CIA did not pass the intelligence on to other branches of the FBI.[76] A lone internal CIA memo in January 2000 claimed that the wider FBI had been fully briefed, but no documentary proof of this could be found.[77]

The common summary of the information-sharing issue surrounding the Malaysia meeting is that the CIA learned of Mihdhar's U.S. visa in January 2000 and did not share that information with the FBI until August 2001. The truth was worse than that. A detailed reading of the record indicates that the CIA *never* shared the visa information with the FBI outside the Counter-Terrorism Center. In August 2001, the Bureau learned of Mihdhar's travel to the United States not from the CIA but from one of its own, an FBI intelligence operations specialist assigned to the CIA's bin Laden unit. In mid-July 2001 this FBI officer, Margarette Gillespie, identified in public reports as "Mary," began a review of cable traffic on the Malaysia meeting dating back to January 2000. She did so at the behest of CIA official Tom Wilshire, a former chief of the bin Laden unit who was, by the summer of 2001, assigned to the FBI's International Terrorism Operations Section. Wilshire had conducted his own review and seized on the reporting indicating that Khallad had been at the Malaysia meeting, calling him "a major league killer" because of his known involvement in the *Cole* bombing. Wilshire did not share the substance of his own research with the FBI but did set Gillespie to work on a review of cable traffic. The key point is that, contrary to claims made to this day by the CIA, Gillespie *found* the cable traffic relating to Mihdhar's U.S. visa; it was not given to her by anyone at the CIA.[78] Gillespie's immediate realization of the implications of this discovery and her alert and proactive response set in motion the search for the terror suspects.

This point is important for reasons that go beyond apportioning blame between the FBI and CIA. There is no doubt that the CIA failed in not sharing the visa information. The CIA inspector general's post-9/11 investigation into the Malaysia meeting found that between fifty and sixty CIA officers read at least one of the Agency cables relating to the travel and visa information on the Malaysia meeting targets during the January–March 2000 timeframe; none saw fit to notify the FBI, whose responsibilities extended to threats within U.S. borders.[79] But we also know from electronic records that five FBI officers assigned to the CTC opened the computerized cables sent in January 2000 from the CIA's Dubai Station in the United Arab Emirates, including the cable reporting visa information from Mihdhar's photocopied passport.[80] In that sense, the FBI was aware of Mihdhar's travel information from the beginning.

The problem was that the intelligence never got beyond those five officers to the wider FBI. The CIA may be partially to blame, but not entirely. One FBI officer wrote a memo, called a Central Intelligence Report, on January 5, 2000, the first day the four al-Qaeda operatives met in Kuala Lumpur and the same day the CIA's counterterrorism officials in Washington viewed the cable from Dubai from the previous day's photocopying of Mihdhar's passport as he traveled to the meeting. Intending to send the memo to other branches of the FBI, the officer included in his report Mihdhar's full identity and passport and U.S. visa information. According to the electronic record, CIA's Wilshire, at that time in charge of the bin Laden unit, ordered this FBI officer to hold off disseminating the report to FBI headquarters, the Bureau's bin Laden unit, and the FBI's New York field office. The author of the report, later identified as Special Agent Doug Miller, checked back with Wilshire eight days later, asking in an e-mail, "Is this a go or should I remake it some way?" Wilshire did not respond, and the Central Intelligence Report was never sent to Miller's FBI colleagues at headquarters or in New York.[81] The CIA inspector general's probe of the matter concluded that Miller's cable was not sent to his colleagues elsewhere in the FBI, "Apparently because it was in the wrong format or needed editing."[82]

Clearly, then, this was an example not simply of passive failure to share information but of the CIA's active thwarting of information-sharing. What is remarkable about the episode is that none of the participants recalled anything about it after the September 11 attacks. Miller could not recall writing the report to his FBI colleagues; Wilshire could not recall ruling that it not be sent and, in retrospect, could come up with no reason why its dissemination should have been blocked. This theme, the inability of harried officers to recall detail, recurs throughout the Justice Department's highly detailed investigation of the Malaysia meeting, and the reason is clear: the particular events related to 9/11 existed in a torrent of information flowing through the counter-terrorism bureaucracies in the three years between the embassy bombings in Africa and the 9/11 attacks. U.S. intelligence realized that the Malaysia meeting was important, as scholar Amy Zegart has noted. But the U.S. visa information, while mentioned in CIA cables, was not seen by either FBI or CIA officers as a critically important element at the time and therefore was neither acted on nor recalled later by the people involved.[83]

Here we encounter a seeming contradiction. The usual reason given for refusal to share information between intelligence agencies has to do with the sensitivity of that information, perhaps the jealous protection of a source or the confidentiality of a sensitive investigation. Mihdhar's travel information seems to have fallen into a different category. The problem was not that the visa information was too sensitive to share, but that it was deemed insufficiently noteworthy to draw the focused attention of overworked counter-terrorism officials.

The official critique of the 9/11 intelligence failures has revolved largely around structural problems—particularly barriers to the sharing of information. And there were indeed substantial barriers. But the difference between what happened with Mihdhar's travel information in January 2000 and what happened in August 2001 is telling.

Between those two dates, there was absolutely no change in intelligence community structure, the "wall," or in the relationship between the FBI and CIA officers working side by side at the CIA's Counter-Terrorism Center. The key difference was that in August of 2001 an FBI analyst who read the same CIA cable traffic generated by the Malaysia meeting twenty months earlier realized its importance and took action. Encountering no obstacles from the CIA, she immediately reported her findings up through the FBI chain of command, and within eight days the belated and ultimately futile search for the future 9/11 hijackers was under way. Such was not the case among either CIA or FBI officers in January 2000. True, one FBI officer, Doug Miller, in January 2000 had tried to alert the wider FBI to the Malaysia intelligence and had been stopped by a CIA officer, Wilshire. But other than one follow-up query, there is no evidence that Miller thought his memo sufficiently important to demand that he be allowed to disseminate the information. And four FBI colleagues of Miller read the same cable traffic and did nothing to notify the Bureau. They, like Miller, could not recall reading it, although the electronic record proves that they opened the cables on their computer screens. The simple explanation is that in January 2000 the possibility that Mihdhar could travel legally to the United States did not stand out as a serious threat. In the summer of 2001, when the same information was read by a different FBI officer, it seemed serious. Working within the same bureaucratic restrictions as her colleagues, that officer notified the wider FBI. Nothing bureaucratic or procedural stood in her way.

The post-9/11 investigative focus on the Malaysia meeting proceeded from a certain line of reasoning: the CIA is responsible for *foreign* intelligence; it may occasionally acquire information pointing to a domestic threat of one kind or another; since domestic threats are not the CIA's responsibility, the Agency has an obligation to pass on such information to the organization that is responsible—in most cases, the FBI. A further assumption flowing from this logic is that if the CIA, with its gaze turned outward, fails to recognize the importance of a particular piece of intelligence pointing to a domestic threat, the FBI will do so since that's where its responsibilities lie. An anecdote from journalism comes to mind. Robert Thomson, a veteran *Washington Post* Metro editor and columnist, once half-seriously compared the area of responsibility of the paper's Metro desk with that of the National desk. "If it happens *outside* a building," he said, "it's ours." A similar assumption informed post-9/11 inquiries into CIA and FBI activities: if it happens outside the country, it's the CIA's; if a foreign threat spills over into the United States, it's the FBI's or, more recently, the Department of Homeland Security's. Having experienced innumerable situations in which one government agency or another failed to share information, the designers of the Counter-Terrorism Center, long before 9/11, placed FBI officers side by side with their CIA counterparts and gave them access to the same cable traffic from overseas. The idea behind the structure of CTC was that no one at the CIA really had to *give* or *share* anything with the FBI; it was right there on the CTC computer screens for the FBI to read.

The voluminous information we have available on the Malaysia meeting strongly suggests that it didn't work that way in practice. True, the CIA had foreign-only responsibilities, but the FBI worked on both foreign terrorism cases—witness its lead role in the embassy bombing and *Cole* investigations—as well as domestic. Investigation of the Malaysia story made it clear that the FBI saw but did not grasp the domestic import of the visa information in January 2000. There was a structural barrier, to be sure: when Miller drafted his Central Intelligence Report for FBI headquarters, including the Mihdhar visa information, he concluded that he needed the approval of CIA officials at the Counter-Terrorism Center's bin Laden unit to distribute CIA-generated information to the FBI. Yet that posed no obstacle twenty months later when the FBI's Gillespie, also assigned to the Counter-Terrorism Center, reviewed the same CIA cable traffic, came across the Mihdhar visa information, recognized its importance, and took immediate action to notify her FBI chain of command without the slightest interference from the CIA.

After the September 11 attacks, FBI officials told the Justice Department inspector general that the Mihdhar visa intelligence "provided a clear domestic nexus" of international terrorism that should have prompted the CIA to share the information with the FBI.[84] This may be so. But one might also ask, who in the Counter-Terrorism Center should have been on the alert for that domestic nexus? The answer is clearly the FBI. And while it is true that one of the five FBI detailees to CTC did try to pass on the information, only to be blocked by the CIA, there is no evidence that the CIA decision to block Miller's Central Intelligence Report touched off any sort of concern within the FBI team working at the CIA, as it should have—*if* the FBI officials had recognized the ominous import of Mihdhar's ability to travel to the United States. The FBI complained that there was no intelligence "push" from CIA relating to the Mihdhar visa. The critical missing ingredient, however, was an intelligence "pull" from the FBI officers who had access to that intelligence and should have had a keener sense of the importance of information about terrorists traveling to the United States.

The CIA reached a divided but, on the whole, harsh judgment as to its own performance in tracking the future hijackers. Tenet, concerned about his own legacy and possessed of a visceral unwillingness to allow himself or the CIA to bear blame for 9/11, has said that the main problem boiled down to the failure to place Mihdhar and Hazmi on the terrorist watch list. CIA Inspector General John L. Helgerson called the consequences of the watch-list failure and the information-sharing lapses "potentially significant":

> Earlier watchlisting of al-Mihdhar could have prevented his re-entry into the United States in July 2001. Informing the FBI and good operational follow-through by CIA and FBI might have resulted in surveillance of both al-Mihdhar and al-Hazmi. Surveillance, in turn, would have had the potential to yield information on flight training, financing, and links to others who were complicit in the 9/11 attacks.[85]

Subsequent CIA directors Porter Goss and Michael Hayden strove to prevent that harsh judgment from coming to light. The CIA-IG's report remained classified TOP SECRET from its completion in June 2005 until August 2007 when, under pressure from Congress, the Agency released nineteen pages from the executive summary. The Department of Justice, by comparison, had long since released its highly detailed inspector general's report covering the Malaysia meeting and related matters running to several hundred pages. Hayden said he resisted releasing the report because he was "deeply concerned about the chilling effect that may follow publication." Helgerson recommended that Hayden order an "accountability review" focusing on key senior officials, including Tenet. Goss refused and Hayden ratified that decision. Mistakes had been made, he said, by leaders and officers who "with inadequate resources" had "worked flat out against a tough, secretive foe." The IG report, Hayden noted, had found no "silver bullet" action that would have prevented the 9/11 attacks, nor was there any "single point of failure" in the intelligence community's response.[86]

THE DCI AND COUNTERTERROR: ACTION AND PARALYSIS

George Tenet, who ran the CIA either as acting director or director for roughly half the period covered by this book, including the period covering the Malaysia meeting, thought of terrorism as primarily an operational problem, not an analytical one. The enemy's goal was clear: kill as many Americans as possible by whatever means available. It was determining the identity of the attackers and the timing and means of attack that posed the critical intelligence problem. The people to answer those questions, in Tenet's view, were on the CIA's operational side. A sketch of Tenet's take on the terrorist threat would begin with the international manhunt for Mir Aimal Kasi, the Pakistani man who opened fire on a line of cars in front of CIA headquarters in January 1993, killing two and wounding three others. The manhunt put the CIA on the ground in Afghanistan and Pakistan in the mid-1990s searching for Kasi, who had fled to the lawless Pakistani-Afghan border region after the shooting. The result for the CIA was the reestablishment of contacts from the Soviet period in a part of the world now home base to al-Qaeda. Those contacts and the experience gained by the CIA officers involved in the search for Kasi would pay dividends in the aftermath of the September 11 attacks, when the CIA's Directorate of Operations, with Tenet at the head of the CIA, led the planning and execution of the fight to topple the Taliban and rout al-Qaeda from its Afghan sanctuary.

The establishment of a bin Laden unit within the D.O. in January 1996 when Tenet, as deputy CIA director, was heavily involved in operational issues, marked a key step in the CIA's emergence as the first U.S. government organization to directly confront the al-Qaeda threat. Five months later, again through its operational activities, the CIA scored its biggest counterterrorism intelligence coup of the pre-9/11 period when Jamal al-Fadl walked into the U.S. embassy in Eritrea and introduced himself as an al-Qaeda member seeking asylum. He had tried to tell his story to the United States before and been turned away at several U.S. embassies before an alert State Department staffer with experience in regional security issues realized that al-Fadl might well be genuine. The CIA began six weeks of questioning, eventually handing al-Fadl over to the FBI, which placed him in the U.S. witness protection program. In private briefings over several years, then later in public in the trial of the embassy bombers, al-Fadl told the story of al-Qaeda, its organizational makeup, goals, and philosophy. "Jamal al-Fadl, in the spring of 1996, is the first window we have into al-Qaeda," said former FBI special agent Jack Cloonan.[87]

Tenet was hardly alone in this view of terrorism as primarily an operational problem. The post–September 11 critique of the intelligence community focused heavily on the Malaysia meeting, the assessment of which centered on the CIA's Counter-Terrorism Center and the bin Laden unit as the Agency tracked, lost, and tracked again two of the future 9/11 hijackers.

Ironically, the operations side of U.S. intelligence may have come in for more criticism because it achieved more than the analytical side did in identifying and monitoring the al-Qaeda terrorists. The intelligence failures relating to the Malaysia meeting followed successes. Shortcomings in intelligence analysis of the terrorist threat were noted after 9/11, but overall the analysis community came in for much less examination and criticism precisely because there was so little to criticize. The emphasis on terrorism as an operational problem proved to be a misjudgment by Tenet and others during the pre-9/11 period. Tenet himself lamented that some of the key mistakes made by his terrorism case officers stemmed from a volume of work so overwhelming that some messages—such as those about al-Qaeda operatives traveling to the United States—went unread.

The post-9/11 critique of the intelligence community also focused on shortcomings in interagency sharing of information. However, the bigger problem was the dearth of analytical work that could have pieced together the many fragments of intelligence relating to the al-Qaeda network into a more coherent picture. An example involving the Africa embassy bombing investigation illustrates the challenge confronting individual intelligence collectors in trying to grasp the sprawling threat of terrorism. The FBI's John Anticev collected the first critical piece of intelligence relating to 9/11—the number of the telephone in Yemen that led the NSA and then the CIA to monitor the Malaysia meeting. Yet Anticev himself was unaware until years later how important that number became. This was not a failure on Anticev's part, but part of the normal, fragmented course of business in tracking terrorism.

The emphasis on terrorism as an operational problem proved to be a critical miscalculation by Tenet during the pre-9/11 period. Lapses such as the failure to respond to intelligence on terrorists with U.S. visas didn't just stem from overwork among counterterrorism officers. What was missing was an analytical overview that could have given harried operators a better idea of what they should be looking for, what kinds of intelligence should be deemed important. The intelligence community's strenuous operational information collection efforts against al-Qaeda, deeply flawed as they were, existed in a larger intelligence milieu in which assessment of the al-Qaeda threat was, in the words of the House-Senate Joint Inquiry Committee, "woefully inadequate." In the 1998–2000 time frame, during which the Malaysia meeting intelligence was being generated, the CIA's Counter-Terrorism Center had only three analysts working on the al-Qaeda problem full time. The FBI had no more than ten analysts working on al-Qaeda during the same period.[88] And what little analysis was being produced did not appear to be getting through to the operational people in the field. The last National Intelligence Estimate presenting the views of the entire U.S. intelligence community on the terrorist threat before 9/11 was issued in April 1997, and even that document contained only a few sentences on al-Qaeda. Former National Counter-Terrorism coordinator Richard Clarke told the congressional Joint Inquiry into the 9/11 attacks that when he visited a half-dozen FBI field offices around the time of the millennium and asked what they were doing to prepare for the al-Qaeda threat, "I got sort of blank looks of 'what is al-Qaeda?' "[89] As the 9/11 Commission found:

> The reams of new information that the CIA's bin Laden unit had been developing since 1996 had not been pulled together and synthesized for the rest of the government. Indeed, analysts in the unit felt that they were viewed as alarmists even within the CIA. A National Intelligence Estimate on terrorism in 1997 had only briefly mentioned bin Laden, and no subsequent national estimate would authoritatively evaluate the terrorism danger until after 9/11.[90]

The CIA inspector general's probe found that prior to and during Tenet's tenure as director, the Counter-Terrorism Center, which performed both analytical and operational functions, provided no comprehensive strategic assessment of al-Qaeda. The CIA-IG found no comprehensive intelligence analysis focusing on bin Laden from 1993 until after the 9/11 attacks. It found no analytical reporting on intelligence suggesting that terrorists might use aircraft as weapons, and limited reporting on the possibility of an attack on the United States.[91] In the 1990s the CIA declassified reams of intelligence reporting on the Soviet Union from the years before the collapse so that the public, media, and academia could engage in an informed debate on how well the Agency had understood the nation's No. 1 threat. A post-9/11 version of that exercise in connection with the new No. 1 threat, al-Qaeda, would not be possible, according to the CIA-IG report, because a comprehensive body of reporting on al-Qaeda in the pre-9/11 files of the CIA simply doesn't exist.

Responding to this criticism after public release of portions of the CIA-IG report in 2007, former director Tenet issued a three-page statement that omitted any discussion of CIA or intelligence community analysis of the terrorist threat prior to 9/11. When confronted with evidence of an across-the-board failure by the analytical community to address a threat that Tenet himself believed worthy of a declaration of war, Tenet had nothing to say. Both his defense and his admission of failure focused entirely on the operational side. The Agency, under his leadership, had pushed hard to bring the terrorist threat to the top of the national security agenda and had built the network of contacts and sources that had made the takedown of al-Qaeda's Afghan sponsor, the Taliban, possible after the 9/11 attacks. "We did not obtain the tactical information which may have allowed us to thwart the 9/11 attacks," Tenet acknowledged. Rather than address the internal Agency critique at length, Tenet evidently preferred to discuss an earlier report by the CIA inspector general. It found that the Counter-Terrorism Center "is a well-managed component that successfully carries out the Agency's responsibilities to collect and analyze intelligence on international terrorism and to undermine the capabilities of terrorist groups." That report was submitted to Tenet a few weeks before the 9/11 attacks.[92]

Reading the narrative of the Malaysia meeting in retrospect is a bit like watching a car drive down the street with a large cup of coffee perched on the roof. You know it's going to end badly, but there's nothing you can do. The impression that figures most prominently is the noise and messiness of intelligence gathering. At the outset, the 2000 Malaysia meeting prompted a nimble, coordinated response by the intelligence community, which learned of the meeting through careful technical work by the NSA based on human-source intelligence gathered by the FBI, and organized on less than a week's notice CIA tracking of two of the 9/11 hijackers and the mastermind of the October 2000 attack on the USS *Cole*. In another sense, the narrative is a frustrating chain of near-misses in which, time after time, the FBI came close to acquiring a critical piece of information but didn't quite manage to do so, or acquired it but failed to fully grasp its importance. Bad luck as well as bureaucratic barriers and individual misjudgments played a role. The tracking of the terrorists began with the CIA following Mihdhar to Malaysia and on to Thailand, where it lost his trail. The CIA didn't know where the man with the U.S. visa had gone. It picked up the trail of Hazmi as the one who had flown to Los Angeles but failed to act on that information. A critical failure occurred in January 2001 in an undisclosed country where the joint CIA-FBI source identified Khallad as one of the Malaysia attendees, a key piece of information because of Khallad's known role as the mastermind of the *Cole* bombing the previous October. However, the information didn't make it into the translation of the interrogation read by the FBI representative.

It seems a remarkable feature of the Malaysia meeting and its aftermath that so many of the intelligence officials who tracked the participants, when asked to recall details of an effort that might have helped prevent 9/11—whether the details were e-mails, cables, meetings, or phone calls—could recall nothing about them. This is indicative of the enormous volume of raw information flowing through the intelligence community, particularly on terrorism, at that time. The CIA's Wilshire, testifying before the House-Senate Joint Inquiry, recalled encounter after encounter with FBI and CIA officers who were "simply overwhelmed" working on the bin Laden issue before September 11, "with a panic-stricken look in their eyes, saying, 'We're going to miss stuff. We're missing stuff.' "[93] On it went, through the June 2001 "wall" meeting, called for the purpose of sharing information and resulting in precisely the opposite. And finally, there was the belated effort in August 2001 under "routine" priority to find Mihdhar, the only perceived urgency being that he should be found before he left the United States. What the CIA and FBI did not understand was that the United States was Mihdhar's final destination.

9 DESERT MIRAGE

AS THE CIA'S MOST EXPENSIVE and sophisticated search engine, a billion-dollar KH-11 "Keyhole" spy satellite, tracked southward over central Iraq on March 17, 2002, on one of its fourteen daily orbits of the Earth, a few computer keystrokes by controllers at a ground station near Washington directed the satellite to aim its powerful light-gathering mirror along a swath of earth that would take in one of Saddam Hussein's hundreds of dusty concrete ammunition bunkers.[1] Images collected from regular passes over Iraq had begun to detect heightened activity at these weapons storage sites around the country. Such activity was fairly routine for an army that conducted periodic exercises. On this day, however, three factors drew the attention of U.S. intelligence. First, the bunker was on a list of storage sites suspected of holding chemical weapons. Second, with the Bush administration stepping up the pressure on Iraq to prove that it had no arsenal of chemical or biological weapons and no nuclear weapons in development, Iraqi efforts to conceal what was going on looked suspicious to U.S. intelligence analysts. Third, other imagery intelligence coming in from Iraq that month indicated that some sort of major military transport operation was under way involving a repositioning of munitions, possibly in preparation for a U.S. invasion.

Spy satellites are better at examining stationary facilities—missile bases, naval shipyards, airstrips, and so on—than at capturing things in motion, such as a truck convoy. Occasionally, however, the intelligence collectors get lucky. So it was on this day, as the KH-11 was passing over the Al Musayyib Storage Depot, adjacent to a barracks of Saddam's elite Republican Guard near the Euphrates River town of Al Musayyib about forty miles southeast of Baghdad. As the satellite's optical gear gathered imagery, Iraqi military crews were in the process of loading flatbed trucks parked next to the bunker, their cargo concealed by canvas. Accompanying the operation was a white tanker truck that the CIA had seen before.[2]

As one peels away the layers in the complex story of how U.S. intelligence came to reach the fateful judgment in 2002 that Iraq was sitting on a viable arsenal of weapons of mass destruction, no single piece of intelligence was more significant than the convoy photographs of March and April 2002.[3]

True, the Bush administration placed great rhetorical weight on the fear that Iraq was developing nuclear weapons. In his State of the Union address of January 2003, Bush amplified a since-discredited British intelligence finding that Iraq had tried to purchase uranium ore from Africa. Vice President Cheney took liberty with the known facts when he said on NBC's *Meet the Press* that the Bush administration knew "with absolute certainty" that Saddam was buying aluminum tubes to build a uranium enrichment plant for nuclear weapons manufacture. National Security Adviser Condoleezza Rice warned skeptics that the Bush administration didn't want the long-sought "smoking-gun" proof of Iraq's guilt to come in the form of a nuclear mushroom cloud. And some of the most compelling, though subsequently refuted, evidence presented by Secretary of State Colin Powell in his February 5, 2003, presentation to the U.N. Security Council concerned Iraq's alleged fleet of mobile biological weapons production trailers. Powell's dramatic and illustrated story was based on a source code-named CURVEBALL, a former Iraqi chemical engineer who had volunteered information to German intelligence. The Defense Intelligence Agency and the CIA strongly suspected even then that CURVEBALL was fabricating his information, most likely to gain relocation assistance for his family. But the flat assertion that Iraq *has*—present tense—weapons of mass destruction rested on chemical weapons. Nuclear weapons, even in the Bush administration's telling, were still under development in Iraq. Biological weapons were more likely to be made in fresh batches during a war. The charge that Iraq had weapons of mass destruction depended on the chemical weapons evidence, and that evidence depended on assumptions drawn from the satellite images of the "transshipment activity" at Al Musayyib in March of 2002. Without that element of immediacy, the case for war could well have unraveled.[4]

For years, a frequent complaint in the policy-making world, whether Democrats or Republicans happened to control the White House, was that too many intelligence reports came laden with caveats, sometimes so many that they were no help to decision-makers. The reporting on Iraq, even in the pressurized political environment of 2002, was no exception. But due almost exclusively to a set of assumptions proceeding from the spy satellite photographs of Iraq collected beginning on March 17, the CIA and the U.S. intelligence community dropped the qualifiers. A dozen years earlier, the CIA had succeeded in gathering evidence on Iraqi weapons activities only to fail to see the full significance of what it had, most notably in the agency's underestimation of Iraq's progress toward a nuclear weapon in the 1980s. It would not make that mistake this time.[5]

A TRUCK COMES TO AREA 58

A bright, late-winter sun and clear desert air on March 17 cast the activities at the munitions bunker in high relief of light and shadow, ideal for imagery intelligence collection. The Keyhole satellite's dish-shaped, precision-milled mirror, nearly the diameter of the entire spacecraft, reflected the incoming light onto an array of light-sensitive pixels, an invention of the defense-intelligence community that was finding a commercial market in digital cameras. The pixels stored the light bouncing off the concave mirror and organized it into digitized bits of information. Computers aboard the bus-sized satellite encoded the data against interception by adversaries, and transmitters beamed the information to receiving stations located in friendly countries around the globe. These stations then relayed the data to an intelligence hub at Fort Belvoir, Virginia, about fourteen miles south of Washington.[6]

Because most of the targets of interest to the CIA are in the Northern Hemisphere, spy satellites are assigned an elliptical polar orbit that brings them closest to Earth—about 140 miles—over the northern half of the planet. The southern half of the orbit is where much of the information collected by the satellites is down-linked to receiving stations in allied countries such as Australia.[7] So it was on March 17, 2002, as on most other days, as information collected by the satellites got to the people who needed it through a series of relays linking the satellite to the computers of a facility opaquely called the Defense Communications Electronic Evaluation Test Activity. In the intelligence community it is known as "Area 58," at Fort Belvoir. Area 58 could be thought of as the optical nerve of U.S. intelligence, the receiving station

of the thousands of images collected by a galaxy of spy satellites in a classified space program, the biggest chunk of the nation's $40 billion intelligence
apparatus.[8]

While the late-morning sun warmed the Iraqi desert, the overnight shift
was still on duty in northern Virginia as computer algorithms at Area 58 un-
scrambled the signals and turned the encoded, digitized bits into recognizable
images. Within hours, military and civilian photo interpreters arriving for the
morning shift fifteen miles north in Bethesda, Maryland, at the gated, fenced,
and heavily guarded National Geospatial Intelligence Agency, would be alerted
to the new imagery.[9] Scanning the pictures on large-screen monitors, the experts immediately saw their significance and alerted Iraq specialists at CIA
headquarters. It was the vehicles that caught their interest. The flatbed trailer
trucks lined up beside the Iraqi storage bunker were under heavy guard, their
cargo concealed by canvas. Parked off to one side was the white tanker truck,
of a type that photo interpreters had first seen during the Iran-Iraq War.

U.S. intelligence had been watching Iraq closely for more than a dozen
years, going back before the Persian Gulf War to Saddam's harrowing conflict
with Iran. The same space-based collection system had photographed Iraqi
troop concentrations near the border with Kuwait in late July 1990, leading to
the CIA's last-minute warning to the White House on August 1 that an invasion was imminent. Thousands of spy satellite photographs of Iraqi military
maneuvers had given intelligence analysts a vast store of knowledge on the
patterns of Iraqi military operations. Iraq used Soviet military equipment,
for the most part, and, with a few variations, followed Red Army procedures
recognizable to the CIA through long experience. In early 2002 the Bush administration was already signaling that a U.S.-led invasion of Iraq was under
consideration. In Baghdad, commanders of the elite Republican Guard responded by ordering their troops to make ready, prompting much of the flurry
of convoys, or "transshipment activity," as the CIA called it. The CIA followed the action from space. In March and April, the three Keyhole satellites
available to the CIA returned photographs of more than 200 Iraqi military
convoys. The assumption was that Iraq was moving munitions out of storage for distribution to frontline troops preparing for battle. Only much later
would U.S. intelligence analysts realize that the dispersal of munitions they
were witnessing would play little role in the conventional war, but would establish a vast network of conventional arms caches to supply insurgent forces.
In early 2002, conventional warfare, not insurgency, led the Pentagon's list of

concerns in Iraq. The intelligence community, recalling criticism it received for less-than-stellar support of U.S. forces in the Persian Gulf War, knew that Iraqi battle preparations would be of prime interest to the U.S. commanders seeking to anticipate Iraqi troop dispositions and armament.

Among this imagery intelligence, photographs of a few of the convoys, beginning with the pictures taken on March 17 and on ten more occasions at different locations in the coming weeks, bore signs of something more serious. These pictures showed extra security covering the operation, efforts to conceal the cargo on open "stake-bed" trucks with canvas, and a trench that intelligence analysts identified as a "decontamination" or "wash-down" trench in case of an accidental release of chemical agent. Analysts checked their voluminous records on Iraq and noted that some of the bunkers where the convoys were seen assembling may have been used up until the Gulf War to store chemical munitions. Others, such as Musayyib, were forward storage areas for easy access by deployed Iraqi troops defending the southern approaches to Baghdad, or to supply troops attacking in the direction of Iran or Kuwait. The clue that most disturbed analysts at Langley was the presence in each of these eleven instances of the squat, white tanker trucks that CIA photo interpreters identified as chemical decontamination vehicles.[10]

AN INTELLIGENCE SIGNATURE

U.S. intelligence already knew a great deal about the "decon" trucks. At the CIA they were called "Samarra Vehicles," after the city that in the 1980s was home to Iraq's only known chemical weapons production plant and where the vehicles had been spotted by spy satellites trained on the Persian Gulf region during the Iran-Iraq War.[11] They had been observed escorting known chemical weapons ammunition convoys to the front, where Iraqi artillery batteries fired mustard gas shells against Iran's human-wave attacks. Other satellite imagery had spotted Iraqi convoys under similarly heavy guard carrying munitions to Kirkuk Airfield, among other places, where they were loaded onto Iraqi warplanes for use in strikes against ethnic Kurds in northern Iraq.

This imagery intelligence from the 1980s received confirmation from the ground following the 1991 Persian Gulf War when Iraqi officers told United Nations inspectors that decontamination trucks always took part in maneuvers involving chemical munitions. If the chemical agent spilled, the hose and spray systems on the tanker trucks would be used to wash down exposed people or equipment. U.S. intelligence learned that the trucks were built by

Mitsubishi and sold to Iraq as multipurpose tankers in the early 1980s—around the time Iraq was first launching mustard gas attacks on Iranian forces. The trucks could carry fuel or water. Mitsubishi sold many to Iraq and other countries as fire trucks. They could also be fitted with supplemental tanks and spray equipment for their supporting role in Saddam's chemical arsenal. During the internal debate at the CIA over the significance of the March 2002 photographs, the winning argument was made by analysts who pointed out that the trucks accompanying the convoys had these extra tanks, presumably carrying the decontamination liquid that would be diluted with water from the larger tank before being used.[12] All of this painstaking intelligence work turned the otherwise unremarkable tanker trucks into what intelligence professionals call a "signature." From the early 1990s on, the CIA believed that if the trucks showed up in a satellite image, there was a good chance that chemical weapons were nearby.

If the trucks proved that Iraq was moving chemical munitions, however, the CIA had a problem. According to the CIA's estimates, Iraq did not have nearly as much chemical agent as was implied by the material seen being loaded onto the flatbed trucks. A debate among CIA analysts ensued as to what the photos showed. The decontamination vehicle might actually be a fire truck or fuel tanker, some argued. But the tide of opinion was shifting in favor of interpreting the convoy activity as chemical weapons–related. Because this conclusion demanded an explanation of where all these additional munitions were coming from, analysts made a fateful assumption. Iraq, they said, must have restarted chemical weapons production and done so within the past year.[13] On May 2, 2002, the National Intelligence Council, a body of advisers to the director of central intelligence based at CIA headquarters and representing the combined views of all fifteen U.S. intelligence agencies, issued a classified report, *Iraq, Unusual Logistical Activities in Preparation for an Anticipated U.S.-Led Campaign*.[14] The report conveyed some of the debate and doubt about the significance of the convoy photos, but concluded that a majority of analysts suspected that the Iraqis were preparing for chemical war.

Despite the use of the imagery intelligence in reaching a definite finding that Iraq had chemical weapons, intelligence reporting throughout the run-up to the war cautioned policymakers that information on Iraqi chemical weapons stockpiles was scant. The October 2002 National Intelligence Estimate issued shortly before Congress voted to authorize the use of force in Iraq said U.S. intelligence had "little specific information on Iraq's CW stockpile." A November addendum to that report said the intelligence community had "almost no information on the size, composition, or location of Iraq's CW stockpile." These words of caution may have been intended primarily for military commanders seeking information on where their troops might encounter chemical weapons, or a chemical weapons attack.[15] They drew virtually no notice in the public debate over whether to invade Iraq from among lawmakers or policymakers privy to these classified reports.

Despite the admitted scarcity of specific intelligence and despite caveats in the supporting material underlying the intelligence reporting, the headline from the CIA and the rest of the U.S. intelligence community was unambiguous. By the fall of 2002, the internal debate had faded, to be replaced by a crucial—and mistaken—conclusion: Saddam definitely possessed stockpiles of weapons of mass destruction.[16] Up until the October 2002 National Intelligence Estimate, the CIA had been careful to say that Iraq *might* have or *was suspected* of having stockpiles of chemical weapons, or CW. In October, the qualifiers were dropped. As the commission on Iraqi WMD intelligence headed by former senator Charles Robb (D-Va.), put it, "The October NIE reflected a shift in the Intelligence Community's judgment about Iraq's CW program in two ways: (1) the NIE assessed that Iraq had large stockpiles of CW; and (2) the NIE unequivocally stated that Iraq had restarted CW production."[17]

Of all the many errors the CIA made in judging the threat posed by Iraq, the one that has received the least attention but was, perhaps, most consequential was the misperception of the Iraqi convoys in March 2002. On the issue of Iraq's nuclear program, the CIA fought the Bush administration internally, at least to some extent, on the evidence of Iraqi efforts to acquire additional uranium from Niger in Africa.[18] And despite irresponsible rhetoric by top Bush administration officials, the intelligence community's bottom line was that while Iraq had restarted its nuclear weapons program, it was not very far along toward acquiring a weapon. On links between al-Qaeda and Saddam's regime, the CIA—at least at the level of rank-and-file analysts—was even more vehement in its refusal to go along with the prevailing view at the White House that these links were close and active. As already noted, CIA officers raised concerns about human intelligence sourcing behind the allegations about mobile biological weapons labs. In addition, most experts guessed that Iraq would make biological weapons in batches rather than stockpile them.

The CIA's chemical weapons finding, in contrast, gave the Bush administration what it needed to make the case for war: intelligence community confirmation from an agency skeptical on other points that Iraq definitely had weapons of mass destruction.[19]

AN INTELLIGENCE CHAIN REACTION

Once intelligence analysts were agreed that the white tanker trucks were for chemical decontamination, a series of other conclusions fell into place. Knowing that the United States was planning for war in Iraq and that this possibility was already being discussed publicly, and therefore known in Baghdad, the CIA interpreted the convoy imagery as part of a flurry of Iraqi war preparations. Because of the number and location of the trucks, analysts assumed that Saddam was deploying chemical munitions to frontline positions for possible use in battle. That assumption meant that Iraq had a large quantity of chemical munitions and led to the conclusion that Saddam must have restarted chemical weapons production within the past year because the amount Iraq was believed to have held over from the Iran-Iraq War and post–Gulf War weapons inspections was relatively small. And if Iraq had restarted chemical weapons production, it was possible that the regime was developing newer, more lethal variants.[20]

The eventual unanimity of the intelligence community over this set of conclusions and the fact that technical intelligence—the most trusted form of information collected by the CIA—underlay the finding added credibility and authority to the Bush administration's case for war. It also helped paper over some of the other disputes within intelligence, and between the CIA and the White House, about the intentions of the Iraqi regime. The intelligence conclusion that most worried a group of senators, including Democrats Bob Graham of Florida and Carl Levin of Michigan who opposed the proposed invasion, was not the chemical weapons finding but the CIA assessment that the scenario in which Iraq would most likely use chemical or biological weapons was the very one the White House was contemplating: an invasion aimed at toppling Saddam's regime. If the administration's principal concern was Iraqi weapons of mass destruction, they argued, why do the one thing the CIA feared would provoke Saddam to use those weapons?[21] That fear, of course, rested on the assumption that Iraq had the weapons to use, an assumption no longer in question. Indeed, while there were furious disputes about the Bush administration's war policy, Iraq's possession of chemical weapons was accepted as fact by the key participants in the debate. Only after the war would it become clear that the intelligence assessment that Iraq had chemical weapons rested on a single strand of evidence, and on a train of logic that proceeded from that strand. The WMD intelligence commission headed by Robb summed up the intelligence failure:

> As this logic train illustrates, the final conclusion regarding restarted CW production was, therefore, fundamentally grounded on the single assessment that the Samarra-type trucks seen on imagery were in fact CW-related. This assessment, however, proved to be incorrect—thereby eliminating the crucial pillar on which the Community's judgment about Iraq's CW program rested.[22]

It was the chemical weapons—the finding that Iraq possessed a stockpile of them—that added a level of urgency to the Bush administration case against Iraq. This firm conclusion then provided the key link in a chain of logic used to intensify the sense of crisis leading up to war. The British talked of the forty-five minutes it would take the Iraqi military to launch a chemical weapons strike. In a White Paper that first raised the forty-five-minute specter, the British sloppily failed to point out that the figure referred to the time it would take to launch a strike within Iraq, presumably against an invading force. To policy-makers or legislators unfamiliar with Iraqi military capabilities, the paper gave the impression that forty-five minutes referred to the time it would take for Iraq to launch a strike on Tel Aviv or London—never mind that Iraq had no missiles capable of reaching London. While Parliament was digesting the White Paper in the fall of 2002, U.S. lawmakers preparing to vote to authorize the use of force against Iraq were receiving alarming reports about the extended range of some of Iraq's unmanned aircraft equipped, the CIA believed, with spray dispensers for releasing chemical or biological agents. One scenario indicated that Iraq could launch a drone from off the U.S. coast against American cities.[23]

To some lawmakers in London and Washington who were being asked to endorse the war policy, it all sounded like the air raid sirens could go off at any time. But the edifice of fear stood on a single pillar: the mistaken assumption that Iraq had chemical weapons that it could put on those missiles or drones. In other words, take away the spy satellite photographs taken in mid-March 2002, a year before the war, and the whole edifice comes tumbling down.

EYE OF THE BEHOLDER

Imagery intelligence signatures, such as the suspected Iraqi decontamination trucks, were among the CIA's most closely guarded secrets because revealing them would enable an adversary to change procedures to hide its weapons.

The Iraqis, it appeared, did not know they were giving themselves away when they brought out the decon trucks, and the CIA wanted to keep it that way. So sensitive was the role of the trucks in helping the CIA track Iraq's arsenal that in February 2003, a month before the U.S.-led invasion, one former CIA official was shocked when Secretary of State Powell included discussion of the trucks in his presentation to the U.N. Security Council. Kenneth Pollack, who had been a CIA Mideast analyst and, more recently, author of a book making the case for war on Iraq, expressed dismay that Powell had given away a highly sensitive piece of classified information.[24] Bush administration officials did not address these concerns directly, but the thinking at the White House was clear enough: why hold back secrets about a regime that would shortly cease to exist?[25]

The logic chain that began with the convoy photographs was part of a larger set of assumptions that informed prewar CIA analysis of Iraqi weapons: Iraq had possessed and used these weapons before; Iraq had failed to account for all the chemical weapons ingredients it was known to have; Saddam's regime lied routinely, so its denials could be dismissed; Iraq had a known set of procedures for handling chemical weapons, and its military could be seen moving munitions using those procedures; a flurry of activity in Iraq was expected because war was expected. Human intelligence reporting from Iraqi defectors tended to support the prewar intelligence community view that Iraq had secretly restarted its chemical weapons program, though this reporting may have been an internally induced error. Postwar investigations found that an intelligence demand-supply cycle had contributed to the magnitude of the misjudgment on Iraq's suspected arsenal. A CIA review conducted in 2005, examining the chemical weapons aspect of the WMD intelligence failure, found that as the possibility of war increased, "intense interest in information on Iraq's WMD capabilities lowered the threshold for reporting such information and increased the volume of reporting from less credible sources."[26] The increased volume of information arose not from an increase in WMD activity in Iraq but from an increase in WMD interest in Washington.

Among the indications that the intelligence underlying the Bush administration's case for war was wrong, in early March 2003, just days before the war began, U.N. weapons inspectors reported to the Security Council that they had not found weapons of mass destruction in a new round of inspections permitted by Saddam under threat of war. Though the overall tone of the report was that fuller cooperation from Iraq was needed and that many questions remained unanswered, the inspectors had been unable in extensive tours of suspect Iraqi weapons sites to confirm recent intelligence suggesting movement of weapons.[27] The Bush administration dismissed this as the result of clever Iraqi concealment, not the absence of weapons themselves.

The most conclusive sign of a major flaw in the case for war came when Saddam's regime did not use chemical or biological weapons against the vastly superior U.S.-led invasion force, even though the survival of the regime was at stake. The coalition forces took control of Iraq in just over a month, executing a lightning push northward slowed more by an epic sandstorm and the sniping of guerrilla forces than by any organized Iraqi defense. Yet they found no caches of chemical munitions. A massive search of the country, involving a team of some 1,200 soldiers, weapons specialists, and intelligence officials—a far larger contingent than the teams of U.N. inspectors who had uncovered so much in the early- and mid-1990s—looked in all the obvious places and some not-so-obvious ones and found nothing. Interrogations revealed not a sinister and secret weapons program but a decrepit regime intent primarily on maintaining its own internal security. In the spring of 2004, chief weapons searcher David Kay stepped down, saying he was as certain as he could be that there were no weapons of mass destruction in Iraq. The interim report of his Iraq Survey Group amounted to a devastating indictment of the Bush administration's case for war. Iraq not only had no arsenal of chemical or biological weapons; it had no facilities with which to make them. What was left of its once considerable nuclear program was a mere vestige. None of the Scud missiles Iraq supposedly had hidden for use against Israel turned up. Excitement over the seizure of two trailers that looked like the mobile biological weapons plants faded when intelligence experts concluded they were for making hydrogen so that Iraqi artillery units could send up weather balloons to help gauge the wind. Aluminum tubes seized by Jordanian authorities with the help of the CIA two years before the war were not for use in a nuclear centrifuge but for making small-caliber conventional rocket tubes. Finally, in late 2004, the search effort by the Iraq Survey Group was quietly disbanded.[28]

Charles Duelfer, Kay's successor, submitted a massive report on the survey group's work. Buried in the multi-volume report was a relatively brief discussion of the satellite imagery of Mussayib and of the suspected decontamination trucks. Officials from the survey group went to Mussayib and ten other sites at which the CIA had suspected weapons transshipment activity in early 2002. Most had been looted beyond the point where any useful information could be gained. Two vehicles of a type seen in the spy satellite images were recovered, but there is no indication in the Duelfer report that they were for chemical decontamination.[29]

Robb's WMD Commission, which explored the CIA's faulty logic in detail, examined the conclusion of U.S. imagery analysts that what they were seeing around the Musayyib bunker was part of a bustle of activity in preparation for war. This, too, proved to be a false assumption. Up until 2000, most of the imagery intelligence collection on Iraq had focused on supporting the U.S. and allied enforcement of the no-fly zones over northern and southern Iraq. Again, the sting of the Gulf War criticism that CIA support for the war-fighter had been lacking helped drive a determination to ensure that U.S. and allied pilots get all the intelligence they needed, particularly about mobile Iraqi air defense batteries. As the Bush administration began to place more emphasis on weapons of mass destruction, imagery collection of strategic targets in Iraq related to WMD more than doubled from 2001 to 2002, according to the WMD Commission. In poring though the greatly expanded take from this surge of collection, intelligence analysts missed an obvious point: It was quite possible that what seemed to them to be a surge of activity in Iraq was merely a reflection of the surge of intelligence collection activity directed at Iraq.[30]

The National Geospatial Intelligence Agency did its own postwar review of its handling of the Musayyib satellite photos. Based on a reexamination of prewar imagery and on interviews with former Iraqi commanders of the site, NGA concluded that the pictures showed routine "maintenance and logistical activity," not shipments of chemical weapons. Captured Iraqis, who insisted that Saddam's chemical arsenal had been destroyed in the years immediately following the 1991 Gulf War, reported that the tanker trucks seen in the convoy photographs were probably carrying extra fuel, or possibly serving as a fire brigade in case some of the conventional munitions exploded. Inspectors found no signs of chemical agent decontamination gear. The trucks that had helped start a war, it turned out, were trucks meant to put out fires.[31]

CLUES AT KAMISIYAH

The CIA had intelligence linking white tanker trucks to Iraqi chemical weapons dating back at least as far as July 1984. Satellite imagery taken that month of the Kamisiyah ammunition depot, then in heavy use supporting Iraqi forces in the war with Iran, showed "a decontamination vehicle normally associated with tactical chemical defense" at the site.[32] This long-buried nugget of intelligence came to light not in 2003, in the wake of the meltdown at the CIA when the U.S. occupying forces in Iraq found no weapons of mass destruction, but in the late 1990s in the shakeout from an earlier intelligence controversy linked to the Persian Gulf War. The issue in this case was Gulf War syndrome, a set of symptoms of mysterious origin experienced by some U.S. veterans of Operation Desert Storm. Beginning in 1993, a growing number of veterans complaining of headaches, chronic fatigue, joint pain, dizziness, and memory loss, among other symptoms, coalesced behind the powerful veterans lobby to push for government assistance and for investigations into what had happened to them in the war. One of the key starting points was a series of hearings by the Senate Banking Committee looking into the export to Iraq of dual-use equipment and technology in the 1980s that might have gone to support Saddam Hussein's weapons programs. The hearings elicited testimony on suspected chemical weapons exposure during the war, prompted in part by weapons-detector alarms that sounded frequently during the conflict and by increasing reports of mysterious illnesses among veterans.[33] The concerns generated extensive media coverage, particularly in the *New York Times*, and sharp congressional criticism of the Pentagon and the CIA. The veterans charged that, contrary to Pentagon and CIA assurances that Iraq had not used chemical weapons during the Gulf War, soldiers were returning home with unexplained illnesses that they believed were linked to hazardous exposures in Kuwait and Iraq during the conflict. The veterans charged that the government was callously forcing them to prove a link between their ailments and their service in the Gulf before it would provide medical treatment and disability payments.

Even after assuring Gulf War veterans that the Veterans Affairs health system would provide for their care regardless of what caused their illnesses, the questions surrounding what had caused the ailments, and whether there had been a cover-up, lingered. The Clinton administration's response was methodical but politically inept. It consisted of a massive document search, beginning in 1994 at the Pentagon and extending to the CIA, for anything that might shed light on whether or how veterans might have been exposed to chemical or biological agents in Iraq and, if they were, whether that exposure could explain the chronic illnesses being reported. Though the search found no conclusive proof of exposure to chemical weapons, it produced significant circumstantial evidence that tended to undermine the government's initial statements and intensify the criticism from veterans.

In 1995 the Pentagon began looking into whether the demolition by U.S. forces of a massive ammunition dump at Kamisiyah in March of 1991, just after the Gulf War, could have inadvertently detonated bombs and shells filled with mustard blistering agent or the nerve agent sarin. On May 14, 1996, U.N. weapons inspectors examined some of the exploded shells at Kamisiyah and found some with internal linings typically used for sarin and mustard gas.[34] The CIA played a small part in the Kamisiyah controversy, but a significant one in light of the judgments the Agency would make seven years later about weapons of mass destruction before the invasion of Iraq. The question confronting the CIA was what it knew before or during the Gulf War about chemical weapons at the ammunition depot and whether it shared its knowledge with the military prior to the demolition of the ammunition stored there. In due course, Agency officials found documents indicating that the CIA indeed had collected information pointing to Kamisiyah as a suspected Iraqi chemical weapons storage site, but had not ensured that the information got to the troops in the field who needed it.

The Gulf War illness issue caught hold during an awkward period for the CIA. The Agency's internal probe began during John Deutch's tenure as CIA director. As in the Ames case, the Guatemala and Honduras investigations, and the intelligence source "scrub," the posture Deutch adopted conveyed the message that the CIA's leadership would insist on investigating and exposing CIA malfeasance. So determined was the CIA under Deutch to show that it was responding to veterans' concerns that it declassified hundreds of Gulf War–related documents and posted them on an Internet site, only to discover that some of them contained sensitive information and had to be temporarily pulled from public view. After Deutch's departure in December 1996, President Clinton nominated National Security Adviser Anthony Lake to replace him. But the nomination foundered in the Senate Intelligence Committee and, on March 17, 1997, had to be withdrawn. Two days later, Clinton would nominate George Tenet for the post. Tenet, who had been Deutch's deputy, was running the CIA as acting director during the period of Lake's foundering nomination. In February 1997 Tenet named Robert Walpole to be his special adviser on a Gulf War Illness Task Force at the CIA. Walpole, an expert in proliferation and weapons of mass destruction, became one of Tenet's most trusted advisers. In 1998, when the Rumsfeld Commission attacked the intelligence community for underestimating the threat of long-range missile attack by a rogue state, Tenet turned to Walpole to direct the CIA's recalibration of its stance on the missile threat, a shift designed to make the criticism go away. And in 2002, Walpole played a key role on the National Intelligence Council, drafting the portion of the October 2002 National Intelligence Estimate that concerned Iraq's supposedly reactivated nuclear weapons program. The result of Walpole's efforts in the Gulf War illness case, issued in April 1997, was a public apology from the CIA.

The timing and sequence here is important to understanding what happened: Deutch departed the CIA in December after undergoing, and in some ways participating in, two years of almost relentless criticism of the Agency for the Ames case, tainted sources in Latin America, and allegations of CIA ties to drug dealers. Deutch's posture had been to bow to critics on Capitol Hill who complained that the CIA doesn't punish its own when wrongdoing is discovered. Deutch departed to high praise from congressional overseers in December of 1996, having begun the probe into the CIA's knowledge of chemical weapons sites that might be related to Gulf War illnesses. After Lake's nomination went down under partisan criticism from the Senate Intelligence Committee, now under Republican control, Tenet named his most trusted fixer to examine the Gulf War illness issue, and the result was a report on April 9, 1997—during the period when Tenet's nomination was still pending and at a time when much congressional attention was focused on the concerns of Gulf War veterans. Under such circumstances, there was no way the CIA was going to issue anything but a report critical of itself and sympathetic to the concerns of veterans. The political pressure was too great.

Tenet ordered a rare public news conference at CIA headquarters on Walpole's report. In an introduction to the report, Tenet wrote that the investigation found nothing to contradict the CIA's pre–Gulf War judgments about Iraq's chemical weapons: that Iraq was likely to distribute chemical munitions to frontline forces in Kuwait and southern Iraq; that there was a possibility they might be used against the coalition but that, in fact, they had not been; and that these munitions might not bear clear markings identifying them as chemical munitions. "The paper does, however, illustrate that intelligence support associated with Operation Desert Shield and Desert Storm—particularly in the areas of information distribution and analysis—should have been better," Tenet wrote. Walpole's report detailed three instances in the years before Iraq's invasion of Kuwait in which the CIA had intelligence indicating that chemical munitions had been stored at Kamisiyah: one in 1984, not shared with the Pentagon, concerned imagery of a decontamination vehicle; another in May

1986 that was shared with the Pentagon was a report from a human source who provided an Iraqi chemical weapons production plan showing that 3,975 mustard-loaded artillery shells may have been distributed to storage sites at Kamisiyah; the third was a November 1986 CIA assessment based on the human intelligence report, which concluded that chemical weapons had been stored at the Kamisiyah site, though it named it Tall al Lahm.

The CIA's first warning about chemical weapons at Kamisiyah went to U.S. Central Command on February 23, 1991, the day before the coalition ground campaign to liberate Kuwait began. The CIA report did not mention Kamisiyah by name but gave the coordinates of the suspected chemical weapons site.[35] Although the information the military was receiving was tenuous, Central Command did order a closer examination of intelligence on seventeen suspected chemical munitions sites. On February 28 the Defense Intelligence Agency notified Central Command that a bunker at a site it identified as Tall al Lahm, but which was also known as Kamisiyah, might contain biological or chemical weapons.[36]

In short, the military had information, albeit incomplete and tenuous, that there might be chemical munitions at Kamisiyah, and it had the information before the munitions demolition operation began on March 4, 1991. Still, the CIA itself determined that this incident amounted to an intelligence failure. The CIA, Walpole's report stated, had failed to "reconcile information in databases to eliminate confusion about facilities"; it had been less than thorough in sharing with the military important information about weapons storage sites; it had fallen into the trap of "tunnel vision" in the assumptions it made about where Iraq would put its chemical weapons; and it failed to include Kamisiyah on prewar lists of suspected chemical weapons sites even though it had prewar intelligence pointing to Kamisiyah as a CW storage site.

"I'll give that apology—we should have gotten more information out sooner," Walpole said at the CIA press conference.[37] "CIA's credibility has suffered in this effort."

Representatives of veterans groups accused Tenet of rushing out a CIA mea culpa to head off tough questioning at his confirmation hearing. And the press had no trouble finding officials willing to heap harsher criticism on the CIA. James Tuite, who had been the staffer in charge of the Senate Banking Committee's 1993–94 probe, called the Walpole report "evidence of an unraveling cover-up of an unprecedented intelligence failure." The *New York Times* portrayed Walpole's findings as providing "dramatic support" to the allegations by Patrick and Robin Eddington, two CIA analysts who had resigned from the Agency and gone public with charges that the CIA had evidence of chemical exposures during the Gulf War.[38] In fact, the Walpole report contained no evidence that Iraq had used chemical weapons, and while it concluded that the demolition of the Kamisiyah bunkers had resulted in the release of mustard and sarin agent, it had no definitive information that anyone had been harmed.

Tenet was confirmed by the Senate and sworn in as CIA director on July 11, 1997. In late July, Walpole was back with an update on the Gulf War illness investigation. This time he reported that a document search had turned up two intelligence community warnings to the military in late February and March 1991—just prior to the demolition of the Kamisiyah munitions—about chemical weapons at that site. "These warnings, unfortunately, did not make their way to the troops who performed the destruction."[39] Walpole showed enough interagency tact not to come right out and say it, but the implication was that the Pentagon, not the CIA, had failed to make sure that the right people got the information about the risks at Kamisiyah.

This episode was one example among many of how the CIA itself contributed to the culture of failure in which it operated virtually throughout the 1990s. Mistakes had been made in the handling of the Kamisiyah intelligence. About that there could be no doubt. But the self-flagellation was built on a false assumption: that because of the CIA's mishandling of important information, U.S. forces out in the field blundered into a mistake that may have been responsible for chronic illness among thousands of Gulf War veterans. This chain of culpability breaks down upon close examination. In October 1997, the Department of the Army inspector general issued a report on the demolition operation at Kamisiyah. The report stated that the commander of the Army's 37th Engineering Battalion had received no specific warning about chemical munitions at Kamisiyah from either the CIA or military intelligence. "Nonetheless, those involved in the demolition mission proceeded on the assumption that chemical munitions could be stored in the facility." The investigation uncovered a growing body of message traffic warning that chemical shells might not bear identifying markers but found "no indication that this information made its way down to the soldiers involved in destroying the Kamisiyah facility. On the contrary, testimony reveals that almost everyone at Kamisiyah was looking for suspiciously marked munitions."[40] The CIA had warned of chemical munitions at Kamisiyah, albeit imperfectly, and it had warned that chemical munitions might not be marked. Neither warning got to the troops in the field, a fault that would appear to lie with Central Command. Yet the troops were alert to the chemical munitions threat anyway, although they made the mistaken assumption that those munitions would have identifying marks.

The first large-scale destruction of munitions occurred on March 4, 1991, after a search of the bunkers found no suspiciously marked munitions. The Army engineers rigged thirty-seven bunkers with high explosives, lit fuses, and moved to an observation area across a canal 2.5 miles away. It wasn't far enough. Some fifteen to twenty minutes after the first detonations, shells and rockets were landing all around the soldiers and far beyond, to distances of more than six miles. At least one chemical weapons alarm sounded during the demolition operation, but the troops in the area responded inconsistently, some donning their protective gear, others not because of a "cry wolf" syndrome that developed in previous frequent false alarms.[41] But subsequent tests in the area of the bunkers turned up negative for chemical release, and no one in the battalion showed any symptoms of exposure. Army investigators interviewed many participants in the demolition operation, including several who had gone up to the bunker site after the demolition. None had suffered any symptoms of chemical exposure in the six years since the incident.[42] The Army investigation found "no empirical evidence that chemical munitions/agents were present during the demolition operation" but rather said that suspicions to that effect were based entirely on "the deductive efforts of intelligence agencies" based on postwar discoveries by U.N. inspectors.[43] The evidence from the inspectors was strong, though circumstantial: in May 1991 they had been told by Iraqi handlers that chemical munitions had been stored at Kamisiyah; in October of that year inspectors had drilled into an unexploded rocket found in an area dubbed "the pit," where remnants of the demolition had been bulldozed, and found it contained sarin nerve agent. And in May 1996, as previously noted, U.N. personnel had found a shell fragment at the site of the destroyed Bunker No. 73 that was consistent with chemical munitions. Based on those findings, along with a study of wind and weather conditions on the day of the demolition as well as troop locations in the region, the Army estimated that some 99,000 U.S. soldiers might have been exposed to low levels of sarin "well below the noticeable health effects level."[44]

Like so many Washington controversies that spawn press attention, the Gulf War illness issue manifested itself in a profusion of investigations—

by the CIA, the Army, congressional committees, and special review panels set up by the Pentagon. Long after the issue had lost steam as a news story, these probes sputtered on and continued to find no evidence that would indicate that the Kamisiyah incident had exposed troops to dangerous chemical agents. In March 2000 the U.S. Army component of Central Command, or ARCENT, issued a "close-out report" on the Kamisiyah incident. The report noted that the entire Gulf War had produced only one confirmed case of chemical agent exposure—a soldier in a scout platoon of the 3rd Armored Division sustained a burn on his upper left arm on February 28, 1991, the day General Schwarzkopf ordered a cessation to offensive action. The incident took place several days before the demolition of the Kamisiyah bunker at a location some seventy-eight miles distant. Central Command medical officials attributed the injury to exposure to liquid mustard agent.[45] With the exception of that one case, the ARCENT report stated, "there have been no reliable reports of soldiers suffering symptoms of chemical or biological warfare agent exposure at or near any of the ARCENT suspected chemical weapons sites," including Kamisiyah.[46]

In April 2002, around the same time that intelligence analysts were debating the satellite imagery showing the suspicious activity at munitions storage bunkers, the CIA issued its final report on Gulf War chemical agent release issues. The report said that the cumulative results of eight years of intensive government research had turned up one incident in which inadvertent release of nerve agent reached U.S. troops deployed for the Gulf War. It had occurred on March 10, 1991, with the destruction of Iraqi rockets in a pit at Kamisiyah, six days after the postwar demolition operations there had begun. The report revised downward the estimated quantity of nerve agent released and concluded that the quantities involved met the Pentagon's definition of low-level exposure—twenty times less than the quantity that would be required to prompt the first noticeable symptoms of exposure. Moreover, the chemical weapons destroyed at Kamisiyah could not explain Gulf War syndrome. The CIA "found no credible evidence that Iraq had substantial amounts of 'exotic' chemical agents that could explain the symptoms experienced by the Gulf War veterans." Finally, the report made no mention of issues relating to the supposed CIA failure to warn the military of what it might find at Kamisiyah.[47]

The Kamisiyah incident, it would appear, was of no consequence to veterans of the Persian Gulf War, but of great consequence to the political standing of the CIA, particularly as it related to its ability to detect and report evidence of Iraqi weapons of mass destruction. The lesson learned at the CIA was simple enough: failure to warn of the presence of weapons of mass destruction in Iraq and to track the movement of chemical munitions among the Iraqi military's various storage facilities will be regarded as a significant intelligence lapse. The presence of a suspected decontamination truck near an Iraqi ammunition bunker was one of the clues the CIA had collected about Kamisiyah, but then forgot about. The Agency would not repeat the mistake.

GROWTH MEDIUM

A strange truth about intelligence on Iraq after the Gulf War is that the last time a Western official saw an actual Iraqi weapon of mass destruction that was part of a viable arsenal was in 1991. Yet seemingly every development on the weapons inspection front throughout the decade worked to intensify a belief in the West that Saddam continued to harbor and develop a secret arsenal.[48] I described in Chapter 4 how the CIA worked with U.N. inspectors in the spring and summer of 1991 to uncover Iraq's secret nuclear weapons program and how that discovery embarrassed the CIA, which had said before the Gulf War that Iraq was up to a decade away from acquiring a nuclear weapon. The guiding assumption that the CIA was seeing only a fraction of what Iraq actually had made it that much more difficult to see the truth later in the decade— that the weapons inspection program had been successful and that Iraq had, in fact, ended its nuclear program. Those 1991 inspections, the dusty chases through the desert, the sifting through junk yards and back lots for buried weapons components, the parking lot standoffs, had an equally profound impact on Iraq's thinking. That impact, like its counterpart at CIA, served to greatly elevate the difficulty of discovering the truth about Iraq's weapons of mass destruction. A CIA retrospective on the weapons of mass destruction intelligence depicts those post–Gulf War inspections as a profound event for the regime in Baghdad. Though the retrospective itself remains classified, it was described extensively in a report by the Senate Intelligence Committee:

> A key event, according to the retrospective, was the U.N.'s aggressive inspections of Iraq in 1991. This shocked the Iraqis, who had believed they would not have to comply and that the inspections would end in a few weeks. This led to what the retrospective characterizes as Iraq's "fateful decision" to covertly dismantle or destroy undeclared WMD items and also destroy the records that could have verified that unilateral destruction.[49]

Between Saddam's destruction of weapons and his destruction of the records that proved he had destroyed them, the latter was almost certainly the more damaging decision for his own long-term interests. Right up to the eve of war in March 2003 it was Iraq's inability to definitively prove what had happened to its pre–Gulf War stockpile that stood in the way of the lifting of international sanctions. Charles Duelfer, who succeeded David Kay in running the post-invasion search for Iraqi weapons of mass destruction, offered a similar assessment of Saddam's motives based on extensive debriefing of regime officials, including Saddam himself. U.N. inspections in "the spring and summer of 1991 were defining moments for Baghdad," according to Duelfer.[50] Saddam wanted to retain the ability to build weapons of mass destruction, but his first priority, after regime survival, was ending economic sanctions. The strategy he chose, Duelfer reported, was "to mix compliance with defiance."[51] Iraq kept its biological program concealed, admitted to the full scope of its nuclear program only under intense U.N. pressure, and destroyed its existing chemical and biological weapons stocks. The destruction of Iraq's weapons happened on two separate tracks, one under U.N. supervision, the other secret. Saddam's reasoning appears to have been to get rid of incriminating weapons without having to divulge to the U.N. and Western intelligence the full scope of Iraq's programs and the state of its weapons technology, in hopes that the programs might someday be revived. It was this secret destruction of weapons that the CIA and other Western intelligence agencies missed—or, when they got wind of it, disbelieved. Saddam faced "internal reluctance" when he ordered the weapons destroyed, particularly from his son-in-law, Hussein Kamel, head of Iraq's Military Industrialization Corporation, a post that put him in charge of WMD programs.[52] But the destruction of weapons went forward, and virtually all were gotten rid of by the end of 1991, though the secret destruction of some biological munitions may have carried over into 1992.[53]

Before Saddam eliminated his chemical arsenal, he put it to use one more time. On March 7, 1991, in the midst of the destruction of the Kamisiyah ammunition dump, Iraqi helicopter forces dropped as many as thirty-two aerial bombs loaded with the nerve agent VX in strikes on Shiite rebels in Karbala. The VX bombs apparently did not detonate properly, leading Iraqi commanders to switch to tear gas strikes on the rebels, who were fighting Iraqi government forces on the ground. Saddam considered but rejected using mustard gas for fear that the coalition would discover that he had done so.[54] Saddam still believed in the utility of weapons of mass destruction. He saw them as the

winning difference in the Iran-Iraq War as crude "human wave" infantry of-
fensives by Iran were cut down with chemical weapons. Saddam also believed
that the decision by the coalition in 1991 to end the Gulf War without marching
on Baghdad stemmed from a fear of Iraq's still-extant weapons stocks.[55] As a
believer in deterrence theory, Saddam had greater faith in these weapons as
a threat to the United States than as a tactical advantage in battle. According
to Kamel, Saddam, in the Gulf War, had "no intention to use chemical weapons, as the Allied force was overwhelming." Moreover, deterrence worked two
ways, and Saddam feared that his use of chemical munitions against the coalition would bring nuclear retaliation.[56]

Four years later, on the night of August 7, 1995, Kamel defected to Jordan
along with his brother, Colonel Saddam Kamel, carrying crates of documents
with hitherto unknown details on Iraqi weapons programs. In particular, the
material provided extensive detail on Iraq's secret biological weapons program,
which had been recently uncovered by U.N. weapons inspectors. On August 22,
1995, Ambassador Rolf Ekeus, then the executive chairman of the U.N. Special
Commission, or UNSCOM, the Iraq inspections organization, debriefed Hussein Kamel in Amman. The Iraqi described the secret decision to destroy chemical and biological weapons and convert production plants to civilian uses, such
as pesticide and medicine production. "All chemical weapons were destroyed. I
ordered destruction of all chemical weapons. All weapons—biological, chemical, missile, nuclear were destroyed."[57] Especially in light of the role weapons of
mass destruction played in the decision to invade Iraq in 2003, this testimony
from Kamel was probably the single most important piece of intelligence on
Iraq obtained by the West in the eleven years between the Gulf War and the
U.S.-led invasion of Iraq. But rather than ease international pressure on Iraq by
providing reassurance that no weapons of mass destruction remained, Kamel's
testimony heightened tension by disclosing new details about the biological
weapons program and the elaborate efforts by Saddam to conceal it from U.N.
inspectors until 1995. "I told [Deputy Prime Minister] Tariq Aziz, 'You've denied bio for years. How can we trust you on anything? This person has been
systematically lying,'" Ekeus recalled.[58] As a result, inspections intensified, reinforcing the belief in Baghdad that there would be no end to them, regardless
of whether Iraq complied. According to the CIA's retrospective, "When Iraq's
revelations were met by added U.N. scrutiny and distrust, frustrated Iraqi leaders deepened their belief that the inspections were politically motivated and
would not lead to the end of sanctions."[59]

It is important to bear in mind that although news of Kamel's defection and his revelation of details of the Iraqi biological weapons program made headlines in 1995, his assertion that he had supervised the destruction of all of Iraq's weapons of mass destruction in 1991 was not disclosed to the public. It would not come to light until late February of 2003—less than a month before the U.S.-led invasion of Iraq—in a *Newsweek* report. The story explained that Kamel's disclosure, given separately to the CIA and Britain's MI-6 as well as the U.N., was kept secret so that the U.N. could continue to press Saddam for more information about the details of his weapons programs.[60] Bill Harlow, the CIA's spokesman at the time the article was published, issued a strong denial, calling the story's assertion that Kamel had revealed that Iraq had destroyed its weapons stocks, "incorrect, bogus, wrong, untrue."[61] But Kamel's statements to Ekeus and other U.N. officials are difficult to read any other way. It appears clear, therefore, that U.S. intelligence knew of Kamel's claim but chose to discount it.

In 1996, Israeli scholar Amos Kovacs wrote about the phenomenon of the "non-use" of intelligence—that is, the collection of vital information that is then discounted, disbelieved, or ignored. "Many so-called 'intelligence failures' are not so much failures of intelligence per se, but rather failures to *use* intelligence," Kovacs wrote. One of the most common causes of the non-use of intelligence is "the mutual estrangement between the intelligence and the decision-making communities."[62] As Kovacs was writing, just such an example of the non-use of vital intelligence was unfolding in connection with the Iraq weapons inspections.

Narratives of the U.N. inspections of Iraq in the 1990s generally credit Kamel with disclosing the existence of a secret biological weapons program. This is not true; it was discovered in the months preceding his defection by U.N. inspectors. The sequence of events is important because it helps explain why intelligence that, in retrospect, was vital—the disclosure that Iraq had destroyed its weapons of mass destruction and converted production plants to civilian purposes—was simply not believed. What was important to the U.N. inspectors and to the CIA was the realization that four years into the inspection process a program to produce an entire line of weapons was only then coming to light. For those charged with watching Iraq, the fact that by the mid-1990s the Iraqi biological weapons program was inactive was considered a secondary issue.

The storyline of the discovery of Iraq's secret biological weapons program served to reinforce the lesson learned in 1991 when U.N. inspectors realized that Iraq was far closer to developing a nuclear weapon than the CIA had predicted. If anything, Iraq's biological weapons program represented a more extreme case. At least there had been *some* intelligence on Iraqi nuclear weapons development efforts before the Gulf War. Terence Taylor, a chief U.N. inspector for Iraq's biological programs, said in an interview that prior to their arrival in Iraq, "We had no information on the biological weapons program other than vague suspicions. I had no information, nothing, clean slate."[63] In the nuclear case, the CIA and other intelligence organizations had been able to direct inspectors to suspected weapons development sites or to the desert stashes where some key components were being buried to prevent their discovery. No such list of suspected sites existed for Iraqi biological programs, so the inspectors built their own list, starting with obvious places of interest such as pesticide or medicine manufacturing plants, a detergent factory, even dairy fermenters that made yogurt. They also began looking for information on Iraqi purchases of growth media. Such material, which is shipped in powdered form, has legitimate uses in hospitals, veterinary medicine, research laboratories, and so forth, but the quantities needed to supply a country the size of Iraq would be modest. The breakthrough for the U.N. inspectors came in March of 1995, five months before Kamel defected, with the discovery that Iraq had imported some forty tons of growth media from companies in Switzerland and Britain. This was a huge amount. "We expected to find evidence of some imports," Taylor said. "We found nearly 40 tons had been shipped to Iraq, enough to keep Iraq going for decades. We thought, 'Uh oh.'" What ensued mirrored the experience of the nuclear inspectors in 1991: initial denial by Iraqi officials followed by reluctant yielding of incomplete information accompanied by obviously false excuses about their inability to document their claims. Taylor recalled: "They cited the allied bombing. There were crazy stories about a fire that destroyed one page, an important missing page, from a particular document. Then they said the box with documents fell off the back of a truck and everything was collected except for that one page."[64] Finally, on July 1, 1995, Iraq admitted it had manufactured biological agent in bulk for weapons purposes but denied having filled shells with biological agent recently and insisted it had destroyed what weapons it had in 1991 and 1992.[65] To Taylor and other U.N. and U.S. officials at the time, the claim that the weapons had been destroyed seemed to be but one small part of the overall Iraq-WMD picture. Of much greater concern was the existence of a continuing secret program, even if it wasn't producing more weapons. "That's the record of the 1990s: Their behavior was repeated lying, repeatedly making it difficult for inspectors. How could you suddenly switch to trusting them?" Taylor asked.[66]

Kamel's defection set in motion a chain of events leading to the discovery of a huge cache of documents on Iraq's secret programs at a chicken farm owned by Kamel at Al Suwayrah, twenty-five miles south of Baghdad. In one of countless decisions by Saddam that backfired, the regime decided to disclose the hidden cache of documents in hopes that it would incriminate Kamel, but not Saddam and his regime. The size of the cache, however, undermined this bogus story: as many as nine trucks were needed to haul the documents from secret storage in Baghdad to the chicken farm. Once again, the vast scale of concealment activity and the assumption that much more remained hidden overrode any notion that the inspection process was succeeding.[67]

This sense of suspicion, though it contributed to the massive intelligence failure of the pre-invasion period in 2002 and 2003, was by no means unfounded. Information collected by Duelfer's Iraq Survey Group after the fall of Baghdad produced testimony that Saddam intended to return to the development and production of weapons of mass destruction once Iraq was free of debilitating economic sanctions. The Iraqi leader's chief concern was not the United States but Iran. Saddam's presidential secretary, 'Abd Hamid Mahmud, wrote while a detainee that Saddam believed that weapons of mass destruction would help "achieve international balance and protect the dignity of Iraq and Iraqis and the Arab nations," an idea that drew on Saddam's belief that Iraq stood as a Sunni-dominated bulwark against Shiite encroachment on the Arab world orchestrated from Tehran. Saddam said to his aides, according to Mahmud, "if only Iraq possessed the nuclear weapon, then no one would commit acts of aggression on it or any other Arab country, and the Palestinian issue would be solved peacefully because of Iraq."

After the fall of Saddam's regime, Tariq Aziz told U.S. interrogators that the Iraqi dictator never explicitly stated his intent but expressed a general belief that other countries in the region should not have weapons of mass destruction if Iraq did not. Saddam himself was somewhat more cryptic in his conversations with his U.S. captors. When asked whether he would have restarted his weapons of mass destruction programs after the lifting of sanctions, he indicated that Iraq would have done what was necessary to protect its security. It was not, at any rate, an outright denial.[68]

THE DESERT FOX

The U.N. Special Commission, or UNSCOM, spurred by the exposure of Iraq's secret biological weapons program in 1995, had embarked on an even more aggressive round of inspections in the ensuing two years. Now it was seeking access to Saddam's presidential palaces, easily big enough to hide not only weapons plans but the weapons themselves. The dictator cast the request as an attempt to humiliate him. By 1997 it had become clear to Saddam that no amount of disclosure would satisfy the U.N., that the real agenda was humiliating Iraq and maintaining crippling sanctions. More to the point, the agenda appeared to be driving him from power. He would tell his subordinates frequently that the choice, as he saw it, was between sanctions with inspections or sanctions without them, and that, in the end, he would prefer the latter.[69] On March 26, 1997, Secretary of State Madeleine Albright made clear in a major policy speech on Iraq at Georgetown University that Iraqi compliance with weapons inspections would not necessarily result in U.S. support for lifting sanctions. "Our view, which is unshakeable, is that Iraq must prove its peaceful intentions," Albright said. "It can only do that by complying with all of the Security Council resolutions to which it is subject. Is it possible to conceive of such a government under Saddam Hussein?" Albright answered her own question: "The evidence is overwhelming that Saddam Hussein's intentions will never be peaceful."[70] The reaction in Baghdad was instantaneous. With Albright's declaration in Washington, the climate for U.N. weapons inspectors in Iraq chilled considerably, according to Ambassador Ekeus. From that point on, Ekeus said in an interview, the Iraqis made clear that they no longer regarded compliance with weapons inspections as a ticket to freedom from international sanctions or from U.S. pressure on Saddam's regime. This change in attitude helps explain what many found hard to understand before the U.S.-led invasion of Iraq in 2003: if Iraq had no weapons of mass destruction, why not just say so and avoid invasion?[71]

There was some irony in Saddam's resignation to the indefinite continuation of sanctions, for in Washington the fear was the opposite, that the harm the sanctions were doing to Iraq would eventually create political conditions under which, with the help of France and Russia, the U.N. would lift the sanctions, and Iraq would be able to use its vast oil revenue to rearm. Saddam's refusal to grant access fueled suspicion that the sprawling palace complexes— some as large as cities—were precisely where Iraq had stashed banned weapons. Saddam charged that the U.S. nationals on the U.N. inspection teams were actually CIA spies, their mission to identify targets for the next war on Iraq. With the Clinton administration denying the espionage charge and urging the U.N. on, the inspectors took the position that they would not allow Saddam to dictate the nationality of their members. In December 1998, when the U.N. and Iraq could not agree on a resumption of "unfettered" inspections, the Clinton administration advised the Security Council that hostilities were imminent and instructed the inspectors to leave Iraq immediately.[72]

In the Gulf War, strike planners knew, U.S. warplanes had bombed a building they thought was involved in conventional weapons development that turned out to be one of Iraq's secret nuclear weapons development sites. The specter also loomed of another "baby milk factory" incident, in which U.S. warplanes in the Gulf War attacked what the coalition claimed was a legitimate military target but which Saddam turned into a propaganda coup by telling Western reporters it was a plant that manufactured infant formula. The possibility of an air strike letting loose a deadly gas plume reminiscent of what some said had happened at Kamisiyah further weighed in Pentagon strike planning. The CIA's ability to identify key weapons-related targets had been called into question in the fall of 1998 in connection with the U.S. cruise missile attack on the Al-Shifa pharmaceutical plant in Khartoum, Sudan, suspected of being used to manufacture nerve agent for the terrorist group al-Qaeda.[73] These concerns about repeating such mishaps generated pressure within the Clinton administration to limit the intensity of the air strikes on Iraq. There was virtually no discussion of the possibility that Iraq had no weapons of mass destruction.[74]

Reporters were also picking up on speculation that the aim was to kill Saddam himself. In background conversations, senior U.S. officers talked about the difficulty of locating Saddam because of his use of doubles and his practice of sleeping in a different location every night. Saddam sought to lessen the risk of assassination by an Iraqi faction, an ever-present danger to Saddam. But the dictator was well aware of the risk of death by air strike. After the fall of his regime, Saddam told his U.S. captors that after 1990 he had used a telephone only twice for fear that an electronic intercept of the call might point U.S. intelligence to his location and lead to an air strike.[75] As the air campaign against Iraq loomed in December 1998, Pentagon officials responded to questions about whether such careful tracking of Saddam's whereabouts implied a change in the long-standing presidential order banning involvement in assassinations by insisting that the commander of an enemy force was a legitimate target in wartime.[76]

Operation Desert Fox, a name that somewhat oddly invoked the nick-name of Erwin Rommel, Hitler's Africakorps commander in World War II, unfolded over four days, December 16–19, 1998. Once the operation was under way, Pentagon reporters ran through a well-established line of questioning for such operations: What had been hit? How much damage was done? What did the attacks accomplish? What was the level of collateral damage? The Pentagon, burned by its experience in the Persian Gulf War with damage claims that later proved unfounded, had a standard reply in response to such after-action questions: "BDA," or bomb-damage assessment, would take some time to complete. Whatever the intent of the strike plan, Saddam remained alive and in power. Nevertheless, the Clinton administration declared Operation Desert Fox a success.[77]

BOMB DAMAGE ASSESSMENT

As days and then weeks went by and more became known about the Desert Fox strikes, it became clearer that there really was no list of weapons-of-mass-destruction targets. The Pentagon press corps could get no clear answer on whether, if at all, Iraq's supposed arsenal had been reduced. The strikes appeared focused initially on Iraqi air defense assets—to eliminate the immediate threat to U.S. warplanes—then shifted to regime leadership targets, tending to confirm the notion that getting Saddam had been a primary aim. Reporters were told vaguely that "dual-use" facilities with possible links to WMD had been hit, along with plants associated with Iraqi rocket and missile development. There were no deadly plumes, no demolished stockpiles.[78]

Only with time would the most important legacy of Operation Desert Fox become clear: the departure of U.N. inspectors. Since no one in policymaking circles, whether Democrat or Republican, questioned Saddam's determination to rearm, the severe gap in U.S. intelligence coverage of Iraq created by the departure of inspectors received little attention. The deep mistrust of the United Nations among Republican lawmakers had eroded confidence in the inspection process. To many Republicans, inspections were a sham, a way for Saddam to rid Iraq of international sanctions while holding on to his weapons. In fact, the departure of inspectors devastated U.S. intelligence collection on Iraq. When the magnitude of the intelligence failure on Iraqi weapons of mass destruction became clear after the U.S.-led invasion in 2003, senior CIA analysts ruefully admitted that the departure of the inspectors five years earlier had led to a virtual blackout of detailed intelligence on Iraqi weapons programs. Through most of the 1990s the CIA had come to rely on U.N. inspection reports to the exclusion of any other human intelligence collection. It seemed there was no need to build a network of spies in Iraq so long as U.N. inspectors had regular high-level access to Iraqi weapons officials.

After 1998 the CIA tried only halfheartedly to build a spy network until the eve of war, when Tenet, suddenly realizing the urgency of the situation, ordered a crash program to penetrate Saddam's regime.[79] It yielded occasional and apparently inaccurate tidbits on the whereabouts of the dictator and little of value on weapons of mass destruction. On March 19, 2003, the opening night of the U.S.-led invasion of Iraq, President Bush approved a massive "decapitation strike" on a site in Baghdad called Dora Farms where Saddam and both of his sons were believed to be staying, possibly in an underground bunker. The intelligence came from the CIA's Directorate of Operations from a spy network inside Iraq codenamed ROCKSTAR. In the post-9/11 environment, CIA reticence about the quality of its targeting information was much diminished; the hesitance seen in the pre-9/11 decisions not to strike at Osama bin Laden was gone. Nevertheless it became apparent soon enough that Saddam had not been killed in the strike.

After the invasion, U.S. forces learned that Saddam had not been there the night the war began. As if that weren't embarrassing enough to the CIA, it turned out that there was no buried bunker at the site.[80] The take from sources reporting on weapons of mass destruction was little better. Tenet told the WMD Commission that the CIA had between thirty and forty sources reporting on chemical weapons in Iraq before the war. None was rated "highly reliable," while six were rated "moderately reliable."[81] Author and journalist James Risen has described a program run by Charles Allen, in 2002 the CIA's assistant director for collection, that involved contacting scientists known to have worked on Iraq's WMD programs. The Agency used family members living outside of Iraq as intermediaries and learned through them that the scientists were reporting that none of the WMD programs were active. According to Risen, the CIA ignored the evidence and never reported it to President Bush.[82]

AN INVISIBLE SUCCESS

Before the U.S. invasion of Iraq in 2003, few were prepared to believe that Iraq had no weapons of mass destruction. Virtually no one in a position of authority, not Bush administration officials, not U.N. officers or members of Congress, was prepared to believe that U.S. and allied intelligence services working with U.N. inspectors on the ground could have rooted out all of the suspect sites, all of the potential hiding places, all the factories, laboratories and dual-use facilities, all the document storage centers and presidential palaces in Iraq that could conceivably conceal something related to weapons of mass destruction. Nothing like that had ever happened before. No international organization had ever successfully disarmed a member state whose government had survived defeat in war. The Versailles Treaty had imposed severe armaments restrictions on Germany, but the victors in World War I had agreed to arms limits on themselves and eventually Germany went ahead and rebuilt its military anyway. In the years after the Gulf War, it seemed impossible to believe that the lying and concealing perpetrated by the Iraqis, some of it crude, some quite sophisticated, had not been done to protect a secret weapons program. Iraq was known to have more chemical weapons than it had destroyed under U.N. supervision, and it was inconceivable that Saddam could have destroyed his additional stocks secretly—seemingly having the worst of both worlds: no weapons of mass destruction but no freedom from sanctions. Yet this, in essence, is what happened in the decade-plus between the Gulf War and the Iraq War. It was an astonishing accomplishment, and not even the CIA, the intelligence organization most centrally involved in the process, was prepared to believe it had succeeded.

The Iraq intelligence failure has been framed as a failure to prove a negative, a failure to prove or conclude that there were no weapons of mass destruction in Iraq. It could just as easily be described as a failure to identify a positive—an accomplishment—a failure to see that policies put in place and carried out by a combination of international agencies, allies, and multiple U.S. administrations through military pressure and intelligence support—could have succeeded in effectively relieving the most powerful nation in the Arab world of its deadliest weapons. Not only had this international intelligence and inspection coalition done so, it had done it in about a year's time. This result was incredible, both because it was difficult to conceive that Saddam would have chosen the disarmament course, and because a decade of budget cuts, espionage fiascos, failures to predict crises, and most vividly, the failure to unravel the 9/11 plot had sapped confidence in the U.S. intelligence community. Under the second Bush administration, it was not only a tendency, it was official policy to view the CIA as incapable of penetrating the most elusive targets. This belief was validated from time to time by intelligence failures, some of them spectacular, but in the case of Iraq, it served mainly as a way to justify a policy course without having to bother to match it up with the available intelligence.

Rumsfeld, Cheney, and other Bush aides who advocated invasion were fully aware that the threat of Iraqi weapons was limited. That is precisely why they felt it safe to invade. Iraq was selected for invasion not because it was dangerous, but because it was vulnerable. The Bush team genuinely believed that Iraq had some banned weapons. U.S. commanders on the march north to Baghdad were surprised when Saddam's troops didn't launch chemical projectiles at the coalition forces, who were equipped for that contingency. But the administration also knew the intelligence underlying the case for war was weak—witness the behind-the-scenes tussles with the CIA over supposed al-Qaeda links to Saddam's regime. The administration overcame this obstacle by adopting Donald Rumsfeld's logic about "unknowns" and "unknowables." The weakness of the intelligence underlying the case for war, in the administration's thinking, strengthened rather than weakened the case for war. And the administration's low regard for the CIA made it easier to use the Agency as a prop in the run-up to war when CIA analysis supported the administration, and to ignore or override the CIA when its analysis did not.

Culminating the decade of declining budgets, declining morale, and declining reputation for the CIA was the September 11 crisis. The Agency's embattled posture amid the criticism over its failure to uncover the September 11 plot greatly weakened the Agency's political position at a time when independence from political pressure and creative thinking was vital to avoiding disaster. As in past intelligence controversies such as the Gulf War, the Soviet collapse and the Ames case, the criticism seemed to be coming from everywhere—the White House, Congress, Republicans, and Democrats, even from the Agency itself. In connection with 9/11, the criticism was uniform and consistent: the CIA had failed to "connect the dots"; it had failed to recognize the critical clues that were lost in a cacophony of intelligence "noise" before the attacks but which loomed so large afterward. This criticism, moreover, was coming at the CIA in the same month when Tenet was orchestrating production of the intelligence assessment of Iraq's ability to mount a catastrophic attack on the United States. It seems that the month of September 2002 must have been dominated at CIA headquarters by the preparation of that fateful October 1 National Intelligence Estimate presenting the intelligence community's views on Iraq's supposed weapons of mass destruction. Perhaps it was for some, but not for the Agency's leadership. The dominant topic that month was the continuing investigation of the House-Senate Joint Inquiry Committee into intelligence failures relating to the September 11, 2001, attacks. Between September 1, 2002, and October 10, the day before Congress voted to authorize force in Iraq, the Joint Inquiry Committee held twelve hearings on 9/11 intelligence failures. As the Agency leadership was being publicly lambasted for missing clues that could have unraveled the deadliest terror plot in history, its senior analysts were sifting through abundant though circumstantial clues about deadly weapons in the hands of a murderous dictator. To the White House, there could be no question how the CIA should respond. The CIA fought the White House on some of the details of the WMD case, but in the end delivered what the Bush administration wanted: a case for war.[83]

The gravitational pull of the 9/11 attacks on strategic thinking in Washington prior to the Iraq War cannot be overstated. It created the political environment in which the Bush administration could embark on a new kind of offensive war. It made the specter of a mass-destruction attack on the U.S. homeland a vivid possibility. It greatly reduced the motivation in Congress and the media to question the case for war. It put the CIA on the defensive for having failed to perceive an impending terrorist threat and contributed to its gross overstatement of the threat posed by Iraq. It also generated a dramatic change of attitude in the CIA's clandestine service—with adverse consequences for the quality of intelligence on Iraq.

GETTING THE ANSWERS YOU WANT

"This is a highly classified area. All I want to say is that there was 'before' 9/11 and 'after' 9/11. After 9/11, the gloves come off."[84]

That colorful statement by Cofer Black, who ran the CIA's Counter-Terrorism Center, was delivered to the House-Senate inquiry committee in September 2002, as senior intelligence analysts were working on their final draft of the National Intelligence Estimate on Iraq. Black's remark provided one of the first glimpses into the coercive and then-secret methods used by the CIA to obtain information from terrorist detainees. The full account would take years to come out, as a few inmates who had won release from the U.S. prison camp at Guantanamo Bay, Cuba, told their stories, and as the military investigation into abuses at the Abu Ghraib prison in Iraq came to light. But even then, in the fall of 2002, coercive interrogation methods were already having an impact, both in the war on terror and in preparing for war in Iraq. For as Black was truculently explaining the new attitude at the CIA to the

House-Senate investigators, analysts at Agency headquarters were working with some of the fruits of that new attitude in putting together the estimate on Iraq's weapons of mass destruction.

In the sixteen months between the 9/11 attacks and the invasion of Iraq, the CIA had made little headway in recruiting human sources in Iraq with valuable information. But it was very busy waging the war on terror, arresting al-Qaeda suspects, and conducting interrogations. As details of this secretive process gradually filtered out, it became clear that once interrogations of "high-value" detainees finished with the obvious priority issues—the organization of al-Qaeda; knowledge of future attacks; the whereabouts of Osama bin Laden; and the techniques used in previous attack operations—the CIA frequently turned to the issue of Iraq. One of the first senior al-Qaeda suspects to be captured after 9/11 was Ibn al-Shaykh al-Libi, who was apprehended in Pakistan exactly two months after the 9/11 attacks on November 11, 2001. Al-Libi ran al-Qaeda's Khalden training camp in Afghanistan before the 9/11 attacks. According to the *Washington Post's* Dana Priest, who has reported authoritatively on detainee treatment issues, it was al-Libi's capture that touched off the first post-9/11 debate within the U.S. government over the interrogation techniques that could be used against al-Qaeda detainees. In a dispute between the CIA, which favored harsher methods, and the FBI, whose senior officers regarded torture as a sure way to elicit bad information, the Bush administration sided with the CIA and, beginning in January 2002, put the Agency in charge of al-Libi's interrogation.[85] The Senate Intelligence Committee's 2006 investigative report on Iraq intelligence failures, quoting from a CIA operational cable, picks up what happened next.

"In early 2002 one of [al-Libi's] American debriefers told him that he had to tell 'where bin Laden was and about future operations or the U.S. would give al-Libi'" to another foreign intelligence service, believed to be Egypt. At this point al-Libi "decided he would fabricate any information the interrogators wanted in order to gain better treatment and avoid being handed over" to a foreign government.[86] It didn't work; al-Libi became one of the first cases of "extraordinary rendition." Once in Egypt, Al-Libi's interrogators "stated that the next topic was al-Qaeda's connections with Iraq. . . . This was a subject about which he said he knew nothing and had difficulty even coming up with a story." The Egyptians, according to the CIA cable, "placed him in a small box approximately 50cm × 50cm." He was then given another opportunity to "tell the truth." When he again did not comply, he was beaten for fifteen minutes. At this point, al-Libi came up with a story about three al-Qaeda operatives traveling to Iraq to receive training about nuclear weapons. The prisoner was taken to a spacious room and fed.[87]

This account was conveyed to CIA headquarters in an operational cable from the field in February 2004, just under a year after the invasion of Iraq. The CIA in 2004 was reexamining al-Libi's prewar statements because the prisoner was now claiming he had made up much of what he told CIA and Egyptian interrogators to avoid being tortured.

But concern that al-Libi was fabricating stories had appeared in multiple intelligence reports before the war. On February 22, 2002, the Defense Intelligence Agency issued a Defense Intelligence Terrorism Summary concerning the issue of Iraq providing weapons training to al-Qaeda. The DIA report recounted the story al-Libi told the Egyptians, presumably without the details about how the information was obtained, but went on to express concern about its accuracy. Al-Libi, the DIA cautioned, "lacks specific details on the Iraqi's [sic] involved, the CBRN (chemical, biological, radiological, nuclear) materials associated with the assistance, and the location where training occurred. It is possible he does not know any further details; it is more likely this individual is intentionally misleading the debriefers." The DIA was elliptical as to why al-Libi would do this, saying his motivation may have been to describe "scenarios to the debriefers that he knows will retain their interest." The DIA went on to make a point that appeared repeatedly in intelligence assessments following 9/11, that Saddam was a secular dictator, "wary of Islamic movements" and unlikely to aid violent groups he could not control.[88] A week later, the DIA revisited the issue, pointing out that despite al-Libi's information, "all-source intelligence has not confirmed Iraq's involvement" in providing weapons training to al-Qaeda operatives.[89]

Concern about the possibility that al-Libi was a fabricator did not prevent the Bush administration from seizing on his information and, without describing the source or the method of obtaining the information, including it in major speeches by President Bush, Vice President Cheney, and others making the case for war against Iraq. Al-Libi's intelligence was featured prominently in Secretary of State Colin Powell's February 5, 2003, presentation to the U.N. Security Council. Powell told the assemblage that "a senior terrorist operative" in detention had "first-hand" information about Iraqi support for al-Qaeda efforts to acquire weapons of mass destruction. Al-Qaeda, Powell said, could not get these programs going by itself: "They had to look outside of Afghanistan for help. Where did they go? Where did they look? They went to Iraq."[90]

In the years since the WMD case against Iraq collapsed, we have seen stories about Powell's dismay over the inaccuracy of the intelligence he presented to the Security Council. He has described an arduous vetting process at CIA headquarters in the days before his presentation in which he, CIA Director Tenet, and senior intelligence community staff pored over documents, sifting out the weak material and including only what they felt they could solidly defend.[91] Somehow this supposedly exhaustive process seems have missed a CIA report distributed just seven days before Powell's presentation. The document, an update of a report titled "Iraqi Support for Terrorism," cautioned that al-Libi's information about training in Iraq might be flawed because "the detainee was not in a position to know if any training took place."[92] More broadly, the CIA assessed that Saddam and bin Laden "are far from being natural partners" and that Saddam's long-standing antipathy toward militant Islamic movements "suggests that any such ties would be rooted in deep suspicion." That feeling was apparently mutual, according to "high-ranking al-Qaeda officials" not identified in the report. According to the CIA, "there was an intense debate within the al-Qaeda leadership in Afghanistan over the risks and benefits of working with Baghdad . . . [and] bin Laden generally opposed collaboration." The report suggested it was possible that their mutual antipathy toward the United States could override their distrust of each other. But the overall tone pointed decidedly away from the notion of a sponsor-client relationship between Iraq and al-Qaeda.[93] Again, keep in mind the timing: the CIA, on Wednesday, January 29, 2003, issued a classified report deeply skeptical that al-Qaeda had ties with Iraq; Powell, Tenet, and a team of senior officers spent the following weekend, February 1 and 2, in a crash effort to assemble the presentation to the U.N. on Wednesday, February 5. Yet none of the doubts expressed by the Agency that helped produce Powell's presentation were shared with the U.N. Powell made only the most elliptical of references to the concerns in his presentation. "Some believe, some claim these contacts do not amount to much," Powell said. "They say Saddam Hussein's secular tyranny and al-Qaeda's religious tyranny do not mix. I am not comforted by this thought." What he didn't say was that "some people" included the CIA, represented there in the Security Council chamber by George Tenet, who was seated directly behind Powell in mute intelligence community endorsement of everything the secretary of state was saying.[94]

As with so many aspects of the case for war in Iraq, doubt, second opinion, and concern about the quality of sources would come to light only after the United States was committed to war. In January 2004, al-Libi told CIA interrogators that his prewar information on Iraq and al-Qaeda had been made up to avoid or curtail torture. The next month, the CIA updated its intelligence reporting on al-Libi to reflect his recanting of his previous statements. The Senate Intelligence Committee report said there were other intelligence sources who spoke about possible chemical and biological weapons training for al-Qaeda operatives in Iraq. But the committee concluded, "No other information has been uncovered in Iraq or from detainees that confirms this reporting."[95] Tenet, in his memoir, claims that al-Libi's recantation came as a shock to him in 2004. Until then Tenet had regarded the information from al-Libi and other sources on Iraq-al-Qaeda ties as "solid." The CIA handed al-Libi over to intelligence officers of another country, also not specified by Tenet, because the Agency believed the prisoner was withholding information about pending terror attacks. But Tenet denies that the purpose of the rendition was to torture al-Libi. Tenet does not mention the January 2003 CIA report or the two DIA reports of 2002, even though those reports raised sharp questions about the validity of information from a source who was, in January 2002, the highest-ranking al-Qaeda operative in U.S. custody. After al-Libi recanted, "there was sharp division" within the CIA about which part of the detainee's story was true. Nevertheless, CIA decided to "recall" intelligence reports that were based on al-Libi's prewar statements. "The fact is," Tenet wrote, "we don't know which story is true, and since we don't know, we can assume nothing."[96]

Of course, as has become abundantly clear since the United States invaded Iraq, the Bush administration and the CIA assumed a great deal.

"ASK THE WHITE HOUSE"

After the September 11 attacks, *USA Today* hired me away from my position as State Department correspondent for the *Chicago Tribune* to fill a newly created beat covering the CIA. As the Bush administration's rhetoric about Iraqi weapons of mass destruction grew more explicit in the summer of 2002, I called Bill Harlow, the CIA's spokesman during Tenet's years as director, and asked what new intelligence had come in to justify the definitive accusations that Iraq had rebuilt its deadly arsenal. The administration statements departed sharply from the heavily qualified tone of the CIA's annual reports on Iraq's suspected weapons programs and of Tenet's yearly "threat briefs" to

Congress. The White House rhetoric on Iraq in late summer of 2002 suggested that the intelligence community had acquired new and highly sensitive information confirming the long-standing suspicions about Saddam's arsenal.

Asked what was behind these bold administration pronouncements, Harlow's response was startling. "We don't know. You'll have to ask the White House," he said.[97]

This was highly unusual. The CIA, despite a streak of independence and occasional disagreements with the White House, nevertheless served the president. Agency officials, though cantankerous and contrarian by nature, knew by survival instinct not to stand in the way of the Official Line coming from the Oval Office. If top administration officials were saying something about intelligence, CIA officials weren't going to undercut it, at least not in conversations with the media.

"Ask the White House."

This was provocative. The implication was: We don't have information to support what the White House is saying; and whatever information the White House has, we either don't have it or don't believe it. It was an early glimpse of the White House–CIA conflict brewing just below the surface. Conversations such as this produced stories that portrayed an administration determined to go to war in Iraq and in search of a *casus belli*, that pointed out the wide gap between the charges being leveled against Iraq and the intelligence to back them up, and that described the concerns among intelligence professionals about the sources providing the Bush administration with its case for war. But stories that raised questions tended to run inside newspapers, while the information being orchestrated by the Bush administration was appearing on front pages. And other than former U.N. weapons inspector Scott Ritter and Saddam Hussein himself, virtually no one in a prominent position in 2002 was saying that Iraq had no weapons of mass destruction.[98]

WAR DRUMS

In subsequent weeks, the basic elements of the conflict between the White House and the CIA came into view. The CIA suspected that Iraq was reviving its banned arsenal. The White House was certain of it. The CIA saw little if any evidence supporting the charge that al-Qaeda was in league with Saddam's regime. The White House saw ample evidence. British intelligence reported that Iraq was trying to buy uranium ore in Africa, and the administration repeated the charge. The CIA's information was that the story could not be confirmed and might be false. And most important, the CIA distrusted the information being peddled by the anti-Saddam Iraqi National Congress and its leader, Ahmed Chalabi, about Iraq's supposed arsenal, while the White House regarded the information and its source as reliable.[99]

As the war drums beat louder, reporters on the defense and intelligence beats clamored for the latest information on Iraq. In December 2002, the Defense Intelligence Agency invited a small group of reporters to a background briefing, much of which focused on the state of Iraqi conventional forces. Iraq's military capability had been more than halved by its overwhelming defeat in the Gulf War, and the ensuing decade of sanctions had afforded little opportunity for repair and improvement, the DIA reported. Message: Defeating Iraq will be relatively easy. On the question of Iraq's weapons of mass destruction, the DIA briefers were equally clear: We have only suspicions, no "smoking gun" proof. This too was remarkable. If an organization directly under the control of a defense secretary as powerful as Donald Rumsfeld was willing to say that, even under the cloak of anonymity, the gaps in intelligence on Iraq must have been considerable indeed.[100]

In the event, the White House and the CIA met somewhere in the middle. U.S. intelligence produced a ninety-page, top-secret National Intelligence Estimate on October 1, 2002, a document filled with caveats, qualifiers, and warnings of incomplete information—and, as it turned out, errors. The caveats were unknown to the press at the time. A summary of the "key points" contained in the estimate would not be made public until July 2003, by which time U.S. forces had been in Iraq for more than four months.[101] Lawmakers, those few who bothered to read it, had access to the debate within the intelligence community over Iraq's arsenal.[102] Most contented themselves with attending briefings that summarized the report. Some read the classified version of the key points, which began with a series of definitive statements that Iraq had chemical and biological weapons, the means to deliver them—even on the United States—and a revived nuclear weapons development program. None of this turned out to be true. The White House, for its part, continued to state flatly that the threat posed by Iraq was clear and present. Its one concession to uncertainty was to say, as Condoleezza Rice put it evocatively in a television interview, that in a post–September 11 world, you did not want to wait to find the smoking gun only to discover that the smoke was a mushroom cloud.[103]

Although the National Intelligence Estimate of October 2002 was deeply flawed, it nevertheless conveyed valuable information to anyone patient enough

to wade through its detailed analysis. To a degree not discernible to those relying exclusively on Bush administration rhetoric, the estimate revealed the
deep divisions within the intelligence community about certain key elements
of the case against Iraq and the uncertain nature of the evidence. Perhaps
aware that such an estimate would reveal intelligence community divisions, the
Bush administration had been prepared to go to war without ordering a full
intelligence-community workup on the weapons-of-mass-destruction assessment. Instead, Congress ordered the report, knowing it would soon be voting
on a war resolution. The intelligence estimate was also notable for what it omitted. Despite the unqualified statement in the key points that "Iraq has chemical . . . weapons," we know from a Senate inquiry that the body of the report,
which remains classified, contains no intelligence information backing up the
chemical weapons assessment. Among lawmakers, who had clearance to read
the document, that absence of supporting evidence went unquestioned in the
congressional debate over war in Iraq.[104]

The failure of the White House to request such a report when it was contemplating full-scale war based, ostensibly, on intelligence; the intelligence community's failure to take up the task on its own initiative until asked, belatedly, by
Congress; and the failure by the vast majority of lawmakers to even read the estimate while preparing to cast one of the most important votes of their careers-
these collectively rank among the most signal failures of the prewar period.

Tenet, in particular, must bear a large share of the blame. While there
was some truth to complaints that the director of central intelligence wielded
insufficient power over intelligence agencies controlled by the Pentagon, the
DCI's authority to order intelligence estimates that would tap the collective
knowledge of the intelligence community was one of the job's most powerful
attributes. In the case of the run-up to war in Iraq, Tenet failed to use this
significant power until far too late in the debate. Here the problem was not
inadequate power in the hands of the director, but the director's failure to use
the power he had available.

The failure of most members of Congress to even read the October estimate
has drawn justified condemnation. Had they done so, they might have noticed
the dissenting views within the intelligence community disputing that Iraq had
been buying aluminum tubes for use as uranium centrifuges and that pilotless
Iraqi aircraft were to be used to dispense chemical and biological weapons.
Still, the few members who read the document seem not to have noticed such
worrisome passages. Such attention as the estimate got from Congress focused

on the CIA's warning that an outright invasion of Iraq presented the one scenario most likely to bring about Iraqi use of its supposed weapons of mass destruction. But it should be noted that Congress got the document on October 1, 2002, and voted for war on October 10; nine days was hardly enough time for hundreds of members of Congress to carefully consider a densely written intelligence report.[105] As in the Persian Gulf War, members who already knew how they were going to vote tended to see a detailed reading of the intelligence estimate as superfluous. Supporters of the war in Congress lined up solidly behind the Bush administration and accepted without question the assertions of top White House officials and the intelligence community about Iraq's arsenal. Opponents largely accepted the WMD assessments as valid, but questioned whether the threat was imminent and raised concerns about the U.S. initiating a war. Senator Carl Levin of Michigan is a case in point. Levin, then the ranking Democrat on the Armed Services Committee and a lawmaker known for doing his homework, said he attended briefings on the intelligence estimate and scanned its key findings. But he said he did not plow through the ninety pages of detailed analysis because he already knew he was going to vote against the authorization to use force. Levin's concern was that the Bush administration was going ahead toward war without the approval of the United Nations, something he regarded as essential to establishing U.S. legitimacy.

DOUBTS AND HUNCHES

From the reporting of author and journalist Bob Woodward, we know that among those with prewar doubts about the quality of WMD intelligence on Iraq was none other than President Bush. In an extraordinary scene in Woodward's book *Plan of Attack*, an account written with extensive White House cooperation, Woodward describes an Oval Office briefing for Bush given by Tenet and his deputy, John McLaughlin, on December 21, 2002. A detailed presentation by McLaughlin that included spy satellite photos and transcripts of electronic intercepts left Bush unimpressed.

"Nice try," the president said. The material was "not something that Joe Public would understand." Turning to Tenet, Bush said, "I've been told all this intelligence about [Iraq] having WMD, and this is the best we've got?"

In a phrase certain to reappear in Tenet's obituaries, the intelligence chief told Bush not to worry: "It's a slam-dunk case."[106]

Oddly, Tenet's half of the conversation has drawn the most attention. How embarrassing, critics have said, for the director of central intelligence to call the Iraq WMD intelligence a slam-dunk case when time would show that Iraq had no weapons of mass destruction and little if anything in the way of infrastructure to make such weapons. The man whose job it was to know, so it appeared, didn't know what he was talking about.

The focus in this scene rightly belongs on Bush. Here, three months before U.S. tanks rolled through a sand berm marking the border between Kuwait and Iraq, we have the president of the United States, the man who would order the attack, stating quite clearly that he found the intelligence underlying his own policy unconvincing. The exchange reveals the evident inadequacy of Bush's previous intelligence briefings on Iraq's alleged arsenal—or perhaps Bush's inattention to the reports he did receive. His remark suggests that the Tenet-McLaughlin briefing was the first detailed presentation on Iraq WMD intelligence that Bush had received and that only at this late date was Bush focusing on the details behind a war policy that he had long since set. Bush clearly saw the weakness of the intelligence and, in private, did not hesitate to say so. But the president's doubts never left the room, and he failed to act on them by slowing the march to war until he was satisfied that the case for war rested on solid ground.

In his "Joe Public" remark, Bush makes clear that the issue wasn't really substance but sales pitch. Tenet himself confirms this point in his memoir, describing the meeting not as an intelligence report to the president but as a rehearsal of a presentation to be made to the United Nations and the American public. "At no time did [Bush] or anyone else in the room suggest that we collect more intelligence to find out if the WMD were there or not," Tenet wrote. "Everyone in the room already believed Saddam possessed WMD. The focus was simply on sharpening the arguments."[107] Tenet offers this explanation in his own defense. Yet it seems all the more damning that neither the intelligence professionals nor the "consumers" of intelligence considered the possibility that the case for war was weak because the intelligence was weak.

THE FAILURE OF IMAGINATION

In 1995, before he ended his defection and returned to Iraq at Saddam's invitation, only to be killed in a shootout that was almost certainly ordered by the dictator, Hussein Kamel had some advice for chief U.N. weapons inspector Rolf Ekeus. "You have an important role in Iraq," Kamel said. "You should not underestimate yourself. You are very effective in Iraq."[108]

The massive intelligence failure prior to the invasion of Iraq can be boiled down to a failure to heed that advice. U.S. intelligence spent more than a decade working with allied security services and multiple international inspection organizations trying to accomplish something, then failed to even consider that their effort had succeeded. During the dozen years between the two wars against Iraq, U.S. intelligence produced not a single analytical report exploring whether Saddam's desire to be out from under international sanctions might have driven him to comply with international demands.[109] In the push and pull with Baghdad over the course of the 1990s, the intelligence community had forgotten one of the key conditions that brought the Gulf crisis to a head back in 1990: deteriorating economic conditions in Iraq. Iraq was on its back after years of bloodletting with Iran, and overproduction of oil by Iraq's Arab neighbors was keeping it there. It was this circumstance, along with Saddam's suspicion that oil prices were being depressed at the behest of the United States, that drove Saddam to invade Kuwait. The CIA saw the controversy as a minor border dispute. In the years after the Gulf War, under the most debilitating sanctions ever imposed on a single country by the international community, Iraq's economy went from bad to worse. By 1995, according to the Duelfer report, Iraq's economy had "hit rock bottom" due to the sanctions. The considerable human suffering stemming from the sanctions, particularly a dramatic rise in infant mortality in Iraq, was becoming harder for the international community to justify. But aside from their toll on the Iraqi people, the sanctions were having precisely the desired effect in Iraq: lifting the sanctions had become Saddam's top priority, even if it meant getting rid of weapons of mass destruction. The trouble was, the people who designed the sanctions simply didn't believe their own success. They stuck with the view that Saddam wanted to revive his weapons of mass destruction programs. Indeed, evidence has emerged since the invasion that Saddam intended to revive those weapons programs. But reviving WMD wasn't Iraq's *top* priority, and this again was a critical intelligence failure.[110]

The pre-invasion intelligence on Iraq that has been declassified also shows a notable absence of discussion of Iran as a motivating factor in Iraq's calculations. The intelligence community duly noted the deterioration of Iraq's conventional military under sanctions that prevented it from importing many key components needed to maintain its weaponry. But it discussed the issue only in the context of a possible conflict with U.S. forces. The CIA failed to consider that Iraq's concern about modernizing its conventional forces to deter or menace Iran would motivate Saddam to try to get the sanctions lifted.

Criticism of the intelligence community's performance prior to the 9/11 attacks often used the phrase "failure of imagination" to describe the inability to envision a massive suicide attack on high-profile U.S. targets, possibly involving aircraft—even though intelligence had been collected pointing in that direction. Lack of imagination characterized the Iraq-WMD intelligence effort as well, but in a different way. In the case of Iraq, the intelligence community failed to consider one of the basic elements of deterrence theory and weapons of mass destruction: if a country, such as Iraq, confronts a much more powerful adversary, such as the United States, the weaker country has no incentive to hide the fact that it has weapons of mass destruction. If it has them, such a country has every incentive to make sure the adversary knows of its capability. Iraq's determined ambiguity was seen uniformly by the CIA as an attempt to hide illegal weapons of mass destruction; no consideration was given to the idea that Iraq might be hiding the fact that it had no such weapons. As the WMD Commission put it:

> Failing to conclude that Saddam had ended his banned weapons programs is one thing—not even considering it as a possibility is another. . . . The absence of such a discussion within the intelligence community is, in our view, indicative of a rut that the Community found itself in throughout the 1990s. Rather than thinking imaginatively, and considering seemingly unlikely and unpopular possibilities, the Intelligence Community instead found itself wedded to a set of assumptions about Iraq, focusing on intelligence reporting that appeared to confirm those assumptions.[111]

. . .

Through much of the CIA's history, overestimating an enemy was the safe course. The Pentagon might spend too much money as a result, but the gigantic U.S. economy could absorb the blow, and the military would avoid unpleasant surprises. The point of worst-case analysis was to avoid war by being abundantly prepared for war. The attitude was ingrained in the thinking of CIA officers from the beginning. Underestimating Japanese naval power had led to the Pearl Harbor intelligence failure, the event that led to the creation of the CIA six years later in 1947. But under the Bush administration's preemption doctrine, there was a worst case on the other side of the equation as well, one the intelligence community failed entirely to consider: what if the United States started a war based on intelligence that proved to be wrong? Not only did the worst-case mentality not work under preemption; it actually worked in reverse. Under the preemption doctrine, worst-case analysis did not avoid war; instead it became a trigger for war, since the idea behind preemption was to strike an enemy first, before the enemy could use his weapons on the United States. Through the late 1990s, a position that Saddam probably had kept stocks of chemical weapons and a secret biological weapons program, as well as nuclear ambitions, was not unreasonable for the purpose of maintaining sanctions on Iraq. Under Bush, that same position was being used in furtherance of a much more radical policy, but with no significant improvement in the quality or quantity of the intelligence. The result has been a great tragedy for the intelligence community, and for the United States.

The consequences of the WMD intelligence failure were far-reaching. In addition to undermining public confidence in the CIA, it seriously undercut the credibility of the Bush administration at home and abroad and raised questions about the legitimacy of the entire war effort. The intelligence failure was so spectacular that some found it hard to believe it could have been anything but a ruse to provide cover for a war waged for other, less salable reasons. Once the main premise became untenable, the Bush administration put forward other reasons for having gone to war, an effort increasingly undermined by the deteriorating situation on the ground in Iraq. Those ever shifting-reasons—spreading democracy, establishing stability, creating an Arab ally, stopping terrorism, ending sectarian violence, holding Iraq together—further undermined public confidence as each, in its turn, proved elusive, resulting in a circumstance in which even supporters of the war could no longer identify what victory or the slightly less ambitious term, success, would look like.

PREWAR ASSESSMENTS OF POSTWAR IRAQ

In January 2003, the National Intelligence Council distributed to senior officials of the Bush administration and key congressional committees two secret reports, *Regional Consequences of Regime Change in Iraq* and *Principal Challenges in Post-Saddam Iraq*. With remarkable foresight, the reports, which received wide distribution among cleared officials across the government, described the risks and pitfalls of what was, by then, the Bush administration's set course toward invading Iraq and overthrowing Saddam Hussein. Coordinated by Paul Pillar, then the national intelligence officer for the Near East and a veteran CIA analyst, the documents, like the October NIE, reflected the collected views of the U.S. intelligence community. Unlike the October NIE, these reports, called Intelligence Community Assessments, were largely validated by subsequent events, a result all the more surprising since the October NIE was based ostensibly on hard intelligence while the January assessments of likely postwar conditions were largely intelligence guesses based on the intelligence community's collected knowledge of the region.

Concerning postwar Iraq, the National Intelligence Council predicted that "the building of an Iraqi democracy would be a long, difficult, and probably turbulent process," and that "a post-Saddam authority would face a deeply divided society with a significant chance that domestic groups would engage in violent conflict with each other unless an occupying force prevented them from doing so." Sunni Arabs would resist yielding power to the majority Shiites, and "score-settling would occur throughout Iraq" as those who suffered under Saddam sought their revenge. A weak government in Baghdad would be unable to prevent al-Qaeda elements from setting up bases in remote areas of Iraq. The assessment quoted the results of a July 2002 simulation that predicted: "Political transformation inside Iraq would require an extremely large, long-term U.S. military presence on the ground and willingness for the United States to go it alone." Iraqi security forces would need to be rebuilt, and the report recommended that, once purged of senior loyalists to Saddam, the Iraqi army should remain intact. Citing long historical experience, the intelligence community assessed that Iraqis have a "deep dislike of occupiers. An indefinite foreign military occupation with ultimate power in the hands of a non-Iraqi officer would be widely unacceptable."[112]

Neither intelligence report was entirely accurate in its predictions. Missing from the description was mention of the aggressive and well-armed insurgency that caught U.S. forces by surprise even before the conventional phase of the conflict was over. The intelligence community's discussion of violence envisioned civil conflict between rival Iraqi groups; it did not describe a coordinated insurgency directed at U.S. occupiers.[113] The assessment of circumstances in the region following the fall of Saddam's regime was overly optimistic in its assumption that the U.S. military occupation would last "at least a year" but then decline steadily. It also suggested that anti-U.S. sentiment in the region would be tempered if there emerged "clear evidence that the Iraqi people welcomed the United States as a liberator." But the report presciently warned of massive refugee flows from Iraq, an intensification of

al-Qaeda activity in the region, and the likelihood that Iran would try to ma-
nipulate the elevation of a Shiite-dominated government in Baghdad to its
advantage.[114]

A notable feature of these assessments, in contrast to the October NIE,
was the absence of significant disagreement within the intelligence community on the subject at hand, in this case the difficulty of the postwar task
facing the United States. But the far more important characteristic of the
reports, despite Pillar's justifiable pride in their overall accuracy, was their
timing, coming as they did three months *after* Congress had voted to authorize force in Iraq. Congress was partly to blame for voting to support Bush's
war policy without demanding a full assessment of the likely consequences.
But the intelligence community served Congress poorly by waiting until the
policy course had already been set before addressing key questions. Neither
lawmakers nor administration officials needed intelligence reports to know
there would be significant challenges associated with the occupation of Iraq.
Such warnings were aired frequently in congressional hearings and floor debate, and duly ignored by the White House. When events bore out the warnings the intelligence community had issued in January, two months before
the war, no one took particular notice. The episode underscored a dynamic
long understood at the CIA: When intelligence analysts accurately predict
that a foreign policy will have adverse results, they win no plaudits from
policymakers.

CONCLUSION

As the January 2003 assessments of postwar Iraq showed, accurate intelligence
is no guarantee of foreign policy success. Nor does intelligence failure necessarily lead to strategic defeat, as the Soviet break-up and victory in the Persian
Gulf War demonstrated. But intelligence failure, and perceived failure, has
long-term consequences beyond the outcome of the crisis or contingency immediately at hand.

Of the intelligence failures that mark the end of this book—the lapses before 9/11 and the misperception of Iraq's weapons of mass destruction before
the invasion of Iraq—the latter now appears to be the more consequential.
Had the intelligence community foiled the 9/11 attacks, it is highly likely that
al-Qaeda would have gone back to its playbook in search of another attack
plan. The invasion and occupation of Iraq by March of 2008 had generated
some 4,000 U.S. battlefield fatalities—well in excess of the loss of life in the

9/11 attacks. The 9/11 attacks exposed intelligence gaps in U.S. defense; the Iraq war was an offensive based ostensibly on intelligence. Al-Qaeda confronted the CIA with a new kind of enemy. Small terrorist bands detached from state affiliation had been encountered before, but none with the global striking power of al-Qaeda. The organization managed to hide its agenda, indeed its very existence, from U.S. intelligence well into the mid-1990s. Small wonder it was able to hide its specific attack plans. Even six years after the devastating 9/11 attacks, its leader remained at large. Despite the high degree of difficulty of coping with such an adversary, we know from the sobering story of the Malaysia meeting that U.S. intelligence and law enforcement came close to penetrating at least part of the circle of attackers.

The Iraq intelligence failure is harder to forgive. Unlike the intelligence community performance prior to 9/11, it cannot be said that the CIA came anywhere near close to seizing on the truth about Iraq's weapons of mass destruction—namely, that there were none. The target was not an elusive terror group but a nation-state, half of whose territory was overflown daily by U.S. warplanes for roughly a decade before the U.S.-led invasion. From 1991 through 1998, U.N. weapons inspectors crisscrossed Iraq, guided by U.S. intelligence in uncovering Iraq's secret weapons programs. The Iraq problem resembled on a much smaller scale the intelligence problem posed by the Soviet Union. It entailed tracking the military forces and weapons, as well as the geopolitical intentions, of a country under a leader who, though capable of severe miscalculation, had a fairly well known set of views, security concerns, and priorities. Iraq even used Soviet-made military equipment and Red Army operational protocol, making the task that much easier for the U.S. intelligence community. Iraq therefore should have been an assignment comfortable to the CIA, with its decades of experience against the Soviets.

The themes I have examined—the politicization of intelligence, the error-prone nature of the business, the tendency of bureaucracies to stumble into new kinds of failure while striving to avoid repeating past mistakes, the gap between the views of line intelligence officers and leaders of the intelligence community—are not unique to the period following the collapse of the Soviet Union. As a predictive enterprise, the intelligence community has failure built into its job description. As an operational enterprise, the CIA and other like organizations are vulnerable not only to their own missteps in hostile environments but to faulty guidance from their commander-in-chief. While there is clearly a sharp break in the history of the CIA marked, in the same year, by the Persian Gulf War and the collapse of the Soviet Union, overriding political pressure on U.S. intelligence dating far back into the Cold War lingered in the post–Cold War period, affecting judgments in unrelated crises in different parts of the world. Political pressure is a difficult force to measure, even approximately. Like a magnetic field, its influence can be seen in events dating back to the Team B assault on the CIA in the 1970s, the triumph of the hard-line anti-Soviet coalition during the Reagan years, the pressure by the Rumsfeld Commission on the CIA to adopt a more alarmist view of the rogue-state missile threat, the attacks on the CIA after the Ames case and the Latin America controversies, and the neoconservative push for intelligence that could justify making war on Iraq.

What, then, makes the post–Cold War period unique? There are two primary factors. The Soviet collapse marked the disappearance of the threat for which the CIA was designed and built, leaving the Agency and the government as a whole questioning its purpose and mission. Second was the emergence of a new and elusive adversary not susceptible to the usual calculations of deterrence. At least during the Cold War there was little or no debate that the Soviet Union was the principal adversary of the United States. That consensus created a political environment for the intelligence community that was stable in comparison with the post–Cold War period when everything was open to debate, including whether the United States even needed a CIA. Elevated uncertainty led to elevated political friction and thus amplified the intensity of scrutiny on the CIA. On numerous occasions there was essentially no constituency with anything to gain by defending the CIA in the wake of a controversy. In such an environment, with even fundamental issues of intelligence priority in question, with budgets declining, with the two major political parties seizing and yielding control of Congress and the White House in asynchronous fashion, with the monolithic Soviet adversary replaced by a global threat environment that James Woolsey described as a "forest full of snakes," the conditions were ripe for the intelligence community to pay dearly not only for its many actual mistakes, but also for situations in which failure was more a perception than a reality.

In intelligence there is no bright line between success and failure, no column of intelligence activities on one side labeled "successes" and another on the other side labeled "failures." The two commingle, often in close proximity. Intelligence failure draws more attention when the CIA fails to reach a correct judgment using information it has successfully collected than when it fails to collect any information in the first place. As often as not, it is the quality of the thinking behind intelligence collection and analysis, rather than the quality of the information collected, that determines the results. A classic example is the CIA's intercept of a shipment of aluminum tubes to Iraq, a notable intelligence coup that was followed up by a far more notorious misjudgment about the intended use of the hardware. It is hard to do much better than capturing a piece of enemy military equipment that can be poked, prodded, tested, and measured. Still, even with the material in hand, the intelligence community wasn't able to reach agreement on what it had. Often too, the line isn't always clear between real intelligence failure and perceived failure. In the Ames case, multiple and spectacular failures of individuals and the system were followed up by a backdraft of exaggerated criticism that created an even greater perception of failure. Woolsey's already problematic position as intelligence chief—his access to the president curtailed and his relations with Congress rocky—was rendered completely untenable by his failure to mete out severe punishment for the Ames debacle. The die was thus cast for Deutch's tenure, characterized by relentless self-criticism of the Agency, to its great detriment—criticism cheered on and thus amplified by Congress.

Tenet's was a stormy tenure marked by significant successes as well as high-profile failures. He must be credited with beginning the process of rebuilding the CIA's human intelligence collection and reviving its morale, brought so low by the Ames debacle and the punitive tone of Deutch's tenure. Unlike Deutch, under whom Tenet worked, Tenet understood the importance of human intelligence in confronting the terrorist threat. His efforts paid dividends in the rapid takedown of the Taliban in Afghanistan after 9/11, though the durability of that achievement is, at this writing, very much in question. But he will be remembered for the "slam dunk" comment to President Bush in December 2002. And the indelible image of his time as the nation's intelligence chief was Tenet seated behind Secretary of State Colin Powell delivering a public recitation of that flawed intelligence, an episode made more embarrassing by the fact that Tenet and Powell appear to have refused to include in the presentation much more material for which the CIA's experts could not vouch. Powell was giving the Security Council only the information the CIA could vouch for—and even that was wrong.

Tenet's inattention to the importance of pulling together a coherent picture of the major security threats facing the United States stands as his most significant failure. The lack of a new or updated community-wide National Intelligence Estimate on al-Qaeda any time after April 1997 is almost unfathomable given the embassy bombings of August 1998 and Tenet's own much-ballyhooed "we are at war" memo on al-Qaeda in December of that year. It is no easier to understand Tenet's failure to order a National Intelligence Estimate on Iraq until Congress demanded one, leading to a rush job that stands as one of the U.S. intelligence community's most flawed analytical products. Without waiting to be asked, Tenet should have made it a basic part of his task as director of central intelligence to keep up a steady flow of community-wide all-source analysis on al-Qaeda and Iraq, the two leading national security issues of the late 1990s. If the quality of intelligence did not change, that by itself would be a telling piece of information, suggesting the need to apply more energy to collection or, alternatively, suggesting a stagnant situation in the adversary camp. And if, as happened in the Iraq case, sharp disagreements emerged among intelligence agencies, Tenet and the administration could have had ample time to factor that uncertainty into decision-making.

One of the leading structural complaints about the intelligence community following 9/11 was the weakness of the position of director of central intelligence. Tenet and his predecessors oversaw the entire intelligence community but controlled no more than about a fifth of its budget. The one exception to this lack of authority lay in the DCI's ability to order up National Intelligence Estimates. Here, Tenet and his predecessors had significant power to define a question, survey the community, and play the lead role in coordinating the resulting report. On al-Qaeda and Iraq, the nation's two principal adversaries in the post–Cold War period, Tenet chose not to exercise that power.

Ultimately, George Tenet may come to be regarded as something of a George McClellan, similar to the Civil War general in his focus on the importance of troop morale and the training of a new generation for a long war, as well as in his reluctance to strike at the enemy in the early years of the war out of fear of the consequences of failure. Like McClellan at Antietam, Tenet had his major victory in the defeat of the Taliban in 2001. But, just as the Army of Northern Virginia slipped from McClellan's grasp and crossed the Potomac after Antietam, so bin Laden slipped from the grasp of U.S. forces at Tora Bora and crossed into Pakistan. In the long run, the improvements in recruiting and training, the mission focus of the Directorate of Operations (since renamed the National Clandestine Service), the honing of the ability to follow hundreds, even thousands of shadowy individuals with multiple aliases across porous borders—all things Tenet set in motion—will not likely begin to pay serious dividends until some time in the next decade. By then, the CIA may be scoring significant successes that owe much to Tenet's initiative, and for which he will receive little if any credit. There will also be the inevitable intelligence failures, brought on in part by the blind spots and biases of today's intelligence community, much as the intelligence misjudgments surrounding 9/11 and the war in Iraq had roots reaching back into the Cold War.

To the extent that the Iraq intelligence disaster resulted from a concerted effort by Donald Rumsfeld and Dick Cheney to undermine confidence in the CIA's ability to discern threats, the damage done by the debacle has hardly been repaired. It remains an open question how the public would react to a proposal by a future president to take preemptive military action against an adversary based on intelligence, but it is likely that such a proposal would be greeted with extreme skepticism. While the Bush administration surely paid a political price for its manipulation of intelligence, the institutional reaction to the 9/11 and Iraq intelligence failures has focused on the intelligence community, and not necessarily in ways likely to restore public confidence. Harsh treatment of prisoners under interrogation by CIA officers and contractors, and National Security Agency access to the phone records and conversations of Americans without a court-approved warrant, were policies instituted by the Bush administration in response to its contention that intelligence failures stemmed from limits on the power of intelligence to collect information. No proof has been offered to demonstrate that these policies produced valuable intelligence. But with each new disclosure the reputation of the intelligence community, and of the United States, eroded further.

The intelligence community today is a hybrid, redesigned out of a perception of the causes of past intelligence failures. The de facto demotion of the CIA by the creation of a new Office of the Director of National Intelligence may prove a healthy development for the Agency. Institutionally, it now falls to the DNI to answer criticism and lead lessons-learned exercises. The CIA, to some extent, has slipped into the shadows, producing all-source intelligence and conducting operations while leaving it to its new master to respond to Congress and the public when things go wrong.

In the wake of the 9/11 and Iraq intelligence disasters, the output of the intelligence community, for a time at least, appeared to be coming out into the open. Intelligence estimates raising concern about continuing violence in Iraq, al-Qaeda's gradual recovery from the post-9/11 U.S. offensive, and Iran's ambiguous nuclear ambitions were declassified in sanitized form, even though they generated negative publicity on the Bush administration.

New bureaucratic structures, however, have done nothing to ease the tension between U.S. intelligence, the architects of U.S. foreign policy, and the American people. The intelligence disasters surrounding 9/11 and the war in Iraq did two things simultaneously: they undermined public confidence in the CIA, and they underscored how much the nation depends on quality intelligence. Despite the new bureaucratic structures, the political pressure—the tension in that gap between the White House and the intelligence community—remains. The gulf of trust between the power centers of U.S. national security and the public at large is widening.

NOTES

All website addresses in the Notes were valid in January 2008.

Notes to Introduction

1. Author's interview with Ambassador Rolf Ekeus, former executive chairman of the United Nations Special Commission, the arms inspection organization sent to Iraq after the Persian Gulf War, October 10, 2007.

2. Reagan's exact words were, "Mr. Gorbachev, tear down this wall!"

3. As of June 2007, there were eighty-seven stars on the CIA's wall of honor. Of those, thirty-three are so-called silent stars, representing officers not yet officially identified by the CIA because of the clandestine nature of their work. In 2000, there were some sixty stars not yet identified by the CIA when former *Washington Post* reporter Ted Gup, through painstaking research, identified twenty-five of them. See Ted Gup, *The Book of Honor: Covert Lives and Classified Deaths at the CIA* (New York: Doubleday, 2000). See also Stephen Barr, "Memorial Service Honors Four Who Fell in Service," *The Washington Post,* May 28, 2007, p. D2.

4. After Congress established the Office of the Director of National Intelligence in 2004, the newly created bureaucracy took over the job of presenting the President's Daily Brief, or PDB, a summary of intelligence developments around the world over the preceding twenty-four hours. But even after the reorganization, the CIA played the critical role in putting together the PDB.

5. Formed in 1975, the Church Committee, named for its chairman, Senator Frank Church (D-Idaho), was formally known as the United States Senate Select Committee to Study Governmental Operations with Respect to Intelligence Activities. The committee investigation was sparked by a December 22, 1974, exposé by Seymour Hersh, then an investigative reporter for the *New York Times,* of a CIA internal compendium of misdeeds known as "The Family Jewels." See Seymour M. Hersh, "Huge CIA Operation

Reported in U.S. Against Antiwar Forces, Other Dissidents in Nixon Years," *The New York Times*, December 22, 1974, p. A1. See also *Final Report of the Select Committee to Study Governmental Operations with Respect to Intelligence Activities*, U.S. Senate, 94th Cong., 2nd sess., April 26, 1976. Headed by Representative Otis G. Pike (D-N.Y.), the Pike Committee, or House Select Committee on Intelligence, conducted a similar probe in 1975; its final report was never published. Both committees were precursors to the House and Senate Select Committees on Intelligence. The CIA declassified the "Family Jewels" document in 2007. Visit the CIA's website or, for more context, see The National Security Archive, George Washington University, http://www.gwu.edu/nsarchiv/NSAEBB/NSAEBB222/index.htm.

6. For a general treatment of CIA relations with Congress in the Agency's early years, see David M. Barrett, *The CIA and Congress: The Untold Story from Truman to Kennedy* (Lawrence: University Press of Kansas, 2005). See also L. Britt Snider, *Sharing Secrets with Lawmakers: Congress as a User of Intelligence*, Studies in Intelligence (Washington, D.C.: Central Intelligence Agency, Center for the Study of Intelligence, Spring 1998), p. 47.

7. Senator Daniel Patrick Moynihan (D-N.Y.) called for the abolition of the CIA after the Soviet collapse, which he said the agency had failed to predict. That failure has become an article of faith among commentators and historians of intelligence. The CIA has disputed the charge. See, for example, Benjamin B. Fischer, ed., *At Cold War's End: U.S. Intelligence on the Soviet Union and Eastern Europe, 1989–1991* (Washington, D.C.: CIA, Center for the Studies of Intelligence, 1999), https://www.cia.gov/library/center-for-the-study-of-intelligence/csi-publications/books-and-monographs/at-cold-wars-end-us-intelligence-on-the-soviet-union-and-eastern-europe-1989-1991/art-1.html.

8. Amy Zegart, an assistant professor of public policy at UCLA, analyzed reform efforts directed at the intelligence community prior to the September 11 attacks. She found that of 340 recommendations for change, only 35 were implemented; of the remainder, 268, or 79 percent of the total, yielded no action at all. See Amy B. Zegart, "September 11 and the Adaptation Failure of U.S. Intelligence Agencies," *International Security* 29, no. 4 (Spring 2005): 88. See also, Amy Zegart, *Spying Blind: The CIA, FBI, and the Origins of 9/11* (Princeton, N.J.: Princeton University Press, 2007).

9. The commission headed by Donald Rumsfeld to examine intelligence on ballistic missile threats advised a new kind of intelligence methodology, recognizing gaps in intelligence and the increasing skill of adversaries at denying access to sensitive information: "This approach requires that analysts extrapolate a program's scope, scale, pace and direction beyond what the hard evidence at hand unequivocally supports." Commission to Assess the Ballistic Missile Threat to the United States, Executive Summary, July 15, 1998 (Washington, D.C.: Government Printing Office, 1998), p. 24, available on the Federation of American Scientists website at http://www.fas.org/irp/threat/missile/rumsfeld/.

10. The decision by Congress in October 2002 to authorize the use of force in Iraq came as a joint House-Senate inquiry was concluding its examination of intelligence failures related to the 9/11 attacks. The investigation involved extensive interaction with the CIA at the highest levels. All summer and fall, the investigation took up substantial quantities of senior executive time during a period when assessing the available intelligence on Iraq should have been the top priority. See U.S. Senate, Select Committee on Intelligence, and U.S. House of Representatives, Permanent Select Committee on Intelligence, *Joint Inquiry into Intelligence Community Activities Before and After the Terrorist Attacks of September 11, 2001,* December 2002 (Washington, D.C.: Government Printing Office, 2002).

11. A book by *New York Times* reporter Tim Weiner makes the case for the CIA as an organization that has failed throughout its sixty-year history. See Tim Weiner, *Legacy of Ashes: The History of the CIA* (New York: Doubleday, 2007). In a rebuttal, CIA historian Nicholas Dujmovic contends that the book minimizes or overlooks many CIA successes, and Dujmovic challenges Weiner on a number of factual points. The wide critical praise for *Legacy of Ashes* underscores the idea that the CIA has been beset by a reputation for bungling throughout its history. The rebuttal, published by the CIA's Center for the Study of Intelligence, is available on the CIA website at https://www.cia .gov/library/center-for-the-study-of-intelligence/csi-publications/csi-studies/studies/ vol51no3/legacy-of-ashes-the-history-of-cia.html.

12. Director of Central Intelligence, National Intelligence Council, *Regional Consequences of Regime Change in Iraq,* Intelligence Community Assessment (Secret), January 2003; and *Principal Challenges in Post-Saddam Iraq* (Secret), January 2003. The documents, declassified in April 2007, are included in an appendix to a report by the U.S. Senate Select Committee on Intelligence, *Prewar Intelligence Assessments About Postwar Iraq,* 110th Cong., 1st sess., May 8, 2007, http://intelligence.senate.gov/prewar.pdf.

Notes to Chapter 1

1. Address by Soviet Premier Mikhail Gorbachev to the 43rd U.N. General Assembly Session, December 7, 1988; excerpts published by the Cold War International History Project, http://www.coldwarfiles.org/files/Documents/1988-1107.Gorbachev.pdf.

2. U.S. Senate Select Committee on Intelligence, Soviet Task Force, December 7, 1988, meeting transcript, p. 3. The transcript of the Soviet Task Force meeting was declassified and reprinted in the record of the U.S. Senate Select Committee on Intelligence, *Hearings on the Nomination of Robert M. Gates to Be Director of Central Intelligence,* 102nd Cong., 1st sess., September–October 1991 (Washington, D.C.: U.S. Government Printing Office, 1992), Vol. II, p. 483; hereafter, *Gates Confirmation Hearings.* The reference to the CIA's having little more than what was in the newspaper appears on p. 485.

3. *Gates Confirmation Hearings,* Vol. II, pp. 520–21. MacEachin's use of the word "publish" in this context refers to the publishing within the government of official analytical

intelligence reports for circulation only to officials cleared to receive them, not to publication for a general readership.

4. Director of Central Intelligence, National Foreign Intelligence Board, National Intelligence Estimate, *Soviet Forces and Capabilities for Strategic Nuclear Conflict through the Late 1990s* (Secret), NIE 11-3/8-88, December 1, 1988, p. 15. The NIE was declassified and published by the CIA in Benjamin B. Fischer, ed., *At Cold War's End: U.S. Intelligence on the Soviet Union and Eastern Europe, 1989–1991* (Washington, D.C.: CIA, Center for the Study of Intelligence 1999), p. 356.

5. Fischer, *At Cold War's End*, p. 347. See also Raymond L. Garthoff, "Estimating Soviet Military Intentions and Capabilities," Chap. 5 in Gerald K. Haines and Robert E. Leggett, eds., *Watching the Bear: Essays on CIA's Analysis of the Soviet Union* (Washington, D.C.: CIA, Center for the Study of Intelligence, 2001), https://www.cia.gov/library/center-for-the-study-of-intelligence/csi-publications/books-and-monographs/watching-the-bear-essays-on-cias-analysis-of-the-soviet-union/index.html.

6. Director of Central Intelligence, National Foreign Intelligence Board, Special National Intelligence Estimate, *Soviet Policy During the Next Phase of Arms Control in Europe* (Top Secret), SNIE 11-16-88, November 16, 1988, p. iv. Reprinted in Fischer, ed., *At Cold War's End*, p. 225. Both this estimate and NIE 11-3/8-88 were partially declassified; in both cases, the summaries and "Key Judgments" sections were made public in 1999. Neither of these declassified documents includes the reference made by MacEachin to the possibility of troop cuts of up to 60,000.

7. Rodman D. Griffin, "The New CIA," *CQ Researcher*, December 11, 1992, p. 1075. Such a statistic is impossible to check, since details of intelligence spending are classified. However, it probably reflects rough approximations given to oversight committees by witnesses from the intelligence community. Senator David Boren (D-Okla.), then-chairman of the Senate Select Committee on Intelligence, said that even in 1991, with the Soviet threat rapidly diminished, "more than half of the agencies of the American intelligence [community] are targeted directly or indirectly at the Soviet military target." *Congressional Record—Senate*, November 4, 1991, p. 29845.

8. CIA Director Robert Gates provided this figure in testimony to House and Senate oversight committees on April 1, 1992. In 1980, Gates said, 58 percent of the "intelligence community's resources," which could refer to dollars or personnel, was devoted to the Soviet threat. See Director of Central Intelligence Robert M. Gates, "Statement on Change in CIA and the Intelligence Community," prepared testimony to House and Senate Intelligence Committees, April 1, 1992, pp. 33–34. Text courtesy of the National Security Archive, George Washington University.

9. *Gates Confirmation Hearings*, Vol. I, p. 424. The 1988 Gates speech was cited by Senator Bill Bradley, who opposed Gates's nomination to be CIA director in 1991.

10. See, for example, Elaine Sciolino, "Soviet Upheaval Injects Urgency in U.S. Debate over Intelligence," *The New York Times*, September 2, 1991, p. A1; and Tom Braden,

"The Spies Who Came in from the Cold War," *Washington Monthly*, March 1992, p. 18. Griffin, in "The New CIA," quotes former CIA counterterrorism chief Vincent Cannistraro as favoring handing over political and economic analysis to the State Department and military intelligence and counterterror functions to the Pentagon.

11. Daniel Patrick Moynihan, "End the 'Torment of Secrecy,'" *The National Interest*, Spring 1992, p. 20.

12. Reuel Marc Gerecht, "A New Clandestine Service: The Case for Creative Destruction," Chap. 4 in Peter Berkowitz, ed., *The Future of American Intelligence* (Stanford, Calif.: Hoover Institution Press, 2005), p. 107 note 2.

13. For post–Cold War arguments in favor of abolishing all or part of the CIA, see Eric Alterman, "A View to Kill," *Rolling Stone*, March 23, 1995, p. 48; Vincent Cannistraro, "The CIA Dinosaur," *Washington Post National Weekly Edition*, September 9–15, 1991, p. 29; Roger Hilsman, "Does the CIA Still Have a Role?" *Foreign Affairs* 74, no. 5 (September–October 1995): p. 104; and Marcus Raskin, "Coming in from the Cold: Let's Terminate the CIA," *The Nation*, June 8, 1992, p. 776. For counterarguments, see Braden, "The Spies Who Came in from the Cold War," p. 18; Richard Pipes, "What to Do About the CIA," *Commentary* 99, no. 3 (March 1995): 36; and Richard Russell, "CIA: A Cold War Relic?" *International Journal of Intelligence and Counterintelligence* 8, no. 1 (Spring 1995): 11.

14. Franklyn D. Holzman, "The CIA's Military Spending Estimates: Deceit and Its Costs," *Challenge* 35, no. 3 (May/June 1992): 28.

15. New York University Professor Stephen F. Cohen has argued that the term "collapse" represents a kind of historical bias, a suggestion that systemic failure rather than conscious political transformation brought about the change. He views the term "breakup" as more neutral.

16. Alan Moorehead, *The Russian Revolution* (New York: Harper & Bros., 1958), pp. 160–61.

17. Bruce D. Berkowitz and Jeffrey T. Richelson, "The CIA Vindicated: The Soviet Collapse Was Predicted," *The National Interest*, Fall 1995, pp. 35–46.

18. Relatives of the many U.S. air crew members killed by Soviet anti-aircraft fire while on sensitive reconnaissance missions over or near Soviet territory will object to this assessment. The point is that there was no direct, large-scale U.S.-Soviet combat that could have escalated into general war.

19. Author's e-mail exchange with Richard Kerr, former CIA deputy director, February 27, 2007.

20. For detailed treatment of accurate predictions of Soviet breakup and reasons why these predictions were rare, see Seymour Martin Lipset and Gyorgy Bence, "Anticipations of the Failure of Communism," *Theory and Society* 23, no. 2 (April 1994): 169; and Randall Collins and David Waller, "What Theories Predicted the State Breakdowns and Revolutions of the Soviet Bloc?" in Louis Kriesberg and David R. Segal, eds., *The Transformation of European Communist Societies* (Greenwich, Conn.: JAI Press, 1992), pp. 31–47.

21. U.S. State Department telegram, George F. Kennan, *The Chargé [d'affaires] in the Soviet Union* [Kennan] *to the Secretary of State* (Secret), Moscow, Feb. 22, 1946, 9 p.m. (known as the "Long Telegram"), available through the National Security Archive at http://www.gwu.edu/nsarchiv/coldwar/documents/episode-1/kennan.htm.

22. X [George F. Kennan], "The Sources of Soviet Conduct," *Foreign Affairs*, July 1947 (known widely as "The Mr. X Article"). Kennan's identity was disclosed publicly not long after the article's publication, giving rise to the view that it was an official policy pronouncement.

23. Daniel Patrick Moynihan, "Will Russia Blow Up?" *Newsweek*, November 19, 1979, pp. 36–39.

24. X, "Sources of Soviet Conduct."

25. Quoted in Moynihan, "End the 'Torment of Secrecy,'" p. 19.

26. Ibid.

27. U.S. National Security Council memorandum, William E. Odom [lieutenant general, U.S. Army; NSC adviser, military-strategic issues], to Zbigniew Brzezinski [NSC adviser], "East-West Relations: A Formula for U.S. Policy in 1981 and Beyond," September 3, 1980, p. 3. Classified CONFIDENTIAL; declassified in 2006; provided by Odom to the author; emphasis in the original.

28. Author's interview with former senator Sam Nunn (D-Ga.), June 26, 2007. Nunn, chairman of the Senate Armed Services Committee at the time, strongly urged the Carter administration to increase defense spending. Michael D. Wormer, ed., *U.S. Defense Policy*, 3rd ed. (Washington, D.C.: Congressional Quarterly, 1983), pp. 7–8.

29. Report of Secretary of Defense Harold Brown to Congress on the FY 1982 Budget, January 19, 1981, p. 16. Obtained at the U.S. Senate Library; for purchase of hard copy, see http://stinet.dtic.mil/oai/oai?verb=getRecord&metadataPrefix=html&identifier=ADA096066.

30. Ibid., p. 18.

31. Odom, NSC memo, "East-West Relations," p. 8.

32. Zbigniew Brzezinski, ed., *Dilemmas of Change in Soviet Politics* (New York: Columbia University Press, 1969). For a review of predictions by scholars and policymakers of Soviet collapse, see also Lipset and Bence, "Anticipations of the Failure of Communism," pp. 169–210.

33. Brzezinski, "Concluding Reflections," in *Dilemmas of Change in Soviet Politics*, pp. 162–63.

34. Olav Njolstad, "The Carter Legacy: Entering the Second Era of the Cold War," Chap. 9 in Njolstad, ed., *The Last Decade of the Cold War: From Conflict Escalation to Conflict Transformation* (London: Taylor & Francis, 2004), p. 198.

35. William E. Odom, "How Far Can Soviet Reform Go?" *Problems of Communism* (November–December 1987): 30.

36. Kirsten Lundberg, "CIA and the Fall of the Soviet Empire: The Politics of 'Get-

ting It Right'" (Case Study, Kennedy School of Government, Case Program, Cambridge, Mass., President and Fellows of Harvard College, 1994), p. 2. Odom is quoted in the case study but the quotation is not referenced. It appears that some unreferenced quotations in the study were from conferences at the Kennedy School.

37. Author's interview with Lt. Gen. William E. Odom (Ret.), senior fellow, Hudson Institute, December 19, 2006.

38. U.S. Senate, Armed Services Committee, *Hearings on the FY 1982 Defense Budget,* 97th Cong., 1st sess., January 28, 1981, p. 11.

39. U.S. Department of Defense, Caspar Weinberger, *Requirements for National Security,* Report of Secretary of Defense Caspar Weinberger to Congress on the FY 1983 Defense Budget, February 8, 1982, p. 149.

40. President Ronald Reagan, Address at Commencement Exercises at the University of Notre Dame, May 17, 1981. Available in the *Public Papers of the Presidents of the United States: Ronald Reagan,* http://www.reagan.utexas.edu/archives/speeches/1981/51781a. htm.

41. President Reagan, speech to the British House of Commons, June 8, 1982. Available in the *Public Papers of the Presidents of the United States: Ronald Reagan,* http://www.reagan.utexas.edu/archives/speeches/1982/60882a.htm.

42. See, for example, Peter Schweizer, *Victory: The Reagan Administration's Secret Strategy That Hastened the Collapse of the Soviet Union* (New York: Atlantic Monthly Press, 1994); and Mark P. Lagon, *The Reagan Doctrine: Sources of American Conduct in the Cold War's Last Chapter* (Westport, Conn.: Praeger, 1994).

43. U.S. Senate, Committee on Appropriations, Defense Subcommittee, testimony of Secretary of Defense Caspar Weinberger, *Budget Hearing,* 97th Cong., 1st sess., March 9, 1981, p. 91.

44. See, for example, comments by President Reagan to the effect that the payoff of the U.S. defense buildup would be willingness on Moscow's part to negotiate meaningful arms reductions. *Public Papers of the Presidents of the United States: Ronald Reagan,* remarks and a question-and-answer session with reporters on announcement of the United States Strategic Weapons Program, October 2, 1981, p. 878, http://www .reagan.utexas.edu/ archives/speeches/1981/100281c.htm; and Radio Address to the Nation on Defense Spending, February 19, 1983, p. 258, http://www.reagan.utexas.edu/archives/speeches/1983/21983a .htm.

45. National Security Decision Directive 75, January 17, 1982, pp. 1, 3, http://www .fas.org/irp/offdocs/nsdd/nsdd-075.htm.

46. Richard Pipes, "Misinterpreting the Cold War: The Hardliners Were Right," *Foreign Affairs* 74, no. 1 (January/February 1995): 154–60.

47. Murray Feshbach, "Population and Manpower Trends in the USSR," paper presented to the Conference on the Soviet Union Today sponsored by the Kennan Institute for Advanced Russian Studies, Woodrow Wilson International Center for Scholars,

Washington, D.C., April 1978. Other demographic work by Feshbach is cited in Lipset and Bence, "Anticipations of the Failure of Communism," p. 205 note 16. For Moynihan's discussion of Feshbach's work, see *Gates Confirmation Hearings*, Vol. 1, p. 428.

48. Hélène d'Encausse, *Decline of an Empire: The Soviet Socialist Republics in Revolt* (New York: Harper & Row, 1979).

49. Andrei Amalrik, *Will the Soviet Union Survive Until 1984?* (New York: Harper & Row, 1970); Randall Collins, *Weberian Sociological Theory* (New York: Cambridge University Press, 1986). For a discussion of Collins's difficulty getting his ideas published, see Lipset and Bence, "Anticipations of the Failure of Communism," p. 178.

50. John Lewis Gaddis, "International Relations Theory and the End of the Cold War," *International Security* 17, no. 3 (Winter 1992/93): 53–58.

51. See Ted Hopf and John Lewis Gaddis, "Correspondence: Getting the End of the Cold War Wrong," *International Security* 18, no. 2 (Fall 1993): 202–15, in which Hopf and Gaddis exchange views on Gaddis's earlier article. The Hopf quote appears on p. 207.

52. Collins and Waller, "What Theories Predicted," in Kriesberg and Segal, eds., *The Transformation of European Communist Societies*, p. 44.

53. Ibid.; and Lipset and Bence, "Anticipations of the Failure of Communism," pp. 172 and 202.

54. Mikhail Gorbachev, *Memoirs* (New York: Doubleday, 1996), Chronology, p. 709.

55. *Gates Confirmation Hearings*, Vol. I, pp. 428–29.

56. Ibid., p. 428.

57. U.S. Senate, Foreign Relations Committee, *Hearing on Estimating the Size and Growth of the Soviet Economy*, 101st Cong., 2nd sess., July 16, 1990, p. 2.

58. Ibid., p. 30.

59. See remarks of Senator Bill Bradley during Senate floor debate on the Gates nomination, *Congressional Record—Senate*, November 4, 1991, p. 29857. Bradley quotes extensively from a soon-to-be-published book that sharply criticized Bush for failing to develop a coherent policy toward the Soviet Union. See Stephen R. Graubard, *Mr. Bush's War: Adventures in the Politics of Illusion* (New York: Hill & Wang, 1992). See also Michael R. Beschloss and Strobe Talbott, *At the Highest Levels: The Inside Story of the End of the Cold War* (Boston: Little, Brown, 1993), p. 31. Beschloss and Talbott also recount the impression among Soviet leaders as well as the American press that Bush was slow to craft a foreign policy in the early months of his administration.

60. Beschloss and Talbott, *At the Highest Levels*, p. 43. The authors note that President Bush wasn't much of a reader and liked his memos kept short, but that he made an exception for reports from the CIA.

61. Stansfield Turner, "Intelligence for a New World Order," *Foreign Affairs* 70, no. 4 (Fall 1991): 162. The passage was also quoted by Moynihan during his appearance before the Senate Select Committee on Intelligence for the Gates confirmation hearings. See *Gates Confirmation Hearings*, Vol. I, p. 429.

62. *Gates Confirmation Hearings*, Vol. II, p. 143.

63. Ibid., p. 172.

64. Robert M. Gates, *From the Shadows: The Ultimate Insider's Story of Five Presidents and How They Won the Cold War* (New York: Simon & Schuster, 1996), pp. 327–28. In the title of his book, Gates displays both his view of how the Soviet breakup came to pass and his skills in bipartisan politics.

65. Ibid., pp. 560–61.

66. Ibid., pp. 328–30.

67. Ibid., p. 332.

68. George P. Shultz, *Turmoil and Triumph: My Years as Secretary of State* (New York: Charles Scribner's Sons, 1993), p. 864.

69. Shultz, *Turmoil and Triumph*, pp. 865–66; Gates, *From the Shadows*, pp. 381, 420–21.

70. *Gates Confirmation Hearings*, Vol. III, p. 36.

71. Ibid., Vol. II, p. 481.

72. Gates, *From the Shadows*, p. 386.

73. *Gates Confirmation Hearings*, Vol. I, p. 511.

74. See James Noren, "CIA's Analysis of the Soviet Economy," Chap. 2 in Haines and Leggett, eds., *Watching the Bear*, available at https://www.cia.gov/library/center-for-the-study-of-intelligence/csi-publications/books-and-monographs/watching-the-bear-essays-on-cias-analysis-of-the-soviet-union/index.html.

75. Kirsten Lundberg, "CIA and the Fall of the Soviet Empire" (Case Study, Harvard University, Kennedy School of Government), p. 11. Details of the CIA's adjusted Soviet defense spending estimate were published in U.S. Congress, Joint Economic Committee (JEC), *Allocation of Resources in the Soviet Union and China-1983* (Washington, D.C.: U.S. Government Printing Office, 1984).

76. CIA Directorate of Intelligence, "Soviet Defense Spending: Recent Trends and Future Prospects, an Intelligence Assessment" (CIA, July 1983).

77. *Gates Confirmation Hearings*, Vol. III, p. 59.

78. Ibid., p. 36.

79. For a particularly gripping account of the Soviet reaction to the secrets it received from Ames, see Milt Bearden and James Risen, *The Main Enemy: The Inside Story of the CIA's Final Showdown with the KGB* (New York: Random House, 2003), esp. Chaps. 1–6.

80. *Congressional Record—Senate*, November 5, 1991, p. S-15949.

81. *Gates Confirmation Hearings*, Vol. II, p. 288.

82. Gates, *From the Shadows*, p. 198.

83. Director of Central Intelligence, National Intelligence Council, National Intelligence Estimate, *Domestic Stresses on the Soviet System*, NIE 11-18-85, November 1985, p. 19, search under document title at http://www.foia.cia.gov/.

84. Lundberg, "CIA and the Fall of the Soviet Empire," Kennedy School case study, p. 13.

85. Director of Central Intelligence, National Intelligence Council, National Intelligence Estimate, *Trends and Developments in Warsaw Pact Theater Forces and Doctrine through the 1990s*, NIE 11-14-89, November 1989, p. vii, available at https://www .cia.gov/ library/center-for-the-study-of-intelligence/csi-publications/books-and-monographs/ at-cold-wars-end-us-intelligence-on-the-soviet-union-and-eastern-europe-1989- 1991/16526pdffiles/NIE11-14-89.pdf.

86. Garthoff, "Estimating Soviet Military Intentions," Chap. 5 in Haines and Leggett, eds., *Watching the Bear*. At the time the volume was published, Garthoff was a guest scholar at the Brookings Institution and a former ambassador to Bulgaria.

87. Albert Wohlstetter, "Is There a Strategic Arms Race?" *Foreign Policy* 15 (Summer 1974): 3–20.

88. Committee on the Present Danger, "What Is the Soviet Union Up To?" pamphlet, Washington, D.C., 1977. General Jones is quoted in Edgar Ulsamer, "The Soviet Juggernaut: Racing Faster Than Ever," *Air Force Magazine*, March 1976, p. 57.

89. Les Aspin, "What Are the Russians Up To?" *International Security* 3, no. 1 (Summer 1978): 49.

90. David Binder, "New CIA Estimate Finds Soviets Seek Superiority in Arms," *The New York Times*, December 26, 1976, p. A14. The press leak came too late to help Gerald Ford, who defeated Reagan in a contentious primary campaign but lost to Jimmy Carter in the general election.

91. Fred Kaplan, "The Rumsfeld Intelligence Agency: How the Hawks Plan to Find a Saddam/Al-Qaeda Connection," *Slate* online magazine, October 28, 2002.

92. U.S. President's Foreign Intelligence Advisory Board, *Intelligence Community Experiment in Competitive Analysis: Soviet Strategic Objectives, an Alternative View, Report of Team "B"* (Washington, D.C.: CIA, 1976), originally classified Top Secret, since declassified. See p. 1 for summary of the mirror-imaging issue. Available at http://www .gwu.edu/nsarchiv/NSAEBB/NSAEBB139/nitze10.pdf. Hereafter, *Team B Report*.

93. Ibid., p. iii.

94. Ibid., p. 2, emphasis in the original.

95. Ibid., pp. 4 and 22.

96. Ibid., p. 4.

97. Richard Kovar, "Mr. Current Intelligence: An Interview with Richard Lehman," *Studies in Intelligence* (CIA)(Summer 2000): 51–63.

98. Raymond L. Garthoff, "On Estimating and Imputing Intentions," *International Security* 2, no. 3 (Winter 1978): 22–32.

99. Richard Pipes, "A 'Worst Case' Analysis?" letter to the editors, *International Security* 2, no. 4 (Spring 1978): 201. In a debate-by-letter exchange, Garthoff countered that Pipes had previously described Team B's assignment as being to provide an alternative

assessment of intelligence on Soviet strategic objectives and stating, "there is no point to another, what you might call optimistic view." In other words, there was no point in having a Team B if the result agreed with Team A, the CIA.

100. Garthoff, "Estimating Soviet Military Intentions," Chap. 5 in Haines and Leggett, eds., *Watching the Bear*.

101. Team B analysis of specific weapons programs begins on p. 19 of the *Team B Report*. For a detailed critique, see Anne Cahn, *Killing Détente: The Right Attacks the CIA* (University Park: Pennsylvania State University Press, 1998), pp. 146–47.

102. Garthoff, "Estimating Soviet Military Intentions," Chap. 5 in Haines and Leggett, eds., *Watching the Bear*

103. Sam Tanenhaus, "The Hard-Liner: Harvard Historian Richard Pipes Shaped the Reagan Administration's Aggressive Approach to the Soviet Union," *Boston Globe*, November 2, 2003, p. 1.

104. Paul C. Warnke, "Killing Détente: The Right Attacks the CIA," *Bulletin of the Atomic Scientists* 55, no. 1 (January 1999): 70.

105. Interview with former CIA director James Woolsey, "Capital Q&A: James Woolsey on Spies and Rogue Missiles," United Press International, March 15, 2001, http://www.newsmax.com/archives/articles/2001/3/14/75527.shtml.

106. Gates, *From the Shadows*, p. 76.

107. Quoted in Lundberg, "CIA and the Fall of the Soviet Empire," Kennedy School case study, p. 2.

108. In his assessment of the record of National Intelligence Estimates on the Soviet Union, Garthoff writes that "the direct impact [of Team B] on the estimating process and on the content of the NIE 11-3/8 estimates was small." On the issue of Soviet objectives, "it made some CIA statements on that subject in the NIEs more cautious and equivocal. But it did not lead to significant changes." See Garthoff, "Estimating Soviet Military Intentions," Chap. 5 in Haines and Leggett, eds., *Watching the Bear*, https://www.cia.gov/library/center-for-the-study-of-intelligence/csi-publications/books-and-monographs/watching-the-bear-essays-on-cias-analysis-of-the-soviet-union/article05.html.

109. Kovar, "Mr. Current Intelligence."

Notes to Chapter 2

1. A facsimile of the Politburo document appears in "From Hesitation to Intervention: Soviet Decisions on Afghanistan, 1979," *Cold War International History Project Bulletin* (Woodrow Wilson International Center for Scholars), no. 4 (Fall 1994): 76. Hereafter, this collection of documents and articles is cited as *CWIHP*.

2. Director of Central Intelligence, Interagency Intelligence Memorandum, "The Soviet Invasion of Afghanistan: Implications for Warning," October 1980, p. 25. Originally Top Secret; declassified in redacted form; hereafter, DCI Memorandum, "Afghanistan: Implications for Warning;" search under document title at http://www .foia.cia.gov/.

3. Director of Central Intelligence, Interagency Intelligence Memorandum, "Soviet Options in Afghanistan," NI IIM 79-100771, September 28, 1979, p. 5. Originally Top Secret; declassified in redacted form. Available at the CIA's Electronic Reading Room, http://www. foia.cia.gov/default.asp. Hereafter, DCI Memorandum, "Soviet Options in Afghanistan."

4. DCI Memorandum, "Afghanistan: Implications for Warning," p. 35. This highly informative self-assessment of the intelligence community's performance prior to the Soviet invasion quoted extensively from products such as the *National Intelligence Daily*, which tracked day-to-day developments in the Afghan crisis for senior U.S. decision-makers. On December 20, 1979, four days before the invasion, a *NID* article reported that "continued Soviet military activity in the Turkestan Military District and the pre-positioning of gasoline and other fuel stockpiles near the Afghan border suggest that the Soviets are preparing a multidivisional force for possible combat operations in Afghanistan," http://www.foia.cia.gov/default.asp.

5. Robert M. Gates, in *From the Shadows: The Ultimate Insider's Story of Five Presidents and How They Won the Cold War* (New York: Simon & Schuster, 1996), p. 131, mentions a March 28, 1979, alert memorandum to Turner warning that the Soviets might provide military assistance to the Afghan government in the face of growing Islamist insurgent pressure. Extensive Soviet archival material can be found in "The Cold War in the Third World and the Collapse of Détente in the 1970s," *CWIHP* 8/9 (Winter 1996): 136–37. The specific reference is to a meeting of the Politburo of the Central Committee of the Communist Party of the Soviet Union, March 17, 1979, working transcript, translated for *CWIHP*; originally classified Top Secret.

6. Douglas MacEachin, *Predicting the Soviet Invasion of Afghanistan: The Intelligence Community's Record* (Washington, D.C.: Central Intelligence Agency, Center for the Study of Intelligence, 2002); see sections, "The Tribes Revolt," and "The Conflict Escalates," https://www.cia.gov/library/center-for-the-study-of-intelligence/csi-publications/books-and-monographs/predicting-the-soviet-invasion-of-afghanistan-the-intelligence-communitys-record/predicting-the-soviet-invasion-of-afghanistan-the-intelligence-communitys-record.html.

7. Gates, *From the Shadows*, pp. 131–34.

8. DCI Memorandum, "Soviet Options in Afghanistan," p. 13.

9. Ibid., pp. 3, 11. Indeed, the Soviets did use the infiltration method to insert forces into Afghanistan in the weeks leading up to the invasion. In late September, U.S. intelligence estimated that there were 6,100 Soviet troops in Afghanistan (p. 6).

10. Ibid., p. 15.

11. *CWIHP* 8/9, p. 137.

12. Ibid., p. 139.

13. Ibid., p. 138. See also Christopher Andrew and Vasili Mitrokhin, *The Sword and the Shield: The Mitrokhin Archive and the Secret History of the KGB* (New York: Basic Books, 1999), p. 12.

14. *CWIHP* 8/9, p. 131.

15. Ibid., p. 130; see also Steve Coll, *Ghost Wars: The Secret History of the CIA, Afghanistan and bin Laden, from the Soviet Invasion to September 10, 2001* (New York: Penguin Press, 2004), p. 47.

16. *CWIHP* 8/9, p. 130; and see p. 132 note 8.

17. *CWIHP* 8/9, p. 159. Andropov may have felt a particular need to press the charge of Amin's tilting to the West to Brezhnev. In October 1979, in a meeting with East German leader Erich Honecker, Brezhnev had complained of Amin's "power-driven" actions and harsh policies toward the Afghan people, but added, "with regard to his basic political platform, he has decidedly confirmed . . . the course of further development of the Revolution, of furthering cooperation with the Soviet Union." *CWIHP* 8/9, p. 157.

18. Ibid., p. 130.

19. Alexander Lyakhovsky, *The Tragedy and Valor of Afghan* (Moscow: GPI Iskon, 1995), p. 109. Translated by Svetlana Savranskaya of the National Security Archive at George Washington University. Lyakhovsky was a commander in Afghanistan who went on to become a major general in the Russian army.

20. Gates, *From the Shadows*, pp. 116–17.

21. Carter Presidency Project, interview with former President Jimmy Carter, Plains, Georgia, November 29, 1982, final edited transcript, an oral history project of the Miller Center for Public Affairs at the University of Virginia, http://www .millercenter.virginia. edu/index.php/scripps/digitalarchive/oralhistories/detail/3260.

22. Bruce J. Amstutz, *Afghanistan: The First Five Years of Soviet Occupation* (Washington, D.C.: National Defense University Press, 1986), pp. 41–45.

23. Ibid., pp. 44–45.

24. Gates, *From the Shadows*, pp. 145–46.

25. Christopher Andrew and Vasili Mitrokhin, *The World Was Going Our Way: The KGB and the Battle for the Third World* (New York: Basic Books, 2005), p. 413; Steve Coll, "Anatomy of a Victory: CIA's Covert Afghan War," *The Washington Post*, July 19, 1992, p. A1; America Abroad Media, interview with former CIA officer Milton Bearden, June 22, 2005, http://www.americaabroadmedia.org/media/On%20line%20extra%20materials/ Afghan-Bearden%20interview.pdf.

26. Gates, *From the Shadows*, p. 145.

27. The public record on CIA analysis of Afghanistan is incomplete and may turn out to contain discussion of Soviet fears of Amin turning to the West. The two principal U.S. intelligence documents on Soviet intervention in Afghanistan that have been made public have already been cited: "Soviet Options in Afghanistan," September 28, 1979, and "The Soviet Invasion of Afghanistan: Implications for Warning," October 1980. The latter document quotes extensively from day-to-day intelligence analysis in classified CIA publications such as the *National Intelligence Daily*. While there are some redactions

from these documents, the key judgments appear intact and do not include discussion of Moscow's fears of a creeping CIA bid for influence in Afghanistan.

28. Andrew and Mitrokhin, *The World Was Going Our Way*, p. 399.

29. Ibid., p. 403.

30. Ibid., pp. 397–99.

31. See MacEachin, *Predicting the Soviet Invasion of Afghanistan*; and Douglas MacEachin and Janne E. Nolan, co-chairs, Working Group Report no. 111, "The Soviet Invasion of Afghanistan in 1979: Failure of Intelligence or of the Policy Process?" September 26, 2005, issued as part of a project conducted by the Institute for the Study of Diplomacy, Edmund A. Walsh School of Foreign Service, Georgetown University, *Discourse, Dissent, and Strategic Surprise: Formulating American Security in an Age of Uncertainty.*

32. *CWIHP* 8/9, p. 130.

33. Interview with Zbigniew Brzezinski, President Carter's national security adviser, *Le Nouvel Observateur*, Paris, January 15–21, 1998, p. 76. Note: A shorter edition distributed in the United States does not include the Brzezinski interview, but the full edition is available at the Library of Congress. The interview has been posted several places online, including, http://www.globalresearch.ca/articles/BRZ110A.html.

34. Memorandum from Zbigniew Brzezinski to President Carter, "Reflections on Soviet Intervention in Afghanistan," December 26, 1979, obtained by the National Security Archive at George Washington University and reprinted at http://www.cnn.com/SPECIALS/cold.war/episodes/20/documents/brez.carter.

35. Ibid.

36. CNN, National Security Archive, interview with Zbigniew Brzezinski, June 13, 1997, http://www.gwu.edu/nsarchiv/coldwar/interviews/episode-17/brzezinski1.html.

37. Brzezinski quoted in Jagmohan Meher, *America's Afghanistan War: The Success That Failed* (New Delhi: Gyan Books, 2004), p. 67.

38. DCI Memorandum, "Afghanistan: Implications for Warning," p. 10.

39. See MacEachin, *Predicting the Soviet Invasion of Afghanistan*, section titled "Another Duel in the Palace." MacEachin reports that the Soviet ambassador may have had a role in sending Amin to a palace meeting at which guards attempted to shoot him; he survived because of the intervention of the chief of the palace guard, who was an Amin supporter and who died in the shootout.

40. Andrew and Mitrokhin, *The World Was Going Our Way*, p. 395. For another first-hand KGB account that indicates genuine suspicion within Soviet intelligence circles of a shift to the West by the Afghan government, see Oleg Kalugin, *Spymaster: My 32 Years in Intelligence and Espionage Against the West* (London: Smith Gryphon, 1994), p. 233.

41. Pavel Simonov and Ulugbek Jraev, "The Afghani Intrigue of the Russian Intelligence," *Axis Information and Analysis* website, November 18, 2005, http://www.axisglobe.com/article.asp?article=442. In light of the disaster that ensued from the Soviet invasion of Afghanistan, the tone of the literature on the episode from the Russian point of

view tends toward the question of who is to blame for the debacle. There seems to be a particular weight of opinion in the direction of Andropov and the KGB. This article, for example, alleges that the KGB sent Moscow deliberately distorted assessments of Amin in hopes of prompting a decision to invade.

42. MacEachin, *Predicting the Soviet Invasion of Afghanistan*, see section "The Tribes Revolt."

43. Meher, *America's Afghanistan War*, p. 68; Amstutz, *Afghanistan: The First Five Years*, p. 44.

44. DCI Memorandum, "Soviet Options in Afghanistan," p. 16.

45. Ibid., p. 9.

46. *CWIHP* 8/9, pp. 159–60.

47. James Phillips, "The Soviet Invasion of Afghanistan," Heritage Foundation "Backgrounder," January 9, 1980, p. 3.

48. ABC News, December 31, 1979, interview with President Carter.

49. Presidential news conference, President Carter, February 13, 1980, The White House, http://www.presidency.ucsb.edu/ws/index.php?pid=32928.

50. Jimmy Carter, *Keeping Faith: Memoirs of a President* (New York: Bantam Books, 1982), p. 471.

51. Memo from Brzezinski to Carter, "Reflections on Soviet Intervention in Afghanistan."

52. President Jimmy Carter, State of the Union Address, January 23, 1980, http://www.jimmycarterlibrary.org/documents/speeches/su80jec.phtml.

53. See, for example, DCI Memorandum, "Soviet Options in Afghanistan," pp. 13–14.

54. William E. Odom, "The Cold War Origins of the U.S. Central Command," *Journal of Cold War Studies* 8, no. 2 (Spring 2006): 57, 61.

55. DCI Memorandum, "Afghanistan: Implications for Warning," pp. 67–68.

56. Meher, *America's Afghanistan War*, p. 67.

57. All of these diplomatic efforts are described in MacEachin, *Predicting the Soviet Invasion of Afghanistan*; see specifically the sections "Another Duel in the Palace" and "The Advance Echelon Deploys."

58. Zbigniew Brzezinski, *Power and Principle: Memoirs of a National Security Adviser* (New York: Farrar, Straus & Giroux, 1983), p. 428; see also MacEachin, *Predicting the Soviet Invasion of Afghanistan*, section titled "Another Duel in the Palace."

59. MacEachin, *Predicting the Soviet Invasion of Afghanistan*, section titled "Intelligence Expectations versus Realities."

60. Ibid., "Introduction."

61. DCI Memorandum, "Afghanistan: Implications for Warning," p. 3.

62. Ibid., p. 65.

63. The quote is from Willis C. Armstrong, William Leonhart, William J. McCaffrey, and Herbert C. Rothenberg, "The Hazards of Single-Outcome Forecasting," *Studies in*

Intelligence (CIA) (Fall 1984): 57. Originally classified Secret, the article has since been declassified and published in H. Bradford Westerfield, ed., *Inside CIA's Private World: Declassified Articles from the Agency's Internal Journal 1955–1992* (New Haven, Conn.: Yale University Press, 1995), pp. 238–54.

64. Armstrong et al., "The Hazards of Single-Outcome Forecasting," quoted in Westerfield, ed., *Inside CIA's Private World*, p. 254.

65. MacEachin, *Predicting the Soviet Invasion of Afghanistan*, see section "Intelligence Expectations versus Realities."

66. MacEachin and Nolan, "The Soviet Invasion of Afghanistan in 1979," pp. 12–13.

67. Gates, *From the Shadows*, p. 131.

68. U.S. Senate Select Committee on Intelligence, *Hearings on the Nomination of Robert M. Gates to Be Director of Central Intelligence*, Oct. 4, 1991, 102nd Cong., 1st sess. (Washington, D.C.: U.S. Government Printing Office, 1992), Vol. III, p. 23; hereafter, *Gates Confirmation Hearings*.

69. Director of Central Intelligence, National Intelligence Estimate, *Warsaw Pact Forces Opposite NATO*, NIE 11-14-81, July 7, 1981, p. 1; originally classified Top Secret, now almost entirely declassified; search under document title at http://www.foia.cia.gov/.

70. Defense Intelligence Agency, *Defense Intelligence History 2007* (Washington, D.C.: Department of Defense, 2007), p. 1. See also *Gates Confirmation Hearings*, Vol. II, p. 211.

71. Douglas J. MacEachin, *U.S. Intelligence and the Polish Crisis, 1980–1981* (Washington, D.C.: CIA, Center for the Study of Intelligence, 2000), https://www.cia.gov/ library/center-for-the-study-of-intelligence/csi-publications/books-and-monographs/ us-intelligence-and-the-polish-crisis-1980-1981/index.htm. This study is available online and in book form. The quotation cited here is from a summary available online but not published as part of the book; subsequent notes provide both the chapter reference, for ease of finding the source material online, and the page number from the book.

72. MacEachin, *Predicting the Soviet Invasion of Afghanistan*, see section "Intelligence Expectations versus Realities"; emphasis in the original.

73. CIA, Directorate of Intelligence, *Probable Soviet Reactions to a Crisis in Poland* (Top Secret), RP 77-10141CX, June 1, 1977, p. I, www.foia.cia.gov.

74. See Cynthia M. Grabo, "Soviet Deception in the Czechoslovak Crisis: A Study in Perspective" (Secret), *Studies in Intelligence* (CIA) (Spring 1970): 19.

75. Director of Central Intelligence, Special National Intelligence Estimate, *Poland's Prospects over the Next Six Months* (Secret), SNIE 12.6-81, Jan. 30, 1981, p. 1.

76. CIA, National Foreign Assessment Center, *Moscow's Polish Problem* (Secret), SR 81-10062, June 1, 1981, p. iii.

77. MacEachin, *U.S. Intelligence and the Polish Crisis*, p. 62.

78. Soviet Union, Cold War archives, Special Dossier (Top Secret), Memorandum to the Communist Party of the Soviet Union (CPSU) Politburo on the situation in Poland, August 28, 1980. Included in the *Cold War International History Project* (*CWIHP*)

Virtual Archive, http://www.wilsoncenter.org/index.cfm?fuseaction=topics.home&topic_id=1409.

79. MacEachin, *U.S. Intelligence and the Polish Crisis*, p. 17.

80. Cold War archives, Special Dossier (Top Secret) Memorandum to the CPSU Politburo "On the development of the situation in Poland and certain steps on our part," April 16, 1981. CWIHP Virtual Archive, http://www.wilsoncenter.org/index.cfm?fuseaction=topics.home&topic_id=1409.

81. *CWIHP* 11, pp. 5, 22.

82. Ibid., p. 121.

83. CIA, message from Ryszard Kuklinski on impending Warsaw Pact invasion, December 4, 1980, reprinted in Andrzej Paczkowski and Malcolm Byrne, eds., *From Solidarity to Martial Law: The Polish Crisis of 1980–1981* (Budapest: Central European Press, 2007), p. 139. The document is also available in the Cold War International History Project archive.

84. Gates, *From the Shadows*, p. 166.

85. MacEachin, *U.S. Intelligence and the Polish Crisis*, p. 38.

86. President Carter, White House Statement: Situation in Poland, December 7, 1980, http://www.presidency.ucsb.edu/ws/index.php?pid=44382&st=&st1.

87. MacEachin, *U.S. Intelligence and the Polish Crisis*, pp. 62–63.

88. The quotation is from a declassified State Department Cable 232803, September 1, 1980, to U.S. embassies in London, Bonn, and Paris, cited in Malcolm Byrne, Pawel Machcewicz, and Christian Ostermann, eds., *Poland 1980–82: Internal Crisis, International Dimensions, a Compendium of Declassified Documents and Chronology of Events* (Washington, D.C.: National Security Archive, 1997); also cited in MacEachin, *U.S. Intelligence and the Confrontation in Poland*, p. 10.

89. CIA, "USSR-Poland: Polish Military Attitudes," *National Intelligence Daily*, June 20, 1981; reprinted in Paczkowski, *From Solidarity to Martial Law*, p. 310.

90. MacEachin, *U.S. Intelligence and the Polish Crisis*, p. 64.

91. Gates, *From the Shadows*, p. 232.

92. Ibid., p. 233. Here Gates is quoting himself from a memo to Casey written April 30, 1981.

93. CIA, *Moscow's Polish Problem*, June 1, 1981, p. 5.

94. Gates, *From the Shadows*, p. 235.

95. Benjamin B. Fischer, "Entangled in History: The Vilification and Vindication of Colonel Kuklinski," *Studies in Intelligence* (CIA) (Summer 2000, unclassified edition): 22.

96. Defense Intelligence Agency Intelligence Appraisal, November 4, 1981, p. 1, reprinted in Byrne, Machcewicz, and Ostermann, *Poland 1980–82*.

97. MacEachin, *U.S. Intelligence and the Polish Crisis*, p. 190.

98. Fischer, "Entangled in History," p. 23. The quote is from an interview with *Journal du Dimanche*, April 21, 1992.

99. *CWIHP* 11 (Winter 1998): 5, 22.

100. Andrew and Mitrokhin, *The Sword and the Shield*, p. 530.

101. Cold War archives, CPSU Politburo transcript, December 10, 1981, CWIHP Virtual Archive, http://www.wilsoncenter.org/index.cfm?fuseaction=topics.home&topic_id=1409.

102. CWIHP Virtual Archive, CPSU Politburo transcript, December 10, 1981.

103. Gates, *From the Shadows*, pp. 450–51.

104. John Lewis Gaddis, *The Cold War: A New History* (New York: Penguin Press, 2006); Matthew J. Ouimet, *The Rise and Fall of the Brezhnev Doctrine in Soviet Foreign Policy* (Durham, N.C.: University of North Carolina Press, 2002).

105. Gates, *From the Shadows*, p. 423. The Brezhnev Doctrine is somewhat problematic. In the view of Cold War historian Malcolm Byrne, the Brezhnev Doctrine was a Western construct, ascribed to the Soviet Union but never articulated as such by Moscow. It dates to the aftermath of the 1968 Soviet invasion of Czechoslovakia to suppress the Prague Spring rising. Brezhnev claimed the right of the Soviet bloc to violate the sovereignty of any member state if that state was seeking to renounce Marxism-Leninism. See, for example, Gaddis, *The Cold War*, p. 150. Hans-Hermann Hertle dates the formal renunciation of the Brezhnev Doctrine to the Bucharest summit of the Warsaw Pact in July 1989. See Hans-Hermann Hertle, "The Fall of the Wall: The Unintended Self-Dissolution of East Germany's Ruling Regime," *CWIHP* 12/13 (Fall/Winter 2001): 133.

106. Gaddis, among others, has argued that the Polish crisis marked the de facto end of the Brezhnev doctrine and a major turning point leading to the end of the Soviet Union. See Gaddis, *The Cold War*.

107. See, for example, Vojtech Mastny, "The Soviet Non-Invasion of Poland in 1980–1981 and the End of the Cold War," *Europe-Asia Studies* 51, no. 2 (March 1999): 189: "With the benefit of hindsight, the irresistible question is whether in 1980–81 Moscow may already have been prepared to give up its control of Poland and perhaps the rest of Eastern Europe with it, for this was the country that eight years later would give the push that brought down communist rule in the region."

108. See, for example, Gerald K. Haines and Robert E. Leggett, eds., *CIA's Analysis of the Soviet Union, 1947–1991* (Washington, D.C.: CIA, Center for the Study of Intelligence, 2001), p. vii. In the preface to this volume, former DCI Robert Gates writes, "I have always believed that the record of actual intelligence assessments represents the best defense of CIA's and the Intelligence Community's analytical performance vis-à-vis the USSR—the good, the bad and the ugly."

109. Douglas J. MacEachin, *CIA Assessments of the Soviet Union: The Record Versus the Charges* (Washington, D.C.: CIA, Center for the Study of Intelligence, 1996), https://www.cia.gov/library/center-for-the-study-of-intelligence/csi-publications/csi-studies/studies/97unclass/soviet.html.

110. MacEachin, *CIA Assessments of the Soviet Union*. The MacEachin study was also published in *Studies in Intelligence* 1, no. 1 (1997).

111. Author's notes from remarks of Stephen F. Cohen, professor of Russian studies and history at New York University, at the forum "The Soviet Collapse, 15 Years Later," hosted by the Woodrow Wilson International Center for Scholars, December 13, 2006.

112. NIE, *Warsaw Pact Forces Opposite NATO*, p. 1.

113. CIA, National Foreign Assessment Center, *Implications of a Soviet Invasion of Poland* (Secret), PA 81-10297, July 24, 1981, p. i.

114. NIE, *Warsaw Pact Forces Opposite NATO*, p. 2.

115. CIA, Directorate of Intelligence, *Readiness of Soviet Forces in Central Europe: Implications for a Rapid Transition to War*, SOV 87100-530D, November 1, 1987, p. v, http://www.foia.cia.gov/princeton.asp.

116. CIA, Directorate of Intelligence, *Instability and Change in Soviet-Dominated Eastern Europe* (Confidential), EUR 82-10124, December 1, 1982, pp. vi, vii, 2, http://www.foia.cia.gov/princeton.asp.

117. Ibid., pp. 13, 14, 16.

118. Ibid., pp. 36, 22, 31.

119. CIA, Directorate of Intelligence, *The Soviet Bloc Financial Problem as a Source of Western Influence* (Secret), NN3-263-94-008, April 1982, p. iii.

120. Director of Central Intelligence, National Intelligence Estimate, *Andropov's Approach to Key U.S.-Soviet Issues* (Top Secret), NIE 11-9-83, August 9, 1983, p. 5, http://www.foia.cia.gov/princeton.asp.

121. NIE, *Andropov's Approach*, p. 20.

122. CIA, Directorate of Intelligence, *Policy Implications of the Slowdown in Soviet Economic Growth, an Intelligence Assessment* (Secret), SOV 84-10104, July 1, 1984, p. 5, http://www.foia.cia.gov/princeton.asp.

123. Ibid., p. vi.

124. Director of Central Intelligence, National Foreign Intelligence Board, National Intelligence Estimate, *Soviet Forces and Capabilities for Strategic Nuclear Conflict through the Late 1990s* (Secret), NIE 11-3/8-87, July 1987, pp. 1, 5.

125. CIA, Directorate of Intelligence, Office of Soviet Analysis, *Intelligence Forecasts of Soviet Intercontinental Attack Forces: An Evaluation of the Record* (Secret), SOV 89-10031, April 1989, p. iv; reprinted in Haines and Leggett, eds., *CIA's Analysis of the Soviet Union*, p. 291.

126. Gates's role as intelligence gatekeeper and his suspicion of Gorbachev's motives were sufficiently well known in policy circles that Gorbachev himself became aware of Gates and actually pushed for his ouster in conversations with Bush.

127. Director of Central Intelligence, National Intelligence Estimate, *Whither Gorbachev: Soviet Policy and Politics in the 1990s* (Secret), NIE 11-18-87, November 1987, pp. 3, 5.

128. Ibid., p. 7, emphasis in the original.

129. Mikhail Gorbachev, *Memoirs* (New York: Doubleday, 1996), see Chronology section.

130. NIE, *Whither Gorbachev*, p. 36.

131. Anatoly Chernyaev, *My Six Years with Gorbachev* (University Park: Pennsylvania State University Press, 2000), Chap. 3.

132. George Bush and Brent Scowcroft, *A World Transformed: The Collapse of the Soviet Empire, the Unification of Germany, Tiananmen Square, the Gulf War* (New York: Alfred A. Knopf, 1998), p. 13.

133. Michael R. Beschloss and Strobe Talbott, *At the Highest Levels: The Inside Story of the End of the Cold War* (New York: Little, Brown, 1993), p. 23.

134. Michael Mandelbaum, "The Bush Foreign Policy," *Foreign Affairs* 70, no. 1 (1990/91), Special Issue, *America and the World*, p. 5.

135. William Webster, speech at Texas A&M University conference "U.S. Intelligence and the End of the Cold War," November 18, 1989, https://www.cia.gov/library/center-for-the-study-of-intelligence/csi-publications/csi-studies/studies/summer00/art02.html.

136. Geir Lundestad, "'Imperial Overstretch,' Mikhail Gorbachev, and the End of the Cold War," *Cold War History* 1, no. 1 (August 2000): 2.

137. George P. Shultz, *Turmoil and Triumph: My Years as Secretary of State* (New York: Charles Scribner's Sons, 1993), pp. 895, 1087.

138. Quoted in Kirsten Lundberg, "CIA and the Fall of the Soviet Empire: The Politics of 'Getting It Right'" (Case Study, Kennedy School of Government, Cambridge, Mass., President and Fellows of Harvard College, 1994), p. 24.

139. National Intelligence Council Memorandum, "The Direction of Change in the Warsaw Pact" (Secret), NIC M 90-10002, April 1990, p. iii.

140. Quoted in Lundberg, "CIA and the Fall of the Soviet Empire," p. 46.

141. Meeting of the CPSU Politburo, October 29, 1980 (Top Secret), available in the *CWIHP* Virtual Archive.

142. *CWIHP* 12/13, p. 11.

143. Director of Central Intelligence, National Foreign Intelligence Board, National Intelligence Estimate, *The Soviet System in Crisis: Prospects for the Next Two Years* (Secret), NIE 11 18-89, November 1989, p. iii. The NIE, available at https://www.cia.gov/library/center-for-the-study-of-intelligence/csi-publications/books-and-monographs/at-cold-wars-end-us-intelligence-on-the-soviet-union-and-eastern-europe-1989-1991/16526pdffiles/NIE11-18-89.pdf, states that it reflects intelligence available as of November 21, 1989; the Berlin Wall fell November 9, 1989.

144. Ibid., pp. vii, 18.

145. Bush and Scowcroft, *A World Transformed*, p. 30.

146. CIA, Directorate of Intelligence, *Gorbachev's Domestic Gambles and Instability in the USSR* (Secret), SOV 89-10077X, September 1989, p. v.

147. Bush and Scowcroft, *A World Transformed*, p. 504.

148. Ibid., p. 154. Bush was probably referring to the findings of the September 1989 CIA report, *Gorbachev's Domestic Gambles.*

149. Quoted in Lundberg, "CIA and the Fall of the Soviet Empire," pp. 46, 47, 52.

150. Author's notes from remarks by Jack F. Matlock Jr., U.S. ambassador to Moscow, 1987–1991, Woodrow Wilson International Center for Scholars, panel discussion, "The Soviet Collapse 15 Years Later," December 13, 2006.

151. Director of Central Intelligence, National Intelligence Estimate, *The Deepening Crisis in the USSR: Prospects for the Next Year* (Secret), NIE 11-18-90, November 1990, p. iii, http://www.milnet.com/cia/Soviet-Fall/art-1.html.

152. Ibid., p. 17.

153. Director of Central Intelligence, National Intelligence Estimate, *Implications of Alternative Soviet Futures* (Secret), NIE 11-18-01, June 1991, p. iii, http://www.milnet.com/cia/Soviet-Fall/art-1.html.

154. Richard Pipes, "The Soviet Union Adrift," *Foreign Affairs* 70, no. 1 (1990/91): 71, 73.

155. *Gates Confirmation Hearings*, Vol. III, p. 59.

156. Olav Njolstad, "The Carter Legacy: Entering the Second Era of the Cold War," in Njolstad, ed., *The Last Decade of the Cold War: Conflict Escalation to Conflict Transformation*, Cold War History Series, Vol. 5 (London: Routledge Taylor & Francis, 2004); see Chap. 9, pp. 196, 206–12.

157. CIA, Directorate of Intelligence, Office of Soviet Analysis, *Soviet Society in the 1980s: Problems and Prospects* (Secret), SOV 82-12026X, December 1982.

158. Coit D. Blacker, "The Collapse of Soviet Power in Europe," *Foreign Affairs* 70, no. 1 (1990/91): 88.

159. Hertle, "The Fall of the Wall," p. 132.

Notes to Chapter 3

1. Author's interview with Bruce Riedel, February 22, 2007. At the time of the interview, Riedel, a career intelligence officer at the CIA and a National Security Council staff member in three presidential administrations, was a senior fellow at the Brookings Institution. After the U.S.-led invasion of Iraq in 2003, Saddam International Airport was renamed Baghdad International Airport.

2. U.S. Department of Defense, *Conduct of the Persian Gulf War: Final Report to Congress* (Washington, D.C.: Department of Defense, April 1992), p. 3.

3. Eliot A. Cohen and staff, *Gulf War Air Power Survey* (Washington, D.C.: U.S. Air Force, 1993), Vol. I, Part I, Chap. 3, p. 59; hereafter, *GWAPS*. The authors cite "fragmentary evidence" of Iraqi invasion planning beginning as early as January, evidence almost certainly collected, or understood, after the invasion. The source they cite (in note 64) is redacted, probably a classified intelligence report and possibly National Security Agency

intercepts of Iraqi military communications. The six-volume report, an indispensable tool for researching the Gulf War, is available online at the Federation of American Scientists website, http://www.fas.org/sgp/library/index.html.

4. U.S. Central Command, *Security Environment 2000: A CENTCOM View* (Secret), May 21, 1990, cited in *GWAPS*, Vol. I, Part I, Chap. 7, p. 202.

5. Riedel interview.

6. Testimony of U.S. Ambassador April Glaspie, U.S. House of Representatives, Committee on Foreign Affairs, Subcommittee on Europe and the Middle East, *United States–Iraqi Relations* (Washington, D.C.: U.S. Government Printing Office, 1991), March 21, 1991, Appendix 1, p. 63. Hereafter, Glaspie House testimony.

7. President Bush, National Security Directive 26, "U.S. Policy toward the Persian Gulf" (Secret), October 2, 1989, p. 2, http://www.fas.org/irp/offdocs/nsd/index.html.

8. Voice of America Editorial 0-03982, "No More Secret Police," February 15, 1990, referenced in Nicholas J. Cull, "'The Perfect War': U.S. Public Diplomacy and International Broadcasting during Desert Shield and Desert Storm, 1990/1991," *Transnational Broadcasting Studies* 15 (Fall/Winter 2006), http://www.tbsjournal.com/Cull.html.

9. Cull, "The Perfect War," pp. 4–5. See also William Safire, "Broadcast to Baghdad," *The New York Times*, September 10, 1990, p. A23.

10. U.S. Senate, Foreign Relations Committee, informal public discussion with U.S. Ambassador April Glaspie, March 20, 1991, p. 12; hereafter, Glaspie Senate testimony. According to the U.S. Senate Library, the "informal" hearing was not published in bound-volume form. Library staff called up the transcript on their internal computer system.

11. Riedel interview.

12. Ibid.

13. CIA, Directorate of Intelligence, *Response to National Security Review-10: U.S. Policy toward the Persian Gulf* (Secret), March 3, 1989, p. 2. Document obtained under the Freedom of Information Act by the National Security Archive, George Washington University.

14. Testimony of Charles Allen, National Intelligence Officer for Warning, before the U.S. Senate Select Committee on Intelligence, *Hearings on the Nomination of Robert M. Gates to Be Director of Central Intelligence*, September–October 1991, 102nd Cong., 1st sess. (Washington, D.C.: U.S. Government Printing Office, 1992), Vol. II, p. 80. Hereafter, *Gates Confirmation Hearings*. Allen testified on Tuesday, September 24, 1991.

15. Alan Cowell, "Iraq Chief, Boasting of Poison Gas, Warns of Disaster If Israelis Strike," *The New York Times*, April 3, 1990, p. A1. In the televised speech, Saddam claimed his scientists had developed a particularly lethal "double chemical" weapon—probably a reference to the binary nerve agent VX. See also Christian Alfonsi, *Circle in the Sand: Why We Went Back to Iraq* (New York: Doubleday, 2006), Chap. 1.

16. Riedel interview. See also *GWAPS*, Vol. I, Part I, Chap. 3, p. 57. The Scud B missile in Iraq's arsenal had a "circular error probable" (CEP) of between three-tenths and

eight-tenths of a mile. CEP is a term with origins in artillery for the radius of a circle into which a given projectile will fall at least half the time. See U.S. Department of Defense, Defense Intelligence Agency, *Scud B Study* (Unclassified), August 1974, p. ix.

17. Author's interview with William Webster, former CIA director, May 10, 2007.

18. Riedel interview.

19. H. Norman Schwarzkopf, with Peter Petre, *It Doesn't Take a Hero: General H. Norman Schwarzkopf, the Autobiography* (New York: Bantam Books, 1992), p. 328. Page citations are from the paperback edition.

20. Ibid., p. 501.

21. U.S. Central Command, *Operation Desert Shield/Desert Storm, Executive Summary*, July 11, 1991, p. 20. The CENTCOM report is heavily redacted in the intelligence section but states that national intelligence analysis, generally understood as a reference to the CIA and DIA, lacked "a methodology to resolve divergent views, opinions and estimates from various intelligence organizations."

22. Defense Department, *Conduct of the Persian Gulf War*, p. 343.

23. U.S. House Armed Services Subcommittee on Oversight and Investigations, *Intelligence Successes and Failures in Operations Desert Shield/Storm*, August 1993, pp. 3, 4, 30–34; hereafter, HASC Report, *Successes and Failures*.

24. Author's interview with members of the National Intelligence Council, December 18, 2003.

25. CIA, Directorate of Intelligence, *Iraq: Nuclear Weapons-Related Procurement Activities* (Top Secret), September 4, 1989, p. 1. Search under document title at the CIA website, http://www.foia.cia.gov/search.asp.

26. According to a Defense Intelligence Agency history, the DIA disseminated its analysis of a possible Iraqi invasion of Kuwait in August 1989, prompting CENTCOM to develop an exercise to test deployment plans for such an eventuality. See U.S. Department of Defense, DIA History Office, *A Chronology of Defense Intelligence in the Gulf War: A Research Aid for Analysts*, July 1997, p. 3; hereafter, Defense Department, *DIA Chronology*.

27. Riedel interview.

28. Defense Department, *DIA Chronology*, p. 5. See also Janice Gross Stein, "Deterrence and Compellence in the Gulf, 1990–91: A Failed or Impossible Task?" *International Security* 17, no. 2 (Fall 1992): 151.

29. Author's interviews with W. Patrick Lang, former Defense Intelligence Agency officer for the Middle East, South Asia, and terrorism, from 1985 to 1992, February 27, 2007, and March 1, 2007; author's e-mail exchange with Richard Kerr, former CIA deputy director, February 27, 2007; Defense Department, *DIA Chronology*, p. 9.

30. George Bush and Brent Scowcroft, *A World Transformed: The Collapse of the Soviet Empire, the Unification of Germany, Tiananmen Square, the Gulf War* (New York: Alfred A. Knopf, 1998), p. 322.

31. *House Armed Services Committee Hearings*, "Crisis in the Persian Gulf: Sanctions,

Diplomacy and War," testimony of CIA Director William H. Webster, December 5, 1990, p. 113; hereafter, *HASC Gulf War Hearings.*

32. *GWAPS*, Vol. I, Part I, Chap. 7, p. 206.

33. Riedel interview.

34. Director of Central Intelligence, National Intelligence Council, *Iraq's Ground Forces: An Assessment* (Secret), Intelligence Memorandum, May 1991, p. iii. The report stated that the Gulf War "significantly reduced the combat power of the Republican Guard, but the Guard tipped the scales in favor of Saddam Husayn's [sic] regime against the insurrections in both northern and southern Iraq. The Guard remains the regime's principal guarantor of internal security, and Baghdad will make its reconstitution a priority."

35. U.S. National Security Council Memorandum, "Saddam's Message of Friend-ship to President Bush" (Secret), July 25, 1990, p. 2. Distributed by the White House Situation Room at 2:46 p.m. and including the verbatim text of a cable that day by U.S. Ambassador to Iraq April Glaspie; hereafter, Glaspie cable.

36. Defense Department, *Conduct of the Persian Gulf War*, p. 5.

37. Defense Department, *DIA Chronology*, p. 5.

38. Colin Powell, with Joseph E. Persico, *My American Journey* (New York: Ballant-ine Books, 1995), p. 447.

39. Lang interviews.

40. Glaspie House testimony, p. 3.

41. Defense Department, *DIA Chronology*, p. 7.

42. Glaspie House testimony, p. 4. Glaspie said Iraqi authorities asked her if it was true that U.S. Navy forces were participating in the UAE exercise. "I hoped I looked suit-ably enigmatic," Glaspie recalled, "because I didn't know whether it was really deployed or not, but I thought it wouldn't do any harm if the Iraqis thought it had."

43. For a detailed examination of the issues surrounding handling of the crisis and lost opportunity to warn Iraq of the consequences of invasion, see Stein, "Deterrence and Compellence," pp. 147–79.

44. Glaspie Senate testimony, p. 9.

45. Glaspie cable.

46. Special to the *New York Times*, "Excerpts from Iraqi Document on Meeting with U.S. Envoy," *The New York Times*, International Section, Sunday, September 23, 1990, p. 19; hereafter, Glaspie-*NYTimes* transcript. ABC News broke the story of the Glaspie transcript; the *Washington Post* followed up with a story; while the *New York Times* was first to publish a transcript of the meeting produced by the Iraqi government. Glaspie had taken extensive notes in the meeting but had been unaccompanied by any other U.S. official; Iraq provided the translator, and presidential aide and Iraqi Foreign Min-ister Tariq Aziz attended. Glaspie claimed there were "many inaccuracies" and "gaps" in the transcript, mainly through editing out certain passages. But the State Department

tacitly legitimized the transcript by issuing no denial of its accuracy. See Glaspie House testimony, pp. 11, 35; and Glaspie Senate testimony, p. 7.

47. Glaspie Senate testimony, p. 8.

48. Bush and Scowcroft, *A World Transformed*, p. 309.

49. Glaspie Senate testimony, p. 9.

50. Glaspie-*NYTimes* transcript.

51. Glaspie cable. As Glaspie assured lawmakers that her "we have no opinion" remark to Saddam was standard, formulaic U.S. diplomatic language presented to the Iraqis many times previously, so she said Saddam's remark about U.S. intolerance of casualties was something Iraqi diplomats had said to her repeatedly, and which had appeared frequently in the Iraqi press.

52. Glaspie cable.

53. Glaspie-*NYTimes* transcript.

54. Glaspie cable.

55. Glaspie Senate testimony, p. 6.

56. Glaspie House testimony, p. 30.

57. The other to have met with Saddam was Deputy Chief-of-Mission Joseph Wilson, who, in 2003, reemerged in the public eye after accusing the Bush administration of lying about Iraq's supposed attempts to buy uranium in Africa. Several U.S. senators had also traveled to Baghdad earlier in the year for meetings with Saddam as part of the Bush administration's attempt to improve relations.

58. Elaine Sciolino, "Confrontation in the Gulf; Deskbound in U.S., the Envoy to Iraq Is Called Scapegoat for a Failed Policy," *The New York Times*, September 12, 1990, p. A1.

59. *GWAPS*, Vol. I, Part I, Chap. 7, p. 202.

60. Kenneth Pollack, *The Threatening Storm: The Case for Invading Iraq* (New York: Random House, 2002), pp. xxii, 34–35.

61. Ibid., p. 34.

62. Defense Department, *DIA Chronology*, pp. 3, 6.

63. *Gates Confirmation Hearings*, Vol. II, p. 81.

64. Riedel interview.

65. Lang interviews.

66. See Michael Slackman, *Target: Pearl Harbor* (Honolulu: University of Hawaii Press, 1990), pp. 10–11; and Stephen Howarth, *To Shining Sea: A History of the United States Navy, 1775–1991* (New York: Random House, 1991), p. 351. For more background on the Fleet Problem exercises, see Samuel Eliot Morison, *The Rising Sun in the Pacific, 1931–April 1942*, Vol. III of *History of United States Naval Operations in World War II* (Boston: Little, Brown, 1948), p. 29. These exercises involved actual fleet maneuvers as well as table-top problems. In the 1930s they often focused on Pacific war scenarios involving Japan; on occasion the exercises were in the Caribbean or Panama Canal area. At all events, the Navy kept the activity east of the International Dateline to avoid antagonizing Japan.

For intelligence issues concerning Pearl Harbor, see Roberta Wohlstetter, *Pearl Harbor: Warning and Decision* (Stanford, Calif.: Stanford University Press, 1962), still regarded by many as the seminal account.

67. For a sampling of this literature, see Willis C. Armstrong, William Leonhart, William J. McCaffrey, and Herbert C. Rothenberg, "The Hazards of Single-Outcome Forecasting," Chap. 19 in H. Bradford Westerfield, ed., *Inside CIA's Private World: Declassified Articles from the Agency's Internal Journal, 1955–1992* (New Haven, Conn.: Yale University Press, 1995), p. 238, drawn from the classified edition of *Studies in Intelligence* 28, no. 3 (Fall 1984): 57–70 (Secret); Richard Betts, "Analysis, War, and Decision: Why Intelligence Failures Are Inevitable," *World Politics* 31, no. 1 (1978): 61–89; Jason D. Ellis and Geoffrey D. Kiefer, *Combating Proliferation: Strategic Intelligence and Security Policy* (Baltimore: Johns Hopkins University Press, 2004); Jack Davis, "Improving CIA Analytic Performance: Strategic Warning," Occasional Papers (CIA, Sherman Kent Center) 1, no. 1 (September 2002); Jack Davis, "Strategic Warning: If Surprise Is Inevitable, What Role for Analysis?" Occasional Papers (CIA, Sherman Kent Center) 2, no. 1 (January 2003); Richard A. Posner, *Preventing Surprise Attacks: Intelligence Reform in the Wake of 9/11* (New York: Rowman & Littlefield, 2006).

68. I. William Zartman, "Preventing State Collapse: The Argument," draft paper, Working Group on Collapsed States, Johns Hopkins University, Washington, D.C., November 1986. The quotation is cited by Alexander L. George and Jane Holl in "The Warning-Response Problem and Missed Opportunities in Preventive Diplomacy," Chap. 2 in Bruce W. Jentleson, ed., *Opportunities Missed, Opportunities Seized: Preventive Diplomacy in the Post–Cold War World* (New York: Carnegie Corporation, 1997), note 28.

69. Author's interview with Douglas MacEachin, former CIA senior analyst, April 19, 2007.

70. *Gates Confirmation Hearings*, Vol. II, p. 83.

71. George and Hall, "Warning-Response Problem," p. 24.

72. Defense Department, *DIA Chronology*, p. 3.

73. *GWAPS*, Vol. I, Part I, Chap. 2, p. 20.

74. Lang interview.

75. Defense Department, *Conduct of the Persian Gulf War*, p. xxvii.

76. U.S. Senate, Committee on Armed Services, *Hearings on the Crisis in the Persian Gulf Region: U.S. Policy Options and Implications* (Washington, D.C.: U.S. Government Printing Office, 1990), testimony of Secretary of Defense Dick Cheney, September 11, 1990, p. 10; hereafter, *SASC Persian Gulf Hearings*.

77. *Gates Confirmation Hearings*, Vol. II, p. 81.

78. Webster interview.

79. Defense Department, *DIA Chronology*, pp. 9–10.

80. CIA Report, "CIA Support to the U.S. Military During the Persian Gulf War,"

June 16, 1997, https://www.cia.gov/library/reports/general-reports-1/gulfwar/061997/support.htm.

81. Author's e-mail exchange with Richard Kerr, former CIA deputy director, February 27, 2007.

82. Stein, "Deterrence and Compellence," p. 160.

83. See, for example, Michael R. Gordon and General Bernard E. Trainor, *The Generals' War: The Inside Story of the Conflict in the Gulf* (Boston: Little, Brown, 1995), p. 4. Trainor and Gordon have the CIA's Charles Allen deciding to "sound the klaxon" on August 1. Powell, in *My American Journey*, p. 448, quotes Schwarzkopf at a Pentagon meeting saying Iraq will invade, but only to grab disputed oil fields; Powell says the CIA's Kerr had already given essentially the same briefing.

84. Powell, *My American Journey*, p. 449.

85. As multiple studies have documented, the U.S. high command regarded a Japanese attack on Pearl Harbor as less likely than an offensive in the Western Pacific. In the Persian Gulf in 1990, as already described, the CIA was watching for hostile Iraqi moves against Israel; obviously, by the time troops were massing on the border of Kuwait, an all-out attack on that country was an evident possibility, but one that U.S. intelligence discounted.

86. See Davis, "Strategic Warning."

87. Schwarzkopf, *It Doesn't Take a Hero*, pp. 457–58.

88. Defense Department, *Conduct of the Persian Gulf War*, pp. 28–29. See also Harry Kreisler, "A Diplomat's Odyssey: Interview with Joseph Wilson IV, Former Acting Ambassador to Iraq," *Conversations with History* series, Institute of International Studies, University of California, Berkeley, May 27, 2005, http://globetrotter.berkeley.edu/people4/Wilson/wilson-cono.html.

89. For a firsthand account of this extraordinary and historic meeting, see Scharzkopf, *It Doesn't Take a Hero*, pp. 351–57; Fahd delivered his one-word agreement to Cheney in English.

90. Schwarzkopf, *It Doesn't Take a Hero*, p. 363.

91. U.S. House of Representatives, Armed Services Committee, *Defense for a New Era: Lessons of the Persian Gulf War*, Interim Report of the Committee on Armed Services, House of Representatives (Washington: U.S. Government Printing Office, 1992), March 30, 1992, p. 14.

92. PBS Television, *Frontline: The Gulf War*, Oral History, interview with former defense secretary Dick Cheney, available on website published as a companion to the January 9, 1996, broadcast, http://www.pbs.org/wgbh/pages/frontline/gulf/. Cheney recounted that he told King Fahd and other top Saudi officials "that they did not have the luxury of waiting until Saddam began an invasion of Saudi Arabia and then ask for help because then it would be too late. We could not get there in time to help them if that were the case."

93. SASC Persian Gulf Hearings, pp. 56, 10–11.

94. HASC Report, *Successes and Failures*, pp. 36–37, 2.

95. *GWAPS*, Vol. I, Part I, Chap. 7, p. 191.

96. For more on the emergence of the Persian Gulf region as a vital U.S. interest and the creation of U.S. Central Command, see William E. Odom, "The Cold War Origins of the U.S. Central Command," *Journal of Cold War Studies* (Harvard and MIT) 8, no. 2 (Spring 2006): 52–82; and W. Scott Thompson, "The Persian Gulf and the Correlation of Forces," *International Security* 7, no. 1 (Summer 1982): 157–80.

97. *Gates Confirmation Hearings*, Vol. I, pp. 577, 578.

98. Ibid., Vol. III, p. 291.

99. Ibid., Vol. I, p. 3.

100. *SASC Persian Gulf Hearings*, p. 9.

Notes to Chapter 4

1. Author's interview with Arnold Punaro, former chief of staff to the Senate Armed Services Committee, April 21, 2007.

2. Colin Powell stated, "No combat commander has ever had as full and complete a view of his adversary as did our field commander. Intelligence support to Operations Desert Shield and Desert Storm was a success story." Norman Schwarzkopf was equally effusive: "The great military victory we achieved in Desert Storm and the minimal losses sustained by U.S. and Coalition forces can be directly attributed to the excellent intelligence picture we had on the Iraqis." See Department of Defense, *Conduct of the Persian Gulf War: Final Report to Congress*, April 1992, Appendix C, "Intelligence," p. 333.

3. Author's interview with Patrick Lang, former Defense Intelligence Agency official, March 1, 2007.

4. Author's interview with Bruce Riedel, former CIA Mideast analyst, February 22, 2007.

5. Author's e-mail exchange with Richard Kerr, former CIA deputy director, February 27, 2007.

6. George Bush and Brent Scowcroft, *A World Transformed: The Collapse of the Soviet Empire, the Unification of Germany, Tiananmen Square, the Gulf War* (New York: Alfred A. Knopf, 1998), p. 322.

7. Defense Department, *Conduct of the Persian Gulf War*, pp. xiii, 9, 71.

8. Author's interview with William Webster, former CIA director, May 10, 2007.

9. Lawrence Freedman and Efraim Karsh, "How Kuwait Was Won: Strategy in the Gulf War," *International Security* 16, no. 2 (Autumn 1991): 7.

10. House Armed Services Committee, *Hearings on the Situation in Iraq and Kuwait*, Webster testimony, December 5, 1990, p. 114; hereafter, *HASC Gulf War Hearings*.

11. Representative Les Aspin (D-Wis.), chairman, House Armed Services Commit-

tee, "The Role of Sanctions in Securing U.S. Interests in the Persian Gulf," December 21, 1991, published as part of *HASC Gulf War Hearings*, p. 853.

12. Senate Foreign Relations Committee, Informal Public Discussion with U.S. Ambassador April Glaspie, March 20, 1991, p. 12; hereafter, Glaspie Senate testimony.

13. Riedel interview.

14. *HASC Gulf War Hearings*, Webster testimony, December 5, 1990, p. 113.

15. *Congressional Record—Senate*, January 10, 1991, pp. 431, 824.

16. Author's notes from interview with Senator Dennis DeConcini, November 2, 1995.

17. *HASC Gulf War Hearings*, p. 905.

18. Ibid.

19. Lang interview.

20. Bush and Scowcroft, *A World Transformed*, p. 389. It is possible that the Democrats made the common mistake of equating casualties with fatalities. Casualties in the military context refer to killed, wounded, and missing.

21. Author's interview with former senator Sam Nunn (D-Ga.), June 26, 2007.

22. Bush and Scowcroft, *A World Transformed*, pp. 425, 445.

23. H. Norman Schwarzkopf, with Peter Petre, *It Doesn't Take a Hero: General H. Norman Schwarzkopf, the Autobiography* (New York: Bantam Books, 1992), p. 414. Page citations are from the paperback edition.

24. Michael Gordon and Bernard Trainor, *The Generals' War: The Inside Story of the Conflict in the Gulf* (Boston: Little, Brown, 1995), pp. 132–33.

25. Testimony of U.S. Ambassador April Glaspie, U.S. House of Representatives, Committee on Foreign Affairs, Subcommittee on Europe and the Middle East, *United States–Iraqi Relations* (Washington, D.C.: U.S. Government Printing Office, 1991), March 21, 1991, p. 37; hereafter, Glaspie House testimony.

26. Eliot A. Cohen and staff, *Gulf War Air Power Survey* (Washington, D.C.: U.S. Air Force, 1993), Vol. I, Part I, Chap. 3, pp. 60–61; hereafter, *GWAPS*. The quotation is from a speech broadcast on Baghdad Radio, August 30, 1990.

27. Ibid., p. 64. The quotation is from the Iraqi News Agency, December 22, 1990.

28. Freedman and Karsh, "How Kuwait Was Won," p. 15.

29. Schwarzkopf, *It Doesn't Take a Hero*, pp. 438–39.

30. *HASC Gulf War Hearings*, pp. 908–9.

31. Ibid., p. 570.

32. Defense Department, *Conduct of the Persian Gulf War*, p. 70. The translation of the operation order into actual number of troops appears in Janice Gross Stein, "Deterrence and Compellence in the Gulf, 1990–91: A Failed or Impossible Task?" *International Security* 17, no. 2 (Fall 1992): 175 note 95.

33. Colin Powell, with Joseph E. Persico, *My American Journey* (New York: Ballantine Books, 1995), p. 485.

34. Ibid.

35. William M. Arkin, *The Gulf War: Secret History*, Weeks 1–30. This series originally ran in *Stars and Stripes* magazine; the website "The Memory Hole" has made it available online at http://www.thememoryhole.org/war/gulf-secret.htm.

36. Freedman and Karsh, "How Kuwait Was Won," p. 12.

37. Defense Department, *Conduct of the Persian Gulf War*, p. 71. The report does not specify which intelligence agency produced these estimates, but presumably the information was all-source intelligence based on satellite imagery, signals intelligence, and analysis conducted certainly at the Defense Intelligence Agency and likely also the CIA.

38. Arkin, *Gulf War*.

39. *GWAPS*, Vol. I, Part I, Chap. 3, p. 77.

40. Ibid., pp. 80–81.

41. CBS, *Face the Nation*, with host Terrence Smith, interview with Secretary of Defense Richard Cheney, Sunday, November 25, 1990.

42. U.S. House of Representatives, Armed Services Committee, *Defense for a New Era: Lessons of the Persian Gulf War*, Interim Report of the Committee on Armed Services, House of Representatives (Washington: U.S. Government Printing Office, 1992), March 30, 1992, p. 30; hereinafter, HASC, *Defense for a New Era*. See also Freedman and Karsh, "How Kuwait Was Won," p. 13.

43. HASC, *Defense for a New Era*, pp. 33–34.

44. *GWAPS*, Vol. I, Part I, Chap. 7, p. 222.

45. HASC, *Defense for a New Era*, p. 31.

46. U.S. House of Representatives, Committee on Armed Services, Subcommittee on Oversight and Investigations, *Intelligence Successes and Failures in Operations Desert Shield/Storm*, August 1993, p. 17; hereafter, HASC Report, *Successes and Failures*.

47. Schwarzkopf, *It Doesn't Take a Hero*, p. 509.

48. Director of Central Intelligence, *Impact and Implications of Chemical Weapons Use in Iran-Iraq War* (Top Secret), April 1988, pp. 1, 7. The document was obtained by the National Security Archive, George Washington University, under the Freedom of Information Act.

49. *HASC Gulf War Hearings*, p. 902.

50. Ibid.

51. Powell, *My American Journey*, pp. 465–66; Gordon and Trainor, *The Generals' War*, p. 130.

52. U.S. Senate, Committee on Armed Services, *Hearings on the Crisis in the Persian Gulf Region: U.S. Policy Options and Implications* (Washington, D.C.: U.S. Government Printing Office, 1990), p. 662; hereafter, *SASC Persian Gulf Hearings*.

53. Gordon and Trainor, *The Generals' War*, p. 179.

54. Powell, *My American Journey*, p. 472; Schwarzkopf, *It Doesn't Take a Hero*, p. 420. Gates's comments got back to Schwarzkopf; it was fortunate that "Stormin' Norman" hadn't been in the room, or there might have been an altercation. A mischievous Powell

relayed to his field commander what Gates had said, "holding the receiver away from my ear" as he did so.

55. HASC Report, *Successes and Failures*, pp. 29, 43.

56. Ibid., p. 4.

57. Riedel interview.

58. Defense Department, *Conduct of the Persian Gulf War*, p. 19.

59. Ibid., p. 74, excerpts from CENTCOM's list of military objectives as laid out in CENTCOM Operations Order 91-001, dated January 17, 1991, parentheses in the original.

60. PBS, *Frontline: The Gulf War*, January 9, 1996, Oral History, interview with Robert Gates.

61. Powell, *My American Journey*, p. 478; Schwarzkopf, *It Doesn't Take a Hero*, p. 460. In 1983 Congress voted under the War Powers Act to authorize a troop deployment to Lebanon already under way, but that mission was framed as a peacekeeping or stabilization operation.

62. *Congressional Record—Senate*, January 11, 1991, pp. 784–88. Readers should be aware that the author was working under contract for the Nuclear Threat Initiative, an organization headed by former senator Nunn, at the time of this writing.

63. Nunn's proposal, Senate Joint Resolution 1, was defeated 46–53 on January 12, 1991.

64. *Congressional Record—Senate*, January 10, 1991, p. 477.

65. *Congressional Record—House*, January 12, 1991, p. 1100.

66. Previously, the closest war vote had been the Senate approval of the Declaration of War against Britain on June 18, 1812, which passed by a six-vote margin, 19–13.

67. *Congressional Record—Senate*, January 12, 1991, p. 1018; *Congressional Record—House*, January 12, 1991, p. 1139.

68. See, for example, Eileen Burgin, "Influences Shaping Members' Decision Making: Congressional Voting on the Persian Gulf War," *Political Behavior* 16, no. 3 (September 1994): 319–42.

69. Ibid., p. 320.

70. Michael Barone, "Looking Back and Forward: How the Democrats Have Changed in the Past 12 Months," *Jewish World Review*, December 21, 2001, available at www.jewishworldreview.com/michael/barone122101.asp.

71. "We would not have won the vote without Geneva. We simply wouldn't," Baker told PBS's *Frontline* program in an interview aired on January 9, 1996.

72. Gordon and Trainor, *The Generals' War*, p. 198.

73. Baker *Frontline* interview.

74. Text of President Bush's letter to President Saddam Hussein of Iraq, January 9, 1991, as released by the White House on January 12, 1991.

75. Senator Alan Cranston (D-Calif.) missed the Senate floor vote but said through colleagues that he would have opposed the war resolution.

76. L. Britt Snider, *Sharing Secrets with Lawmakers: Congress as a User of Intelligence,* an Intelligence Monograph (Washington, D.C.: CIA, Center for the Study of Intelligence, 1997), p. 49. Snider quotes an anonymous intelligence officer: "The Intelligence Community knew how poorly trained the Iraqi forces were. Some of them had been dragged out of dancehalls in Baghdad in their Bermuda shorts. But, for some reason, it wasn't highlighted to the Congress . . . perhaps because they were concerned this information would leak out and it might suggest which Iraqi forces were the softest targets."

77. Riedel interview.

78. Snider, *Sharing Secrets with Lawmakers,* p. 49.

79. Author's interview with L. Britt Snider, former staff counsel, Senate Select Committee on Intelligence, September 26, 2006.

80. Author's conversation with former senator David Boren, June 24, 2002.

81. Nunn interview.

82. Ibid.

83. Ibid.

84. Michael Crowley, "The Stuff Sam Nunn's Nightmares Are Made Of," *The New York Times Magazine,* February 25, 2007.

85. Nunn interview; Snider, *Sharing Secrets,* p. 49. See also "Nunn Regrets Vote on Gulf War," *The Washington Post,* December 26, 1996, p. A12.

86. Riedel interview.

87. See John Zaller, "Elite Leadership of Mass Opinion: New Evidence from the Gulf War," Chap. 9 in W. Lance Bennett and David L. Patetz, *Taken by Storm: The Media, Public Opinion, and U.S. Foreign Policy in the Gulf War* (Chicago: University of Chicago Press, 1994).

88. Nunn interview.

89. S.J. Res. 1, "A Joint Resolution Regarding United States Policy to Reverse Iraq's Occupation of Kuwait," was defeated January 12, 1991, 53–46, shortly before the Senate authorized the use of force. The measure, with Nunn as the chief sponsor, "supports the continued application of international sanctions and diplomatic efforts to pressure Iraq to leave Kuwait, but does not rule out declaring war or authorizing the use of force at a later time."

90. Nunn interview.

91. John Zaller, "Strategic Politicians, Public Opinion and the Gulf Crisis," Center for American Politics and Public Policy, Occasional Paper Series, February 4, 1993. Zaller has shown how the jump in President Bush's popularity as a result of his handling of the war and the dip in support for Democratic members of Congress did not carry over into the 1992 election. By June 1991, a nationwide poll found 60 percent of respondents saying that both major parties supported the use of force equally. As Zaller points out, "With most of the public unable to remember the Democratic Party's position on the war just five months after the vote occurred, it is hardly surprising that Bush had trouble making an issue of it in the election."

92. Readers may quibble with my use of the phrase "voted for war," since the language of the authorization urged the president to try means short of force to resolve the crisis and not to use force until he could certify to Congress that other means would not be successful. I simply reject this strict-constructionist interpretation of the vote. It was a vote for war and was understood as such by everyone voting in the House and Senate.

93. In the House, the party breakdown on the authorizations to use force was as follows: for the vote on the Persian Gulf War, January 1991: 86 Democrats and 164 Republicans for; 179 Democrats, one Independent and three Republicans against; two Democrats not voting. For the vote on the Iraq War, October 2002: 81 Democrats and 215 Republicans for; 126 Democrats, one Independent, and six Republicans against; one Democrat and two Republicans not voting. See *Washington Post* website, Votes Database at http://projects .washingtonpost.com/congress/.

94. Crowley, "The Stuff Sam Nunn's Nightmares Are Made Of."

95. Author's analysis of roll call votes.

96. Commission on the Intelligence Capabilities of the United States Regarding Weapons of Mass Destruction, *Report to the President of the United States*, March 31, 2005, p. 151. The report cites two intelligence community documents: Director of Central Intelligence, National Intelligence Council, National Intelligence Estimate, *Iraqi Military Capabilities Through 2003*, NIE 99-04/II, April 1999 at p. 6; and Director of Central Intelligence, National Intelligence Council, Intelligence Community Assessment, *Stability of the Iraqi Regime: Significant Vulnerabilities Offset by Repression*, ICA 2002-02HC, April 2002, p. 5.

97. U.S. House Armed Services Committee, testimony of General Richard B. Myers, United States Air Force, chairman, Joint Chiefs of Staff, September 18, 2002, p. 3 of prepared statement, http://www.globalsecurity.org/military/library/congress/2002_hr/02-09-18myers.htm.

98. Ibid., p. 5 of prepared statement.

99. U.S. Senate, Armed Services Committee, testimony of Secretary of Defense Donald Rumsfeld, September 19, 2002, pp. 8, 18, 19 of prepared testimony, http://www .globalsecurity.org/military/library/congress/2002_hr/rumsfeld919.pdf.

100. Director of Central Intelligence, National Intelligence Council, *Regional Consequences of Regime Change in Iraq*, Intelligence Community Assessment (Secret), January 2003; and *Principal Challenges in Post-Saddam Iraq* (Secret), January 2003. The documents, declassified in April 2007, are included in an appendix to a report by the U.S. Senate Select Committee on Intelligence, *Prewar Intelligence Assessments About Postwar Iraq*, 110th Cong., 1st sess., May 8, 2007, http://intelligence.senate.gov/prewar.pdf.

101. CIA, Director George Tenet's unclassified responses to Questions for the Record by the Senate Select Committee on Intelligence, April 8, 2002, http://www.fas.org/irp/congress/2002_hr/020602cia.html.

102. *Congressional Record—House*, October 10, 2002, p. H7767–H7778.

103. *Congressional Record—Senate*, October 10, 2002, p. S10250.

104. See U.N. Security Council Resolution 687 of April 3, 1991, http://www.fas.org/

news/un/iraq/sres/sres0687.htm. The resolution establishes the terms of the ceasefire but does not explicitly state what would happen if Iraq failed to comply.

105. *Congressional Record—Senate,* October 10, 2002, p. S10306.

106. U.S. Senate Select Committee on Intelligence, *Hearing on Current and Projected National Security Threats to the United States* (Washington, D.C.: U.S. Government Printing Office, 2003), February 11, 2003, p. 73.

107. Ibid., p. 74.

108. Ibid., pp. 157, 193–95. Carl Ford's written responses to the committee were submitted on April 30, 2003; Admiral Jacoby's came in on June 30; Tenet's on August 18. The Iraq War began on March 19, 2003.

109. Based on author's interviews with House and Senate members.

110. *GWAPS,* Vol. II, Part II, Chap. 6, p. 314.

111. CIA, Directorate of Intelligence, *Response to National Security Review-10: U.S. Policy Toward the Persian Gulf* (Secret), March 3, 1989, p. 3. Document obtained under the Freedom of Information Act by the National Security Archive, George Washington University.

112. CIA, Directorate of Intelligence, *Iraq: Nuclear Weapons–Related Procurement Activities* (Top Secret), September 4, 1989, p. 7. Document obtained under the Freedom of Information Act by the National Security Archive, George Washington Unviersity.

113. CIA, Directorate of Intelligence, memo to Richard Haass, special assistant to the president for Near East and South Asian Affairs, "Analysis on Iraqi Attempt to Procure Furnaces" (Secret), July 19, 1990, p. 1. Document obtained under the Freedom of Information Act by the National Security Archive, George Washington University.

114. President Bush, remarks to allied armed forces near Dhahran, Saudi Arabia, November 22, 1990, http://bushlibrary.tamu.edu/research/public_papers.php?id=2485& year=1990&month=11.

115. Opponents of going to war immediately did not agree among themselves as to how much longer sanctions should be imposed before going to war. Senator Nunn said he envisioned trying sanctions for three or four more months after the mid-January 1991 deadline set by the Security Council for Iraq to quit Kuwait. Other members were talking in the range of a year or more. The resolution Nunn sponsored to continue sanctions did not specify a time frame.

116. ABC, *This Week with David Brinkley,* interview with National Security Adviser Brent Scowcroft, November 25, 1990.

117. *SASC Persian Gulf Hearings,* p. 518.

118. Ibid., p. 523.

119. Ibid., p. 560.

120. British House of Commons, Report of a Committee of Privy Counselors, *Review of Intelligence on Weapons of Mass Destruction* (London: The Stationery Office, 2004), July 14, 2004, pp. 42 and 43. The report, an examination of intelligence failures

concerning Iraq and weapons of mass destruction before the U.S.- and British-led invasion of Iraq in March 2003, includes quotations from the JIC report, and other intelligence reporting on Iraqi weapons, dating back to the time of the first Gulf War; hereafter, British *Review of Intelligence*.

121. Ibid., p. 43.

122. See, for example, testimony of Gary Milhollin, Director, Wisconsin Project on Nuclear Arms Control, in *SASC Persian Gulf Hearings*, September 13, 1990, p. 519; see also International Institute for Strategic Studies, *Iraq's Weapons of Mass Destruction: A Net Assessment* (London: IISS, September 9, 2002).

123. Congressional Research Service, *CRS Issue Brief: Iraq and Nuclear Weapons*, updated November 28, 1990, by Warren H. Donnelly, Senior Specialist, pp. 1, 4, 6.

124. *Senate Persian Gulf Hearings*, p. 582. For more on the shortcomings of U.S. intelligence in tracking nuclear developments in adversary states, see Jeffrey T. Richelson, *Spying on the Bomb: American Nuclear Intelligence from Nazi Germany to Iran and North Korea* (New York: W. W. Norton, 2006).

125. HASC, *Successes and Failures*, p. 36.

126. *GWAPS*, Vol. II, Part I, Chap. 5, p. 225.

127. Author's interview with David Kay, former U.N. weapons inspector, March 13, 2007; *GWAPS*, Vol. II, Part I, Chap. 5, p. 227. For a slightly different account of this incident, see also James Risen, *State of War: The Secret History of the CIA and the Bush Administration* (New York: Free Press, 2006), pp. 100–101.

128. *GWAPS*, Vol. II, Part II, Chap. 6, p. 345.

129. Kay interview. See also Jay C. Davis and David A. Kay, "Iraq's Secret Nuclear Weapons Program," *Physics Today*, July 1992, p. 21. See also, Richelson, *Spying on the Bomb*, pp. 318–20, 351–56, and 447–57.

130. Kay interview. See also Davis and Kay, "Iraq's Secret Nuclear Weapons Program," p. 24.

131. Kay interview. See also Davis and Kay, "Iraq's Secret Nuclear Weapons Program," p. 24. Another account of the incident outside Fallujah appears in Barton Gellman, "Foiled by Saddam's Concealment Strategy. Shell Games: The Hunt for Iraq's Forbidden Weapons," *The Washington Post*, October 11, 1998, p. A1.

132. Kay interview.

133. Davis and Kay, "Iraq's Secret Nuclear Weapons Program," p. 26.

134. British *Review of Intelligence*, pp. 44, 45.

135. Federation of American Scientists, "Iraqi Nuclear Weapons," http://www.fas.org/nuke/guide/iraq/nuke/program.htm.

136. United Nations Security Council, Fourth Consolidated Report of the Director of the International Atomic Energy Agency under Paragraph 16 of Security Council Resolution 1051, October 8, 1997, p. 21.

137. *GWAPS*, Vol. II, Part II, p. 316.

138. Davis and Kay, "Iraq's Secret Nuclear Weapons Program," p. 21.

139. Author's interview with members of the National Intelligence Council, December 18, 2003. Participants were: Stuart Cohen, vice chairman; General John Landry, chemical weapons specialist; Larry Gershwin, biological weapons and denial and deception expert; Robert Walpole, nuclear weapons. Only Cohen would speak for attribution. For an account based on these interviews, see John Diamond, "A Desert Mirage: How U.S. Misjudged Iraq's Arsenal," *USA Today*, February 3, 2004, p. 1A.

140. Kay interview.

Notes to Chapter 5

1. The embassy bugging situation was discussed in detail by Representative Henry J. Hyde (R-Ill.) in remarks for the record in 1990. See Representative Henry J. Hyde, "Embassy Moscow: Paying the Bill," extension of remarks, *Congressional Record*, October 26, 1990, p. E3555.

2. The CIA's Directorate of Operations refers to foreigners it has recruited as sources of intelligence as "assets" or "agents." Most people think a CIA agent is an employee of the CIA; in fact, an agent is a foreigner, paid or engaged by the CIA to provide CIA employees, who are called field officers or case officers, with intelligence.

3. Robert Gates, *From the Shadows: The Ultimate Insider's Story of Five Presidents and How They Won the Cold War* (New York: Touchstone Books, 1997), pp. 363–64.

4. The Senate Select Committee on Intelligence's staff trip to Moscow and subsequent inquiries was described to the author by L. Britt Snider, then the general counsel to the committee and one of the participants in the Moscow trip, in a conversation on October 28, 1996. Snider discussed the trip and the Ames case at greater length in a formal interview on September 26, 2006. Some details, such as the identity of Downing as the CIA chief-of-station at the time, were obtained through separate research. A brief account of the Senate staff trip appeared in Tim Weiner, David Johnston, and Neil Lewis, *Betrayal: The Story of Aldrich Ames, an American Spy* (New York: Random House, 1995), p. 138.

5. Precisely how many Soviets working for the CIA Ames compromised may never be known. The number most often cited is twenty-five. See, for example, Pete Earley's *Confessions of a Spy: The Real Story of Aldrich Ames* (New York: G. P. Putnam's Sons, 1997). In some cases, Ames confirmed KGB suspicions about spies it had learned about from other sources, such as fired CIA employee Edward Lee Howard or FBI turncoat Robert Hanssen. The number of agents executed as a result of Ames also depends on which ones are attributed to him and which to Howard, Hanssen, or other sources. In December 1995, then–CIA Director John Deutch said "at least nine" were executed as a result of Ames. See Director of Central Intelligence John Deutch, *Statement on the Clandestine Services and the Damage Caused by Aldrich Ames*, December 7, 1995; hereafter, Deutch statement on Ames damage, December 1995. Former CIA director Gates

has also said that "at least nine" executions were attributable to Ames. See Gates, *From the Shadows*, p. 17. James Woolsey, DCI at the time of Ames's arrest, puts the number executed as a result of Ames at "between 10 and 13." See interview with James Woolsey, "Capital Q&A: James Woolsey on Spies and Rogue Missiles," United Press International, March 15, 2001, http://www.newsmax.com/archives/articles/2001/3/14/75527.shtml. The Senate Select Committee on Intelligence reported that ten Soviet sources of the CIA and FBI were executed as a result of Ames. See U.S. Senate Select Committee on Intelligence, *An Assessment of the Aldrich H. Ames Espionage Case and Its Implications for U.S. Intelligence*, November 1, 1994, p. 85; hereafter, Senate Ames Report.

6. The best account of the KGB's roll-up of agents working for the CIA appears in Milt Bearden and James Risen, *The Main Enemy: The Inside Story of the CIA's Final Showdown with the KGB* (New York: Random House, 2003). Bearden was a veteran CIA operations officer who was chief of the Soviet–East European Division in the Directorate of Operations at the time of the Soviet collapse; earlier he ran CIA operations supporting the Mujahadin in Afghanistan. Risen is a reporter for the *New York Times*. The recall of Soviet officers to Moscow was something the CIA and FBI routinely tracked. For example, the FBI had a surveillance team on hand at Dulles International Airport when Valery Martynov, fingered by Ames, departed for Moscow in November 1985.

7. For example, the Soviet government announced the execution of Adolph G. Tolkachev, a Soviet military expert on radar-evading aircraft, on October 22, 1986. Such announcements were immediately noticed by the CIA but not by the Western press. Thus, while there was publicly available evidence of a major intelligence breach, knowledge of the problem remained confined to the CIA. Tolkachev had been betrayed by Edward Lee Howard, a disgruntled former CIA employee fired for giving problematic answers in a routine polygraph investigation. Ames confirmed to the KGB that Tolkachev was a spy in June 1985 when, in a single meeting, he betrayed virtually all of the CIA's human sources in the Soviet government. See David Wise, *Nightmover: How Aldrich Ames Sold the CIA to the KGB for $4.6 Million* (New York: Harper Collins, 1995), p. 124.

8. U.S. House of Representatives, Permanent Select Committee on Intelligence, *Report of Investigation: The Aldrich Ames Espionage Case* (Washington, D.C.: U.S. Government Printing Office, November 30, 1994), p. 14; hereafter, House Ames Report.

9. Bearden and Risen, *The Main Enemy*, p. 303.

10. Snider interview (see note 4 above).

11. House Ames Report, p. 4; see also CIA Inspector General Frederick P. Hitz, "The Aldrich Ames Case: An Assessment of CIA's Role in Identifying Ames as an Intelligence Penetration of the Agency," Abstract of Report Investigation, October 21, 1994, unclassified summary, para. 3. The report was made public in the House Ames Report; the information cited appears on p. 14, http://www.loyola.edu/dept/politics/intel/hitzrept.html.

12. Several published accounts have described Ames's arrest. The most detailed appears in Earley's *Confessions of a Spy*, pp. 321–26. See also Wise's *Nightmover*, pp. 1–5. The

KGB paid Ames $2.5 million in cash over nearly a decade of spying and set aside $2.1 million in overseas accounts for his use upon what was expected to be a comfortable retirement in the Soviet Union. See Senate Ames Report, pp. 38, 41.

13. For a highly informative discussion of the dynamics of the relationship between Congress and the intelligence community, see L. Britt Snider, "Sharing Secrets with Lawmakers," *Studies in Intelligence* (CIA)(February 1997).

14. House Ames Report, p. 41.

15. Ibid., p. 43.

16. U.S. House of Representatives, Representative Larry Combest, Chairman, House Permanent Select Committee on Intelligence, "Aldrich Ames Spy Case," extension of remarks, *Congressional Record*, May 16, 1995, p. E1047.

17. For example, the committee published a report in 1987 on the problem. It began, "Over the past several years, a dangerous upward trend in successful espionage operations against the United States has occurred." See U.S. House of Representatives, Permanent Select Committee on Intelligence, *Report: United States Counterintelligence and Security Concerns—1986* (Washington, D.C.: U.S. Government Printing Office, 1987), 100th Cong., 1st sess., February 4, 1987, p. 1. The report is reprinted as Appendix 4 in House Ames Report.

18. The House Ames Report, pp. 43–44, stated, "It does not appear that the DCI [Webster] was even fully informed about the losses at the time." See also p. 49. Gates said in a November 2, 1995, interview with the *New York Times* that some CIA officials suspected Ames was a spy as early as 1992 but did not tell Gates during his tenure as CIA director: "This is a group of people in 1992 who knew that Aldrich Ames was the mole, and they didn't tell me." The record on CIA-FBI cooperation over the 1985–86 agent losses is mixed. The House Ames Report, pp. 46–47, says the CIA promptly shared information with FBI counterintelligence investigators but adds that "the FBI never had full access to the CIA files." Britain's Intelligence and Security Committee reported that Ames "may have caused untold damage to British security interests" and said it was "unsatisfied" with the level of cooperation from the CIA in assessing that damage. See Philip Johnson, "MPs Fear 'Untold Damage' Caused by CIA Traitor Ames," *Electronic Telegraph*, March 29, 1996.

19. U.S. Department of Justice, Inspector General Michael R. Bromwich, *A Review of the FBI's Performance in Uncovering the Espionage Activities of Aldrich Hazen Ames*, April 21, 1997, unclassified executive summary, Section III, "The FBI's Performance in Uncovering Ames."

20. Senate Ames Report, p. 38. The full transcript of the DeConcini interview of Ames, which took place on August 5, 1994, is reprinted in the report.

21. Gorbachev was elected general secretary of the Communist Party on March 10, 1985; Ames walked into the Soviet embassy and volunteered to spy for the KGB on April 16, 1985.

22. U.S. National Commission on Terrorist Attacks Upon the United States (9/11

Commission), testimony of former CIA director John Deutch, public hearing, Tuesday, October 14, 2003, http://govinfo.library.unt.edu/911/archive/hearing4/index.htm.

23. Quoted by Maureen Dowd in "Lies and Kisses," Liberties column, *The New York Times*, November 2, 1995.

24. House Ames Report, p. 19.

25. Earley, *Confessions of a Spy*, p. 139. Earley provides a highly detailed account of Ames's opening moves in his approach to the KGB in April 1985, pp. 137–45.

26. Senate Ames Report, Appendix 3, Ames interview, p. 78.

27. Senate Ames Report, pp. 13, 17, 40.

28. House Ames Report. A transcript of the interview of Ames by Representative Dan Glickman (D-Kan.), chairman of the House Intelligence Committee, and Larry Combest (R-Tex.), its ranking member, appears in Appendix 3 of the report. The quote is on p. 34 of the interview. The interview took place on August 8, 1994. The location is not provided, but presumably it was in the Alexandria city jail, the same place that the Senate committee interview took place a few days earlier.

29. CIA Inspector General Frederick Hitz, *The Aldrich H. Ames Case: An Assessment of CIA's Role in Identifying Ames as an Intelligence Penetration of the Agency*, unclassified abstract of the report of investigation, October 21, 1994, reprinted in House Ames Report, p. 13; hereafter, CIA-IG Report, *Identifying Ames*.

30. United States District Court, Eastern District of Virginia, Alexandria Division, Statement of Aldrich Hazen Ames in *United States of America v. Aldrich Hazen Ames*, Criminal Case No. 94-64-A, April 28, 1994, p. 3, appended to government's Statement of Facts. Document provided courtesy of the National Security Archive, George Washington University; hereafter, *U.S. v. Ames*, Statement of Facts, Ames Statement.

31. Ames told House Intelligence Committee members, "The KGB has a much tighter tradition of compartmentation and paper. They don't believe in Xerox machines, much less automated cable distribution systems. But, they gradually came to believe, they had to believe, that it was as I said, that I could walk out every two months, say, I could walk out of the embassy in Rome with a stack of cable traffic like that that was unaccountable." House Ames Report, p. 42.

32. Senate Ames Report, p. 22.

33. Statement of the Director of Central Intelligence, John Deutch, on the Clandestine Services and the Damage Caused by Aldrich Ames, December 7, 1995. Precisely how Ames could have managed this particular feat physically, Deutch did not say. Deutch's phrase, "during one assignment" may mean that Ames was carrying out a particular request by the KGB in several parts. Ames also gave a great deal of material to the KGB on computer disks; investigators may have done a rough calculation of how high a stack of paper this material would have made.

34. House Ames Report, p. 43.

35. Senate Ames Report, Appendix 3, Ames interview, pp. 14–15.

36. Senate Ames Report, p. 18. For a description of Rosario's role as a CIA asset, or source, in Mexico City, see Wise, *Nightmover*, pp. 23–26, 29–30.

37. House Ames Report, p. 24.

38. Ames said that, for the most part, he did not give the KGB the actual names of the Soviets spying on behalf of the CIA but rather "codenames or traffic from our field stations that could unerringly identify them." House Ames Report, Appendix 3, Ames interview, p. 15.

39. Ibid., p. 31.

40. In his interviews with House and Senate Intelligence Committee members, Ames rarely missed an opportunity to boast of his deep knowledge of the KGB. Describing his first approach to the Soviets in April 1985, Ames said he was not worried that his espionage would somehow be detected by the CIA: "I was aware, through my knowledge of the KGB, [of] the tremendous extent and care that the KGB took to compartment" information about spies. Senate Ames Report, Ames interview, p. 18.

41. Ibid., p. 27.

42. Senate Ames Report, p. 76.

43. Ames claimed he gave only innocuous information to the KGB when he walked into the Soviet chancery on 16th Street in Washington, D.C., on April 16, 1985. This account is contradicted by KGB Colonel Cherkashin, who said Ames's first approach included the revelation of Martynov and Motorin's treachery on behalf of the CIA. See Peter Earley, "The Price of Treason," *U.S. News & World Report*, February 17, 1997, p. 33.

44. U.S. Department of Justice, Office of Inspector General, *A Review of the FBI's Performance in Deterring, Detecting, and Investigating the Espionage Activities of Robert Philip Hanssen*, August 2003, unclassified executive summary, p. 18.

45. U.S. Department of Justice, Office of Inspector General, *A Review of the FBI's Performance in Uncovering the Espionage Activities of Aldrich Hazen Ames*, April 21, 1997, Section III, A, Findings.

46. Earley, *Confessions of a Spy*, p. 179, gives the figure seven. Victor Cherkashin says the number was "probably closer [to] twenty." Cherkashin clearly was in a position to know. Even the higher figure compares favorably with the numbers at the CIA and FBI, which had similar access. Victor Cherkashin, with Gregory Feifer, *Spy Handler: Memoir of a KGB Officer. The True Story of the Man Who Recruited Robert Hanssen and Aldrich Ames* (New York: Basic Books, 2005), p. 252.

47. Ames did not name Mechulayev in his debriefings after his guilty plea, but the FBI was able to determine his identity through information Ames provided. See Wise, *Nightmover*, p. 151.

48. House Ames Report, Appendix 3, Ames interview, p. 32. Ames's regular handler in Rome was Aleksey Khrenkov (Senate Ames Report, p. 36), but Mechulayev, codenamed VLAD, was the officer who met with Ames in Rome with the story about the Politburo insisting on immediate roll-up of the CIA's spy network.

49. Cherkashin, *Spy Handler*, p. 191.

50. Earley, *Confessions of a Spy*, p. 186.

51. *U.S. v. Ames*, Statement of Facts, Ames Statement, p. 3.

52. Earley, *Confessions of a Spy*, p. 121.

53. House Ames Report, Appendix 3, Ames interview, pp. 46–47.

54. Ibid., p. 76. Ames tried to appear humble and contrite in his interviews, particularly with lawmakers, but could not contain his vanity. He noted repeatedly that he was not a disgruntled employee; indeed, why should he have been, having been reassigned and promoted through years of lackluster performance. Rather, it appears that a desire to feel important was one of his motivations. He appears frustrated with his inability to get anyone at the CIA to pay attention to his ideas; in his work for the KGB, he had that spy service's undivided attention.

55. House Ames Report, Appendix 3, Ames interview, pp. 55, 69. Representatives Dan Glickman of Kansas, the House Intelligence Committee chairman, and Larry Combest of Texas, its ranking member, conducted the interview.

56. U.S. House of Representatives, Permanent Select Committee on Intelligence, testimony of Richard J. Kerr, former deputy director of central intelligence, November 16, 1995, hearing on the management of the U.S. intelligence community; available at http://www.fas.org/irp/congress/1995_hr/kerr1116.htm. While observing that the D.O. "got too big," Kerr also recommended against cutting back on the number of CIA stations overseas because "our ability to predict where the next crisis will occur is not particularly good."

57. U.S. House of Representatives, Permanent Select Committee on Intelligence, *IC21: The Intelligence Community in the 21st Century* (Washington, D.C.: U.S. Government Printing Office, 1996), Chapter IX, "Clandestine Service," Finding 10; hereafter, *IC21*, Chap. IX, "Clandestine Service."

58. Bearden and Risen, *The Main Enemy*, pp. 45–48. Gordievsky has written his own account of his escape in *Next Stop Execution* (London: Macmillan, 1995). How the KGB first learned that Gordievsky was spying for Britain out of the KGB's London residence is somewhat murky. Gordievsky was recalled abruptly to Moscow in mid-May 1985 and subjected to hostile interrogation. This was one month *after* Ames first approached the KGB in Washington with an offer to spy but one month *before* Ames's "big dump" betraying a long list of Soviet assets run by the KGB, a list that included Gordievsky. By coincidence, Ames had learned in March that Gordievsky was spying for the British. Ames had been assigned the task of identifying a source the British had refused to divulge to the CIA, but one that the CIA knew was providing highly valuable intelligence. Ames insists he did not compromise Gordievsky until June, indicating to the CIA that the KGB had another source. Neither Edward Lee Howard nor Robert Hanssen could have known about Gordievsky, the FBI determined, and U.S. counterintelligence investigators believed Ames was telling the truth. Who, then, told the KGB about Gordievsky?

KGB Colonel Cherkashin claims that a British journalist based in Washington who had assisted the KGB on occasion had first divulged to the KGB Gordievsky's work for the British. See Cherkashin, *Spy Handler*, p. 25.

59. John Walcott and Brian Duffy, "Special Report, Cover Story: The CIA's Darkest Secrets," *U.S. News & World Report,* July 4, 1994, p. 34.

60. Andrew quoted in ibid., p. 34.

61. Cherkashin, *Spy Handler*, p. 193.

62. Bearden and Risen, *The Main Enemy,* pp. 168–69; Cherkashin, *Spy Handler*, pp. 194–95.

63. For example, author Jeffrey Richelson reports that in the early 1980s a number of Eastern European intelligence services, notably Bulgaria's, had discovered CIA sensors disguised as tree limbs and other natural objects near military installations. Such discoveries were undoubtedly shared among Warsaw Pact intelligence services. See Jeffrey T. Richelson, *The Wizards of Langley: Inside the CIA's Directorate of Science and Technology* (Boulder, Colo.: Westview Press, 2001), p. 241.

64. U.S. Department of Justice, Commission for Review of FBI Security Programs, *A Review of FBI Security Programs,* March 2002, p. 19; hereafter, DOJ, *Review of FBI Security Programs*. For example, Hanssen betrayed Soviet General Dimitri Polyakov, code-named TOPHAT, in 1979; Ames confirmed Polyakov to the Soviets as a CIA spy in the "big dump" of June 1985. Polyakov was arrested on July 4, 1986, interrogated for twenty months, and shot. The Soviets did not reveal his arrest publicly until 1990. Ibid., p. 8; see also, David Wise, *Spy: The Inside Story of How the FBI's Robert Hanssen Betrayed America* (New York: Random House, 2003), p. 24. Conversely, Ames gave up Boris Yuzhin, Sergei Motorin, and Valery Martynov in the spring of 1985; Hanssen confirmed them to the Soviets as spies in October 1985. Yuzhin was imprisoned; Motorin and Martynov were executed. DOJ, *Review of FBI Security Programs,* p. 9. See also Senate Ames Report, p. 85; and "An Assessment of the Aldrich H. Ames Espionage Case and Its Implications for U.S. Intelligence," *Security Awareness Bulletin,* April 1994, http://www.loyola.edu/dept/politics/intel/sab4.html.

65. Markus Wolf, *Man Without a Face: The Autobiography of Communism's Greatest Spymaster* (New York: Public Affairs, 1999), p. 17. Cherkashin, Ames's KGB handler, offered an almost identical analysis: "Catching even sloppy moles is incredibly difficult, notwithstanding the many mistakes of the FBI and CIA. . . . The public was bombarded with lists of obvious signs of espionage *after* the arrests of Ames and Hanssen." Cherkashin, *Spy Handler*, p. 255.

66. CIA-IG Report, *Identifying Ames*, in House Ames Report, p. 15; Earley, *Confessions of a Spy*, pp. 251, 257–58.

67. Wolf, *Man Without a Face*, pp. 9–19.

68. Director of Central Intelligence, Counter-Intelligence Center, memorandum for CIA Office of Security, December 5, 1990, requesting investigation of Aldrich Ames, in House Ames Report, Appendix 8.

69. Senate Ames Report, pp. 71–73.

70. Ibid., p. 80.

71. Ibid., p. 82; Earley, *Confessions of a Spy*, p. 316. The note read, "I am ready to meet at B on 1 Oct. I cannot read North 13–19 Sept. If you *will meet* at B on 1 Oct. pls signal north w[eek] of 20 Sept. to confi[rm]. *No* message at pipe. If you *cannot* mee[t] 1 Oct, signal north after 27 Sept with message at pipe." The note was a draft of a message Ames had left for the SVR, or Russian intelligence, successor to the KGB, in September 1993 proposing a meeting in "B" or Bogota, Colombia, where Ames traveled occasionally on the pretext of meeting Rosario's family. Emphasis in the original; for more detail, see Wise, *Nightmover*, p. 237.

72. For more on the Soviet spy theory of Ames's capture, see interview with retired KGB Lieutenant General Nikolay Leonov, "KGB Lieutenant General Nikolay Leonov: Failure by Ames in the United States Was Impossible: He Was Betrayed in Moscow," *Komsomolskaya Pravda*, December 22, 1994, in Foreign Broadcast Information Service, SOV-94-248 (December 27, 1994), pp. 17–19. See also Ronald Kessler, *The CIA at War: Inside the Secret Campaign Against Terror* (New York: St. Martin's Press, 2003), p. 12. The Stasi archives issue is addressed in Walter Pincus, R. Jeffrey Smith, and Pierre Thomas, "East German Files Helped in Ames Arrest," *The Washington Post*, March 6, 1994, p. A1. See also Wolf, *Man Without a Face*, p. 371. Cherkashin, in *Spy Handler*, pp. 250–53, appears to endorse the idea that a KGB source betrayed Ames to the CIA. Bearden, in *The Main Enemy*, p. 438, says the Stasi files accessed by Western intelligence in 1990 did not include the most sensitive files on joint Stasi-KGB espionage operations against the West. He does not mention AVENGER.

73. Bearden and Risen, *The Main Enemy*, pp. 159–61.

74. Wise, *Nightmover*, p. 128.

75. Senate Ames Report, p. 23.

76. For the definitive account of IVY BELLS, see Sherry Sontag and Christopher Drew, *Blind Man's Bluff: The Untold Story of American Submarine Espionage* (New York: Public Affairs, 1998).

77. For more on the Lonetree case as a distraction from Ames, see Rodney Barker, *Dancing with the Devil: Sex, Espionage and the U.S. Marine: The Clayton Lonetree Story* (New York: Simon & Schuster, 1996).

78. Senate Ames Report, p. 47.

79. For summary descriptions of these and other espionage cases, see Richard M. Bennett, *Espionage: An Encyclopedia of Spies and Secrets* (London: Virgin Books, 2002).

80. Senate Ames Report, p. 48.

81. Ibid., p. 29.

82. Bearden and Risen, *The Main Enemy*, pp. 70–83, 141–50.

83. Department of Justice, Office of Inspector General Glenn A. Fine, *A Review of the FBI's Performance in Deterring, Detecting, and Investigating the Espionage Activities of Robert Philip Hanssen*, unclassified executive summary, August 2003, pp. 4, 13.

84. Ibid., p. 19.

85. Clinton himself played no significant role in the Ames investigation, other than receiving a weekly briefing on the probe. In the weeks before Ames was arrested, the FBI became concerned about a planned official trip to Moscow that Ames was scheduled to make. The FBI's lead investigator on the case, Special Agent Leslie G. Wiser, suggested that the CIA make up a story that Clinton wanted a briefing on Black Sea security issues that Ames was working on as part of his government work. The White House refused to let Clinton be used as part of a ploy and so Ames was given the story that he was to brief National Security Adviser Anthony Lake. This delayed the Moscow trip and gave investigators more time to prepare for Ames's arrest. See Earley, *Confessions of a Spy*, p. 321.

86. House Ames Report, pp. 53–55.

87. Senate Ames Report, p. 78; see also Statement of R. James Woolsey, Director of Central Intelligence, to the House Permanent Select Committee on Intelligence, September 28, 1994, pp. 12–13, included in House Ames Report, Appendix 2.

88. Snider interview.

89. Author's interview with former CIA director R. James Woolsey, March 13, 2007.

90. Dennis DeConcini and Jack August Jr., *Senator Dennis DeConcini: From the Center of the Aisle* (Tucson: University of Arizona Press, 2006), pp. 198–99. Woolsey told the author that Vice President Al Gore and National Security Adviser Anthony Lake did try to protect the intelligence community budget from deep post–Cold War cuts, but with limited success.

91. Thomas Powers, "Computer Security: The Whiz Kid vs. the Old Boys," *The New York Times Magazine*, December 3, 2000.

92. U.S. House of Representatives, Permanent Select Committee on Intelligence, *Report of the Guatemala Review* (Washington, D.C.: U.S. Government Printing Office, March 17, 1997), Appendix A, letter from U.S. Representative Robert Torricelli to President Clinton, March 22, 1995.

93. Central Intelligence Agency, Office of Inspector General Frederick P. Hitz, *Report of Investigation: Selected Issues Relating to CIA Activities in Honduras in the 1980s*, originally classified Secret, August 27, 1997, p. 1; hereafter CIA-IG, *CIA Activities in Honduras*. The report was declassified in September 1998 as a result of efforts by members of Congress and the National Security Archive. Made available courtesy of the National Security Archive, George Washington University, http://www.gwu.edu/nsarchiv/latin_america/honduras/cia_ig_report/. See also Gary Cohn and Ginger Thompson, "Unearthed: Fatal Secrets," Baltimore *Sun*, June 11, 1995, p. 1A. The inspector general's report mentions the *Sun* series, but the CIA's investigation was also prompted by a series of stories on human rights abuses in Honduras by James Lemoyne, foreign correspondent for the *New York Times*.

94. U.S. Senate Select Committee on Intelligence, testimony of Acting Director of Central Intelligence William O. Studeman on Guatemala, April 4, 1995.

95. Speech by Director of Central Intelligence John Deutch, "The Future of U.S.

Intelligence—Charting a Course for Change," July 11, 1995, https://www.cia.gov/news-information/speeches-testimony/1995/index.html.

96. President's Intelligence Oversight Board (IOB), *Report of the Guatemala Review,* June 28, 1996, p. 22; hereafter IOB, *Guatemala Review.* The full report is available at http://www.ciponline.org/iob.htm. Selected pages of the printed report are available at http://www.gwu.edu/nsarchiv/NSAEBB/NSAEBB27/04-01.htm.

97. IOB, *Guatemala Review,* pp. 21–22, 24.

98. CIA-IG, *CIA Activities in Honduras,* p. 29.

99. Ibid., pp. 126, 200.

100. Powers, "Computer Security."

101. Snider interview.

102. Senate Ames Report, Ames interview, pp. 16–18. Ames has been somewhat inconsistent in his description of the double agents. In an interview with author Pete Earley, Ames talked about "two or three" double agents and later referred to "three." Another reference to two came in his Senate Intelligence Committee interview, which occurred a few months after his arrest and seems to be the more reliable recollection. See Earley, *Confessions of a Spy,* p. 139.

103. Senate Ames Report, p. 20. See also Earley, *Confessions of a Spy,* p. 178.

104. Earley, *Confessions of a Spy,* p. 92.

105. Ibid., p. 139.

106. Senate Ames Report, Ames interview, p. 16.

107. One of those was KGB officer Aleksandr Zhomov, code-named PROLOGUE, who approached the CIA's Moscow Station chief Jack Downing on the Moscow–Leningrad train in May 1987. Although the CIA didn't determine conclusively until July 1990 that he was a double agent who remained under Moscow's control, PROLOGUE provided the CIA with valuable information, particularly confirmation of the extent of the 1985–86 asset losses. See Bearden and Risen, *The Main Enemy,* pp. 297, 447–48.

108. Director of Central Intelligence John Deutch, Statement to the Public on the Ames Damage Assessment, October 31, 1995; hereafter, Deutch statement on Ames damage, October 31, 1995.

109. A 1994 survey by the CIA inspector general found that only 9 percent of the Directorate of Operations personnel surveyed believed that promotion review panels rewarded quality work in validating assets. See IOB, *Guatemala Review,* "Asset Validation System" section.

110. Author's notes from Senate Intelligence Committee news conference, Hart Senate Office Building, Washington, D.C., October 31, 1995.

111. Ibid.

112. Tim Weiner, "CIA Tells Panels It Failed to Sift Tainted Spy Data," *The New York Times,* November 1, 1995, p. A1.

113. U.S. Senate Select Committee on Intelligence (SSCI), Statement of Frederick P. Hitz, CIA Inspector General, November 9, 1995; hereafter, Hitz SSCI testimony.

114. Letter from former directors of Central Intelligence William Webster, Robert Gates, and R. James Woolsey to Director of Central Intelligence John Deutch, October 10, 1995. Letter made available courtesy of the National Security Archive, George Washington University.

115. Earley, *Confessions of a Spy*, p. 201.

116. Hitz SSCI testimony, emphasis added.

117. Author's contemporaneous interview with Senator Dennis DeConcini, November 2, 1995.

118. Author's contemporaneous interview with Anthony Cordesman, Center for Strategic and International Studies, November 2, 1995.

119. Author's contemporaneous interview with Bill Lee, at that time a former Defense Intelligence Agency analyst who had specialized in Soviet military capability, November 7, 1995.

120. Author's contemporaneous interview with U.S. Air Force General Joseph Ralston, commander, Air Combat Command, November 7, 1995.

121. Author's contemporaneous interview with Donald Yockey, former Pentagon acquisitions chief during the first Bush administration, November 10, 1995. See also John Diamond, "Pentagon Decision-Making Said Unaffected by Tainted Spy Reports," Associated Press, November 17, 1995.

122. Christopher Andrew and Vasili Mitrokhin, *The World Was Going Our Way: The KGB and the Battle for the Third World* (New York: Basic Books, 2005), p. 489. Andrew and Mitrokhin write that a Pentagon study in the early 1980s estimated that 70 percent of all Warsaw Pact weapons were based on Western technology.

123. Deutch statement on Ames damage, December 1995.

124. Author's contemporaneous interview with Charles Horner, November 1, 1995. See also John Diamond, "Pentagon Examining Whether Tainted Information Influenced Weapons Programs," Associated Press, November 1, 1995.

125. Author's e-mail exchange with former CIA deputy director Richard Kerr, July 9, 2007. Kerr observed: "I think we were quite conscious of that [disinformation] problem. My impression is that [the] Sov[iets] did not try to inflate their capability beyond what [the CIA] might expect. Also, trying to figure out if you are being fed information is a tough process."

126. Deutch statement on Ames damage, December 1995.

127. Ibid.

128. Department of Defense news briefing, Captain Michael Doubleday, November 2, 1995, Pentagon briefing room.

129. E-mail exchange with Richard Kerr, July 9, 2007.

130. Author's interview with former deputy defense secretary John White, June 11, 2007.

131. Author's interviews with a former Directorate of Operations official who spoke on condition of anonymity, June 4, 2007, and with former D.O. Soviet–East European division chief Milton Bearden, June 1, 2007.

132. Lee interview.

133. Author's e-mail exchange with Kerr, July 3, 2007.

134. Author's interview with former CIA inspector general Frederick Hitz, June 7, 2007.

135. Hitz interview.

136. U.S. Senate, Committee on Armed Services, testimony of Acting Director of Central Intelligence John McLaughlin, intelligence reform hearing, August 17, 2004.

137. Director of Central Intelligence George Tenet, Written Statement for the Record before the House-Senate Joint Inquiry Committee, October 17, 2002. According to the 9/11 Commission report, "The nadir for the Clandestine Service was 1995, when only 25 trainees became new officers." See National Commission on Terrorist Attacks Upon the United States, *The 9/11 Commission Report* (New York: W.W. Norton, 2004), p. 90. The reference to twelve graduates in one of the 1995 CIA case officer classes appears in George Tenet, with Bill Harlow, *At the Center of the Storm: My Years at the CIA* (New York: Harper Collins, 2007), p. 14.

138. CIA Deputy Director for Operations James L. Pavitt, Written Statement for the Record before the National Commission on Terrorist Attacks Upon the United States (9/11 Commission), April 14, 2004. Pavitt's testimony to the 9/11 Commission marked the first time in CIA history that an operations chief had testified publicly.

139. Congressional Research Service, Stephen Daggett, national defense specialist, "The U.S. Intelligence Budget: A Basic Overview," *CRS Report for Congress*, September 24, 2004, pp. 2–3. The "top-line" budget for U.S. intelligence has been classified through most of the decades since World War II. The overall figures were disclosed for fiscal 1997, $26.6 billion, and fiscal 1998, $26.7 billion. Steve Aftergood of the Federation of American Scientists notes that while the breakdown of intelligence spending has remained classified, the report of the Aspin-Brown Commission on intelligence reform inadvertently showed that the CIA's fiscal 1996 budget was $3.2 billion. The report had a chart showing the relative size of the various intelligence community budgets, though not the actual dollar amounts, but included the dollar figure for the Defense Mapping Agency, which made it possible to extrapolate other intelligence community budgets. See U.S. Commission on Roles and Capabilities of the U.S. Intelligence Community, *Preparing for the 21st Century: An Appraisal of U.S. Intelligence*, March 1, 1996, http://www.gpoaccess.gov/int/report.html.

140. *IC21*, Chap. IX, Clandestine Service, Finding 10.

141. National Commission on Terrorist Attacks Upon the United States (9/11 Commission), Staff Statement No. 11, public hearing, April 14, 2004, p. 3. The Bush administration was responsible for intelligence budget preparation for fiscal years 1990 to 1993; Clinton for fiscal 1994 through 2002.

142. CIA Deputy Director for Operations James Pavitt, Address to Duke University Law School Conference, April 11, 2002, https://www.cia.gov/news-information/speeches-testimony/2002/pavitt_04262002.html.

143. Tenet, *At the Center of the Storm*, pp. 13–16.

144. *IC21*, Chap. IX, Clandestine Service, Finding 10.

145. CIA news conference, Deputy CIA Director John McLaughlin, remarks to reporters, July 9, 2004, http://transcripts.cnn.com/TRANSCRIPTS/0407/09/acd.00.html.

146. Tenet, 9/11 Commission testimony, April 14, 2004.

147. House Armed Services Committee, testimony of Deputy Defense Secretary Paul Wolfowitz, August 10, 2004; for Wolfowitz's prepared statement, see http://www.GlobalSecurity.org/security/library/congress/2004_h/040810-wolfowitz/pdf; an audio transcript of the entire hearing, including the quoted remarks, is available at http://armedservices.house.gov/comdocs/schedules/2004.shtml.

148. For an example of Tenet offering this defense, see *9/11 Commission Report*, p. 140.

149. Author's interview with Richard L. Russell, September 14, 2004. See also Richard L. Russell, "Spies Like Them," *National Interest*, Fall 2004; and Richard L. Russell, *Sharpening Strategic Intelligence: Why the CIA Gets It Wrong and What Needs to Be Done to Get It Right* (New York: Cambridge University Press, 2007).

150. Reuel Marc Gerecht, "A New Clandestine Service: The Case for Creative Destruction," Chap. 4 in Peter Berkowitz, ed., *The Future of American Intelligence* (Washington, D.C.: Hoover Institution Press, 2005), p. 109.

151. Reuel Marc Gerecht, "The Sorry State of the CIA," *On the Issues* (Washington, D.C.: American Enterprise Institute for Public Policy Research, July 2004), p. 3.

152. Gary Webb, "Dark Alliance: America's 'Crack' Plague Has Roots in Nicaragua War," *San Jose Mercury News*, August 18, 1996, p. A1, was the first of a series of articles that caused a sensation, particularly in the African American community that had been ravaged by the crack scourge. Other mainstream news organizations later challenged many of the findings of the series, and the newspaper's own editor-in-chief, Jerry Ceppos, apologized in an editorial published May 11, 1997, for what he described as four key flaws in the series, including oversimplification of the crack epidemic and the presentation of only one interpretation of complex evidence. In the main, media criticism focused on weak links in the available evidence between the CIA, crack traffickers, and the Contras. For an overview of the series itself and the media criticism that followed, see Peter Kornbluh, "Anatomy of a Story. Crack, the Contras, and the CIA: The Storm over 'Dark Alliance,'" *Columbia Journalism Review* (January/February 1997).

153. CIA Inspector General Frederick P. Hitz, statement before the House Permanent Select Committee on Intelligence, March 16, 1998. The CIA-IG produced a two-volume report on the probe: Volume I: *Report of Investigation Concerning Allegations of Connections Between the CIA and the Contras in Cocaine Trafficking to the United States* (96-0143-IG) (Washington, D.C.: January 29, 1998); and Volume II: *Report of Investiga-*

tion Concerning Allegations of Connections Between CIA and the Contras in Cocaine Trafficking to the United States (Washington, D.C.: October 8, 1998).

154. U.S. Senate Select Committee on Intelligence, testimony of Director of Central Intelligence John Deutch, September 19, 1996.

155. Gerecht, "A New Clandestine Service," p. 105. See also Walcott and Duffy, "The CIA's Darkest Secrets," p. 34.

156. CIA Inspector General L. Britt Snider, *Report of Investigation: Improper Handling of Classified Information by John M. Deutch,* February 18, 2000. See especially paragraphs 179–89 for the criminal referral issue, and paragraphs 230–43 for details on the role of senior CIA officers in impeding the progress of the investigation. Available at www.fas.org/irp/cia/product/ig_deutch.html. See also James Risen, "CIA Inquiry of Its Ex-Director Was Stalled at Top, Report Says," *The New York Times,* February 1, 2000, p. A1.

157. John Solomon, "Clinton Grants Pardons to 140, Including Brother," Associated Press, January 21, 2001. The AP dispatch states that Deutch "had been discussing a possible plea deal with prosecutors to settle allegations he mishandled classified government information when the pardon muted his case." As previously noted, Deutch declined to be interviewed.

158. R. Jeffrey Smith, "CIA Drops Over 1,000 Informants," *The Washington Post,* March 2, 1997, p. A1; Tim Weiner, "CIA Severs Ties to 100 Foreign Agents," *The New York Times,* March 3, 1997, p. A1. The figure 100 is a reference to sources the CIA concluded were implicated in major crimes overseas and whose intelligence was not worth the risk of dealing with them. The larger figure refers to the total number of sources stripped from the rolls because they were no longer providing quality intelligence or had become irrelevant after the end of the Cold War.

159. For example, see Lindsay Moran's account of her brief career as a D.O. officer in the late 1990s, including a detailed description of her 1999 training regimen at "The Farm," the CIA's paramilitary training center near Williamsburg, Virginia. See Lindsay Moran, *Blowing My Cover: My Life as a CIA Spy* (New York: G.P. Putnam's Sons, 2005); also, author's interview with Moran, December 18, 2004.

Notes to Chapter 6

1. Joseph S. Bermudez Jr., "A History of Ballistic Missile Development in the DPRK" (Democratic People's Republic of Korea, or North Korea), Monitoring Proliferation Threats Project, Occasional Paper No. 2, 1999, Monterey Institute of International Studies, Center for Nonproliferation Studies, p. 29.

2. David C. Wright, "Backgrounder: Assessment of the North Korea Missile Program," Union of Concerned Scientists, February 25, 2003. Wright was co-director and senior scientist of UCS's Global Security Program.

3. Bermudez, "History of Ballistic Missile Development," p. 30; Wright, "Assessment of the North Korea Missile Program."

4. Korean Central News Agency, "Successful Launch of First Satellite in DPRK," September 4, 1998, http://www.kcna.co.jp/item/1998/9809/news09/04.htm. Lt. Col. Clayton K. S. Chun, USAF, "Shooting Down a 'Star': Program 437, the U.S. Nuclear ASAT System and Present-Day Copycat Killers," *The Cadre Papers*, No. 6, Institute of National Security Studies, College of Aerospace Doctrine, Research and Education, Air University Press, Maxwell Air Force Base, Ala., April 2000, pp. 42, 46.

5. Bermudez, "History of Ballistic Missile Development," p. 30; Wright, "Assessment of the North Korean Missile Program."

6. Bermudez, "History of Ballistic Missile Development," p. 30.

7. Timothy M. Beard and Ivan Eland, "Ballistic Missile Proliferation: Does the Clinton Administration Understand the Threat?" Cato Institute, Foreign Policy Briefing, February 11, 1999.

8. See *Congressional Record—House*, debate and votes on H.R. 7, Roll Call No. 136, February 15, 1995, pp. H1780–H1846; Public Broadcasting Service, "Timeline: Missile Defense, 1944–2002," *Frontline*, p. 7, http://www.pbs.org/wgbh/pages/frontline/shows/missile/etc/cron.html. The role of Republican "deficit hawks" in blocking initial attempts to fund a national missile-defense program was described by Joseph Cirincione of the Carnegie Endowment for International Peace in "The Persistence of the Missile Defense Illusion," presentation to the Conference on Nuclear Disarmament: Safe Disposal of Nuclear Materials or New Weapons Development? Como, Italy, July 2–4, 1998.

9. Director of Central Intelligence, National Intelligence Council, declassified excerpts from the National Intelligence Estimate "Emerging Missile Threats to North America During the Next 15 Years," NIE 95-19, President's Summary, November 1995, available at Federation of American Scientists website, http://www.fas.org/spp/starwars/offdocs/nie9519.htm.

10. Maria Ryan, "Filling in the 'Unknowns': Hypothesis-Based Intelligence and the Rumsfeld Commission," *Intelligence and National Security* 21, no. 2 (April 2006): 286.

11. Ibid., p. 287, emphasis in the original.

12. Author's interview with John McLaughlin, December 21, 2006. McLaughlin was a senior CIA analyst in 1995; from 1997 to 2000, the deputy director for intelligence, the Agency's top analyst post; and from 2000 to 2004, the CIA's deputy director. At the time of the interview he was a professor at the Johns Hopkins University School of Advanced International Studies.

13. Bill Gertz, "Intelligence Report Warns of Missile Launches Against U.S.," *The Washington Times*, May 14, 1996, p. A3.

14. While it is understood that the National Intelligence Council, which produced intelligence estimates, is an organization distinct from the CIA that seeks opinions from all intelligence agencies, National Intelligence Estimates must nevertheless be seen as heavily influenced by the CIA. Before the intelligence reorganization legislation of 2005, the council operated out of CIA headquarters and reported to the CIA director in his

role as the director of central intelligence, a title carrying supervisory authority over the entire intelligence community. Most of the senior analysts on the council were drawn from the ranks of the CIA's Directorate of Intelligence.

15. United States General Accounting Office, *Foreign Missile Threats: Analytic Soundness of National Intelligence Estimate 95-19*, statement of Richard Davis, director, National Security Analysis, National Security and International Affairs Division, before the Senate Select Committee on Intelligence, Dec. 4, 1996, p. 4.

16. John E. McLaughlin, vice chairman, National Intelligence Council, "Emerging Missile Threats to North America During the Next 15 Years," prepared statement for the record to the Senate Select Committee on Intelligence, December 4, 1996, p. 1. McLaughlin's latter point was dropped from his oral testimony but remains part of the official record. He told the committee that eight intelligence agencies contributed to the estimate and that "differences among experts were not great." See hearing transcript, Intelligence Analysis on the Long-Range Missile Threat to the United States, U.S. Senate Select Committee on Intelligence, Dec. 4, 1996.

17. McLaughlin testimony, p. 3.

18. McLaughlin interview.

19. Independent Panel Review of "Emerging Missile Threats to North America During the Next 15 Years," NIE 95-19, panel headed by former CIA director Robert Gates; hereafter, Gates panel. Declassified summary released by the CIA, December 23, 1996, p. 6.

20. Gates panel, p. 5.

21. Gates panel, p. 2.

22. Opening statement of Representative Curt Weldon (R-Pa.), chairman of the House Armed Services Research and Development Subcommittee, *Hearing on North Korean, Iranian and Worldwide Missile Threats*, May 7, 1997.

23. The Commission to Assess the Ballistic Missile Threat to the United States, informally called the Rumsfeld Commission, was established pursuant to Public Law 104-201, the National Defense Authorization Act for Fiscal Year 1997, Section 1321.

24. *Report of the Commission to Assess the Ballistic Missile Threat to the United States*, Pursuant to Public Law 201, 104th Congress, July 15, 1998; hereafter, Rumsfeld Commission Report (Washington: Government Printing Office, 1998).

25. Author's interview with Dr. Barry Blechman, April 23, 2007. The author had a brief conversation with Rumsfeld in summer 2007; the former defense secretary declined a request for a formal interview.

26. Blechman interview.

27. In a hastily arranged news conference the Indian government said the tests had occurred at 3:45 p.m., local time. International seismic monitoring data, however, placed the precise time at 3:43:44.2 p.m. See "India's Nuclear Weapons Program: Operation Shakti—1998," updated March 30, 2001, available online at http://nuclearweaponarchive.org/India/IndiaShakti.html.

28. Jeffrey T. Richelson, *Spying on the Bomb: American Nuclear Intelligence from Nazi Germany to Iran and North Korea* (New York: W. W. Norton, 2006), p. 434.

29. Evan Thomas, John Barry, and Melinda Liu, "Ground Zero: India's Blasts Dramatize the Nuclear Age," *Newsweek*, May 25, 1998, p. 28. One of the shafts used in the May 11 test had been designated "White House" by Indian officials.

30. Richelson, *Spying on the Bomb*, p. 427.

31. David L. Marcus, "India Holds Underground Nuclear Tests," *The Boston Globe*, May 12, 1998, p. A1.

32. Richard Shelby, "Sen. Shelby Comments on 'Colossal Intelligence Failure of the Decade,'" press release, May 12, 1998.

33. Bill Gertz, "India Blasts Take U.S. Intelligence by Surprise," *The Washington Times*, May 12, 1998, p. A1. The Comprehensive Test Ban Treaty became open for signature in 1996. The Clinton administration, which had led the effort for the treaty, made the United States the first nation to sign. But in 1999 the Senate, whose consent is required to ratify U.S. participation, voted against ratification.

34. Richelson, *Spying on the Bomb*, p. 435. The author is grateful to Bruce Riedel, senior fellow for political transitions in the Middle East and South Asia at the Brookings Institution, for providing a prepublication manuscript of his article, "South Asia's Nuclear Decade" written for the spring 2008 edition of the journal *Survival: Global Politics and Strategy*. At the time of India's nuclear test, Riedel was a CIA analyst.

35. The author covered these events while reporting for the Associated Press. For the reference to sandstorms, for example, see John Diamond, "CIA Searching for Answers Behind Its India-Nuclear Failure," Associated Press, May 16, 1998; and Thomas et al., "Ground Zero."

36. CIA Public Affairs Staff, Admiral David Jeremiah, transcript of news conference, CIA headquarters, June 2, 1998, https://www.cia.gov/news-information/press-releases-statements/press-release-archive-1998/jeremiah.html.

37. James Risen, Steven Lee Myers, and Tim Weiner, "U.S. May Have Helped India Hide Its Nuclear Activity," *The New York Times*, May 25, 1998, p. A1.

38. See Tim Weiner, "U.S. Suspects India Prepares to Conduct Nuclear Test," *The New York Times*, December 16, 1995, p. A1; and R. Jeffrey Smith, "Possible Nuclear Arms Test by India Concerns U.S.," *The Washington Post*, December 16, 1995, p. A1.

39. Sumit Ganguly, "India's Pathway to Pokhran II: The Prospects and Sources of New Delhi's Nuclear Weapons Program," *International Security* 23, no. 4 (Spring 1999): 168.

40. Jeremiah news conference, June 2, 1998.

41. Raj Chengappa, *Weapons of Peace: The Secret Story of India's Quest to Be a Nuclear Power* (New Delhi: Harper Collins India, 2000), 256–57.

42. Jeffrey T. Richelson, ed., "U.S. Intelligence and the Bomb," National Security Archive Briefing Book No. 187, a compendium of newly declassified intelligence documents on India's nuclear weapons programs, posted on the National Security Archive

website April 13, 2003. The reference is to Document 22 in the compendium: Intelligence Community Staff, Post Mortem Report, *An Examination of the Intelligence Community's Performance Before the Indian Nuclear Test of May 1974* (Top Secret), July 1974, http://www.gwu.edu/nsarchiv/NSAEBB/NSAEBB187/index.htm.

43. John Pike, "Pokhran—The Intelligence Failure," undated, http://www.Global Security.org/wmd/world/india/pokharan-intell.htm.

44. Jeremiah news conference, p. 6.

45. John Diamond, "CIA Searching for Answers Behind Its India-Nuclear Failure," Associated Press, May 16, 1998. For more detail on denial and deception efforts, see Richelson, *Spying on the Bomb*, p. 444.

46. Pike, "Pokhran—The Intelligence Failure."

47. John Diamond, "Review Raps CIA for Failing to Learn of India's Nuclear Tests," Associated Press, June 2, 1998.

48. Author's interview with L. Britt Snider, former counsel to the Senate Select Committee on Intelligence and CIA inspector general, September 26, 1996.

49. Author's interview with Linda Millis, former CIA senior analyst, October 31, 2006.

50. McLaughlin interview.

51. Polly Nayak, "The Indian Nuclear Tests—Parsing the U.S. Intelligence Failure," November 2004, paper presented at Stanford University's Center for International Security and Cooperation, p. 2.

52. Ibid., p. 10. Nayak's paper is based entirely on open sources, mainly contemporaneous media accounts. The CIA letter to Jeremiah, for example, was cited in *Armed Forces Newswire*, "Tenet Asks for Assessment of Indian Nuclear Testing" (Phillips Business Information Inc.), May 14, 1998. But her access to classified information concerning India and nuclear issues can be reasonably taken as indication that the information she cites from open sources conforms with what she knew internally at the Agency.

53. CIA, Office of Near Eastern, South Asian, and African Analysis, *India: Problems and Prospects for the BJP Government*, Intelligence Report (Secret), April 13, 1998, p. 4. The report was obtained by Jeffrey T. Richelson and the National Security Archive at George Washington University, under the Freedom of Information Act.

54. CIA, *India: Problems and Prospects*, p. 8.

55. Jeremiah news conference, June 2, 1998, p. 1.

56. The CIA focused on BJP's truculent national security stance in a report three weeks after the Pokhran test. See, CIA, Office of Near Eastern, South Asian, and African Analysis, *India: BJP Flexing Muscles, But How Far Will It Go?* (Secret), Intelligence Report, May 29, 1998, p. 13. Obtained by Jeffrey T. Richelson and the National Security Archive at George Washington University, under the Freedom of Information Act.

57. Nayak, "Indian Nuclear Tests," p. 2.

58. Tim Weiner, "Nuclear Anxiety: The Blunders," *The New York Times*, May 13, 1998, p. A1.

59. John Diamond, "CIA Searching for Answers Behind Its India-Nuclear Failure," *Associated Press*, May 16, 1998.

60. Nayak, "Indian Nuclear Tests," pp. 6, 4–5.

61. "Nuclear Issue Not Raised in Clinton Talks," *The Hindu*, March 22, 1998.

62. Risen, Myers, and Weiner, "U.S. May Have Helped India." This article in the *New York Times* says Berger raised only the issue of Indian missile testing and did so to praise the Indian government for its restraint in the wake of the Ghauri test by Pakistan. Nayak, "Indian Nuclear Tests," p. 7, says the nuclear issue came up briefly.

63. Richelson, *Spying on the Bomb*, p. 433. Richelson dates the decision to April 8; other accounts date it to April 9.

64. The polling results were mentioned in the CIA's post-test report, *India: BJP Flexing Muscles*, May 29, 1998, p. 3.

65. Nayak, "Indian Nuclear Tests," p. 17. The same point appears in CIA's *India: BJP Flexing Muscles*, May 29, 1998, p. 5, to which Nayak almost certainly contributed.

66. In an interview the day after India's test, Pakistani physics professor Pervez Hoodbhoy, asked about the state of Pakistan's nuclear capability, replied, "Nobody really knows. I suppose that in the next few days or perhaps the next few weeks or months, we shall know better." It was testimony to the shroud of uncertainty surrounding Pakistan's nuclear program as well as the well-understood likelihood that India's test would provoke tests-in-kind by Pakistan. See PBS, *The NewsHour with Jim Lehrer*, transcript, "Growing Nuclear Family," interview with Pervez Hoodbhoy, professor of nuclear physics at Quaid-I-Azam University, Islamabad, Pakistan, May 12, 1998.

67. CIA Director George Tenet, prepared statement before the 9/11 Commission, March 24, 2004, p. 19. Pakistani general Pervez Musharraf ousted elected prime minister Nawaz Sharif in a coup on October 12, 1999, further straining U.S.-Pakistani relations.

68. Rumsfeld Commission Report, Executive Summary, p. 21.

69. Ibid.

70. Rumsfeld Commission, Intelligence Side Letter to the Rumsfeld Report; hereafter, Rumsfeld Side Letter, March 1, 1999, p. 5.

71. Rumsfeld Commission Report, Executive Summary, p. 24.

72. Ibid. Rumsfeld made his famous "known unknowns" remark at a Pentagon news conference in 2002. See Department of Defense News Briefing, Secretary Donald Rumsfeld and Air Force General Richard Myers, February 12, 2002, http://www.defenselink.mil/transcripts/transcript.aspx?transcriptid=2636. See also Rumsfeld's discussion of the link between the quote and the Rumsfeld Commission in Jeffrey Goldberg, "The Unknown: The CIA and the Pentagon Take Another Look at Al Qaeda and Iraq," *The New Yorker*, February 10, 2003, http://www.newyorker.com/archive/2003/02/10/030210fa_fact.

73. Bob Woodward, "Two Months Before 9/11, an Urgent Warning to Rice," *The Washington Post*, October 1, 2006, p. A17.

74. Robert D. Walpole, National Intelligence Officer for Strategic and Nuclear Programs, "The Rumsfeld Report on Ballistic Missile Threats," presentation to the Carnegie Endowment for International Peace, September 17, 1998.

75. Walpole, Carnegie presentation.

76. Ibid.

77. Bradley Graham, *Hit to Kill: The New Battle over Shielding America from Missile Attack* (New York: Public Affairs, 2001), p. 148.

78. Ryan, "Filling in the 'Unknowns,'" p. 307.

79. National Intelligence Council, "Foreign Missile Developments and the Ballistic Missile Threat to the United States Through 2015," September 1999; hereafter, September 1999 NIE. Declassified excerpts from the 1999 National Intelligence Estimate, published in James M. Lindsay and Michael E. O'Hanlon, *Defending America: The Case for Limited National Missile Defense* (Washington, D.C.: Brookings Institution Press, 2001), Appendix D, p. 218. Lindsay had been a member of Clinton's National Security Council staff in 1996 and 1997 and evidently supported the administration's move away from outright opposition to national missile defense.

80. Michael Dobbs, "How Politics Helped Redefine the Threat," *The Washington Post*, January 14, 2002, and quoted in a profile of the politics behind missile defense in an analysis by the policy website Right Web at the Interhemispheric Resource Center, May 21, 2004.

81. September 1999 NIE.

82. Rumsfeld Commission Report, pp. 5, 8.

83. President George W. Bush, *The National Security Strategy of the United States of America*, September 17, 2002, http://www.whitehouse.gov/nsc/nssall.html.

84. Testimony of Robert G. Joseph before the House Armed Services Committee, June 28, 2000, p. 3, http://www.ndu.edu/WMDCenter/docUploaded/Joseph%20Testimony%2028%20June%202000.pdf; hereafter, Joseph, HASC testimony.

85. Ibid., pp. 3–4.

86. Ibid., p. 4.

87. Joseph Cirincione, "Assessing the Assessment: The 1999 National Intelligence Estimate of the Ballistic Missile Threat," *Nonproliferation Review* (Spring 2000): 125.

88. See Robert S. Litwak, *Rogue States and U.S. Foreign Policy: Containment After the Cold War* (Washington, D.C.: Woodrow Wilson Center Press, 2000).

89. President William J. Clinton, "Remarks to Future Leaders of Europe in Brussels," January 9, 1994, *Public Papers of the Presidents, William J. Clinton*, Vol. 1 (1994) p. 11; Anthony Lake, "From Containment to Enlargement," Dispatch, (U.S. Department of State) 4, No. 39 (Sept. 27, 1993), pp. 658–64; and Anthony Lake, "Confronting Backlash States," *Foreign Affairs* 73 (1993): 45. See also Petra Minnerop, "Rogue States—State Sponsors of Terrorism?" *German Law Journal* (September 1, 2002).

90. See Defense Department briefing, November 22, 1999. Also quoted in John Pike,

"National Missile Defense: Rushing to Failure," *F.A.S. Public Interest Report* (Federation of American Scientists) 52, no. 6 (November/December 1999): 3.

91. Nathan Voegeli, Center for Nonproliferation Studies, Monterey Institute of International Studies, "Issue Brief: A look at National Missile Defense and the Ground-Based Midcourse Defense System," Nuclear Threat Initiative, December 2005, p. 8.

92. Congressional Research Service, Amy Belasco, "The Cost of Iraq, Afghanistan and Advanced Base Security Since 9/11," *CRS Report for Congress*, October 7, 2005, summary page. Unattributed, "U.S. Stages Missile Defense 'War Games' for Congress," Reuters dispatch, January 24, 2006; David Ruppe, "Annual U.S. Missile Defense Spending Could Double," Global Security Newswire, January 24, 2006.

93. Defense Department Operational Update Briefing, Secretary of Defense Donald Rumsfeld and Richard Myers, Chairman of the Joint Chiefs of Staff, Dec. 22, 2004, http://www.defenselink.mil/transcripts/transcript.aspx?transcript=2046.

94. 9/11 Commission, Staff Statement No. 6, March 23, 2004, p. 6. The charge that al-Qaeda is not described by name in intelligence community documents was made by the 9/11 Commission in Staff Statement No. 11, April 14, 2004, p. 3. U.S. intelligence officials, speaking anonymously, denied that charge, saying that al-Qaeda appears by name as early as 1993 in a CIA report. For more details on the content of the 1995 estimate, entitled "The Foreign Terrorist Threat in the United States," see "A Scapegoat Is Not a Solution," Paul R. Pillar, (then) National Intelligence Officer for Near East and South Asia, op-ed, *The New York Times*, June 4, 2004.

95. U.S. House Committee on International Relations, The President's International Affairs Request for Fiscal Year 2005, 108th Cong., 2nd sess., February 11, 2004, opening statement of Representative Henry Hyde (R-Ill.), chairman, http://commdocs.house.gov/committees/intlrel/hfa91796.000/hfa91796_of.htm; emphasis added.

96. Ibid.

Notes to Chapter 7

1. United States District Court, Southern District of New York, *United States v. Usama bin Laden et al.*, S(7) Cr. 1023, (Day 26) trial transcript, April 3, 2001, p. 3781, available at http://cryptome.org/usa-v-ubl-dt.htm. Hereafter, *U.S. v. bin Laden.* Odeh's lawyers at the embassy bombings trial sought to suppress statements by their client allegedly made under duress. They claimed that "Pakistani authorities subjected Mr. Odeh to constant abuse, including threats of torture, physical assaults, sleep deprivation, and other inhumane treatment." Kenyan authorities, who questioned Odeh outside the presence of the FBI, "told [Odeh] that if he didn't talk they would take him to a forest and hang him upside down until he told them what they wanted to hear." Judge Leonard B. Sand rejected the motion. In the above-referenced case, see Document 232, Notice of Motion to Suppress Statements and Evidence, filed July 7, 2000, http://cryptome.org/usa-v-qaeda-ms.htm.

2. For a detailed official description of the embassy bombings, see U.S. Department

of State, Accountability Review Boards, *Bombings of the U.S. Embassies in Nairobi, Kenya and Dar es Salaam, Tanzania on August 7, 1998, Report of the Accountability Review Boards*, January 8, 1999. Secretary of State Colin Powell, in testimony before the 9/11 Commission on March 23, 2004, called the attacks the worst in State Department history. The effect of the stun grenade in drawing people to windows may have been a deliberate al-Qaeda tactic. See Lawrence Wright, *The Looming Tower: Al-Qaeda and the Road to 9/11* (New York: Alfred A. Knopf, 2006), p. 271.

3. *U.S. v. bin Laden*, (Day 12) trial transcript, February 28, 2001, p. 1699.

4. United States District Court, Southern District of New York, *United States v. Mohamed Sadeek Odeh*, Complaint, Sworn Statement of FBI Special Agent Daniel J. Coleman, August 26, 1998, p. 5, http://jya.com/usa-v-qaeda.htm. See also *U.S. v. bin Laden*, May 2, 2001, p. 5487.

5. Kamran Khan, "Pakistan Gears to Midwife 'Get Osama' Operation," *News International Pakistan*, August 17, 1998, p. 1.

6. National Commission on Terrorist Attacks upon the United States, *The 9/11 Commission Report* (New York: W. W. Norton, 2004), p. 116.

7. George Tenet (with Bill Harlow), *At the Center of the Storm: My Years at the CIA* (New York: HarperCollins, 2007), p. 115.

8. University of Pittsburgh, Matthew B. Ridgeway Center, "Anatomy of a Terrorist Attack: An In-Depth Investigation into the 1998 Bombings of the U.S. Embassies in Kenya and Tanzania," working paper, Spring 2005, p. 83.

9. *U.S. v. bin Laden*, (Day 11) trial transcript, February 27, 2001, pp. 1619–32, and (Day 12) trial transcript, February 28, 2001, pp. 1640–44, 1648–52, 1663. FBI Special Agent John Anticev, who interrogated Odeh in Kenya after the embassy bombings, provided a detailed narrative of Odeh's background and al-Qaeda activities in this trial testimony.

10. Ibid., p. 1684. FBI Special Agent John Anticev is quoting Odeh's recollection of what Saleh told him.

11. *U.S. v. bin Laden*, (Day 38) trial transcript, May 2, 2001, p. 5438.

12. Ibid., (Day 12) trial transcript, February 28, 2001, pp. 1679, 1684, and 1713.

13. Routine eavesdropping by the National Security Agency on a satellite phone used by bin Laden and his lieutenants not only provided information about plans for the meeting but also helped establish the link between al-Qaeda and the embassy bombings. When the *Washington Times* mentioned these intercepts the day after the Sudan and Afghan strikes, bin Laden immediately stopped using the phone. See *9/11 Commission Report*, p. 127; and Martin Sieff, "Terrorist Is Driven by Hatred for U.S., Israel," *The Washington Times*, August 21, 1998, p. A1.

14. Ken Silverstein, "Made for TV: Bill Clinton's Flawed Record on Terrorism," *Harper's Magazine*, posted on Harpers.org on September 11, 2006. Silverstein is Washington editor of *Harper's*. A similar account, different in detail, appears in Wright, *The Looming Tower*, pp. 281–82.

15. *9/11 Commission Report*, p. 117; Steve Coll, *Ghost Wars: The Secret History of the*

CIA, Afghanistan, and bin Laden, from the Soviet Invasion to September 10, 2001 (New York: Penguin Press, 2004), p. 411; U.S. Senate Select Committee on Intelligence and U.S. House of Representatives Permanent Select Committee on Intelligence, *Joint Inquiry into Intelligence Community Activities Before and After the Terrorist Attacks of September 11, 2001*, hearing, testimony of White House counterterrorism coordinator Richard Clarke, June 11, 2002, p. 48; hereafter, Joint Inquiry Committee. Wright, in *The Looming Tower*, p. 285, suggests the strikes may have killed as few as five.

16. Wright, *The Looming Tower*, pp. 283–84. Wright bases the story about the crossroads decision on Khalid al-Hammadi's "The Inside Story of al-Qa'ida, as Told by Abu-Jandal (Nasir al-Bahri), bin Laden's Personal Guard," *Al-Quds al-Arabi*, translated by the U.S. Foreign Broadcast Information Service.

17. 9/11 Commission *Staff Statement No. 6*, "The Military," March 23, 2004, p. 6, emphasis added. Coll, in *Ghost Wars*, p. 410, reports that the Zhawar Kili meeting "was not much of a secret" among members of Pakistani intelligence, known to have close ties to bin Laden. He does not allege that Pakistani authorities alerted the Taliban or al-Qaeda, but raises the possibility.

18. Richard A. Clarke, *Against All Enemies: Inside America's War on Terror* (New York: Free Press, 2004), p. 189.

19. Coll, *Ghost Wars*, p. 410.

20. Khan, "Pakistan Gears to Midwife 'Get Osama' Operation"; Kamran Khan and Pamela Constable, "Bomb Suspect Details Anti-U.S. Terror Ring," *The Washington Post*, August 19, 1998, p. A1. (In a common arrangement, Khan was reporting for the *Post* as well as his own Pakistani newspaper.) The *Post* reported: "In Islamabad today, speculation intensified that the United States may be planning a military strike at bin Laden's compound in eastern Afghanistan, possibly using Pakistan as a base."

21. Author's interview with former ambassador William B. Milam, December 18, 2006. Milam, a senior policy scholar at the Woodrow Wilson International Center for Scholars at the time of the interview, arrived in Islamabad as the new U.S. ambassador to Pakistan just after the U.S. strikes of August 1998. See also Seymour M. Hersh, "The Missiles of August," *The New Yorker*, October 12, 1998, p. 39.

22. Daniel Benjamin and Steven Simon, *The Age of Sacred Terror* (New York: Random House, 2002), p. 280.

23. 9/11 Commission, Eighth Public Hearing, remarks of Commissioner Robert Kerrey to former secretary of state Madeleine Albright. See also Joint Inquiry Staff Statement, Eleanor Hill, October 8, 2002, p. 13.

24. Ridgeway Center, "Anatomy of a Terrorist Attack," p. 97. Albright, in an appearance on CNN's *Larry King Live* the day of the strikes, said, "The president, who was deeply involved in the planning of this whole thing, was very concerned about collateral damage." Secretary of State Madeleine K. Albright, interview on CNN, *Larry King Live*, August 20, 1998, State Department transcript, http://secretary.state.gov/www/

statements/1998/980820a.html. The 9/11 Commission reported that Central Command had developed a target list for Afghanistan the previous July, at a time when the White House was becoming frustrated with the use of Afghan surrogates in covert action against al-Qaeda and sought direct military options. See *9/11 Commission Report*, p. 116. The third country was probably Yemen.

25. George Tenet, *Written Statement for the Record of the Director of Central Intelligence Before the National Commission on Terrorist Attacks Upon the United States*, March 24, 2004, p. 6.

26. Joint Inquiry Committee, Hearing on the Intelligence Community's Response to Past Terrorist Attacks Against the United States from February 1993 to September 2001, Joint Inquiry Staff Statement, Eleanor Hill, staff director, Joint Inquiry Staff, October 8, 2002, p. 4.

27. The Small Group consisted of six senior officials: Clinton; Secretary of State Madeleine Albright; National Security Adviser Sandy Berger; Secretary of Defense William Cohen; General Henry H. Shelton, chairman of the Joint Chiefs of Staff; and CIA Director George Tenet. The day of the U.S. strikes, Berger made clear that the Small Group had been his idea, not Clinton's. See White House press briefing, Secretary of State Madeleine Albright and National Security Adviser Samuel "Sandy" Berger, August 20, 1998. For an account of the Counterterrorism Security Group meeting, see Clarke, *Against All Enemies*, p. 181.

28. Ridgeway Center, "Anatomy of a Terrorist Attack," p. 97.

29. Kerrey recalled the scene during an appearance by Tenet six years later before the 9/11 Commission. See National Commission on Terrorist Attacks Upon the United States, Ninth Public Hearing, March 24, 2004.

30. Albright-Berger press conference, August 20, 1998.

31. Reporter Hersh contends that the Joint Chiefs of Staff, below the level of General Henry H. Shelton, the chairman, were cut out of the planning for Infinite Reach until the eve of the strikes. See Hersh, "The Missiles of August." Counterterrorism coordinator Clarke wrote that the targets were nominated by "CIA and the Joint Chiefs"; see *Against All Enemies*, p. 186. But the *9/11 Commission Report*, p. 116, indicates that Central Command did the staff work on the targets. It is possible that the Pentagon's Joint Staff was involved in planning without the knowledge of the Joint Chiefs below Shelton.

32. Albright-Berger press conference, August 20, 1998. Berger sketched a timeline of the decision-making: embassies bombed, August 7; Pentagon presents Clinton with strike options, August 12; blame for bombings fixed on al-Qaeda and strikes approved in principle, August 14; final go-ahead from Clinton, morning of August 20. A fax, evidently from al-Qaeda, claiming responsibility for the attack, but not intended as a public announcement, was found on a fax machine in London. See Benjamin and Simon, *Age of Sacred Terror*, p. 258.

33. Clarke, *Against All Enemies*, p. 184. The "slam dunk" comment to Bush was first

reported by Bob Woodward in *Plan of Attack* (New York: Simon & Schuster, 2004), pp. 247–50.

34. *9/11 Commission Report*, p. 116, says Tenet had word of the planned August 20 bin Laden gathering on August 8, the day after the embassies were bombed. The report's endnotes and other testimony indicate the intelligence on the meeting may have come somewhat later; Chap. 4, p. 481 note 40, for example, cites a "CIA memo, 'Khowst and the Meeting of Islamic Extremist Leaders on 20 Aug.,' August 17, 1998." The first report may have been included in another still-classified document, CIA Briefing Materials, "Bombings in Nairobi and Dar es Salaam—An Update," August 14, 1998, referenced in Chap. 4, p. 481 note 37. Clarke recalls first hearing about the meeting on August 14 in a CIA report and discussing it with Tenet. See Clarke, *Against All Enemies*, p. 184.

35. Albright-Berger news conference, August 20, 1998.

36. *9/11 Commission Report*, p. 117, cites a memo by an NSC staffer on "Shifa" written August 11, 1998; see Chap. 4, p. 481 note 44.

37. Michael Barletta, "Chemical Weapons in the Sudan: Allegations and Evidence," *Nonproliferation Review* (Fall 1998): 122. Russell Watson and John Barry, "Our Target Was Terror," *Newsweek*, August 31, 1998, p. 28.

38. State Department spokesman James B. Foley said, "The main purpose of the strikes was to prevent further terrorist attacks against American targets, not a retaliation." This was not just posturing to international law governing the use of military force. Foley in the same briefing noted that the U.S. embassy in Tirana, Albania, had been evacuated a week after the African embassy bombings because of a specific terrorist threat. See U.S. Department of State, Daily Press Briefing, August 21, 1998, http://secretary.state.gov/www/briefings/9808/980821db.html. See also Ridgeway Center, "Anatomy of a Terrorist Attack," p. 99. Benjamin and Simon, in *The Age of Sacred Terror*, p. 261, report that the threat was quite real: the Albanian government broke up a plot on the U.S. embassy in Tirana later that August.

39. On the Pentagon's request for simultaneous attacks, see Clarke's testimony to the Joint Inquiry Committee, June 11, 2002, p. 47. In the same transcript, p. 91, Senator Richard Shelby suggests that waiting for the shift-change in Khartoum may have cost the U.S. military the opportunity to kill bin Laden in Afghanistan.

40. Barletta, "Chemical Weapons in the Sudan," p. 117.

41. Tim Weiner and James Risen, "Decision to Strike Factory in Sudan Based Partly on Surmise," *The New York Times*, September 21, 1998, p. A1.

42. Tim Weiner and Steven Lee Myers, "Flaws in U.S. Account Raise Questions on Strike in Sudan," *The New York Times*, August 28, 1998, p. A1.

43. Clarke, *Against All Enemies*, p. 148.

44. See *U.S. v. bin Laden*, testimony of prosecution witness Jamal Ahmad Al-Fadl, (Day 4) trial transcript, February 13, 2001, p. 524. Al Fadl's three days of testimony—essential reading for a firsthand account of al-Qaeda's development—are available at

the Center for Nonproliferation Study's website, http://cns.miis.edu/pubs/reports/bin-laden.htm. It is clear from the context of the direct examination that the government is questioning al-Fadl on information he has already provided in closed-door debriefs.

45. Weiner and Risen, "Decision to Strike Factory in Sudan."

46. Joint Inquiry Committee, Briefing by Staff on U.S. Government Counterterrorism Organizations (before September 11, 2001) and on the Evolution of the Terrorist Threat and U.S. Response: 1986–2001, testimony of Richard A. Clarke, Counterterrorism Coordinator for the National Security Council from 1993 to 2001, June 11, 2002, hearing transcript, p. 17.

47. Joint Inquiry Committee, Clarke testimony, June 11, 2002, p. 41.

48. *U.S. v. bin Laden*, (Day 4) trial transcript, February 13, 2001, p. 524.

49. Karl Vick, "U.S., Sudan Trade Claims on Factory," *The Washington Post*, August 25, 1998, p. A1; Robert S. Greenberger and Nikhil Deogun, "Officials Say Soil Sample Buttressed U.S. Suspicions about Sudan Plant," *The Wall Street Journal*, August 25, 1998, p. 16. The soil sample was first discussed in public by a Clinton administration official the day these news accounts appeared. See U.S. State Department transcript, Thomas R. Pickering, undersecretary of state for political affairs, U.S. Sudan, Afghanistan Strikes, August 25, 1998. The Egyptian nationality of the CIA operative is in Coll, *Ghost Wars*, p. 411. The December date for the taking of the soil sample is from James Risen, "To Bomb Sudan Plant, or Not: A Year Later, Debate Rankles," *The New York Times*, October 27, 1999, p. A1.

50. The *9/11 Commission Report* cites the memo by Clarke's staff, p. 117.

51. Risen, "To Bomb Sudan Plant, or Not."

52. Barletta, "Chemical Weapons in the Sudan," p. 121; see also Tim Weiner, "Pentagon and CIA Defend Sudan Missile Attack," *The New York Times*, September 2, 1998, p. A5.

53. Joint Inquiry Committee, Clarke testimony, June 11, 2002, p. 48.

54. Ryan C. Hendrickson, "The Clinton Administration's Strikes on Usama Bin Laden: Limits to Power," in Ralph G. Carter, ed., *Contemporary Cases in U.S. Foreign Policy* (Washington, D.C.: CQ Press, 2002), pp. 196–216.

55. U.S. Department of Defense Background Briefing, August 20, 1998, attributable to a "senior intelligence official." Available at http://www.defenselink.mil/news/Aug1998/x08201998_x820bomb.html.

56. Author's interview with Lee Hamilton, president of the Woodrow Wilson International Center for Scholars, Washington, D.C., October 31, 2006.

57. DoD Background Briefing, August 20, 1998.

58. Guo Guangquin, "U.S. Air Strike on Pharmaceutical Factory in Sudan," Xinhua Domestic Service news agency, August 21, 1998, retrieved by U.S. Foreign Broadcast Information Service (FBIS). See also "Sudan Bans U.S. Aircraft from Its Airspace," Agence France-Press, August 22, 1998, FBIS.

59. The Pentagon did not identify the ships involved in the strikes, but some

information leaked. See Ridgeway Center, "Anatomy of a Terrorist Attack," p. 25. Various reports identified the USS *Abraham Lincoln* Carrier Battle Group as the force involved. Based on reports of the strike and on which ships were Tomahawk-capable, it's likely that the Indian Ocean force launching on Afghanistan included the Aegis cruisers USS *Valley Forge* and *Shiloh*, the Aegis destroyer USS *Elliot*, and a Los Angeles–class submarine, either the USS *Jefferson City* or *Columbia*; the Red Sea force likely would have involved two of three Aegis destroyers, USS *Milius*, *Briscoe*, and *Hayler*. See G. D. Bakshi, "Mono-Ethnic Solutions: The Taliban's Cheque Book Campaign, Autumn 1998," *Strategic Analysis* 22, no. 9 (December 1998).

60. James Bennet, "U.S. Cruise Missiles Strike Sudan and Afghan Targets Tied to Terrorist Network," *The New York Times*, August 21, 1998, p. A1. Different sources have provided different figures for the number of cruise missiles involved in the strike. Coll in *Ghost Wars* says thirteen missiles were fired at Al-Shifa, seventy-five at the Afghan targets. Clarke in *Against All Enemies* cites seventy-five against Afghanistan but no figure for the Al-Shifa strike. *Anatomy of a Terrorist Attack* said twenty were fired at Shifa and fifty-six at Afghanistan. Timothy Naftali's *Blind Spot* cites seventy-nine missiles total against Sudan and Afghanistan. Lawrence Wright's *The Looming Tower* also has seventy-nine: thirteen at Al-Shifa and sixteen at the Afghan targets. This last breakdown seems the most definitive.

61. DoD Background Briefing, August 20, 1998.

62. *9/11 Commission Report*, p. 117, citing a memo, McCarthy to Berger, re Shifa, August 11, 1998. See also Chap. 4, pp. 482–83 note 45. Reno's concern about attacking Muslim countries is reported by the 9/11 Commission; her plea for delay to get better intelligence is reported by Hersh in "The Missiles of August," pp. 35–36. Her concern about legal justification and the Berger quote appear in Benjamin and Simon, *The Age of Sacred Terror*, p. 260.

63. DoD Background Briefing, August 20, 1998; Barletta, "Chemical Weapons in the Sudan," p. 118; Tim Weiner and Steven Lee Myers, "Flaws in U.S. Accounts Raise Questions on Strike in Sudan," *The New York Times*, August 29, 1998, p. A1; U.S. Department of State Daily Press Briefing, August 24, 1998, http://secretary.state.gov/www/briefings/9808/980824db.html.

64. Ridgeway Center, "Anatomy of a Terrorist Attack," p. 101; Weiner and Risen, "Decision to Strike Factory in Sudan"; U.S. Congressional Research Service, Ted Dagne, "Sudan: Humanitarian Crisis, Peace Talks, Terrorism, and U.S. Policy," CRS-Issue Brief for Congress, March 19, 2002, p. 13; Risen, "To Bomb Sudan Plant, or Not." The embassy was partly reopened in October 1997, but with locally hired staff.

65. Barletta, "Chemical Weapons in the Sudan," p. 118.

66. Hersh, "The Missiles of August." Dr. Mohammed Haque, member of an independent delegation to Khartoum following the missile attacks, said Al-Shifa was used primarily for packaging medicines or taking imported medicine in powder form and

processing it into pills or capsules. See report by delegation members Richard Becker, Sara Flounders, and John Parker, "Sudan: Diversionary Bombing," (undated), posted on the website Covertaction.org. Haque was part of the International Action Center group headed by former Attorney General Ramsey Clark. IAC, a radical group, has been highly critical of U.S. policy in the Middle East.

67. Editorial, "Intelligence Lapse?" *The Washington Post*, September 6, 1998, p. C6.

68. Human Rights Watch Executive Director Kenneth Roth, letter to President William J. Clinton, September 15, 1998, released by HRW, http://hrw.org/press/98/sept/sudan915.htm. See also *Sudan: Global Trade, Local Impact, Arms Transfers to All Sides in the Civil War in Sudan*, Human Rights Watch Report 10, no. 4 (August 1998), Part III, "Armed Forces and Armaments," http://www.hrw.org/reports98/sudan/.

69. DoD Background Briefing, August 20, 1998.

70. Steven Lee Myers and Tim Weiner, "The Chemicals: Possible Benign Use Is Seen for Chemical at Factory in Sudan," *The New York Times*, August 27, 1998, p. A1.

71. Patrick Eddington, "Get Ready for More Targeting Disasters," *Los Angeles Times*, July 5, 1999, p. 5.

72. The senior intelligence official who briefed reporters at the Pentagon said the precursor chemical EMPTA, which spells out as O-ethyl methylphosphonothioic acid, "is unique to the production of VX." See also Barletta, "Chemical Weapons in the Sudan," p. 124. The two additional processes required to make VX are mentioned in William Broad, Barbara Crossette, Judith Miller, and Steven Lee Myers, "U.S. Says Iraq Aided Production of Chemical Weapons in Sudan," *The New York Times*, August 25, 1998, p. A1. Reference to FOFONOS appears in Myers and Weiner, "Possible Benign Use Is Seen for Chemical."

73. Broad et al., "U.S. Says Iraq Aided Production of Chemical Weapons."

74. State Department transcript, Pickering, August 25, 1998.

75. National Commission on Terrorist Attacks Upon the United States (9/11 Commission), Eighth Public Hearing, transcript, March 23, 2004.

76. Risen, "To Bomb Sudan Plant, or Not."

77. Prepared statement of William S. Cohen to the National Commission on Terrorist Attacks Upon the United States, March 23, 2004, p. 9.

78. Clarke testimony to 9/11 Commission, March 24, 2004.

79. Declassified versions of PDD-39 available as of this writing do not explicitly say that there is a lower threshold of evidence for aggressive U.S. action against terrorists possibly using weapons of mass destruction. The directive does say that preventing terrorists from obtaining WMD is a top national security priority. See the version of Presidential Decision Directive 39, July 21, 1995, posted by the Department of Justice, http://www.ojp.usdoj.gov/odp/docs/pdd39.htm.

80. Werner Daum, "Universalism and the West: An Agenda for Understanding," *Harvard International Review*, Special Issue, *The Future of War* 23, no. 2 (Summer 2001).

81. See, for example, Richard Becker, "Report on IAC [International Action Center] Fact-Finding Delegation to the Sudan, September 1998," http://iacenter.org/Africa/sudanrt.htm. Becker was part of a delegation to Sudan from the International Action Center (IAC). Becker reported that ordinary Sudanese asked the delegation why America would bomb a medicine factory. IAC founder Ramsey Clark alleged that the Al-Shifa strike was part of a U.S. "strategy" of bullying Muslim countries and was intended to "punish the Sudanese for their independence." See International Action Center press release, "U.S. Delegation Led by Ramsey Clark Returns from Fact-Finding Mission in Sudan; Ramsey Calls for Restitution in Destruction of Factory," September 21, 1998, http://www.commondreams.org/pressreleases/Sept98/092198d.htm; and Ramsey Clark, letter to H. E. Sir John Weston, Permanent Mission of the United Kingdom to the United Nations, November 11, 1998, http://www.casi.org.uk/discuss/1998/msg00300.html. On the Chinese embassy bombing as a deliberate act, see John Sweeney, Jen Holsoe, and Ed Vulliamy, "NATO Bombed Chinese Deliberately: NATO Hit Embassy on Purpose, Kosovo: Special Report," *The Observer* (London), October 17, 1999.

82. Tenet testified before the 9/11 Commission that he had no recollection of being the one who shut down get-bin-Laden operations at the last minute. But other key participants identify Tenet as the official who, in three key instances, told the White House that intelligence about bin Laden's whereabouts, though tantalizing, wasn't solid enough to justify an air strike. *9/11 Commission Report*, p. 140.

83. Executive Order 11905 sec. 5(g), 41 Federal Register (FR) 7703, 7733, signed by President Gerald Ford, February 19, 1976. The order was renewed in revised form by President Reagan on December 4, 1981, in language that remains in effect. See Executive Order 12333, 46 FR 59941, 3 CFR, December 4, 1981. Section 2.11 of the order provides: "*Prohibition on Assassination.* No person employed by or acting on behalf of the United States Government shall engage in, or conspire to engage in, assassination." Section 2.12 bars "*Indirect participation.* No agency of the Intelligence Community shall participate in or request any person to undertake activities forbidden by this order." For a discussion of the history of the assassination ban, see Library of Congress, Congressional Research Service, Elizabeth B. Bazan, "Assassination Ban and E.O. 12333: A Brief Summary," *CRS Report for Congress*, January 4, 2002.

84. *9/11 Commission Report*, p. 116.

85. Berger-Albright press conference, August 20, 1998.

86. U.S. Department of Defense news briefing, Secretary of Defense William S. Cohen, General Henry H. Shelton, chairman, Joint Chiefs of Staff, Pentagon Briefing Room, August 20, 1998.

87. 9/11 Commission, Eighth Public Hearing, transcript, March 23, 2004.

88. 9/11 Commission, Ninth Public Hearing, transcript, March 24, 2004.

89. Barletta, "Chemical Weapons in the Sudan," p. 116.

90. 9/11 Commission hearing, March 23, 2004.

91. U.S. States Senate Select Committee on Intelligence and U.S. House of Representatives Permanent Select Committee on Intelligence, Joint Inquiry Committee, Briefing by Staff on U.S. Government Counterterrorism Organizations before September 11, 2001, and the Evolution of the Terrorist Threat and U.S. Response: 1986–2001, June 11, 2002, declassified hearing transcript, p. 32.

92. See CIA, Unclassified Report to Congress on the Acquisition of Technology Relating to Weapons of Mass Destruction and Advanced Conventional Munitions, for the years 1997–2003 on the CIA website, www.cia.gov, under Reports.

93. With reference to "UBL," note that the U.S. Government transliteration of the al-Qaeda leader's name is Usama bin Laden. For this book, I have opted for the more commonly used Osama bin Laden.

94. 9/11 Commission Report, p. 130. See report endnotes 117 and 119 for references to e-mails.

95. Clarke, Against All Enemies, p. 199.

96. See, for example, the Federation of American Scientists website for specifications of the Tomahawk Land-Attack Cruise Missile and variants, http://www.fas.org/man/dod-101/sys/smart/bgm-109.htm.

97. 9/11 Commission Report, p. 131; see p. 485 note 118, for Maher's remark.

98. Dr. Marijcke Jongbloed, "Houbara Bustard Conservation," Al Shingdagah, January–February 2003, http://www.alshindagah.com/janfeb2003/houbara.html.

99. Mary Anne Weaver, "Of Birds and Bombs," APF Reporter 20, no. 4 (2004), a publication of the Alicia Patterson Foundation, http://www.aliciapatterson.org/APF2004/Weaver01/Weaver01.html.

100. 9/11 Commission Report, p. 486 note 151, refers to a CIA "UBL Situation Report" of February 2, 1999.

101. Ibid., p. 486 note 152, refers to a CIA cable, "Update on Location of an Activity at Sheikh Ali's Camps," February 7, 1999.

102. Ibid., pp. 137–39; see in particular p. 486 note 164, for reference to the security guard subsource.

103. Coll, Ghost Wars, p. 446.

104. Wright, The Looming Tower, pp. 290–91.

105. 9/11 Commission hearing, March 24, 2004, testimony of Richard A. Clarke, former national coordinator for counterterrorism, p. 84.

106. 9/11 Commission Report, p. 140.

107. Testimony of CIA Director George Tenet Before the 9/11 Commission, March 24, 2004.

108. Tenet, At the Center of the Storm: My Years at the CIA, p. 124.

109. 9/11 Commission Report, p. 138; see p. 486 notes 163, 164.

110. For the UAE assertion that bin Laden had not been at camps, see Coll, Ghost

Wars, p. 448; for the UAE denial that royals were at the camp, see *9/11 Commission Report*, Chap. 4, p. 486 note 163. Clarke, in *Against All Enemies*, p. 200, says an after-action report by the CIA showed that in only one of three instances in which the administration considered launching cruise missiles to kill bin Laden was the terror leader actually there, and the desert camp incident was not the one.

111. 9/11 Commission hearing, March 23, 2004, testimony of William Cohen, former secretary of defense, p. 99.

112. 9/11 Commission hearing, March 24, 2004, testimony of Sandy Berger, former national security adviser, p. 75.

113. Author's interview with former Senator Robert Kerrey (D-Neb.), November 29, 2006; at the time of the interview, Kerrey was president of the New School for Social Research in New York.

114. National Commission on Terrorist Attacks Upon the United States (9/11 Commission), written statement for the record of Director of Central Intelligence George Tenet, March 24, 2004, p. 16.

115. 9/11 Commission hearing, March 24, 2006, transcript, p. 14.

116. Ibid., p. 20.

117. Ibid., p. 62.

118. Ibid., p. 74.

119. 9/11 Commission Staff Statement No. 6, "The Military," March 23, 2004, p. 3.

120. 9/11 Commission, Staff Statement No. 7, "Intelligence Policy," March 24, 2004, p. 6.

121. Anonymous Navy planner involved in planning Kosovo air campaign, quoted in Michael D. Snoderly, Lt. Cdr., USN, "Compressing the Levels of War: Operation Desert Storm and Operation Allied Force Case Study," paper submitted to the Naval War College, Newport, R.I., May 15, 2001, p. 1.

122. The March timeframe of the CIA's initial targeting efforts was included in an oral presentation by Undersecretary of State Thomas R. Pickering to representatives of the Chinese government in Beijing. See U.S. Department of State, Report on Accidental Bombing of Chinese Embassy, presented to the Chinese government by Undersecretary of State Thomas R. Pickering in Beijing, June 17, 1999, transcript released by the State Department July 6, 1999, http://canberra.usembassy.gov/hyper/1999/WF990706/epf202. htm; hereafter, Pickering Beijing presentation. The lack of Balkan expertise in the CIA's Counter-Proliferation Division is discussed in Steven Lee Myers, "Fateful Choice: Chinese Embassy Bombing: A Wide Net of Blame," *The New York Times*, April 17, 2000, p. A1.

123. William M. Arkin, "Q&A on Chinese Embassy Bombing," Washingtonpost. com, May 5, 2000.

124. U.S. Department of Defense, "Kosovo/Operation Allied Force After-Action Report," Report to Congress, January 31, 2000, p. 23, http://www.GlobalSecurity.org/ military/ops/allied_force.htm.

125. Paul C. Strickland, "USAF Aerospace-Power Doctrine: Decisive or Coercive?—NATO's war over Kosovo, Yugoslavia: The Role of Air Power," *Aerospace Power Journal*, Fall 2000, http://www.findarticles.com/p/articles/mi_m0ICK/is_3_14/ai_68507680/print. Strickland, an Air Force lieutenant colonel at the time the article was written, served in the combined air operations center, or CAOC, during the Kosovo campaign and interviewed Lieutenant General Short for his article.

126. Richard A. Hand, "Who Should Call the Shots? Resolving Friction in the Targeting Process," thesis presented to the School of Advanced Airpower Studies, Air University, Maxwell Air Force Base, Alabama, June 2001, p. 67.

127. Myers, "Fateful Choice."

128. Strickland, "USAF Aerospace-Power Doctrine," p. 26.

129. U.S. House Permanent Select Committee on Intelligence, Hearing on the Bombing of the Chinese Embassy, July 22, 1999, prepared testimony of Deputy Defense Secretary John Hamre, http://www.GlobalSecurity.org/intell/library/congress/1999_hr/990722-hamre.htm.

130. U.S. House Permanent Select Committee on Intelligence, hearing on the Chinese embassy bombing, July 22, 1999, remarks by Hamre during question-and-answer session with Representative Julian Dixon (D-Calif.). The hearing occurred in open session, but a transcript of the session was not published by the committee. The author obtained the transcript via Nexus search in the "legis" subcategory with the date and keyword "embassy." A transcript is also available through the Federal Document Clearing House.

131. Ibid. CIA Director George Tenet told the committee, "It was the only target we nominated." According to the *New York Times*, the CIA proposed two or three other targets, but in the wake of the embassy bombing the Pentagon refused to consider them. In any case, the CIA was not overburdened with target selection chores. See Myers, "Fateful Choice."

132. Pickering Beijing presentation.

133. See, for example, Bradley Graham and Steven Pearlstein, "Belgrade Target Never Verified on Outdated Map," *The Washington Post*, May 10, 1999, p. A1; and Eric Schmitt, "Pentagon Admits Its Maps of Belgrade Are Out of Date," *The New York Times*, May 11, 1999, p. A1.

134. U.S. House Permanent Select Committee on Intelligence, prepared testimony of Deputy Secretary of Defense John Hamre on the inadvertent bombing of the Chinese embassy in Belgrade, Yugoslavia, May 7, 1999, July 22, 1999.

135. David A. Fulghum and Robert Wall, "Operation Allied Force: Intel Mistakes Trigger Chinese Embassy Bombing," *Aviation Week & Space Technology*, May 17, 1999, p. 55.

136. Patrick G. Eddington, "Get Ready for More Targeting Disasters," *Los Angeles Times*, July 5, 1999, p. 15.

137. House Intelligence Committee, Tenet testimony, July 22, 1999.

138. Benjamin S. Lambeth, *NATO's Air War for Kosovo: A Strategic and Operational*

Assessment (Washington, D.C.: Rand, 2003), pp. 144–45. See also Fulghum and Wall, "Intel Mistakes Trigger Chinese Embassy Bombing."

139. Department of Defense Background Briefing on China Embassy Bombing, May 10, 1999, The Pentagon, www.defenselink.mil. The briefers were identified as a senior official from the CIA and a senior official from the Defense Intelligence Agency.

140. Pickering Beijing presentation.

141. Ibid.

142. Myers, "Fateful Choice."

143. House Intelligence Committee, CIA Director George Tenet, DCI Statement on the Belgrade Chinese Embassy Bombing, July 22, 1999. Tenet's prepared testimony in which he refers to the intended target being 300 meters, or 328 yards, away from the Chinese embassy appears on the CIA website at www.cia.gov; it is also in the hearing transcript of the intelligence committee.

144. Tenet, House Intelligence Committee, July 22, 1999.

145. U.S. Department of Defense news briefing, Kenneth Bacon, assistant secretary of defense for public affairs, June 24, 1999, available in the transcript archive of the Defense Department website, www.defenselink.com.

146. Tenet, House Intelligence Committee, July 22, 1999. Bacon, DoD briefing, June 24, 2006.

147. The takeoff time is an estimate based on a precise figure released by the U.S. government for the strike: 2146-Zulu, or 9:46 p.m. Greenwich time, which, in Belgrade, was fourteen minutes before midnight. The precise attack time is included in Pickering's Beijing presentation.

148. John Pike, "B-2 Production," GlobalSecurity.org website; the specific page is http://www.GlobalSecurity.org/wmd/systems/b-2production.htm.

149. John A. Tirpak, "With Stealth in the Balkans," *Air Force Magazine Online*, October 1999, http://www.afa.org/magazine/oct1999/1099stealth.asp.

150. Ibid.; see also http://www.GlobalSecurity.org/military/systems/munitions/jdam.htm.

151. Tirpak, "With Stealth in the Balkans."

152. The JDAM has a "circular error probable" (CEP) of 13 meters, or 42.65 feet. CEP in military terminology is the radius of the circle within which half of a given type of missile or bomb will fall. If the GPS equipment on the JDAM fails, the inertial navigation system takes over; it has a CEP of 30 meters, or 98.43 feet.

153. The precise drop-time and the number of bombs released were included in Pickering's Beijing presentation.

154. Arkin, "Q&A on Chinese Embassy Bombing," Washingtonpost.com, May 5, 2000.

155. "Further on 3 Killed by Missile Attack," Xinhua News Agency, Beijing, May 8, 1999; "Xinhua Feature on NATO Bombing of Chinese Embassy," Xinhua News Agency,

May 8, 1999; foreign media reports via the Foreign Broadcast Information Service.

156. Myers, "Fateful Choice." The Myers article reports that all three victims were intelligence officers; an earlier article in the same newspaper said two of the three were spies, not journalists. See Eric Schmitt, "In a Fatal Error, CIA Picked a Bombing Target Only Once: The Chinese Embassy," *The New York Times*, July 23, 1999, p. A1.

157. Author's interview with Thomas R. Pickering, former undersecretary of state for political affairs, U.S. Department of State, April 24, 2007.

158. Author's interview with L. Britt Snider, former CIA inspector general, October 2006.

159. John Sweeney and Jens Holsoe in Copenhagen and Ed Vulliamy in Washington, "NATO Bombed Chinese Deliberately; NATO Hit Embassy on Purpose," *The Guardian* (United Kingdom), October 17, 1999, p. 1.

160. Bill Gertz, "Spies Tell China: Embassy Attack Was No Accident," *The Washington Times*, May 24, 1999, p. A1.

161. James D. Perry, "Operation Allied Force," *Aerospace Power Journal* 14, no. 2 (Summer 2000): 79, provides a detailed examination of reaction in China to the Kosovo campaign in general and the Chinese embassy bombing in particular.

162. Sweeney, "NATO Bombed Chinese Deliberately"; Myers, "Chinese Embassy Bombing"; author's phone interview with William Arkin, December 21, 2006.

163. Myers, "Chinese Embassy Bombing"; Schmitt, "In a Fatal Error, CIA Picked a Bombing Target Only Once."

164. Department of Defense, "Kosovo/Operation Allied Force," p. xx. See also Snoderly, "Compressing the Levels of War," pp. 6–8.

165. *The NewsHour with Jim Lehrer*, transcript of PBS broadcast report, "The Wrong Target," Online Focus, Online NewsHour, May 10, 1999, http://www.pbs.org/newshour/bb/europe/jan-june99/bombing_5-10.html.

166. White House transcript, President Clinton, remarks at the White House strategy meeting on children, violence, and responsibility, May 10, 1999, http://frwebgate3.access.gpo.gov/cgi-bin/waisgate.cgi?WAISdocID=9426737141+21+0+0&WAISaction=retrieve.

167. Pickering interview.

168. Hamre testimony, House Select Committee on Intelligence, July 22, 1999.

169. Department of Defense, "Kosovo/Operation Allied Force," p. xiii.

170. Statement by Bill Harlow, CIA Director of Public Affairs, on the inadvertent bombing of the Chinese embassy, April 10, 2000, https://www.cia.gov/news-information/press-releases-statements/press-release-archive-2000/pr04102000.html.

171. Tenet, House Intelligence Committee testimony, July 22, 1999.

172. *9/11 Commission Report*, p. 140; see also Chap. 4, p. 487 note 173, which references a still-classified CIA memo, Jeff to Tenet, "Tracking Usama Bin Ladin, 14–20 May, 1999," dated May 21, 1999.

173. PBS *Frontline* program, "The Dark Side," interview with Gary Schroen, January 20, 2006, posted on *Frontline's* website: http://www.pbs.org/wgbh/pages/frontline/darkside/interviews/schroen.html.

174. *9/11 Commission Report*, p. 140.

175. Statement of William S. Cohen to the 9/11 Commission, March 23, 2004.

176. Albright, 9/11 Commission testimony, March 23, 2004.

Notes to Chapter 8

1. For biographical background on Owhali, see Jason Burke, "Dead Man Walking," *The Observer* (London), August 5, 2001.

2. Author's interview with former CIA analyst and 9/11 Commission staff member Douglas MacEachin, April 19, 2007.

3. Owhali's actions on August 7, 1998, and the attack plan were detailed in the summation of Assistant U.S. Attorney Kenneth Karas in the embassy bombings trial. See United States District Court, Southern District of New York, *United States v. Usama bin Laden et al.*, defendants, S(7) 98 Cr. 1023, (Day 37) trial transcript, May 1, 2001, esp. pp. 5431–46. Hereafter, *U.S. v. bin Laden.* See also University of Pittsburgh, Matthew B. Ridgeway Center, "Anatomy of a Terrorist Attack: An In-Depth Investigation into the 1998 Bombings of the U.S. Embassies in Kenya and Tanzania," working paper, Spring 2005. Hereafter, Ridgeway Center, "Anatomy of a Terrorist Attack."

4. The casualty figures are from U.S. Department of State, Accountability Review Boards, *Bombings of the U.S. Embassies in Nairobi, Kenya and Dar es Salaam, Tanzania on August 7, 1998, Report of the Accountability Review Boards*, January 8, 1999.

5. Other critical lines of inquiry before 9/11, along with a detailed recounting of the Malaysia meeting operation, are discussed in U.S. Senate Select Committee on Intelligence, and House of Representatives, Permanent Select Committee on Intelligence, *Joint Inquiry into Intelligence Community Activities Before and After the Terrorist Attacks of September 11, 2001,* 107th Cong., 2nd sess., December 2002, pp. xii–xiv. Hereafter, Joint Inquiry Committee.

6. Ibid., p. xvii.

7. U.S. National Commission on Terrorist Attacks Upon the United States, *The 9/11 Commission Report* (New York: W. W. Norton, 2004), p. 400. Hereafter, *9/11 Commission Report.*

8. Michael Isikoff and Daniel Klaidman, "The Hijackers We Let Escape," *Newsweek*, June 2, 2002.

9. Amy B. Zegart, "'CNN with Secrets': 9/11, the CIA, and the Organizational Roots of Failure," *International Journal of Intelligence and Counterintelligence* 20, no. 1 (2007): 18.

10. *U.S. v. bin Laden*, (Day 14) trial transcript, March 7, 2001, p. 2036. There is no indication in the trial transcript that the Khalid described to the FBI by Owhali as a Saudi who was his contact in Pakistan was Khalid al-Mihdhar, the Saudi national who would become a 9/11 hijacker. But by 1998, Mihdhar had gone to Pakistan and Afghanistan and sworn allegiance to bin Laden.

11. Joint Inquiry Committee, p. 129.

12. For a detailed description of the FBI response to the bombing, see David E. Kaplan, "On Terrorism's Trail: How the FBI Unraveled the Africa Embassy Bombings," *U.S. News & World Report*, November 23, 1998.

13. For profiles of Qutb and Azzam, see Lawrence Wright, *The Looming Tower: Al-Qaeda and the Road to 9/11* (New York: Alfred A. Knopf, 2006), pp. 7 and 95.

14. Author's interview with FBI Special Agent John Anticev, March 20, 2007.

15. Author's e-mail exchange with FBI Special Agent John Anticev, April 23, 2007.

16. *U.S. v. bin Laden*, testimony of FBI Special Agent Stephen Gaudin, (Day 14) trial transcript, March 7, 2001, pp. 2026, 2035; Wright, *The Looming Tower*, p. 277.

17. Anticev interview.

18. MacEachin interview. See also Ridgeway Center, "Anatomy of a Terrorist Attack," p. 83.

19. Author's interview with a former 9/11 Commission staff investigator who requested anonymity, June 10, 2007.

20. Testimony of Cofer Black, former director, CIA Counter-Terrorism Center, before the Joint Inquiry Committee, September 26, 2002.

21. The primary source for details about the Malaysia meeting is the report of U.S. Department of Justice Inspector General Glenn A. Fine, *A Review of the FBI's Handling of Intelligence Information Related to the September 11 Attacks*, November 2004, Chap. 5. Hereafter, DOJ-IG *FBI 9/11 Review*.

22. Joint Inquiry Committee, p. 129.

23. *9/11 Commission Report*, p. 181; see also Chap. 6, p. 502 note 41.

24. Joint Inquiry Committee, pp. 11, 145.

25. DOJ-IG *FBI 9/11 Review*, pp. 231, 234; *9/11 Commission Report*, Chap. 6, p. 502 note 45; author's e-mail exchange with former CIA spokesman Bill Harlow, August 3, 2007.

26. DOJ-IG *FBI 9/11 Review*, p. 231.

27. MacEachin interview; Joint Inquiry Committee, p. 144.

28. DOJ-IG *FBI 9/11 Review*, p. 239; *9/11 Commission Report*, Chap. 6, p. 502 note 53.

29. Lawrence Wright, "A Reporter at Large: The Agent, Did the CIA Stop an FBI Detective from Preventing 9/11?" *The New Yorker*, July 10 and 17, 2006, p. 67.

30. DOJ-IG *FBI 9/11 Review*, pp. 229 note 163; 240.

31. Ibid., pp. 255, 260.

32. *9/11 Commission Report*, p. 266.

33. DOJ-IG *FBI 9/11 Review*, p. 292.

34. Ibid., p. 294.

35. Ibid., p. 301.

36. Some accounts of the Malaysia meeting have it that the CIA broke into Mihdhar's hotel room in Dubai and photographed the passport. The reality was not so cloak-and-dagger. Through NSA intercepts, the CIA had Mihdhar's travel itinerary, including his plan to transit through Dubai en route to Malaysia. CIA's Dubai Station contacted

Dubai authorities and requested they look for a "Khalid" arriving on a specific flight from Yemen and bound for Malaysia. Former CIA spokesman Bill Harlow said it was not a difficult match to make. Author's e-mail exchange with Bill Harlow, August 3, 2007. While Harlow did not name the cooperating country, Dubai has been publicly disclosed in official reports as the place Mihdhar transited. For the hotel break-in version, see Wright, *The Looming Tower*, p. 311.

37. Joint Inquiry Committee, p. 50.

38. The initial NSA intelligence on the Malaysia meeting in December 1999 indicated a "Salem," thought to be a younger brother of "Nawaf," would also be attending the Malaysia meeting. The principal official U.S. accounts of the meeting do not place Salem in Kuala Lumpur, and Khalid Sheikh Mohammed's account to CIA interrogators does not include Salem as a participant. His attendance in Malaysia has not been ruled out but appears unlikely. He was, however, a hijacker.

39. Joint Inquiry Committee, pp. 131–32.

40. *9/11 Commission Report*, p. 155. The CIA's main post-9/11 sources of information on the Malaysia meeting were Khalid Sheikh Mohammed and Khallad in interrogations. See, for example, *9/11 Commission Report*, Chap. 5, p. 492 note 41.

41. Ibid., pp. 155–57, Chap. 5, p. 493 note 54.

42. Ibid., pp. 494–95 note 59.

43. Ibid., p. 159.

44. Central Intelligence Agency transcript, background briefing for reporters, July 21, 2004, by three CIA officials speaking on background as "senior CIA officials." The briefing, attended by the author, was timed one day in advance of the release of *The 9/11 Commission Report* and was intended to provide the Agency's views on issues that would be treated at length by the commission.

45. CIA background briefing, July 21, 2004.

46. *9/11 Commission Report*, p. 241.

47. DOJ-IG *FBI 9/11 Review*, p. 248.

48. Joint Inquiry Committee, 138.

49. *9/11 Commission Report*, p. 269.

50. DOJ-IG *FBI 9/11 Review*, p. 293. The FBI intelligence officer is identified only as "Donna" in the report, a procedure used for several of the key figures in the U.S. tracking of the Malaysia meeting, because of the continued operational status of some of the intelligence and law enforcement officers. Through the reporting of Lawrence Wright, several of these individuals, given cover names in the DOJ-IG report, have been identified; Wright identifies Donna as Dina Corsi. See Wright, *The Looming Tower*, p. 340. It should be noted that despite Corsi's incorrect assumption that Hazmi had left the United States, he was placed on the terrorism watch list at the end of August along with Mihdhar.

51. DOJ-IG *FBI 9/11 Review*, pp. 261–66.

52. Ibid., p. 290.

53. Joint Inquiry Committee, p. 196.

54. DOJ-IG *FBI 9/11 Review*, p. 295; Joint Inquiry Committee, pp. 152–53.

55. DOJ-IG *FBI 9/11 Review*, pp. 297, 305.

56. Pete Earley, *Confessions of a Spy: The Real Story of Aldrich Ames* (New York: G. P. Putnam's Sons, 1997), p. 317; Tim Weiner, David Johnston, and Neil A. Lewis, *Betrayal: The Story of Aldrich Ames, an American Spy* (New York: Random House, 1995), pp. 239–44.

57. Major Louis A. Chiarella and Major Michael A. Newton, both military lawyers, discuss this issue in, "'So Judge, How Do I Get That FISA Warrant?': The Policy and Procedure for Conducting Electronic Surveillance," *Army Lawyer*, October 1997, p. 29 note 31. See also David Wise, *Nightmover: How Aldrich Ames Sold the CIA to the KGB for $4.6 Million* (New York: Harper Collins, 1995), p. 220.

58. DOJ-IG *FBI 9/11 Review*, p. 25.

59. Author's e-mail exchange with L. Britt Snider, former chief counsel, Senate Select Committee on Intelligence, August 2, 2007.

60. Wise, *Nightmover*, p. 280.

61. Earley, *Confessions of a Spy*, p. 331.

62. Chiarella and Newton, "How Do I Get That FISA Warrant?" p. 29 note 31.

63. Snider e-mail exchange.

64. DOJ-IG *FBI 9/11 Review*, p. 25. The phrase "Chinese wall" is quoted from a 1994 memo by Scruggs and, according to the inspector general's report, was the first time "wall" had been used in this context. See also *9/11 Commission Report*, p. 78.

65. DOJ-IG *FBI 9/11 Review*, p. 28.

66. Ibid., pp. 33, 41.

67. Ibid., pp. 281–87.

68. Ibid., p. 344.

69. Ibid., p. 257.

70. Ibid., p. 273; MacEachin interview; Wright, *The Looming Tower*, pp. 343–44.

71. DOJ-IG *FBI 9/11 Review*, p. 273. Bongardt is identified as "Scott" in the DOJ-IG review. Through the reporting of Lawrence Wright, Scott, a cover name given in the DOJ-IG report, has been identified as Bongardt. See Wright, *The Looming Tower*, p. 341.

72. DOJ-IG *FBI 9/11 Review*, p. 300.

73. Rolince's and Levin's comments drawn from U.S. House and Senate Intelligence Committees Joint Hearing, Malaysia Hijackers at September 11th, September 20, 2002.

74. CIA, Office of Inspector General, John L. Helgerson, *Report on CIA Accountability with Respect to the 9/11 Attacks*, June 2005, originally classified Top Secret; nineteen-page executive summary approved for release August 2007, p. xvi; hereafter, CIA-IG *9/11 Accountability Report*.

75. Joint Inquiry Committee, pp. 81, 86.

76. DOJ-IG *FBI 9/11 Review*, p. 226.

77. Ibid., p. 235. CIA-IG *9/11 Accountability Report*, p. xv.

78. *9/11 Commission Report*, pp. 267–70; DOJ-IG *FBI 9/11 Review*, pp. 291–92. The CIA-IG *9/11 Accountability Report*, p. xiv, claims, "Ultimately, the two terrorists were watchlisted in late August 2001 as a result of questions raised in May 2001 by a CIA officer on assignment at the FBI." This is a reference to the CIA's Wilshire, whose own review of the Malaysia meeting cable traffic prompted his suggestion that the FBI's Mary do the same. But it was Mary, an FBI officer on assignment to the CIA, who sounded the alarm that led to the watch-listing of Mihdhar and Hazmi. Through the reporting of Lawrence Wright, Mary, a cover name given in the DOJ-IG report, has been identified by name as Margarette Gillespie. See Wright, *The Looming Tower*, p. 340.

79. CIA-IG *9/11 Accountability Report*, p. xiv.

80. DOJ-IG *FBI 9/11 Review*, p. 244.

81. Ibid., pp. 231–33; Wright, *The Looming Tower*, p. 311.

82. CIA-IG *9/11 Accountability Report*, p. xv.

83. Post-9/11 reviews frequently pointed out the advantage of 20/20 hindsight and the way in which events loom large in retrospect that were lost in a sea of other seemingly equally important events at the time. Zegart notes that this was not the case with the Malaysia meeting: "CIA officials knew this al-Qaeda meeting was important. They treated it as important." Key intelligence was not lost in a fog of unimportant intelligence, "It was found and then lost." But Zegart's analysis pays too little note of the intelligence community's erroneous assumption that the meeting had something to do with foreign terrorism, not an attack on the United States. See Zegart, "CNN with Secrets," p. 32.

84. DOJ-IG *FBI 9/11 Review*, p. 241.

85. CIA-IG *9/11 Accountability Report*, p. xv.

86. CIA, General Michael V. Hayden, "Director's Statement on the Release of the 9/11 IG Report Executive Summary," August 21, 2007.

87. Public Broadcasting System, *Frontline*, "The Torture Question," interview with former FBI special agent Jack Cloonan, July 13, 2005, http://www.pbs.org/wgbh/pages/frontline/torture/interviews/clloian.html; see also Jane Mayer, "Junior: The Clandestine Life of America's Top Al Qaeda Source," *New Yorker*, September 11, 2006.

88. Joint Inquiry Committee, p. 59.

89. Ibid., p. 38.

90. *9/11 Commission Report*, p. 118.

91. CIA-IG *9/11 Accountability Report*, p. xvii.

92. Statement by George J. Tenet on CIA Report, August 21, 2007. Statement issued by the former CIA director in response to the declassification and release of the CIA inspector general's executive summary of its *9/11 Accountability Report*.

93. Joint Inquiry Committee, testimony of "CIA Officer," September 20, 2002. As previously noted, the officer, identified as "John" in the Justice Department IG investigation and as a "CIA Officer" in the Joint Inquiry public hearing, was identified as Tom Wilshire by Wright in *The Looming Tower*, p. 311.

Notes to Chapter 9

1. Much of the material in this section is drawn from the author's interviews with members of the National Intelligence Council, the organization that produced a National Intelligence Estimate examining the threat of Iraqi weapons of mass destruction in October 2002, days before Congress voted to authorize the use of force in Iraq. The interviews were conducted at CIA headquarters on December 18, 2003, and January 23, 2004, at a time of increasing pressure on the U.S. intelligence community to explain why no significant stocks of weapons of mass destruction were being found in Iraq. Hereafter, Author's NIC interviews.

2. U.S. Senate Select Committee on Intelligence (SSCI), *U.S. Intelligence Community's Prewar Intelligence Assessments on Iraq*, July 9, 2004, p. 200. Hereafter, SSCI, *Prewar Intelligence on Iraq*.

3. Director of Central Intelligence, National Intelligence Council, *Key Judgments: Iraq's Continuing Programs for Weapons of Mass Destruction*, excerpts from October 1, 2002, National Intelligence Estimate, declassified July 18, 2003, http://www.fas.org/irp/cia/product/iraq-wmd.html. Hereafter, October 2002 NIE. The estimate, like all NIEs at that time, was written by the National Intelligence Council, a body that advised the director of central intelligence on important intelligence questions, often by pooling the wisdom of all 15 U.S. intelligence agencies. The National Geospatial Intelligence Agency (NGA) is the main entity responsible for imagery analysis, but according to interviews with NIC members, the March 2002 satellite imagery went to both the NGA and the CIA.

4. President George W. Bush, State of the Union address, January 28, 2003, http://www.whitehouse.gov/news/releases/2003/01/20030128-19.html. Vice President Cheney on NBC's *Meet the Press*, September 8, 2002. NBC posts transcripts only back to 2003, but see transcript at http://www.mtholyoke.edu/acad/intrel/bush/meet.htm. National Security Adviser Condoleezza Rice on CNN's *Late Edition with Wolf Blitzer*, September 8, 2002, http://transcripts.cnn.com/TRANSCRIPTS/0209/08/le.00.html. Secretary of State Colin Powell, address to the U.N. Security Council, February 5, 2003, http://www.whitehouse.gov/news/releases/2003/02/20030205-1.html. Hereafter, Powell, UNSC address, February 2003.

5. The October 2002 NIE stated, "Baghdad has chemical . . . weapons," only in the opening "key findings" section, not in the body of the ninety-plus page report. Most of the report is classified, but the Senate Select Committee on Intelligence disclosed in its investigative report that the unqualified assertion, "Baghdad has," is supported nowhere in the body of the estimate. See SSCI, *Prewar Intelligence on Iraq*, p. 199.

6. The description of the weather and lighting conditions are based on the relevant satellite images of the Samarra Vehicle that the author was shown at National Intelligence Council headquarters in December 2004. The images have not been made public. Elements of U.S. imagery satellite intelligence are described in detail in Jeffrey T. Richelson, *The U.S. Intelligence Community*, 3rd edition (Boulder, Colo.: Westview Press,

1995), p. 153. See also Jeffrey Richelson, "The Future of Space Reconnaissance," *Scientific American*, January 1991, p. 41. The evolution of the Keyhole satellite program is described in William E. Burrows, *Deep Black: Space Espionage and National Security* (New York: Random House, 1986).

7. Interview with U.S. Defense Intelligence Agency official, speaking on condition of anonymity, January 2005.

8. Jim Wolf, "U.S. Recovers Spy System Hit by Y2K Glitch," Reuters, January 3, 2000; Richard Lardner, "Technical Woes Were Not Disclosed by DoD; Pre-Y2K Problems Undercut Operation of U.S. Satellite Imagery Network," *Inside the Pentagon*, January 13, 2000. A detailed breakdown of U.S. intelligence spending is classified, but the Commission on Roles and Capabilities of the United States Intelligence Community, known as the Aspin-Brown Commission, reported percentage breakdowns among the various branches. See *Preparing for the 21st Century, an Appraisal of U.S. Intelligence* (Washington, D.C.: U.S. Government Printing Office, 1995), p. 132.

9. The National Geospatial Intelligence Agency, or NGA, is technically part of the Department of Defense but is one of the three so-called national intelligence agencies, along with the National Security Agency and National Reconnaissance Office, that run the nation's spy satellites.

10. Author's NIC interviews. See also Powell, UNSC address, February 2003; and Director of Central Intelligence, *Comprehensive Report of the Special Advisor to the Director of Central Intelligence on Iraq's Weapons of Mass Destruction*, Special Advisor Charles Duelfer, September 30, 2004, Vol. III, "Iraq's Chemical Warfare Program," p. 37. Hereafter, Duelfer, *Comprehensive Report.*

11. A reference to Samarra as the only chemical weapons agent production site in Iraq appears in a Defense Intelligence Agency memo to the U.S. Central Command's Air Force headquarters in the weeks prior to the beginning of the Gulf War air campaign. See "Defense Intelligence Agency memo to CENTAF, Subject: Iraqi Chemical Warfare (CW) Facilities and Storage Areas," December 28, 1990. The memo is part of a collection of Gulf War illness documents at www.gulflink.osd.mil.

12. Author's NIC interviews. See also Commission on the Intelligence Capabilities of the United States Regarding Weapons of Mass Destruction, *Report to the President of the United States* (Washington, D.C.: U.S. Government Printing Office, 2005), Chap. 1, p. 230 note 507. Hereafter, WMD Commission, *Report to the President.*

13. WMD Commission, *Report to the President*, p. 123.

14. Ibid., Chap. 1, p. 230 note 505.

15. October 2002 NIE; WMD Commission, *Report to the President*, p. 119; see also p. 228 note 474. The commission cites a classified report by the National Intelligence Council titled *Iraq's Chemical Warfare Capabilities: Potential for Dusty and Fourth-Generation Agents: Memorandum to Holders of NIE 2002-16HC* (the October NIE), November 2002. This memorandum was requested by U.S. Central Command, the military headquarters

in charge of the Iraq invasion mission, to explore the "CW implications for any U.S.-led military operations against Iraq."

16. SSCI, *Prewar Intelligence on Iraq*, pp. 200–201. See also WMD Commission, *Report to the President*, pp. 116–17.

17. Ibid., p. 115.

18. Before the war, the Bush administration said only that British intelligence had evidence of Iraqi attempts to acquire uranium somewhere in Africa; after the war, Niger was specified as the country in question.

19. Some of these debates, such as the dispute over the level of al-Qaeda interaction with Saddam's regime, were known to journalists and reported publicly before the war. Others were not disclosed until July 18, 2003, four months after the U.S.-led invasion of Iraq, with the declassification and release by the White House of the opening pages of the October 2002 NIE. See also David Barstow, William J. Broad, and Jeff Gerth, "How White House Embraced Suspect Iraq Arms Intelligence," *The New York Times*, October 3, 2004, p. A1; Walter Pincus, "CIA Asked Britain to Drop Iraq Claim," *The Washington Post*, July 11, 2003, p. A1; and David Albright, "Iraq's Aluminum Tubes: Separating Fact from Fiction," Institute for Science and International Security, December 5, 2003.

20. WMD Commission, *Report to the President*, pp. 122–23.

21. On October 7, 2002, four days before the Senate voted to authorize the use of force in Iraq, then–Deputy CIA Director John McLaughlin wrote to Graham that Saddam might team up with terrorists in a WMD attack on the United States as "his last chance to exact vengeance by taking a large number of victims with him." The letter also included an exchange between Levin and an unidentified "senior intelligence witness"— most likely CIA Director George Tenet—in which Levin asked about the likelihood Saddam would use WMD if the United States invaded and threatened the survival of his regime. "Pretty high," the witness responded. See McLaughlin letter in the *Congressional Record—Senate*, October 9, 2002, p. S10154. The episode illustrates the point that, even among war skeptics such as Graham and Levin, the assumption was that Iraq possessed weapons of mass destruction. One reason for their opposition to the use of force was that they believed a U.S.-led invasion would bring about the very WMD attack the invasion was intended to thwart.

22. WMD Commission, Report to the President, p. 123.

23. Britain, "Iraq's Weapons of Mass Destruction, The Assessment of the British Government," September 24, 2002, p. 19, http://www.number-10.gov.uk/output/Page271. asp. The report was released the day Parliament began major prewar debate on Iraq policy. Senator Bill Nelson (D-Fla.) recalled being told in classified briefings that Iraq's unmanned aerial vehicles could conceivably be launched from a barge or a neighboring country to deliver weapons of mass destruction on U.S. targets. Author's interview with Senator Nelson, July 2004.

24. Author's interview with Kenneth Pollack, February 5, 2003.

25. Author's NIC interviews.

26. The passage is quoted in U.S. Senate Select Committee on Intelligence, *Postwar Findings About Iraq's WMD Programs and Links to Terrorism and How They Compare with Prewar Assessments*, together with additional views, 109th Cong., 2nd sess., September 8, 2006, p. 42. Hereafter SSCI, *Iraq Postwar Findings*. The quotation itself is from an internal CIA report, "Iraq: No Large-Scale Chemical Warfare Efforts Seen Since Early 1990s," January 18, 2005, pp. 4–5.

27. U.N. Monitoring Verification and Inspection Commission (UNMOVIC), "Unresolved Disarmament Issues, Iraq's Proscribed Weapons Programmes," working document submitted to the U.N. Security Council by UNMOVIC, March 6, 2003, p. 14, http://www.un.org/Depts/unmovic/new/documents/cluster_document.pdf.

28. Statement by David Kay on the Interim Progress Report on the Activities of the Iraq Survey Group (ISG), before the House Permanent Select Committee on Intelligence and the Senate Select Committee on Intelligence, October 2, 2003, http://www.thenti.com/e_research/official_docs/cia/cia100203.pdf. Unclassified key findings of the report are available at http://www.issues2000.org/transcripts/100604_iraq_survey_group_Comp_Report_Key_Findings.pdf. See also testimony of David Kay, former head of the Iraq Survey Group, before the Senate Armed Services Committee, January 28, 2004, Hearing on Iraqi Weapons of Mass Destruction Programs, http://www.cnn.com/2004/US/01/28/kay.transcript/. The Carnegie Endowment for International Peace has assembled most of the key documents on Iraq and weapons of mass destruction on its website, www.ceip.org.

29. Duelfer, *Comprehensive Report*, Vol. III, "Iraq's Chemical Warfare Program," pp. 33–34, 37,

30. WMD Commission, *Report to the President*, p. 167.

31. Duelfer, *Comprehensive Report*, Vol. III, "Iraq's Chemical Warfare Program," p. 37. See also WMD Commission, *Report to the President*, p. 123 and notes 504–13. The classified NGA report is cited as National Geospatial Intelligence Agency, *Reassessment of Activity at Al Musayyib Barracks Brigade Headquarters and Ammunition Depot, 1998–2004* (June 15, 2004).

32. Director of Central Intelligence (DCI), Persian Gulf War Illnesses Task Force, *Khamisiyah: A Historical Perspective on Related Intelligence*, April 9, 1997, p. 3. Hereafter, DCI, *Khamisiyah*, April 1997 report. Note: U.S. government documents on Iraq spell Kamisiyah in a variety of ways; I have chosen to use the Pentagon's transliteration in the text.

33. U.S. Senate, Committee on Banking, Housing and Urban Affairs, report: *U.S. Chemical and Biological Warfare-Related Dual Use Exports to Iraq and Their Possible Impact on the Health Consequences of the Gulf War*, also known as "The Riegle Report," 103rd Cong., 2nd sess., May 25, 1994, http://www.gulfweb.org/bigdoc/report/riegle1.html.

34. DCI, *Khamisiyah*, April 1997 report, p. 20.

35. Ibid., p. 6.

36. Ibid., p. 19.

37. Philip Shenon, "CIA Says It Failed to Give Data on Iraqi Arms," *The New York Times*, April 10, 1997, p. A1.

38. Ibid.

39. Robert D. Walpole, Special Assistant to the DCI [Director of Central Intelligence] for Persian Gulf War Illnesses Issues, Central Intelligence Agency, statement for the record to the Presidential Advisory Committee on Gulf War Veterans' Illnesses, "17 Suspect CW/BW Storage Sites Identified in 28 February 1991 CENTCOM Message," July 29–30, 1997, p. 2, http://www.gulflink.osd.mil/17SuspectCW_BWStorageSites.pdf.

40. Department of the Army, Inspector General, *Inquiry into Demolition of Iraq Ammunition*, October 10, 1997 (redacted copy), p. 18, www.gulflink.osd.mil/army_ig/.

41. Ibid., p. 20.

42. Ibid., pp. 11, 13.

43. Ibid., pp. 20–21.

44. Ibid., p. 4.

45. Ibid., p. 9.

46. U.S. Army-Central Command (ARCENT), *Close-Out Report: ARCENT Suspected Chemical Weapons Sites Investigation*, March 9, 2000, overview section, www.gulflink. osd.mil/arcent/arcent_s01.htm.

47. Central Intelligence Agency, Persian Gulf War Illnesses Task Force, *Intelligence Update: Chemical Warfare Agent Issues During the Persian Gulf War*, April 2002, https://www .cia.gov/library/reports/general-reports-1/gulfwar/cwagents/index.htm#appendixb1; see sections titled "Key Findings," "Iraqi Chemical Agents and Gulf War Illnesses," and "What Is Low-Level Nerve Agent Exposure?"

48. The report of the Iraq Survey Group states: "While a small number of old, abandoned chemical munitions have been discovered, ISG judges that Iraq unilaterally destroyed its undeclared chemical weapons stockpile in 1991. There are no credible indications that Baghdad resumed production of chemical munitions thereafter." See Duelfer, *Comprehensive Report*, Vol. III, "Iraq's Chemical Warfare Program," p. 1. UNSCOM supervised destruction of Iraq's chemical weapons stocks in 1991. A biological weapons *program*, but not an arsenal of biological weapons, was uncovered by U.N. inspectors in 1995. And, as we saw in the Kamisiyah episode, a small number of live chemical munitions were found in the mid-1990s mixed in haphazardly with conventional munitions, not part of a concerted Iraqi WMD program.

49. SSCI, *Iraq Postwar Findings*, pp. 130–31.

50. Duelfer, *Comprehensive Report*, Vol. I, "Transmittal Message," p. 8.

51. Ibid., p. 9.

52. Ibid.

53. Ibid., Vol. II, "Biological Warfare," p. 2.

54. Ibid., Vol. I, "Regime Strategic Intent," p. 25.

55. Ibid., "Transmittal Message," p. 8.

56. U.N. Special Commission, International Atomic Energy Agency, Note for File: Transcript of interview of General Hussein Kamal (classified "Sensitive"; since released), Amman, Jordan, August 22, 1995, pp. 12–13. Note: The document spells the Iraqi general's name "Kamal;" most Western media organizations spell it Kamel, as I do in the text.

57. Ibid., p. 13.

58. Author's interview with Ambassador Rolf Ekeus, former executive chairman of the United Nations Special Commission, the arms inspection organization sent to Iraq after the Persian Gulf War, October 10, 2007.

59. SSCI, *Iraq Postwar Findings*, p. 131.

60. John Barry, "The Defector's Secrets," *Newsweek*, March 3, 2003. The issue was published February 24, 2003.

61. "U.S., Britain Deny *Newsweek* Defector Report," Reuters, February 24, 2003.

62. Amos Kovacs, *The Uses and Nonuses of Intelligence*, monograph, Stanford University, Center for International Security and Arms Control, October 1996, pp. 1–2, emphasis in the original.

63. Author's interview with Terence Taylor, a former United Nations Special Commission chief inspector for biological weapons programs in Iraq, May 23, 2007.

64. Ibid.

65. Duelfer, *Comprehensive Report*, Vol. I, "Regime Strategic Intent," p. 47.

66. Taylor interview.

67. Duelfer, *Comprehensive Report*, Vol. I, "Regime Strategic Intent," pp. 50–51.

68. Ibid., p. 51.

69. Ibid., p. 61.

70. Secretary of State Madeleine Albright, policy speech on Iraq, March 26, 1997, Georgetown University.

71. Ekeus interview.

72. For a summary of Clinton administration and U.N. views on the inspections controversy, see "Inspecting the Deal," *Online NewsHour*, PBS, February 25, 1998, http://www.pbs.org/newshour/bb/middle_east/jan-june98/iraq_2-25.html.

73. For a U.S. intelligence community perspective on the much-debated baby milk factory controversy, see "Iraqi Deception and Denial," Foreign Press Center Briefing, John Yurechko, Defense Intelligence Agency Officer, October 11, 2002, http://fpc.state.gov/14337.htm. The point of the briefing, coming on the day the Senate voted to authorize the use of force in Iraq, was to undermine Iraqi denials that it had maintained an arsenal of weapons of mass destruction. For links to news reports on the pharmaceutical plant issue, see Mark Barletta and Erik Jorgensen, "Al-Shifa Pharmaceutical Plant: Key Reports & Analyses of the U.S. Attack and CW Allegations, 20 August 1998 to 15 April 1999," Center for Nonproliferation Studies and Monterey Institute of International

Studies, April 1999, a the Center for Nonproliferation Studies website, http://cns.miis. edu/research/wmdme/biblio.htm.

74. Rick Atkinson and Vernon Loeb, "Limited Campaign Could Limit Success," *The Washington Post*, December 17, 1998, p. A1.

75. Duelfer, *Comprehensive Report*, Vol. I, "Regime Strategic Intent," p. 11.

76. William Arkin, "The Difference Was in the Details," *The Washington Post*, January 17, 1999, p. B1.

77. The author was covering the Pentagon for the Associated Press at the time. See Department of Defense news briefings, December 18–19, 1998, Subject: Operation Desert Fox, http://www.defenselink.mil/transcripts/transcript.aspx?transcriptid=1789 and http://www.defenselink.mil/transcripts/transcript.aspx?transcriptid=1790.

78. The Federation of American Scientists obtained and posted briefing slides prepared by the U.S. Central Command, which ran the operation. See BDA Assessment Summary, as of December 19, 1998, http://www.fas.org/news/iraq/1998/12/19/bda2/ slide08.htm. See also Dr. Mark J. Conversino, "Operation DESERT FOX: Effectiveness with Unintended Effects," in *Air & Space Power Chronicles* (United States Air Force), July 13, 2005. Conversino effectively rejects suggestions by some after the invasion of Iraq that Operation Desert Fox had succeeded in destroying all of Iraq's weapons of mass destruction.

79. Then–CIA Director George Tenet described the agency's efforts to penetrate Iraq after the departure of inspectors, but conceded that the record was "mixed." See Tenet's speech, "Iraq and Weapons of Mass Destruction," at Georgetown University, February 5, 2004, on the CIA's website at https://www.cia.gov/news-information/speeches-testimony/2004/tenet_georgetownspeech_02052004.html. But the Senate Intelligence Committee's report on Iraq-related intelligence states flatly, "The CIA [material redacted] did not have any WMD sources in Iraq after 1998." See SSCI, *Prewar Intelligence Assessments on Iraq*, p. 260. A more extensive special commission investigation found that the CIA did have some sources but they were of poor quality and the agency was slow to flag decision-makers to their unreliability. See WMD Commission, *Report to the President*, pp. 127–30.

80. A detailed description of the attempt to kill Saddam on the opening night of the war appears in Michael R. Gordon and Bernard E. Trainor, *Cobra II: The Inside Story of the Invasion and Occupation of Iraq* (New York: Pantheon, 2006), pp. 168–77. Details of the ROCKSTAR spy network were first reported by Bob Woodward in a *Washington Post* series accompanying his book on the Iraq War. See Bob Woodward, "U.S. Aimed for Hussein as War Began," *The Washington Post*, April 22, 2004, p. A1; and Bob Woodward, *Plan of Attack* (New York: Simon & Schuster, 2004), pp. 373–75, 417–18.

81. WMD Commission, *Report to the President*, p. 117, and Chap. 1, p. 227 note 457. The commission attributed the information to a Statement for the Record provided in closed session by then–CIA Director George Tenet.

82. James Risen, *State of War: The Secret History of the CIA and the Bush Administration* (New York: Free Press, 2006), pp. 89–91, 106.

83. The decision by Congress in October 2002 to authorize the use of force in Iraq came as a joint House-Senate inquiry was concluding its examination of intelligence failures related to the September 11, 2001, attacks. The investigation involved extensive interaction with the CIA at the highest levels. All summer and fall it took up substantial quantities of intelligence community senior executive time during a period when assessing the available intelligence on Iraq should have been the top priority. See U.S. Senate Select Committee on Intelligence and U.S. House of Representatives Permanent Select Committee on Intelligence, *Joint Inquiry into Intelligence Community Activities Before and After the Terrorist Attacks of September 11, 2001*, December 2002 (Washington, D.C.: Government Printing Office, 2002). Hereafter, Joint Inquiry Committee.

84. Testimony of Cofer Black, former chief, CIA Counter-Terrorism Center, before the Joint Inquiry Committee, September 26, 2002.

85. Dana Priest, "Al Qaeda-Iraq Link Recanted: Captured Libyan Reverses Previous Statement to CIA, Officials Say," *The Washington Post*, August 1, 2004, p. A20.

86. SSCI, *Iraq Postwar Findings*, p. 80. The Senate Intelligence Committee report cites a "CIA Operational Cable" dated February 5, 2004. The report does not identify Egypt as the country to which al-Libi was sent. *Newsweek* reporters Michael Isikoff and Mark Hosenball identified Egypt in a November 2005 report. See Michael Isikoff and Mark Hosenball, "New CIA Paper Shows Pre-War Intel Flaws," *Newsweek*, Web Exclusive, posted November 10, 2005, http://www.msnbc.msn.com/id/9991919/site/newsweek/print/1/displaymode/1098/.

87. SSCI, *Iraq Postwar Findings*, pp. 80–81.

88. The quotations are declassified excerpts of Defense Intelligence Agency Terrorism Summary, DITSUM #044-02 of February 2002. Several paragraphs of the classified document were declassified in 2005 at the request of Senators Jay Rockefeller and Carl Levin, the ranking Democrats, respectively, on the Senate Intelligence and Senate Armed Services committees. The material was made public by Levin on November 5, 2005. The DIA report is also quoted in SSCI, *Iraq Postwar Findings*, p. 77.

89. Defense Intelligence Agency, Special Analysis, February 28, 2002, p. 1, quoted in SSCI, *Iraq Postwar Findings*, p. 77.

90. Powell, UNSC address, February 2003.

91. See, for example, the account in Karen DeYoung, *Soldier: The Life of Colin Powell* (New York: Alfred A. Knopf, 2006).

92. This passage from the document is quoted in Isikoff and Hosenball, "New CIA Paper Shows Pre-War Intel Flaws."

93. SSCI, *Iraq Postwar Findings*, pp. 64–65. The underlying CIA report quoted here is cited as CIA, *Iraqi Support for Terrorism*, January 29, 2003.

94. The best account of the behind-the-scenes debate at the CIA during the prepara-

tion of Powell's U.N. Security Council presentation appears in Karen De Young's *Soldier*.

95. SSCI, *Iraq Postwar Findings*, p. 82.

96. George Tenet, *At the Center of the Storm: My Years at the CIA* (New York: Harper Collins, 2007), pp. 353–54.

97. Harlow spoke on background at the time, but granted the author permission to identify him in this recounting.

98. See, for example, John Diamond, "CIA's Evidence of Iraqi Threat Lacks 'Smoking Gun,'" *USA Today*, August 16, 2002, p. 6A; John Diamond and Dave Moniz, "Finding Saddam, 'Chem-Bio' Arms Slows U.S.: Cloudy Intelligence Complicates Planning of Potential War on Iraq," *USA Today*, August 23, 2002, p. 10A; John Diamond, "U.S. Assertions Go Beyond Its Intelligence: Questions Raised on Iraq Evidence," *USA Today*, September 17, 2002, p. 4A; and Barbara Slavin and John Diamond, "Experts Skeptical of Al-Qaeda–Iraq Tie: Link Could Help the Case for War, But Some Say It's Weak," *USA Today*, September 27, 2002, p. 4A.

99. Most of the points in this paragraph were known to the author at the time through reporting. The CIA–White House rift over the allegations of Iraq shopping for uranium in Africa were first reported by Walter Pincus and Mike Allen, "CIA Got Uranium Reference Cut in Oct., Why Bush Cited It in Jan. Is Unclear," *The Washington Post*, July 13, 2003, p. A1.

100. Defense Intelligence Agency background briefing, Pentagon, Washington, attended by the author, December 18, 2002. Details of this briefing are also discussed in Chap. 4.

101. October 2002 NIE.

102. Author's reporting, March and April 2004. The *Washington Post* reported that as few as six senators and a handful of House members read the full report. There are no declassified log sheets that would indicate which members went to the secure rooms of the House and Senate Intelligence committees to read the document. See Dana Priest, "Congressional Oversight of Intelligence Criticized: Committee Members, Others Cite Lack of Attention to Reports on Iraqi Arms, Al Qaeda Threat," *The Washington Post*, April 27, 2004, p. A1. Former senior CIA intelligence analyst Paul Pillar cited the same figure—six senators—based on information from congressional aides responsible for safeguarding access to such classified reports. See Paul R. Pillar, "Intelligence, Policy and the War in Iraq," *Foreign Affairs* 85, no. 2 (March/April 2006).

103. Interview with National Security Adviser Condoleezza Rice conducted by Wolf Blitzer, *CNN Late Edition*, September 8, 2002, http://www.mtholyoke.edu/acad/intrel/bush/wolf.htm.

104. SSCI, *Prewar Intelligence on Iraq*, p. 199.

105. The Senate vote came at 1:15 a.m. on October 11, 2002, the late-night session resulting from the desire of many senators to speak on the issue.

106. Woodward, *Plan of Attack*, pp. 247–50.

107. Tenet, *At the Center of the Storm*, pp. 361–62.

108. Transcript of Hussein Kamal debrief, p. 7.

109. The WMD Commission, which had total access to U.S. intelligence products on Iraq-WMD, makes this assertion on pp. 155–56.

110. Duelfer, *Comprehensive Report*, Vol. III, "Biological," p. 15.

111. WMD Commission, *Report to the President*, p. 155.

112. Director of Central Intelligence, National Intelligence Council (NIC), *Regional Consequences of Regime Change in Iraq*, Intelligence Community Assessment (SECRET), January 2003; and *Principal Challenges in Post-Saddam Iraq*, (SECRET), January 2003. The documents, declassified in April 2007, are included in an appendix to a report by the U.S. Senate Select Committee on Intelligence, *Prewar Intelligence Assessments About Postwar Iraq*, 110th Cong., 1st sess., May 8, 2007, http://intelligence.senate.gov/prewar. pdf. The cited quotations are from *Principal Challenges*, pp. 5, 6, 10, 20, and 37.

113. U.S. forces advancing toward Baghdad from Kuwait were prepared for weapons of mass destruction but not for guerrilla attacks. For an account of one of the initial attacks on U.S. forces by Iraqi irregulars, a sign of things to come, see Col. Gregory Fontenon, U.S. Army (Ret.); Lt. Col. E. J. Degen, U.S. Army; and Lt. Col. David Tohn, U.S. Army, *On Point: The United States Army in Operation Iraqi Freedom* (Fort Leavenworth, Kan.: Combat Studies Institute Press, 2004), an official study conducted under the auspices of the Army Chief of Staff, pp. 123–35.

114. NIC, *Regional Consequences of Regime Change in Iraq*, pp. 1, 5, 6, 16.

BIBLIOGRAPHY

All website addresses in the Bibliography were valid in January 2008.

Books, Periodicals, and Other Secondary Sources

Adams, James. *Sellout: Aldrich Ames and the Corruption of the CIA*. New York: Viking, 1995.

Alfonsi, Christian. *Circle in the Sand: Why We Went Back to Iraq*. New York: Doubleday, 2006.

Amalrik, Andrei. *Will the Soviet Union Survive Until 1984?* New York: Harper and Row, 1970.

Amstutz, J. Bruce. *Afghanistan: The First Five Years of Soviet Occupation*. Washington, D.C.: National Defense University Press, 1986.

Andrew, Christopher, and Vasili Mitrokhin. *The Sword and the Shield: The Mitrokhin Archive and the Secret History of the KGB*. New York: Basic Books, 1999.

———. *The World Was Going Our Way: The KGB and the Battle for the Third World*. New York: Basic Books, 2005.

Anonymous. *Imperial Hubris: Why the West Is Losing the War on Terror*. Washington, D.C.: Brassey's, 2004. Note: After publication, the author was revealed to be then–CIA officer Michael Scheuer.

Atkinson, Rick. *Crusade: The Untold Story of the Persian Gulf War*. Boston: Houghton Mifflin, 1993.

Baer, Robert. *See No Evil: The True Story of a Ground Soldier in the CIA's War on Terrorism*. New York: Crown, 2002.

Bamford, James. *Body of Secrets: Anatomy of the Ultra-Secret National Security Agency*. New York: Doubleday, 2001.

Barker, Rodney. *Dancing with the Devil: Sex, Espionage and the U.S. Marine: The Clayton Lonetree Story*. New York: Simon and Schuster, 1996.

Barrett, David M. *The CIA and Congress: The Untold Story from Truman to Kennedy.* Lawrence: University Press of Kansas, 2005.

Bearden, Milt, and James Risen. *The Main Enemy: The Inside Story of the CIA's Final Showdown with the KGB.* New York: Random House, 2003.

Bennett, Richard M. *Espionage: An Encyclopedia of Spies and Secrets.* London: Virgin Books, 2002.

Bennett, W. Lance, and David L. Paletz, eds. *Taken by Storm: The Media, Public Opinion, and U.S. Foreign Policy in the Gulf War.* Chicago: University of Chicago Press, 1994.

Berkowitz, Peter, ed. *The Future of American Intelligence.* Stanford, Calif.: Hoover Institution Press, 2005.

Bermudez, Joseph S. Jr. "A History of Ballistic Missile Development in the DPRK" [Democratic People's Republic of Korea, or North Korea]. Monitoring Proliferation Threats Project. Occasional Paper No. 2. Monterey Institute of International Studies, Center for Nonproliferation Studies, 1999.

Beschloss, Michael, and Strobe Talbott. *At the Highest Levels.* Boston: Little, Brown, 1993.

Bodansky, Yossef. *Bin Laden: The Man Who Declared War on America.* New York: Prima/Random House, 2001.

Brugioni, Dino A. *Eyeball to Eyeball: The Inside Story of the Cuban Missile Crisis.* New York: Random House, 1990.

Brzezinski, Zbigniew. *Power and Principle: Memoirs of a National Security Adviser.* New York: Farrar, Straus & Giroux, 1983.

———, ed. *Dilemmas of Change in Soviet Politics.* New York: Columbia University Press, 1969.

Burgin, Eileen. "Influences Shaping Members' Decision Making: Congressional Voting on the Persian Gulf War." *Political Behavior* 16, no. 3 (September 1994): 319–42.

Burrows, William E. *By Any Means Necessary: America's Secret Air War in the Cold War.* New York: Farrar, Straus & Giroux, 2001.

———. *Deep Black: Space Espionage and National Security.* New York: Random House, 1986.

Bush, George, and Brent Scowcroft. *A World Transformed: The Collapse of the Soviet Empire, the Unification of Germany, Tiananmen Square, the Gulf War.* New York: Alfred A. Knopf, 1998.

Byrne, Malcolm, Pavel Machcewicz, and Christian Osterman, eds. *Poland 1980–82: Internal Crisis, International Dimensions, a Compendium of Declassified Documents and Chronology of Events.* Washington, D.C.: National Security Archive, 1997.

Cahn, Anne. *Killing Détente: The Right Attacks the CIA.* University Park: Pennsylvania State University Press, 1998.

Carter, Jimmy. *Keeping Faith: Memoirs of a President.* New York: Bantam Books, 1982.

Cerf, Christopher, and Micah L. Sifry, eds. *The Gulf War Reader*. New York: Times Books, 1991.

Cerulo, Karen A. *Never Saw It Coming: Cultural Challenges to Envisioning the Worst*. Chicago: University of Chicago Press, 2006.

Chengappa, Raj. *Weapons of Peace: The Secret Story of India's Quest to Be a Nuclear Power*. New Delhi: Harper Collins India, 2000.

Cherkashin, Victor, with Gregory Feifer. *Spy Handler: Memoir of a KGB Officer. The True Story of the Man Who Recruited Robert Hanssen and Aldrich Ames*. New York: Basic Books, 2005.

Chernyaev, Anatoly. *My Six Years with Gorbachev*. University Park: Pennsylvania State University Press, 2000.

Clark, Wesley. *Waging Modern War*. New York: Public Affairs, 2001.

Clarke, Richard A. *Against All Enemies: Inside America's War on Terror*. New York: Free Press, 2004.

Cohen, Eliot A., and staff. *Gulf War Air Power Survey*. Washington, D.C.: U.S. Air Force, 1993.

Coll, Steve. *Ghost Wars: The Secret History of the CIA, Afghanistan, and bin Laden, from the Soviet Invasion to September 10, 2001*. New York: Penguin, 2004.

Collins, Randall. *Weberian Sociological Theory*. New York: Cambridge University Press, 1986.

Cordesman, Anthony H. *After the Storm: The Changing Military Balance in the Middle East*. Boulder, Colo.: Westview Press, 1993.

———. *The Iraq War: Strategy, Tactics, and Military Lessons*. Washington, D.C.: CSIS Press, 2006.

Cull, Nicholas J. "'The Perfect War': U.S. Public Diplomacy and International Broadcasting During Desert Shield and Desert Storm, 1990/1991." *Transnational Broadcasting Studies* 15 (Fall/Winter 2006).

Daalder, Ivo H., and Michael E. O'Hanlon. *Winning Ugly: NATO's War to Save Kosovo*. Washington, D.C.: Brookings Institution Press, 2000.

Davis, Jay C., David A. Kay. "Iraq's Secret Nuclear Weapons Program." *Physics Today* (July 1992).

DeConcini, Dennis, and Jack L. August Jr. *Senator Dennis DeConcini: From the Center of the Aisle*. Tucson: University of Arizona Press, 2006.

DeYoung, Karen. *Soldier: The Life of Colin Powell*. New York: Alfred A. Knopf, 2006.

Dunlop, John B. *The Rise of Russia and the Fall of the Soviet Empire*. Princeton, N.J.: Princeton University Press, 1993.

Earley, Pete. *Confessions of a Spy: The Real Story of Aldrich Ames*. New York: G. P. Putnam's Sons, 1997.

d'Encausse, Hélène. *Decline of an Empire: The Soviet Socialist Republics in Revolt*. New York: Harper & Row, 1979.

Fischer, Benjamin B., ed. *At Cold War's End: U.S. Intelligence on the Soviet Union and Eastern Europe, 1989–1991*. Washington, D.C.: CIA, Center for the Study of Intelligence, 1999.

Fontenot, Col. Gregory, U.S. Army (Ret.); Lt. Col. E. J. Degen, U.S. Army; and Lt. Col. David Tohn, U.S. Army. *On Point: The United States Army in Operation Iraqi Freedom*. Washington, D.C.: Office of the Chief of Staff of the Army / Fort Leavenworth, Kan.: Combat Studies Institute Press, 2004.

Ford, Harold P., *CIA and the Vietnam Policymakers: Three Episodes, 1962–1968*. Washington, D.C.: CIA, Center for the Study of Intelligence, 1998.

Freedman, Lawrence, and Efraim Karsh, *The Gulf Conflict 1990–1991*. Princeton, N.J.: Princeton University Press, 1993.

———. "How Kuwait Was Won: Strategy in the Gulf War." *International Security* 16, no. 2 (Autumn 1991): 5–41.

Funigiello, Philip J. *American-Soviet Trade in the Cold War*. Chapel Hill, N.C.: University of North Carolina Press, 1988.

Gaddis, John Lewis. *The Cold War: A New History*. New York: Penguin, 2006.

———. *Surprise, Security, and the American Experience*. Cambridge, Mass.: Harvard University Press, 2004.

———. *The United States and the End of the Cold War: Implications, Reconsiderations, Provocations*. Oxford: Oxford University Press, 1992.

Gates, Robert M. *From the Shadows: The Ultimate Insider's Story of Five Presidents and How They Won the Cold War*. New York: Simon & Schuster, 1996.

Garthoff, Raymond L. *The Great Transition: American-Soviet Relations and the End of the Cold War*. Washington, D.C.: Brookings Institution Press, 1994.

George, Roger Z., and Robert D. Kline. *Intelligence and the National Security Strategist: Enduring Issues and Challenges*. Washington, D.C.: National Defense University Press, 2004.

Godson, Roy, Ernest R. May, and Gary Schmitt, eds. *U.S. Intelligence at the Crossroads: Agendas for Reform*. Washington, D.C.: Brassey's, 1995.

Gorbachev, Mikhail. *Memoirs*. New York: Doubleday, 1996.

Gordievsky, Oleg. *Next Stop Execution*. London: Macmillan, 1995.

Gordon, Michael R., and Bernard E. Trainor. *Cobra II: The Inside Story of the Invasion and Occupation of Iraq*. New York: Pantheon Books, 2006.

———. *The Generals' War: The Inside Story of the Conflict in the Gulf*. Boston: Little, Brown, 1995.

Graham, Bob. *Intelligence Matters: The CIA, the FBI, Saudi Arabia and the Failure of America's War on Terror*. New York: Random House, 2004.

Graham, Bradley. *Hit to Kill: The New Battle over Shielding America from Missile Attack*. New York: Public Affairs, 2001.

Graubard, Stephen R. *Mr. Bush's War: Adventures in the Politics of Illusion*. New York: Hill & Wang, 1992.

Gup, Ted. *The Book of Honor: Covert Lives and Classified Deaths at the CIA*. New York: Doubleday, 2000.

Haines, Gerald K., and Robert E. Leggett, eds. *CIA's Analysis of the Soviet Union, 1947–1991*. Washington, D.C.: CIA, Center for the Study of Intelligence, 2001.

————. *Watching the Bear: Essays on CIA's Analysis of the Soviet Union*. Washington, D.C.: CIA, Center for the Study of Intelligence, 2001.

History Staff, Center for the Study of Intelligence. *At Cold War's End: U.S. Intelligence on the Soviet Union and Eastern Europe, 1989–1991*. Washington, D.C.: CIA, Center for the Study of Intelligence, 1999.

International Institute for Strategic Studies. *Iraq's Weapons of Mass Destruction: A Net Assessment*. London: IISS, September 9, 2002.

Isikoff, Michael, and David Corn. *Hubris: The Inside Story of Spin, Scandal, and the Selling of the Iraq War*. New York: Crown, 2006.

Jentleson, Bruce W. *With Friends Like These: Reagan, Bush, and Saddam, 1982–1990*. New York: W. W. Norton, 1994.

————, ed. *Opportunities Missed, Opportunities Seized: Preventive Diplomacy in the Post–Cold War World*. New York: Carnegie Corporation of New York, Rowman & Littlefield, 2000.

Johnson, Dominic. *Overconfidence and War: The Havoc and Glory of Positive Illusions*. Cambridge, Mass.: Harvard University Press, 2004.

Johnson, Loch K. *Secret Agencies: U.S. Intelligence in a Hostile World*. New Haven, Conn.: Yale University Press, 1996.

Kalugin, Oleg. *Spymaster: My 32 Years in Intelligence and Espionage Against the West*. London: Smith Gryphon, 1994.

Keaney, Thomas A., and Eliot A. Cohen. *Revolution in Warfare? Air Power in the Persian Gulf*. Annapolis, Md.: Naval Institute Press, 1993.

Kessler, Ronald. *The CIA at War: Inside the Secret Campaign Against Terror*. New York: St. Martin's Press, 2003.

Kriesberg, Louis, and David R. Segal, eds. *The Transformation of European Communist Societies*. Greenwich, Conn.: JAI Press, 1992.

Lagon, Mark P. *The Reagan Doctrine: Sources of American Conduct in the Cold War's Last Chapter*. Westport, Conn.: Praeger, 1994.

Lambeth, Benjamin S. *NATO's Air War for Kosovo: A Strategic and Operational Assessment*. Washington, D.C.: Rand, 2003.

Lindsay, James M., and Michael E. O'Hanlon. *Defending America: The Case for Limited National Missile Defense*. Washington, D.C.: Brookings Institution Press, 2001.

Litwak, Robert S. *Rogue States and U.S. Foreign Policy: Containment after the Cold War*. Washington, D.C.: Woodrow Wilson Center Press, 2000.

Lowenthal, Mark M. *Intelligence: From Secrets to Policy*. 2nd ed. Washington, D.C.: CQ Press, 2003.

Maas, Peter. *Killer Spy: The Inside Story of the FBI's Pursuit and Capture of Aldrich Ames, America's Deadliest Spy.* New York: Warner Books, 1995.

MacEachin, Douglas J. *CIA Assessments of the Soviet Union: The Record Versus the Charges.* Washington, D.C.: CIA, Center for the Study of Intelligence, 1996.

———. *Predicting the Soviet Invasion of Afghanistan: The Intelligence Community's Record.* Washington, D.C.: CIA, Center for the Study of Intelligence, 2002.

———. *U.S. Intelligence and the Confrontation in Poland, 1980–81.* University Park: Pennsylvania State University Press, 2002.

Mahle, Melissa Boyle. *Denial and Deception: An Insider's View of the CIA from Iran Contra to 9/11.* New York: Nation Books, 2004.

Mann, James. *Rise of the Vulcans: The History of Bush's War Cabinet.* New York: Viking, 2004.

Meher, Jagmohan. *America's Afghanistan War: The Success That Failed.* Delhi: Kalpaz Publications, 2004.

Moorehead, Alan. *The Russian Revolution.* New York: Harper & Bros., 1958.

Moran, Lindsay. *Blowing My Cover: My Life as a CIA Spy.* New York: G. P. Putnam's Sons, 2005.

Moynihan, Daniel Patrick. *Secrecy: The American Experience.* New Haven, Conn.: Yale University Press, 1998.

Naftali, Timothy. *Blind Spot: The Secret History of American Counterterrorism.* New York: Basic Books, 2005.

Njolstad, Olav, ed. *The Last Decade of the Cold War: From Conflict Escalation to Conflict Transformation.* London: Taylor & Francis, 2004.

Ouimet, Matthew J. *The Rise and Fall of the Brezhnev Doctrine in Soviet Foreign Policy.* Durham, N.C.: University of North Carolina Press, 2002.

Paceman, Floyd L. *A Spy's Journey: A CIA Memoir.* St. Paul, Minn.: Zenith Press, 2004.

Packer, George. *The Assassins' Gate: America in Iraq.* New York: Farrar, Straus & Giroux, 2005.

Paczkowski, Andrzej, and Malcolm Byrne, eds. *From Solidarity to Martial Law: The Polish Crisis of 1980–1981.* Budapest: Central European University Press, 2007.

Penkovskiy, Oleg. *The Penkovskiy Papers.* New York: Doubleday, 1965.

Persico, Joseph E. *Casey: From the OSS to the CIA.* New York: Viking, 1990.

Pillar, Paul R. *Terrorism and U.S. Foreign Policy.* Washington, D.C.: Brookings Institution Press, 2002.

Pipes, Richard. "Misinterpreting the Cold War: The Hardliners Were Right." *Foreign Affairs* 74, no. 1 (January/February 1995).

———. "The Soviet Union Adrift." *Foreign Affairs* 70, no. 1 (1990/91).

Pollack, Kenneth M. *The Threatening Storm: The Case for Invading Iraq.* New York: Random House, 2002.

Posner, Richard A. *Preventing Surprise Attacks: Intelligence Reform in the Wake of 9/11.* Lanham, Md.: Rowman & Littlefield, 2005.

Powell, Colin, with Joseph E. Persico. *My American Journey.* New York: Ballantine Books, 1995.

Ranelagh, John. *The Agency: The Rise and Decline of the CIA.* New York: Touchstone Books, 1986.

Reeve, Simon. *The New Jackals: Ramzi Youssef, Osama bin Laden and the Future of Terrorism.* Boston: Northeastern University Press, 2002.

Remnick, David. *Lenin's Tomb: The Last Days of the Soviet Empire.* New York: Random House, 1994.

Richelson, Jeffrey T. *A Century of Spies: Intelligence in the Twentieth Century.* New York: Oxford University Press, 1995.

————. *Spying on the Bomb: American Nuclear Intelligence from Nazi Germany to Iran and North Korea.* New York: W. W. Norton, 2006.

————. *The Wizards of Langley: Inside the CIA's Directorate of Science and Technology.* Boulder, Colo.: Westview Press, 2001.

Ricks, Thomas E. *Fiasco: The American Military Adventure in Iraq.* New York: Penguin, 2006.

Risen, James. *State of War: The Secret History of the CIA and the Bush Administration.* New York: Free Press, 2006.

Russell, Richard L. *Sharpening Strategic Intelligence: Why the CIA Gets It Wrong and What Needs to Be Done to Get It Right.* New York: Cambridge University Press, 2007.

Scheuer, Michael. *Through Our Enemies' Eyes: Osama bin Laden, Radical Islam and the Future of America.* Washington, D.C.: Potomac Books, 2006.

Schwarzkopf, H. Norman, with Peter Petre. *It Doesn't Take a Hero: General H. Norman Schwarzkopf, the Autobiography.* Paperback edition. New York: Bantam Books, 1992.

Schweizer, Peter. *Victory: The Reagan Administration's Secret Strategy That Hastened the Collapse of the Soviet Union.* New York: Atlantic Monthly Press, 1994.

Shultz, George. *Turmoil and Triumph: My Years as Secretary of State.* Macmillan, New York 1993.

Sims, Jennifer, and Burton Gerber, eds. *Transforming U.S. Intelligence.* Washington, D.C.: Georgetown University Press, 2005.

L. Britt Snider. "Sharing Secrets with Lawmakers: Congress as a User of Intelligence." *Studies in Intelligence* (CIA). February 1997.

Sontag, Sherry, and Christopher Drew. *Blind Man's Bluff: The Untold Story of American Submarine Espionage.* New York: Public Affairs, 1998.

Spector, Leonard S. *Nuclear Ambitions.* Boulder, Colo.: Westview Press, 1990.

Stein, Janice Gross. "Deterrence and Compellence in the Gulf, 1990–91: A Failed or Impossible Task?" *International Security* 17, no. 2 (Fall 1992): 147–79.

Suskind, Ron. *The One Percent Doctrine: Deep Inside America's Pursuit of Its Enemies Since 9/11.* New York: Simon & Schuster, 2006.

———. *The Price of Loyalty: George W. Bush, the White House, and the Education of Paul O'Neill.* New York: Simon & Schuster, 2004.

Tenet, George, with Bill Harlow. *At the Center of the Storm: My Years at the CIA.* New York: Harper Collins, 2007.

Treverton, Gregory F. *Reshaping National Intelligence for an Age of Information.* Cambridge: Cambridge University Press, 2001.

Turner, Stansfield. "Intelligence for a New World Order." *Foreign Affairs* 70, no. 4 (Fall 1991).

Watson, William E. *The Collapse of Communism in the Soviet Union.* Westport, Conn.: Greenwood Press, 1998.

Weiner, Tim. *Blank Check: The Pentagon's Black Budget.* New York: Warner Books, 1990.

———. *Legacy of Ashes: The History of the CIA.* New York: Doubleday, 2007.

Weiner, Tim, David Johnston, and Neil Lewis. *Betrayal: The Story of Aldrich Ames, an American Spy.* New York: Random House, 1995.

Westerfield, H. Bradford, ed. *Inside CIA's Private World: Declassified Articles from the Agency's Internal Journal, 1955–1992.* New Haven, Conn.: Yale University Press, 1995.

Wirls, Daniel. *Buildup: The Politics of Defense in the Reagan Era.* Ithaca, N.Y.: Cornell University Press, 1992.

Wise, David. *Spy: The Inside Story of How the FBI's Robert Hanssen Betrayed America.* New York: Random House, 2003.

———. *Molehunt: The Secret Search for Traitors That Shattered the CIA.* New York: Random House, 1992.

———. *Nightmover: How Aldrich Ames Sold the CIA to the KGB for $4.6 Million.* New York: Harper Collins, 1995.

Wohlstetter, Roberta. *Pearl Harbor: Warning and Decision.* Stanford, Calif.: Stanford University Press, 1962.

Wolf, Markus, with Anne McElvoy. *Man Without a Face: The Autobiography of Communism's Greatest Spymaster.* New York: Public Affairs, 1997.

Woodward, Bob. *Plan of Attack.* New York: Simon & Schuster, 2004.

———. *State of Denial: Bush at War Part III.* New York: Simon & Schuster, 2006.

Wright, Lawrence. *The Looming Tower: Al-Qaeda and the Road to 9/11.* New York: Alfred A. Knopf, 2006.

Zaller, John. "Elite Leadership of Mass Opinion: New Evidence from the Gulf War." In W. Lance Bennett and David L. Paletz, eds., *Taken by Storm: The Media, Public Opinion, and U.S. Foreign Policy in the Gulf War.* Chicago: University of Chicago Press, 1994.

————. "Strategic Politicians, Public Opinion and the Gulf Crisis." Occasional Paper. Seattle: Center for American Politics and Public Policy, February 4, 1993.

Zegart, Amy B. "September 11 and the Adaptation Failure of U.S. Intelligence Agencies." *International Security* 29, no. 4 (Spring 2005).

————. *Spying Blind: The CIA, FBI, and the Origins of 9/11*. Princeton, N.J.: Princeton University Press, 2007.

Zinni, Anthony C., and Tony Koltz. *The Battle for Peace: A Frontline Vision of America's Power and Purpose*. New York: Palgrave Macmillan, 2006.

Selected Reports and Primary Sources

Unless otherwise noted, government reports are U.S. government.

Army—Central Command (ARCENT). *Close-Out Report: ARCENT Suspected Chemical Weapons Sites Investigation*. March 9, 2000. www.gulflink.osd.mil/arcent/arcent_s01.htm.

British House of Commons. Report of a Committee of Privy Counselors, *Review of Intelligence on Weapons of Mass Destruction*. London: The Stationery Office, 2004.

CIA, Directorate of Intelligence. *Iraq: Nuclear Weapons–Related Procurement Activities* (Top Secret), September 4, 1989. Document obtained under the Freedom of Information Act by the National Security Archive, George Washington University.

————. Memo to Richard Haass, special assistant to the president for Near East and South Asian Affairs, "Analysis on Iraqi Attempt to Procure Furnaces" (Secret), July 19, 1990. Document obtained under the Freedom of Information Act by the National Security Archive, George Washington University.

————. *Response to National Security Review-10: U.S. Policy Toward the Persian Gulf* (Secret), March 3, 1989. Document obtained under the Freedom of Information Act by the National Security Archive, George Washington University.

CIA, Independent Panel Review. *Emerging Missile Threats to North America During the Next 15 Years, NIE 95-19*. Panel headed by former CIA director Robert Gates. Washington, D.C.: U.S. Government Printing Office, December 1996.

CIA, Office of Inspector General John L. Helgerson. *Report on CIA Accountability with Respect to the 9/11 Attacks*. June 2005, declassified executive summary approved for release August 2007.

Cold War International History Project Bulletin (CWIHP). Washington, D.C.: Woodrow Wilson International Center for Scholars, Issues 1–15, Spring 1992 through Spring 2004.

Commission to Assess the Ballistic Missile Threat to the United States (Rumsfeld Commission). *Report*. Washington, D.C.: Government Printing Office, 1998. http://www.fas.org/irp/threat/missile/rumsfeld/.

————. Executive Summary. Washington, D.C.: Government Printing Office, 1998.

Commission on the Intelligence Capabilities of the United States Regarding Weapons of

Mass Destruction (Robb Commission). *Report to the President of the United States.* Washington, D.C.: U.S. Government Printing Office, 2005.

Defense Intelligence Agency History Office. *A Chronology of Defense Intelligence in the Gulf War: A Research Aid for Analysts.* Washington, D.C.: Department of Defense, July 1997.

Department of the Army, Office of Inspector General. *Inquiry into Demolition of Iraq Ammunition.* October 10, 1997. www.gulflink.osd.mil/army_ig/.

Department of Defense. *Conduct of the Persian Gulf War: Final Report to Congress.* Washington, D.C.: Department of Defense, April 1992.

———. Kosovo/Operation Allied Force After-Action Report: *Report to Congress.* Washington, D.C.: Department of Defense, January 31, 2000.

Department of Justice, Commission for Review of FBI Security Programs. *A Review of FBI Security Programs.* Washington, D.C.: Department of Justice, March 2002.

Department of Justice, Office of Inspector General Glenn A. Fine. *A Review of the FBI's Handling of Intelligence Information Related to the September 11 Attacks.* Washington, D.C.: Department of Justice, November 2004.

———. *A Review of the FBI's Performance in Deterring, Detecting, and Investigating the Espionage Activities of Robert Philip Hanssen.* Unclassified executive summary. Washington, D.C.: Department of Justice, August 2003.

Department of State, Accountability Review Boards. *Bombings of the U.S. Embassies in Nairobi, Kenya and Dar es Salaam, Tanzania on August 7, 1998: Report of the Accountability Review Boards.* Washington, D.C.: Department of State, January 8, 1999.

Director of Central Intelligence. *Comprehensive Report of the Special Advisor to the Director of Central Intelligence on Iraq's Weapons of Mass Destruction*, Special Advisor Charles Duelfer. September 30, 2004.

———. "The Soviet Invasion of Afghanistan: Implications for Warning." Interagency Intelligence Memorandum, October 1980.

———. "Soviet Options in Afghanistan." Interagency Intelligence Memorandum, NI IIM 79-100771, September 28, 1979. http://www.foia.cia.gov/default.asp.

———. *Impact and Implications of Chemical Weapons Use in Iran-Iraq War* (Top Secret). Interagency Intelligence Memorandum, April 1988.

Director of Central Intelligence, National Intelligence Council. *Emerging Missile Threats to North America During the Next 15 Years.* Declassified excerpts from the National Intelligence Estimate, NIE 95-19, President's Summary, November 1995.

———. *Foreign Missile Developments and the Ballistic Missile Threat to the United States Through 2015.* National Intelligence Estimate, September 1999.

———. *Key Judgments: Iraq's Continuing Programs for Weapons of Mass Destruction.* Excerpts from October 1, 2002, National Intelligence Estimate, declassified July 18, 2003.

Director of Central Intelligence, Persian Gulf War Illnesses Task Force. *Khamisiyah: A Historical Perspective on Related Intelligence.* April 9, 1997.

Director of Central Intelligence John Deutch. *Statement of the Director of Central Intelligence on the Clandestine Services and the Damage Caused by Aldrich Ames.* December 7, 1995.

———. *Statement to the Public on the Ames Damage Assessment.* CIA, October 31, 1995.

Executive Office of the President, National Security Council Memorandum. *Saddam's Message of Friendship to President Bush.* July 25, 1990.

National Commission on Terrorist Attacks Upon the United States. *The 9/11 Commission Report.* New York: W. W. Norton, 2004.

President's Foreign Intelligence Advisory Board. *Intelligence Community Experiment in Competitive Analysis: Soviet Strategic Objectives, an Alternative View, Report of Team "B."* Washington, D.C.: CIA, 1976.

President's Intelligence Oversight Board. *Report of the Guatemala Review.* Washington, D.C.: U.S. Government Printing Office, June 28, 1996.

United States District Court, Eastern District of Virginia, Alexandria Division. Statement of Aldrich Hazen Ames in *United States of America v. Aldrich Hazen Ames,* Criminal Case No. 94-64-A, 1994.

United States District Court, Southern District of New York. *United States v. Usama bin Laden et al.,* S(7) Cr. 1023, 2001.

U.S. House of Representatives, Committee on Armed Services. *Hearings on the Crisis in the Persian Gulf: Sanctions, Diplomacy and War.* Washington, D.C.: U.S. Government Printing Office, 1990.

———. *Defense for a New Era: Lessons of the Persian Gulf War.* Interim Report of the Committee on Armed Services. Washington, D.C.: U.S. Government Printing Office, March 30, 1992.

U.S. House of Representatives, Committee on Armed Services, Subcommittee on Oversight and Investigations. *Intelligence Successes and Failures in Operations Desert Shield/Storm.* Washington, D.C.: U.S. Government Printing Office, August 1993.

U.S. House of Representatives, Committee on Foreign Affairs, Subcommittee on Europe and the Middle East. *United States-Iraqi Relations.* Washington, D.C.: U.S. Government Printing Office, 1991.

U.S. House of Representatives, Permanent Select Committee on Intelligence. *IC21: The Intelligence Community in the 21st Century.* Washington, D.C.: U.S. Government Printing Office, 1996.

U.S. House of Representatives, Permanent Select Committee on Intelligence. *Report of the Guatemala Review.* Washington, D.C.: U.S. Government Printing Office, March 17, 1997.

———. *Report of Investigation: The Aldrich Ames Espionage Case*. Washington, D.C.: U.S. Government Printing Office, November 30, 1994.

U.S. Senate, Select Committee to Study Governmental Operations with Respect to Intelligence Activities (the Church Committee), *Final Report of the Select Committee to Study Governmental Operations with Respect to Intelligence Activities*, U.S. Senate, 94th Cong., 2nd sess., April 26, 1976.

U.S. Senate, Committee on Armed Services. *Hearings on the Crisis in the Persian Gulf Region: U.S. Policy Options and Implications*. Washington, D.C.: U.S. Government Printing Office, 1990.

U.S. Senate, Committee on Banking, Housing and Urban Affairs. *U.S. Chemical and Biological Warfare-Related Dual Use Exports to Iraq and Their Possible Impact on the Health Consequences of the Gulf War* (The Riegle Report). Washington, D.C.: U.S. Government Printing Office, May 25, 1994. http://www.gulfweb.org/bigdoc/report/riegle1.html.

U.S. Senate Select Committee on Intelligence. *An Assessment of the Aldrich H. Ames Espionage Case and Its Implications for U.S. Intelligence*. Washington, D.C., November 1, 1994.

———. *Hearing on Current and Projected National Security Threats to the United States*. 109th Cong., 2nd sess., February 11, 2003. Washington, D.C.: U.S. Government Printing Office, 2003.

———. *Hearings on the Nomination of Robert M. Gates to be Director of Central Intelligence*. 102nd Cong., 1st sess., September–October 1991. Washington, D.C.: U.S. Government Printing Office, 1992.

———. *Prewar Intelligence Assessments About Postwar Iraq*. 110th Cong., 1st sess., May 8, 2007. Washington, D.C.: U.S. Government Printing Office, 2007. http://intelligence.senate.gov/prewar.pdf.

———. *U.S. Intelligence Community's Prewar Intelligence Assessments on Iraq*. 108th Cong., 2nd sess, July 9, 2004.

———. *Postwar Findings About Iraq's WMD Programs and Links to Terrorism and How They Compare with Prewar Assessments*, together with additional views. Washington, D.C.: U.S. Government Printing Office, September 8, 2006.

U.S. Senate Select Committee on Intelligence, and U.S. House of Representatives Permanent Select Committee on Intelligence. *Joint Inquiry into Intelligence Community Activities Before and After the Terrorist Attacks of September 11, 2001*. Washington, D.C.: U.S. Government Printing Office, 2002.

University of Pittsburgh, Matthew B. Ridgeway Center. *Anatomy of a Terrorist Attack: An In-Depth Investigation into the 1998 Bombings of the U.S. Embassies in Kenya and Tanzania*. Working paper, Spring 2005.

INDEX

Note: Page numbers in italic type indicate illustrations.